S0-AYH-061

Austria	Hungary*
Belgium and Luxembourg	Ireland
California*	Morocco
Channel Islands	Northern Italy
China*	Portugal
Corsica	Scotland
Crete	Sicily
Cyprus	Southern Italy
Egypt	Spain
England	Switzerland
France	Turkey
Germany	Wales
Greece	Yugoslavia
Holland	

Boston and Cambridge
Florence
Istanbul
Jerusalem
London
Moscow and Leningrad
New York
Oxford and Cambridge
Paris and Versailles
Rome and Environs
Venice

Cathedrals and Abbeys of England and Wales
Churches and Chapels of England*
Literary Britain and Ireland
Museums and Galleries of London
Victorian Architecture in Britain

*in preparation

The Annunciation by Petrus Christus (1452), the Groeninge Museum, Bruges (Hugo Martens)

BLUE GUIDE

BELGIUM
AND LUXEMBOURG

John Tomes

Maps and plans by John Flower

A & C Black
London

WW Norton
New York

Seventh edition 1989

Published by A & C Black (Publishers) Limited
35 Bedford Row, London, WC1R 4JH

© A & C Black (Publishers) Limited 1989

Published in the United States of America by
WW Norton & Company, Incorporated
500 Fifth Avenue, New York, NY 10110

Published simultaneously in Canada by
Penguin Books Limited,
2801 John Street, Markham, Ontario L3R 1B4

British Library Cataloguing in Publication Data

Belgium and Luxembourg.—7th ed.—(Blue guide).
    1. Belgium—Visitors' guides 2. Luxembourg—
Visitors' guides
    I. Tomes, John
    914.93'0443

    ISBN   0–7136–2822–7

ISBN 0-393-30483-3 USA

Printed and bound in Great Britain by
William Clowes Limited, Beccles and London

Biographical Note

Educated at Oxford, where he gained his degree in Modern
Languages, and after careers in the Royal Air Force and the aero
engine industry, John Tomes was invited to update the Blue Guides to
'Greece' and 'Sicily'. Subsequently, he became author of Blue Guides
'Scotland', 'Wales', 'Belgium and Luxembourg' and 'Holland', a
group which he has now seen through several editions. A number of
his short stories have been published and broadcast, and his other
travel books include the 'Shell Book of Exploring Britain' (A & C
Black), of which he is co-author with the late Garry Hogg.

PREFACE

To many people Belgium is simply a transit country; many others, though, take rewarding advantage of special-offer weekends in cities such as Brussels, Antwerp, Ghent and Bruges; and others, and especially those with children, enjoy the splendid beaches and the cheerful resorts which go with them. But, by comparison, only a few appear to tour and explore; to find that rich and often surprising other Belgium—and Luxembourg too—far removed from the conventional beat yet never far removed from those three essentials, a comfortable bed and good food and drink. This Seventh Edition of **Blue Guide Belgium and Luxembourg** gives priority of course to thorough coverage of all the prime tourist areas. But it also ranges farther afield throughout Belgium and Luxembourg—two countries (three, in fact, if one views Flanders and Wallonia through the same separatist spectacles as worn by so many of their inhabitants) which together provide an often astonishing variety of people and language, of culture and custom, of architecture and scenery, all within a compact area in which the farthest point is under 350km from the coast—by roads along and to either side of which there is much that will both surprise and repay the touring explorer.

Not that there is need to travel anything like that far, for the visitor has only to step ashore to be welcomed by a string of coastal resorts, large and small and catering for most tastes, while at Bruges, a mere 15km inland, and at Ghent only a short distance farther, will be found all the charm and the splendour of old Flanders as well as many of Belgium's finest and justly famed art galleries. Antwerp, despite its huge modern port still a most Flemish of cities and a place where Rubens never seems far away, lines the Scheldt, while cosmopolitan Brussels, both national and international capital and as renowned for its ancient and glorious Grand-Place as for the controversial modern architecture which surrounds but never encroaches upon it, lies little more than an hour away from the coast. And lastly, for those in search of quiet and scenery, there wait the romantic Ardennes—land of forest and grottoes and fairies, of high moor, deep valleys, meandering rivers and perched castles—building up beyond the Meuse to embrace the historic and lovely little Grand-Duchy of Luxembourg and then reach beyond the vineyards and the Moselle into the marches of western Germany.

Acknowledgements are due first to all who over the years have contributed to the compilation and high reputation of this Guide since its first edition (as 'Belgium and the Western Front') in 1920.

For this new edition, as on previous occasions, invaluable and comprehensive background information has been generously provided by the numerous and excellent publications of the two national tourist offices, as also by the tourist offices of the various provinces and of many towns, especial thanks, for both encouragement and help, being due to Mr P.J. Claus, director of the London office. Especial appreciation, too, to the author's wife, for her range of contributory skills—secretarial, research, critical and, certainly not least, navigational.

Comments and Suggestions. A continually evolving guide such as this can profit immensely from the contributions of its users, and the author takes this opportunity to thank the several people who have taken the trouble to provide comments and suggestions. Such—whether on fact, on the general layout and style of the book, or, most valuable of all, new material resulting from personal discovery—will always be most welcome.

Background Sources. The editor has found the undermentioned most valuable for reference and background: *Encyclopaedia Britannica*. For the Battle of Waterloo, and for events before and after the battle, *Waterloo, A Guide to the Battlefield*, by David Howarth (Library of Imperial History, for the Waterloo Committee), and *Wellington, The Years of the Sword*, by Elizabeth Longford (Weidenfeld and Nicolson). For information on the archaeological site at Montauban, *The Buried Past*, by Henri-Paul Eydoux (Weidenfeld and Nicolson). For military events, *History of the First World War* and *History of the Second World War*, by B.H. Liddell Hart (Cassell). Also *Before Endeavours Fade*, by Rose E.B.Coombs, and *After the Battle (No. 4)*, edited by Winston G. Ramsey, both published by Battle of Britain Prints International Ltd; and *Massacre at Malmédy*, by Charles Whiting (Leo Cooper). For background on several Châteaux, *Châteaux de Belgique à Visiter*, by Chevalier Joseph de Ghellinck d'Elseghem (Rossel Edition, Brussels). For information on artists, *Dictionnaire des Peintres, Sculpteurs, Dessinateurs et Graveurs* by E. Bénézit and successors (Librairie Gründ).

Acknowledgements

Thanks are due to the Belgian National Tourist Office and to the following organisations and individuals for permission to reproduce illustrations:

Groeninge Museum, Bruges, page 2

CGT, Sergysels, page 40

CGT—CRCH—UCL, page 52

CGT, Delrance, page 58

CGT, V.D. Bremt, page 138

CGT, Van Rafelghem, page 155

The Imperial War Museum, page 156

A. De Belder, page 264

CGT, Desutter, page 277

CGT, Dédé, pages 291, 340

Weidenfeld & Nicolson Archives, J.
   Mertens/Weidenfeld & Nicolson, page 377

Luxembourg National Tourist and Trade Office, pages 405, 407

A NOTE ON BLUE GUIDES

The Blue Guide series began in 1918 when Muirhead Guide-Books Limited published 'Blue Guide London and its Environs'. Finlay and James Muirhead already had extensive experience of guide-book publishing: before the First World War they had been the editors of the English editions of the German Baedekers, and by 1915 they had acquired the copyright of most of the famous 'Red' Handbooks from John Murray.

An agreement made with the French publishing house Hachette et Cie in 1917 led to the translation of Muirhead's London Guide, which became the first 'Guide Bleu'—Hachette had previously published the blue-covered 'Guides Joannes'. Subsequently, Hachette's 'Guide Bleu Paris et ses Environs' was adapted and published in London by Muirhead. The collaboration between the two publishing houses continued until 1933.

In 1931 Ernest Benn Limited took over the Blue Guides, appointing Russell Muirhead, Finlay Muirhead's son editor in 1934. The Muirheads' connection with Blue Guides ended in 1963 when Stuart Rossiter, who had been working on the Guides since 1954, became house editor, revising and compiling several of the books himself.

The Blue Guides are now published by A & C Black, who acquired Ernest Benn Limited in 1984, so continuing the tradition of guide-book publishing which began in 1826 with 'Black's Economical Tourist of Scotland'. The Blue Guide series continues to grow: there are now more than 30 titles in print with revised editions appearing regularly and many new Blue Guides in preparation.

'Blue Guides' is a registered trade mark.

NOTES ON USING THE GUIDE

The Guide is in three main parts. The first gives background and practical information on Belgium, this including a history and a survey of art. The second part describes Belgium under 39 Routes: of these No. 1 is Brussels and its environs; Nos 2 to 21, preceded by an Introduction, cover North, or Flemish, Belgium; and Nos 22 to 39, also with an Introduction, cover South, or Walloon, Belgium. The last part of the Guide (Introduction and Routes 40 to 44) describes the Grand-Duchy of Luxembourg. Each of the above three Introductions is accompanied by a Plan of Routes.

Town and District Names. Many places, especially near the Language Frontier, have Flemish and French, and in the E of the country also German names, and road signs change, sometimes unrecognisably, as soon as this frontier is crossed. In general the rule followed in this Guide has been to use the English version of a name where such exists (e.g. Brussels, Antwerp, Ghent) but otherwise to use the local version. For places near the Language Frontier, or in other cases where there might be confusion, the alternative names are also given. A list of principal places with the various renderings of their names appears on p 85.

Distances. The preamble to each Route gives its total distance. In both the preambles and texts italicised distances are those between points along the Route, i.e. each italicised distance represents the distance from the previous one. Other distances (e.g. along diversions) are, though with one or two exceptions, in Roman print. For a number of reasons distances can only be approximate.

Maps and General Index. Maps at the end of the Guide cover the whole of Belgium and the Grand-Duchy of Luxembourg and include all places of principal interest. Since Routes sometimes cross or run close to one another, it is advisable to consult the General Index for places lying either side of the road being travelled, this ensuring that places within easy reach but perhaps described under another Route are not missed.

Index of Artists. Artists (painters, sculptors, architects, etc.) appear under a special index and are not included under the General Index.

Asterisks (*) draw attention to sites and works of art of special importance, interest or attraction.

Opening Times are given wherever available and judged reasonably reliable, the times being those provided by the responsible tourist authorities. The warning must, though, be given that neither these authorities, nor individual sites, care to commit themselves and that times can and do change without notice. More often than not sites will be visited on an opportunist basis. However, when a site is a positive objective, to avoid possible disappointment intending visitors should always first check with Tourist Information.

Particulars given are normally inclusive, e.g. April–September means 1 April–30 September. In most cases the closing time shown is the actual closing time, but, and particularly in the case of larger sites, last entry may well be a half hour or more before this. A charge is made for many sites; many, however, offer a reduced fee to students

and pensioners and some are open free on one day in the week.
   See also Access to Sites (Churches, Museums and Art Galleries, Castles and Châteaux) on pp 70 and 71.

Town Plans. Pedestrianised roads are indicated by line shading.
Important parking areas are indicated by the symbol [P].
Information centres are indicated by the symbol 𝒊 .

CONTENTS

MAPS AND PLANS

ROUTE MAPS

PLANS

BACKGROUND INFORMATION

Introduction to Belgium

The visitor to Belgium (population around ten million) can in fact enjoy two countries in one, for although constitutionally one (now federal) nation North and South Belgium are two very different places. North Belgium (for detail, see p 131) is Flemish in language, culture and attitude, scenically flat but rich in historic cities, their splendid architecture and famed museums and art galleries a legacy from centuries of struggle for independence and an equally long tradition of vigorous civic pride. North Belgium also offers the coast with its sands and resorts, and, not far inland, the great battlefields of the First World War. South Belgium (for detail, see p 298), likewise strong in its own culture and tradition, is Walloon French-speaking Belgium; not without some interesting towns, though these cannot compare with those of the North, and known too for its heavy industry around Mons and Charleroi, Walloon Belgium is visited mainly for the scenery of the Ardennes. The capital of these two 'countries' is the bilingual and cosmopolitan city of Brussels, famous above all for its breathtaking Grand-Place; notable too as the 'capital' of Europe, for its art galleries and museums, for the variety and elegance of its shops, and as a gastronomic city second to none.

Aspects of Belgium

Communities and Languages. The division of Belgium into Flemish (c 60 per cent) and French-speaking (c 40 per cent) communities—with all that this inflicts in cultural, political, language, social and other problems, now hopefully ameliorated by the new federal constitution (see below)—has its origins partly in the separation as far back as the 3C between the lands colonised by the Germanic Franks and those of the Wala, the Romanised Celts; partly in the story of the Revolt of the Netherlands (1555–1648); and partly in the fact that the French language, which until the revolution of 1830 had been that of the nobility and ruling class whether Flemish or Walloon, after the revolution began increasingly to be questioned as Flemish importance and aspirations grew. The border between the two communities—popularly called the Language Frontier though it is of course far more than this—was officially drawn in 1962 and is now confirmed by the detailed provisions of the new constitution; the 'Frontiers' are shown on the map of the Provinces on p 16. To the N of this line the language, though called Flemish, is to all intents and purposes Dutch, if with local variations and accents. Along the Language Frontier itself and in the larger towns French is also widely understood. But Regional susceptibilities are never far below the surface and it is a solecism to assume that French will be understood; if one does not speak Flemish, then it is both courteous and sensible either to try English, which is widely understood and often preferred, or to inquire if French may be spoken. To the S of the frontier the language is French, though again with local accents and variations (e.g. 'septante' and 'nonante' for 'soixante-dix' and 'quatre-vingt-dix').

Belgium has also two other communities, one being the city of Brussels; officially bilingual, and with both Flemish and French-speaking communes, although in practice French predominates, at any rate in those districts most visited by tourists. The other community is that of the German-speaking Cantons de l'Est.

The **Royal Family**. For the royal line prior to the accession in 1951 of King Baudouin, see History of Belgium, p 28 et seq. Baudouin (born 1930) married in 1960 the Spanish noblewoman Fabiola de Mora y Aragon (born 1928). The couple are childless, the heir to the throne being the King's brother Prince Albert (born 1934; Prince de Liège) who in 1959 married the Italian Princess Paola Ruffo di Calabria. Albert and Paola have three children, Philippe (born 1960), Astrid (born 1962) and Laurent (born 1963).

National Anthem and Flag. The first French-language version of the national anthem was written in August 1830 by the Frenchman L.A. Dechet ('Jenneval'), an actor at the Théâtre de la Monnaie, birthplace of the revolution of 1830. Fighting with the revolutionaries, Dechet was killed at Lier some six weeks later. François van Campenhout, a violinist at the same theatre, composed the music and named the song 'La Brabançonne' since it was in Brussels in the province of Brabant that the revolution started. For the same reason the national flag uses the colours of Brabant (vertical black, gold, red). In 1860 Charles Rogier rewrote the French words and his is the version in use today. There have been several Flemish texts, but the current one received official approval in 1938.

National Constitution. The Belgian constitution officially became federal in 1980, although at least a decade is being allowed to bring what is in practice a formula of considerable and splintered complexity into effect. Basically the country is a federation over which reigns a constitutional monarch. Below the Crown are the various levels of the federation, each with its defined powers, at the top being a bicameral national government, responsible for, for example, foreign policy, defence and communications, but subject also to many checks and balances to ensure fair representation as between the nation's communities. Below this level the scene becomes complex because the split is into three Communities (Flemish, French and German speaking) and also four Regions (Flemish, Walloon, German and Brussels), while—as an added complication—on the Flemish side the Community and Region function as one, while on the French side they function separately. None of this is likely, however, noticeably to affect the tourist and, in the interests of simplicity, it can be said that, whatever may be called, the levels below the national government are Flemish, Walloon, the German-speaking Cantons de l'Est and Brussels, and that their responsibilities embrace such fields as education, culture (including tourism), health, and environment and planning.

For long it seemed that the Provinces would disappear, or at any rate become subordinate to the Regions. Opposition to abolition was, though, both vocal and effective and, for the present anyway, the Provinces survive somewhat unhappily on the sidelines.

Folklore. No one can be long in Belgium without meeting the word 'Folklore' (Flem. Volkskunde), loosely used in a variety of contexts. Museums of local customs, crafts and history, whether modest village

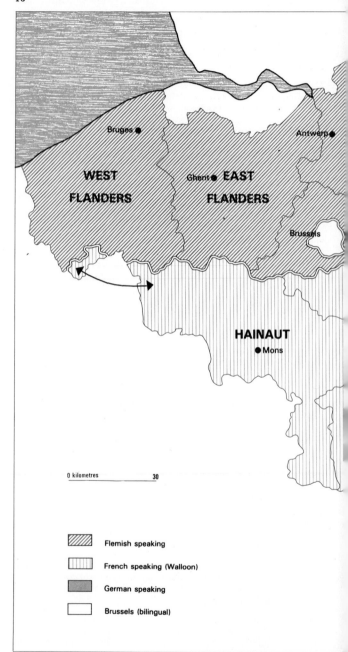

Flemish speaking

French speaking (Walloon)

German speaking

Brussels (bilingual)

Belgium : Provinces and Communities

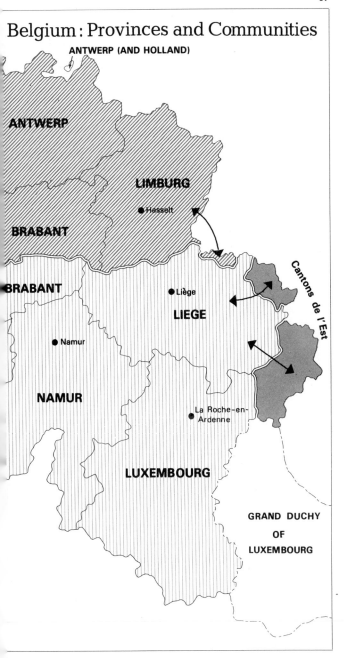

ANTWERP (AND HOLLAND)

ANTWERP

LIMBURG

● Hasselt

BRABANT

BRABANT

● Liège

LIEGE

● Namur

NAMUR

La Roche-en-
Ardenne

Cantons de l'Est

LUXEMBOURG

GRAND DUCHY

OF

LUXEMBOURG

rooms or distinguished collections such as those in Ghent or Antwerp, are classed as folklore museums. Local 'citizens' (Manneken-Pis in Brussels, Op-Signor in Mechelen, Jean de Nivelles high on his church turret, and many others) are folklore characters. Folklore legend appears also in the traditional pieces shown at Belgium's puppet theatres (e.g. Toone in Brussels). Above all, perhaps, folklore provides the roots for the infinitely varied and almost countless processions and festivals, both religious and secular, that crowd the Belgian calendar. These range from simple village affairs, through widely known festivals such as the carnival at Binche, the Lumeçon at Mons, or the Kattestoet at Ypres, to the stately pageants of the Golden Tree at Bruges and the aristocratic Ommegang staged in the Grand-Place in Brussels. Although many are carnivals held prior to Lent, folklore occasions, often with varying dates, cover the year. The National tourist organisation annually publishes a comprehensive Calendar of Touristic Events which, in addition to all the principal folklore events, includes dates for sports meetings, music and art festivals, trade fairs, flower shows, etc.

Carillons, in their various forms very much a feature of many Flemish and also of some Walloon towns, originated with the early belfries in which small bells were struck with a hammer to signal the hours. At first there were always four bells, known as the 'Quadrilloner' whence derives today's 'carillon', among the oldest belfries being those of Bruges, Ghent and Mechelen. Carillons of six or eight bells did not appear until the beginning of the 16C; at about the same time the mallet was replaced by the clavier, Oudenaarde in 1510 boasting the first keyboard and Mechelen in 1583 claiming to have the first with pedals. Modern times have seen the installation of electric and automatic carillons. There is a carillon school and museum at Mechelen.

Gastronomy. Belgium enjoys a gastronomic reputation second to none, this applying to all regions and to restaurants of all categories; it is rare to be served a poor meal, even rarer to be offered insufficient quantity. For more detail, see p 73.

History of Belgium

Today's independent Kingdom of Belgium dates only from 1831. Thus much of this History is that of the lands and peoples out of which Belgium, as also Holland and the Grand-Duchy of Luxembourg, grew. Constant changes of sovereignty brought corresponding and confusing changes of name. In this History nomenclature has generally been simplified as below.

Netherlands. The combined areas of roughly present-day Belgium and Holland, with also the Grand-Duchy of Luxembourg and parts of northern France. The term is politically valid until the de facto separation of North and South at the end of the 16C.

Spanish Netherlands. The southern part of the Netherlands from its subjection by the Duke of Parma subsequent to the Union of Arras (1579) until the Treaty of Utrecht (1713).—**Belgium**. Roughly this same territory from the Treaty of Utrecht to the present day. Over this period Belgium was successively the Austrian Netherlands; briefly the United States of Belgium; again the Austrian Netherlands; incorporated into France; a part of the United Kingdom of the Netherlands; and finally the Kingdom of Belgium.

United Provinces. The northern and Protestant part of the Netherlands, which Parma failed to subdue and which declared its independence under the Union of Utrecht (1579).—**Holland** (the Dutch). Roughly this same territory subsequent to the recognition of its independence by the Peace of Münster (1648). *Note*. 1. The name United Provinces in fact continued in use until the republic fell to the French in 1795. 2. Modern Holland is officially the Kingdom of the Netherlands. 'Holland' is simply a popular name deriving from the ancient county, the nucleus from which today's state grew and now forming two of its provinces, and references early in this History to 'Holland' are to this county or province.

Luxembourg. Until 1815 roughly the combined area of today's Grand-Duchy and of the Belgian province of Luxembourg; after 1839 only the Belgian province.—**Grand-Duchy of Luxembourg**. The independent Grand-Duchy created in 1815, but whose territories were much changed in 1839. (See also p 391.)

Roman and Frankish Period (BC to AD 843)

Between 57 and 50 BC that part of northern Gaul lying in the basins of the Scheldt and the Meuse was conquered by Julius Caesar. At that time the territory now known as Belgium was inhabited by Gallo-Celtic tribes (Belgae). In 15 BC these conquered lands became the imperial province of Gallia Belgica and the Roman occupation lasted until the 5C. During the 3C, however, as Rome began to weaken, Frankish penetration began (Franks being the generic name for the loose federation of several Germanic tribes), these early Franks being accepted by the Romans as 'foederati', or mercenaries who fought for Rome under their own chiefs. By about 431, under Chlodio, leader of the dominant Salii tribe, Tournai became the capital of the Frankish Merovingian kings, a dynasty named after Meroveus, successor to Chlodio. Meroveus was followed by Childeric I (died 481), who threw off the Roman association, and he by Clovis who declared himself Christian, thus gaining Church support and conquering all Gaul except for Burgundy and Provence. Farther north, the eventual withdrawal of the Romans led to the completion of Frankish colonisation of the lower Scheldt and the Lys. The 'Silva Carbonaria', a belt of forest stretching from the Scheldt to the Ardennes, separated these Franks from the Wala (Walloons) or Romanised Celts, thus defining, at least in part, the ethnic and language frontier that persists today. On the death of Clovis in c 511, his realm splintered, what is now Belgium becoming a neglected corner.

The Frankish lands developed into two 'kingdoms': Austrasia (capital Metz) in the E, and Neustria (Merovingian) to the S and west. Dagobert, a child who became King of Austrasia in 623, was under the domination of Pepin (I) of Landen, who was 'Mayor of the Palace', the title enjoyed by the chief court official. In 629 Pepin fell out of favour, returning however on Dagobert's death in 638 and governing Austrasia until his own death the following year. Pepin II (of Herstal), son of a daughter of Pepin of Landen (possibly Begga of Andenne), led Austrasia against Neustria, in 687 winning a battle which marked the beginning of the end for the Merovingian line. The son of Pepin II, Charles Martel, became ruler in effect if not in name of all the Frankish lands, on his death in 741 being succeeded by his younger son, Pepin (III), the Short, who by 751 had deposed the last Merovingian (Childeric III) and had himself crowned King of the Franks. He died in 768, one of his sons being Charlemagne.

Charlemagne reigned from 768 to 814, in 800 being declared by the Pope to be Emperor of the West, at the head of an empire which extended from Denmark to southern Italy and from northern Spain to the Oder. 'Belgium' occupied an important position in this empire and also one adjacent to Charlemagne's favourite residence at Aachen (Aix-la-Chapelle). Charlemagne's reign was one which saw great progress—one aspect being the start of the real use of the waterways, today so important an aspect of Belgium's industrial communications system—but on his death his lands were partitioned and in 843, after bitter fighting between his grandsons, the Treaty of Verdun divided the area of 'Belgium' between Charles the Bald and Lothair. The former, becoming King of West Francia (roughly today's France), received the narrow strip W of the Scheldt (i.e. Flanders); the latter, with lands along the Rhine and the Rhône (Middle Kingdom), received the remainder, this later becoming the Duchy of Lower Lotharingia (Lorraine). To the E was East Francia out of which would grow Germany.

Feudal and Burgundian Period (843 to 1482)

During the 9C and 10C the Norsemen appeared, raiding and settling, a threat which fostered the growth of defensive feudalism and the emergence in the West of the powerful counts of Flanders. Although nominally vassals of the kings of France, the counts took over more and more land and by the middle of the 11C had become virtually independent.

The first count was Baldwin Iron Arm, who carried off and married a daughter of Charles the Bald, Judith by name, who had already been the wife of two English princes; in c 867 he built his great stronghold at Ghent. Baldwin II, child of this marriage, built the walls of Bruges and Ypres and married a daughter of England's Alfred the Great. The daughter of Baldwin V (1036–67), Matilda, shared the English throne with William the Conqueror; Baldwin's son married the widow of the Count of Hainaut, thus becoming ruler of that province, and the son of this marriage, Robert the Frisian, ruled over Holland and Friesland. Count Robert II (1093–1119) was famous for his exploits in the First Crusade, acquiring the title of 'Lance and Sword of Christendom'. Baldwin IX (1172–1206), another Crusader, became, as Baldwin I, the first king of the Latin empire of Constantinople; his pious daughters, the countesses Margaret and Joanna (or Joan), are known for the number of religious houses they founded.

Although Flanders thus became strong and unified, Lotharingia fared differently, breaking up into several minor countships and principalities.

With the wane of feudalism during the 12C and 13C came the rise of the towns, the clothworking Flanders (Flemish) towns of Ghent, Bruges and Ypres attaining an economic prosperity and civic dignity surpassed only by a few Italian cities. With England as their chief wool-supplier, these and many other towns became the principal markets of north-western Europe and maintained an almost complete independence of France.

This autonomy, won and preserved only through great struggle and sacrifice, was the ancestor of today's still fiercely defended local government level of communes. In the North *Belfries* and, in the South, *Perrons* (usually a decorated column on a platform) now and later became the symbols of civic independence. The former, durable and practical as well as symbolic, served as watch-towers with warning bells, refuges, meeting-places, and jails. Perrons, mainly found in

Liège, and often destroyed or carried off by new rulers, stood as focal spots for meetings, the reading of proclamations, the exercise of justice, etc.

But the French were determined to reassert their authority, and the nobles to regain their privileges, and although during the reign of France's Philip the Fair the towns routed the French nobility at the Battle of the Golden Spurs (near Kortrijk, 1302), by 1322 the franco-phile Count Louis of Flanders and Nevers had succeeded in reducing Flanders to being virtually a French province. Local rivalries, the jealousies of the guilds (protective associations which may be regarded as the ancestors of the trade unions), the tyranny of the urban oligarchy over the country people, and, later, changing trade routes and the emigration of many weavers to England, all combined to bring about a long period of instability leading first to Burgundian supremacy under Philip the Good (1419) and eventually to Habsburg rule (1477). The confusing events, in Flanders and elsewhere, up to the accession of Philip the Good are summarised below.

1338. Jacob van Artevelde of Ghent allied the Flemish towns with England's Edward III during the opening stages of the Hundred Years War.

1345. Death of William II, Count of Hainaut, his lands being divided between his sister, the Empress Margaret, who got Hainaut, and her son William, to whom went the provinces of Holland and Zeeland.

1346. Louis de Male, son of Louis of Nevers, became Count of Flanders. As francophile as his father, much of his countship was a struggle with the towns, in which he largely relied on French backing.

1355. Death of John of Brabant. His daughter Joanna, and her husband, Wenceslas of Luxembourg, became rulers of Brabant and Limburg. In 1356 they were forced to sign the Joyeuse Entrée, a declaration of rights that became a form of charter for Brabant.

1357. Louis de Male invaded Brabant, acquiring Mechelen and Antwerp.

1369. Marriage between Margaret, heiress of Louis de Male, and Philip the Bold of Burgundy.

1382. Philip van Artevelde (son of Jacob) defeated Louis de Male and took Bruges, but later the same year was defeated and killed by the French at Westrozebeke (between Ypres and Roeselare).

1383. The English, with assistance from Ghent, unsuccessfully besieged Ypres.—At Louvain the citizens surrendered to Wenceslas; as a result many weavers were forced to emigrate and, with the move of Wenceslas to Vilvoorde, Brussels began to supplant Louvain as capital of Brabant.

1384. Death of Louis de Male. Margaret and Philip the Bold of Burgundy inherited Flanders, Mechelen, and Antwerp; also Artois and other territories in France. This year thus marked the end of Flanders as a separate state and the start of the Burgundian period.

1390. Joanna ceded Brabant and Limburg to Philip the Bold.

1404. Philip the Bold was succeeded by John the Fearless, but in Brabant and Limburg by Philip's second son, Antoine.

1411. Antoine acquired Luxembourg by marriage.

1415. Antoine was killed at Agincourt, being succeeded by John IV of Brabant, who married Jacqueline, Countess of Hainaut, Zeeland, and Holland.

In 1419 Duke Philip the Good of Burgundy (grandson of Philip the Bold) succeeded to the countship of Flanders. He ruled until 1467 and consolidated Burgundian power. In 1421 he bought Namur; in 1430 he inherited Brabant, Limburg, and Antwerp; in 1433 he caused Jacqueline of Hainaut to be deposed and took over Hainaut, Holland, and Zeeland; in 1443 he bought Luxembourg; in 1456 he had his nephew, Louis de Bourbon, elected Bishop of Liège, and he also made his bastard son Bishop of Utrecht.

Philip the Good was determined to assert monarchical authority. In 1438 he forced Bruges to surrender many of its privileges, and in 1453, after an unsuccessful revolt, Ghent suffered the same fate. At the same time Philip tried to foster the towns' economic prosperity, amongst other things prohibiting the import of English cloth and encouraging the Antwerp fairs. Two other dates are important. In 1430, in Bruges, he established the Order of the Golden Fleece, partly in compliment to the Flanders wool-weavers and partly in glorification of his own house and court; and in 1465 he summoned representatives of all the provinces (or States) to a States General in Brussels.

Philip was succeeded in 1467 by his son, Charles the Bold. He imposed absolute rule on Liège, acquired Alsace, and, by marrying Margaret of York, cemented his alliance with her brother, Edward IV of England. Disappointed in his efforts to be declared a king, he undertook a disastrous campaign in Lorraine and was killed at Nancy in 1477, leaving his lands in turmoil. His successor, his daughter Mary, held virtually a prisoner in Flanders, was forced to sign the Great Privilege, a charter conferring far-reaching rights on the provinces. In the same year she married Maximilian of Austria, the Burgundian federation created by Philip the Good thus passing to the Habsburgs. Mary died in 1482.

The Holy Roman Emperors Maximilian and Charles V (1482 to 1555)

On Mary's death, Maximilian became regent. He made peace with France and subdued the whole of the Netherlands which, on his election as Holy Roman Emperor in 1494, he handed over to his son, Philip the Handsome. Philip married Joanna of Castile, but died in 1506, his Burgundian lands passing to his six-year-old son Charles, for whom his aunt, Margaret of Austria, acted as governor. From 1513 to 1519 England's Henry VIII occupied Tournai in the course of his war with France. In 1515 the States General declared Charles of age, in 1516 he became King of Spain, and in 1519 Emperor (as Charles V, or Quint), thus succeeding to all the Habsburg dominions. Although he relinquished the Austrian territories to his brother, he still held Spain, Sardinia, Naples, Sicily, and Milan; Burgundy and the Habsburg lands in Alsace; and the Netherlands, which he extended to include Friesland, Utrecht, and Groningen. In 1530 Charles appointed his sister, Mary of Hungary, to be regent of the Netherlands, now but a part of a scattered empire and heavily taxed to support the wars of their usually absent ruler. Ghent rebelled in 1540, but Charles personally suppressed the uprising, cancelling the city's privileges and imposing a huge fine. Charles's reign also saw the rapid spread of Protestantism, particularly in the northern Netherlands, despite severe persecution such as under the Edict of Blood which decreed death for all convicted of heresy. Charles abdicated in 1555.

The Revolt of the Netherlands (1555 to 1585. Reign of Philip II of Spain)

Charles V was followed by his son Philip II of Spain, married the previous year to Queen Mary of England. His Catholic bigotry, his ruthless persecution of heretics, his introduction into the Netherlands of the Jesuits, and his Spanish garrisons, all led to increasing opposition, revolt, and the further spread of Protestantism. Allied to this popular opposition, springing from religious and social grievances, was the more selfish opposition of the nobles (some of them 'stadholders', or provincial governors), resentful of the increasing centralisation of power into Spanish hands and of the loss of their power of patronage under Philip's plans for the reorganisation of the Church. Philip's reign also saw the separation of the North from the South (i.e., between what would become modern Holland and Belgium) and the emergence of the House of Orange.

Orange, today a town and district on the Rhône in southern France, was an independent principality at the time of Charlemagne. Prince Philibert (1502–30) served Charles V and was rewarded with extensive lands in the Netherlands, lands which became more important to the family than Orange. In 1544 William (the Silent) succeeded to the principality and to the Netherlands territories, later to have his place in history as leader of the Revolt of the Netherlands and as founder of Holland. Having been seized by Louis XIV in 1672, the principality of Orange was officially transferred to France by the Treaty of Ryswick in 1697, thereafter only the princely title surviving.

Start of the revolt (1558–67). Forced to grant a demand by the States General that all Spanish troops be withdrawn, Philip retired to Spain, leaving Margaret of Parma (natural daughter of Charles V) as governor, with, as chief councillors, Cardinal Granvelle (a French adviser to Philip, made Archbishop of Mechelen) and Berlaymont (a Walloon noble). Opposition hardened, being headed by William of Orange, the Inquisition was defied, Protestantism (in particular Calvinism) spread to the nobility, and in 1564 Granvelle was recalled. The following year the League of the Nobility was formed, as both a religious and a political opposition, and petitioned for moderation of the anti-Protestant edicts. Berlaymont rejected the petition, contemptuously referring to the League as 'ces gueux' ('those beggars'), a taunt which the leaguers accepted as an honorific title. The year 1566 saw the rapid growth of extreme Calvinism, with fanatics rioting and destroying Church property, particularly in Antwerp. But this development, the 'Iconoclastic Fury', split the opposition to Spain, and Margaret, seizing the opportunity to play off the popular party against the aristocratic, regained the support of many of the nobles. William of Orange and Count Egmont (governor of Flanders) attempted to steer a middle course, but failed as the result of a Calvinist uprising in Flanders, and William retired to his estates (Nassau) in Germany.

Rule by the Duke of Alva (1568–73). Determined on the absolute suppression of heresy, Philip sent the Duke of Alva and an army of 10,000 to the Netherlands. Alva promptly ushered in a period of terrorism, setting up the so-called Council of Blood to deal with heretics and insurgents, outlawing William, and executing Egmont, Horn, and many other nobles. In Nassau, William attempted to raise an army, but he had no money and in any case gained no support from the towns, all now strongly garrisoned by Alva's troops. But in 1572 the tide began to turn when the Sea Beggars (privateers commissioned by William and hitherto operating from England or East Friesland) captured Brielle at the mouth of the Meuse (Maas). This, and the capture of Flushing (Vlissingen) soon after, gave the rebels footholds in the Netherlands and was the key to the success from now on of the revolt in the North. By the end of the year the rebels controlled most of the province of Holland and William was declared stadholder. Alva, without sea power, could do little in the North, but he put down the simultaneous uprising in the South, retaking Mons which had been seized by William's brother, Louis of Nassau. He then brutally sacked Mechelen, while his son Frederick dealt similarly with Zutphen. But neither Alva nor his son could defeat the now thoroughly aroused heroism of the northern townspeople; the dykes were cut, Frederick had to withdraw, and Alva, his fleet defeated in the Zuider Zee and his army now unpaid and mutinous, left for Spain.

Separation of North from South(1573–85). Alva was replaced by Luis de Requesens and the fighting continued, with the North determined on religious freedom but the South ready for compromise. Although there were setbacks—amongst these the defeat and death of Louis of Nassau near Nijmegen—the North virtually shook off the Spanish hold and Catholicism was even officially forbidden in the province of Holland. When Requesens died in 1576, William, now stadholder of the combined provinces of Holland and Zeeland, saw his opportunity, advancing into Flanders, occupying Ghent, and starting negotiations with the States General. On 8 November 1576 the Pacification of Ghent was signed, the final impetus to agreement being the arrival of the news of the 'Spanish Fury', the barbarous sacking of Antwerp by mutinous Spanish soldiery. The Pacification aimed at securing religious freedom and accepted in principle union between North and South.

The new governor was Philip's bastard brother, Don John of Austria, who, at the time of the signing of the Pacification, was at Luxembourg with a new Spanish army. William persuaded the States General to withhold recognition until Don John accepted the terms of the Pacification. This led to deadlock, until William's hand was strengthened in 1577 by the signing of the Union of Brussels, under which all provinces represented in the States General demanded the departure of foreign troops and the implementation of the Pacification, but at the same time recognised Philip's sovereignty. At this Don John yielded, signing the Perpetual Edict, which accepted most of William's demands. But the unity apparently achieved was shortlived—largely because the growth of Calvinism was alarming the Catholics, and especially the Catholic nobles—and confusion at once followed. Accompanied by Walloon troops Don John withdrew to Namur, which he successfully assaulted; the States General repudiated William; and, secretly helped by southern Catholic nobles, the Archduke Mathias (brother of the emperor, and later emperor himself) arrived in Brussels and in January 1578 declared himself governor.

Philip now sent Alexander Farnese, Duke of Parma, with yet another large army, and helped by this Don John asserted his authority over much of the South; Gembloux, Louvain, Tienen, Bouvignes, Nivelles, Soignies, Binche, Beaumont, and Chimay all capitulated to him before his death in 1578. Three months later the last hope for unity between North and South disappeared when the deputies of Hainaut, Artois, and Douai signed the Union of Arras (5 January 1579) declaring faith in Catholicism and allegiance to Philip. The North replied with the Union of Utrecht and continued the struggle. But Parma's rear had now been secured by the Union of Arras and between 1580 and 1585 (William of Orange was assassinated in 1584) he made himself master of Tournai, Ypres, Bruges, Ghent, and finally Antwerp which, under Marnix van St. Aldegonde, capitulated only after a two years siege. Here, though, Parma's progress halted. The United Provinces (as the northern provinces were now termed) were supported by France and England; Philip's resources were weakened by the destruction of the Spanish Armada (1588); and Parma had to move S to fight the French.

The Spanish Netherlands (1579 to 1713)

Although the southern Netherlands (Spanish Netherlands) recognised the Spanish king as their sovereign, there was no longer any question of Spanish domination. There was a Spanish governor in Brussels, but the country was virtually independent, and even if the king did control the army and foreign policy, his hands were tied because only the provinces could levy taxes. On religious matters, though, the king remained supreme and the Spanish Netherlands became exclusively Catholic.

Parma died in 1592, and Philip, just before his own death in 1598, handed over the whole of the Netherlands to his daughter Isabella (created 'archduke' in her own right) and her husband Archduke Albert, in the hope that as independent sovereigns they might be able to regain the United Provinces. This hope foundered on the insistence that Catholicism was to be the only religion, and after more years of generally indecisive fighting (during which Spain's Admiral Spinola took Ostend, still holding out for the United Provinces) the Twelve Years Truce was agreed in 1609. The 'archdukes' profited by the truce to consolidate Catholicism, in this being much helped by the Jesuits whose influence now became predominant. This was also a period of intellectual and artistic brilliance, with Rubens and Moretus in Antwerp and Justus Lipsius teaching at Louvain.

The Thirty Years War broke out in 1618, and in 1621 Albert and Isabella resumed their campaign against the United Provinces, the fighting dragging on until 1648. The main events, virtually all unfavourable to Spain, are outlined below.

1621. Archduke Albert died. Isabella became governor for Spain's Philip IV.
1625. Spinola took Breda.
1629–32. Frederick Henry of Nassau took 's Hertogenbosch, Venlo, Roermond, and Maastricht.
1633. Death of Isabella, succeeded as governor by the Infante Ferdinand. France concluded an alliance with the United Provinces.
1635. The United Provinces invaded Brabant, sacking Tienen.
1636–45. Frederick Henry took Breda (1636) and Admiral Tromp destroyed the Spanish fleet (1639). In 1641 Frederick Henry married his son William (II) to Mary of England (daughter of Charles I), a direct attempt to establish a semi-royal dynasty in the United Provinces. In the South, Arras was taken by the French (1640), who also beat the Spanish at Rocroi (1643). In 1644 the United Provinces captured Hulst, thus gaining control of the whole left bank of the Scheldt estuary. Frederick Henry died in 1647, being succeeded by William II.

In 1648 Philip IV, compelled by the need to concentrate against France, signed the Peace of Münster. Not only was the independence of the United Provinces recognised, but Philip also gave in to their insistence that the Scheldt be closed. Antwerp was thus ruined, not to recover until the reopening of the estuary in 1795, and commercial prosperity shifted from the South to the North.

Henceforward the story of the Spanish Netherlands became that of Spain's and other countries' successive wars with France. Despite the sacrifices made under the Peace of Münster, Spain was not successful and her influence steadily declined.

Peace of the Pyrenees (1659). France gained most of Artois and several fortresses in the S of the Spanish Netherlands.

War of Devolution(1667–68). Louis XIV ascended the French throne in 1643, coming of age, marrying the Spanish Infanta, and assuming power in 1659. It soon became a constant tenet of his foreign policy that the Spanish Netherlands should be subject to France. He used the death of his father-in-law, Philip IV (succeeded by Charles II), as the excuse to claim Flanders for his queen. Turenne conquered Flanders, but the Dutch, fearful of France as a neighbour, organised the Triple Alliance with England and Sweden. Louis partially yielded, but under the Peace of Aix-la-Chapelle nevertheless received Charleroi, Binche, Ath, Tournai, and Kortrijk, which Vauban set about fortifying.

Dutch War (1672–78). Knowing that he had to eliminate the Dutch, Louis invaded Holland. But, led by William III, the Dutch cut the dykes, flooding their country, and then formed a coalition which included Spain. Louis had to withdraw, and under the Peace of Nijmegen Spain recovered Kortrijk, Charleroi, and Binche, but lost Poperinge, Ypres, and a number of places further south.

Chambres de Réunion (1679–84). Under a cloak of legality Louis unilaterally annexed several places, including Luxembourg, which Vauban at once fortified.

War of the Grand Alliance (1690–97). The Dutch stadholder, William III, became King of England in 1689, England thus turning into an active opponent of France. He formed the Grand Alliance (or League of Augsburg), embracing most of both Protestant and Catholic Europe, and war broke out in 1690. Namur was taken by Louis in 1692, but retaken by William in 1695. By the Peace of Ryswick Spain recovered Mons, Luxembourg, and Kortrijk.

War of the Spanish Succession (1702–13). In 1700 Charles II, the last of the Spanish Habsburgs, died. Childless, he willed the crown of Spain and the Spanish Netherlands to Philip of Anjou, grandson of Louis XIV. Quickly seizing his opportunity, Louis forced his grandson to hand the Spanish Netherlands over to France, whereupon England and Holland, both led by William III, went to war, thus starting a drawn-out struggle which covered much of Europe.

In the Spanish Netherlands the forces opposing France were commanded by the Duke of Marlborough and Prince Eugene of Savoy. 1702: Marlborough advanced S from Holland, taking the Meuse fortresses, including Liège and Huy. 1704: Marlborough's and Eugene's campaign on the Danube, ending with the destruction of a French army at Blenheim. 1705: the French retook Huy. Marlborough broke through the French lines at Tienen, but could not continue because of lack of Dutch support. 1706: Marlborough's victory at Ramillies (NE of Namur) led to French evacuation of most of the Spanish Netherlands. 1708: the French overran Flanders, taking Ghent and Bruges. Marlborough defeated the French at Oudenaarde, retaking Ghent and Bruges. 1709: Marlborough took Tournai, and then, after near defeat at Malplaquet, Mons.

The Treaty of Utrecht was signed in 1713, France abandoning all claim to the Spanish Netherlands which were placed under the sovereignty of the Emperor Charles VI of Austria.

The Austrian Habsburgs (1713 to 1794)

Belgium, now the Austrian Netherlands, had merely undergone a change of sovereignty, the country remaining as independent under Austria as it had been under Spain since the Union of Arras. Under the Barrier Treaty (1715), though, aimed at discouraging any further French ideas of annexation, Belgium had to accept Dutch garrisons at Namur, Dendermonde, Tournai, Menen, and Veurne.

Charles VI died in 1740, leaving no male heir. He had long sought support for his succession by his daughter Maria Theresa, but many of the powers refused to accept her and the **War of the Austrian Succession** broke out. This war came to Belgium in 1744 when the country was invaded by the French under Maurice de Saxe; the Dutch-manned Barrier Treaty forts surrendered, the English were beaten at Fontenoy (near Tournai), and Louis XV occupied Belgium until the war was settled by the Peace of Aix-la-Chapelle (1748), which returned the country to Austria.

Maria Theresa reigned until 1765. Under her enlightened and popular governor, Charles of Lorraine, roads and waterways were built, agriculture modernised, and industry (notably coal and glass) encouraged. Maria Theresa's successor, Joseph II (died 1790), was well-meaning, but autocratic and impatient when faced by stubborn Belgian conservatism. He succeeded in getting rid of the Dutch Barrier Treaty garrisons, but his attempt to open the Scheldt simply by using it nearly led to war (the Dutch fired on his ships), and his plans for internal reforms—logical, humane, and modern though they were—merely aroused opposition and bitterness. This was particularly the case with the Edict of Toleration (1781), recognising religious freedom, and the proposals to modernise the country's antiquated administrative system. Encouraged by the revolution in France, there was a local uprising in 1789 which defeated the Austrians at Turnhout. Within weeks the whole country was in revolt (the Brabançon Revolt) and in January 1790 the United States of Belgium was declared. Two Belgian factions now faced one another: the democrats who wanted a revolutionary constitution, and the nobles, supported by the clergy and the majority of the country, who wanted no significant change. Anarchy followed failure to agree, and by the end of the year the Emperor (now Leopold II) subdued the country by force of arms. Wisely, Leopold dropped Joseph's reforms.

In 1792 war broke out between revolutionary France and Austria, the French general Dumouriez winning the battle of Jemappes near Tournai and occupying Belgium. His success was shortlived and a few months later (March 1793) the Austrians defeated him at Neerwinden (Landen). But Austrian days were numbered, and in June 1794 the French under Jourdan defeated them at Fleurus, Belgium again finding herself under French occupation.

Belgium annexed to France (1794 to 1814)

After a little over a year of military occupation Belgium was formally annexed as a part of revolutionary France (October 1795). The measures now pushed through, going far beyond anything proposed by Joseph II and ruthlessly enforced, did at least have the effect of transforming Belgium into a modern state. The Church, hitherto so powerful, was persecuted and its buildings everywhere despoiled; the national administration was centralised and rationalised; ancient privileges were abolished; conscription was introduced. All this was highly unpopular and led in October 1798 to the Peasants' Revolt, which was brutally suppressed. Under Napoleon (after 1799) the process continued, though in more constructive and acceptable form. A modern legal system (Code Napoléon) was established; metric systems were introduced; industry was encouraged and profited from the many markets available within the French empire; the Church and government became reconciled. Most important perhaps was the reopening of the Scheldt and the start of the revival of Antwerp; here Napoleon also boosted recovery by constructing the docks and naval harbour which he described as 'a pistol aimed at the heart of England'.

But despite all their improvements the French remained unpopular, and the occupation of the country by the Allies on Napoleon's fall in 1814 was welcomed with relief.

United Kingdom of the Netherlands (1815 to 1831)

The Allies' main objective in 1815 was to establish a deterrent to any future French northward expansion. Therefore, paying scant regard to the wishes of the people—with their differing customs, economic outlook, and religion—they amalgamated Belgium and Holland into the United Kingdom of the Netherlands under Prince William of Orange, who ascended the throne as William I. (At the same time the Allies established the Grand-Duchy of Luxembourg, with William as its first Grand-Duke.) William faced a near-impossible task, not made any easier by his obstinately pro-Dutch character. Nevertheless initially he was not unsuccessful; industry flourished, enjoying Dutch colonial markets, Antwerp prospered, and education advanced as new (lay) schools and universities were founded. But there was much the Belgians would not accept—equality of representation in the States General when Belgium's population was nearly double that of Holland; the wide authority assumed by a Protestant and foreign king; the insistence on Dutch as the official language—nor did the Church willingly adapt to the principle of religious liberty. By 1828 Belgium was approaching revolution, and William's continuing obstinacy and his suppression of the opposition press ensured that it broke out in 1830.

The Revolution. On 25 August Auber's opera 'La Muette de Portici' was played in Brussels, and on hearing the duet 'Amour sacré de la Patrie' the audience left the theatre and the flag of Brabant was hoisted. Similar revolts at once followed in the provinces, and the Belgians were defeated at Hasselt. William sent his elder son to Brussels to negotiate, then, when this failed, his second son Frederick, backed by troops. After some fighting Frederick withdrew, a provisional government was formed, and national independence proclaimed.

Kingdom of Belgium

On 20 January 1831 the London Conference recognised Belgium as an independent and 'perpetually neutral' state. The crown was accepted by Prince Leopold of Saxe-Coburg.

Leopold (1790–1865) was a son of the Duke of Saxe-Coburg-Saalfeld and uncle of Queen Victoria, over whom he long exercised a strong influence. As a youth he saw service in the Russian army, and later he fought in the campaigns of

1813–14, after Napoleon's fall entering Paris with the Allied leaders. In 1816 he married Charlotte, only child of the Prince Regent and heiress presumptive to the British throne; she died in childbirth the following year. In 1830 he was offered but declined the throne of Greece. His second marriage (1832) was to Louise-Marie, daughter of King Louis-Philippe of the French. Their daughter, Charlotte, married Maximilian (of Austria), who became Emperor of Mexico where he was shot by rebels in 1867.

The Dutch did not easily give way. William invaded within days of Leopold's taking the oath, only retreating when faced by French troops who arrived in response to an appeal by the latter. William next refused to accept the Twenty-Four Articles, setting out the terms of the separation of two countries, and held on in the citadel of Antwerp, which he only evacuated after assault by the French and a blockade of the Dutch ports. Only in 1839 did William finally accept defeat, the independence and neutrality of Belgium now being guaranteed by the Treaty of London (later to become historic as the 'scrap of paper'), signed by Austria, Great Britain, Prussia, France, and Russia. (See also p 392 regarding the territorial adjustments with the Grand-Duchy of Luxembourg under this treaty.)

The new Belgian constitution ensured maximum rights for the people, the King receiving only minor executive powers. Thanks to this, and to a king who was both cultured and wise, Belgium made great economic progress, keeping clear of the general European revolutionary disturbances of 1848. In 1865 Leopold I was succeeded by his son, Leopold II. A man of strong personality and considerable business acumen, he successfully steered neutral Belgium through the hazards of the Franco-Prussian war (1870) and did much to foster the growth of commerce and transport. Politically the reign saw the official recognition of the Flemish language, with the founding (1886) of the Flemish Academy and the passing of a law (1898) establishing Flemish equality with French. In 1893 universal suffrage was introduced, though with qualifications.

Belgian Congo. Leopold II had always been interested in colonial possibilities, in particular in the Congo. In 1878 he formed the Comité des Etudes du Haut Congo, this developing into the International Association of the Congo, and the following year, at Leopold's instigation, H.M. Stanley opened trading stations and made agreements with the chiefs. In 1884–85 the powers recognised the International (but effectively Belgian) Association as an independent state, the Belgian government at the same time authorising Leopold to be sovereign but also declaring that the link between Belgium and the Congo was 'exclusively personal'. The venture brought Leopold great wealth, especially from the Domaine de la Couronne, a vast territory treated as the King's personal property. In 1890, in return for financial investment, the Belgian government was given the right of annexation, a right which it exercised in 1908 under the pressure of serious international charges of gross maladministration (seizure of native land, monopolistic exploitation, and even atrocities). The territory was granted independence in 1962.

Leopold II died in 1909, being succeeded by his nephew Albert, the main event of whose reign was the First World War.

First World War (1914 to 1918)

Opening Phase. In July 1914, with war imminent, the British government formally drew the attention of France and Germany to the neutrality of Belgium guaranteed under the Treaty of London of 1839. Dismissing the treaty as a 'scrap of paper', Germany demanded that Belgium allow her troops free passage. Belgium refused on 3 August and that night Germany invaded, the first units crossing the frontier near Malmédy. Under the undaunted leadership of their King Belgian resistance was stubborn and heroic, though they could hardly hope to hold the German army. Liège fell on 9 August opening the way to German columns to pour across the plains of Limburg and Brabant. Between 20 and 23 August the French were defeated near Charleroi and the British at Mons, both then falling back into France. Namur, Louvain, and Brussels fell by the end of the month, by which time the Germans were in occupation of most of central and southern Belgium. Antwerp had to surrender on 9 October, after which the Belgian army retreated through Flanders. By 15 October an Allied line had been established along the Yser, where the Belgians opened the sluices, creating a vast lake between Nieuwpoort and Diksmuide. In November the Germans took Diksmuide, but this was the limit of their advance and they transferred their main effort towards Ypres, where, despite vast superiority, they were unable to break through the small British army. Both sides dug in and for some three years there was trench warfare from Nieuwpoort to the French frontier on the Lys, and thence to Switzerland. In the small strip of their country still free the Belgians established their headquarters at Veurne, while the King made nearby De Panne his 'capital'.

German Occupation. The many memorials throughout Belgium are testimony enough to the ruthlessness of the enemy and the stubborn heroism of the Belgian people. Among their leaders were men such as Cardinal Mercier, whose pastoral letter 'Patriotism and Endurance' protested against German excesses and defined what should be the people's attitude towards the invader; and the indomitable Burgomaster Adolphe Max of Brussels who defied the German governor and was deported.

The occupation was administered by German governors, and among the many repressive measures were the merging of executive and judicial powers; the edict that the family was responsible for the actions of its individuals; general property confiscation; mass labour deportation to Germany and the front. German efforts to exploit the differences between Flemings and Walloons met with little success. In the economic field the occupation was disastrous; raw materials were seized, exports ceased, and Belgian factories were stripped of everything which could be of use in Germany. Despite all this, thousands of Belgians escaped and throughout the war the army kept an average strength of 150,000.

Closing Phase. The tide began to turn in June 1917 when British and Commonwealth troops took the ridge at Mesen, 9km S of Ypres, though this was followed by the bloody and inconclusive Third Battle of Ypres which ended in the mud of Passchendaele. In March 1918, with troops freed by the collapse of Russia, the Germans launched their last and nearly successful offensive, but by June American troops and British reinforcements were pouring into France. The Belgian army took Diksmuide in September and by October had liberated West Flanders. On 11 November, Armistice Day, the Canadians had entered Mons while the Belgians had reached beyond Ghent.

Between the Wars (1919 to 1940)

By the Treaty of Versailles Belgium was granted reparations and gained from Germany the eastern territories of Moresnet, Eupen, and Malmédy. The neutrality which had proved so valueless was abolished and Belgium thus became free to make her own defensive alliances, in 1920 concluding a military convention with France.

Unqualified universal suffrage was introduced soon after the war's end. One effect of this was to sharpen the Flemish question, and in 1921 Flemish was made the official language of that part of the country. The same year also saw the signing of a customs, consular, and railway union with the Grand-Duchy of Luxembourg.

1929–31. Like other countries Belgium's economic foundations and political institutions were badly shaken by the Depression, and foreign trade, the country's main livelihood, virtually disappeared.

In 1934 King Albert, the much-loved and respected 'Soldier King', was killed in a climbing accident. He was succeeded by his son, Leopold III, whose reign started with tragedy when the following year his Queen, Astrid of Sweden, was killed in a motor accident while Leopold was driving.

The years 1933–39 were the run-up years to the Second World War. The Nazis supported the Belgian fascists, the Rexists, and in 1936, when Germany militarily reoccupied the Rhineland, Leopold, announcing that Belgium's policy was once again one of strict neutrality, renounced all agreements on military aid.

Second World War (1939 to 1945)

Opening Phase. Belgium's reiterated but fragile neutrality lasted only eight months, during which period, despite evidence of German intentions, she refused British and French requests that she should accept their troops or at least hold staff talks. Early on 10 May 1940 Germany attacked Belgium and Holland, in Belgium sweeping past the Liège forts, taking bridges over the Albert Canal, and destroying the 'impregnable' Meuse fort of Eben-Emael. As the Belgians retired to their main line of defence between Louvain and Antwerp, the British and French moved in, the British reinforcing positions between Wavre and Louvain while the French advanced to the line Huy-Tienen. By 13–14 May the French collapsed at Sedan (France), leaving the way open to the sea which the Germans reached near Abbeville by 20 May. Meanwhile in Belgium, despite meeting stubborn resistance, the Germans pressed inexorably forward, superbly prepared and equipped and enjoying an air superiority which they used as ruthlessly against military targets as against the streams of refugees now clogging the roads. Louvain, Brussels, and Antwerp all fell and the Allies faced the danger of being surrounded and cut off from the sea by a German pincer movement from Abbeville in the S and Antwerp in the north. An attempt was made to break out of the trap by an offensive against the still thin German line between Sedan and Abbeville, but when this failed a retreat to the coast was the only course open.

It was agreed with King Leopold that his army would cover this retreat. But the enemy broke through the Belgian line either side of Kortrijk and on 28 May Leopold surrendered—an action which only history can judge but which was inevitably contrasted with the behaviour of his father in 1914. The immediate practical result was the disappearance of the Allies' northern flank. The British commander (Gort) at once established his final perimeter on the line Gravelines–Bergues–Veurne–Nieuwpoort in preparation for evacuation, and, after a stand by the British between Ypres and Comines and by an isolated French group near Lille, all the British divisions and many of the French were within this perimeter by 30 May. By 4 June the evacuation from the beaches between Dunkirk in France and De Panne in Belgium had been achieved. The Belgian government escaped first to France and then to England, but the King, considering himself a prisoner-of-war, refused to desert his army.

German Occupation followed substantially the same pattern as that of the First World War, though this time not even a corner of Belgium remained free, nor was it possible to escape over the border into Holland. Resistance again was often heroic, despite such added Nazi refinements as anti-semitism, concentration camps, and the Gestapo. The King, a prisoner in his Brussels palace of Laeken, did what he could to help his people, even meeting Hitler at Berchtesgaden and negotiating the return of 50,000 prisoners and some improvement in the allocation of food supplies to Belgium. In 1941 he married Lilian Baels, a commoner who received the title of Princesse de Réthy, and on 7 June 1944 he and his family were deported to Germany.

Closing Phase. The invasion of France started on 6 June 1944 and by the end of August the Allies were on the Belgian and German borders. The liberation of Belgium began at the beginning of September, the forces in the N being largely British and Canadian (under Montgomery), those in the S American (under Bradley). In the N, Brussels was reached on 3 September, followed swiftly by Ghent, Ostend, Bruges, and Antwerp. In the S the Americans freed Charleroi, Mons, and Namur on 3 September and, by 10 September, Liège and Luxembourg. By the end of the month the Canadians had forced the enemy back into the Breskens corner at the mouth of the Scheldt, while E of Antwerp the British crossed the Antwerp–Turnhout canal. Soon Belgium was free of the enemy, the front line running along the German frontier from Aachen to Wasserbillig in the Grand-Duchy of Luxembourg at the confluence of the Sûre and Moselle. The Allies now paused to regroup, the plan being to strike into Germany through Aachen in the N and through Alsace in the south. This, though, left the centre very thin, a weakness Hitler was not slow to exploit, on 16 December launching his counter-offensive under Von Rundstedt. For this Battle of the Ardennes (or Battle of the Bulge), see p 301. By the end of January 1945 the Germans were again behind their frontier.

After the Second World War

When the Allies invaded France in June 1944, King Leopold was deported with his family first to Germany and then to Austria. Although freed in May 1945 the King (who soon moved to Switzerland) found that he could not return to Belgium, so high ran feeling about his surrender and, less justifiably, about his relations with the Germans and even about his second marriage. His brother Prince Charles was therefore appointed regent. When in 1950 a referendum on whether he should retain the throne gave Leopold only just over 57 per cent he abdicated in favour of his son Baudouin who ascended the throne in 1951 (see also Royal Family, p 415).

Important post-war events have been the formation of the Benelux Union with Holland and Luxembourg (actually signed in London in 1944 by the governments in exile); the granting of independence to the Congo in 1962; the formal establishment of the 'Language Frontier' in 1962; the growth of Brussels (as home of the EEC, NATO, and other international concerns) into being the 'capital' of Europe;

and the continuing and widening tension between the Flemings and the Walloons, culminating in 1980 with the formal change from a centralised constitution to a federal one.

Religious Houses and Begijnhofs

The founding of Religious Houses (abbeys, monasteries, convents, etc.) and Begijnhofs—the former throughout Belgium, the latter mainly in the North—forms a part of the pattern of Belgium's history. Both represent the urge, often on the part of members of noble families and dating from the early Middle Ages, to proclaim the Faith in visible and practical terms. Genuine piousness apart, individual motives were various, e.g. thanks for the granting of some prayer, to mark some miracle or great event, or even simply as a form of religious insurance.

Religious Houses. In the early years of Christianity there were lone hermits, first in the deserts of the East, then in western Europe. Gradually these holy men banded into communities, compelled by the demands of survival to clear the forest, practise primitive drainage and irrigation, and to become, in fact, the pioneers of Belgian agriculture up to about the time of Charlemagne. These monks were also the only literate people in the land, this automatically bringing power and influence as advisers, teachers, and administrators. Abbeys and their rich revenues soon became the reward, not only for genuinely pious monks but increasingly for court favourites who treated them as comfortable and lucrative sinecures. The Norse raids of the 9C and 10C helped to foster the growth of defensive feudalism, many religious houses in the process becoming secular feudal estates. Canons' Chapters, also developing at this period, were communities (or colleges, hence collegiate churches) of priests rather than monks; while not fully feudal, the chapters did enjoy important local rights.

The 10C, however, also saw the start of the monastic age proper, impetus being given by the Lateran Synod of 1059 which urged the clergy to live together as communities. The movement reached its peak in the 12C, flourishing in the 13–14C and exercising a considerable influence on Netherlands social, commercial, and artistic life. The religious houses, both directly and by example, taught the peasants the techniques of agriculture; they functioned as shrewd and vigorous commercial concerns; they worked the mines, developed forges, and became skilled in metalwork; and, through their orders for church furnishings, they were practical patrons of the arts. Many of the monks, too, were artists of genius, responsible for delicate illuminated manuscripts, metalwork, painting, and sculpture. But the wars and violent dissensions which for so long plagued Belgium did not spare the religious houses, and some survive now only as medieval ruins. Of the buildings in use today, whether for religious or other purposes, the majority are of the 17–19C, this being due not only to earlier destruction but also to the worldly and wealthy abbots of the period. The houses were disestablished and their treasures scattered at the French Revolution. During the 19C many of the great abbey churches were reconsecrated, serving then as now as parish and other churches, often still loosely called 'abbey' although the abbey as such may have long since disappeared. Several abbeys did, however, start up again, and new ones have been founded, Belgium today thus still having many flourishing houses.

Augustinians is the name given to various orders which follow the 'Rule of St. Augustine'. In fact St. Augustine (354–430), a Roman of North Africa and Bishop of Hippo, and not to be confused with the later saint who brought Christianity to England, laid down no rule as such, but left practical advice in letters and sermons, this providing the earliest guidelines for community religious life and later formulated into a 'rule'. Among Augustinian orders are Augustinian Canons (or Austin Friars, or Canons Regular); Augustinian Hermits (Black Friars), and Premonstratensians (see below).—**Benedictines** (Black Monks) follow the rule of St. Benedict (c 480–c 543). Born in Umbria (Italy) he established no fewer than 12 monasteries in the district around Subiaco, S of Rome. Perhaps his most famous foundation was the monastery of Monte Cassino, between Rome and Naples, from where his rule spread. The rule was not one of great austerity. One feature is that there is no real overall authority, each monastery being independent and monks belonging to their monastery rather than to an order; another is that the day is divided into fixed periods allotted to worship, labour, and study. Education has long been an important Benedictine activity. St. Benedict's sister, Scholastica, is regarded as the patroness of Benedictine nuns.—**Capuchins** are an offshoot of the Franciscans, originating in c 1520 when the monk Matteo di Bassi became convinced that the Franciscan habit was not truly similar to that worn by St. Francis and designed himself a pointed hood (capuce). In 1619 the Capuchins were officially granted the status of an independent order.—**Carmelites** originated by tradition as a Jewish order in pre-Christian times but historically in the 12C when a Crusader from Calabria and ten companions established themselves as hermits on Mount Carmel. In 1220 the Order moved to Cyprus, and thence to Sicily, France and elsewhere. The Order changed from hermit to mendicant in 1247, but in 1562 St. Theresa and St. John of the Cross founded houses which returned to the original austere and contemplative rule, their adherents becoming known as the Discalced Carmelites because, unlike the others (the Calced), they went either barefoot or simply with sandals. This split survives today.—**Carthusians** are an order founded by St. Bruno in 1084 at the then desolate spot in France called Chartreuse where Bruno and some companions began to lead a life as hermits. Bruno later founded other monasteries and the Carthusian rule has survived virtually unchanged to the present day. When after the French Revolution the Order was able to return to Chartreuse, practical problems such as the need to pay rent led to the invention and marketing of the now famous liqueur.—**Cistercians** (Grey, or White Monks) were originally Benedictines, but in 1098 the monk Robert of Molesmes, dissatisfied with what he felt to be the laxness of Benedictine life, migrated with twenty followers to Cîteaux, near Dijon, where the Count of Burgundy provided a monastery. In 1112 the energetic and popular St. Bernard (1090–1153) joined the community, infusing it with new life. When he died there were 280 Cistercian houses; by the end of the century over 500, and the Order enjoyed great influence. The Cistercian rule was a strict adherence to those originally offered by St. Benedict, a main feature being emphasis on manual work. As a result the Cistercians became renowned as farmers, in Belgium building large farms and granges and being responsible for much of the country's early land clearance. A feature of this labour-intensive way of life was the large numbers of lay-brothers.—**Dominicans** (Friars Preachers) belong to the Order founded by St. Dominic (1170–1221) in 1216 at Toulouse; this started from a group of followers who accompanied St. Dominic while he was preaching to the heretical Albigenses. St. Dominic always travelled in poverty and simplicity, and, from this example, the Order adopted an austere discipline in which the rule of poverty extended beyond the individual friars to the monasteries themselves. The Order was thus mendicant until the rules were relaxed in the second half of the 15C. Dominican influence soon became, and remained, virtually worldwide, university theological teaching being one of the Order's main activities. Dominican nuns specialise in teaching, nursing, and missionary work.—**Franciscans** (Friars Minor. Fr.: *Frères Mineurs*. Flem.: *Minderbroeders*) are members of the Order founded in Assisi in 1209 by St. Francis (1181–1226). Devoted to absolute poverty and the service of the poor and the sick, the movement spread fast, eventually, in spite of frequent internal divisions, becoming worldwide and the most numerous of all the religious orders. Although a mendicant order, the rule was that begging was only permitted if bread could not be earned by work. The Franciscan nuns are the

Poor Clares (Flem.: *Grauwe Zusters*, Grey Sisters), named for their founder St. Clare, also of Assisi, where St. Francis received her vows in 1212.—**Jesuits**are members of the Society of Jesus, founded in Spain in 1540 by Ignatius Loyola. The spiritual background is purification from worldly standards and identification of the individual mind with God. The Society has always been concerned with preaching, missionary, charitable, and above all educational work. It has produced many scholars and scientists. With its unswerving and often ruthless Catholic attitudes, the Society was encouraged to go to the Netherlands by Philip II, there playing its part in sparking the Revolt of the Netherlands; later its influence became predominant when the 'archdukes' were profiting by the Twelve Years Truce (1609–21) to consolidate Catholicism in the Spanish Netherlands. Suppressed in 1773 on a number of grounds, but mainly because it had become too powerful, the Society was restored in 1814.—**Premonstratensians**, or **Norbertines**, are not monks, but an order of Augustinian Canons (see above), founded in 1120 by St. Norbert at Prémontré in northern France, his aim being to establish a strict form of canonical life. Although following the Rule of St. Augustine, the Order added conditions designed to ensure a much greater austerity. Today the main Premonstratensian abbey is in Belgium at Tongerlo.—**Trappists** are closely associated with the Cistercians and since 1892 have officially been called the Reformed Cistercians. In 1664 the abbot of La Trappe in Normandy, Armand de Rancé, initiated a reform which involved a way of life far stricter than the Cistercian and even included various vows of silence. The Order did not spread far and the community was dispersed at the French Revolution. However, twenty monks settled in Switzerland, and from here houses were founded in Belgium, England, Italy, Spain, and Canada. La Trappe itself reopened in 1817, and in 1898 the Trappists recovered Cîteaux, the mother-house (1098) of the Cistercians. There are now Trappist houses, including some nunneries, in many parts of the world, those in Belgium being known for their beer.—**Trinitarians**, following an austere version of the Augustinian rule, date from the founding of a movement in 1198 which sought the release of Christian slaves held by the Moors and the Saracens, if necessary by the offering of oneself in substitute. Over the centuries many thousands of slaves have owed their freedom to the Order.

Begijnhofs (Béguinages) were self-contained lay sisterhoods devoting themselves largely to charitable work. The word may derive from St. Begga, daughter of Pepin of Landen, but more probably comes from a Liège priest, Lambert le Bègue (died 1187), whose activities in caring for the bereaved families of Crusaders led him to encourage associations of widows and other women who while enjoying the refuge and companionship of pious community life were not bound by vows. Lambert is thought to have founded the first such community at Liège in c 1189, and the countesses Margaret and Joanna, daughters of Baldwin I of Constantinople, founded others a few years later. The movement soon spread around Europe, notably in the Rhineland, but later, as it came under the influence of the various religious orders, fell into disrepute and in Protestant countries was suppressed at the Reformation. The movement continued however to flourish in the Netherlands where most towns of any importance had a begijnhof and it is virtually only in Flemish Belgium that begijnhofs survive today.

Architecturally two main types developed, one being a 'village' of small streets (e.g. Lier, Louvain), the other surrounding a court or field (e.g. Bruges, Ghent). There was always a church, other important buildings being the infirmary and the weaving centre; although there were community rooms, most of the women lived in little, individual houses. Although some begijnhofs are still occupied by religious and charitable communities, most today serve other purposes, e.g. almshouses, municipal homes, or, as at Louvain, university residences. With their quaint streets and little houses, normally quiet oases within busy towns, the better preserved begijnhofs well merit a visit. In many cases houses have been preserved as museums of begijnhof life.

ART IN BELGIUM

By *Joanna Woodall*, Courtauld Institute of Art

Note: Belgium's wealth of paintings and sculpture, from about the 12C to modern times, can be seen throughout the country, though mainly in the North, in numerous churches, museums and galleries. A special index lists most of the artists, including architects, page references showing where their works are mentioned in the text.

Art to the end of the 7C: Palaeolithic to Merovingian.

Until about the end of the 7C Belgium largely shares her history and her art with much of the rest of northern Europe. Artefacts from the Palaeolithic to the Carolingian period are displayed in the Musée d'Art et d'Histoire in Brussels, while surviving monuments include the ancient Pierre Brunehault standing-stone near Tournai, the Roman-wall at Tongeren and the Merovingian chapel in the Collégiale Ste. Gertrude at Nivelles, a product of the great monastic building programme initiated after the conversion of Clovis to Christianity in the 6C.

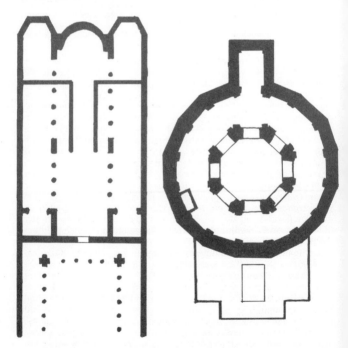

Plans of (left) a typical basilican church and (right) a centralised or circular church.

Architecture, 8–13C: Carolingian and Romanesque.

After the Emperor Charlemagne established his court at Aachen, Belgium, and especially the Meuse region, acquired greater importance as 'the outskirts of the capital of the Empire'. The major architectural innovation of the period, the centralised or circular church plan, is epitomised by the Palatine chapel at Aachen, but its many Belgian derivations are now known only through excavations. Although all that can be seen today is a re-erected fragment, excavations during the 1950s revealed that the plan of St. Donatian at Bruges was inspired by the circular chapel at Aachen. The traditional basilican or hall church with aisles and apse, which had been used from ancient Christian times, also underwent radical changes during the Carolingian period. The church of St. Ursmer at Lobbes is a surviving example of this type of church which in part probably dates from this time.

The Treaty of Verdun (843) divided present-day Belgium politically and culturally at the river Scheldt. Two distinct Romanesque styles emerged: the 'Scaldian style' (from the river Scheldt) to the west, and the 'Mosan style' (from the Meuse) to the east. Since the Meuse region soon came to form part of the Ottonian Empire it is not surprising that Mosan architecture, which centred on Liège and Maastricht (Holland), represents a natural development of Carolingian traditions and is closely connected to contemporary Rhenish architecture. The style is characterised, both in construction and decoration, by simplicity, austerity and strength. Although much altered and restored, the church of St. Gertrude at Nivelles remains the most striking example of the Mosan basilica. The rural churches of St. Hadelin at Celles and Notre-Dame d'Hastière-par-Delà typify the style, with their fortress-like west ends (called *westwork*), characteristic square piers with imposts but no bases, low transepts, flat timberwork ceilings and crypts. The centralised plan also survived, and, although no example is fully extant, the rebuilt church of St. Jean in Liège reflects an original Romanesque rotunda.

French control of the valley of the Scheldt meant that Scaldian Romanesque, although ultimately deriving from Carolingian precedents, was related to Norman (and consequently sometimes English) developments. On the whole, the Scaldian style is more elaborate than the Mosan, paving the way for the Gothic (the pointed arches in the Scaldian church of St. Brice in Tournai are among the first in Belgium). Indeed, while the Mosan style was established in the 11C, the Scaldian did not blossom until the 12th. The oldest surviving monument of the style is probably the church of St. Vincent at Soignies (?11C) but its apotheosis is Tournai cathedral (nave 12C), which has been called 'the cradle of Scaldian Gothic art'. Towers above the crossing are characteristic of the style—Tournai has five, but there is usually only one. The nave is often multi-storeyed with complex piers and sometimes alternating supports. Outside, the decoration may become more ornate towards the top, and any *westwerk* is, in contrast to the Mosan practice, pierced by an entrance.

The earliest surviving secular architecture dates from this period—notably the early 13C Koornstapelhuis on the Graslei in Ghent, and parts of the Steen and Gravensteen in Antwerp and Ghent respectively.

Architecture, 13–16C: Gothic

Architecture during this period reveals a gradually increasing tendency towards local interpretations and variations of what were originally northern French innovations. These innovations, such as pointed arches, flying buttresses and lofty piers, have little significance on their own, but they are indicative of a new aspiration to create buildings which minimise their own weight and mass, emphasising rather light and space. In Belgium the result was a number of remarkable achievements in both ecclesiastic and secular architecture which reflect the growing wealth and municipal and regional consciousness of the area. The Belgians were understandably reluctant to abandon this rich and splendid style and it lasted well into the 16C.

Ecclesiastic Building

The first Gothic churches are basically French buildings transplanted onto Flemish soil. Gothic forms were soon incorporated at Tournai (cathedral choir 1243–55) and monks, especially Cistercians, favoured a simple, severe Gothic (e.g. the ruined abbey church of Villers-la-Ville). Regional variations became established during the 13C and three broad distinctions are discernable: Scaldian, Mosan, and Brabantine. The two former obviously derive from previous stylistic divisions. Features of Scheldt Gothic, which flourished mainly in the 13C, include foliated capitals, called 'Tournai capitals', polygonal apses, crossing towers flanked by four small stair towers, and chapels placed obliquely between transepts and choir. St. Niklaas, Ghent and Onze Lieve Vrouw, Oudenaarde, are outstanding. Churches of the Meuse region, of which Notre-Dame at Huy is quite typical, often have rectilinear apses. Columns tend to be cylindrical at the bottom but polygonal at the top, with banded decoration, and there is often a high gallery above the triforium.

During the 14C Brabantine Gothic gradually became pre-eminent. Louvain was the first major centre, with a number of important buildings (especially the Groot Begijnhof, in part 14C, and St. Pieter of 1425). Subsequently the Brabantine Gothic spread throughout the Scheldt valley and it can be broadly equated with the late Gothic or 'Flamboyant' style. The cathedrals of Brussels, Mechelen, Ghent and Antwerp are all, in part at least, interpretations of this Brabantine theme. Splendid western towers epitomise the aims and achievements of ecclesiastical Gothic in Belgium.

Secular Building

Towers are also characteristic of secular architecture of which 'no other country possesses as rich a heritage...from such an early date' (Yarwood, 'Architecture in Europe'). The wealth of such architecture can be directly related to the rise of towns and the increasing influence of their merchant citizens. Civic pride was expressed in the building of elaborate town halls, market and cloth halls and belfries. The earliest surviving buildings come from the Scheldt valley where the cloth halls at Ypres and Bruges date originally from the 13C (Ypres is largely rebuilt, but to the original design). Both these buildings incorporate central belfries, crenelated wings and small corner turrets—features which reappear again and again. A series of superb 15th and 16C town halls bear witness to the sheer exuberance of Belgian secular architecture by this time. The grandeur of Brussels, though somewhat restored, testifies to the growing importance of the city; Louvain is as ornate as a church reliquary, while Oudenaarde (early 16C) is more typical. The stepped gabling which we have seen even in the Romanesque period is characteristic of some guild-halls, such as the Groot Vleeshuis in Ghent (1408) and the Vleeshuis in Antwerp, and private houses, many of which survive in Bruges.

Architecture: 16C

16C architecture in Belgium is characterised by a strange marriage between superficial innovation and a deep underlying conservatism. The style of building which had been developed and enriched in Brabant during the previous two centuries (e.g. the Stadhuis, Louvain, and the church of Notre-Dame du Sablon, Brussels) was both successful and highly popular. During a period when government by foreigners was relatively new and felt by some to be oppressive, this indigenous style was not likely to be discarded lightly. At the same time, however, Habsburg rule meant that the Netherlands were, as never before, at the hub of international trade and politics. As a consequence, the region was open to external artistic influences to an unprecedented degree at precisely the time when Italian art was becoming established as the acme of creative achievement. Patrons anxious to be in the forefront of fashion demanded Italianising buildings and architects were quick to respond by introducing Renaissance motifs, easily accessible by means of engravings. As early as 1515 the decoration of the traditional triumphal arches erected for Charles V's solemn entry into Bruges included classically inspired grotesques and medallions.

But men brought up in the absence of any real classical architecture were understandably slower to assimilate the basic principles of Renaissance proportion and some of their buildings have consequently been described as 'Gothic in fancy dress'. A number of palaces built or renovated during the first half of the 16C, such as Margaret of Austria's residence at Mechelen, the palace of the Prince-Bishops at Liège and Cardinal Granvelle's magnificent palace in Brussels (now destroyed) represent variations on the fertile theme of an amalgamation of contemporary Italian with traditional, native elements. Knowledge of Renaissance architecture increased as the century progressed: visits to Italy by young artists became commonplace and books and engravings of Italian architecture became more accurate and more readily available. *Cornelis Floris*'s Stadhuis at Antwerp (1561–66) reveals a sophisticated understanding of Italian principles combined with a conscious determination, interesting in the context of Antwerp's resistance to Philip II, to retain traditional characteristics.

Antwerp Stadhuis (1551–66), designed by Cornelis Floris and combining Flemish traditional and Italian Renaissance influences with its emphatically vertical belfry incorporated in a classically-inspired façade

Architecture: 17C

The penchant for traditional structures thinly masked by innovative decoration survived into the 17C. The main developments occurred in ecclesiastical architecture and they should be seen in the context of a counter-reformation promoted by the Spanish 'archdukes' and the Jesuits. St. Carolus Borromeüs, the former Jesuit church of Antwerp (begun 1615, designed by the Jesuit *Pieter Huyssens*), has been described as the first Baroque church in Belgium. The impressive bell-tower, which was built slightly later, the façade and the interior, decorated by *Rubens*, certainly gave the church a rich Baroque flavour, but the destruction of Rubens's work in 1718 revealed that the basic plan remained entirely traditional: a nave with two aisles but no transept. The architect did not consider spatial organisation, in addition to decoration, to be integral to a truly Baroque effect. Huyssens and his contemporaries *Jacob Franckaert* and *Wenceslas Coeberger* designed a number of such 'semi-Baroque' churches during the first half of the century. They are often attractive and interesting in their varied solutions to the problem of reconciling tradition with fashion. Coeberger's church of Scherpenheuvel, NW of Louvain, is a brave attempt at a centralised plan and Franckaert's façade architecture, as for example in the Begijnhof church in Mechelen, is lively and progressive. However, the outstanding example of a more integrated, although still characteristically Belgian Baroque is the church of St. Pieter in Ghent, where the unknown designer has made exciting use of light and space.

The two principal figures of the second half of the century were the Jesuit *Willem Hessius* and *Luc Fayd'herbe*. The former's church of St. Michiel in Louvain (begun in 1650), together with the Abbey Church of St. Servaas in Grimbergen, illustrate the continuing tendency to produce charming but skin-deep Baroque, while the latter's church of Onze Lieve Vrouw van Hanswijk in Mechelen (begun 1663) mistakes the bizarre for the Baroque.

In secular architecture Baroque ornamentation (often very fine) was generally applied to traditional forms. Rubens's house, although restored, can be fitted into this pattern, while Jordaens's house, also in Antwerp, is somewhat more daring. Even at the very end of the century the guild houses of the Grand-Place in Brussels, rebuilt after the bombardment of 1695, retain their traditional high and narrow format. This was partly, admittedly, for reasons of space, but opportunities for innovation in the composition of the façade, as opposed to its ornamentation, were rarely taken.

Architecture: 18C

The 18C, although a period of stylistic variety, reveals as a whole a gradual weakening of native architectural traditions in the face of foreign influences. The transfer of control of the provinces from the Spanish to the Austrian Habsburgs was significant in this process. The date 1700 for the church of the Minimes in Brussels, where, for the first time, characteristically Belgian features are replaced by an international Baroque, seems almost symbolic. But, by contrast with the 17C, the major examples of 18C Baroque in Belgium occur in secular building. There was an important difference between the restrained, elegant style of the Meuse districts (e.g. *J.A. Anneessens*'s wing for the Palace of The Prince-Bishops at Liège), where French influence was skilfully blended with local tradition, and the more flamboyant, partly Austrian-inspired Baroque of Flanders. The latter was practised in Antwerp by *J.P. Baurscheit the Younger* and in Ghent by *Bernard de Wilde* (the Hôtel Falignan) and *David 't Kindt*, although these two soon incorporate lighter 'Rococo' elements into their façades.

Namur Cathedral, begun in 1751, is another landmark in the internationalisation of architecture in the southern Netherlands. Designed by the Milanese *Gaetano Pizzoni*, who was, significantly, commissioned through the Court at Vienna, the design is completely Italian and a hint of classicism, that international style *par excellence*, is evident in the still basically Baroque interior.

Laurent Benoit Dewez (1731–1812), who had received an international training and was the chief architect to the governor, Charles of Lorraine, from 1766–82, was primarily responsible for the establishment of classicism. His château at Seneffe of c 1760, reminiscent of an 18C English country house, is a remarkable achievement. The urban development of Brussels towards the end of the century provided great opportunities for the practitioners of classicism, and the Place des Martyrs (1775, by *Claude Fisco*), the Place and Parc Royale (begun 1775, designed by *BarnabéGuimard*), and the Palais de la Nation (Guimard) are important products of this originally French style.

CASTLES AND CHÂTEAUX, are found all over Belgium. From feudal times on defence was a powerful building motive, at one end of the scale being great fortresses, serving only secondarily as the homes of their owners, and at the other private manors and farms, used primarily as homes but at the same time fortified in case of trouble. The oldest and most impressive of the great castles is that of the counts of Flanders at Ghent, fragments of which date back to the 9C. Solre-sur-Sambre and Spontin are examples of fortified manors, and fortified farms (château-ferme), many of them most attractive, will be found in many districts, notably in Namur. For the most part the true fortresses of the past survive only as romantic ruins, or as later restorations or rebuildings, often massively impressive. In the 16C, warfare changed and the defensive requirement gave way to the aristocratic urge for palatial, comfortable, and elegantly furnished homes; castles became châteaux, these being either new buildings or adaptations of the old around the defensive moat and keep (donjon). A distinctive Belgian style developed; one of mixed brick and stone, of towers of all shapes and sizes, with pepper-pot turrets and often a bulbous crown. This style lasted through until the 18C, and despite the French, Baroque, and Neo-Classical influences which then appeared, it remains the basic style of most of the châteaux seen today.

Painting to the end of the 15C

Flemish painting during this period is overwhelmingly religious in content. The development of landscape can, however, be traced in the backgrounds of many works, andwduring the 15C portraiture became increasingly important. In this century Flemish painting as a whole is characterised by technical excellence, a coherent vision and a wonderfully rich pictorial language. The very nature of these qualities implies that *Jan* and *Hubert van Eyck*, the first 'personalities' in the history of Flemish painting, could not have emerged from an artistic void. Their background is, however, international and knowledge of their antecedents in Belgium is limited, largely because long critical neglect and Belgium's turbulent history and damp climate have dealt harshly with early Flemish painting. Surviving pre-Eyckian work bears witness to the close links between Flanders and the courts of northern France at Paris and Dijon. Outstanding examples of early fresco painting are preserved in the Bijloke Museum in Ghent. The Calvary of the Tanners in the Bruges Cathedral Museum is a rare instance of a 14C panel painting remaining in Belgium.

The true ancestors of the Van Eycks seem, however, to have been the miniature painters—at least the bulk of our evidence about the Flemish pictorial tradition before the 15C comes from this type of work. Masterpieces such as *Jacquemart de Hesdin*'s Très Belles Heures du Duc de Berry in the Bibliothèque Royale, Brussels, well repay study. It is worth remembering that the Van Eycks almost certainly originated from the Limburg region in eastern Belgium, which gave its name to the brothers who produced the famous Très Riches Heures at Chantilly.

Jan van Eyck's life is relatively well documented—he was employed by John of Bavaria at The Hague in the early 1420s and by Philip of Burgundy from 1425. From 1430 until his death in 1441 he lived mostly in Bruges where some of his works can still be seen. He signed a number of paintings, an apparently unusual step which may have been prompted by his immediate fame. Hubert is known primarily from an inscription on the back of the brothers' most famous painting, the Adoration of the Mystic Lamb in Ghent Cathedral. The precise contribution of each brother and the meaning of these panels are subjects of endless debate. 15C Flemish painters certainly employed 'disguised symbolism'—the deliberate concealing of usually religious meaning within apparently ordinary elements of the painting—but the extent and nature of the symbolism is hotly debated. The Van Eycks perfected a complex technique of oil painting which still retains its brilliant, transparent effect. Their style is notable for its minute and convincing articulation of surface and space by means of colour and light.

Friedländer has said that 'in the 15C the painter worked modestly, in the spirit of the craftsman, but the artist of genius by his very nature—though not as his aim—produced personal and individual achievements'. Hence we have the apparent paradox of a few individuals standing out against a large crowd of anonymous imitators whose often high quality works can be seen throughout Belgium. They were concerned not with originality but with making a living and they were confirmed in this attitude by the conservatism of most patrons. Among the outstanding figures was the *Master of Flémalle* (probably Robert Campin of Tournai, died 1444), whose work combines intense realism with a concern for decorative values. His influence was widespread, and there are two works attributed to him in the Brussels Fine Arts Museum, but none of his greatest masterpieces remains in Belgium. The brilliant *Roger van der Weyden* (died 1464), who worked in Tournai and Brussels, turned the Van Eycks' technical achievements to the service of his own subjective and dramatic vision. As no one before, he exploited the emotional potential of colours and abstract form. His portraits have a nobility and spirituality which was highly popular with patrons. Again the major works are mainly outside Belgium, but there is an early copy (1440) of his masterpiece, the Deposition, in Louvain and accepted works in the Fine Arts Museums of Antwerp, Brussels and Tournai.

Van der Weyden's influence is evident in the work of *Dirk Bouts* (died 1475) the Haarlem painter who settled in Louvain before 1460. There are major works in the Fine Arts Museum, Brussels ('The Judgement of the Emperor Otto'), Louvain (Church of St. Pieter), and Bruges (Cathedral Museum). The isolation of Bouts's elongated and angular figures within his often deep but simplified space and the contrast between his lovely landscapes and his horrific subjects are emotive and disturbing. The influence of both Van der Weyden and the Van Eycks can be traced in the works of Bouts's contemporary in Bruges, *Petrus Christus* (died 1472). His Lamentation (in the Brussels Museum) is quietly effective. A more original artist, who breaks out of the conventional 'craftsman' mould if only by reason of his ultimate insanity, is *Hugo van der Goes* of Ghent (died 1482). The emotional intensity of his approach is conveyed by a cavalier attitude to space and scale, an ability to intimate movement, a unique palette and, sometimes, an explicit awareness of the viewers' presence. The Death of the Virgin (Groeninge museum, Bruges) is a masterpiece.

By contrast the technically superb paintings of *Hans Memling* are balanced and rational. The bulk of his work remains in a charming museum in his adopted home of Bruges. Their derivation from Van der Weyden is clear, but they are gentler, more idealised, more homely.

Memling's most important successor was *Gerard David* (died 1523) who came to Bruges from Oudewater in 1484. David's style remains solemn and reticent, but his figures have an animation and suppleness which look towards the 16C. Some of his major works remain in Bruges, for instance the Unjust Judge panels in the Groeninge museum. A complete contrast to David's gentle approach is the macabre vision of his contemporary *Hieronymous Bosch* (died 1516). Although not stictly a Belgian artist (he spent his life in his home town of 's Hertogenbosch in Holland), Bosch is always linked to the Flemish school and had a profound influence on artists such as Brueghel and Patinir. Bosch's fantastic assemblages of grotesque motifs, all the more horrifying because they derive ultimately from natural phenomena, are not fully understood but they probably relate to popular culture, both secular and religious. Most of Bosch's major works are in Spain—he was a great favourite with Philip II—but there are examples in the Brussels (a fairly orthodox Crucifixion), and Ghent Museums.

Painting: 16C

Overall, this period does not achieve the standard of those immediately preceding or succeeding it. It did, however, produce artists of exceptional talent and presents a fascinating record of the development of new genres and of a confrontation between two artistic traditions—the Flemish and the Italian. The term 'Renaissance' is often misleading in a country whose great heritage was not classical art but the still vigorous and highly decorative traditions of the indigenous 'gothic'. Despite the Italian orientation of most Flemish artists of this period, what seems to have occurred was the assimilation of certain Italian elements and ideals into the native vocabulary of form and style and into the syntax of traditional notions of the role of the artist and the work of art. The result was a distinctive, if sometimes slightly garbled, new language—a prerequisite for the emergence of the 17C masters.

The period sees the rise of Antwerp to economic and artistic pre-eminence. Among the most important artists at the turn of the century was *Quinten Metsys* (died 1530), whose refined and sophisticated sacred works attempted to combine the best of the Flemish tradition with new Italian—chiefly Leonardoesque—ideas, and whose animated portraits and satirical genre scenes were highly influential. Also influenced by Leonardo was *Joos van Cleef*, who astutely adopted many of Metsys's formulae, but whose winsome Madonnas are more frankly charming and decorative. A more vigorous, not to say virile, talent was *Jan Gossaert*(or *Mabuse*) whose visit to Italy in 1508 led to an innovatory concern with the monumental nude in secular, mythological contexts (as exemplified by the Venus and Cupid in Brussels).

The Reliquary of St. Ursula (dedicated 1489), centrepiece of the Memling Museum in Bruges. In this piece Memling adapted the traditional iconography of the Virgin of the Misericord to show St. Ursula as protectress of the 11,000 virgins who, according to legend, voyaged with her

The work of these artists is related to 'Antwerp Mannerism', a decorative and anti-naturalistic style produced between c 1515 and 1535 by numerous, often anonymous artists. Incorporating Italian, Dutch and Flemish elements, it is more akin to late Gothic Brabantine architecture than to contemporary Italian art.

Outside Antwerp, *Jan Provoost* was creating lively works in Bruges and in Brussels the painter and designer of tapestry and glass *Bernard van Orley* successfully appropriated Raphaelesque ideas—but it is Raphael at second hand, divorced from nature. The preoccupation with Italy was more comprehensively indulged by a second generation of artists, calling themselves Romanists. Among them were *Michiel Coxie, Pieter Coecke, Lambert Lombard* (died 1566), who was almost a caricature of the Renaissance artist, and Lombard's immensely successful pupil *Frans Floris* (died 1570). Floris reveals a broader knowledge of Italian art than Lombard, in particular familiarity with Venetian and northern Italian techniques. Among Floris's many pupils was *Martin de Vos*, whose work reflects his collaboration with Tintoretto and knowledge of Veronese.

The period sees a gradual but highly significant trend towards secular subject matter. One aspect of this was the establishment of landscape, of which *Joachim Patinir* (died c 1524) was an early practitioner. His airy pictures, with their unnatural 'birds-eye' view, high horizons and visionary mountains, established a convention which dominated until the end of the century and is reflected in the works of *Herri met de Bles, Bruegel the Elder* and, later, *Gillis van Coninxloo*. It was only finally abandoned by *Paul Bril*. Another flourishing genre was portraiture, and here observation never succumbed to pretension. Until c 1530 extrovert, sometimes rhetorical half length figures were fashionable; later Lombard, Van Heemskerk and Floris created free, direct images. After c 1550 specialist portraitists, aware of, but not dominated by Italy, produced more reticent, often three-quarters length and usually three-quarters view depictions of bourgeois sitters. *Pieter* and *Frans Pourbus the Elder, W.* and *Adriaen Key* are fairly typical, while *Antonio Moro*, painter to the Habsburg court, gained international status and helped to formulate the European court portrait. *Frans Pourbus the Younger* was also important.

In the field of genre painting the lead of Quinten Metsys was followed by *Jan Sanders* and the Dutchman *Marius van Reymerswael*. *Pieter Aertsen* and his nephew *Beuckelaer* later developed a novel type of kitchen or peasant scene executed broadly in the style of the 'Romanists'.

The most significant painter of the 16C was, however, *Pieter Bruegel the Elder* (c 1525–69). Painting for a limited circle of intellectual connoisseurs, Bruegel's works (of which there are good examples in Brussels and Antwerp) combine acute observation of peasant physiognomies and customs with Bosch-like fantasy and rich allegorical and symbolic content. His transparent colour, brilliant sense of design and incisive drawing serve an objective yet deeply sympathetic view of humanity. *Pieter Brueghel the Younger* painted attractive copies of his father's work which, however, lack the delicacy and sensitivity of the originals. More significant was the younger son *Jan* (known as 'Velvet') whose small, exquisite genre works and flower paintings were highly prized.

Painting: 17C

The period is dominated by a single figure, *Pieter Paul Rubens* (born 1577) gentleman artist, scholar and diplomat *extraordinaire*. Rubens's significance lies partly in what has been termed his 'creative eclecticism' (Jaffé)—his ability to fuse highly disparate elements into a coherent, attractive and intensely personal idiom. Rubens largely acquired his huge formal vocabulary when, in his twenties, he spent eight years in Italy in the service of the Duke of Mantua and, in 1603, visited Spain. His eager eye assimilated all he saw, from classical antiquity to the Carracci and Caravaggio, and he was at this period perhaps particularly impressed with the 16C Venetians. Rubens's earlier training in Antwerp, especially the time he spent in the studio of Otto van Veen (Venius), was not, however, wasted. Reminiscences of Van Veen and other Flemings often appear in Rubens's works and, at a more fundamental level, the enthusiastic but sometimes awkward reorientation of Flemish art towards Italy in the 16C was essential to the synthesis achieved by Rubens in the 17th.

Even before Rubens burst upon the Antwerp scene artists such as *A. Janssens* (died 1632) were producing fairly sophisticated interpretations of Italian ideas which reveal knowledge of Caravaggio and the Bolognese school. But Janssens, like so many others, ultimately joined the tide of emulation created by Rubens's enormous success. Two masterpieces, executed soon after his return from Italy and both today in Antwerp Cathedral, heralded Rubens's fame. The Raising of the Cross, rent by a fierce diagonal, is a picture of tremendous, calculated verve and passion which fully merits the label 'Baroque', while the Descent from the Cross is a calmer composition of great pathos. Three Adorations of the Magi, also executed in the 1610s (today in the Fine Arts Museums in Brussels and Antwerp and St. Jan, Mechelen) reveal how Rubens could revitalise a traditional Flemish subject and how he continuously developed and refined his ideas. Paintings such as these and Rubens's position as court painter to Albert and Isabella quickly established him as Antwerp's leading artist, with a large and highly efficient workshop. The price of a 'Rubens' varied according to how much of the picture had been executed by the master himself. The small oil sketches by Rubens from which his assistants worked have always been highly valued as 'autograph', but it is worth remembering that they were not primarily intended as independent works of art; their compositions must be visualised on a much larger scale.

Rubens was an artist of many parts: portraitist, landscapist, painter of mythologies, political eulogies and grand religious works, he was ideally suited to serve the 17C Church and State. A large number of his works remain in Belgium and any selection is inevitably a personal one. There are, for instance, the splendid altarpieces from Antwerp churches and, very different in purpose and effect, the series of hunting scenes designed for tapestries to decorate Philip IV's hunting lodge which are now in the Brussels Museum. Another masterpiece is the utterly confident portrait of Gaspard Gevartius in the Antwerp Fine Arts Museum and, also in Antwerp and in stark contrast, there is the Last Communion of St. Francis where all Rubens's skills are marshalled to express a single truth—the mystery of faith.

*Rubens's 'Last Communion of St. Francis' (1619) in Antwerp
Fine Arts Museum. A picture infused with the spirit of the
Counter Reformation*

Although they share a formal idiom and their styles sometimes
converge, Rubens and his great contemporaries *Antoon van Dyck*
(1599–1641) and *Jacob Jordaens* (1593–1678) are fundamentally
different artistic personalities. Van Dyck, who collaborated so closely
with Rubens in the late 1610s that connoisseurs find difficulty in
separating their work, ultimately developed a more exclusive
preoccupation with grace, elegance and emotional sensibility and
formulated a different technique and palette. Two works from the
series of Mysteries of the Rosary in St. Paulus, Antwerp, provide a
splendid opportunity to compare the two masters at the moment of
their closest collaboration. Although the types and bold movements of
the figures in Van Dyck's Carrying of the Cross recall Rubens, who is
represented by the neighbouring Scourging of Christ, the unstable
composition, flickering light, elements of unrestrained pathos and
rapid, sketchy technique are Van Dyck's own. Van Dyck spent the
years from 1621–27 in Italy and after 1632 his career was pursued
mostly in England, where he concentrated on portraiture. There are
some excellent portraits in Belgium, especially in the Brussels
Museum (the sculptor François Duquesnoy—painted in Italy), but the
country is particularly rich in Van Dyck's religious works, usually

from the period after his return from Italy. A recurrent theme is the Crucifixion (Mechelen cathedral, St. Michielskerk, Ghent, Onze Lieve Vrouwe, Dendermonde), a subject which this hypersensitive artist interpreted in terms of despair and pathos. Two Lamentations in the Antwerp Museum also invite a comparison between Van Dyck's earlier and later styles.

Jacob Jordaens was a pupil of *Adam van Noort*, who was also one of Rubens's teachers. He may have co-operated with Van Dyck in the 1610s and from about 1635 on was certainly commissioned to complete works left unfinished by Rubens. Despite these close contacts Jordaens was a highly original artist: the 'Encyclopedia of World Art' characterisation of 17C Flemish painting as deeply affected by the assimilation of Italian art but remaining always 'within the context of Flemish sensibility—naturalistic, sensual, anti-intellectual in a certain sense and devoted to the visual transcription of life perceived as energy and enthusiasm and rendered in the evocative manner of the Flemish tradition' is particularly applicable to him. Jordaens's early style is robust, firm, illusionistic and boldly executed. Complex influences, including Caravaggism (although he never went to Italy), 16C Flemish art and, of course, Rubens combine to produce an entirely personal approach exemplified by the Allegory of Fertility (1620s) in the Brussels Museum. Jordaens's Martyrdom of St. Apollonia in St. Augustinus, Antwerp (1628), which seems almost to burst with movement and form, can be compared with Van Dyck's St. Augustine in the same church, and Jordaens also contributed to the Mysteries of the Rosary series, mentioned above. It seems paradoxical that this painter, famed for his exuberant depictions of revels (including the specifically Flemish theme 'The King Drinks') should have become a Calvinist. His conversion, when aged about fifty, was one cause or consequence of a new moderation and restraint in his religious pictures which, particularly when he relied on the services of his large workshop, lack the energy and verve of earlier works.

The presence of Rubens and his two outstanding followers Van Dyck and Jordaens meant that Antwerp, despite its relative economic decline, remained the centre of Belgian artistic production. The works of innumerable minor Antwerp masters testify to this trio's dominating influence, although painters such as *Gerard Seghers* and *Theodoor Rombouts* were also impressed by Caravaggio and his followers. Some of the more talented artists of the day understandably preferred to work outside Antwerp, but all remained ultimately within Rubens's sphere of influence. In Bruges *Jacob van Oost the Elder* produced sensitive works incorporating Venetian and Dutch elements, while the masterpiece of *Theodoor van Loon* of Brussels was the powerful, Caravaggesque decoration of the church at Scherpenheuvel. *Gaspard de Crayer*, who worked in Brussels and received numerous commissions from Ghent churches (e.g. St. Michiel) profited greatly from the examples of Rubens and Van Dyck but always managed to retain his own identity. In Liège a relatively independent group of artists led by *Gerard Douffet* and including *Bartholomé Flémalle* were influenced by Caravaggism but were also conscious of the impact of Poussin in France.

The 17C saw a proliferation of different genres skilfully practised by numerous artists and often reflecting contemporary Dutch influence. The career of *Adriaen Brouwer*, a painter of landscapes and scenes from everyday life, was short but brilliant. His brushwork is direct and free, his pictures naturalistic yet lyrical. The Fine Arts Museum in Brussels provides a good opportunity to compare Brouwer with his contemporary *David Teniers the Younger* (1610–90). The peasant scenes of the court artist Teniers are also sensitive in treatment, but they are much more detatched and cool in expression. Brouwers and Teniers were the leading figures among the so-called 'kleinmeister', although Belgium's galleries are rich in attractive and amusing scenes of work and play in the 17C by other hands. These two were also, along with Rubens, the major land-scapists of the period, but it would be a pity if the greater emotional and formal integration of their landscapes were allowed to obscure the decorative beauty of works by predecessors such as *Joos de Momper* (died 1635), *Kerstiaen de Keuninck* (died c 1632–35) and *Denis van Alsloot* (died c 1628). Later, *Lucas van Uden* and *Jan Wildens* were excellent interpreters of 'the Rubens landscape' and *Jacques d'Arthois* of Brussels managed to combine Baroque grand-eur with the decorative charm of his fellow citizen Van Alsloot. *Jan Siberechts* (1627–1700/03) was more independent. The best of his pictures achieve a bold and entirely personal monumentality.

In the field of still-life *Frans Snyders* (1579–1657) expanded the tradition of large kitchen and market subjects established by Aertsen and Beuckelaer in the 16C to encompass subjects of hunting and game. *Paul de Vos* (1596–1678) produced pictures which are close in style and theme and equal in quality to those of his brother-in-law Snyders. *Jan Fyt* (1611–61), a pupil of Snyders, preferred to contemplate the trophies of the hunt rather than evoking the frenzy of the hunt itself. His works are striking and decorative, with an impressive feeling for surface textures. The art of flower painting was given its independence at the very beginning of the 17C by Jan Breughel; it achieved greater sophistication in the work of his pupil, the Jesuit *Daniel Seghers* (1590–1661). Both Seghers's paintings and the still-lifes of his influential contemporary *Jan Davidz de Heem* (1616–83/84) have a symbolic as well as a decorative purpose. Among the portraitists *Cornelis de Vos* (brother of Paul) created charming and elegant representations, especially of children, and, later in :the century, *Gonzales Coques* achieved great success in Brussels with his fashionable conversation pieces.

Painting: 18C

In the 18C two themes are clear: the continuation and imitation of the ideas and styles of the previous century and the ever-increasing influence of foreign, and especially French, models and ideas. It was natural, for instance, that many artists should hark back to the 'golden age' of religious and history painting in Belgium. The worst productions of this type are merely pallid imitations of Rubens, but the Louvain artist Pieter Verhaghen produced works in the spirit of Jordaens which are, nevertheless, vigorous, attractive and original. On the other hand, a slightly younger artist, *Andreas Cornelis Lens* (1739–1822), reveals a conciousness of French developments in his graceful, classical pictures and *Piat Sauvage*'s sculptural trompe l'oeils in the Cathedral and gallery at Tournai are both fashionably decorative and inspired by Poussin's second seven sacraments series.

The status of genre painting was extremely high during this period—a situation which reflects both contemporary French taste and the brilliant example of the 17C. David Teniers was particularly admired by artists such as *Balthasar van den Bossche* and the talented *Jan Joseph Horemans I.* Despite their aspirations to elegance, Van den Bossche and Horemans adhered firmly to the Flemish tradition. The perspective of other genre artists, such as *Pieter Snayers* and *Pieter van Angelis*, extended to France and Italy, while still others, including *Frans Xaver Henri Verbeek* and *Jacob de Roore* looked north to Holland, and especially to Leiden, for inspiration. The increasing 'internationalisation' of painting during this period can be traced in the development of *Jan Anton Garemijn* of Bruges (1712–99). He began by painting village genre entirely in the tradition of Teniers, later adopted a French-inspired 'Rococo' style and finally (c 1790) was influenced by the wave of classicism which was sweeping Europe. The career of *Léonard Defrance* (1735–1805) provides a contrasting example of what is essentially the same process: the weakening of the independent Flemish tradition. The classicism of Defrance's earlier works betrays the proximity of his home to France and his studies in Italy and the south of France. His conversion to the recreation of 17C Leiden genre in 1773 seems to have been partly a result of personal conviction (his works always remain individual) and in part a consquence of his consciousness of a lucrative Parisian market—to which he responded by introducing French elements into his pictures.

In the fields of landscape and flowers the native tradition was also abandoned for French and Dutch models. The landscapist *Karel van Falens*, for example, was inspired by the Dutch painter Wouwerman, while later in the century *Henricus Josephus Antonissen* and *Balthasar Paul Ommeganck* chose Wynants and Berchem as exemplars.

Romanesque Sculpture

The local stone of the low countries is not ideal for sculpture—it is either soft and crumbly sandstone or the exceptionally hard black marble of Tournai. The relative paucity of monumental sculpture of this period and the excellence of work in other media are in part consequences of this problem. There are superb Mosan ivories dating from the 10th and 11C in the treasury of Onze Lieve Vrouw, Tongeren, the Musée Curtius, Liège, and the Musée d'Art et d'Histoire, Brussels (where, indeed, all kinds of Romanesque sculpture can be seen). During the 12C excellent champlevé enamel was produced, also in the Meuse region, and the work of *Godefroid de Huy* was outstanding. His reliquary of Pope Alexander (1145) is in the museum in Brussels. High quality metalwork from this period also survives, for example the wonderful bronze font at St. Barthélemy, Liège (1107–18), attributed to *Renier de Huy*. This work has been called 'a Christian resurrection of Classic Hellenism' (Lejeune), so directly do its graceful figures reflect their classical ancestry. It forms a startling contrast with the approximately contemporary (1149) font from St. Germanus at Tienen, now in Brussels, where Renier's grace and refinement are countered by primitive vigour and an innate sense of design. At the end of the 12C *Nicholas of Verdun* produced the lovely Reliquary of Notre-Dame at Tournai, and there are many other beautiful but anonymous works of this period (e.g. the Châsse St. Hadelin at Visé (12C) and the Châsse St. Remaclus at Stavelot (13C). In wood the seated Madonna, known as *Sedes Sapientae*, and the crucifix are the dominant forms. Once again a contrast between a popular and a more aristocratic art is highlighted by the primitive but powerful Virgin from Evegnée, now in the Diocesan Museum, Liège, and the more elegant, gentler image in the Brussels Fine Arts Museum. Simple but eloquent crucifixes survive at Tongeren, Tancremont and Liège.

Bronze baptismal font (1107–18) in the Eglise Saint Barthélemy, Liège, the masterpiece of Renier de Huy

The architectural division between Mosan and Scaldian styles is also tenable for that monumental sculpture which does survive. In the Meuse region there is the mysterious iconography of the ancient doorways of Ste. Gertrude at Nivelles and the lovely Virgin of Dom Rupert originally from the Abbey of St. Laurent, Liège, and now in the Musée Curtius. She is suckling her child—a motif which is to be endlessly repeated in Flemish art. A direct comparison between the Scaldian and Mosan styles is, however, best made by means of the various stone fonts which survive from both regions. By far the richest source for Scaldian architectural sculpture is Tournai cathedral, with its impressive doorways and decorated capitals.

Gothic Sculpture: 13th and 14C

The decisive influence upon Belgian Gothic sculpture was French. This determining factor was common to all the centres—the Meuse, the Scheldt, Brabant—but previous local traditions and the different routes of diffusion of French influence (some French ideas reached the Meuse region via Germany, for instance) produced different results in each area. In Tournai the direct impact of France, and in particular Notre-Dame, Paris, is evident in the reliquary of St. Eleutherius of 1247 (Cathedral Treasury) and the Genesis story and Prophets from the Cathedral W façade. But Tournai was by no means merely a provincial outpost of the French style. During the 14C a flourishing school of funerary sculpture developed. Much of the work was for export, but many reliefs can still be seen in the cathedral (e.g. the monument to Jean de Bos) and local churches. Other important works of the Scheldt region are the portal of the hospital of St. Jan in Bruges (c 1270), again reminiscent of French prototypes, and the monument of Hugo II, castellan of Ghent, in the Ghent Bijloke Museum.

Detail from the Reliquary of St. Eleutherius (1247) in the Cathédrale Notre-Dame, Tournai

Reflections of French developments are also to be found in the Meuse region after c 1250, as for instance at the churches in Tongeren and Dinant. The lovely 13C Sedes Sapientae of St. Jean, Liège is a good example of Romanesque iconography translated into the Gothic idiom. In the 14C French influence on Mosan sculpture becomes even more marked and it is sometimes difficult to decide the precise origin of isolated works. However, the Porte de Bethléem at Notre-Dame, Huy, is, despite its international character, likely to be local work. Two outstanding Mosan sculptors of the end of the 14C were *Jean Pepin de Huy* and *Jean de Liège*. Both these artists worked mostly for French courts, providing further evidence of the close relationship between these regions. Mosan goldsmiths' work continued to be important, although its quality declined somewhat in relation to the superb production of the Romanesque period. The outstanding name of the 14C was *Hugo d'Oignies*, many of whose exquisite creations are today in the treasury of the convent of Notre-Dame at Namur. There are other important, though anonymous reliquaries at Stavelot, Amay and the cathedral at Namur.

In sculpture as in architecture the 14C saw the rise of Brabant to pre-eminence. The region was certainly not immune to French influence, as the Black Madonna of Halle clearly illustrates. It was not, however, dominated by France, but rather reacted fruitfully to the stimulus of French influence. *Walter Paris*'s Virgin from OLV Tienen, of the 1360s, for instance, reveals elements of the new vital realism which was to be most fully developed by Claus Sluter.

Sculpture: late 14C to 1500

A comprehensive history of Belgian sculpture of this period has yet to be written. This is partly because of the complexity of the subject: works ranged from precious metal objects to monumental architectural decoration, and the design and execution of a single item often involved many people. It is also in part a result of the uneven survival of sculpture from this time. Iconoclasm has meant that, until about 1450, so little work remains in Belgium that it is difficult to trace a coherent line of development, while later, although metalwork and monumental sculpture are still relatively rare, there is a proliferation, and ultimately a glut, of small carved altarpieces. These painted wooden retables, produced on a massive scale usually by anonymous craftsmen, largely defy analysis according to the conventional criteria of individual contributions and stylistic progression. What is clear, however, is that the sculpture and sculptors of northern France and the Netherlands exercised international influence and it has been argued that the significance of this sculpture originally rivalled that of Flemish painting of the same period.

Initially, the revolutionary work of the Dutchman *Claus Sluter* was the decisive influence in Belgium. Although Sluter worked principally at the Burgundian court at Dijon, the political union of Flanders and Burgundy (1384) meant that echoes of his realistic, autonomous and vital individuals quickly reverberated throughout Belgium. In addition, Sluter's style may in part originate from the southern Netherlands. Notable works in his idiom are the eight prophets from Brussels Town Hall (now in the Musée Communal), some of the sculpture at the church of Onze Lieve Vrouw at Halle and the Coronation of the Virgin at St. Jacques, Liège. The retable of the church of St. Salvator, Hakendover, reveals, however, a more conservative approach, perhaps particularly appropriate to small-scale works.

A dominant and fascinating theme throughout the period is the mutual interaction between painting and sculpture. Interesting parallels have been drawn between early 15C alabasters and metal reliefs (of which few remain in Belgium) and contemporary miniature painting. There is also evidence that Robert Campin and Roger van der Weyden (among many other painters) polychromed, if they did not actually design, sculpture. Both artists came from Tournai, a centre of the production of marble reliefs, some of which can still be seen in the cathedral, and it has been suggested that their styles may have been influenced by these reliefs. Certainly Roger's style, in particular, had an enormous impact on sculpture, as is revealed by the characteristic tension between line and volume of the Entombment in St. Vincent, Soignies. Some measure of what has been lost from this period is provided by the stone St. Adrian in the Musée d'Art et d'Histoire in Brussels, which evokes tantalising thoughts of the brilliant Leyden sculptor *Nicolaus Gerhaerts*; by the restrained and beautiful effigy of Isabella of Bourbon, now in Antwerp cathedral; and by the Paschal candelabrum of 1482–83 cast by *Renier van Thienen*, at Zoutleeuw. On a small scale, the reliquary group of Charles the Bold, made by *Gérard Loyet* of Lille in 1467 (and now in the treasury of St. Paul's church, Liège) testifies to the continued vitality and refinement of goldsmiths' work.

Such sculptures contrast sharply in function and style with the innumerable wooden altarpieces produced in the latter half of the century, mostly in Brussels. Crowded, clear-cut and richly decorated, often including genre elements, these works are designed to be appreciated in detail and are, at best, highly expressive and dramatic—still echoing the preoccupations of Roger van der Weyden. Outstanding examples are the *Claudio de Villa* altar (c 1470) in the Musée d'Art et d'Histoire, Brussels, the altar of St. Leonard (1479) in the church of St. Leonardus at Zoutleeuw, and the altarpiece of the Passion in St. Dympna at Geel (c 1480–90).

At the end of the century the emotional grip of the age of Van de Weyden at last relaxes and an unprecedented diversity results. In Brussels the leading master, *Jan Borman the Elder*, produced the St. George altar of 1493 (now in the Musée d'Art et d'Histoire, Brussels). A work of superb, if slightly impersonal technique, this retable is notable for the naturalistic elegance of its figures, calm and clear composition and perfection of detail. The choir stalls at St. Sulpitius, Diest, are products of similar concerns. In Antwerp the standard of the best craftsmanship was also excellent and here there was a marked tendency towards vivid characterisation and anecdotal detail. Some indication of the richness of this decade can be seen from two almost random examples: the Crucifixion group in St. Pieter's Louvain, where traditional forms and emotional values are revitalised and make a stark contrast to the humour of Antwerp, which looks towards the 16C, and the bronze effigy of Mary of Burgundy in Notre-Dame, Bruges, where exquisite decoration and a freer naturalism bear witness to the two decades which divide it from the equally beautiful but more austere effigy of Isabella of Bourbon in Antwerp cathedral.

Sculpture: 16C

In sculpture, as in painting and architecture, the overall impression is of a struggle to assimilate the fundamentally alien concepts of the Italian Renaissance. The attempt certainly produced some approximations to High Renaissance classicism, but it also engendered other fruits which in their decorative extravagence and material richness both perpetuate Flemish traditions and unconciously anticipate some aspects of the 17C Baroque.

Mass production of wooden altarpieces reached its apogee at the beginning of the 16C, creating what has been described as an 'embarrassing plenitude' of works (T. Müller). In Brussels *Jan Borman* and his school remained important (e.g. the Auderghem altar in the Musée d'Art et d'Histoire, Brussels), while in Antwerp exaggeration of the local traditions of humour and characterisation led after c 1515 to distortions of form which can be compared to the 'Mannerism' current in painting. The Lamentation altar from Averbode, now in the Vleeshuis, Antwerp, is an example of such work. An apparently new centre of production was Mechelen, where the style was typically more tranquil and subdued (e.g. the St. Dympna altarpiece in the church at Geel, by *Jan van Waver*). Fashionable italianate elements were absorbed into the traditional formats, by the French immigrant *Robert Moreau*, for instance, in his Oplinter altar of c 1530 in the Musée d'Art et d'Histoire in Brussels. The advent of the Reformation, however, destroyed many markets and ultimately reduced the significance of devotional wooden sculpture.

Meanwhile, the inclusion of the Burgundian heritage in Charles V's huge domain meant that the Netherlandish court tended to attract artists from further afield. These men were often imbued with Renaissance ideas and eagerly responded to their patrons' increasing preoccupation with Italy—an attitude neatly symbolised by the presence of Michelangelo's Virgin in the church of Onze Lieve Vrouw in Bruges from 1506. Outstanding among the foreigners was *Conrad Meit* from Worms (died 1550/51) whose marble Virgin and Child in Ste. Gudule, Brussels, reveals a personal but profound understanding of the forms and the concepts of the Renaissance. Another immigrant was *Jean Mone* of Metz. Mone specialised in alabaster work and the translucent surface and inherent delicacy of this medium seem entirely appropriate to a master who tended to concentrate upon the external forms rather than the principles of the Renaissance, and who delighted in the slender decorative motifs of the Italian Quattrocento. His alabaster altar at Onze Lieve Vrouw in Halle, with its lovely, pure details, is like a gorgeous wedding cake. *Jacques Du Broeucq* (died 1584) was another important 'italianist'. His masterpiece, the decoration of the church of St. Waudru in Mons, was badly damaged in 1797, but a number of fragments remain. Here Gothic and Renaissance meet: the decoration of traditional church furnishings is conceived in wholly Italian terms.

The most influential of these 'progressive' sculptors, *Cornelis Floris*, was also a distinguished architect. Floris's most important works in Belgium are the tabernacle of St. Leonardus in Zoutleeuw (1550–52)—an enormously tall Gothic structure adorned with italianate motifs—and the much more restrained tomb of Jan III Mérode at Geel and rood screen in Tournai cathedral. But Floris's influence, like that of his rival *Hans Vredeman de Vries*, was exercised chiefly through his engraved designs for decorative ornament (particularly strapwork and grotesques)—designs that were endlessly copied and repeated throughout Belgium and beyond.

The Chimneypiece in the Vrije Museum at Bruges epitomises many of the major themes of Flemish 16C sculpture. Commissioned by Margaret of Austria to commemorate the Peace of Cambrai (1529) and largely executed by a foreigner, *Guyot de Beaugrant* of Lorraine, it is a symbol of the new international context of the Netherlandish court. The production of the work by a team of collaborating sculptors to designs by the painter *L. Blondeel* reflects, however, Flemish practice dating at least from the 15C. The lavish decoration and use of contrasting materials have been called a 'Mannerism of abundance' (Vey and Von der Osten), but they can also be seen as a partial translation into Italian of the Flemish 'late Gothic' delight in ornament and rich effects. The work has even been described as 'avant-Baroque' (Fierens), partly because of its sheer extravagence, but also because it is an integrated decorative scheme employed to make a political point: the glorification of the House of Habsburg.

Sculpture: 17th and 18C

After the iconoclasm and uncertainty of the second half of the 16C, the establishment of the 'Archdukes' Albert and Isabella and the Catholic Church's reassertion of itself in the southern Netherlands were a boon for all artists, but particularly for sculptors, whose work remained to a greater extent than painters' dependent on public and religious commissions. Several excellent artists rose to the challenge of furnishing the new churches and refurbishing the old.

Initially, the most influential figure was, paradoxically, a man who spent his career in Rome and by whose hand only two putti (on the monument of Bishop Triest) are thought to survive in Belgium. This was *François Duquesnoy* (son of Jérôme Duquesnoy The Elder, creator of Manneken-Pis in Brussels), who achieved the remarkable feat of retaining his artistic individuality in Bernini's Rome, and who was the inspiration of his brother *Jérôme II* and of the prolific *Artus Quellin the Elder*. Jérôme the Younger's works (e.g. the rest of Bishop Triest's monument in Ghent and statues in Notre-Dame du Sablon and the cathedral in Brussels) are rather eclectic, but technically accomplished and stylistically up to the minute. Artus Quellin the Elder was more original. A master of the formal repertory of the Baroque, Artus nevertheless created personal works which are characterised by a vigorous grasp of observed reality. Although the main commission of his life was for the Town Hall in Amsterdam, good examples of his sculpture remain in Belgium, particularly in Antwerp. Quellin's nephew *Artus the Younger* was also an able sculptor with a fresh approach to the conventions of the Baroque style. Rome and François Duquesnoy were the sources of his art, but his later works are themselves innovative: the St. Rose of Lima (St. Paulus, Antwerp) anticipates the greater refinement and delicacy of the Rococo, while the dramatic Creator at Bruges cathedral fully exploits the possibilities of the Baroque.

The sculpture of *Luc Fayd'herbe* was sometimes highly successful, sometimes less so. Among the numerous examples of his work which can be seen in Mechelen, for example, there is the monument to Bishop Andreas Cruesen in the cathedral, where the vitality and power of the dead cleric contrasts rather inappropriately with the relatively insipid Christ and Father Time. Meanwhile *Jean Del Cour* of Liège (died 1707) produced his interpretation of the Baroque in reserved, dignified and highly accomplished works such as the monument of Bishop Allamont in Ghent cathedral (commissioned 1667). Del Cour's figures are aristocratic and sensitive, and his beautiful draperies were a speciality which ultimately became a recognisable mannerism. His most popular and influential work is the Fontaine de la Vièrge in Liège.

A detail of Hendrik Verbruggen's elaborate wooden pulpit in the Cathédrale Saint Michel, Brussels (1699). The detail and decorative exuberance of this and similar works can be seen as late expressions of the traditional concerns of Flemish wood sculptors

In the 18C sculpture, like architecture, loses its recognisably Belgian Baroque character and assumes an international, classical aspect. Perhaps the region's transformation from its early 16C position as the economic, political and cultural hub of Charles V's empire to its more peripheral, relatively insignificant 18C role can be seen as having some effect on art. Certainly large commissions declined and a number of sculptors (e.g. *Gabriel Grupello*) went abroad in search of more lucrative markets.

In the first half of the century a series of extraordinary pulpits in wood—the traditional Flemish medium—can be seen as representing a final Flemish flourish in the face of encroaching classicism. Of course such a view is slightly frivolous in its blatant hindsight, but works such as *Hendrik Verbruggen's* pulpit in Brussels cathedral of 1699 (which set the trend), *M. van der Voort's* creation in Mechelen cathedral of 1721–23 and *Verhaeghen's* fantasy in O.L.V. van Hanswijk, also in Mechelen, do incorporate characteristics, such as profuse decoration with little concern for basic structure, vigour and virtuosity in execution and a naturalism which sometimes verges on the anecdotal, which can be associated with previous Flemish sculpture. Love them or loathe them, these pulpits, and other church furnishings in a similar vein, certainly make an impact.

Stone sculpture, which at the turn of the century is still recognisably related to the Quellins and the Duquesnoys (e.g. Grupello's numerous charming works in Brussels), later becomes characterised by a cool classicism. *Laurent Delvaux* (died 1778) and *Pieter Verschaffelt* (died 1793), who had both spent long years in Rome, were fully committed to the new, international style, but earlier artists, such as *M. van der Voort* (died 1737), managed to keep a foot in both the Baroque and the classical camps. As we have seen, Van der Voort was responsible for the Mechelen pulpit, but his two earlier monuments in the same cathedral are distinctly classical in feeling. The ultimate triumph of classicism is represented by Delvaux's pupil *G.L. Godecharle*, who, significantly, later studied in Paris. Some of his work is routine, but occasionally, as in the portrait of his wife in Brussels (Musée Communal), he makes a more personal statement.

Art in the 19th and 20C

By *Tania Jones,* Courtauld Institute of Art

In this period the process of 'internationalism' which we have observed in the 18C was completed. After the domination of Neo-Classicism, individualism reigned, in a country already divided by language, and the art of this time did not have a national identity. This development, which was intimately connected with the enormous social political and economic changes occurring, meant that Belgium, for the first time politically independent, became, artistically speaking, a province of Europe. There were distinguished Belgian artists throughout this period, eclectic in style, although maintaining their own artistic personalities, who while being participants in broad European movements and ready to absorb strong artistic influences from abroad, were also part of a distinct tradition of Belgian art. They had an eye for detail, an interest in human subjects, and they focused on the depiction of light and colour, which had been the particular characteristics of art in Flanders for centuries. There is an obvious line of descent in emotive works of art from the early primitives and the 17C Baroque to the Romantics, Symbolists, Expressionists, Surrealists of the 19th and early 20C and up to the Social Realists and Hyper-realists of today.

The political annexation of Belgium by France was preceded by an artistic conquest of the country. Thus, by the end of the 18C classicism reigned supreme in all spheres of Belgian art, although many of the artists gained their recognition abroad, for example *Josef Suvée* (1743–1807), *Frans Jozef Kinsoen* (1771–1839) and *Jozef Odevaere* (1775–1830). Although much architecture was destroyed during the

French occupation and very little created, classicism remained the dominant style after 1815. Its chief practitioner was the court architect *Charles van der Straeten* (1771–1834), whose masterpiece is the sober Palais Ducale (1826; now the Palais des Académies) in Brussels. The expansion of the universities during this period created opportunities for architects, as for example the division of Louvain University in this century has done for the architect Lucien Kroll and others. Examples of classicist work can be found at Ghent (Louis Roelandt) and Liège (J.N. Chevron).

The outstanding figure among the numerous followers of the French painter Jacques Louis David was *François Joseph Navez* (1787–1869). Navez had trained with David in Paris. He also visited Rome before in 1830, when he became the director of the Brussels Academy and the head of the Neo-Classical movement there. His best works are portraits: 'The de Hemptinne Family' (Brussels Museum), approaches the quality of his master. *Mathieu-Ignace van Bree* (1773–1839) was another important link with France: after his training with François-André Vincent, he taught his pupils at the Antwerp Academy (where he became head in 1827) to concentrate simultaneously on the declamatory and the naturalistic aspects of classicism. The result was a type of nationalistic history painting produced by a school of Belgian artists, working mainly in Antwerp, after the country's independence from Holland in 1830. This group, led by *Gustave Wappers* (1807–74), who succeeded Bree at the Antwerp Academy in 1839, *Ferdinand de Braekeleer* (1792–1883) and *Nicaise de Keyser* (1813–87), dominated the scene until sometime after 1850. No longer classicist in style, their works are a glorification of their country in a sort of romantic history painting or patriotic allegory. Wappers' 'Episode during the Belgian Revolt of 1830' (1834; Brussels Museum), de Keyser's 'La Bataille des Eperons d'or' (1836; Brussels Museum), Louis Gallait's 'Les Têtes Coupées' (1857; Tournai Museum), or 'The Plague at Tournai in 1092' (Tournai Museum) and Emile Wauters' 'The Madness of Hugo van der Goes' (1872; Brussels Museum) are energetic and forceful works, which provide a glamourised view of the past.

Belgian romantic painting consists primarily of historical costume pieces, represented on a grand scale, which sometimes verge on melodrama. The exemplar of this style, and almost a caricature of the 'romantic artist' was *Antoine Wiertz* (1806–65), who trained in Antwerp. His passionate, sometimes hysterical works, reminiscent of Goya, can be seen in the Wiertz Museum in Brussels, which was specially built by the government of the time to house his immense canvases. This period also had a calmer, less grandiose aspect. The important murals painted by *Hendrik Leys* (1815–69) for the Stadhuis in Antwerp look back, nostalgically, to Flemish art before Rubens, in a way which is rather analogous to the Pre-Raphaelites in England. Somewhat later, *Henri de Braekeleer* (1840–88), inspired by the Netherlandish artists of the 17C, produced beautifully painted tranquil interiors and landscapes.

From c 1830 until the end of the 19C architecture in Belgium, as in the rest of Europe, was characterised by eclecticism. The rapid growth of the cities, which demanded massive building programmes, inevitably produced some banal and lifeless work but there were also some remarkable achievements. *Joseph Poelaert*'s vast, domed, Palais de Justice (1866–83), which stands on a hill overlooking Brussels, is impressive, while J.P. Cluysenaer's Galeries St. Hubert (1846), also in Brussels, are graceful. The Brussels Bourse (1873) by Leon Suys and the

Musée de l'Art Ancien (1875–85) by Alphonse Balat, who redesigned the façades and the staircase of the Palais Royal for the King and also designed the botanical hothouses at the Château Royal at Laeken, are notable buildings, as is also the National Bank in Antwerp (1879) by *Henri Beyaert* (1823–94).

Just as David's presence in Belgium had a profound impact on painting so for sculpture did the presence of François Rude, the major French sculptor of the early 19C, who lived in exile in Brussels between 1815 and 1827. The influence of French sculpture was continued later in the century by Auguste Rodin, who worked in Brussels, with his master Carrier-Belleuse, on the decoration of the Bourse.

Rude's emphasis on the direct observation of nature undoubtedly influenced the Belgian *Willem Geefs* (1805–83), whose Mausoleum of Frédéric de Mérode in Ste. Gudule, Brussels, was regarded by his contemporaries as boldly realistic. In sculpture, as in architecture and painting, eclecticism was a central and often fruitful element. With the growth of the cities sculpture became increasingly important, particularly in public commissions: typical commissions would be for the enrichment of the façades of buildings, sometimes commemorative sometimes decorative in theme, and for statues to be placed at the end of the long avenues. Among notable works of the period are *Eugène Simonis'* (1810–92) equestrian statue 'Godefroid de Bouillon' (1848), Place Royale, Brussels, and Paul de Vigne's 'The Triumph of Art' and Charles van der Stappen's 'The Teaching of Art', grand allegorical figure groups on the façade of the Musée des Beaux Arts (1880s). *Charles Fraikin* (1817–93) who has a museum devoted to his work at Herentals (outside Antwerp) was admired for his mythological marble groups like 'L'Amour captif' (1845; Brussels Museum), and 'Vénus Anadyomène', Palais Royal, Brussels (1861), *Thomas Vinçotte* (1850–1925) received recognition for his pediment group of 'Belgium between Agriculture and Industry' on the Palais Royal, Brussels, and *Jacques de Lalaing* (1858–1917) was noted for his majestic tomb to the English killed at the battle of Waterloo at Evere cemetery near Brussels.

The Botanical Gardens in Brussels includes works by most of the important Belgian sculptors of the 19C. Among these was *Constantin Meunier* (1831–1905), whose sculptures of heroic workers express a romantic concept of labour which struck a deep chord within newly industrialised Europe. His works reflect a general increase in social awareness, and they still have the power to move. Much of Meunier's material was derived from the mining district of the Borinage, where the deplorable conditions also shocked the Dutch painter van Gogh in his early career. The best collections of Meunier's works are in the Brussels museum and the museum devoted to his work which is also in Brussels and has been recently restored.

Paul de Vigne's works have an Italianate, almost Donatellesque quality; while the powerful, lusty productions of *Jef Lambeaux* (1852–1908), the Fleming, may inspire thoughts of Rubens or Jordaens, as well as of Giambologna, the Renaissance sculptor whose work Lambeaux had seen in Florence and who himself was Flemish. 'The Merry Song' (Antwerp Museum) and the fountain (1887) in the Grote Markt at Antwerp show this strength. *Julien Dillens* (1849–1904) and *Jules Lagae*, the latter best known for his 'Expiation' (Ghent Museum), showing pathos in the representation of struggling prisoners, were also sculptors. Dillens's sculpture is symbolist or even Art Nouveau in style; this affinity was strengthened by his use of ivory which was imported from the Belgian Congo in the 1890s. Others of note are Achille Chainaye, G. Charlier and Victor Rousseau whose small-scale figural sculpture in bronze and marble using classical forms gains a greater sensibility and grace after the influence of Rodin. George Minne, best known for his elongated kneeling figures, especially those in the fountain outside the cathedral of St. Bavo in Ghent, was also an illustrator. The use of line developed in his graphic work was important for his work in sculpture, particularly in the creation of emotive subjects. *Rik Wouters* (1882–1916), a painter as well as a sculptor, *Ernest Wijnants* (1878–1964; museum devoted to his work in Mechelen) and *Oscar Jespers* (1887–1970) looked towards modernism by depicting simplified, primitive and almost abstract forms. There is a large collection of late 19C and 20C sculpture at the open air museum at Middelheim, Antwerp.

From 1850 a new impetus can be seen in the paintings of *Florent Willems* (1823–1905) and, particularly, *Alfred Stevens* (1923–1906), a pupil of Navez who later lived almost exclusively in Paris. In their paintings these artists populated interiors with attractive women: 'Women with a Mirror' (Groeninge museum, Bruges), by Willems, reminds one of a Dutch 17C genre piece like those of Gerard ter Borch. 'Autumn Flowers' (1867 Brussels museum); is a good example of Stevens's depiction of women in all their finery, contemporary with the mode of the Second Empire in France. Alfred's older brother *Joseph Stevens* (1819–92) and *Jan Stobbaerts* (1838–1914) specialised in painting animals—especially dogs, sometimes satirically, for example Stevens's 'Brussels-the Morning' (1848; Brussels Museum)—and rural life, with a vitality worthy of their Flemish heritage.

The establishment of the Société Libre des Beaux-Arts in 1868 marked the end of the acceptance of the government-sponsored Academies and Salons, held triennially in Ghent, Antwerp and Brussels, and the beginning of avant-gardism in Belgium. Having been inspired by Courbet's 'Stone Breakers', which was exhibited in Belgium in 1851, *Charles de Groux* (1825–70) and Constantin Meunier (already mentioned as a sculptor) were both at the centre of the Realist movement. They were founding members of this group who wished to concentrate on depicting the lives of the poor. *Eugène Laermans* (1864–1940), working almost thirty years later, continued to depict enobled labourers returning from their daily struggle in derelict landscapes analogous to their suffering. A large proportion of the group were landscape painters who wished to paint free from the confines of the studio. Members of the SLBA, including *Louis Dubois* (1830–80), *Alfred Verwee* (1838–1895), *Edouard Agneessens* (1842–85), *Felicien Rops* (1833–98), who started as a landscape painter but became most famous for his erotic graphic work (museum devoted to his work in Namur), and *Eugène Smits* (1826–1912), chose to exhibit with French artists to give the group a more European flavour. By the 1870s there was less opposition to Realism, as paintings by these artists were being accepted in the Salons. The success of *Charles Herman*'s painting 'A l'Aube' (1875) was an important turning point in the struggles against Neo-Classical and romantic painting. His 'realism', like that of Willems and Stevens, was the depiction of the bourgeoisie.

Landscape, which in Belgium as elsewhere in Europe had achieved a position of primary importance around 1865, was well represented by *Théodore Fourmois* (1814–71), *Alphonse Asselbergs* (1839–1916), *Joseph Coosemans* (1828–1904), and *Eugène Huberti* (1819–80), who were friends with the Barbizon painters in France, and by *Hippolyte Boulenger* (1837–74), painter of the Ardennes and the forests of Tervuren. Perhaps the most interesting landscape painters of the late 19C are *Paul-Jean Clays*(1819–1900), *Louis Artan* (1837–90), *Guillaume Vogels* (1836–96), *A.-J. Heymans* (1839–1921) working at Kalmthout, and *Theodoor Baron* (1840–1899) and *Frans Courtens* (1854–1943) working at Dendermonde, who to some extent resisted the seductive appeal of the French Impressionists' style and adopted an atmospheric, translucent style characteristic of Belgian art. An early work by *Emile Claus* (1849–1924), 'The Leie at Astene', (Groeninge museum, Bruges), marked the transition to yet another kind of impressionism which was called Luminism after the name of the group Vie et Lumière. This group, whose art vibrated with sunlight, was formed by Claus in 1904, with artists like *A.-J. Heymans*, *George Buysse* (1864–1916) and *Georges Morren* (1868–1941), some thirty years later than the start of Impressionism in France.

The immediate heirs to the Société Libre des Beaux-Arts were the groups La Chrysalide (1875–81) and L'Essor (1876–91), who also organised their own exhibitions. The former comprised artists such as Louis Artan, Guillaume Vogels and others from SLBA; and the latter included the sculptor Julien Dillens, *Jean Delville* (1867–1953), *Léon Frederic* (1856–1940) and *Fernand Khnopff* (1858–1921), who were Symbolists. *Xavier Mellery* (1845–1921), Khnopff's teacher, *William Degouve de Nunques* (1867–1935), *Emile Fabry* (1865–1966) and to some extent *Léon Spilliaert* (1881–1946), who came from Ostend, followed closely in their wake. The ideas of these and future groups were disseminated by the various art journals that came into existence at the same time, initiated by literary as well as professional figures. Their success was partly due to the prevailing atmosphere of liberalism, which kings Leopold I and II upheld. Brussels, which was French-speaking, became the artistic capital of Belgium, international in its outlook and ready to absorb new ideas, while Ghent and Antwerp remained with their Flemish heritage most prominent, only to become important again in the 20C.

Of Belgian painters of this period the most widely known is *James Ensor* (1860–1949). Macabre and fantastic, he is known for his use of skeletons and masks to make social comment in works such as 'The Entry into Brussels 1889'. In the best tradition of Bosch, these pictures still have the capacity to shock, and to fascinate. Even in his early works Ensor is penetrating. The 'Sombre Lady' (Brussels Museum) and the 'Mangeuse d'Huitres' (Antwerp Museum), provoke a response from the viewer.

Although very much an individual Ensor was also a participator. He contributed to both L'Essor and La Chrysalide, and was one of the founding members of the group Les XX (Les Vingt; 1883–94), which was established following the activity of the previously mentioned groups. Les XX, named because of its twenty members and twenty invited exhibitors, and its sucessor La Libre Esthetique (1894–1914), were, again, eclectic in their outlook and recognised the importance of combining all the arts and styles of art. In their exhibitions, held annually, they also had poetry readings and concerts as well as displays of Impressionist, Neo-Impressionist, Symbolist, Art Nouveau and Decorative works of art from abroad, especially France and England, as well as from Belgium. The Belgian artists were very receptive to these styles. Seurat's famous pointillist painting 'La Grande Jatte', depicting Parisians out on a Sunday afternoon on the

Seine, was exhibited at Les XX in 1887 and had the most immediate and profound effect on some of the group's members, especially *Théo van Rysselberghe* (1862–1926), *Georges Lemmen* (1865–1916), *Alfred 'Willy' Finch*(1854–1930), *Anna Boch* (1848–1933) and Henry van der Velde, who all immediately adopted pointillism. Théo van Rysselberghe, however, continued to paint psychological portraiture but using the pointillist technique. In Belgium the approach to pointillisim was less scientific then it had been in France but it also became more widespread.

Henri Evenepoel (1872–99) was an individualist. He painted portraits in a style inspired by Manet. Their poster-like quality looks forward to posters of *Jules van Biesbroeck* (1850–1920).

The end of the century saw the emergence of two extremely important architects: *Victor Horta* (1861–1947) and *Henry van de Velde* (1863–1957). Both were seminal figures in the development of Art Nouveau. This style had been imported partly from England with the works of William Morris, Walter Crane and Aubrey Beardsley that had been shown at exhibitions such as La Libre Esthétique. The two-dimensional arabesque lines of Art Nouveau were developed by the architects and designers of Belgium into three dimensions. *Gustave Serrurier-Bovy* (1858–1910), from Liège, designed Art Nouveau furniture. The surviving works of Horta, who used modern materials such as glass and steel to create buildings of an organic and supple grace, are in Brussels. His most famous building, the 'Maison du Peuple' (1896–99) for the Socialist Workers' Party, in Place Emile van de Velde, with its famous wall of glass, was destroyed in the 1960s. His house and studio (1898) is now a museum, and the Hotel Tassel (1892), now used by the Mexican Embassy, was recently restored to its former glory. A more simplified form of Art Nouveau was created by him in the Palais des Beaux Arts in Brussels (1922–29) and also the Museum of Fine Arts, Tournai (1928). Van de Velde, painter, craftsman and influential critic, as well as architect and interior designer, invites comparison with Charles Rennie Mackintosh. Both aimed at creating a total artistic movement. Van de Velde spent many years in Weimar. There he became the director of the Arts and Crafts School, which he designed himself in 1901 and which became in 1919 the first Bauhaus under the direction of Walter Gropius. The concept of unity of the arts, which Les XX had subscribed to, led, eventually, to these achievements. Little of Van de Velde's architectural work remains in Belgium except for 'Bloemenwerf' (1895), his own house in Uccle on the outskirts of Brussels. Façades in the Art Nouveau style remain prominent in the streets of Belgium, particularly in Ghent (Horta's birthplace) and on and around the Avenue Louise in Brussels. *Paul Hankar* (1859–1901) was another architect who had succumbed to the style, although he was less concerned with spatial unity than with decoration. His Ciamberlani house (1897), 40 Boulevard de la Cambre, shows his use of multi-coloured brickwork.

One of van de Velde's most famous buildings, although not in the curvilinear style of the fin-de-siècle but in the style of the international modern movement, is the Kröller-Müller Museum in Otterlo, Holland. His influence can be felt in the austerity and refinement of the best early 20C Belgian architecture. *Victor Bourgeois* (1897–1962), who created the Cité Moderne (1922–25), Berchem-Ste. Agathe, Brussels, and the studio of Oscar Jespers (1928), used clean white forms. *Louis Herman de Koninck* (1896–1985) was a modernist

who after the Bauhaus was forced to close in 1933 taught func-
tionalism at the School of Art and Architecture at Le Cambre,
Brussels. This school had been founded in 1926 by Henry van de
Velde and is still strong today for visual art and design. De Koninck
created his own house in Uccle, where he used his rationalist
philosophy of minimum interiors with maximum spatial impact. The
work of *Antoine Pompe* (1873–1980), on the other hand, represented a
new rationalised way of building in brick, as seen in the Clinic for Dr
van Neck (1910), No. 55 Rue Wafelaerts, Brussels. In the early 20C
monumental architecture in Belgium became international in character, revealing the influence of contemporary developments in
Holland, France and Germany. Amongst the vast quantity of 20C
architecture the new universities sited at Louvain-le-Neuve and Sart
Tilman near Liège are interesting and original designs. However,
architecture after 1945 was not really part of a movement, in fact
individualism reigned, unlike in Holland where planning dominated
the overall look of the houses and the layout of the cities. For this
reason it has been said that Belgium's architecture was a 'splendid and
full-blooded chaos', and on the one hand it has been pessimistically
interpreted as the 'ugliest country in the world', and on the other as
having meaning and freedom admired in the architecture of today.
The protagonists of the functionalist movement were, as mentioned
above, L.H. de Koninck, Victor Bourgeois and Hoste. The anti-
functionalists are Bob van Reeth, Charles Vandenhove, Lucien
Kroll—particularly for his Alma metro station, which is Gaudi-like in
its biomorphic plasticity—André Loits, Luc Schuiten, Marcel
Raymaekers, Jacques Sequaris and Marc Dessauvage. The disparate
individualistic styles of these architects, although referring through
the use of materials such as brick to the vernacular heritage of
building, provide an immensely varied modern geometry within the
towns and cities of Belgium and exhibit this country's eclectic tastes.

The marked preference of the early 20C painters and sculptors for
surrealism and expressionism can perhaps be interpreted in terms of
traditional Flemish tastes for the bizarre, the exuberant and the
tactile, as well as the influence of groups like the Symbolists who were
exploring the imagination in art. This is first expressed in the
religious-pastoral scenes painted by *Jacob Smits* (1856–1928), who
was born in Holland and influenced by Rembrandt. The source and
centre of Flemish expressionism was the School of Sint Martens-
Latem, a village outside Ghent, in which the leading figures were,
from the first group established around 1905, sculptor *George Minne*
(1866–1941), and artists *Albert Servaes* (1883–1966), *Valerius de
Sadeleer* (1867–1941), *Gustave van de Woestyne* (1881–1947) and
Albijn van den Abeele (1835–1918), whose work shows a certain
gothic mysticism. They were influenced by Symbolist painters in
Brussels and writers of the time, a few of whom came from Ghent, but
they also depicted religous subjects. Minne's sculpture 'Three Maries
at the Tomb', Servaes' series of the 'Chemin de Croix' and de
Woestyne's 'Crucifixion' are all representative examples. De
Saedeleer and Abeele painted landscapes in Flanders with a cold
stillness and contemplation about them comparable with Bruegel.
From the second group, established around 1909, were *Constant
Permeke* (1886–1952), master of emotional realism, *Gustave de
Smet* (1877–1943) and *Frits van den Berghe* (1883–1939). Their work
shows slight Cubist influence but they are figurative paintings using
cubic forms. Flemish expressionism developed independently from

that in Germany. It was more humane, evoking pathos by depicting fishermen and peasants in predominantly earthy colours. The Permeke Museum is in Jabbeke and the Gustave and Leon de Smet museums are at Deurle, 3km SE of Sint Martens-Latem.

Meanwhile, *Leon de Smet* (1881–1966; Gustave's brother), *Edgard Tytgat* (1879–1957), *Jean Brusselmans* (1884–1953) from Dilbeek, *Hippolyte Daeye* (1873–1952), *Fernand Schirren* (1872–1944), *Auguste Oleffe* (1867–1931), *Louis Thevenet* (1874–1930), *Willem Paerels* (1878–1962), *Henri Wolvens* (1896–1977) and *Rik Wouters* 1882–1916) developed their styles. In broad terms these artists are known as Brabant Fauvists because of their use of bold outlines and bright blocks of colour.

René Magritte (1898–1967), one of the most important Surrealist painters, was born and trained in Belgium. His unexpected juxtaposition of motifs, which, while essentially ordinary, are of unnatural scale and remoteness, has been extremely influential. One of his most famous paintings 'The Empire of Lights' (1952; Brussels Museum) is reminiscent of Willem Degouve de Nuncques' 'House of Mystery' (1892; Brussels Museum). After participating in the birth of the movement in Paris, between 1927 and 1930, Magritte returned to Brussels. Although Surrealism has been regarded as French it has an affinity with the peculiar in Belgian painting. In Brussels Magritte painted murals for public buildings, something which *Paul Delvaux* (1897–?), another Belgian Surrealist, also did. From 1935 Delvaux produced obsessional and unforgettable images of sexuality, travel and death. One of his murals can be seen on the exit of the Bourse metro station in Brussels (1978) and there is a museum of his works at Sint Idesbald. Another contributor to the Surrealist movement in Belgium was E.L.T. Mesens who developed the style in collage.

Louis Buisseret (1888–1956), *Anto Carte* (1886–1954) and *Leon Devos* (1897–1974) started a group called Nervia in 1928, which was centred around the town of Mons. The idea was to represent Walloon art. The styles of the artists vary but the paintings contain religious, allegorical and genre images in a lyrical almost Graeco-Roman manner. A few of these works can be seen in the museum at Charleroi.

Before the Second World War Belgian art was dominated by the two main movements: Expressionism and Surrealism. The exceptions were *Jules Scmalzigaug* (1886–1917), who was touched by the Futurist style and whose canvases depicting speed and light are influenced by the Italians Severini and Boccioni, and Marthe Donas, who was a Cubist painter and spent most of her life abroad. Between the wars saw the first experiments in abstraction, with artists like *Paul Joostens* (1889–1960), *Jozef Peeters* (1895–1960), *Michel Seuphor, Karel Maes* and *Joseph Lacasse*. The main protagonist was *Victor Severanckx* (1897–1965). These artists were aware of the developments in Holland through the Belgian George Vantongerloo, who was a friend of Théo van Doesburg. After 1945 the art world was fragmented. Two major groups having particular connections with Belgium were La Jeune Peinture (1945–50) and Cobra (1948–51). La Jeune Peinture, influenced in part by the lyrical and geometrical abstractions of Victor Severanckx, paved the way for the fully-fledged abstract art of the 1950s and numbered among its adherents Gaston Bertrand, Louis van Lint and Anne Bonnet, Marc Mendelson, Lismonde, Jan Cox and Jo Delahaut. The artists of Cobra, whose name is an acronym of Copenhagen, Brussels and Amsterdam, questioned the distinction between painting and writing and laid great emphasis on spontaneity. The most notable Belgian member of the group was *Pierre Aleckinsky*. Their exhibition at Liège in 1951 had a great influence on future Belgian artists. Prosper de Troyer and Felix de Boeck (museum devoted to his work in Brussels) painted abstractions that were a development from expressionism without any structured forms. After this it is difficult to mention one name without mentioning many, but perhaps Raoul Ubac, Octave Landuyt and Bram Bogart might be picked out. Pol Mara and Pol Bury were influenced by the Pop or Op art movement. Since the 1960s art has moved back to figuration and a new realism, social or hyperrealism, with artists like Roger Somville, Roger Raveel, Etienne Elias, Raoul de Keyser, Guy Degobert, Marcel Maeyer, Roger Wittevrongel, Marcel Broodthaers and Panamarenko. Here the use of photography becomes important and real objects are exploited to appeal to the imagination. Although in a modern contemporary idiom, the objects and their bizarre juxtapositions have a timelessness and remind us of 'the soul of things' or the expression of 'the invisible through the visible', which was the basis of the art of the symbolists and surrealists before them.

Today there are two divided ministries of culture, one for the Flemish, another for the Walloons, and the artistic character of the country is made up of small local communities with a multitude of museums. However, what is certain is that as always Belgium continues actively to contribute to the development of Western art.

PRACTICAL INFORMATION

Tourist Information. The national organisation is at 61 Rue Marché aux Herbes, 1000 Brussels. Tel: (02) 5123030. Although tourist visitors are served by a single reception office at this address, this office in fact represents two parallel and autonomous community organisations: the Office de Promotion du Tourisme de la Communauté Française (OPT) and the Vlaams Commissariaat-Generaal voor Toerisme (VGGT). Each of these organisations publishes its own brochures, but some of common interest (e.g. accommodation, events) are published jointly. Representation abroad is also joint, such offices including *United Kingdom*: 38 Dover Street, London W1X 3RB. Tel: (01) 4995379.—*USA*: 745 Fifth Avenue, New York, NY 10151. Tel: (212) 7588130.—*Germany*: 47 Berliner Allee, D-4000 Düsseldorf. Tel: (0211) 326008.—*France*: 21 Boulevard des Capucines, 75002 Paris. Tel: (1) 4742 4118.—*Holland* 435 Herengracht, 1017-PR Amsterdam. Tel: (020) 251251.

Below national level the offices most likely to interest the visitor are the provincial ones, listed below in alphabetical order of provinces.

Antwerp: 11 Karel Oomsstraat, 2018 Antwerp. Tel: (03) 2162810.—*Brabant*: 61 Rue Marché aux Herbes, 1000 Brussels. Tel: (02) 5130750.—*East Flanders*: 64 Koningin Maria-Hendrikaplein, 9000 Ghent. Tel: (091) 221637.—*Hainaut*: 31 Rue des Clercs, 7000 Mons. Tel: (065) 316101.—*Liège*: 77 Boulevard de la Sauvenière, 4000 Liège. Tel: (041) 224210.—*Limburg*: Domein Bokrijk, 3600 Genk. Tel: (011) 222958.—*Luxembourg*: 9 Quai de l'Ourthe, 6980 La Roche-en-Ardenne. Tel: (084) 411012.—*Namur*: 3 Rue Notre-Dame, 5000 Namur. Tel: (081) 222998.—*West Flanders*: Kasteel Tillegem, B-8200 Bruges 2. Tel: (050) 380296 or 337344.

Additionally all large towns, as also many smaller places, have individual tourist information offices, though the latter are in many cases open only in summer. It is worth bearing in mind that province and town offices provide detailed local literature and advice that may well not be available elsewhere.

Sea and Air Servces from England. The principal *Sea Crossings* (all carrying cars) are from Dover to Zeebrugge or Ostend, operated in partnership by P and O European Ferries (Zeebrugge) and the Belgian Regie voor Maritiem Transport (Ostend). Crossing times are 3¾–4 hours to Ostend and about half an hour longer to Zeebrugge. P and O European Ferries also operate a service from Felixstowe to Zeebrugge, crossing time 5¼hours on day sailings or about 8 hours by night. Another service (P and O North Sea Ferries) links Hull and Zeebrugge (drive on c 17.00; drive off c 09.00).

For those without cars there is the Regie voor Maritiem Transport Jetfoil crossing from Dover to Ostend in 1 hour 40 minutes. An alternative for car owners is to use one of the shorter sea crossings to France, continuing into Belgium by road.

Some addresses. P and O European Ferries, Channel House, Channel View Road, Dover CT17 9TJ. Tel (0304) 203388.—P and O European Ferries, 127 Regent Street, London W1R 8LB. Tel: (01) 7344431.—P and O European Ferries, Car Ferry Terminal, 8380 Zeebrugge. Tel: (05) 542222.—P and O European Ferries, Car Ferry Terminal, Felixstowe. IP11 8TB. Tel: (0394) 604802.—Regie voor Maritiem Transport, 5 Natienkaai, B-8400 Ostend. Tel: (059) 707601. —P and O North Sea Ferries, King George Dock, Hedon Road, Hull.

HU9 5QA. Tel: (0482) 795141 or Leopold II Dam, 8380 Zeebrugge. Tel: (050) 543430.

The principal *Air Services* are operated by British Airways and the Belgian SABENA (Société Anonyme Belge d'Eploitation de la Navigation Aérienne) between London-Heathrow and Brussels-Zaventem. Other lines provide services to Antwerp, Ostend and on to Liège.

Tour Operators. A number of tour operators in different parts of the United Kingdom offer competitively priced tours to Belgium. An up-to-date list of such operators is available from the Belgian National Tourist Office in London.

Motoring in Belgium. In some towns and rural areas the motorist will meet cobbles and rough stretches, and notices warning that the next few kilometres are in indifferent condition are quite commonplace, but for the most part Belgium has an excellent network of motorways and other roads, the traffic laws and signs generally conforming to western European continental practice. Motorways, and some other major through roads, are designated A followed by a national number and also E with a European number where the road, or a section of it, officially forms part of the European system. Other major roads have an N (National) designation. The E signs, often without an accompanying placename, are widely used on major highways and whatever is required should always be in the driver's mind. The numbering system was changed during 1986–87 and care should therefore be taken not to be using out-of-date maps. Michelin sheets 212, 213 and 214 (1cm: 2km) can be recommended, as can also sheet 409 (1cm: 3.5km) covering the whole of Belgium and the Grand-Duchy of Luxembourg.

It is advisable to be a member of a home motoring club, such membership in most cases carrying reciprocal right to the use of the facilities of affiliated Belgian clubs, including their road patrol breakdown services. In Belgium there are two principal clubs: the Touring Club Royal de Belgique (TCB), 44 Rue de la Loi, Brussels (tel: 02–2332211) is affiliated to the British Automobile Assocation, while the Royal Automobile Club de Belgique (RACB), 49 Avenue du Globe, Brussels (Tel: 02–3430008) is affiliated to the British Royal Automobile Club. Home clubs provide specialised publications with up-to-date and detailed information on local laws, and, since there are variations between British, and even more so United States', and continental practice, it is as well to be properly briefed. A few selected points are mentioned below.

Accidents. In the event of an accident of any significance, and always if there has been a personal injury, the police should be informed before any vehicle involved is moved. They must also be informed in the case of damage to an unoccupied stationary vehicle. In the case of minor accidents vehicles must be moved as soon as drivers have exchanged particulars. For Police, dial 901 (or 906 in Antwerp, Bruges, Brussels, Charleroi, Ghent or Mechelen). For Fire or Ambulance, dial 900).

Bicycles can be a hazard. Cycle tracks—sometimes marked only by a painted line—may run along one or both sides of the road, and motorists have to be as aware of these as of the road itself; this applies particularly when turning, bicycles continuing ahead normally having priority.

Insurance is compulsory. Normal British car policies should provide cover for the miniumum legal requirement, but this does not necessarily mean that full home cover is automatically extended abroad. Motorists are advised to consult their company or broker, and will always be wise to arrange for a Green Card extending the home policy to use abroad for a specified period. Motorists are also advised to travel under the protection of one of the comprehensive breakdown, get-you-home, medical and other cover schemes offered by the home motoring clubs.

Licences. A national or international driving licence is required, but the minimum age for local validity is eighteen. Vehicle registration documentation should be carried, and vehicles must also show GB or other appropriate registration identification.

Speed Limits. In built-up areas (which generally means between place name signs), 60 km/h. Other roads, 90km/h or 120km/h on motorways and some 4-lane roads. Lower limits are frequently imposed.

Traffic Signs. Signs (Flemish and French) include the following:

Alle Richtingen
Toutes Directions   } = All Directions

Weg Omlegging
Déviation. Route Déviée   } = Diversion

Werk in Uitvoering
Chantier   } = Roadworks

Moeilijke Doorgang
Passage Difficile   } = Difficult road stretch

Uitgezondert Plaatselijk Verkeer
Excepté Circulation Locale   } = Entry only for locally resident or business traffic

Doorgaand Verkeer
Toutes Directions   } = Through traffic

Schijf Verplicht
Disque Obligatoire   } = Parking disc must be shown

Warning Triangles must be carried by all vehicles. In the event of accident or breakdown, the triangle must be displayed behind the vehicle (100 metres on motorways; 30 metres on other roads) and must also be visible at a distance of 50 metres.

Travel by Train. Belgium has a dense and efficient rail network which offers a variety of reduced fares (groups, tourist period-tickets, weekend tickets, Benelux pass and others), while other facilities include prearranged car and bicycle hire at a number of stations, and combined train, bus and even boat excursions to many places of interest. Information: *Belgium*. Any station. Or Tel: (02) 2192640. *United Kingdom*. 22–25A Sackville Street, London W1X 1DE. Tel: (01) 7341491.

Access to Sites (see also Notes on Using the Guide, Opening Times). *Churches* which are an important tourist attraction are generally open throughout the day, though many close between about noon and 14.00. Other than for worship, Sundays should be avoided since several services are likely to be held during which visitors are asked not to walk around. Saturday afternoon can also be risky, this being a popular time for weddings. Entry to churches is normally free, but a charge is often made for treasuries, crypts and towers, or to see special works of art. Many churches not in the above category will be found to be closed, among the reasons being restoration (sometimes a matter of many years) and also the difficulty in finding custodians, essential in view of the theft and vandalism plaguing our times. Nevertheless, in case it should sooner or later prove possible to open such churches, this Guide gives a brief indication of what may be found in them. There are also churches which normally open only for services; in many such cases, though, these can be visited by applying to the sacristan or other local key-holder whose address is often on the door.

Museums and Art Galleries. In Belgium the word museum has a broad use, covering not only museums proper but also what in the United Kingdom would more properly be called an art gallery. The word is also used for areas of architectural, archaeological or other interest. Museums of many kinds abound in Belgium, many small towns and villages boasting one (normally local history, bygones, folklore and crafts). Though the number included is large, only selected museums are mentioned in this Guide. Others (with capricious opening times and sometimes short-lived) may be the result of one man's or one school's enthusiasm. The fact that some such museums do not find a place here does not mean that they are not worth a visit; indeed a browse around may well prove a rewarding experience.

As regards the larger museums and galleries, some points are worth bearing in mind. First, specialised temporary exhibitions are becoming an increasingly popular feature of museum management, these sometimes being on a scale which ousts a part of the permanent collections. Second, more and more museums are undergoing extensive restoration and rearrangement, this in some cases likely to last over a period of several years. Third, most of the larger museums, and especially the art galleries, have insufficient display space for the size of their collections, and increasingly the policy is to rotate material rather than overcrowd. For the above and other reasons (financial restrictions; difficulty in recruiting suitable staff) not only may important sections be closed for periods ranging from certain days up to several years, but also the allocation of material to specific rooms can be subject to not infrequent change.

Castles and Châteaux, although usually with beautiful, rich and interesting interiors, are often just as worth visiting for their settings and exteriors. In the majority of cases these can be well seen from a nearby road and visitors should not necessarily be deterred by the fact that a castle or château may not be 'Open'.

Accommodation. Hotels in Belgium embrace the same range of standards as in other West European countries. The national tourist organisation publishes annually a list of hotels, motels and pensions, and the use of this is recommended; all establishments included must conform to a legal standard, the more important establishments are placed within one of five Benelux categories, and the list also contains up-to-date information on facilities and prices. By law prices have to be displayed in each room. Prices may vary according to the season, the expensive months normally being July and August.—There is a useful free nationwide hotel reservation service operated by BTR (Belgium Tourist Reservations). The address is PO Box 41, 1000 Brussels 23. Tel: from UK dial 010–32–2–2305029. From USA dial 011–32–2–2305029.

Banking and Currency. Banks are normally open Monday–Friday, 09.15 to 15.30, some closing for lunch and some with an extension on Friday to 16.00. In the larger cities there are exchanges open over much longer periods, and there are also special facilities at Brussels Gare du Nord, Gare du Midi and Zaventem airport. The cashing of Travellers' Cheques can be expensive since a high service charge is made by the Belgian banks for each transaction; this charge is not though levied in the case of Thomas Cook's or American Express cheques exchanged at their own offices. Holders of a UK Banker's Eurocheque Card can cash personal cheques up to the current permitted limit at any bank showing the Eurocheque sign.

The monetary unit is the Belgian franc, divided into 100 centimes, though due to inflation these latter have for all practical purposes disappeared. Banknotes are of 50, 100, 500, 1000 and 5000 francs.

Except for copper ones of 20 francs and 50 centimes, coins are nickel, the values being 50 francs, 5 francs and one franc.

Camping and Caravanning. The national tourist organisation publishes an annual list of officially approved sites, these being placed within categories (stars). Several unofficial sites will also be found, especially in popular touring districts.

Commonwealth War Graves. More than 204,000 servicemen from the countries of the Commonwealth died in Belgium during the two World Wars and are buried or commemorated there. The greater number of graves are in war cemeteries in the immediate neighbourhood of the battlefields of 1914–18, and the largest (Tyne Cot Cemetery, Passchendaele, 11,900 graves; Lijssenthoek Military Cemetery, 9900 graves; Poelcapelle British Cemetery, 7400 graves; Hooge Crater Cemetery, 5900 graves) are in the neighbourhood of Ypres. Other large cemeteries, principally of the 1939–45 war, are situated elsewhere in Belgium at, for instance, Adegem, Heverlee near Louvain, Schoonselhof at Antwerp, Leopoldsburg, Brussels, and Hotton in the Ardennes. In all there are some 175 Commonwealth war cemeteries, but war graves, in large plots or small groups, are also situated in some 460 other burial grounds.

Those who have no known grave, of which there are more than 102,000, are commemorated by name on the Menin Gate Memorial at Ypres or on a number of other memorials to the missing such as those at Tyne Cot, or the Ploegsteert Memorial in Berks Cemetery Extension.

The war graves, cemeteries, and memorials are maintained by the Commonwealth War Graves Commission, whose head office is at 2 Marlow Road, Maidenhead, Berks SL6 7DX. Tel: (0628) 34221. The land on which they are situated was generously provided by the Belgian government under the terms of war graves agreements signed after the two world wars.

The Commonwealth war cemeteries vary greatly in size, but in general design they resemble each other. Within an enclosure bounded by a low wall or hedge and planted with trees, flowers, and grass plots, the orderly rows of graves are marked by simple headstones of uniform design, bearing the name, rank, unit, and date of death of the soldier lying below, his regimental crest, the symbol of his faith, and in many cases a personal inscription chosen by the next-of-kin. Officers and men lie side by side as they fought in life. In each cemetery stands a Cross of Sacrifice, and in each of the larger cemeteries is also an altar-like Stone of Remembrance inscribed with the words 'Their Name liveth for Evermore'.

Relatives and friends wishing to visit a grave will find a printed register near the entrance to the cemetery. Those who are uncertain of the location of a grave, cemetery or memorial are advised to obtain this information from the Commission's head office in Maidenhead (see above), or from its North-West Europe headquarters at 82 Elverdingestraat, Ypres, Belgium. Tel: (057) 200118. The locations of the war cemeteries and memorials in southwestern Belgium and northern France of the First World War are shown on a special overprinted edition of Michelin Map Sheet 51 obtainable from the Commission, who also publish other material of interest and who can obtain photographs of war graves at a small charge. The Royal British Legion (49 Pall Mall, London

SW1. Tel: 930 8131) can arrange for poppy wreaths to be laid, also at a reasonable charge.

British Embassy (Consulate). 28 Rue Joseph II, Brussels, with Consular Section at No. 32. Tel: (02) 2179000.

Entry Formalities. A passport or other internationally recognised identification must be shown on entry to Belgium. Subsequent registration with the police is covered by hotel, campsite etc registration. Visitors wishing to stay longer than three months should obtain a permit before entering Belgium.

Food and Drink. Belgium justly enjoys gastronomic fame both as to the quality and the quantity of what is offered throughout the country. That appreciation of food and drink was long ago a national characteristic is clear from the paintings of such artists as the Brueghels and Teniers with their scenes of robust eating, or from those of Snyders and others who portrayed kitchens and still-life; and that the tradition is as alive today will surely be agreed by anyone who has had a meal in Belgium.

In general Belgian food tends to be rich—much use is made of fat and pig in various forms—and herbs play a large part in its preparation. Nationally, but especially in Liège, soup is popular and in some of its forms (e.g. chervil) a speciality, large bowls amounting to whole meals in themselves being served in many cafés. The region of the Ardennes offers its famous pâté and smoked ham, as also game which includes young boar, venison and hare. Several dishes are prepared or served with prunes (rabbit is perhaps the best known), and beer is also much used for cooking (e.g. braised beef, rabbit). Brussels is known for its chicory ('witloof' meaning white leaf) as also for the hothouse grapes grown in the district near Tervuren. From the sea and rivers come mussels, served in various ways; the famous oysters of Ostend; eels, particularly 'au vert' (young); the trout of the Ardennes; and 'waterzooi', fish (or chicken) boiled with herbs. Confectionary and baking are also Belgian specialities, Brussels in particular being known for its richly filled chocolates (pralines) and several other towns for their local biscuits and cookies. 'Gaufres' (Flem. 'wafel'), a form of waffle, are often baked to order at street stalls. But perhaps the most ubiquitous food in Belgium is the potato in the simple form of fried chips, served not only with most meals but also from special vans and stalls (Friture. Frituur). Offered blazing hot (with or without a dressing) in containers of varying size, 'frites' can be a delicious and satisfying meal, in towns and villages usually easily found at any time of the day.

Beer has been the Belgian national drink since at least the time of the Gallo-Celtic Belgae. In the Middle Ages the abbeys did much to foster the art and commerce of brewing, notably by the introduction of hops, and the 14C saw the spread of the trade to lay brewers and the foundation of the brewers' guilds which by the 16C became among the most powerful in the land. During the 19C the discovery of pasteurisation and other technical progress led to a proliferation of breweries, so that today the country boasts some 355 brands of beer (most of lager type) and it has been calculated that the national consumption amounts to 126 litres per Belgian per year.

Medical. British Department of Health and Social Security pamphlets SA28 and SA30 detail the medical cover available under reciprocal arrangements. However, it is important to note that not everyone qualifies and that even those who do should obtain and take with them a Certificate of Entitlement (Form E111). Intending visitors are also advised to consider what private insurance may be desirable; in this connection attention is drawn to the cover provided under the motoring clubs' comprehensive schemes referred to above.

Post. Post Offices are usually open Monday to Friday 09.00 to 16.00 or 17.00, the smaller ones often closing for lunch. Except for the office in Avenue Fonsny, Brussels, most post offices are closed on Saturdays, Sundays and public holidays.

Public Holidays. New Year's Day (1 January). Easter Monday. Labour Day (1 May). Ascension Day. Whit Monday. National Day (21 July). Assumption Day (15 August). All Saints' Day (1 November). Armistice Day (11 November). King's Birthday or Fête de la Dynastie (15 November; partial holiday, government and official). Christmas Day (25 December). If one of the above falls on a Sunday, the following day becomes the holiday.

Telephone. Prices are indicated in kiosks. International calls cannot be made from all kiosks, but only from those bearing 'hats' of different countries and which exhibit instructions in a number of languages.

Time. Belgium is on Central European time, i.e. Greenwich Mean time plus one hour in winter, or plus two hours in summer (roughly early April to end September).

Tipping. In hotels and restaurants service and VAT should always be included on the bill and there is no requirement for an additional tip. Service and VAT are also normally included in taximeter readings. Tips are expected by theatre and cinema usherettes (10 per cent) and hairdressers (20 per cent); also by public toilet attendants (say, 20 francs) if no fixed price is indicated. Porters at stations and airports are entitled to an official fee per item.

'Tourist Trains' abound throughout Belgium but especially around the Ardennes. Running along roads these 'trains' are made up of simple semi-open carriages drawn by an (often battery-powered) 'engine'. Plying regularly around many popular tourist areas, they provide a pleasant and undemanding way of gaining a general local impression.

Glossaries

The Flemish-English and French-English glossaries below list words which in one way or another appear in the text, the meaning given here being that of the context.

FLEMISH-ENGLISH

Aan	On. Upon	*Burcht*	Castle.
Aarde	Earth		Fortress
Abdij	Abbey	*Bureel*	Office
Achter	Behind. Rear	*Burg*	Castle.
	of	*Burgemeester*	Burgomaster.
Akker	Field		Mayor
Andries	Andrew		
Appel	Apple	*Carmer* (old	Carmelite
Athenëum	High School	form for	
		modern	
Baan	Road. Way	*Karmeliet)*	
Bal	Ball		
Basiliek	Basilica	*Dal*	Valley
Beek	Brook. Stream	*De*	The
Begijnhof	(see p35)	*Denijs*	Denis
Beiaard	Carillon.	*Dienst*	Service
	Chimes	*Dier*	Animal
Belfort	Belfry	*Dijk*	Dike
Berg	Hill	*Dok*	Dock
Beuk	Beech tree	*Domein*	Domain.
Beurs	Exchange		Estate
Beest (dialect:	Animal.	*Donker*	Dark.
Biest)	Cattle		Obscure
Blekker	Dunes	*Doorn*	Thorn
(dialect)	hillock	*Dorp*	Village
Bloed	Blood	*Duin*	Dune
Bloot (dialect:	Bare.	*Duivel*	Devil
Blote)	Naked		
Boog	Bow	*Ei* (genitive =	Egg
	(weapon)	*eier)*	
Boom	Tree	*Eik*	Oak
Boomgaard	Orchard	*En*	And
Bos	A wood	*Engel*	Angel
Boter	Butter		
Boudewijn	Baldwin	*Feest*	Festival
Bourgondie	Burgundy	*Fontein*	Fountain
(Bourgonje)		*Frankrijk*	France
Boven	Upper. Above		
Brand	Fire	*Gang*	Passage.
Broek (old	Brook.		Way
word)	Stream	*Gasthuis*	Hospice.
Broer	Brother		Almshouse
Bron	Fountain.	*Gat*	Gap.
	Spring		Opening
Brood	Bread		(of a water
Brouwer	Brewer		inlet)
Brug	Bridge	*Gebouw*	Building
Buiten	Outer.	*Gedenkteken*	Memorial
	Outside	*Geest*	Ghost. Spirit

Gefusilleerd	Shot (executed)	*Hotel*	Hotel. Large private townhouse
Geld	Money		
Geldmunt	Mint (of money)	*Hout*	Wood
		Huidevetter	Tanner
Gemeente	Commune. Local government district	*Huis*	House
		Inlichtingen	Information
Gemeentehuis	Town Hall	*Jan*	John
Gerechtshof	Law Courts	*-je*	(diminutive suffix)
Gild	Guild		
Gillis	Giles	*Jong*	Young
Godshuis	Hospice. Almshouse	*Joris*	George
		Justitiepaleis	Law Courts
Goed	Good		
Goud	Gold	*Kaai*	Quay. Wharf
Graaf	Count (title)	*Kamer*	Chamber. Room
Graan	Grain. Corn		
Gracht	Moat. Canal	*Kammen*	Comb
Gravin	Countess	*Kamp*	Camp
Griet	Margaret. Peg	*Kanaal*	Canal
		Kant	Lace
Groente	Vegetable	*Kantoor*	Office
Groot (grote)	Large. Principal	*Kapel (adj = Kapelle)*	Chapel
		Karthuizer	Carthusian
		Kasteel	Castle
		Kat	Cat
Haan	Cock	*Katelijne*	Katherine
Hal (old form = Halle)	Hall (Cloth, Market)	*Kathedraal*	Cathedral
		Kei	Boulder. Pebble
Halen	To fetch		
Handboog	Hand bow (weapon)	*Kerk*	Church
		Ketel	Boiler. Cauldron
Handel	Commerce		
Handschoen	Glove	*Kip*	Hen. Chicken
Haven	Harbour. Port	*Klein*	Small
Haver	Oats	*Klooster*	Cloister. Religious House
Hedenags	Nowadays. Contemporary		
		Koe	Cow
Heide	Heath. Moor	*Koning*	King
Heilig	Holy	*Koningin*	Queen
Hengelen	To angle, fish	*Koninklijk*	Royal
Hertog	Duke	*Koorn*	Corn. Grain
Het	The	*Kraan*	Crane
Heuvel	Hill	*Kruid*	Herb
Hoed	Hat	*Kruis*	Cross
Hoek	Corner	*Kultuur*	Culture
Hof	Court. Yard. House. Property	*Kunst*	Art
		Laan	Avenue. Boulevard
Holle (dialect)	Mad		
Hoofd	Head	*Lakenhal (old form = halle)*	Cloth Hall
Hoog (hoge)	High		

Lam	Lamb
Lang	Long
Laurentius	Lawrence
Leen	Loan. Fief
Leder (old form = *Leer*)	Leather
Leeuw	Lion
Lei	Avenue. Boulevard. Quayside
Leven	Life
Lichttoren	Lighthouse
Lodewijk	Ludwig
Loge	Lodge
Luchthaven	Airport
Maagd	Maiden. Girl
Maand	Month
Markt	Market
Meer (old dialect form = *Meir*)	Lake. Marsh
Meter	Measurer. Inspector
Metser	Mason
Mevrouw	Mrs
Minderbroeder	Friar Minor (Franciscan)
Moere	Moor. Undrained land
Molen	Mill
Mond	Mouth
Mortier	Mortar
Munt	Coin. Mint (money)
Naald	Needle
Nachtegaal	Nightingale
Natie	Nation
Neder (old form = *Neer*)	Lower. Down
Nieuw	New
Niklaas	Nicholas
Noord	North
Ommegang	Procession
Onthoofden	Beheaded
Onvrij	Not free
Onze Lieve Vrouw (OLV)	Our Dear Lady
Oost	East
Op	On. Upon
Openlucht	Open-air
Os	Ox
Oud (oude)	Old

Over	Over. Across. Beyond
Paard	Horse
Paleis	Palace
Pand	Premises
Panne	Depression (of land)
Paradijs	Paradise
Pastorie	Parsonage
Pauwel	Paul
Paviljoen	Pavilion
Peper	Pepper
Peterselie	Parsley
Pieter	Peter
Plaats	Place. Square (in a town)
Plantentuin	Botanic Garden
Plantsoen	Public gardens
Plein	Square (in a town)
Poeder	Powder
Poel	Pool
Poelje (old dialect)	Chicken. Poultry
Polder	Reclaimed land
Poort	Gate
Predikheer	Dominican friar
Prelaat	Prelate
Prins	Prince
Punt	Point
Raad	Council
Raap	Rape (seed)
Rei	Quayside
Reiger	Heron
Ridder	Knight
Rijk(s)	Kingdom (National)
Saai	Cloth of the Aldermen's hall
's (= des) Schepenzaal	
Schild	Shield
Schipper	Master of a ship
Schoen	Shoe
Schone Kunsten	Fine Arts
Schout	Sheriff
Schouwburg	Theatre
Schutter	Marksman
Sierkunst	Decorative Art

Sint	Saint	*Vlaanderen*	Flanders
Sluis	Sluice. Lock (of a waterway)	*Vlaming*	Fleming
		Vlas	Flax
		Vlees	Flesh. Meat
Spaans	Spanish	*Vlies*	Fleece
Speelkaart	Playing card	*Vliet*	Stream. Small waterway
Spiegel	Mirror		
Spoor	Track (e.g. railway)		
		Vogelenzang	Birdsong
Stad	Town	*Volder*	A fuller
Stadhuis	Town Hall	*Voor*	Before. In front of. For
Stedelijk	Municipal		
Steeg	Lane. Alley		
Steen	Stone (= Castle. Prison)	*Vorming*	Marshalling
		Vrees	Fear
		Vrij	Free
Steenhouwer	Stonemason	*Vrouw*	Woman
Steenweg	Highway		
Ster (old dialect = Sterre)	Star	*Wacht*	Watch. Guard. Police
Stoet	Pageant	*Wafel*	Waffle
Straat	Street	*Wal*	Wall. Rampart
Strand	Beach		
Streek	District	*Wapen*	Weapon. Arms. Coat-of-arms
Suiker	Sugar		
Sweet (old form)	Sword		
		Weg	Road. Way
't (= het)	The	*Werf*	Wharf
Techniek	Technology	*Werk*	Work
Ten. Ter	At the	*Wetenschap*	Science. Technology
Thermen	Hot springs		
Tol	Customs. Toll		
Toreken	Small tower	*Wied*	Weed
Toren	Tower	*Wijk*	District
Trein	Train	*Wijn*	Wine
Troon	Throne	*Wijngaard*	Vineyard
Trouwzaal	Wedding Room	*Wissel*	Exchange
Tuin	Garden	*Wol* (dialect = *Wolle*)	Wool
Turkije	Turkey (country)		
		Zaal	Hall
Vaart	Canal. Navigation	*Zand*	Sand
		Zee	Sea
Van	Of	*Zeevaart*	Navigation
Vee	Cattle	*Zijl*	Watercourse
Veld	Field	*Zilver*	Silver
Verschansing	Entrenchment	*Zonder*	Without
		Zout	Salt
Veste	Fortification	*Zuid*	South
Vijver	Pond	*Zuivel*	Dairy produce
Vis	Fish		
Visser	Fisherman	*Zuster*	Sister

Numbers

1	*Een*	1st	=	*eerst*	
2	*Twee*	2nd	=	*tweede*	
3	*Drie*	3rd	=	*derde*	
4	*Vier*	4th	=	*vierde*	
5	*Vijf*	5th	=	*vijfde*	
6	*Zes*	6th	=	*zeste*	
7	*Zeven*	7th	=	*zevende*	
8	*Acht*	8th	=	*achtste*	
9	*Negen*	9th	=	*negende*	
10	*Tien*	10th	=	*tiende*	
11	*Elf*	11th	=	*elfde*	
12	*Twaalf*	12th	=	*twaalfde*	
13	*Dertien*	13th	=	*dertiende*	
14	*Veertien*	14th	=	*veertiende*	
15	*Vijftien*	15th	=	*vijftiende*	
16	*Zestien*	16th	=	*zestiende*	
17	*Zeventien*	17th	=	*zeventiende*	
18	*Achttien*	18th	=	*achttiende*	
19	*Negentien*	19th	=	*negentiende*	
20	*Twintig*	20th	=	*Twintigste*	
21	*Eenentwintig*				
22	*Tweeëntwintig*				
30	*Dertig*				
40	*Veertig*				
50	*Vijftig*				
60	*Zestig*				
70	*Zeventig*				
80	*Tachtig*				
90	*Negentig*				
100	*Honderd*				
1000	*Duizend*				

Days

Maandag	Monday	*Zondag*	Sunday
Dinsdag	Tuesday	*Hemelvaart*	Ascension
Woensdag	Wednesday	*Kerstmis*	Christmas
Donderdag	Thursday	*Nieuwjaar*	New Year
Vrijdag	Friday	*Pasen (paas-)*	Easter
Zaterdag	Saturday	*Pinksteren*	Whitsun

Months

Januari	January	*Juli*	July
Februari	February	*Augustus*	August
Maart	March	*September*	September
April	April	*Oktober*	October
Mei	May	*November*	November
Juni	June	*December*	December

Colours

Blauw	Blue	*Mauve*	Mauve
Bruin	Brown	*Paars*	Purple
Geel (gele-)	Yellow	*Rood (rode-)*	Red
Goud	Gold	*Roze*	Pink
Grijs	Grey	*Wit*	White
Groen	Green	*Zwart*	Black

FRENCH-ENGLISH

Abattoir	Slaughter-house
Abbaye	Abbey
Abîme	Abyss
Aérien (ne)	Aerial
Affligé	Afflicted. Sick
Agglomération	Conurbation
Aigle	Eagle
Allée	Road. Lane. Avenue
Amour	Love
Ancien (ancienne)	Former
Ange	Angel
Angle	Corner
Anonyme	Limited (of a commercial company)
Argent	Silver. Money
Armée	Army
Armes	Weapons. Coat-of-Arms
Armure	Armour
Athénée	High School
Aubépine	Hawthorn
Auberge	Inn
Audace	Courage
Autrefois	Former times
Bain	Bath. Spa
Balle	Ball
Banque	Bank
Baraque	Hut
Barrage	Dam
Barrière	Barrier. Toll-gate
Bas (basse)	Low
Bassin	Reservoir. Low-lying district
Basilique	Basilica
Baudouin	Baldwin
Beau (belle)	Beautiful. Fine
Beaux-Arts	Fine Arts
Béguinage	(See p 35)
Belvédère	View-point
Beurre	Butter
Bibliothèque	Library
Blanchisserie	Laundry
Blé	Corn. Grain
Bois	Wood
Bois à brûler	Wood for burning
Bon (bonne)	Good
Bord de l'Eau	Water's edge
Botte	Boot
Boucher	Butcher
Boucherie	Meat market
Bourse	Exchange
Brasserie	Brewery. Bar
Brasseur	Brewer
Brique	Brick
Bruyère	Heath
Butte	Mound
Cahier	Sketch book
Caillou	Stone. Pebble
Canotier	Oarsman
Carmes	Carmelites
Carpe	Carp (fish)
Carrefour	Crossroads
Caves	Wine cellars
Cendres	Cinders
Centenaire	Centenary
Cerf	Stag
Chanoine	Canon
Chantoir	Pothole
Chapelier	Hat maker
Chapelle	Chapel
Chapitre	Chapter (ecclesiastical)
Charbon	Coal
Châsse	Reliquary
Chaussée	Highway
Chemin-de-fer	Railway
Chêne	Oak
Cheval marin	Seahorse
Cinquantenaire	Jubilee
Cire	Wax
Cité	Large urban building, or group of buildings, serving a common purpose
Clerc	Cleric
Cloître	Cloister. Religious House
Collégiale	Collegiate church
Colonne	Column. Pillar

Commune	Local government-nt district
Comte	Count (title)
Congrès	Congress
Counseil	Counsel. Council
Convers	Lay (of monks)
Coticule	Hone-stone
Cour	Courtyard
Couronne	Crown
Couvent	Convent
Crèvecoeur	Heartbreak
Croisiers	Crutched Friars
Croix	Cross
Cygne	Swan
Cyprés	Cypress
De (du, des)	Of
Demeure	Residence
Dentelle	Lace
Dieu	God
Digue	Dike
Domaine	Estate (of land)
Donjon	Keep of a castle
Duc	Duke
Duchesse	Duchess
Dynastie	Royal line
Eau	Water
Echevin	Alderman. Deputy mayor
Ecluse	Lock (of a waterway)
Eglise	Church
Enfant	Child
Epave	Wrecked ship
Escalier	Stairway
Espagne	Spain
Espagnole	Spanish
Espérance	Hope
Esprit	Spirit (Holy)
Est	East
Estampe	Print. Engraving
Etang	Pond
Etat	The State
Etude	Study
Etuve	Bath-house
Evêché	Bishop's palace
Exposition	Exhibition
Fabrique	Factory
Fagne	Upland moss-hag
Fée	Fairy
Fer	Iron
Ferme	Farm
Ferronier	Worker in iron
Fierté	Pride
Fils	Son
Flandre	Flanders
Fontaine	Fountain. Spring
Forêt	Forest
Fosse	Pit. Ditch
Foulon	Fuller (of textiles)
Frère	Brother
Frère Convers	Lay Brother
Fusillé (e)	Shot (executed) person
Gare	Station
Gauche	Left (direction)
Gaufre	Waffle
Géant	Giant
Gendarmerie	National police
Gibier	Game animals
Gland	Acorn
Godefroid	Godfrey
Grand	Large. Principal
Grand-Place	Main square
Grès	Sandstone
Grisaille	Grey representation of objects in relief (of art)
Grotte	Grotto. Cave
Halle aux Draps	Cloth Hall
Haut (haute)	High
Herbes	Herbs
Histoire	History
Homme	Man
Hôpital	Hospital
Hors	Outside. Beyond
Hôtel	Hotel. Large private town house
Hôtel de Ville	Town Hall
Impératrice	Empress
Ingénieur	Engineer

Japonais	Japanese	*Neuf (neuve)*	New
Jardin	Garden	*Nord*	North
Jeu de balle	Ball game	*Notre-Dame*	Our Lady
Jonction	Junction		
		Or	Gold
Lac	Lake	*Palais*	Palace
Ladrerie	Lazer (leper) house	*Palais de Justice*	Law Courts
Lapidaire	Lapidary (adj)	*Parc*	Park
Le (la, les)	The	*Patrie*	Country
Légumes	Vegetables	*Pauvre*	Poor
Lez	Near (of place names)	*Pays*	District
		Perdu	Lost. Ruined
Libre	Free	*Petit (e)*	Small. Little
Livre	Book	*Pierre*	Peter. Stone
Logis	Lodging	*Pitié*	Compassion
Loi	Law	*Place*	Square (of a town)
Loup	Wolf		
Lumière	Light	*Plage*	Beach
		Poisson	Fish
Maison	House	*Pont*	Bridge
Malade	Sick	*Porte*	Gate
Manège	Riding school	*Presse*	The Press
Marais	Marsh	*Printemps*	Spring (season)
Marché	Market		
Maux	Sick people	*Pris*	Taken
Medaille	Medal. Medallion	*Profond*	Deep
		Poulets	Poultry
Métier	Trade. Occupation	*Praline*	Richly filled chocolate
Midi	South (noun)	*Pré*	Field. Meadow
Militaire	Military		
Mineurs	Franciscans (Friars Minor)	*Quai*	Quay. Wharf
		Quartier	District of a town
Minier	Mining (adj)	*Quatre-Bras*	'Four Arms' (Frequent name for crossroads)
Monastère	Monastery		
Monde	World		
Monnaie	Mint (noun, of money)		
Mont (Montagne)	Hill	*Rampe*	Slope
		Réduit	Refuge. Retreat. Redoubt
Mont de Piété	Public pawnshop		
		Reine	Queen
Mort (morte)	Dead	*Remparts*	Ramparts
Mosan	Of the Meuse area (art, archaeology)	*Rends nous*	Restore to us
		Renseignements	Information
		Rocher	Rock
Moulin	Mill	*Roi*	King
Muette	Dumb person (fem)	*Romain*	Roman
		Roman	Romanesque
Mur	Wall	*Rond Point*	Roundabout (road system)
Musée	Museum. Art gallery		

Route	Road	*Templier*	Member of the Order of Templars
Rue	Street		
Ruelle	Lane. Alley		
Ry (old word)	King	*Temps de chien*	Awful weather
Sabbat	Sabbath	*Tête*	Head
Sablon	Sand	*Théâtre*	Theatre
Sacré	Holy	*Thermes*	Hot springs
Saint (Sainte)	Saint. Holy	*Toison d'Or*	Golden Fleece
Salle	Hall		
Sanctuaire	Sanctuary. Holy place	*Tombeau*	Tomb
		Tonnelet	Small barrel
Sang	Blood	*Tortillard*	Meandering local railway
Sciences Naturelles	Natural History		
Secours	Help	*Tour*	Tower
Sentier	Path. Track	*Trône*	Throne
Serment	Oath	*Tour*	Hole. Cave
Serre	Glasshouse		
Sions	Jews	*Val. Vallon*	Valley
Société	Company (commercial)	*Vent*	Wind (weather)
		Verre	Glass
Soeur	Sister	*Viande*	Meat
Source	Spring. Source of a river	*Vicinal*	Local railway
		Vie	Life
Souterrain	Basement. Underground	*Vieil (vieille, vieux)*	Old
		Ville	Town
Sud	South	*Vin*	Wine
Syndicat d'Initiative	Local promotion and information organisation	*Vivant*	Living
		Wallonie	Wallonia. Walloon Belgium

Numbers

1	*Un*	1st	=	*premier (première)*
2	*Deux*	2nd	=	*deuxième*
3	*Trois*	3rd	=	*troisième*
4	*Quatre*	4th	=	*quatrième*
5	*Cinq*	5th	=	*cinquième*
6	*Six*	6th	=	*sixième*
7	*Sept*	7th	=	*septième*
8	*Huit*	8th	=	*huitième*
9	*Neuf*	9th	=	*neuvième*
10	*Dix*	10th	=	*dixième*
11	*Onze*	11th	=	*onzième*
12	*Douze*	12th	=	*douzième*
13	*Treize*	13th	=	*treizième*
14	*Quatorze*	14th	=	*quatorzième*
15	*Quinze*	15th	=	*quinzième*
16	*Seize*	16th	=	*seizième*
17	*Dix-sept*	17th	=	*dix-septième*
18	*Dix-huit*	18th	=	*dix-huitième*

Numbers (cont.)

19	*Dix-neuf*		19th =	*dix-neuvième*
20	*Vingt*		20th =	*Vingtième*
21	*Vingt-et-un*			
22	*Vingt-deux*			
30	*Trente*			
40	*Quarante*			
50	*Cinquante*			
60	*Soixante*			
70	*Septante* (Belgian form)			
80	*Quatre-vingt*			
90	*Nonante* (Belgian form)			
100	*Cent*			
1000	*Mille*			

Days

Lundi	Monday	*Dimanchè*	Sunday
Mardi	Tuesday	*Ascension*	Ascension
Mercredi	Wednesday	*Noël*	Christmas
Jeudi	Thursday	*Nouvel An*	New Year
Vendredi	Friday	*Pâques*	Easter
Samedi	Saturday	*Pentecôte*	Whitsun

Months

Janvier	January	*Juillet*	July
Février	February	*Août*	August
Mars	March	*Septembre*	September
Avril	April	*Octobre*	October
Mai	May	*Novembre*	November
Juin	June	*Décembre*	December

Colours

Blanc	White	*Noir*	Black
Bleu	Blue	*Or (Couleur*	Gold
Brun	Brown	*d'or)*	
Gris	Grey	*Pourpre*	Purple
Jaune	Yellow	*Rosé*	Pink
Mauve	Mauve	*Rouge*	Red
		Vert	Green

Alternative Place Names
(Flemish, French and Other)

Selected names below are listed alphabetically under North (Flemish) Belgium, South (Walloon) Belgium, and Cantons de l'Est and Various.
Belgium = België or La Belgique
Brussels = Brussel or Bruxelles

North (Flemish) Belgium

Flemish	French	Other
Aalst	*Alost*	
Albert Strand	*Albert Plage*	
Antwerpen	*Anvers*	Eng: Antwerp

North (Flemish) Belgium (cont.)

Flemish	French	Other
Baarle-Hertog	*Baarle-Duc*	
Brugge	*Bruges*	
Borgloon	*Looz*	
De Haan	*Le Coq*	
De Panne	*La Panne*	
Diksmuide	*Dixsmude*	
Gent	*Gand*	Eng: Ghent
Geraardsbergen	*Grammont*	
Halle	*Hal*	
Haspengouw	*Hesbaye*	
Ieper	*Ypres*	
Ijzer	*Yser*	
Kempen	*Campine*	
Koksijde	*Coxyde*	
Kortrijk	*Courtrai*	
Leie	*Lys*	
Leuven	*Louvain*	
Lier	*Lierre*	
Maas	*Meuse*	
Mechelen	*Malines*	
Menen	*Menin*	
Mesen	*Messines*	
Neerheylissem	*Hélécine*	
Oostende	*Ostende*	Eng: Ostend
Oudenaarde	*Audenarde*	
Roeselare	*Roulers*	
Ronse	*Renaix*	
Schelde	*Escaut*	Eng: Scheldt
Scherpenheuvel	*Montaigu*	
Sint Truiden	*Saint Trond*	
Temse	*Tamise*	
Tienen	*Tirlemont*	
Tongeren	*Tongres*	
Torhout	*Thourout*	
Veurne	*Furnes*	
Vlaanderen	*La Flandre*	Eng: Flanders
-Voeren	*Fourons-*	
Zeebrugge	*Zeebruges*	
Zoutleeuw	*Léau*	

South (Walloon) Belgium

French	Flemish	Other
Ath	*Aat*	
Braine-le-Château	*Kasteelbrakel*	
Braine-le-Comte	*'s Gravenbrakel*	
Clabecq	*Klabbeek*	
Comines	*Komen*	
Enghien	*Edingen*	
Escaut	*Schelde*	Eng: Scheldt
Hainaut	*Henegouwen*	
Jodoigne	*Geldenaken*	

South (Walloon) Belgium (cont.)

French	Flemish	Other
La Hulpe	*Ter Hulpen*	
Lessines	*Lessen*	
Liège	*Luik*	Ger: Lüttich
Lys	*Leie*	
Meuse	*Maas*	
Mons	*Bergen*	
Mouscron	*Moeskroen*	
Namur	*Namen*	
Nivelles	*Nijvel*	
Oreye	*Oerle*	
Othée	*Elch*	
Saintes	*Sint Renelde*	
Soignies	*Zinnik*	
Tournai	*Doornik*	
Tubize	*Tubeke*	
Waremme	*Borgworm*	
Wavre	*Waver*	

Cantons de l'Est and Various

German	French	Flemish
Aachen	*Aix-la-Chapelle*	Aken
Büllingen	*Bullange*	
	Dunkerque	Duinkerke
	Lille	Rijsel
Monschau	*Montjoie*	
Mosel	*Moselle*	
Reinhardstein	*Rénastène*	
Sankt-Vith	*Saint-Vith*	
Trier	*Trèves*	
Weismes	*Waimes*	

1   Brussels and Environs

BRUSSELS (Fr. **Bruxelles**; Flem. **Brussel**), with about a million inhabitants, is both the national capital as also that of the two parts of the Province of Brabant and of each of the new federal Regions, one of these being the city itself. However, whatever changes the new constitution may be bringing, the city seems likely to remain one comprising 19 communes—some Flemish, some Walloon, some mixed—and as such officially bilingual with all street names, official notices and suchlike in both French and Flemish. The former, however, tends to predominate, particularly in the central area, and is also generally understood elsewhere even though Flemish or the mixed Brussels dialect may be the local language; French is normally used in the text below. Always cosmopolitan, and home now to the European Economic Community (EEC; Common Market) and the North Atlantic Treaty Organisation (NATO)—each with its own diplomatic representation quite separate from that to the Belgian Crown—and home also to many other international organisations and business concerns, Brussels, with good justification, also regards itself as the capital of Europe.

A roughly hexagonal belt of very wide boulevards, some 8km in circumference and laid out in 1818–71 along the course of the 14C ramparts, marks the boundary of ancient Brussels and still encloses the heart of the city. Within this area the LOWER TOWN, with the Grand-Place and the Place de Brouckère as its centre and also with the main shopping streets, will be of principal interest to visitors. Along the high ground to the E and S sprawls the UPPER TOWN; here, both within and beyond the ring boulevards, are the great museums and art galleries, the Palais du Roi with the Parc de Bruxelles, the huge Palais de Justice, many embassies, and the headquarters of the EEC. On the slope between the upper and lower towns an intermediate strip contains the cathedral, the central station, and the broad flight of steps that, as the Mont des Arts, ascends to the Place Royale.

Architecturally, the superb Grand-Place and its adjacent narrow streets survive from the past, as do also a number of 18C and 19C districts and individual buildings. Generally, though, the trend during the post-war decades—and this was particularly the case in the central lower town and along the boulevards—was in favour of massive high-rise or other modern blocks, many of these dubbed 'Centres' and including restaurants, hotels and extensive shopping precincts. Whether this policy has given Brussels an excitingly modern and progressive individuality, or whether it has robbed the city of heart and warmth of character is still much debated by both residents and visitors. What can be said is that the 1980s have witnessed a vigorous revival of interest in conservation and that more and more the emphasis is now on restoration rather than total redevelopment.

For the visitor the capital's main attractions are its famed Grand-Place, its wealth and variety of museums and art galleries, its

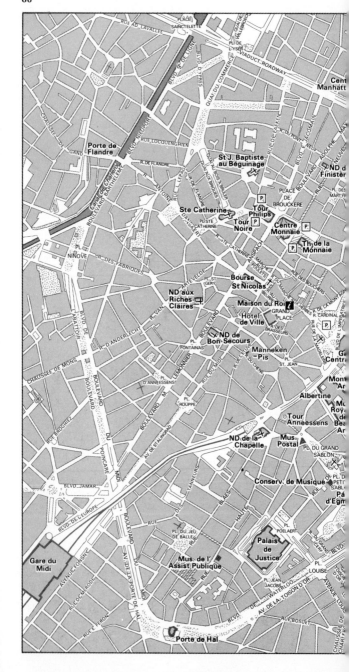

89

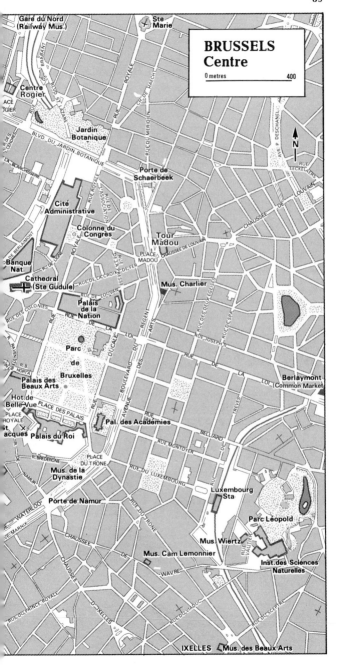

excellent restaurants (the two Rues des Bouchers near the Grand-Place have the most 'popular' concentration), and its many excellent shops, these ranging from large stores along the main streets to a rich choice of smaller shops in the older streets, in the elegant 19C arcades ('galeries') or within the modern warrens of the 'Centres'. Also meriting mention are the floodlighting and the Metro, both examples of modern civic pride and both mentioned in more detail below.

Tourist Information. There are two offices in central Brussels; that at 61 Rue du Marché aux Herbes, immediately N of the Grand-Place and on the site of a meat market with origins reaching back to the 12C, being concerned not only with Brussels but also with Belgium as a whole and, more specifically, the two parts of the Province of Brabant. (June–September: 09.00 to 20.00 or 19.00 on Saturday and Sunday. November–February: Monday–Saturday, 09.00 to 18.00. Sunday, 13.00 to 17.00 but closed 25 December and 1 January. March–May, and October: 09.00 to 18.00 Tel: 5123030.).—Tourist Information Brussels (TIB), concerned solely with Brussels and offering many detailed services, is at the Hôtel de Ville in the Grand-Place. The Guide (with map), published annually by TIB, provides some 100 pages of wide-ranging information. (April–September: 09.00 to 18.00 or 17.00 on Sunday. October–March: Monday–Saturday, 09.00 to 18.00. Closed 25 December and 1 January. Tel: 5138940.)

Public Transport. On the whole moving around Brussels is not difficult, with a good bus, tram and Metro network, plenty of taxis (service included in the metred price), and even several and convenient central parking facilities. The bus, tram and Metro services are controlled by STIB (Société des Transports Intercommunaux Bruxellois). Map and other information from either of the Tourist Information offices, or STIB stations (Porte de Namur. Rogier, Midi), the Midi Information Centre also covering local and national rail and associated bus services. Various carnets can be bought giving substantial reduction for multiple journeys.—The *Metro* is a continuing achievement of the 1970s and 1980s, the first section having been opened in 1976. Justly claiming to be not only a transport achievement but also an artistic one, the stations are decorated with mosaics, murals, sculpture, and marble and tile designs, the work of contemporary Belgian artists. Among the better-known names may be mentioned Paul Delvaux (a mural at the Bourse) and Octave Landuyt (four bas-reliefs at the Porte de Namur). A leaflet is obtainable from information offices.

Airport. Zaventem, 14km NE. Special train between the airport, the Gare du Nord and the Gare Centrale, with connection to the Gare du Midi. 20 to 25 minutes. Service half-hourly between about 05.30 to 23.00 outward and 06.00 to 23.45 inwards. It is worth noting that the rates charged by taxis based at the airport are considerably higher than those charged by city taxis. There is a Tourist Information office in the airport baggage hall.

Stations. *Nord*, to the N of Place Rogier. *Centrale*, at the Carrefour de l'Europe (Boulevard de l'Impératrice) above the Grand-Place. *Midi*, off the SW ring boulevard.

Main Post Offices (normally Monday–Friday, 09.00 to 17.00; some offices open until later on Friday and also Saturday morning). Centre Monnaie. Gare Centrale. Centre de Communication Nord (Gare du Nord), 80 Rue du Progrès. Bourse. Palais de Justice, 1 Boulevard Charlemagne. Brussels X (Gare du Midi), 48A Avenue Fonsny (always open).

Telephone. Telegram. Telex. *Telephone*. Kiosks showing international flags accept international calls and telegrams. Some main offices: Gare du Midi, Avenue Fonsny. No. 17 Boulevard de l'Impératice. No. 23A Rue de Brabant (near Gare du Nord). Place de Luxembourg. Zaventem Airport.—*Telegrams*. Dial 905 for Europe; 986 for elsewhere. Or use above telephone offices.—*Telex*. No. 13 Boulevard de l'Impératrice. Tel: 5134490. Daily 08.00 to 21.30.

Money Exchange. Outside normal banking hours (Monday–Friday, 09.15 to 15.30 but with some branches open Saturday morning), money can be changed at various downtown offices with wider hours or at the three main stations (Midi and Nord: daily, including Holidays, 07.00 to 23.00. Centrale: Monday–Saturday, 08.00 to 20.00. Sunday 09.00 to 17.00). Also, close to the Grand-Place, Paul Laloy, 6 Rue de la Montagne (Monday–Friday, 09.00 to 18.00. Saturday, 10.00 to 18.00. Sunday in June–September, 11.00 to 13.00).

Tours. Local agencies offer a variety of city and environs tours, these including Laeken, the Atomium and Waterloo. Also tours throughout Belgium.

English Bookshop. W.H. Smith, 71–75 Boulevard Adophe Max.

Theatres. *Théâtre Royal de la Monnaie*, the historic opera House, Place de la Monnaie. *Toone* puppet theatre, Petite Rue des Bouchers. Also many other theatres and auditoriums, normally playing in Flemish or French.

Markets. Brussels offers a wide choice of picturesque markets, the long list filling over two pages of the official city (TIB) guide. Some of the more interesting are given below. *Birds*. Grand-Place. Sunday, 07.00 to 14.00. *Flowers*. Grand-Place. Daily, 08.00 to 18.00. *Antiques and Books*: Place du Grand Sablon. Saturday, 09.00 to 18.00. Sunday, 09.00 to 14.00. Place du Jeu de Balle. Daily, 07.00 to 14.00. *Flea Market*: Place du Jeu de Balle. Daily, 07.00 to 14.00. *Fruit and Vegetable*: Place Sainte Catherine. Daily, 07.00 to 17.00. *Domestic Animals*. Rue Dropsy Chaudron, Anderlecht. Sunday, 08.00 to 12.00. *Horses*: Place de la Duchesse de Brabant, Molenbeek. Friday, 08.00 to 15.00.

Floodlighting. Among the many parts of the City which are floodlit (dark until 00.30) are the Grand-Place (until 02.00); the Baroque Eglise Saint Jean Baptiste au Béguinage; the Eglise Sainte Catherine; the Bourse; the Cathédrale Saint Michel; and most of the stretch between and including the Parc de Bruxelles and the Place Royale and the Palais de Justice, particularly attractive being Notre-Dame du Sablon.

History. In the early centuries the river Senne, now canalised and covered along its course through the city, formed an extensive area of marsh in which the Gallo-Roman population took refuge when harried by the Franks after the withdrawal of the Romans. Hence perhaps the city's name, which probably derives from Bruocsella (Broekzele) meaning a village of the marsh. There follows a shadowy connection with St. Géry (6C) who is said to have founded a chapel on one of the islands (today's Place Saint Géry), but the first recorded mention of Brussels is in a document of 966. The village grew, largely because it provided a river crossing on the trade route between Cologne and Ghent and Bruges (this old route can still be traced as the succession of streets following the course of the ancient Steenweg, see p 93), and it is known that by 979 the dukes of Lower Lotharingia were living on the island, that in 1041 the then duke moved to higher ground (the Coudenberg, his castle, occupying a part of what is now the Parc de Bruxelles, later becoming the chief palace of the Netherlands), and that six years later a church was dedicated to St. Michael. In the early 12C the first fortified wall was built, fragments of this still surviving as three small towers (Noire, Villers, Anneessens). As the village grew into a town the merchants established a market out of which later grew the Grand-Place, and in 1312 the town was granted its first charter, the Charter of Cortenberg, this being confirmed in 1356 on the occasion of the 'Joyeuse Entrée' of Wenceslas of Luxembourg and Joanna of Brabant, now rulers of Brabant, the dukedom in which Brussels lay. New walls enclosing a wider area were raised between 1357 and 1383; strengthened in the 16C, these defences stood until the 19C when they gave way to the ring boulevards, the Porte de Hal being all that survived. In 1402 work started on the Hôtel de Ville as Brussels prospered, acquiring a trade in luxury articles such as lace, tapestry, jewellery, and church furnishings, notably retables. Then in 1531 the seat of the government of the Netherlands was finally transferred from Mechelen to Brussels, the latter soon afterwards (1568) witnessing the execution in the Grand-Place of the patriot leaders, Egmont and Horn.

Under the Archdukes Albert and Isabella (1598–1621) the Spanish régime was milder and the arts flourished, but disaster came with the War of the Grand Alliance during which in 1695 Louis XIV's Marshal Villeroi bombarded the city for 36 hours, destroying 16 churches and nearly 4000 houses, much of this damage occurring in and around the Grand-Place. In 1706, during the War of the Spanish Succession, Brussels opened its gates to Marlborough, but when this war ended in 1713 with the Treaty of Utrecht Belgium was awarded to the Austrian Habsburgs and six years later the leader of the city guilds, Frans Anneessens, was beheaded in the Grand-Place for defending the privileges of Brussels against the encroachments of its Austrian rulers. The Coudenberg palace burnt down in 1731. Although occupied by the French under Marshal Saxe in 1746 (War of the Austrian Succession), Belgium was soon restored to Austria and Brussels now enjoyed a period of prosperity under the cultured and enlightened Charles of Lorraine, appointed governor by his sister-in-law Maria

Theresa. Inspired by Charles, who wanted to make Brussels a northern Vienna, the second half of the 18C saw the building of the Palais du Roi (partly on the site of the old Coudenberg palace), the Palais de la Nation and the Place Royale, while the gates of the city wall were demolished.

During the years under revolutionary France, Brussels, now no more than the capital of the French department of the Dyle, saw the completion of the demolition of its walls and the start of the conversion of their course into boulevards. In 1815 the Battle of Waterloo, fought only 20km from the city, saved Brussels from a renewed French occupation, and from now until 1830, during which period Belgium was an unwilling partner in the United Kingdom of the Netherlands, Brussels alternated with The Hague as the royal residence of King William I. The revolution that finally secured Belgian independence started in Brussels, in the Théâtre de la Monnaie, on 24 August 1830.

The 19C saw the start of the transformation of Brussels into a modern city, the work on the ring boulevards (finally inaugurated in 1871) opening the way for the spread of the Upper Town, notably towards today's Parc du Cinquantenaire and along the Avenue Louise. Landmarks of the 19C included the inauguration of continental Europe's first passenger train service between Brussels and Mechelen (1835); the founding of the Free University in 1834; the opening of the Galeries Saint Hubert in 1846; the building of the Palais de Justice between 1866 and 1883; the covering of the Senne in 1871 and at the same time the replacement of extensive slums by main streets, much of this achievement thanks to the drive of Burgomaster Anspach; and the great Jubilee exhibition of 1880 in the Parc du Cinquantenaire.

At the start of the First World War Brussels was left undefended and the German army entered on 20 August 1914. The passive resistance of the people was encouraged by their burgomaster, Adolphe Max, who refused to cooperate with the invader and was deported. The underground newspaper 'La Libre Belgique' was produced in Brussels, and in 1915 the English nurse Edith Cavell was shot here for helping fugitive soldiers to escape to neutral Holland. The Belgian heroine Gabrielle Petit was shot the following year. Occupied again during the Second World War (May 1940–September 1944), the city repeated its open and underground resistance and much help was given to Allied airmen and others.

The post-war years were the years of vigorous modernisation, impetus being given by the World Fair of 1958, the symbol of which, the Atomium, still dominates the city's northwestern outskirts; it was at this time too that the ring boulevards were given the system of tunnels which has served as a model for many other cities. These were also the years of progress towards acceptance as the capital of Europe, with Brussels chosen as the headquarters of the EEC in 1959 and of NATO in 1967. Modernisation continues—if more tempered now by the claims of conservation—features of the 1970s and 1980s being the fine Metro and the ambitious outer ring motorway. Finally, the 1980s have seen the administrative changes brought about by Belgium's new federal constitution, Brussels adding to its titles that of 'capital' of each of the new Regions, of which Brussels itself ranks as one.

Routes from Brussels. To *Ostend*, see Rte 8; to *Ronse, Oudenaarde* and *Kortrijk(Courtrai)*, see Rte 12; to *Mechelen* and *Antwerp*, see Rte 15; to *Louvain* (*Leuven*) and *Liège*, see Rte 21; to *Tournai*, see Rte 22; to *Mons*, see Rte 23; to *Charleroi*, see Rte 24; to *Namur*, see Rte 27.

Central Brussels is described below by four districts: A. The Lower Town; B. The Upper Town; C. The Ring Boulevards; and D. The Parc du Cinquantenaire and Parc Léopold. Section E. covers the Musées Royaux des Beaux Arts (Art Ancien and Art Moderne), and further sections describe the Outer City and Suburbs (F.) and Waterloo and Tervuren (G.).

A. The Lower Town

The Lower Town has two centres, 400m apart: the relatively modern Place de Brouckère and the ancient Grand-Place. Today the main streets are Boulevards Anspach and Adolphe Max, running roughly S and N out of the Place de Brouckère, and the Rue Neuve, parallel to Boulevard Adolphe Max. These streets date from after the covering of the Senne and the slum clearance of the second half of the 19C.

Before this, from at least as early as the 10C, the main artery was the Steenweg, the Brussels section of the trade route between the Rhine and Ghent and Bruges; this ran roughly E to W, passing just N of the Grand-Place. Interest can be added to time spent in the older parts of the Lower Town by bearing in mind, perhaps even retracing, the course of this ancient way. From the E one approach to Brussels was through the Porte de Schaerbeek in what is now the Upper Town, then down past the cathedral and the Rue de la Montagne; the other approach was through the Porte de Namur, then by way of the Mont des Arts down to the Rue de la Madeleine. In the Lower Town the two approaches met at the E end of the Rue du Marché aux Herbes, which the Steenweg then followed. In early times the Rue du Marché aux Herbes was beside a rivulet which came off the Coudenberg and joined the Senne somewhere near where the Bourse now stands. Flanked by stalls and markets, the Steenweg crossed the Senne, near the town wharf which functioned here until the 16C, then followed the line of the Rue Sainte Catherine and the Rue de Flandre to leave the town by the Porte de Flandre.

The Grand-Place

The ****GRAND-PLACE** (Grote Markt) is generally accepted to be the finest of Europe's historic city squares. With, facing one another, the great Gothic Hôtel de Ville and the Maison du Roi, and surrounded by elaborately decorated guild houses, it is both a place of great dignity and beauty and also an epitome of the history of the city. The square—now for all practical purposes reserved for pedestrians—should be seen not only by day but also when floodlit. Colour is added by the daily flower market and the Sunday morning cage-bird market. Several ceremonies are held here throughout the year, the best known being the 'Ommegang' (first Thursday in July, and in future perhaps twice yearly), a historic and aristocratic pageant with origins reaching directly back to 1549 and indirectly to 1348.

The site, originally a part of the Senne marsh, was drained in the 12C and named the Nedermerct (Lower Market). The name Grand-Place was first used in 1380. In the 15C splendid tournaments were staged here, in one of which (1438) Philip the Good fought in the lists. On 5 June 1568 Counts Egmont and Horn were beheaded here by order of Alva, who watched the executions from the Maison du Roi. Villeroi bombarded in 1695, causing immense damage which was however made good within less than four years, an achievement which even today remains a source of civic pride. In 1719 another patriot, Frans Anneessens, was executed here.

The ****Hôtel de Ville** (Tuesday–Friday, 09.30 to 17.00. Sunday and some Holidays, 10.00 to 16.00. Guided tours, with last departure 30 minutes before closing time. No visits during meetings of or receptions by City Council. Closed 1 January, 1 May, 1 and 11 November, 25 December), with its Gothic façade one of the noblest buildings in Belgium, occupies most of the SW side of the Grand-Place. It is known that a stone building was erected here in c 1353—a fragment of its porch is incorporated in the base of the tower—but the present building was started in 1402, this earliest part, by Jacob van Thienen, being the eastern wing. In 1455 Jan van Ruysbroeck completed the tower, a marvel of lightness 96m high and topped by a figure of St. Michael (Martin van Rode, 1455; restored) serving as a weathervane. The western wing was built in c 1444–80, the first stone being laid by the future Charles the Bold, then the nine-years-old heir. This wing is shorter than the other because of the instructions given to the architect (unknown) that he must not encroach upon the Rue Tête

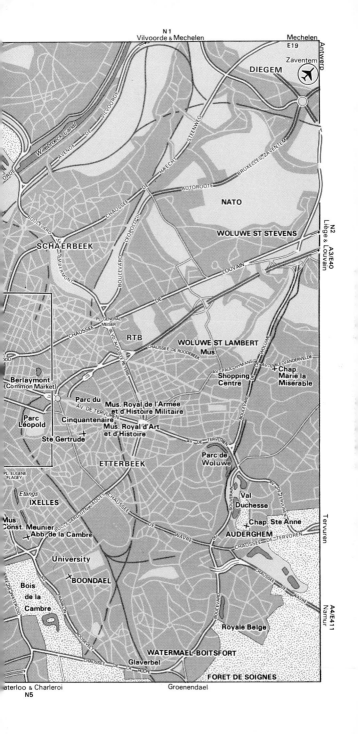

Brussels, Hôtel de Ville

d'Or. The statues, representing prominent local personalities from the 14C onwards, are of the 19C, but fragments of the older sculpture can be seen in the Musée Communal in the Maison du Roi. The courtyard, with fountains representing the rivers Meuse and Scheldt, and the rear portion on the site of the cloth hall destroyed in 1695, are of 1705–17.—The Salle du Conseil Communal, once the council room of the States of Brabant, displays 18C tapestries, after designs by Abraham Janssens, who painted also the ceiling (Gods in Olympus). The next room visited is the Salle Maximilienne, with, above the chimneypiece, portraits by André Cluysenaer of Maximilian of Austria and Mary of Burgundy. On the walls hang 18C Brussels tapestries. In the Portrait Gallery are full-length portraits of Charles V,

Philip the Handsome, Philip IV. Albert and Isabella, Charles II and Philip II, all by Louis Grangé (1718). The Antechamber contains interesting views of old Brussels by J.B. van Moer. The Salle Gothique, with fine woodcarving, shows 19C Mechelen tapestries of figures representative of the guilds. On the Escalier des Lions there are two paintings by Emile Wauters: John of Brabant granting a charter in 1421, and Mary of Burgundy swearing (1477) to protect the liberties of Brussels. On the ceiling of the Salle des Mariages the escutcheons of the guilds are reproduced, and on the Escalier d'Honneur are busts of burgomasters, allegorical wallpaintings by Jacques de Lalaing, and, at the foot, a fountain with a figure of St. Michael (Charles van der Stappen, 1890).

Across the Grand-Place from the Hôtel de Ville stands the **Maison du Roi**. In the 14C or earlier a wooden building here was the bread market, and in the 16C the Duke of Brabant used a later stone building to house various officials, the name being changed from Broodhuis (Bread house) to Maison du Duc. Charles V ordered a complete rebuilding (by Antoon and Rombout Keldermans, Hendrik van Pede and others), the fine new house then being given its present name although it has never in fact been a royal residence. Much damaged by the bombardment of 1695, restored in 1763 but thereafter neglected, the Maison du Roi was virtually demolished and rebuilt in the 1870s by Victor Jamaer who based his work on old engravings and on Van Pede's town hall at Oudenaarde but added the galleries on the façade and the tower.

The Maison du Roi now houses the **Musée Communal** (Monday, Tuesday, Wednesday, Friday, 10.00 to 12.30, 13.30 to 17.00. Thursday, 10.00 to 17.00. Saturday, Sunday, and some Holidays, 10.00 to 13.00. Closes at 16.00 in October–March. Closed 1 January, 1 May, 1 and 11 November, 25 December), where paintings, plans, furniture and sculpture combine to reflect the city's past, the two most popular exhibits being Pieter Brueghel the Elder's entertaining *Marriage Procession (normally in the first room to the right of the entrance) and, contrastingly, the Wardrobe of Manneken-Pis (see below), usually to be found on the upper floor. Also noteworthy, in the rooms to the right of the entrance, are two retables (15C and 16C), 16C and 17C tapestries, including one based on a cartoon by Rubens, and porcelain and silver of the 18C and 19C. The rooms to the left of the entrance show faience and pewter, but principally stone and wood sculpture, notably stonework (14C and 15C) from such buildings as the Hôtel de Ville, Notre-Dame du Sablon and Notre-Dame de la Chapelle, while a pleasing touch of rather more recent history is provided by a statue (1725) of St. John Nepomuk, which once stood on the last bridge over the Senne, demolished in 1868.

A large room upstairs is normally devoted to the city as such; plans and models of various periods, a wealth of interesting pictures, and illustrations for some spectacular late 19C schemes to link the lower and upper districts, these including an aerial gallery of 1898 and a soaring funicular of 1890. The second floor, reached by a stair with a stained-glass window showing the arms of the far-flung lands of Charles V, consists mainly of a fine hall, the theme in which is the story of the people of Brussels. Here too, in another room, is the Wardrobe of Manneken-Pis, showing a selection of the 400 or so suits donated since Louis XV's first gift of 1747.

The magnificent ***Guild Houses**, used by the guilds as official and social meeting-places and bearing popular names generally taken from some decorative feature, are described clockwise starting from the Rue de la Tête d'Or.

Brussels, Guild Houses on the Grand-Place

No. 7 is the *Maison du Renard* (fox), the House of the Haberdashers. A 14C wooden building here later became the property of the guild and was replaced by today's stone building in the 17C. The bas-reliefs (by Marc de Vos and Jan van Delen) represent trade activities, and the statue on top is of St. Nicolas, patron saint of merchants.—No. 6, the *Maison du Cornet* (horn), the House of the Boatmen, is a rebuilding of 1697 by Antoon Pastorana. The gable takes the form of the stern of a 17C ship.—No. 5 is the *Maison de la Louve* (she-wolf). This House of the Archers, completed in 1691 to plans by Pieter

Herbosch, was virtually untouched by the bombardment four years later.—No. 4, the *Maison du Sac* (sack), the House of the Joiners and Coopers, dates from 1644 (gable rebuilt by Pastorana in 1697). The guild moved to this site in the 15C, their earlier house having been razed to make way for the new Hôtel de Ville.—No. 3 was the House of the Tallow Merchants. The guild bought the site in 1439. The stone house built in 1644 was damaged in the bombardment and restored in 1697 by Jan Cosyns; the house is known as the *Maison de la Brouette* (wheelbarrow), and the guild's patron, St. Gilles, stands in the gable.—Nos 1 and 2, the *Maison du Roi d'Espagne* (King of Spain), from a statue of Charles II, was the House of the Bakers, a bronze bust of whose patron, St. Aubert, decorates the façade. The building (attributed to Jan Cosyns) dates from 1697.

Six rather simpler houses, not all belonging to guilds, stand to the W of the Maison du Roi. These are No. 39 *L'Ane* (donkey); No. 38 *Sainte Barbe*, also known as *La Ronce Couronnée* (the Crowned Blackberry Bush); No. 37 *Le Chêne* (oak), the House of the Hosiery Makers; No. 36 *Le Petit Renard* (small fox); No. 35 *Le Paon* (peacock), always privately owned; No. 34 *Le Heaume* (helmet).

To the E of the Maison du Roi No. 28 is *Ammanskamerke* (magistrate's room).—Nos 26 and 27 are the *Maison du Pigeon*, also known as the *Maison des Peintres* (painters). Their house having been destroyed in 1695, the site was sold by the painters' guild to the architect Pierre Simon who probably put up the present building. Victor Hugo lived here in 1852.—*La Maison des Tailleurs* (tailors) occupies Nos 24 and 25. Originally there were two houses here; No. 24 (*La Maison de la Taupe*, the mole) being owned by the De Mol family and No. 25 being called *La Chaloupe d'Or* (golden boat). After 1695 the houses were made into one for the tailors and given a single façade by Willem de Bruyn.—No. 23 *L'Ange* (angel) was also rebuilt by De Bruyn, who gave it Ionic and Corinthian columns.—Nos 22 and 21 join to form the *Maison Joseph et Anne*, and No. 20 is *Le Cerf* (stag).

The E side of the square is occupied by the *Maison des Ducs de Brabant*, a mansion with a pilastered front, a rounded pediment, three pairs of steps, and the busts of the dukes from which the house gets its name. The building (Willem de Bruyn) was early divided into six houses. From N to S these are *La Bourse; La Colline* (hill), the home of the Guild of Masons; *Le Pot d'Etain* (pewter pot), belonging to the Guild of Cabinet Makers; *Le Moulin à Vent* (windmill), belonging to the millers; *La Fortune*, belonging to the tanners; *L'Hermitage*, used at different times by wine and vegetable merchants.

Five fine houses stand E of the Hôtel de Ville. Nos 12 and 11, the *Maison du Mont-Thabor* (1699) and *La Rose* (1702), were both private houses, the latter being owned by the Van der Rosen family.—No. 10 is *L'Arbre d'Or* (golden tree), better known as the Brewers' House and still in use as such. It contains a small Museum (Monday–Friday, 10.00 to 12.00, 14.00 to 17.00. Saturday in April–September 10.00 to 12.00. Closed 1 January and 25 December), in part arranged as a 17C brasserie. The house (1698), surmounted by a statue of Charles of Lorraine, is a rebuilding by Van Bruyn.—The *Maison du Cygne* at No.9 was rebuilt in 1698 by C. van Nerven for Pieter Fariseau, a founder of the Brussels opera. Later (1720) Le Cygne became the house of the butchers' guild, and later still (1885) the Belgian Labour party was founded here.—No. 8 is *L'Etoile* (star), one of the oldest in origin and historically most interesting houses in the Grand-Place. Its name goes back to the 13C; after destruction in 1695 it was rebuilt, only to be demolished in 1850 to ease access to the Grand-Place. However in 1897 Charles Buls, the burgomaster, had the house built again, this time over a pedestrian arcade. In the arcade is a memorial to the Brussels alderman Everard 't Serclaes, leader of the guilds in the 14C in their struggle against the francophile Count of Flanders, Louis de Male. Attacked by the count's allies from Gaasbeek in 1388, he died in L'Etoile; the tradition has grown that good fortune will follow from stroking the arm of the effigy. Another memorial here honours Charles Buls (died 1914), who restored L'Etoile and did much else to preserve old Brussels.

Around the Grand-Place

The visit to the Grand-Place can conveniently be combined with a stroll around the nearby narrow streets—many of their names recalling past markets and trades—and through the elegant arcades (galeries).

To the NORTH, across the Rue du Marché aux Herbes, are the Petite Rue des Bouchers and the Rue des Bouchers, recalling the nearby meat hall which stood on the site of today's Tourist Information building. These two streets form a compact and animated picturesque quarter largely given over to restaurants. Off the Petite Rue des Bouchers is the *Toone* puppet theatre, continuing a tradition dating from Spanish times; incensed at open criticism and insults from the stage, the Spanish closed all the theatres, puppets then taking over as a popular, effective and easily hidden means of reviling the foreign occupiers. Today's theatre was founded in 1835 by one Antoine (Toone), the 'plays' now staged being a strange mixture based on various classics (Hamlet, Carmen, the Passion, etc.), played in Brussels dialect and larded with popular local and topical allusions, something of this past being recalled by a small museum, open during performance intervals. The Rue des Bouchers cuts across the **Galeries Saint Hubert**, which divide into the Galerie de la Reine and the Galerie du Roi. These light and attractive arcades, with some good shops, were built by J.P. Cluysenaer in 1846 as the first of their kind in Europe.

There are several places of interest off the SOUTH side of the Grand-Place. The Rue Charles Buls, beside the Hôtel de Ville, soon passes (E) the Rue des Brasseurs which was in 1873 the scene of the strange shooting affair between the poet Verlaine and his protégé Rimbaud; for this Verlaine was imprisoned for six months at Mons. The **Musée de Costume et Dentelle** (Monday, Tuesday, Wednesday, Friday, 10.00 to 12.30, 13.30 to 17.00. Thursday, 10.00 to 17.00. Saturday, Sunday and some Holidays, 14.00 to 16.00. Closes at 16.00 in October–March. Closed 1 January, 1 May, 1 and 11 November, 25 December), at 6 Rue de la Violette, the next road leading SE, shows lace, both old and modern, and clothing spanning the 17C to modern times. Rue Charles Buls is extended by the Rue de l'Etuve, soon crossing the Rue de Lombard with, at No. 30A, the fascinating three-dimensional attractions of the **Musée de l'Holographie** (Tuesday–Sunday, 11.00 to 18.00), while a short way farther along the Rue de l'Etuve, on the corner with the Rue du Chêne, stands the fountain of **Manneken-Pis**, a bronze statuette designed in 1619 by the elder Jérôme Duquesnoy; stolen in 1817 and found smashed, the fragments were reassembled to form the mould in which today's figure was cast. Quickly becoming a folklore character, Manneken-Pis (or 'Petit Julien') is known for his varied wardrobe, the first contribution to which was made in 1698 by the Elector of Bavaria. Another contributor (1747) was Louis XV who gave a costume and conferred a decoration in compensation for Manneken's ill-treatment by his soldiers. The suits, now numbering some 400, are held in the Musée Communal.

From Manneken-Pis the Rue du Chêne ascends SE to pass provincial government buildings, roughly opposite which, at the end of the Rue de Villers, the **Tour Villers** survives as a fragment of the 12C walls. Rue du Chêne curves into the Place Saint Jean in which a memorial honours Gabrielle Petit, shot by the Germans in 1916. Endowed with a photographic memory she was active in the underground resistance, on one occasion even entering a barracks disguised as a German soldier. When condemned to death she was told (so strong had been the international outcry over the shooting of Edith Cavell) that if she appealed she would almost certainly be reprieved, but this she scorned to do, proudly replying that she would show how a Belgian woman could die.

WEST of the Grand-Place the Rue au Beurre soon reaches the **Eglise Saint Nicolas** (09.00 to 18.30. Closed most Holidays), dedic-ated, appropriately for this district of shops, to the patron of merchants and attractive for the way in which, as was the old custom, small shops still abut the exterior. On an ancient church site, the present fabric dates from the 14–15C (choir 1381), but there was major reconstruction in 1955 and the façade is effectively of this date. Among the church's paintings are works by Bernard van Orley and Antoon Sallaert as well as one attributed to Rubens. Also noteworthy are the Vladimir Ikon (1131) and the striking modern blue window over the W porch.—For the Bourse, just beyond, see below.

Other Parts of the Lower Town

As already noted, the busy PLACE DE BROUCKERE (pavement cafés) is the modern centre of the Lower Town. It is named after Charles de Brouckère (1796–1860) who held various ministries, founded the Banque de Belgique, and was burgomaster of Brussels from 1848–60. Three districts are described below: South, West, and North of the square.

SOUTH OF PLACE DE BROUCKERE. To the S the Place de Brouckère is overhung by two huge modern blocks, that to the W being the *Tour Philips* and that to the E the soaring, winged **Centre Monnaie**, housing the city administration, the main post office, shops, Metro station and underground car park. The name derives from the mint which once stood here. Immediately E of the Centre Monnaie, across an open pedestrian space, stands the **Théâtre de la Monnaie**, mainly used for opera and ballet. The theatre was rebuilt by Joseph Poelaert after a fire of 1855. It was in the previous theatre that the signal for the revolution of 1830 was given during a performance of Auber's

'La Muette de Portici'; on the words of the duet 'Amour sacré de la Patrie, Rends-nous l'audace et la fierté', the audience rushed out and the old flag of Brabant was hoisted on the Hôtel de Ville.

It was in the Rue d'Assaut, a short way behind and above the theatre, that Fanny d'Arblay (Burney), the diarist, lodged for a while in June 1815 after her failure to find a barge to take her to Antwerp when convinced, as were most of her friends, by the ever louder sound of the guns at Waterloo that Napoleon would soon enter the city. Later, hearing cries of 'Bonaparte est pris! le voilà', she watched from a window 'a general in the splendid uniform of France' led prisoner tied to his 'noble war-horse'. This prisoner turned out to be Count Lobau.

The **Centre Anspach**, immediately SW of the Centre Monnaie, houses two museums. The *Musée du Jouet* (Toys. Daily, 10.00 to 18.00. Closed 1 January, 25 December) shows toys from the mid 19C onwards, while the *Musée de Cire* (Waxworks. Wednesday–Monday, 10.00 to 18.00. Closed 1 January, 25 December) portrays events of the history of Belgium. Boulevard Anspach, named after the burgomaster (died 1879) who did so much for the modernisation of this part of Brussels, leads S to the **Bourse**, designed by the younger Suys and completed in 1873; the site was previously occupied by a convent. It is well worth going down into the concourse of the Bourse Metro station to see the large work by Paul Delvaux illustrating past forms of municipal transport. Beyond the 17C **Eglise Notre-Dame de Bon Secours** (E), by Jan Cortvriendt, Place Fontainas is one convenient starting-point for a walk through the old quarters to the W (see below). The street now becomes Boulevard M. Lemonnier, off the W side of which is the Place d'Anneessens with a statue of the patriot by Vinçotte. Roughly opposite, the Rue de Tournai runs into the Place Roupe, named for N.J. Roupe (1769–1839), known for his opposition to the French authorities during the annexation, as a leader of the revolution of 1830, and as the first post-revolution burgomaster of Brussels. The bus (W) for Waterloo starts here.

Boulevard M. Lemonnier from Place Fontainas, or Avenue de Stalingrad from Place Roupe, traverse a rather dreary district to reach the Boulevard du Midi (nearly 1 km away), the western of the ring boulevards, across which is the Gare du Midi.

WEST OF PLACE DE BROUCKERE. Some of the older parts of Brussels lie to the W and SW of the Place de Brouckère; long drab and run-down, the district is in process of restoration.—The **Eglise Saint Jean Baptiste au Béguinage** (Tuesday, Thursday, Friday, Saturday, 09.00 to 17.00. Sunday, 10.00 to 17.00), about 300m NW of the Place de Brouckère across the Rue de Laeken, was built in 1657–76 by Luc Fayd'herbe. The Baroque façade (floodlit), one of the finest in Belgium, has three gables, and the interior contains works by Theodoor van Loon and a Crucifixion by De Crayer. The béguinage had disappeared by the mid 19C. The Place Sainte Catherine, with a fruit and vegetable market, is about 200m S by way of the Rue du Cyprès and the Place du Samedi. Here stands the **Eglise Sainte Catherine**(1854), a large building in a mixture of styles by Joseph Poelaert; the belfry of the church's 17C predecessor stands on the S, while just E of the church the little *Tour Noire* survives from the 12C town walls. Two parallel streets running northwards from the church, the Quai au Bois à Brûler and the Quai aux Briques, were once busy quays either side of a waterway; well away from the traffic and towering buildings around Place de Brouckère, flanked by small, mainly 19C houses many of which are seafood restaurants, and separated by an open space with water and fountains, the two quays today form a restful and pleasing rectangle in which survives something of the ambience of a Brussels that was. The *Cheval Marin*, at the N end of the Quai aux Briques, is a fine building of 1680, much restored and now a restaurant. From the Quai aux Briques several alleys connect to the Rue de Flandre, once a section of the old Steenweg but today lacking in character, the only building of note being the *Maison de la Bellone* (No. 46), a patrician house of the late 17C, once the headquarters of the Ommegang and now used for exhibitions, largely of the entertainment arts; it owes its name to the figure above the door of Bellona, the Roman goddess of war. At its N end the Rue de Flandre ends at the Canal de Charleroi, but of the Porte de Flandre which once stood here no trace survives.

Followed S, Rue de Flandre returns to the Place Sainte Catherine, whence the course of the Steenweg is continued by Rue Sainte Catherine and the Marché aux Poulets, the latter crossing Boulevard Anspach near the site of the old Senne wharf. The Rue des Poissoniers, S out of Rue Sainte Catherine, and then the short Pont de la Carpe, lead to the **Place Saint Géry**, generally accepted as the site of the island on which this saint built his chapel in the 6C. Later (979) there was a residence and chapel here of the dukes of Lower Lorraine, this eventually followed in the 16C by a church which was demolished in 1798 and in 1881 by the *Marché Saint Géry* which still stands; a plaque on the E end of the market outlines the island as it may once have been. The **Eglise Notre-Dame aux Riches Claires** (08.00 to 18.00. Closed Sunday afternoon and all Holidays), just S of Place Saint Géry, is a good Flemish Renaissance work by Luc Fayd'herbe (1665; enlarged in the 19C).

NORTH FROM PLACE DE BROUCKERE. Two important parallel shopping streets run NE, the broad Boulevard Adolphe Max and the much more interesting, narrow, crowded and pedestrian Rue Neuve. Just to the E of the latter, about halfway along its length, is the contrasting **Place des Martyrs**, a quiet and dignified square surrounded by uniform buildings (1775) by Claude Fisco. In the centre of the square there is a monument above the graves of those who fell in the revolution of 1830; also a personal memorial to Count Frédéric de Mérode who fell in the same cause, and one to the author of the words of the 'Brabançonne', the Belgian national anthem. Farther along the Rue Neuve, the little **Eglise Notre-Dame de Finistère** (1708), with a Baroque interior, is known for its much venerated figure of Notre-Dame du Bon Succès, brought here from Aberdeen in 1625. The adjacent Rue du Pont Neuf recalls by its name the course of the Senne. The last street E out of the Rue Neuve is the Rue de la Blanchisserie, off which the Rue des Cendres soon bears N; it was in a house within the angle of the two streets that on 15 June 1815, just before Waterloo, the Duchess of Richmond (Charlotte Gordon, wife of the 4th Duke) held her famous ball, a brilliant occasion hard to picture in today's setting of back streets. Here Wellington, on hearing that the French were already at Quatre-Bras, calmly finished his supper before inquiring of his host 'Have you a good map in the house?'. *City 2*, at the N end of Rue Neuve, is a shopping complex.

Boulevard Adolphe Max and Rue Neuve both end at the northern ring boulevard opposite Place Rogier. Beyond Place Rogier is the Gare du Nord, with the museum of the Belgian railways. (For these places see C. The Ring Boulevards.)

B. The Upper Town

This section describes the Upper Town within the ring boulevards.
For the boulevards themselves, and the Upper Town beyond them,
see Sections C. and D.

East of the Grand-Place, the Rue du Marché aux Herbes ends as the
apex at the foot of the large, open, sloping triangle which separates
the Lower Town from the Upper Town proper. The arms of the
triangle are the Rue de la Madeleine and the Rue de la Montagne,
both with old or restored houses, while above, forming the base of the
triangle, is the Boulevard de l'Impératrice, a contrasting strip of rather
characterless buildings behind which rise (far left) the towers of the
cathedral. From NE to SW the buildings along the Boulevard de
l'Impératrice are the telephone exchange, the air terminal, the Gare
Centrale, and the contrastingly more attractive steps and buildings of
the Mont des Arts. The broad Rue Cardinal Mercier climbs across the
centre of the triangle and the intersection at the top is called the
Carrefour de l'Europe.

Formerly thickly covered by small houses, this part of Brussels was transformed
by the 'Jonction' scheme for linking the Gare du Nord via a Gare Centrale to the
Gare du Midi. Involving a series of tunnels and cuttings, the scheme, started in
1911, was only completed with the opening of the Gare Centrale in 1952.

The Rue de la Montagne, the northern arm of the triangle, ascends
towards the cathedral, allowing a view to the left along the modern
Boulevard de Berlaimont, flanked by the long uniform building of the
Banque Nationale and, beyond, the even longer and uglier slab of the
Cité Administrative, the home of many government departments.

The Gothic *Cathédrale Saint Michel*, often called simply **Sainte
Gudule**, is the national church of Belgium (07.00 to 19.00 or 18.00 in
winter).

From Carolingian times or earlier a succession of chapels or churches stood on
this site, one of the first being dedicated to St. Gudule, a maiden of the Pepin
family who, it is told, persisted in her piety despite discouragement by the devil
who amused himself by blowing out her candle whenever she made her way
across the marsh to pray. In 1047 her remains (they disappeared during the 16C)
were brought to the church that stood here on that date and which was then
dedicated to St. Michael. This church appears to have burnt down in 1072 and
the foundations of a Rheno-Mosan church, now exposed in the nave, may be of
this or, more probably, of a successor. By the 12C the church here was dedicated
to both St. Gudule and St. Michael. The building of today's church started in the
early 13C (choir) and continued into the 15C, and there was a good deal of later
rebuilding; the towers date from the 15C and are in part the work of Jan van
Ruysbroeck. The glittering religious ceremonies of the Order of the Golden
Fleece were held here, notably by Philip the Good and Charles the Bold. The
church suffered severely during the troubles of the 16C and again at the time of
the French Revolution, but it was Napoleon who made the first donation towards
restoration. A new carillon of 49 bells was installed in 1975.

The NAVE is of the 14th and 15C, the S side being the older. On the
piers the statues of the Apostles date from 1634–54 and are by Luc
Fayd'herbe (James the major and Simon), Jan van Mildert (Philip,
Andrew, Peter), Jérôme Duquesnoy the Younger (Paul, Thomas,
Thadaeus, Bartholomew), and Tobias de Lelis (Matthew, James the
minor, John). The pulpit (1699) was made by Hendrik Verbruggen for

the Jesuit church at Louvain and transferred here in 1776 on the suppression of the Order. Also noteworthy are the huge W window (1528, Last Judgement, by an unknown Antwerp master) and the glimpse of the foundations of an earlier church. The TRANSEPTS, dating from the late 13th and early 14C (S) and the late 14C (N), contain two triptychs painted by Michiel Coxie when aged 89 and 92. The windows are from designs by Bernard van Orley and represent (S) Louis of Hungary and his wife Mary, sister of Charles V, with their patron saints, and (N) Charles V and his wife Isabella of Portugal. In the CHOIR (1215–65; triforium 1273) lie, amongst others, Duke John II of Brabant (died 1312) and his wife Margaret of York (died 1322), daughter of King Edward I of England. The high windows above the altar are a heraldic glorification of the Habsburgs. The three central ones, by Nicolas Rombouts, represent Maximilian of Austria and Mary of Burgundy in the centre, with their son Philip the Handsome and his wife Joanna of Castile (left) and their grandsons Charles V and Ferdinand of Austria (right). The outer windows show (left) Philip III of Spain and his wife Margaret of Austria (attributed to Jan Ofhuys) and (right) Philibert of Savoy and Margaret of Austria, aunt of Charles V (attribributed to Nicolas Mertens). Immediately behind the high altar (1887) are (N) the Mausoleum of the Dukes of Brabant, by Robert de Nole from designs by Josse de Beckberghe, surmounted by a lion in gilt copper cast in 1610 from the design of Jean de Montfort; and (S) the Mausoleum of Archduke Ernst of Austria (died 1595), also by Robert de Nole and Josse de Beckberghe. Off the AMBULATORY (early 13C) the apsidal chapel, in origin of 1282, was rebuilt in 1675 by Leo van Heil; its main feature is an alabaster retable of 1538 by Jean Mone, originally in the Abbaye de la Cambre. Also in the ambulatory (N side) is a memorial of 1957 to the painter Roger van der Weyden who is buried in the church.

The two large chapels either side of the choir date from the 16th and 17C and superseded the seven chapels and chapter-room which formerly surrounded the ambulatory. The CHAPELLE DE NOTRE-DAME DE LA DELIVERANCE (S, 1649–55) was built from drawings by Jérôme Duquesnoy the Younger. The windows, executed by Jan de la Baer of Antwerp from designs by Theodoor van Thulden, represent, above, scenes from the life of the Virgin, and, below, the various donors. Also in this chapel are the tomb of Count Frédéric de Mérode by Charles Fraikin and a retable of 1666 by Jan Voorspoel with a painting of the Assumption by J.B. de Champaigne. The CHAPELLE DU SAINT SACREMENT DE MIRACLE (N), built in 1534–39, commemorates and owes its construction to the 14C legend of the Miracle of the Host.

The story well illustrates the kind of murderous myth widespread at the time, but long since totally discredited by historical research and in 1968 officially declared unfounded. In 1369, it was said, a Jew living in Enghien arranged for the theft of the consecrated Host. Soon after, he was murdered and his wife fled to Brussels, bringing the Host with her. In the synagogue here on Good Friday the assembled Jews stabbed the Host with their daggers, whereupon blood spurted. In great fear the Jews then instructed a woman to get rid of the Host, but instead she returned it to the church where it became a precious relic under the protection of the cathedral. By the 16C the veneration of the Host had become such that it was judged necessary to build this special chapel.

The chapel's windows, the first three (from W to E) executed by Jan Haeck from designs by Bernard van Orley and (central window of the three) Michiel Coxie, represent, above, incidents from the story and, below, the donors (John III of Portugal and Catherine of Aragon, Louis II and Mary of Hungary, and Francis I of France and Eleanor of Austria, all three ladies being sisters of Charles V). In the next window the donors are Ferdinand, brother of Charles V, and Anna of Poland. The window above the altar (Adoration of the Sacrament), replacing a window by Bernard van Orley which was destroyed in 1772, is a good copy (1848) by J.B. Capronnier of the earlier style. Behind the altar (1849) a piece may be seen of the beam in which the Host was hidden during the turbulent times of the 16C. In the crypt lie the Archdukes Albert and Isabella, Charles of Lorraine and others.

The cathedral is a convenient point from which to visit the **Palais de la Nation** in the Rue de la Loi a short way to the SE across the Rue Royale (10.00 to 16.00 when parliament not sitting. Closed Holidays, and Saturday and Sunday in November–March). Built in 1783 for the States of Brabant from plans by the French architect Barnabé Guimard, and with a sculptured pediment by Gilles Godecharle, this has since 1830 been the meeting-place of the Belgian Parliament. In 1815–30 the building alternated with the Binnenhof at The Hague as the seat of the States General of the United Kingdom of the Netherlands, and during this period one wing was the residence of the Crown Prince of the Netherlands, William III (of Holland) being born here in 1817. Edith Cavell was tried here in 1915.—For the adjacent Parc de Bruxelles and the other buildings around it, see below.

From the cathedral the **Colonne du Congrès** (300m NE) may be reached by the Rue de Ligne. The column (47m), designed by Joseph Poelaert and surmounted by a statue of Leopold I by Willem Geefs, was erected in 1850–59 to commemorate the National Congress of 1831 which proclaimed the constitution after the revolution. Bronze figures at the angles typify Freedom of the Press and Education (both by Jan Geefs), of Association (by Charles Fraikin), and of Religion (by Eugène Simonis). The two lions are also by Simonis. Unknown soldiers of the First and Second World Wars are buried at the foot of the column, where an eternal flame burns.—To the W of the column is the mass of the *Cité Administrative* (government departments).

Below the cathedral, the Boulevard de l'Impératrice followed S passes first the air terminal and then the **Gare Centrale** (1952), inside which, above the entrance, there is a wallpainting by J. Hayez, while, outside, reliefs either side of the entrance recall the old quarters demolished as part of the 'Jonction' scheme (see above). Below the station, to the W in the Rue de la Madeleine, can be seen the **Eglise La Madeleine**, a 15C Gothic building restored in 1958; against it has been placed the Baroque façade of the Chapelle Sainte Anne, previously in the nearby Rue de la Montagne.

From the Gare Centrale there is a choice of ascents to the level of the Place Royale.

VIA THE GALERIE RAVENSTEIN. Behind the station, reached either by a subway or by an entrance off the Rue Cantersteen, will be found the spacious **Galerie Ravenstein** with a rotunda (restaurants, cafés). The arcade ends at the Rue Ravenstein, a part of Brussels which will be of interest to readers of Charlotte Brontë. The Rue Baron Horta, which ascends out of Rue Ravenstein, replaced the Escallier Belliard; here stood the Pensionnat Heger to which Charlotte came in 1842 and 1843, first as a pupil and then as a teacher, falling unrequitedly in love with Monsieur Heger. Her stay here provided the background for 'Villette' and 'The Professor'. The **Palais des Beaux Arts** (by Victor Horta), used for various cultural purposes, stands within the angle of Rue Ravenstein and Rue Baron Horta; the building was restricted to one storey in order not to obstruct the view from the royal palace above. The *Musée du Cinéma* (normally evenings), in Rue Baron Horta, is both a museum and a cinema for the showing of old films. In Rue Ravenstein (formerly Rue Isabelle, Charlotte Brontë's 'Rue

Fossette') the picturesque 15C *Hôtel Ravenstein*, the last survivor of the Burgundian period patrician mansions of Brussels, now houses learned societies.

VIA THE MONT DES ARTS. The rising ground to the S of the Gare Centrale is the **Mont des Arts** (Albertine), a focus for cultural, educational and conference interests conceived in 1934 as a memorial to King Albert and completed between 1954 and 1965, except for the Musées Royaux des Beaux Arts, completed in the mid 1980s. On the left a street ascends through an arch formed by a conference building (Dynastie), on the upper side of the arch being a clock and carillon (1964) with many small figures who are identified below, while on top an elegant gentleman strikes the hour with his stick. In the centre, starting from a statue of the King, a broad sweep of steps rises through gardens, once the steep Rue Montagne de la Cour, to the *Palais des Congrès*.

The impressive **Bibliothèque Royale Albert I**, forming the western side of the complex, houses libraries, reading rooms, lecture halls, and several departments most of which are of specialised concern. Visitors are most likely to be interested by the early 16C Gothic *Chapelle Saint Georges*, or *Chapelle de Nassau* (during exhibitions or on request. Closed Sunday, Holidays and last week of August), incorporated in the E wall of the library. Used now for exhibitions, this chapel is the only surviving part of the mansion here which was predecessor to the splendid Hôtel de Nassau (p 115). This latter is depicted in a bas-relief (G. Dobbels, 1969) on the outside wall, and the chapel's stepped windows are a reminder of the steepness of the Rue Montagne de la Cour beside which it stood.

There are five principal departments (or, as they are frequently called, museums) of the Bibliothèque Royale; all are closed Sunday, Holidays, and during the last week of August. The *Musée du Livre* (Monday, Wednesday, Saturday, 14.00 to 17.00) offers a survey of the history of books. Interesting also are reproductions of the studies in which notable Belgian men of letters worked. The *Musée de l'Imprimerie* (Monday–Friday, 09.00 to 17.00) reviews typography, lithography and bookbinding, the emphasis being on the 19th and early 20C. The *Archives and Literature Museum* (Monday–Friday, 09.00 to 12.00, 14.00 to 17.00) houses documents, recordings and tapes relating mainly to Belgian literature in French, while the *Chalcography Department* (same times) offers a collection of some 5000 engraved wood and copper plates. Finally, there is the Library's Museum and Historical Section, open only to approved researchers.

The steps of the Mont des Arts end at the Rue Coudenberg, opposite the Hôtel Ravenstein (see above), continued by the short surviving stretch of the Rue Montagne de la Cour into the Place Royale. On the right, filling the angle with the Rue de la Régence, are the **Musées Royaux des Beaux Arts** (Ancient Art and Modern Art), for which, as also for the Apartments of Charles of Lorraine, see Section E.

The PLACE ROYALE, built during 1772–85 from designs by Barnabé Guimard, forms a Neo-Classical ensemble inspired by Charles of Lorraine whose statue stood in the square until removed at the time of the French Revolution; the present statue (Eugène Simonis, 1848) is of Godfrey de Bouillon raising the standard for the First Crusade. The church here is that of **Saint Jacques sur Coudenberg** (1776–85), standing on the site of the chapel of the chaplains of the dukes; the

interior contains sculptures by Laurent Delvaux and Gilles Godecharle (Tel: 5117836). Beside the church ascends the Rue de Namur, a
section of the ancient Steenweg; off it, in Rue Bréderode, the **Musée
de la Dynastie** tells the story of the royal family from 1830 until the
present day (Wednesday–Saturday, 14.00 to 17.00. Also at same times
when Palais Royal open, though not Sunday and Monday. Closed 1
January, 21 July, 25 December).

The PARC DE BRUXELLES, immediately NE of the Place Royale, was
laid out in its present French formal style in 1835. Much of the
Coudenberg palace (burnt 1731) stood here and in 1830 the park was
the scene of some of the earliest and fiercest fighting of the revolution.
Among the sculptures scattered around the park are a Diana by
Gabriel Grupello and a monument by Vinçotte to the sculptor
Godecharle. For the Palais de la Nation, on the N side of the park, see
p 106. The Rue Ducale, along the E side, presents a line of once
aristocratic mansions, one of which (No. 51) was occupied by Byron in
1816 who had, according to the plaque, left his country which had
failed to recognise his genius. The *Palais des Académies*, at the
street's S end, was built in 1823 for the Crown Prince of Orange and in
1876 became the seat of the Académie Royale de Belgique. The
grandiose **Palais du Roi** (open in summer), just NE of the Place Royale
and overlooking the park from the south, is the successor of the early
Coudenberg palace of the dukes of Brabant and of later rulers such as
Philip the Good and Charles V, the latter signing his abdication here
in 1555. Coudenberg burnt down in 1731 and the present palace grew
between 1740 and 1827, but was transformed in 1904–12 from plans
by Jean Maquet, with a pediment group (Belgium between Agriculture and Industry) by Vinçotte. The palace is the sovereign's official
town residence. The pavilion at the W end is the **Hôtel de Belle-Vue**,
long a residence for members of the royal family but today a museum
(a department of the Musée d'Art et d'Histoire) displaying, in period
rooms, furniture of the 18th and 19C, glassware, porcelain, etc., much
of the collection belonging to the royal family (10.00 to 17.00. Closed
Friday, 1 January, 1 May, 1 and 11 November, 25 December).

The Rue de la Régence, with (N) the entrance to the Musée d'Art
Ancien (see Section E.), soon reaches the **Eglise Notre-Dame du
Sablon** (Monday–Friday, 07.30 to 18.30. Saturday, Sunday, Holidays,
09.00 to 19.00).

In 1304 the Guild of Crossbowmen built a chapel here, and in 1348 occurred a
curious incident when a pious woman of Antwerp was told by the Virgin to take
to Brussels a neglected wooden Madonna before which she regularly prayed.
Installed in the Sablon chapel, the statue, later destroyed by Calvinists, became
so venerated that the crossbowmen decided to build what grew into the present
church. During the 17C this part of Brussels became the aristocratic quarter, as
can be judged from the memorials in the church. In 1615 the governor Isabella
succeeded in shooting down the guild's target bird on the church, a feat which
led to much acclaim.

The lavishly decorated Gothic church, largely of the 15–16C, has a
good W portal. In the interior the oldest part (c 1400) is the two great
piers supporting the crossing, but the choir dates from only about ten
years later. Especially noteworthy are the beautiful slim choir lancets;
at the W end of the S aisle the curious skeletal monument of Claude
Bouton (died 1556), chamberlain to Charles V; in the S transept a
triptych by Michiel Coxie; and, on either side of the choir, the Baroque
burial chapels of the Tour et Taxis family, that on the left containing
sculpture by Jérôme Duquesnoy the Younger and Gabriel Grupello.

The church stands above the PLACE DU GRAND SABLON, the name reminding that this was once a sandy patch amid the marshes. Today, the sloping square, surrounded by old or restored houses, is known for its antiques shops and for its antiques and books market (Saturday and Sunday). A fountain (Jacques Bergé, 1775) records the gratitude of Thomas Bruce, 3rd Earl of Elgin and 2nd Earl of Ailesbury, a friend of James II, to the city in which as a Jacobite exile he lived for many years (1696–1741). The **Musée Postal**, at No. 40, records the story of the Belgian postal service; it also shows large collections of stamps and much interesting tele-communications equipment (Tuesday–Saturday, 10.00 to 16.00. Sunday and Holidays, 10.00 to 12.30. Closed 1 January, 25 December).

Across the Rue de la Régence rises the PLACE DU PETIT SABLON, a formal garden laid out in 1890, with a fountain-group of Counts Egmont and Horn, ten statues of famous Netherlanders of the 16C, and, on the fine wrought-iron balustrade, 48 statuettes representing the medieval guilds. The building overlooking the garden is the **Palais d'Egmont**, also known as the **Palais d'Arenberg**, the name of the family who owned it during the 18C. Built in c 1548 for Françoise of Luxembourg, mother of the Count Egmont executed by Alva, the palace was rebuilt in 1750 and again after a fire in 1891. Sold to the state in 1964, it is now used by the Ministry of Foreign Affairs; it was here that Great Britain, Ireland and Denmark signed the agreements (22 January 1972) under which they became members of the EEC. The best view of the palace is from the garden, entered either from the ring Boulevard de Waterloo or from the Rue du Grand Cerf along its W side; the garden contains a replica of Frampton's 'Peter Pan' in London's Kensington Gardens.

The **Conservatoire de Musique**, on the corner of the Rue de la Régence and the Plaçe du Petit Sablon, was built by J.P. Cluysenaer in 1876 on the site of the Tour et Taxis mansion where in 1516 the Prince de Taxis founded the first international postal system. The building houses the **Musée Instrumental**, a unique collection of musical instruments from all over the world and covering from the Bronze Age onwards (Tuesday, Thursday, Saturday, 14.30 to 16.30. Wednesday, 16.00 to 18.00. Sunday, 10.30 to 12.30. Closed all Holidays. The museum may move to a new address).

The immense **Palais de Justice** (Monday–Friday, 09.00 to 15.00. Closed all Holidays), in Graeco-Roman style, was built by Joseph Poelaert in 1866–83; it stands on a raised plateau dominating much of Brussels, the site, perhaps not inappropriately, of the medieval Galgenberg, or gallows hill. The dome, over 100m in height, was rebuilt after fire damage in 1944; around its colonnade are figures representing Justice, Law, Mercy and Strength. The portico is flanked by Doric colonnades in front of two open vestibules between which a stairway ascends to the grandiose hall which forms the centre of the building.

The large open space in front of the Palais de Justice is the PLACE POELAERT, off which descends a road tunnel to the Avenue Louise. A British monument in gratitude for Belgian help during the First World War, unveiled by the Prince of Wales in 1923, stands against the SE side of the square, and another monument, on the terrace, is to the Belgian infantry. The terrace (orientation table, binoculars) commands a view of the Lower Town; the tower to the right is that of the church of the Minimes (1700–15), the now vanished convent of which stood partly on the site of the house of Andreas Vesalius, the anatomist, born in Brussels in 1514.

The QUARTIER DES MAROLLES, below and to the W of the Palais de Justice, is a cheerful, thickly populated district, still, if decreasingly, the home of the true native of Brussels, speaking a mixed dialect. The main street is the Rue Haute, close to the upper end of which is the Porte de Hal (see C.). The **Musée de l'Assistance Publique** (Wednesday, 14.00 to 17.00) is at 298A; rather misleadingly named—for this is no museum of social security—the museum in fact houses art treasures from former charitable institutions, notably gold and silverware, furniture, and some 16C and 17C paintings. No. 132 Rue Haute was the home of Pieter Brueghel the Elder. So honoured was Brueghel that he was exempted from having to provide billets here for Spanish troops. The Place du Jeu de Balle, in the parallel Rue Blaes, is the scene of the daily Vieux Marché (flea market).

The Rue Haute and the Rue Blaes drop down to the **Eglise Notre-Dame de la Chapelle**, always a people's rather than a nobles' church. A chapel founded here in 1134 was replaced by the present part Romanesque and part Gothic church which grew between 1210 and the end of the century. The nave and aisles were, though, destroyed by fire in 1405 and then rebuilt, while the tower, badly damaged by the French bombardment of 1695, was replaced by one by Antoon Pastorana in 1708. In the tympanum of the main portal the bas-relief of the Trinity is by Constantin Meunier. The church is best known for containing the tomb of Pieter Brueghel the Elder, in the third chapel off the S aisle; the memorial was erected by his son, Pieter, and bore a painting by Rubens, now in a private collection. Other features of interest are the pulpit (1721) by Pierre Plumier, who also carved the Spinola family memorial in the Chapelle du Saint Sacrement, and, in the same chapel, a monument of 1834 to Frans Anneessens who lies in the church. The 19C choir stalls retain their original stone seats.

The **Tour Anneessens**, or **Tour d'Angle**, a remnant of the 12C fortifications, stands just E of Notre-Dame de la Chapelle. Once attached to the Steenpoort, the tower survived as a prison and it was here that Frans Anneessens was held in 1719 prior to his execution.

C. The Ring Boulevards

As already noted, the ring boulevards were laid out in 1818–71 along the course of the 14C walls. Since then they have become a very wide multi-lane swathe of fast motor roads provided with a system of tunnels. Over several stretches there are, above tunnels, central roads in each direction, with small roads at the sides, these last often called 'avenues' and bearing names different to their companion boulevards. The ring is broken by 'places' (Madou, Louise, etc.), but these are more busy traffic intersections than conventional squares; they generally correspond to the old gates and still mark the city's main entrances and exits. The circumference of the ring is c 8km, but, other than for the Gare du Midi, visitors are unlikely to be much interested in the 4km western stretch between the Porte de Hal and Place Sainctelette and then along the N to Place Rogier. A drive around the ring has little to recommend it, but a walk along the outer side of the southern ring) passes good shops (Avenue de la Toison d'Or and at Place Louise).

The main features described below may generally be reached by extending tours of the Upper or, to a lesser extent, the Lower Town. The arc of the ring likely to be of most concern to visitors (Place Rogier clockwise to Place Louise) is served by Metro with frequent stations.

PLACE ROGIER, at the end of Boulevard Adolphe Max and halfway along the northern ring, is named after Charles Rogier, a leader of the 1830 revolution and later the minister primarily responsible for starting Belgium's railways and for negotiating freedom of navigation on the Scheldt. On the edge of a district of redevelopment, especially to the NW, the square is dominated by two 'centres', *Rogier* and **Manhattan**, the latter with the entrance to the Metro. To the W a viaduct carries a main road past the prominent Basilique Nationale to join the Ostend and ring motorways.

At the **Gare du Nord**, behind the Centre Rogier, will be found the **Musée des Chemins-de-Fer Belges** (Monday–Friday, 09.00 to 16.30. Closed Holidays) covering the story of Belgium's railways since 5 May 1835 when continental Europe's first passenger train ran from the Allée Verte station to Mechelen. In fact three trains made the run that day, carrying a total of 900 passengers, the third being pulled by the engine 'L'Eléphant' which can be seen here. The occasion is recorded by a large picture. Upstairs there are several panels of prints, photographs, etc., particularly attractive being aquarelles by James Thiriar showing typical 19C railway workers in the uniforms of their time.

Le Botanique (Metro), now a cultural centre, occupies the high ground E of Place Rogier; the sculpture in the grounds includes works by Constantin Meunier. Here (Porte de Schaerbeek) the Rue Royale crosses the ring boulevard, opposite Le Botanique being the Jesuit church and, at the N end of the Rue Royale, the **Eglise Sainte Marie**, a conspicuous octagonal building in Byzantine style built in 1844 by Hendrik van Overstraeten. At the top of the rise the ring curves S, soon reaching PLACE MADOU (Metro) whence the Chaussée de Louvain leads E, in 2km reaching Place Général Meiser (p 122). Beyond the SE corner of Place Madou, at 16 Avenue des Arts, the **Musée Charlier** (Monday–Friday, 13.00 to 17.00) shows the collections of the sculptor Guillaume Charlier; with fine furniture and silver, there are also pictures by such 19C artists as Constantin Meunier, James Ensor, Jacob Smits and Henri de Braekeleer, as also sculpture by Charlier himself. Soon the Rue de la Loi is crossed (one-way E–W), at the far end of which are the headquarters of the EEC and the Parc du Cinquantenaire (Section D.), both of which can be reached by Metro from here. The main W–E artery is the parallel Rue Belliard, 300m farther along the ring, leading past the Parc Léopold (Section D.) and then becoming the Avenue de Tervuren, the city's finest exit and approach road. At the PLACE DU TRONE (Metro Luxembourg), with a statue of Leopold II standing near a side entrance to the royal palace, the ring bears SW, soon reaching the PORTE DE NAMUR (Metro). Here the Chaussée de Wavre leads away SE, at No. 150 being the *Musée Camille Lemonnier* (Wednesday, 13.00 to 15.00. Closed June to August), home of this writer (1844–1913). From the Porte de Namur to the PLACE LOUISE (metro), the centre of the ring is the Boulevard de Waterloo while the outer side is the Avenue de la Toison d'Or, off which is the long **Galerie de la**

Toison d'Or, extending some 200m eastwards across the Rue de Stassart to the Chaussée d'Ixelles, whence the **Galerie d'Ixelles** and the **Galerie de la Porte de Namur** return N to the Porte de Namur. These arcades, with the northern part of Avenue Louise and its adjacent **Galerie Louise**, form an attractive and in part elegant shopping district. Across the ring there is an entrance to the garden of the **Palais d'Egmont**, and farther W on this N side, in the Place Jean Jacobs, a memorial honours the victims of the wreck (1908) of the first Belgian training ship.

The **Porte de Hal**, on the curve where the ring turns N, is all that remains of the 14C defences; because it was used as a prison it escaped the fate of the other gates destroyed in the early 19C. The Chaussée de Waterloo, behind, leads out to the battlefield, while opposite, across the boulevard, is the start of the Rue Haute (p 110).

From the Porte de Hal the ring, now the Boulèvard du Midi, runs N, passing the **Gare du Midi** and reaching the Porte d'Anderlecht (1.5km from the Porte de Hal). Between mid July and mid August this length of the ring becomes the Midi Fairground (roundabouts, roller-coaster, etc., and much local atmosphere). Beyond the Porte d'Anderlecht the boulevard (now de l'Abattoir) reaches Place Ninove, here meeting the Canal de Charleroi which is followed for 1km to the PLACE SAINCTELETTE, a busy intersection below the viaduct from Place Rogier.

The Quai de Willebroeck, leading NE off the adjacent Place de l'Yser, soon becomes the Allée Verte, in the 18C a fashionable residential district and in the 19C site of continental Europe's first railway station for passenger services.

D. Parc du Cinquantenaire and Parc Léopold

The Parc du Cinquantenaire and the Parc Léopold are close to one another rather over 1km E of the eastern ring boulevard, the former being at the head of the Rue de la Loi and the latter beside the parallel Rue Belliard. The parks are important for their museums, the Musée Royal d'Art et d'Histoire, the Musée Royal de l'Armée et d'Histoire Militaire and Autoworld being at the Cinquantenaire, while by the Parc Léopold are the Institut des Sciences Naturelles and the Musée Wiertz. The Berlaymont, headquarters of the EEC, is just W of the Parc du Cinquantenaire.

The easiest approach is by Metro. Motorists should note that the Rue de la Loi is one-way from the Cinquantenaire to the ring and that the parks are reached from the W by the Rue Belliard.

Parc du Cinquantenaire

The rather characterless Parc du Cinquantenaire was laid out for the exhibition of 1880 which celebrated the 50th anniversary of the founding of the modern state of Belgium. Beneath runs the road tunnel linking the Rue de la Loi and the Rue Belliard with the Avenue de Tervuren. The Brussels mosque is in the NW corner, and a short way to the S of it there is a memorial of 1921 by Vinçotte to Belgium's explorers and missionaries. The dominant feature of the park is the **Palais du Cinquantenaire**, originally the main building of the exhibition but since enlarged to house museums. Semicircular colonnaded wings lead up to a triumphal arch (by Charles Girault) with a quadriga by Vinçotte, and on either side there are figures representing the provinces of Belgium, the two provinces of Flanders being treated as one.

The **Musée Royal de l'Armée et d'Histoire Militaire** (Tuesday–Sunday, 09.00 to 12.00, 13.00 to 16.45, but with some variations between sections. Closed 1 January, 1 May, 1 November, 25 December), occupying the N wing of the Palais du Cinquantenaire, comprises three principal sections, the first, the historial rooms, showing over-crowded and overpowering collections illustrating the history of the Belgian army from 1789 up to the present day. Amidst weapons, uniforms, medals and varied equipment, here are also many portraits of flamboyant military figures and several theatrically dramatic battle pictures, some emphasis being placed on Waterloo. Beyond, a large hall, essentially for Armoured Vehicles, shows also artillery and much else, while the Air Section offers a fine collection of both civil and military aircraft and their associated air and ground equipment.

Autoworld (Daily, 10.00 to 17.00 or 18.00 in April to October. Closed 1 January, 25 December), in the N part of the S wing of the palace, is for the veteran car enthusiast. The ground floor covers the period from about 1885 onwards, and includes the De Pauw Collection and also a section telling the story of tyres; the upper level shows the Mahy and other collections and is used also for temporary exhibitions.

The remainder of the S wing of the palace is filled by the ****Musée Royal d'Art et d'Histoire** (the entrance being on the W flank), with distinguished collections of antiquities and of many and worldwide forms of the decorative arts, while the extensive range of other departments embraces such fields as folklore, lace, textiles, precision instruments, ceramics, carriages and much else. The museums of the Hôtel de Belle-Vue and the Pavillon Chinois are both dependencies of this museum.

The museum is open Tuesday–Friday, 09.30 to 12.30, 13.30 to 16.45. Saturday, Sunday, some Holidays, 10.00 to 16.45. Closed 1 January, 1 May, 1 and 11 November, 25 December. This does not, however, apply all the time to all departments and an Odd and Even dates system operates. In principle Odd Dates are the opening days for Glass, Sculpture and Decorative Art, Lace, Ceramic, Precision Instruments, Delftware and the Special Museum for the Blind; Even Dates are the opening days for Antiquities, Islamic and Christian Oriental Art, Far East, India, Southeast Asia, Pre-Columban America, Polynesia. The Folklore and Carriages departments open only on Wednesday.

But even the foregoing is accompanied by the official caveat 'Subject to modification', and experience is that despite the above format there frequently seems some reason why quite large areas are closed, a state of affairs seemingly accepted as more or less permanent because there is a large illuminated plan at the entrance on which green and red lights indicate which departments are open and which closed.

The main departments and sub-departments are outlined below, together with an indication of their contents. Some visitors will have particular interests and will head straight for their choice, though, to avoid disappointment, such visitors would be wise to consult Tourist Information or telephone 7339610 to confirm that the department chosen is in fact open. Most visitors, however, will be content to accept and enjoy whatever they may find on a meander through the areas which happen to be open.

ANTIQUITY. 1. *Egypt*, from prehistory to Christianity. Reconstruction of an Old Kingdom tomb (mastaba). Attractive figure-groups of

Middle Kingdom boating and agricultural activities. A length of the Book of the Dead. 2. *Near and Middle East*. Material from Cyprus, Syria, Palestine, Anatolia, Mesopotamia (finds from Ur), Iran and Phoenicia. 3. *Greece*. A fine collection of vases and other ceramic work. Sculpture. *Gold cup from Argos. Tanagra figures. 4. *Rome*, including Roman Africa, Syria and Asia Minor. 5. *Model of Ancient Rome*(4C). 6. *Portico and Mosaics from Apamea*, a Syrian town destroyed by the Persians in the 7C. Note especially the large *Hunting mosaic.—NATIONAL ARCHAEOLOGY, with material spanning from palaeolithic through Gallo-Roman to Carolingian times.

EUROPEAN DECORATIVE ARTS. 1. *Sculpture, Furniture, Tapestries, etc.* and 2. *Mosan (Meuse) Art*. The rich collections under these two sub-departments include several ancient wooden figures; retables of the 15C and 16C; stone sculpture such as fonts and graveslabs; religious and lay furniture up to the 19C, one item being the cradle of Charles V; Art Nouveau material; Brussels and Tournai tapestry (15–17C). 3. *Silver and Metalwork. Scientific Instruments*. Within the former category, examples of the superb Mosan work of the 12C and 13C including articles by Godefroid de Huy; Limoges enamels (13C); bronze church furnishings. Within the latter category, globes of the 17C; clocks of 1800 and 1804, the latter with a small tellurion; three London orreries (18C); astrolabes (16C and 17C). 4. *Ceramics*. Examples of work of Brussels and Tournai and of most European producers, including a *Collection of Delftware of some 2000 pieces. Art Deco, and contemporary Belgian ceramics. 5. *Lace*. Collection spanning the 16–20C. 6. *Textiles*. Exhibits covering from the start of the Christian era up to the 19C, including oriental, Egyptian, Persian, Byzantine, French, English, etc. 7. *Glass*. History of glassware— NATIONAL FOLKLORE. Old pharmacy. Small popular religious art. Silver and other metal objects, collars, badges, etc., mostly associated with the guilds. Toys, games, dolls' houses.—EUROPEAN HANDICRAFTS.—CARRIAGES. Mainly of the 18C and 19C, including a Coupé de Gala of Louis XV. Also sleighs.

NON-EUROPEAN CIVILISATIONS. 1. *Islam*. 2.*Christian Art of the East*. 3. *South-East Asia*. 4. *Far East*. 5. *Pre-Columban America*. Outstanding collections from North, Central and South America. 6. *Oceania*.—MUSEUM FOR THE BLIND. The theme is the chronological study of materials and of the techniques relative to them, the exhibits used being those that can be appreciated by touch.

The **European Economic Community**, or **Common Market**, occupies the huge four-winged *Berlaymont* building off the W edge of the Parc du Cinquantenaire. The building (L. de Vestel, J. Gilson, A. and J. Polak), named after a monastery which once occupied this site, stands on the Rond Point Schuman, commemorating the Frenchman Robert Schuman, promoter of the plan for pooling Europe's steel and coal resources (1951) out of which the EEC eventually grew. The founder members (Treaty of Rome, 1957) were Belgium, France, Germany, Italy, Holland and Luxembourg. The United Kingdom, Ireland and Denmark acceded in 1972, Greece in 1981, and Spain and Portugal in 1985.

The **Eglise Sainte Gertrude**, off the Place Van Meyel 200m S of the Musée d'Art et d'Histoire, contains a beautiful late 15C *Statue of St. Gertrude, found in the loft in 1935.

Parc Léopold

The Parc Léopold, in which are the buildings of a number of scientific institutions, is an attractive steep-sided park with a small lake at the foot of its hill. The Institut des Sciences Naturelles (entered from the park or from the Rue Vautier) tops the hill, and the Musée Wiertz is just opposite in the Rue Vautier.

The **Institut des Sciences Naturelles** (09.30 to 12.30, 13.30 to 16.45. Closed 1 January, 25 December) is best known for its palaeontological collections, which include a famous *Series of 250-million-years-old fossil iguanodons discovered in 1875 at Bernissart in Hainaut. Also worth noting are a mammoth from Lier, skeletons of Stone Age miners, and the collection of prehistoric tools.

The **Musée Wiertz** (Tuesday–Sunday, 10.00 to 17.00 or 16.00 in November–March. Closed 1 January, 1 May, 21 July, 1 and 11 November, 25 December) is in the studio built by the government for the painter Antoine Joseph Wiertz (1806–65). The pictures are not only sensational but also gruesome (e.g. Hunger, Madness and Crime. Vision of an executed Criminal. Premature Burial). While the collection is dominated by the artist's huge canvases, which he refused to sell, many of the smaller and often quieter pictures both in the main hall and the side rooms merit attention.

E. Musées Royaux des Beaux Arts

The Musées Royaux des Beaux Arts, two separate but linked galleries for ancient and modern art, form the upper part of the Mont des Arts (or Albertine) complex. A long-term programme of modernisation and extensions completed by the mid 1980s has embraced part of the 18C buildings (by Jan Folte) down today's narrow Rue du Musée, known collectively as the *Ancienne Cour* and occupying much of the site of the former Hôtel de Nassau.

The Duvenvoorde mansion here (c 1344) passed by marriage to the Nassau family in 1404. At the close of the 15C Englebert of Nassau rebuilt the house, as also its Chapelle Saint Georges, now incorporated in the Bibliothèque Royale Albert I and more generally known as the Chapelle de Nassau. Again destroyed and rebuilt, the mansion became the property of William III of England, Marlborough living here in 1706. After 1731, when the Coudenberg palace burnt down, the Hôtel de Nassau became the residence of the Austrian governors, being almost entirely rebuilt by Charles of Lorraine after 1756. Here in 1763 Mozart, aged eight, performed before the governor. Charles of Lorraine's apartments, with a monumental staircase and sculpture by Laurent Delvaux, have been restored and are shown to groups on request (Tel: 5195357).

Although with individual main entrances, the two galleries are internally linked by escalator and visitors may thus use either entrance. Opening times are: *Musée d'Art Ancien*: Tuesday–Sunday, 10.00 to 12.00, 13.00 to 17.00. *Musée d'Art Moderne*: Tuesday–Sunday, 10.00 to 13.00, 14.00 to 17.00. There is thus a staggered lunch break, although it is hoped to do away with this and offer continuous opening.

The ****Musée d'Art Ancien** occupies a Neo-Classical building (1875–85) by Alphonse Balat, modernised inside and with a long extension at the rear. The four pillars at the entrance support statues by Guillaume de Groot of Painting, Sculpture, Architecture and Music; above the door are busts of Rubens, Giambologna and Van Ruysbroeck, while on either side are allegorical reliefs, some by

Thomas de Vinçotte, and groups by Charles van der Stappen (left) and Paul de Vigne (right).

The Old Masters collection dates back to the French Revolution when the 'Muséum de Bruxelles' was opened, mainly exhibiting works looted from churches and religious houses. The first curator, G.J.J. Bosschaert (1737–1815), made every effort to recover other such works as had already been carried off to France and successfully laid his hands on most soon after the fall of Napoleon. In 1842 the collection was enlarged by the pictures which had been collected by Charles of Lorraine in the Ancienne Cour, and further acquisitions after 1860 made necessary the construction of today's building.

Beyond the large rectangular hall, usually showing sculpture, the paintings are arranged around three coloured circuits. Blue (Rooms 10 to 34) shows works of the 15C and 16C and also includes the Delporte Bequest (Rooms 37 to 45). Brown (Rooms 50 to 62) is devoted to the 17C and 18C. Yellow (Rooms 69 to 91) covers the 19C. Additionally, a Red Circuit is for temporary exhibitions, while the Green Circuit is that of the Musée d'Art Moderne.

Selected pictures—only a fraction of the museum's rich collections—are mentioned below, generally in the order of the rooms visited.

The BLUE CIRCUIT, ROOMS 10 to 34 (15C and 16C), shows works of the Old Netherlands School (Flemish Primitives and Flemish 16C), Pieter Brueghel the Elder, and the Northern Netherlands.

Notable among the works of the Flemish Primitives are: *Early Netherlands Master*: Retable of the Life of the Virgin, dated to the late 14C and the oldest work in the museum; damaged, especially on the right. *Petrus Christus*: Pietà. *Master of the Aix Annunciation*: Jeremiah (c 1449), the subject shown as savant rather than prophet; possibly a portrait of René of Anjou. The central panel of this triptych is at Aix-en-Provence. *Master of Flémalle* (? Robert Campin): Annunciation, in a Flemish interior. Mass of St. Gregory. *Master of the Legend of St. Catherine*: Nativity, a part of a triptych. *Roger van der Weyden*: *Man with an Arrow (1456), possibly John of Coimbra, nephew of Philip the Good; he wears the collar of the Golden Fleece, and two years later, aged 25, he died, possibly by poisoning. Portrait of Laurent Froimont, a nobleman; a panel of a diptych of which the other half is at Caen. *Hugo van der Goes*: St. Anne, Virgin and Child, with a Franciscan donor. *Dirk Bouts*: *Judgement of the Emperor Otto; in two fascinating paintings, one being the Punishment of the Innocent, the other Ordeal by Fire. Bouts died while working on the former which was very likely completed by his sons. The story is that the Emperor Otto executed a nobleman, falsely accused by the Empress; appealing to God to prove her husband's innocence, the widow successfully underwent the ordeal by fire, whereupon Otto sent his Empress to the stake. The pictures were commissioned for the town hall of Louvain. *Master of 1473*: Triptych of Jan de Witte, a leading citizen of Bruges, and his wife, probably commissioned to celebrate their marriage. *Hans Memling*: Martyrdom of St. Sebastian, painted in c 1470 for the archers' guild of Bruges. Portraits of Willem Moreel, burgomaster of Bruges, and of his wife (c 1478), painted for the hospital of which Moreel was a governor; a later (1484) portrait of Moreel and his wife hangs in the Groeninge museum in Bruges. *Jean Hey*: Ecce Homo (1494), the only known work by this French artist.

Also works by the *Master of the Legend of St. Barbara*, the *Master of the Legend of the Madeleine*, the *Master of the Vue de Sainte*

Gudule, and the *Master of the Life of Joseph*, with portraits of Philip the Handsome and Joanna the Mad.

Moving towards and into the 16C, representative Old Netherlands artists and works include: *Albert Bouts*: Several works. *Marten van Heemskerk*: Triptych with Entombment. *Hieronymus Bosch*: Christ on the Cross, a conformist work with a background believed to be Bosch's home town of 's Hertogenbosch. *Lucas Cranach the Elder*: Several works. *Gerard David*: *Virgin feeding the Child (à la Soupe au Lait), a tranquil and delightful picture which is far more genre than religious. *Quinten Metsys*: Triptych of the Life of St. Anne, dated and signed 1509 and commissioned for the altar of St. Anne in the church of Sint Pieter at Louvain. *Anon. (Netherlands School)*: *Child with a dead Bird, a masterly insight into a child's emotion. *Jan Gossaert (Mabuse)*: Venus and Cupid (Gossaert studied in Italy and this is one of the earliest Netherlands pictures with a mythological subject; in its original frame, the picture is dated 1521). *Two portraits of Donors, wings of a triptych of which the centre is lost; far removed from the formalised piety of conventional donors, this unidentified man and woman survive as sensitive portraits of two very human beings. *Lucas van Leyden*: Temptation of St. Anthony, painted when the artist was aged about seventeen. *Bernard van Orley*: Several works, including portraits and the triptych The Virtue of Patience; illustrating the trials of Job, the triptych (1521) was commissioned by Margaret of Austria, herself author of a poem with the same title. Portraits of Georges de Zelle (1519), a doctor who lived in the Place Saint Géry, and of Margaret of Austria. *Pieter Huys*: Last Judgement (1554), a strange work meriting detailed study and reminiscent of Bosch. *Pieter Aertsen*: The Cook (1559), a daunting portrayal.

A *Section (Room 31) is devoted to *Pieter Brueghel the Elder*, a leaflet being provided which sketches the artist's life and elaborates on the principal pictures here. Pictures normally on show include the Fall of the Rebel Angels; Adoration of the Kings; Census at Bethlehem, but in an uncompromisingly Flemish and winter setting, the picture thus more a contemporary social portrayal rather than religious; Landscape with the Fall of Icarus, a painting conveying, through the inattention of the peasants, the indifference of man to tragedy not personally affecting him; Man Yawning.

Among 16C artists and works from the more northern Netherlands (largely Antwerp) are *Antonio Moro*: Portrait of Hubert Goltzius (1576), the painter and antiquary; this was probably Moro's last work before his death. Portrait of the (?) the Duke of Alva. *Pieter Pourbus*: Portrait of Jacob van der Gheenste (1583), an alderman of Bruges. *Martin de Vos*: St. Paul at Ephesus (1568), a picture notable for its animated crowd. *Frans Pourbus the Elder*: the Marriage of Hoefnagel, a painter and humanist who was a friend of the artist; the work gives a charming if perhaps stilted picture of a Protestant family occasion (Pourbus and Hoefnagel were both Antwerp Protestants).

The Blue Circuit traverses also the rooms (37–45) of the DELPORTE BEQUEST, the collections of Dr Franz Delporte (died 1973). The collections include paintings, sculpture, ceramic and objets d'art of the 13–18C. Among the paintings are works by *Abel Grimmer, Adriaen Key, Joachim Patinir, Pieter Brueghel the Elder* (*Winter landscape with Skaters), *Pieter Brueghel the Younger* and *Marten van Heemskerk*. As well as material from Europe, there are ceramics and objets d'art from Persia, Egypt, Mexico, China, Japan and West Africa.

Around the BROWN CIRCUIT, ROOMS 50 to 62, covering the 17C and 18C, primary interest is likely to focus on the museum's renowned **Collection of pictures by *Pieter Paul Rubens* (normally mostly in the adjoining Rooms 52 and 62), the pictures ranging from huge canvases to small works, including portraits and sketches.

Among the large canvases are: Coronation of Mary. Pietà with St. Francis. Mary and St. Francis interceding. Calvary; dating from 1636–37, this large, crowded and almost heroic scene was painted (for the abbey of Afflighem) at the late period in the artist's life when he suffered from rheumatism in his right hand. The Martyrdom of St. Livinius, another great dramatic work of the same period, this one commissioned for the Jesuit church in Ghent. Adoration of the Magi, painted for the church of the Capucines at Tournai.

Smaller works include: The Woman taken in Adultery. Studies of a Negro's Head, a masterpiece of observant portraiture, the model for which was used elsewhere by Rubens (e.g. Adoration of the Magi) and also by Van Dyck. Madonna with Forget-me-nots. Landscape with the hunt of Atalanta, a picture which influenced both Gainsborough and Constable. The Martyrdom of St. Ursula (sketch); this vigorous, almost theatrical portrayal of the story of the murder of the saint and her 11,000 virgins may be compared with the calmer, naive versions of earlier centuries, notably Memling's painted reliquary of 1489 at Bruges.

Among the portrait subjects are: the Archduke Ernst, Governor of the Netherlands. Peter Pecquius, man of letters and chancellor of Brabant. Hélène Fourment, the artist's second wife. The Archdukes Albert and Isabella, painted for one of the triumphal arches erected when the Infante Ferdinand made his entry into Antwerp in 1635.

Most of the other rooms of this circuit surround the upper level of the splendid central hall, among the artists and works to be found here being (artists in alphabetical order): *Adriaen Brouwer*: Drinkers at a Table. The Flute Player. *Jan Both*: Landscapes. *Antoon van Dyck*: Several portraits, including A Genoese Lady and her Daughter; François Duquesnoy (the sculptor; painted in Rome in 1622–23); Jean Charles della Faille (c 1629. Della Faille was a distinguished Jesuit and professor of mathematics at Madrid). Rinaldo and Armida, sketch copy of the artist's painting now in Baltimore. St. Francis. St. Felix. Martyrdom of St. Peter. *Jan Fyt*: Cock and Turkey. The Dog Cart. *Jan van Goyen*: View of Dordrecht, a work vividly conveying wind and cold. River Mouth. *Frans Hals*: Portraits. *Group of children, a part of a large picture of a family in a garden. *Meindert Hobbema*: Landscapes. *Jacob Jordaens*: Several works, including *Allegory of Fecundity (c 1625), held to be among the finest of this artist's works. Satyr and Peasant (two versions). The King Drinks. Pan and Syrinx. *Nicolas Maes*: *Old Woman Dreaming, a touching study of old age. *Rembrandt:* Portrait of N. van Bambeeck. Dead Woman. *Jan van Ruisdael* and *Salomon van Ruysdael*: Landscapes. *Frans Snyders*: Fish Market. Dogs fighting over a Bone. Oysters and Fish. Deer Hunt. *Jan Steen*: The Rhetoroticians. *David Teniers the Younger*: Several works, including Card Players; Flanders Kermesse, a cheerful scene with in the background the château which Teniers had rented; *Village Doctor. *Lucas van Uden*: On the way to Market, a work giving a good picture of contemporary life. *Cornelis de Vos*: Portraits, notably the Artist and his Family (1621).

Other schools represented in this area are the Spanish (Room 50) with *Ribera* and *Murillo*; the Italian, 14–18C (Rooms 50 and 51) with *Francesco Guardi*, *Tiepolo* and *Tintoretto*; and the French (Room 61) with Philippe de Champaigne (Presentation in the Temple) and *Nicolas de Largillière* (Portrait of a Man).—Rooms 55 and 56 house the Della Faille Bequest.

The YELLOW CIRCUIT, ROOMS 69 to 91, showing works of the 19C, is in two parts, with Rooms 69 to 71 detached from the remainder. In principle the subject matter of rooms and groups of rooms should be as below; in practice there is a good deal of overlapping and interchange, both within this Circuit and also as between this Circuit and the Green Circuit of the Musée d'Art Moderne.

Rooms 69 to 71. Neo-Classicism. Romanticism. *Jacques Louis David*: The Assassination of Marat, an historical if unattractive work. In total contrast there is the same artist's Mars disarmed by Venus, a thoroughly entertaining picture if only for its prudishly tactical ingenuity. This bright and cheerful work in turn contrasts with *François Joseph Navez's* subdued Agar and Ishmael in the Desert. Also some portraits by Navez. *Louis Gallait* is prominent here too, with several individual portraits and groups including his charming *Portrait of Simonne Bucheron, aged three.

Leaving these detached three rooms, the Yellow Circuit offers Realism as the basic theme of Rooms 72 to 80. Here, for instance, are *Charles de Groux* with his Pilgrimage of St. Guido, The Gleaners and Benedicite; *Louis Dubois* with Roulette, and The Storks; and *François Lamorinière* with Pond at Putte. Here too is *Emile Wauters's* Hugo van der Goes at the Convent (after the latter had gone mad), a picture which, to quote this Guide's article on 'Art in Belgium', provides 'a fascinating glimpse of the past through the rose-tinted spectacles of the 19C'. *Louis Artan* provides several typical sea scenes, notably L'Epave (The Wreck), *Edouard Agneessens* *At the Theatre and *Sleeping Adolescent, and *Joseph Stevens* Marché aux Chiens. A whole room is devoted largely to portraits by *Alfred Stevens*, notably the touching The Widow and her Children, a portrayal of what strikes as an almost elegant despair if compared with the powerful canvases of *Eugène Laermans* which so brutally project the grinding hopelessness of the lives of so many of the lower orders.

Constantin Meunier, one of the most prolific and best known of the artists of the turn of the century, has his own room here (79) in which his pictures and sculptures, and especially the latter, convincingly record both the dignity and the pathos of manual labour (see also Constantin Meunier Museum). In the next room hang several works by *Henri de Braekeleer*, including typical interestingly detailed interiors, their occupants usually intimately absorbed in whatever they are doing, while *Jacob Smits* is represented by portraits, one being the deeply sobering Father of the Condemned.

Symbolism follows, the first work to hit the visitor being *Léon Frederic's* astonishing great triptych (The Cascade, The Stream, The Lake) teeming with its multitude of pink, nude children. By contrast—and, many might judge, a lot more attractive—the same artist's *The Ages of the Peasant perceptively traces its theme through a series of five groups from The Little Girls to The Aged. Other artists represented here include *Fernand Khnopff* with Memories, and Lawn Tennis; *Jean Delville* with The Treasures of Satan; and *Jan Verhas* with School Procession, 1878, a glorious study of the faces, characters and attitudes of a procession of small girls, each one of whom claims individual notice.

Beyond, Luminism is represented largely by *Frans Courtens* and *Emile Claus*, the latter with typical gentle landscapes; *Henri Even-*

epoel has a room to himself (88); and the room beyond is largely given over to the first artists of Sint Martens-Latem with, for example, *Albert Servaes* (his gloomy Pietà and Peasants in the Fields), *Gustave van de Woestyne* (Sunday Afternoon. Crucifixion, with grotesque expressions) and drawings and sculptures by *George Minne*.

The Yellow Circuit continues past Impressionism, with works by, for example, *Renoir, Boudin, Sisley, Gauguin, Seurat, Fantin-Latour* and *Monet*, to close with the Hess Vandenbroek Bequest in Room 91.

The **Musée d'Art Moderne**, in its present form a creation of the 1980s, has its main entrance on the W side of the Place Royale but may also be reached by escalator and passage from the Musée d'Art Ancien, along the passage being a row of busts by *Gilles Godecharle* (Homer, Racine, Milton, Washington, Fénélon, Schiller, Wieland and Senecca).

An imaginative architectural achievement, the galleries drop through eight subterranean semicircular levels, within these being, to quote an official description, '1200 arches sheltering more than 11,000 mostly Belgian modern art pieces', this last word well chosen because in addition to pictures and sculpture there are all manner of collages and assemblages in wood, metal, plastic and other materials. Some visitors will doubtless appreciate everything here; others, with specialist understanding and taste, will head for their chosen level; most seem content to descend from level to level, admiring, hating, scoffing, or simply baffled, but assuredly never bored. The levels are reasonably clearly defined and signed, although they tend to merge both thematically and physically and it is easy to stray unaware from one to another.

LEVEL–1 is Contemporary Tendencies (temporary exhibitions), and LEVELS–2 and –3 are for the most part reception areas.

LEVEL–4 (James Ensor. Leon Spillaert. Neo-Impressionism. Nabis. Fauvism). On this Level perhaps the most immediately striking work is *Théo Rysselberghe's* dramatic Arabian Fantasy, this contrasting with his calm Portrait of Madame Charles Maus and his blue-tinted The Promenade and Woman Reading to a Small Girl. *Rik Wouters* is also well represented with, for example, The Flautist and Lady with a Yellow Neckband and his sculpture Domestic Cares. *Jan Cox* is another here, showing his wild and garish Fight for the Body of Patroclus, Battle of the Gods, and Finis. And, in addition to *James Ensor* and *Leon Spillaert*, other artists include *Pierre Bonnard*: Nu à Contre-jour. *Kess van Dongen*: Portrait of Louis Barthou. *Raoul Dufy*: View of Marseille. *Ossip Zadkine*: Three very different sculptures; a symbolic City Destroyed (Rotterdam, see 'Blue Guide Holland'), a towering wood Diana, and a sober bust of AndréGide.

On LEVEL–5 (Nervia. Expressionism) the most obvious works are those by *Constant Permeke*, nudes and other somewhat gloomy pictures which achieve strength through deformity and exaggeration. Also here, *Jean van den Eeckhoudt*: Several works including Self-portrait with the Artist's Wife. *Alice Frey*: Girl Dreaming. *Albert Crommelynck*: Self-portrait.—LEVEL–6 (Expressionism. Cubism. Pure Plasticism. Surrealism). *Gustave de Smet*: Several individual portraits and groups. *Frits van den Berghe*: Man in the Clouds. Sunday. *Salvador Dali*: The Temptation of St. Anthony. *Paul Delvaux* provides three contrasts; the conventional Evening Train, the grotesque agony of Crucifixion, and the more typical eerie fantasy of the dreamy ladies of La Voix Publique.—LEVEL–7 (Realism. Animism.

Jeune Peinture Belge, 1945–48). *Isidore Opsomer*: Portrait of Camille Huysmans. *Jan Cox*: Self-portrait. Also works by *Leon de Smet*, *Henri Wolvens* and *Ossip Zadkine*.—LEVEL–8 is for Cobra, Surrealism after 1940, Lyric Abstract, Geometric Abstract, and New Figuration, five themes combining to offer a bewildering choice of medium, colour and design. Notable among the paintings are *Francis Bacon's* Pope with Owls, a Self-portrait by *Jan Cox*, and, dominating one section, *Octave Landuyt's* desperate L'Englouti.

F. Outer City and Suburbs

Northern Districts

LAEKEN, with its conspicuous church, the royal palace and the Atomium, is the northern district likely to be of most interest to the tourist. From the Lower Town it may be reached by a choice of roads all converging at Square Jules de Trooz on the canal (Charleroi to Antwerp) which with its basins serves as the port of Brussels.

The **Eglise Notre-Dame de Laeken** (Joseph Poelaert, 1870) was erected in memory of Louise-Marie, the first Queen of the Belgians. It contains a 13C figure of the Virgin and in the royal crypt rest Leopold I, Leopold II, Albert I and Queen Astrid. Outside, on the N, are a monument to Marshal Foch and a memorial of 1927 to a French Unknown Soldier, while in the cemetery stands the Gothic choir of the earlier church (17C). From the church the Avenue du Parc Royal skirts the park (Domaine Royal) surrounding the **Palais Royal**, well seen from the road. There is no admittance to the palace but the hothouses (*Serres Royales*) are sometimes open, usually in May.

An old manor here was bought by the governors Maria Christina of Austria and Albert of Saxe-Teschen who in 1782–84 had this palace built by the architects Louis Montoyer and Antoine Payen. Restored in 1802 by Napoleon, who here signed the order for the advance of his armies into Russia, the palace was largely rebuilt in 1890 after a fire.

In the public PARC DE LAEKEN, opposite the palace entrance and stretching away towards the Atomium, are the Neo-Gothic *Monument Leopold I* (1881) and the *Villa Belvédère*, residence of the heir to the throne. The Avenue du Parc Royal ends at a busy traffic complex within which stands the *Fontaine de Neptune*, a replica of the 16C fountain by Giambologna in Bologna's Piazza Nettuno. The **Pavillon Chinois**, on the opposite side of the road to the right, was started for Leopold II in 1906 and now houses a collection of Chinese porcelain (Tuesday–Saturday, 09.30 to 12.30, 13.30 to 16.30. Closed 1 January, 1 May, 1 and 11 November, 25 December). The *Tour Japonais*, opposite, was bought by Leopold II at the Paris exhibition of 1900.

There is a choice of approaches to the **Atomium** (Eugène Waterkeyn), an aluminium structure 120m high, symbol of the 1958 World Fair and symbolising the atom in the form of an iron crystal molecule, that of the central cubic system, enlarged 165 billion times. There is a fast lift to the top and escalators link the spheres, in three of which there is an exhibition (Easter–mid September: 09.30 to 22.00. Winter: 09.30 to 18.00) on the peaceful use of nuclear energy. Beside the adjacent roundabout a memorial to Burgomaster Adolphe Max bears his calm yet defiant words of 1914. The Atomium stands within the PARC DES EXPOSITIONS, a complex for trade fairs, a short way to the N being the large **Brussels International Trade Markt** (John Portman, 1975) and farther N the even larger **Palais du Centenaire**, built in 1935, celebrating the centenary of Belgian independence, and a major feature of the exhibitions of 1935 and 1958. A short distance SW of the Atomium is the **Planetarium** (for opening times, and times of English commentary, ask Tourist Information).

In the commune of JETTE, to the SW of the Atomium, the 18C buildings of the abbot's palace (14 Rue Jean Tiebackx) are all that survives of the Abbey of Dieleghem, a Premonstratensian house founded in 1100. The building now houses two museums, the *Musée Communal* and the *Musée Nationale de la Figurine Historique*, the latter exhibiting hundreds of statuettes and also with dioramas tracing the story of civilisation (both Tuesday–Friday, 10.00 to 12.00, 14.00 to 16.00).

The northeastern commune of EVERE is the home of the **North Atlantic Treaty Organisation (NATO)**, the headquarters of which are beside the road to Zaventem airport. Originally in Paris, the headquarters moved to Brussels in 1967.—At DIEGEM, to the NE, the **Eglise Sainte Catherine** has a striking 'wedding cake' tower of 1654 and, inside, the shrine of St. Cornelius with a painting of the saint by Jan van Houbraken (1643). Below the church stands the small *Châtelet* (15C, restored) of the former manor house.—In ZAVENTEM, the village which gives its name to Brussels's airport, the church contains a painting of St. Martin by Van Dyck. While on his way to Rome the painter is said to have stayed in Zaventem (in the Café Van Dyck of 1624 in the square adjacent to the church) and to have fallen in love with one of his host's daughters, but his request for her hand was refused. The church also has a work by De Crayer.

Eastern Districts

The Chaussée de Louvain leaves the ring boulevard at Place Madou and after 2km reaches Place Général Meiser in the commune of SCHAERBEEK. For the motorist this square can be important; the main approach to the airport and the Mechelen and Antwerp motorway heads NE from here, while the start of the motorway to Louvain, Liège and Germany is only 400m to the south east.

Just S of Place Général Meiser are the tower and buildings of the Belgian radio and television service, occupying the site of former military rifle ranges. In the Place des Carabiniers, between the buildings and Boulevard Auguste Reyers, the *Monument des Fusillés* commemorates those shot here by the Germans, among these being Nurse Cavell.

The smart residential commune of WOLUWE SAINT LAMBERT is known for its fine **Shopping Centre**which fills the angle between Avenue Paul Hymans and the main N–S Boulevard de la Woluwe. Just E of the Shopping Centre along Avenue Emile Vandervelde the sadly named *Chapelle Marie la Misérable* honours a pious girl of the 13C who refused the advances of a nobleman, whereupon the latter hid a valuable cup in her hovel and accused her of theft. She was then condemned to death and buried alive, the site later becoming a place of miracles. The Boulevard de la Woluwe leads S to cross the Avenue de Tervuren at the pleasant **Parc de Woluwe** with hills, trees and lakes.

AUDERGHEM, to the S, is reached by the Boulevard du Souverain, on the E side of which can be glimpsed the estate of **Val Duchesse**, site of the first Dominican community in the Netherlands (13C). The Romanesque *Chapelle Sainte Anne*(12C, restored) is a short way up the adjacent Avenue Valduchesse (Wednesday in July–September, 26 July which is the saint's day, 14.00 to 17.00). Farther SE, lying between the Chaussée de Tervuren and the Chaussée de Wavre, some of the 14C buildings of the *Abbaye du Rouge Cloître* survive (S wing, now a restaurant, and parts of the farm; art exhibitions). Here too is an Information Centre for the Forêt de Soignes (Tuesday, Wednesday, Thursday, Saturday, Sunday, 10.00 to 12.00, 14.00 to 17.00. Closed July and all Holidays).

Southern Districts

The elegant AVENUE LOUISE links the ring boulevard with the Bois de la Cambre, on the way passing (E) the Abbaye de la Cambre. The description that follows covers in turn the abbey; the Bois de la Cambre and the Forêt de Soignes beyond; then the districts either side of Avenue Louise (Ixelles on both sides, and Uccle, Forest and Drogenbos on the west).

The **Abbaye de la Cambre**, originally a Cistercian nunnery founded in 1201, now comprises mainly 18C buildings forming two quadrangles. The church however dates in part from the 14C, with a N transept added in the 15C and containing the shrine of St. Boniface of Lausanne (died 1260), a pupil of the nuns who retired from his see at Lausanne to end his days at La Cambre. A painting by Albert Bouts hangs in the nave. The cloister of the 13th and 14C was destroyed in 1578, rebuilt the following year and restored in 1933; it has modern windows with the arms of the abbesses (including Mary Scott of Buccleuch, Scotland) and also murals of 1957 by Irene van den Linden telling the story of St. Adelaide; a nun of La Cambre, she uncomplainingly suffered many illnesses and believed that by so doing she saved souls from damnation.

The **Bois de la Cambre**, immediately S of the abbey, was once a part of the Forêt de Soignes but was acquired by the city in 1862 and landscaped as a particularly attractive park, today with a number of restaurants. The FORET DE SOIGNES, a survival of the ancient Silva Carbonaria, with magnificent trees, and cycle, walking and riding tracks, spreads around the SE arc of Brussels. The road separating the forest from the Bois de la Cambre is the Chaussée de la Hulpe which curves SE to cross the forest and meet the main Tervuren to Waterloo road at a major intersection. Just S of here a small road (Avenue Dubois) wanders W into the forest, soon passing the *Château de Groenendael*, today a restaurant occupying an 18C priory which was successor to an Augustinian priory founded here in c 1340. Beyond are the priory fishponds and a bench with a medallion memorial to the first prior, Jan van Ruysbroeck (1294–1381), a mystic and precursor of the Reformation. A forest museum (in Avenue Dubois) is housed in an 18C farm which once belonged to the priory (May, June, September, October: 13.30 to 17.30). Avenue Dubois continues W to join the Chaussée de Waterloo which skirts the W side of the forest.

A part of the commune of IXELLES lies to the E of Avenue Louise. Here the **Musée des Beaux Arts** (1892), at 71 Rue Jean de Volsem, houses objets d'art, sculpture, and a distinguished collection of paintings spanning from the 16C to modern times, the emphasis being on the 19th and 20C (works by De Braekeleer, Van Ryssel-berghe, Jacob Smits, Delacroix, Courbet and Joshua Reynolds). There is also an interesting collection of illustrated posters from many nations, including one almost complete set signed by Toulouse-Lautrec (Tuesday–Friday, 13.00 to 19.30. Saturday, Sunday, 10.00 to 17.00. Closed all Holidays). The heart of this part of Ixelles is the Place Eugène Flagey, with, by the lake, a memorial to Charles de Coster (1827–79), author of a well-known modernisation of the legend of Till Eulenspiegel (see also p 191). From here roads beside the lakes (Etangs d'Ixelles) reach the Abbaye de la Cambre. Visitors with an interest in police work may visit the *Centre d'Histoire et de Traditions de la Gendarmerie* at 98 Rue Juliette Wytmans to the E of the lakes.

The E side of the Bois de la Cambre is bounded by the Avenue Franklin Roosevelt, a fashionable residential district with the buildings (1924–30) of the **Université Libre de Bruxelles (ULB)**, founded in 1834 in the Ancienne Cour (p 115) by Theodoor Verhaeghen whose statue stands here. There is another large and modern university complex about 1km to the NE beyond Avenue de la Couronne.

Four museums are associated with the university. The *Musée de l'Histoire de l'Art et Archéologie* (Building D, 9th Floor, 30 Avenue Antoine Depage. During term: Monday–Thursday, 14.00 to 17.00; closed Holidays) shows full-size replicas of Greek and Roman sculpture; material on the restoration of medieval paintings; and information on and material from the university's archaeological department's excavations. The *Musée de Minéralogie* (30 Avenue Antoine Depage. During terms: Monday–Friday, 09.00 to 12.00, 14.00 to 16.00. Closed Holidays) shows over 1000 samples of worldwide provenance. Additionally, *Museum of Scientific Instruments* (Tel: 6422111) and *Museum of Zoology* (Tel: 6423678).

To the W of Avenue Louise, about halfway down its length, the Rue du Bailli leads to the **Eglise de la Sainte Trinité** which incorporates the Baroque façade of the Augustinian church (Jacob Franckaert, 1642) formerly in the Place de Brouckère. A short way SW of the church, at 25 Rue Americaine, the **Musée Horta**, occupying the house of the architect Victor Horta, contains archives, photographs etc (Tuesday–Sunday, 14.00 to 17.30. Closed all Holidays). The *Musée Constantin Meunier (Tuesday–Sunday, 10.00 to 12.00, 13.00 to 17.00. Closed 1 January, 1 May, 1 and 11 November, 25 December), in the artist's home at 59 Rue de l'Abbaye which branches W off Avenue Louise towards its southern end, exhibits a rich collection comprising some 170 of Meunier's sculptures and 120 of his paintings and drawings.

The **Musée David et Alice van Buuren**, at 41 Avenue Leo Errera in the commune of UCCLE to the W of the Bois de la Cambre, contains a magnificent private art collection (16–20C) which includes paintings, drawings, sculpture and Delftware. Among the artists represented are Fantin-Latour, Patinir, Ensor, Permeke, Rik Wouters and Van de Woestyne (Monday, 14.00 to 16.00). A short way to the E of this museum runs the Rue Edith Cavell in which stands (a little N of Avenue Winston Churchill) the *Institut Edith Cavell*.

Nurse Edith Cavell (1865–1915) was head of a large school for nurses founded by herself and Marie Depage who was lost with the 'Lusitania'. When war broke out in 1914 she actively helped fugitive soldiers to escape to Holland. Arrested, she was held at the prison of Saint Gilles (c 1km to the N) before being tried in the Palais de la Nation, sentenced to death and shot on 12 October 1915. Her calm words, 'Patriotism is not enough', are inscribed on her memorial in

London's St. Martin's Place. The Institute bears a memorial to the two founders and an adjacent street is named after Marie Depage.

In the Rue de Stalle, in the SW part of the commune, the little *Chapelle Notre-Dame des Affligés* (also known as Notre-Dame du Bon Secours, or simply as the Chapelle de Stalle) dates from the 14th and 15C.

The commune of FOREST is immediately NW of that of Uccle. The *Abbaye Saint Denis* here was founded in 1238 as a retreat for noblewomen, later becoming Benedictine, but today's buildings are reconstruction of the 18C and are now used for cultural purposes. The adjacent mainly 13C early Gothic church has a Romanesque 12C chapel containing the tomb of St. Alène, a noble lady whose conversion to Christianity so enraged her father that he cut off her arm, the limb however afterwards working so many miracles that eventually the father too was converted.

At DROGENBOS, to the SW of Forest, the **Museum Felix de Boeck** at 222 Grote Baan shows around sixty canvases by this artist (born 1898 at Drogenbos) whose work represents many of the trends of his period.

Western Districts

In ANDERLECHT a number of places merit a visit, some being to the E of the railway and others to the west. To the E of the railway there are two museums, one being the *Musée Gueuze* at 56 Rue Gheude, just S of the Chausée de Mons (Mid October–April: Saturday, 11.00, 14.00, 15.30); the museum describes the typical methods of brewing beer in Brussels. To the SW (600m), at 14 Rue van Lint, the *Musée de la Résistance* (Tuesday, Wednesday, Thursday, 09.00 to 12.00, 13.00 to 16.00. Closed all Holidays) recalls the gallant underground of two world wars. To the W of the railway, there are three sites close to one another around the Place de la Vaillance. The ***Maison d'Erasme** (Daily except Tuesday and Friday, 10.00 to 12.00, 14.00 to 17.00. Closed 1 January), dating from 1515, was not in fact the home of Desiderius Erasmus, but the guest house of the chapter of Anderlecht where he used to stay (in c 1520 when visiting his friend Canon Wijkman). The beautiful rooms have been arranged in 16C style and contain material on Erasmus's life and works and also a small but good collection of 15C and 16C paintings, the principal artists being Roger van der Weyden, Dirk Bouts, Hugo van der Goes, Cornelis Metsys and Hieronymus Bosch (*Tryptych, Epiphany).

Desiderius Erasmus (?1466–1536), born in Rotterdam or perhaps Gouda, was a Renaissance humanist and theologian with a passion for learning. His attitude was one of reason and commonsense, opposed to ignorance, superstition and extremism; because of this he was unjustly accused of being lukewarm to Catholicism and even of sympathy with Martin Luther. He enjoyed a succession of generous patrons and spent long periods in England where he was an intimate of Thomas More. In 1516 he came to Belgium as adviser to the young Charles V, and later he lived at Louvain where he helped found the Collegium Trilingue, at this time being at the peak of his fame and conducting witty and erudite correspondence with admirers all over Europe. In 1521, with the increasing hysteria about Lutheranism, he settled at Basle in Switzerland. His considerable literary output included a translation of the New Testament, but he is probably best known for his correspondence, the 3000 letters of which, several written from this house, provide a unique picture of his times.

The nearby very fine **Eglise Saint Pierre et Saint Guidon** (Monday–Saturday, 09.30 to 12.00, 14.30 to 19.00. Sunday and Holidays, 09.00 to 12.30, 16.00 to 19.00) is a foundation dating back to prior to the 11C.

The present church was built between 1470 and 1515 by Jan van Ruysbroeck and Hendrik de Mol; the tower, designed in 1517 by Mathias Keldermans, was never finished, but a spire was added in 1898. The interior has some 15C wallpaintings (restored), and an 11C crypt which is one of the oldest in Belgium and which contains the tomb (11–12C) of St. Guidon; a native of Brabant and at one time sacristan of Notre-Dame de Laeken, he spent seven years as a pilgrim in the Holy Land. A small *Béguinage*, founded in 1252 and recently restored (some rooms open), is immediately N of the church.

It was from the ridge of MOLENBEEK-SAINT-JEAN to the N that Villeroi bombarded Brussels in 1695. *Karreveld*, in the northern part of the commune, is a fortified farm with origins reaching back to the 13C although today's buildings are of the 16th and 17C. To the N again (commune of KOEKELBERG) stands the **Basilique Nationale du Sacré Coeur** (09.00 to 17.00), a vast edifice begun in 1905 to the grandiose design of P. Langerock (he envisaged six towers, each 90m in height) and completed in 1970 to a more modest plan by A. van Huffel and P. Rome. The basilica is a national memorial to all those who have given their lives for their country, and the interior with its richness in marble and stained-glass is impressive.

G. Waterloo and Tervuren

Waterloo

The battlefield of Waterloo (18 June 1815) is 20km S of Brussels on the Charleroi road (N5), the town of Waterloo, 3km N of the battlefield, being reached first. Public transport Route W from Place Rouppe roughly every half-hour. In summer many agencies run coach excursions.

One way in which to enjoy the essence of the battlefield is by the sightseeing 'train' which plies between Waterloo station, the Musée Wellington and the Butte du Lion (Late June–August. Roughly hourly. Duration, including visits, at least 3 hours).

At the battlefield, apart from obvious modern features such as the motorway, there have been two major landscape changes since 1815, both of them along the line held by Wellington. The first is the *Butte du Lion*, built 1824; where this and the buildings below now stand was previously open farmland. The other change is that in 1815 the road now leading from N5 to the Butte was a narrow sunken lane. It is also worth remembering that the valley was planted with rye, which, allowed to grow much higher in the 19C, at least at the start gave good cover. The Butte offers a good general view and most of the places mentioned in the battle description below can be readily identified from here, though it should be remembered that the ridges and folds, so vital to the soldiers, cannot be appreciated from this height. The main points of interest can also be reached by car. The visitor is likely to be surprised by the small size of the stage on which one of the most decisive events of Europe's history took place, and on which some 140,000 men fought, 39,000 of them meeting their deaths.

Before the Battle (see also Rtes 24 and 27). On 1 March 1815 Napoleon landed in France after his escape from Elba and the 'Hundred Days' began. By 20 March he was in Paris, reassembling his army with astonishing speed. The rest of Europe mobilised, but only two armies, both in Belgium, were a threat: Blücher's Prussians, and Wellington's mixed force of British, Belgians, Dutch, and Germans. Knowing that, combined, these two would have overwhelming superiority, Napoleon determined to separate them, crossing the frontier near

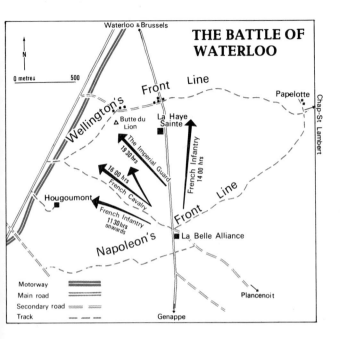

Charleroi on 15 June and the next day mauling Blücher at Ligny, while Wellington stood at Quatre-Bras. Blücher fell back towards Wavre, forcing Wellington to retire to the area just S of Waterloo which he had already chosen for his defence of Brussels. Early in the morning of 18 June Wellington received an assurance from Blücher that he would join him as soon as he could. This, though, turned out to be not possible until the evening, so the French attack had to be met by Wellington alone.

The Battle. Napoleon had about 72,000 men and 246 guns; Wellington, with about 68,000 men (24,000 British) and 150 guns, was apprehensive about both the steadfastness and even the loyalty of some of his non-British contingents. These two armies were drawn up only some 1500m apart, the French facing N with the farm of La Belle Alliance as their centre, while Wellington occupied the ridge to the N, his centre being roughly where the Butte du Lion stands today. Throughout the night of 17–18 June there had been heavy rain. The sodden ground favoured the defenders, while the attacking French had to advance uphill over mud, despite Napoleon's having postponed his main attack from dawn until early afternoon in the hope that the ground would dry. The fighting divides into distinct phases (times are approximate).

Phase 1. 11.30. French attack on Hougoumont, vital for the defence of Wellington's right. The attack failed both as such and in its purpose of forcing Wellington to divert reinforcements here. Hougoumont continued under fierce attack throughout the day.—*13.00.* The Prussians reached the area of Chapelle St. Lambert, 6km NE of La Belle Alliance, and Napoleon detached Lobau to meet this threat.

Phase 2. 14.00. After a half-hour artillery barrage the French infantry attacked Wellington's left (E of today's N5). The Scots infantry charged and engaged the French hand-to-hand, and when, soon after, the British cavalry charged through the infantry, the French broke. But the cavalry charged too far and were driven back by French cavalry.

Phase 3. 16.00. Led by Marshal Ney, the French cavalry attacked Wellington's centre (towards and just W of the Butte), but, having failed to break Wellington's infantry squares, were driven back down the slope by Allied cavalry. Further French cavalry waves met the same fate.—*16.30.* In the SE the Prussians forced Lobau back through Plancenoit, but failed to hold the village when Lobau was reinforced by Napoleon's Young Guard.

Phase 4. 18.00. The French stormed and took La Haye Sainte, but only after its Hanoverian defenders had run out of ammunition; only 41 out of 350 survived.—*19.30.* The French Imperial Guard attacked Wellington's centre, struggling up the slope already churned to mud by the earlier cavalry assaults. Met by devastating fire from Allied infantry (kept lying down and hidden until the last moment), for the first time in its history the Guard broke and fled.—To the SE the Prussians finally defeated Lobau. At about *21.15* Wellington and Blücher met at La Belle Alliance.

After the Battle. Wellington handed over the pursuit to the Prussians. Napoleon, fleeing in his coach, reached Genappe, where he just had time to change to a horse. At 05.00 he reached Charleroi. Thence he fled to Paris, a second abdication, fruitless negotiations for sanctuary in America or England, and finally exile and death on St. Helena.

The town of **Waterloo** was Wellington's rear headquarters, and here he spent the night of 17–18 June before riding forward to the battle area. The headquarters house, in 1815 an inn and thus an obvious choice, is now the *Musée Wellington* (April–mid November: daily, 09.30 to 18.30. Mid November–March: daily, 10.30 to 17.00. Closed 25 December and 1 January). The museum is in three parts, one of which, a circuit signed in green, is concerned with local history, with some emphasis on local people, and thus of only limited interest to the foreign visitor. The second part (Room 14), probably the best starting point, is an imaginatively arranged small hall in which a series of admirably clear illuminated plans, together with tableaux, trace the various phases of the battle (English Text). The museum's third part is a tour (signed in red) through the building's several rooms, all with appropriate small souvenirs and many interesting contemporary, or nearly so, pictures. Room 4 is Gordon's Room, the room in which Alexander Gordon, Wellington's aide-de-camp from Peninsular days, died; his bed and somewhat bulky correspondence box are shown. Room 6, with a fine copy of Lawrence's famous portrait, is the Duke's Room, while 7, 8 and 10 are for the Netherlands, the Prussians and the French, the last with several souvenirs of Napoleon. Room 11 explains the various measures being taken to conserve the battlefield area.

Opposite the museum is the church, only the late-17C round portion of which was in existence in 1815. Both church and graveyard are full of memorials, and just N of the church, in a garden beside the Brussels road, a monument commemorates the amputated leg of Lord Uxbridge, commander of the British cavalry. At *Mont St. Jean* (1.5km S of Waterloo) the Hôtel des Colonnes is where Victor Hugo wrote the Waterloo chapter of 'Les Misérables'.

The battlefield is reached at the crossroads sometimes called 'Waterloo-Gordon'. Here there are three memorials: Belgian, Hanoverian, and one to Sir Alexander Gordon, Wellington's aide-de-camp who was killed in the battle. The top of the mound on which this last stands marks the original height of the ridge before the earth was removed to build the Butte du Lion. Here also, in the SW angle, a tree is successor to the one which marked Wellington's command-post and which in the years after the battle was destroyed by souvenir hunters. The road to the E marks the line of Wellington's left, while that to the W leads along his centre to the **Butte du Lion**, built by the government of the United Netherlands in 1826 on the spot where the Prince of Orange was wounded (May–August: 08.30 to 19.00. September, October, March, April: 09.30 to 17.00. November–

February: 10.00 to 15.00. Closed 12.30 to 13.30). Around the foot of the mound cluster car parks, cafés and souvenir shops. Here also are the *Panorama de la Bataille* (daily, 09.30 to 18.00 or 18.30 on Sunday and Holidays) and the *Musée de Cires* (Easter–October: daily, 09.00 to 18.30. Winter: daily, 10.15 to 16.45) with wax figures of important people associated with the battle. The road continues W along the famous ridge (target of the French cavalry and Imperial Guard attacks, and along which Wellington rode to and fro during much of the day) to reach N27, a short way S down which is the farm of *Hougoumont* (signed 'Goumont', across a motorway bridge; memorials). At the time of the battle this was a fortified farm immediately N of a wood, but most of the building was burnt down during the fighting and the wood has disappeared.

The main road S from 'Waterloo-Gordon' passes (W 200m) the farm of *La Haye Sainte*, rebuilt after the battle and little changed since. In the second attack the French crept along the wall beside the road and actually seized the barrels of the defenders' rifles poking out of loopholes. *La Belle Alliance*, also little changed since 1815, is 1km farther south. Here, during the morning of the battle, in a scene of splendour and enthusiasm, Napoleon reviewed his troops, and here in the evening Wellington met Blücher.

From La Belle Alliance a road bears SE for Plancenoit, passing in 400m *Napoleon's Viewpoint* from mid afternoon onwards and in about another 500m reaching the *Prussian Monument*. On the main road, just S of La Belle Alliance, are (E) a monument to Victor Hugo and (W) the *French Monument* of 1905, a wounded bronze eagle by Jean Gérôme. Napoleon's headquarters was at the *Ferme du Caillou*, about 2km S of La Belle Alliance. Here before the battle he breakfasted off crested silver plate, confidently asserting that the fighting would amount to no more than a cannonade and a cavalry charge, after which he would lead the Imperial Guard against the English. The farm, of 1757, is now a museum (April–October: Tuesday–Sunday, 10.30 to 18.00. November–March, but closed January: Tuesday–Sunday, 13.30 to 17.00) showing weapons, the table on which Napoleon spread his maps, Napoleon's bed, and paintings, etchings and plans.

Tervuren

Tervuren, 13km from central Brussels, is reached by the fine Avenue de Tervuren which passes by tunnel below the Parc du Cinquantenaire and, soon after, either under or through Square Montgomery in which there is a statue of the Field Marshal. Farther E, No. 281 on the right (the Stoclet house) is a striking building clad in white marble framed by gilded mouldings, the work (1911) of the Austrian architect Joseph Hoffman and a precursor of Art Deco. At No. 364 the *Musée du Transport Urbain Bruxellois*(first Saturday in April to first Sunday in October: Saturday, Sunday, Holidays, 13.30 to 19.00. Vintage tram rides 14.00 to 18.00) shows a collection of public transport vehicles from horse-drawn days to recent times.

Pleasantly situated at the NE corner of the Forêt de Soignes, Tervuren is best known for the *Musée **Royal de l'Afrique Centrale** to the E of the town on the Louvain road (Mid March–mid October: daily, 09.00 to 17.30. Mid October–Mid March: daily, 10.00 to 16.30). This fine museum (which is also a distinguished scientific institution) started as an African outstation of the Brussels Universal Exhibition of

1898, the following year becoming the Musée du Congo. The present building (by Charles Girault) was opened in 1910, and in 1960, the year of Congo's independence, the museum formally extended its scope to cover the whole of Africa and, in some fields, beyond.

The museum is arranged as some 20 exhibition areas, or rooms, around a central court, these being outlined clockwise.—ROOM 1, *Agriculture, Mining, Wood*, of particular importance being the large wood collection, surveying the various commercial woods.—ROOM 2. *African Mountain Scenery*, with good dioramas of the various levels of Ruwenzori.—ROOM 3 is the *Memorial Hall*, while ROOM 4, *History: Europe and Central Africa*, shows several souvenirs of the great explorers.—ROOM 5. *Jewellery and Ornaments.*—ROOM 6. *Ethnography and Art outside Central Africa*, the exhibits generally in a cultural context and the emphasis being on Black Africa.—ROOM 7. *Sculpture, Central Africa* is of particular interest for its representation of the various ethnic groups.—ROOM 8. *Temporary Exhibitions.*—ROOM 9. *Ethnography of Central Africa*, covering a vast area embracing Zaire, northern Angola, Rwanda and Burundi.—ROOM 10 is the *Rotunda*, offering views of the park. Among the many statues some date back to the 1897 Exhibition.

ROOM 11 is concerned with *Comparative Ethnography*, both material culture such as food production and handwork, and social and spiritual culture as evidenced in social structure, religion and custom.—ROOM 12. Large *Zoological Dioramas* of the northern savannah, equatorial forest and southern savannah, showing typical mammals and birds. —ROOM 13 is devoted to *Insects*, ROOM 14 to *Fishes and Reptiles* and ROOM 15 to *Birds*, shown both systematically and in natural settings.—In ROOM 17 *Mammals* are displayed in some excellent dioramas.—ROOM 18. *Prehistory and Archaeology*, with material resulting from recent museum excavations.—ROOM 19. *Geology and Mineralogy.*

In Tervuren itself, what is left of the early 19C *Château*, destroyed by fire in 1879, stands above the roundabout at the entrance to the town. This was successor to a castle which from the 13C had been a hunting-lodge of the rulers of Brabant. Charles of Lorraine died here in 1780. The castle chapel of Saint Hubert (Wenceslas Coeberger, 1617) survives and is said to occupy the site where the saint died in 727; it will be found just inside the park, behind the town and some barracks. The large park includes a well-known French formal garden. In the town the ducal *Eglise Saint Jean* (13–15C) contains a reconstructed choir-gallery of 1517 attributed to Mathias Keldermans.

To the S of Tervuren, reached by Jezus Eiklaan, is the *Arboretum*, laid out in 1902 on land given by Leopold II.—*Duisberg*, 3km E of Tervuren, is the centre of a grape-growing district and is surrounded by hothouses. The church has a 13C nave and choir.

NORTH BELGIUM

(Provinces of West and East Flanders, Antwerp, northern Brabant and Limburg)

North Belgium is Flemish Belgium; that is, the Belgium of Flanders. The people, language, and culture (all Frankish in origin) are Flemish, and the history reaches back to the powerful counts of Flanders, who emerged from the void left by the death of Charlemagne and in due course absorbed Antwerp, Brabant, and Limburg. This history continues through the growth of the towns, their continual struggle for independence, their prosperity from the cloth trade, and, with the start of the Burgundian period in 1384, the end of Flanders as a separate state, though certainly not as an ethnic and, above all, a civic culture. It was this vigorous civic pride that led to the construction of the many splendid buildings, both religious and secular, that are such a feature of northern Belgium, and to the patronage of the arts which has left such a rich legacy.

For the visitor other than the holidaymaker on the coast North Belgium essentially means *Antwerp*, *Bruges* and *Ghent*, all historic towns, all famous for the charm and beauty of their old buildings and canals, and all offering superb art treasures, especially the works of Flemish Old Masters, in their museums, galleries and churches. These are the principal centres, but to them may be added a list of more modest towns, most with at least a good Grote Markt (market square), if not other old buildings, and many also with museums and galleries of distinction. Among many such towns are *Oudenaarde*, with its spacious Grote Markt and elegant town hall; *Kortrijk*, where old buildings stand close to modern pedestrians' shopping streets; *Mechelen*, famed for its great cathedral tower; *Louvain*, with notable Gothic architecture, a historic university, and an outstanding museum; *Lier*, a picturesque small town, known for its elaborate astronomical clocks; *Diest*, also picturesque, and with a good museum housed in medieval cellars; and *Tongeren*, the oldest town in Belgium, offering Roman remains and an imaginative Gallo-Roman museum.

The great BATTLEFIELDS (*Yser* and *Ypres*) of the First World War attract many visitors. These are described under Routes 4, 5, 6, and 7, all traversing a region of evocative names, and of war cemeteries, memorials, and campaign museums.

First World War. After the fall of Antwerp on 9 October 1914 the Belgian army retreated through Flanders, support being given by a Royal Navy flotilla. A front, with its left protected by the sea at Nieuwpoort, was eventually established along the *Yser*, the scene of heavy fighting between 18 and 30 October, ended only when the Belgians opened the sluices and flooded the area between the river and the railway. From now until 1918 the front stabilised from *Nieuwpoort*, southwards behind the flooded zone to about *Boezinge*, then round what would soon become the notorious salient of *Ypres*. Thus a large part of this corner of Belgium became total devastation. After the war much of the rebuilding was in the old style, so that many towns were reborn with their original character. Ypres, with its great Cloth Hall, is the outstanding example—In the **Second World War** the invading Germans once again quickly forced their way to the sea. This time though there was no Allied stand, and between 27 May and 4 June

1940 the great evacuation took place from the beaches between *De Panne* and *Dunkirk* (France). The damage was negligible compared to 1914–18, but much rebuilding was again in the old style.

Scenically the greater part of North Belgium is flat. Nevertheless, there are districts which have some individuality.

COAST AND POLDERS. The **Coast**, some 60km between the French and the Dutch frontiers, comprises a string of resorts, usually backed by dunes. Many are virtually joined to one another, and superficially each looks much the same as its neighbour: a perimeter of villas and other buildings in the dunes, enclosing a town area ending in a seafront esplanade. Inland from some of the resorts will be found the parent village or small town (the 'dorp'). The dunes, while still a distinctive part of the landscape, are fast being built over, so that once prominent features no longer appear as such. The resorts, with magnificent sands, casinos (which are as much cultural and entertainment centres as gambling rooms), and standards and facilities to suit most tastes, are as lively and overcrowded in summer as some of them can be bleak and empty out of season. *Ostend*, the principal town, is halfway along the coast, and *Zeebrugge*, with its historic mole, further to the east. A tram covers the whole stretch from De Panne to Knokke (c 2 hours), but because of dunes and high buildings not a lot is seen of the sea.—Behind the coastal strip are the **Polders**, a reclaimed plain drained by canals and protected by dykes, where the scattered villages can be counted by their church steeples, while, in between, the plain is dotted with large farms. The most attractive polder district is between Bruges and Holland; here the canals are lined by trees, and, with cottages restored and converted into restaurants, this has become a corner of some gastronomic repute.

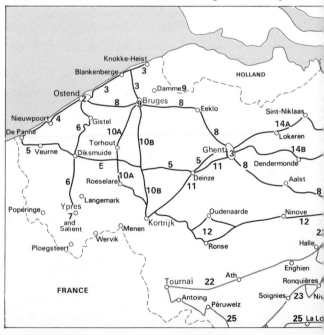

FLEMISH ARDENNES is the name given to a small range of hills running through *Ronse*. Several high points allow extensive views over the Flanders plain and into Hainaut and northern France. Eastwards from here the country is undulating.

WAASLAND. With *Sint Niklaas* as its principal town, this district is bounded by the Ghent-Terneuzen canal in the W, by the Dutch frontier in the N, and by the river Scheldt on the S and east. Basically sand and clay, the addition of richer soil and the application of scientific farming have turned this into a land of exceptional fertility. A feature are the poplars bordering the roads and the many irrigation ditches.

The KEMPEN, a large district covering more than half of the provinces of Antwerp and Limburg, occupies the NE corner of Belgium. Starting just E of Antwerp, and bordered on the N by Holland, it stretches E to the Maas (Meuse) and S to the road through Aarschot and Hasselt. The *Albert Canal*, with the E313 motorway parallel to its S, cuts W–E through the centre. Features are heath, moor, dunes, and pines, but these occur in large patches rather than overall, and motorways, spreading towns, and industry are combining to change hitherto remote and unspoilt landscapes. A good picture of the old Kempen (village, farm, etc.) can be got by visiting the *Bokrijk* estate and open-air museum between Hasselt and Genk. The Kempen contains a number of large recreational parks, and several districts are signed for walking. It is also known for its historic and thriving abbeys, notably *Averbode*; *Postel*, in typical Kempen landscape; and *Tongerlo*, with a special 'theatre' exhibiting a famous copy, by a pupil, of Da Vinci's Last Supper. The district is crossed by Routes 18 and 19, while Route 20, skirting the southern edge, links interesting towns such as *Lier*, *Aarschot*, and *Diest*.

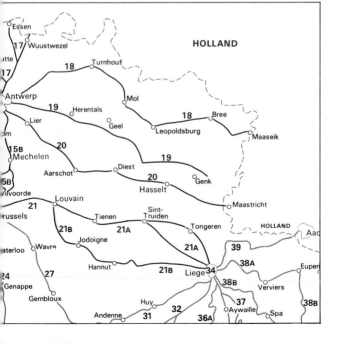

2 Ostend

OSTEND (Oostende. 69,000 inhab.) is the principal town along Belgium's coast. A renowned resort, thermal spa and conference centre with some 8km of beaches, offering plenty of entertainment and a good cultural choice, and served by an important and historic harbour (general, fishing, yachts, ferry services to Dover), Ostend is a lively place throughout the year. After Brussels (Zaventem) the airport ranks as Belgium's second most active, international trains leave for all parts of Europe, and the E40 motorway leads into the heart of the Continent.

Centre. Wapenplein.

Tourist Information. Wapenplein. Open Easter and Whitsun. Also late June–mid September: daily, 09.00 to 13.00, 14.00 to 20.00. Other periods: Monday–Friday, 08.00 to 12.00, 13.45 to 17.45. Saturday, 09.00 to 12.00, 14.00 to 17.00. Tel: 701199.—In July and August there is also Information at the station (daily, 10.00 to 12.30, 14.00 to 18.00).

Station. On E of the town adjoining the quays.

Post Office. Hendrik Serruyslaan.

Airport. *Middelkerke*, 3km west.

Beaches. There are five official beaches. *Kleinstrand* (small beach) is by the harbour entrance; *Grootstrand* (large, or main beach) stretches from the Casino to the Thermen; *Mariakerke* extends from the Thermen to Dorpstraat, and *Raversijde* continues to the west. The fifth beach is *Oosterstrand* to the E of the harbour entrance. Access to all beaches is free although a charge is made for some (Lido) sections. Bathing is only permitted at the above beaches and the flag signals should be noted (Green = Safe. Yellow = Dangerous. Red = Bathing forbidden).

History. An 11C fishing village, once known as Oostende-ter-Streepe (the E end of the strip), was in 1267 given a charter as a town by Margaret of Const-antinople. From this point on the port grew in importance, becoming a main departure point for the crusades and, until the start of the construction of Zeebrugge during the 19C, the only significant harbour along the coast. During the Revolt of the Netherlands Ostend held out for the United Provinces until taken by the Spanish commander Spinola in 1604, though only after a bitter siege lasting three years. In 1273 the Ostend Company was formed for the purpose of trade with the Indies and, although under pressure from England and Holland its charter was later revoked, it none the less opened the way to increasing prosperity, and increasingly also Ostend became the port for sailings between England and the Continent. The town first became a royal residence in 1834, and four years later Leopold I inaugurated the Ostend–Brussels railway. The first Casino-Kursaal was opened in 1852, and after the dismantling of the fortifications in 1860–70 the town began to spread.

In 1914 the Belgian government briefly had its seat here (7–13 October), but the Germans marched in on 15 October and from then on the harbour was used as a destroyer and submarine base. On the night of 22–23 April 1918 an attempt (simultaneous with that on Zeebrugge) was made to block the harbour. This failed, but the crews volunteered for a second attack, successfully carried out on 9–10 May when the 'Vindictive', used the previous month at Zeebrugge, was sunk across the port entrance. The Germans evacuated Ostend on 17 October 1918 after blowing up the station and harbour facilities. In the Second World War, serving as a German coastal fortress, the town suffered considerably under air attack until liberated by the Canadians on 9 September 1944.

Some important events have been the opening of the Palais des Thermes (1933); the opening of the new Casino-Kursaal (1953); the completion of the motorway to Brussels (1958); and the extension of the airport since 1976.

The town divides into two parts. The eastern part, bounded by the harbour, Vindictivelaan, Hendrik Serruyslaan and the shore, is the animated 'popular' quarter. The western part, starting from the broad, gardened Leopold II Laan, is more spacious and elegant in character.

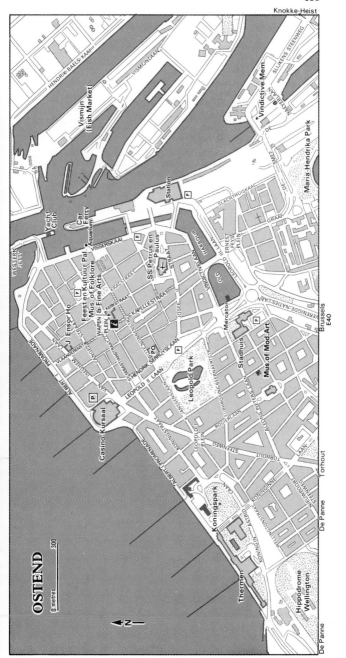

Knokke-Heist

OSTEND

0 metres 300

N

Vismijn (Fish Market)

Yacht Club

Car Ferry

Aquarium

WESTERN JETTY

Station

P

HENDRIK BAELS-KAAI

VISMIJNLAAN

SLIJKENS STEENWEG

Vindictive Mem.

Maria-Hendrika Park

MAKELLAAN

DE SMET

GRAAF

SLACHTHUISKAAI

DE

ERNEST FEYS PLEIN

VERENIGDE-NATIES-LAAN

Brussels E40

Mercator

OLD LEOPOLD HARBOUR

VINDICTIVELAAN

VISSERSKAAI

Feest en Kultuur Pal

Mus. of Folklore

& Fine Arts

J. Ensor Ho

PROMENADE

ALBERT

KAPELLESTRAAT

KERKSTRAAT

VAN ISEGHEMLAAN

WAPEN PLEIN

SS Petrus en Paulus

JOSEF II STRAAT

Stadhuis

P

Mus of Mod. Art

KONINGINNELAAN

PO

HENDRIK SERRUYSLAAN

LEOPOLD I LAAN

Leopold Park

P

P

VLAANDERENSTR

ROGIER LAAN

ALFONS PIETERS LAAN

EUPHROSINE BEERNAERTSTR

TORHOUT STEENWEG

Torhout

Casino Kursaal

P

KONINGSTRAAT

LEOPOLD II LAAN

ALBERT PROMENADE

Koningspark

NIEUWPOORT STEENWEG

KONINGINNELAAN

WELLINGTONSTR

De Panne

Thermen

Hippodrome Wellington

De Panne

The **Sint Petrus en Sint Pieterkerk** (1905–07), across the Visserskaai from the station, contains a monument by Fraikin to Queen Louise-Marie, the first Queen of the Belgians, who died in Ostend in 1850. Adjoining the church is the tower of its predecessor, almost completely destroyed by fire in 1896; it was preserved as being the only building in Ostend dating back to the siege of 1601–04. Visserskaai, running N from here between the town and the Montgomerydok, is a wide thoroughfare with many restaurants and, on its E side, the former shrimp market, now housing the **Aquarium** (April–September: daily, 10.00 to 12.00, 14.00 to 17.00. Other months: Saturday, Sunday, same times).

Leading W from the station, Vindictivelaan skirts the old harbour in which is moored the 'Mercator', a three-masted merchant fleet training ship built in 1932; taken out of service in 1960, the ship is now a museum largely of material collected on voyages to 54 different lands (January, February, November, December: Sunday and Holidays, 10.00 to 12.00, 13.00 to 16.00. Closed 1 January and 25 December. March and October: Saturday, Sunday, 10.00 to 12.00, 13.00 to 17.00. April and May: Saturday, Sunday, Holidays, 09.00 to 12.00, 13.00 to 18.00. Easter and June–September: daily, 09.00 to 12.00, 13.00 to 18.00).

Kapellestraat, for pedestrians only and one of the liveliest streets in Ostend, connects from Vindictivelaan to the WAPENPLEIN, the town centre, with on the square's S side the **Feest en Kultuur Paleis**, completed in 1958 on the site of the town hall and museum destroyed by bombing during the last war. Features are the large clock with the signs of the zodiac and the carillon of 1965 with 49 bells; concerts are regularly given and a melody is played automatically each half-hour. The building houses *Tourist Information* and two museums. The **Museum voor Schone Kunsten** (daily except Tuesday, 10.00 to 12.00, 14.00 to 17.00.Closed 1 January, 1 May, all October, 25 December) exhibits international and Flemish pictures of the 19C and 20C, some emphasis being on Spillaert and Ensor. Among several other artists represented are Henri Victor Wolvens, Constant Permeke, Floris Jespers, Gustave de Smet and Edgard Tytgat. The **Museum De Plate**, devoted to local history and custom, includes prehistoric and Roman material, costumes, interiors, and a section on wooden shipbuilding (Easter, Whitsun, July, August: daily except Tuesday and Sunday, 10.00 to 12.00, 15.00 to 17.00. Other months: Saturday, 10.00 to 12.00, 15.00 to 17.00).

There are two other museums in this part of the town. At 41 Sebastiaanstraat (W out of Wapenplein) the **Museum voor Religieuze Kunst**(Easter–May, July–September and Christmas period: daily except Tuesday and Wednesday, 11.00 to 12.00, 15.00 to 18.00. June: Saturday, Sunday, 11.00 to 12.00, 15.00 to 18.00) occupies a former chapel. The varied and interesting collection of religious pictures and sculpture, covering the period from Impressionism to the present day and including works by James Ensor, is periodically changed with special exhibitions in spring and summer. The **James Ensorhuis**, at 27 Vlaanderenstraat which runs N out of Wapenplein, was the home of this artist (1860–1949), born here of an English father and an Ostend mother. The house contains some of the curios which he and his uncle and aunt collected, notably shells; there is documentation on the first floor and the second is Ensor's studio (Easter, Whitsun, June–September: daily except Tuesday, 10.00 to 12.00, 14.00 to 17.00.)

Vlaanderenstraat continues to the Albert I Promenade. To the E is the monument (1953) to seamen who lost their lives during the war, just beyond being the western jetty, embarkation point for sea excursions and with a footpath out to the end. The North Sea Yacht Club is near the base of the jetty.

The **Casino-Kursaal**, to the W along the Albert I Promenade, was built in 1953 as successor to the first casino of 1852. Offering opera, ballet, concerts and light entertainment as well as a restaurant, night club and gaming rooms (one of these with murals by Paul Delvaux), the Casino-Kursaal is Ostend's principal centre for entertainment.

Farther W are the **Koningspark**, the gardens of the former royal residence; the **Thermen**, with Turkish baths, a medical centre and a hotel; and the **Hippodrome Wellington**, scene of flat racing and trotting. To the W of the racecourse extends the suburb of MARIAKERKE, in the western part of which (Dorpstraat) will be found the **Onze Lieve Vrouw ter Duinen Kerk** much of which dates from the second half of the 14C; the interior contains Baroque furnishing, and the grave of James Ensor is in the churchyard.

From the Casino-Kursaal the broad Leopold II Laan, either side of gardens, leads S, soon reaching a floral clock and the small Leopold Park. Opposite the floral clock and set back in Hendrik Serruyslaan, the **Post Office** (1939–after 45) bears a large and striking symbolic sculpture by Joseph Cantré. The **Stadhuis** (Victor Bourgeois, 1956–60), well placed at the end of Leopold II Laan and facing the old harbour, is successor to the 17C town hall in the Wapenplein, destroyed by bombing in 1940. Ostend's arms, carved by A. Michiels, are on the S façade and the interior contains pictures by Alice Frey. The **Provincial Museum for Modern Art**, at 11 Romestraat, two blocks W of the Stadhuis, uses paintings, sculpture, graphics and film to provide a survey of Begian modern art (April, May, September, October: daily except Monday, 10.00 to 12.30, 13.30 to 18.00. June–August: daily except Monday, 10.00 to 13.30, 17.00 to 20.30. November–March: daily except Monday, 10.00 to 12.30, 13.30 to 17.00).

The **Maria Hendrika Park** (boating, fishing) is immediately S of the Stadhuis.— The *'Vindictive' Memorial*, incorporating the bows of the ship and the masts of HMS 'Thetis' and 'Iphigenia', is in a small garden below the Blankenberge road where it splits to cross the inner docks. This road crosses more docks (c 1km farther), immediately after which a road bears NW for the *Vissersdok* with the fish market.

For Ostend to *Blankenberge* and *Knokke-Heist*, see Rte 3; to *Nieuwpoort* and *De Panne*, see Rte 4; to *Ypres*, see Rte 6; to *Bruges, Ghent* and *Brussels*, see Rte 8.

3   Ostend to Knokke-Heist

Total distance 32km.—*20km***Blankenberge**.—*4km***Zeebrugge**.—*8km* **Knokke-Heist**.—For most of the way the main road runs through dunes and the inland parts of the towns, little therefore being seen of the sea. From Ostend the tram takes some 26 minutes to Blankenberge, 45 minutes to Zeebrugge, and 70 minutes to Knokke.

Ostend, see Rte 2. The road rounds the sunken garden of the 'Vindictive' memorial, crosses the head of the fishing docks, and then turns parallel with the coast to pass *Bredene*, a village lying behind coastal dunes.—*11km* **De Haan**, a small resort with wooded dunes, is said to owe its name to the legend about some fishermen who during a storm were unknowingly being driven towards the shore but were alerted to their danger by the sound of a cock crowing.—*9km* **Blankenberge**(15,000 inhab. Tourist Information: Koning Leopold III Plein, by the station) is a cheerful resort with at its W end a picturesque harbour of 1862–76. On the SE of the town near the station are the modern *Stadhuis*, the fifth in Blankenberge's history, and the *Sint Antoonskerk*, dating from 1335–58, though much restored, and containing 17C and 18C paintings, amongst these a Temptation of St. Anthony by Jan Maes, Storm and Sea attributed to Jacob van Oost the Younger, and Flight into Egypt attributed to David Vinckeboons. Kerkstraat runs NW from the station passing the *Oude Stadhuis* (1680, the fourth in the series) to reach the shore near the *Casino*. To the E is the pier on which *Aquarama* shows local and tropical fish, fluorescent minerals, shells and ship models (Easter–mid September: daily, 10.00 to 19.00 or 22.00 in July and August).

4km **Zeebrugge** is a huge, still expanding artificial port which originated behind a mole built by Baron de Maere between 1895 and 1907 at the same time as the Boudwijn Kanaal linking Zeebrugge with Bruges. The road arrives at a crossroads with (S) the road to Bruges (see below) and, opposite, the short approach to the small resort district, the base of the original mole, and the western side of the harbour with the ferry services to England and, around the quays, a lively array of windmills, generating sufficient power to operate many of the port installations.

Baron de Maere's Mole is famous in the annals of the First World War and will long be associated with the heroic St. George's Day raid of 1918.

Lissewege, Great Barn of the Abbey of Ter Doest

Under German occupation Zeebrugge and the canal became an important submarine base, and it was decided that the entrance must be blocked. The attack, under Vice Admiral Roger Keyes, was launched on the night of 22–23

April, the force comprising three blockships; the old cruiser 'Vindictive'; two Liverpool ferries, 'Daffodil' and 'Iris II'; the submarine 'C3'; and several smokescreen and rescue craft. At midnight 'Vindictive' reached position on the seaward side of the mole, her task being to land a party to attack the German batteries and prevent their firing on the blockships. Because of the tide and current 'Vindictive' was unable to hold close enough, but was rammed and locked into position by 'Daffodil'. In the dark, under heavy fire, and meeting unexpected barbed wire, the landing-party had great difficulty in finding the batteries. Meanwhile 'C3' rammed the wooden viaduct forming the first part of the mole and blew herself up, her crew having escaped by collapsible boat. The approaching blockships came under heavy shelling, 'Thetis' running aground just clear of the mole but 'Intrepid' and 'Iphigenia' being sunk across the channel and their crews rescued by launches. 'Vindictive' recalled her landing-party and the force returned to Dover. Although not as decisive as hoped, the partial closing of the port reduced German submarine operations at a crucial period of the war.—For the simultaneous attack on Ostend, and the later operation there by 'Vindictive', see Rte 2.

During the Second World War Zeebrugge was blocked in May 1940, and blown up by the Germans in 1944. The port was finally reopened in 1957 when the last of the 1918 blockships ('Thetis') was removed.

Contained within, and dwarfed by, massive new harbour arms thrusting seaward, the original mole has today lost its identity. But the raid of 1918 is remembered by the *St. George's Day Memorial*. This, a replacement of the original destroyed by the Germans during World War II, has now been placed at the E end of Zeedijk (the promenade of the resort part of Zeebrugge), effectively at the base of the mole, the line of the first part of which is traced by a path also named for St. George's Day. The memorial, in part a bas-relief of the plan of the raid, incorporates a plaque honouring the part played by the submarine C3.

The port extends S, a huge area here being under development, while the modest town (as distinct from the beach area) lies either side of the road heading E, to the N being the fishing port and market (Port boat tours. Easter–mid September: daily except Friday, which is normally reserved for groups, 11.00 and 14.30. Duration 1½ hours).

ZEEBRUGGE TO BRUGES (13km). The main road is uninteresting and it is pleasanter to leave it at (4km) *Lissewege* and reach Bruges by the small road to the E of the Boudewijn Kanaal. The little polder village of Lissewege is known for its large 13C church with a huge brick tower, well worth climbing (265 steps) for the view offered across the polders. One explanation offered as to why such a large edifice should have been built here is that it was to honour a miraculous Madonna found in a local stream and which returned to the stream every time it was removed: so a chapel, then later this church, was built over the stream which, indeed, still flows below. The church interior, much of it the work of Walram Rombout, a local worker in wood and stone, contains a Visitation by Jacob van Oost the Elder (1652) and a St. James of Campostela by Jan Maes (1665): also noteworthy are the 17C graveslabs set in the walls just inside the church, many of these of particular interest for their clear portrayal of the clothing of the period.

Just S of Lissewege, between the main road and the canal, is the site of the abbey of *Ter Doest*, founded in 1106 (to be near the chapel sheltering the miraculous Madonna) and destroyed by iconoclasts in 1571, all that survived being the great *Barn of c 1250 (apply to adjacent restaurant for entry). Below the immense roof, with some 38,000 tiles, the interior is divided into three naves by two rows of oak piers resting on stone bases. The strange little chapel at the entrance to the estate dates from 1687 and was built by an abbot in gratitude for winning a law suit against Louis XIV.—*Dudzele*, 3km S of Lissewege, across the canal, preserves the Romanesque tower of its former 12C church.

Beyond Zeebrugge the road crosses the adjacent Schipdonk and Leopold canals, draining the polders bordering the Dutch frontier, to reach (*8km* from Zeebrugge) **Knokke-Heist** (30,000 inhab. Tourist Information: Lichttorenplein, Knokke), the collective name given to the 7km-long string of beaches made up of Heist, Duinbergen, Albert Strand, Knokke and Het Zoute, each claiming a character of its own—*Heist*, relaxed and for the family; *Duinbergen*, quiet and residential; *Albert Strand*, lively and with the Casino; *Knokke*, the busy heart of the strip; *Het Zoute*, residentially elegant. Knokke-Heist prides itself on being something more than just a summer resort, attention being drawn to the town's many sculptures as also to the variety of festivals, theatre, ballet, film galas and exhibitions, these including the annual firework and flower festivals, and also the World Cartoon Exhibition held here each year since 1962. The Casino at Albert Strand, the main centre for cultural and entertainment activity, is something of an art focus in itself, with, outside, a statue (the Poet) by Ossip Zadkine and, inside, murals and paintings by René Magritte, Paul Delvaux and others.

   Het Zwin, 3km E of Het Zoute, was the estuary which, until it silted up towards the end of the 15C, gave Sluis (in Holland), Damme and Bruges much of their early prosperity. In 1340 the fleet of England's Edward III, commanded by Edward in person, sailed up the estuary, he and his Flemish allies then almost totally destroying the French Fleet assembled in the roadstead in preparation for an invasion of England. Some idea of the size of the estuary can be gained from the fact that the English are said to have had 250 sail and the French 200. Today the reclaimed land has for the most part been cultivated, but 150ha of dune and marsh near the sea (including 25ha on the Dutch side) have been preserved as a nature reserve and bird sanctuary. Over half of this area is open to the public, among the birds that may be seen being oyster catchers, avocets, storks, greylag geese, golden orioles and collared doves. The reserve is open April–September: daily, 09.00 to 19.00. In summer there is a bus service from Knokke and Het Zoute.

4   Ostend to De Panne

Total distance 29km.—*8km* **Middelkerke**.—*8km***Nieuwpoort**.— *9km***Koksijde-Bad**.—*4km* **De Panne**.—As far as Nieuwpoort there is a choice between N34 close to the shore, or the older N318 which keeps parallel about 1km inland. From Ostend the tram, mostly running inland, takes 35 minutes to Nieuwpoort or 70 minutes to De Panne.

Ostend, see Rte 2.—*3km* **Mariakerke**, see p 137.—*Ostend Airport* is on N318 between Mariakerke and (*5km*) **Middelkerke**, with a casino and where the modern church incorporates an early Gothic belfry once used as a lighthouse.—*4km* **Westende** was during the First World War just within range of the Allied guns behind the Yser (Ijzer). From here westwards was devastation.—*2km***Lombardsijde**, on the right bank of the Yser near its mouth, twice changed hands in October and November 1914, what was left thereafter virtually becoming the German front line for four years. The Allied sentry in the dunes to the W of the village was known as 'l'homme de l'extrême gauche', the first man along a front that stretched from here to Switzerland.

Lombardsijde is a place of ancient origin, some historians tracing the name to the Lombards, a tribe once inhabiting the lower Elbe, who are said to have established a harbour on the estuary of the Yser, formerly much broader than today. The river silted up in about the 12C, leaving Lombardsijde high and dry and Nieuwpoort ('Novus portus' as described in its charter) took its place.

At the Yser bridge, just before Nieuwpoort, three waterways meet the estuary in a group of six sluices arranged in an arc; three allow access to canals, and three are for the flow of excess water. Here stand a group of memorials, the most prominent of which is the *Koning Albert Monument* (1938), a rotunda designed by Julien de Ridder with an equestrian statue by Karel Aubroeck and an interior encirlced by some resounding French verse by Maurice Gauchez as also Flemish lines by Auguste van Cauwelaert. Albert's queen (Elisabeth, died 1968) is remembered too, by a tablet, and steps (fee) ascend to the top gallery with its orientation tables. Adjacent, and guarded by defiant lions, a more modest but perhaps more moving British monument lists by units the 566 men missing after the Antwerp fighting of 1914 and along this coast during the following years, while, just across the canals, are a French monument and, on the right in trees, the Yser Memorial by the sculptor Pierre Braecke.

Battle of the Yser (see also Rte 5). By 18 October 1914 an Allied line had been established across the NW corner of Belgium, from the coast up the Yser to Ypres, the Belgians holding the northern 35km between Nieuwpoort and Steenstraat on the Yser–Ypres canal. The Battle of the Yser was fought at the same time as the opening phase of the First Battle of Ypres. For two days, despite heavy attack, the Belgians held, but on the night of 21–22 October the Germans got a force across the Yser at Tervate, reinforcing their position the following night in the face of gallant Belgian counter-attacks. On 24 October a major German offensive broke through the front at this point, only to find that the Belgians, reinforced now by a French division, had retired and were strongly deployed along the embankment of the Nieuwpoort–Diksmuide railway. Checked, the Germans turned their attention to Diksmuide, making a burning ruin of the town and then attacking through the rubble at midnight, 24–25 October This attack, and another the following night, were both repulsed. Exhausted now, and fast running out of ammunition, the Belgians decided to use the sea. First, to safeguard their own positions, they blocked all the culverts along the railway, then on the 27th, and again on 28 and 29 October, the Veurne canal sluices were opened at high tide. The result was disappointing, and it became clear that the sluices of the Noordvaart (the N canal) must also be opened, despite the fact that they lay in No Man's Land. The daring operation was successful (night 29 October) and the sea water poured through, spreading as large lagoons over the flat meadows between the river and the railway. Three German divisions which had taken Ramskapelle and Pervijze were forced into hasty retreat, the Battle of the Yser was won, and a front was established which would not significantly change for nearly four years.

Visitors in search of a closer identification with the First World War may divert to two places, one just SE and one just south. To the SE, in 3km, N367 crosses the Yser by the *Uniebrug* where, to the N and oblivious of the motorway, a figure of a soldier stands lone watch, while on the right a tablet records that it was here on 22 to 24 August 1914 that the Belgian 14th Régiment de Ligne defended the last shreds of its country, in so doing sacrificing 900 of its members. *Ramskapelle*, just 2km S of Nieuwpoort, was a key place along the railway immediately to its E; its rails now lifted, this historic line nevertheless survives as a low embankment still well showing those culverts, once so heroically blocked, as also vestiges of concrete defences. When, during the night of 29 October 1914, the area to the E was finally successfully flooded, two regiments, one Belgian and one French, retook Ramskapelle by bayonet charge, an exploit commemorated by a joint memorial on the village churchyard wall. For *Pervijze*, 4km S of Ramskapelle, see Rte 5.

Leaving the Koning Albert Monument, the road crosses the Yser, with (left) a memorial to the Resistance and, farther along the waterfront, the national memorial to Belgium's fishermen (1958).

2km **Nieuwpoort** (8000 inhab.), on the left bank of the Yser estuary, is an interesting small town and port, the centre of a municipality which includes *Nieuwpoort aan Zee*, known for its large marina, and also the inland village of *Ramskapelle*.

History. The 'novus portus' which received its charter in 1163 was to suffer much from war, being besieged nine times between the 13C and the 18C. One historic occasion was the battle of 1600, fought on the sands, when Maurice of Nassau, helped by an English contingent under the brothers Sir Francis and Sir Horace Vere, defeated the Spanish under Archduke Albert. The town was fortified until 1862. Throughout the First World War Nieuwpoort remained in Allied hands, but what little had survived the Yser battle and the bombardments of the following years was destroyed in the fighting of 1918.

Boat Excursions. Two interesting boat excursions can be made during the summer, one to Diksmuide and another to Ypres (apply Fishing Centre Vieren, 90 Albert I Laan).

The town centre is the Grote Markt on which there are a number of buildings of interest. The *Onze Lieve Vrouwkerk* was dedicated over 800 years ago in 1163 but has since been several times destroyed, though always rebuilt generally in the original style. It had a succession of towers but in 1539 was given a detached *Belfry*; destroyed in 1914, this was replaced in 1952 and now houses a chromatic carillon of 67 bells (concerts in mid June–mid September: Wednesday and Saturday, 20.30; also Friday, 11.15. Mid September–mid June: Sunday and Friday, 11.15). Immediately E are the adjoining *Stadhuis*, a Neo-Renaissance building of 1922, and the *Halle*, a rebuilding also of 1922 in the style of its corn exchange predecessor of c 1280. Here are the town's two museums, one of ornithology and the other of local history (Easter. July–August: daily except Sunday, 09.30 to 12.00, 14.00 to 17.30). In the E part of the town, to the S of the sluices, survives the *Laurentiustoren*, known also as the 'Duivelstoren' because it was here that a witch came to meet the devil. First built in c 1281 as part of a church (of Sint Laurentius), the tower was later incorporated into a fortress built by Philip the Bold and continued as part of the ramparts until they were demolished in 1862. During the First World War the tower again saw military use, as an observation post, as a result being largely destroyed.

Beyond *Nieuwpoort aan Zee* the road skirts the shore to reach (*6km*) **Oostduinkerke-Bad** (15,000 inhab. Tourist Information: Astrid Plein), a resort with a magnificent beach and known for its shrimps, caught by fishermen who wade out on horseback and sweep the breakers with their nets spread out on each side. Leopold II Laan leads S to the inland village, passing (1.5km from the sea) the modern *Sint Niklaaskerk* (J. Gilson, 1955) bearing a huge Crucifix by Arnost Gause. Some 500m farther on, to the E in P. Schmitzstraat, will be found the *Nationaal Visserijmuseum* (daily, 10.00 to 12.00, 14.00 to 18.00. Closed 1 January, 1 November, 25 December) with ship models, fishing equipment, a reconstruction of a fisherman's home and café, and paintings and carvings of fishing subjects.

3km **Koksijde-Bad** (15,500 inhab. Tourist Information: Gemeentehuis), another resort, boasts the highest dune along the Belgian coast. This, the *Hoge Blekker* (33m), is off the SW corner of the dunes nature reserve of *Doornpanne* which lies to the E of the town. From the town centre, Jaak van Buggenhoutlaan leads past (right) the modern *Onze Lieve Vrouw ten Duinenkerk* (J. Landsoght, 1964) to the site of the abbey of *Ter Duinen*, well signed off the main coastal road, with a museum housed in a modern and imaginative setting and devoted to local history and flora and fauna, emphasis being on the abbey the ruins of which can be visited in the adjacent park (Easter. July–September: daily, 10.00 to 18.00. Other months, but closed January: 09.00 to 12.30, 13.30 to 17.00).

The Cistercian abbey was founded in 1108, rebuilt after a flood of 1237, and finally destroyed by the Sea Beggars in 1566. In 1597 some of the monks re-established themselves in their grange of *Ten Bogaerde*, 1.5km S, of which the present buildings date mainly from 1612, though part of the 12–13C barn survives. The abbey was transferred to Bruges in 1627 and suppressed in 1796.

Close to the museum are a windmill (1773; built at Veurne and brought here in 1954) and, beside J. van Buggenhoutlaan, a chapel of 1819 marking the grave of St. Idesbald (died 1167), the third abbot (but see p 189).

In **Sint Idesbald**, the W extension of Koksijde-Bad, signs off the main coastal road direct to the *Musée Paul Delvaux* (April–September: daily except Monday, but open Monday in July and August, 10.30 to 18.30. October–December: Saturday, Sunday, 11.00 to 17.00. Closed some Holidays), not to be missed by connoisseurs of this artist who achieved much of his work in Koksijde. The large and well-displayed collection here covers a long and stylistically varied period and, for example, includes View of the Quartier Léopold station, Brussels (1922), a conventional if slightly impressionistic picture; The Red Chair (1936), with a somewhat less ethereal model than typical later; the Dream of Constantine (1955), far removed from the typical; *The Sabbath (1962), notable for its lighting and draped cloth; *The Procession (1963), in which a passing train contrasts brutally with the nine nudes processing seemingly in a trance through a grove; the Bride's Dress (1969); *La Petite Mariée (1976); On the Way to Rome (1979); The Dioscuri (1982).

4km **De Panne** (9500 inhab. Tourist Information: Gemeentehuis, Zeelaan) is so called from the slight depression (panne) of dunes and woods among which this popular resort lies. It was here in 1831 that King Leopold I first set foot on Belgian soil (memorial at W of Zeedijk), and during 1914–18 De Panne was 'capital' of this, the only unconquered corner of Belgium, King Albert and Queen Elisabeth living at the Villa Maskens, the latter working as a nurse in a field hospital. In May 1940 the retreating British army reached the sea here, the subsequent historic evacuation (monument on Leopold I Esplanade) being from the beaches between De Panne and Dunkirk in France. The French frontier is only 2km to the W, the land between being a dunes nature reserve of 340ha known as the *Westhoek*; there are waymarked paths and a guide to local flora is available from Tourist Information. Just S of De Panne, on the road to Adinkerke, *Meli* is a recreational park with many attractions for children (April–September: daily from 09.30).

For De Panne to *Diksmuide* and *Ghent*, see Rte 5.

5   De Panne to Ghent

Total distance 86km.—*6km* **Veurne.**—*17km*
Diksmuide.—*34km* **Tielt.**—*13km* **Deinze.**—*4km* **Ooidonk.**—*12km*
Ghent.

De Panne, see Rte 4.—*6km* **Veurne** (**Furnes**. 11,500 inhab. Tourist
Information: Grote Markt) is an agricultural centre at the junction of
several canals which form a moat encircling the course of the old
ramparts. The large and outstandingly attractive Grote Markt contains several interesting buildings in Flemish and Spanish style.

Veurne, the Stadhuis

Veurne traces its origin to a fortified place built here against the Norse raids of
the 9th and 10C. The ramparts were demolished in 1771. During the First World
War the town, 9km behind the Yser front, was the Belgian military headquarters
and suffered much damage from intermittent bombardment. Damage was again
suffered in May 1940.
    The 'Boet Processie' (Penitents' Procession) takes place on the last Sunday in
July. Successor to a 12C ceremony in honour of the True Cross (see below), the
procession in its present form dates from 1644.

Most places of note are around the Grote Markt, on the N side of which is a neat row of 17C gabled houses. The *Stadhuis* (Guided tours), at the NW corner, is a mixed Gothic and Renaissance building of 1596–1612 by Lieven Lucas, with a loggia by Jérôme Stalpaert in front and an octagonal turret behind. The building connects with the more severe *Gerechtshof*, built in 1613–18 mainly by Sylvanus Boullain and with a chimneypiece by Stalpaert in the hall. It was in these adjoining buildings that King Albert had his headquarters in 1914. Behind is the *Belfry* of 1628. The *Sint Walburgakerk*, behind the Gerechtshof, according to tradition stands on the site of a pagan temple to Wotan. It consists of a choir of 1230–80, rebuilt after a fire in 1353, and transepts begun in c 1300 but only completed, together with the short nave, in 1902–04; the ruined 14C tower, in the park, was never completed. Within the church are choir stalls of 1596 by Osmaer van Ommen, a pulpit of 1727 by Hendrik Pulincx, and a Descent from the Cross attributed to Pieter Pourbus. The sacristy contains the 16C reliquary of the True Cross.

In 1099 Count Robert II of Flanders, returning from Jerusalem with a piece of the True Cross, was caught by a gale and vowed to offer the relic to the first church he should see. This being Sint Walburga, the gift was duly made and a brotherhood was formed to honour it with an annual procession.

On the W side of the Grote Markt the house next to the Stadhuis dates from 1624, while on the S side the *Hoge Wacht*, once the house of the night watch, was in 1636 enlarged into a main guard headquarters. The Ooststraat leads E out of the square, here on either side being the former *Vleeshuis* or meat hall (1615) with a graceful façade and now a public library and cultural centre, and the *Spaans Paviljoen* (c 1450, enlarged 1528–30) which served as town hall until 1586 and later was occupied by officers of the Spanish garrison; it is now used by the magistracy.

The *Sint Niklaaskerk*, in the Appelmarkt off the SE corner of the Grote Markt, is a late 15C hall-church with a choir of 1773. The massive brick tower, of the 13C and thus considerably older than the church proper, contains a huge bell of 1379, one of the oldest in Belgium. The modernised interior exhibits (restored, and well lit above the altar) a triptych of 1534 ascribed to either Pieter Coecke or Bernard van Orley.

Another attraction in Veurne (Albert I Laan) is the *Bakery Museum*, demonstrating the preparation of bread, cakes, tarts and much else (April–September: Monday–Friday, 10.00 to 12.00, 14.00 to 18.00, Saturday, Sunday, Holidays, 14.00 to 18.00. October–March: Monday–Friday, 14.00 to 17.00).

The château of **Beauvoorde** (June–September: daily except Monday, 14.00 to 17.00), 7km S of Veurne, was rebuilt in c 1591–1617, probably by Boullain, on the site of an old castle by then in ruins. Inside are some good chimneypieces (one attributed to Stalpaert), paintings, ceramic, glass and silverware.—*Houtem*, 3km W of Beauvoorde, was King Albert's headquarters in 1915–18. To the N from here stretches the polder of *De Moeren*, drained in 1627 by Wenceslas Coeberger using windmills.

The small town of **Lo** (2000 inhab.), 12km SE of Veurne, was once important because of its Augustinian abbey, founded in the 12C and suppressed at the time of the French Revolution. Of this, all that survives is the attractive *Dovecot* (1710) behind the church, this latter being a 19–20C successor to the abbey church; it contains Baroque stalls and a pulpit of 1626 by Urbain Taillebert. The *Westpoort*, with two pepperpot turrets, dates back to the 14C and the *Stadhuis* is a restoration of a 16C building. Tradition holds that Julius Caesar tethered his horse to the ancient yew by the Westpoort. Near the Stadhuis is the restored 15–16C convent of the Grauwe Zusters (the Grey Sisters, or Poor Clares).

9km Pervijze was briefly taken by the Germans on 28 October 1914, but almost immediately evacuated when the Belgians flooded the area. A tower in this small town (to the SW of the central crossroads) long served as a 1914–18 observation post; in today's built-up setting, and probably only glimpsed from a speeding car, the tower may seem of little significance, though, if viewed from the S, its tactical value is more striking. In *3km* a minor road (signed OLV Hoekje and Dodengang) forks E, with, almost immediately, another even smaller road heading N for *OLV Hoekje*, representing an exposed and remote point along the Belgian front. Today—still flat, bleak and exposed— this rather unreal spot preserves a miscellany of 1914–18 memories: regimental memorial stones around a monument; a plaque honouring a Franciscan monk turned artillery officer who set up his observation post in the ruin of the old chapel; immediately beyond the chapel, a demarkation stone recording the bald but always dramatic fact that here the invader was halted; a bunker; and, inside the chapel, some vivid stained glass of war scenes as also some fast deteriorating wartime pictures and maps. The *Dodengang* (or Boyau du Mort, or Trench of Death) is reached by returning S and then bearing E along the original minor road off N35. Near the entrance there are some interesting 1914–18 photographs, and the upper floor of the entrance building affords an overall view and some tactical appreciation of a section of 1914–18 trench complex, but on the whole this quite extensive system along the Yser is, with its neat concrete sandbags and immaculate duckboards, altogether too clean and tidy to be convincing (April–September: daily, 09.00 to 17.00 in April and September, 18.00 in May and 19.00 in July–August. October 1–15: Sunday, 09.00 to 17.00).

Returning to N35, the bridge over the Yser is reached in rather under *4km*, to the right rising the *Ijzertoren*, essentially a Flemish nationalist tower built in 1930 as a combined war memorial and cry for peace; blown up by an unknown hand in 1946, another tower was built close to the ruins of the original. The vertical AVV stands for All for Flanders; the horizontal VVK for Flanders for the King. In front are the Heroes' Gate and the Pasepoort (Peace Gate), erected from the ruins of the original tower, and in the crypt there are memorials to Flemish patriots. The tower(lift) houses a museum, with some emphasis on Flemish nationalism but also explanatory material on the fighting around Diksmuide (March, April, October, November: daily, 09.00 to 17.00. May, June, September: daily, 09.00 to 19.00. July and August: daily, 08.00 to 20.00).

1km **Diksmuide** (15,000 inhab. Tourist Information: Grote Markt) is a typical rebuilt town, much of it in the old style.

In the 9–10C fortifications protected a settlement here against the Norse raiders. Later, the Spanish garrisoned what had by then become a small town, and in 1680 it was one of the several places arbitrarily annexed by Louis XIV. In the First World War Diksmuide bore the brunt of the German attacks during the Yser fighting, thereafter becoming part of the front line and being so totally destroyed that it was identified only by a board bearing its name.

The spacious Grote Markt is surrounded by many old-style houses, while above rises the tower of the *Sint Niklaaskerk*, in origin of the 14C, rebuilt in the 17C and again after both world wars. The *Begijnhof*, founded during the 13C and in use as such until the First

Diksmuide, the Begijnhof Church

World War, has been rebuilt; the approach alley from the canal bridge bears the name of St. Thomas, recalling a tradition that Thomas à Becket once stayed here.—*20km Lichtervelde*, where the Sint Jacobskerk contains a late Romanesque font.

14km **Tielt** (19,000 inhab. Tourist Information: Stadhuis), long associated with textiles and shoes, was the birthplace of Olivier le Daim, a wandering barber who became the powerful confidant of France's Louis XI; one year after the King's death in 1484 he was hanged. During the First World War the town was for a period the German headquarters on the Flanders front and here on 1 November 1914 the Kaiser narrowly escaped bombs dropped by British aircraft. The town's central and most attractive feature, on the Markt, is the *Belfry* of 1275 (spire 1620) and the adjacent *Halle*, or trades hall, largely of the early 17C; the coats-of-arms below the windows are of various local lords, and a plaque on the S façade commemorates the Peasants' Revolt of 1798. Also of interest are the *Stadhuis*, essentially of the 19C but with a wing along Tramstraat in part dating back to a 13C convent hospice; the modern (1937) *Onze Lieve Vrouwkerk* known for its sculpture and bronze Stations of the Cross; the *Sint Pieterskerk*, founded in the 11C (tower 1646) and with notable furnishing which includes a Rococo pulpit of 1857; the 17C *Stockt Chapel* where stained-glass windows depict the affliction of the plague; and the *Minderbroederskerk*, with Baroque altars and the 17C cloisters of its monastery.

Meulebeke, 5km S of Tielt, was the birthplace of Karel van Mander (1548–1606), the Dutch painter, best known for his biographical work on artists.

The border into East Flanders is crossed beyond (*6km*) *Aarsele*, where there are a Romanesque church and a restored windmill.—*7km* **Deinze** (25,000 inhab.), on the river Lȳs (Leie), has a 13–14C church and, at No. 1 L. Matthyslaan, the modern, purpose-built *Museum van Deinze en De Leiestreek* (Monday and Wednesday–Friday, 14.00 to 17.30; Saturday, Sunday, Holidays, 10.00 to 12.00, 14.00 to 17.00), a town and district museum in two distinct parts. The first is an art gallery showing works of all kinds by just about all the artists associated with the Leie, or Lys, district, among the many names being Emile Claus, George Minne, Constant Permeke, A. Servaes and Leon and Gustave de Smet. The other part of the museum is devoted to the archaeology, history and folklore of Deinze.

There is now a choice of roads, that S of the Lys through Deurle being described in Rte 11. This Rte continues N of the river to (*4km*) the château of **Ooidonk**, just S of the village of Bachte-Maria-Leerne (Ascension. Whitsun and Whitmon. July—mid September: Sunday and Holidays, 14.00 to 18.00. Park open daily). In wooded parkland and standing at the end of a long copper-beech avenue, this elaborate moated château originated as a 13C fortress. Burnt down by the citizens of Ghent in 1501, because the then owner supported Philip the Handsome, and again in 1578 by Ghent Calvinists, the castle was rebuilt at the end of the 16C as a residential château, the corner towers being the only significant survival from the earlier fortress. The mainly 19C interior contains furniture, porcelain, Beauvais tapestries, and a collection of royal portraits.—*8km* **Drongen** is known for its abbey. Founded by Premonstratensians in 1138 on an even earlier Benedictine site, the abbey was dissolved by the French at the end of the 18C, the buildings soon afterwards being used by Lieven Bauwens (see Ghent history) as Belgium's first cotton-mill. Occupied since 1837 by Jesuits, the abbey as seen today is mainly 17th and 18C, the church being of 1736 and housing a Pietà of the school of Roger van der Weyden. Erasmus was a frequent visitor here.—*4km***Ghent**, see Rte 13.

6   Ostend to Ypres

Total distance 45km.—*9km***Gistel**.—*6km Sint Pieters Kapelle*.— *10km* **Diksmuide**.—*15km Boezinge*.—*5km* **Ypres**.—Between Sint Pieters Kapelle and Boezinge the road follows the line of the 1914– 18 front, and from Boezinge to Ypres the base of the Ypres salient (Rte 7B).

Ostend (see Rte 2) is left by the Torhoutsesteenweg and in 5km the road crosses the Ostend-Nieuwpoort canal.

A road running E along the S bank in 7km reaches **Oudenburg**, once on an arm of the sea and occupying the site of a large Roman coastal fortress, with a correspondingly large burial area, and later of a medieval port. No significant Roman remains survive above ground, but finds are shown in a museum close to the Markt Plein in the town centre.

The main road continues SE, crossing the E–W arm of the E40 motorway.—*9km* **Gistel** (6000 inhab.) is an ancient place the name of which may derive from the stables (stallingen) of the counts of Flanders. The town is associated with St. Godeleva, strangled in 1070 by her husband, the lord of Gistel, because he could not accept her religious convictions. Her shrine is in the church (c 1500). The abbey of *Ten Putte* (3km W) is the 19C successor to a Benedictine nunnery founded soon after the saint's death, reputedly on the site of the castle in which she was strangled.— This Rte now bears SW on N367 across a district called *Moere Blote*, marshland largely drained in 1620–23 by Wenceslas Coeberger; at (*6km*) *Sint Pieters Kapelle* the Rte turns S on N369 for (*5km*) *Keiem*. Much of the country to the W of the road between Sint Pieters Kapelle and Keiem was flooded in 1914–18, the outposts of the opposing armies being in places 3km apart and patrolling being carried out in boats. *Tervate*, 3km W of Keiem, is where the Germans first got across the Yser in strength.—*5km* **Diksmuide**, see Rte 5.

Passing, just beyond Woumen, the lake of *Blankaart*, today a nature reserve but long a part of the Yser front flooding, N369 in *13km* crosses the Ypres–Yser canal near the village of *Steenstraat*, for which, as also for the road continuing to (*2km*) *Boezinge* and (*5km*) **Ypres** (Rte 7A) see Rte 7B, Northern Salient.

7   Ypres and the Salient

A. Ypres

YPRES is the English and French name for the Flemish town of **Ieper** (34,500 inhab.), at the S end of the canal from the Yser and 12km from the French border. In the 13–15C a powerful place, ranking first among the ancient cloth-working towns of Flanders and thus rich in fine buildings, today Ypres is known principally in the context of the fighting of 1914–18 which early reduced the town, on the base of the notorious salient, to ruins. Immediately behind the front line, the traffic routes through the town were continuously shelled long after the buildings had disappeared, and the junction of the Grote Markt with the Menen road became known as 'the most dangerous corner in Europe' (the British always used the French spelling, Menin, and this will be used below where it seems more appropriate). The original lines of the cobbled streets nevertheless survived, and the town was rebuilt to the former plan, many of the buildings, notably the great cloth hall and the cathedral, being faithful copies of their predecessors. Within and around the town numerous memorials and military cemeteries remind that over half a million men of both sides gave their lives here.

Tourist Information. Stadhuis, Grote Markt.

Post Office. Rijselstraat.

Commonwealth War Graves Commission. 82 Elverdingestraat. There are some
40 British military cemeteries within 3km of the Grote Markt, and 130 others
around the Salient. At the Commission maps can be consulted and directions
obtained. Many cemeteries can be reached by bus. Open Monday–Friday, 08.30
to 12.30, 13.30 to 17.00 or 16.30 on Friday.

English Church. Memorial church of *St. George*; corner of Elverdingestraat, just
NW of the cathedral.

Festival. 'Kattestoet'. Procession of cats, giants, etc., on second Sunday in May
(see below).

History. Starting in the 10C as the point where the Paris to Bruges trade road
crossed the river Ieperlee (in those days navigable, now canalised underground),
Ypres grew to become a powerful centre, deriving great wealth from its weaving
and sharing with Bruges and Ghent the effective control of Flanders. In the 13C,
when the Cloth Hall was built (c 1260–1304), it boasted a population of some
200,000, but the tide began to turn in the following century, from 1383 onwards,
this being the year in which the English, aided by troops from Ghent, besieged the
town (see picture in the cathedral). Ypres held out, but the surrounding district
was ravaged and the weavers were forced to emigrate. Chaucer's description of
the skill of the Wife of Bath as surpassing that of the weavers of 'Ipres and Gaunt'
dates from about this time. This dispersion marked the beginning of the end.
Rivalries between the towns and the rigid traditionalism of their guilds hastened
the decline and by the close of the 16C the population had dwindled to 5000.

But in strategic terms Ypres remained important, sacked by Parma in 1584 and
throughout the next century continually fought over by France and Spain. In 1678,
under the Peace of Nijmegen, Ypres became French and Vauban strengthened
the defences. But peace did not last long and, after surviving the War of the Grand
Alliance (1690–97), Ypres changed hands several times during the War of the
Spanish Succession (1702–13), during that of the Austrian Succession (1744–48)
and during the war which broke out in 1792 beween revolutionary France and
Austria, finally once again becoming a French town in 1794.

In October 1914 Ypres was briefly occupied by German cavalry, who, however,
withdrew the next day (14 October) when the British Expeditionary Force arrived.
For the Salient for which Ypres then became the soon devastated pivot, see Rte 7B.
On 1 May 1920 the town was awarded the British Military Cross.

In the Second World War Ypres escaped direct attack other than from the air.

Along the N side of the Grote Markt stretches the famous **Cloth Hall*
(Lakenhalle), long the most splendid Gothic public building in
Belgium and a proud monument to the wealth and power of the
medieval guilds. Built originally during the 13C (c 1260–1304) along
the river Ieperlee, in those days busy with shipping, the hall was
essentially a combined market, warehouse and covered quay. (During
winter wool was stored on the upper floor, cats being introduced to
keep down the mice. In spring the cats, no longer required, were
thrown down to the people below, a custom which—symbolising the
killing of evil spirits—continued until 1817 as part of the 'Kattestoet'
festival, still celebrated on the second Sunday in May, but the cats now
being cloth replicas.)

After surviving centuries of war, the hall was totally destroyed in
1914, largely by an artillery barrage of 22 November, but was rebuilt,
externally to the old design, largely in the 1930s, though it was not until
1967, and after yet another war, that King Baudouin performed the
final opening ceremony. The façade, 130m long, has at the centre a
superb square belfry (70m; carillon with concerts on most Sundays in
June–September between 21.00 to 22.00; ascent in summer), the lower
courses of which incorporate something of the original 13C building. It
bears figures of Baldwin IX and his queen (said to have laid the
building's first stone), of Albert I and Queen Elisabeth, and of Our Lady

Ypres, the Cloth Hall and Cathedral

of Thuin, protectress of Ypres since the English siege of 1383. On the right of the entrance a tablet remembers the French victims of 1914–18.

The *Nieuwwerk*, housing part of the town hall, abuts the E end of the Cloth Hall, this elegant Renaissance building above a vaulted gallery being a reconstruction (1950s) of an original of 1619–24, destroyed in 1914. In the gallery are *Tourist Information* and the **Salient** or **Memorial Museum** (Easter–mid November: daily, 09.30 to 12.15, 13.30 to 17.30), a very professional and comprehensive museum as compared to some of the rather opportunist ones around the Salient. The material, Allied and German, includes pictures and photographs, civil and military; a section devoted to war cemeteries; some excellent dioramas, all of the conditions of 1917 (Passchendaele, Menin Gate, Lille Gate); a large *Model of devastated Ypres and another of an aerodrome of 1917–18; trench signs and examples of trench art; official proclamations; instructive maps; a mock-up of a section of trench; and many personal mementoes.

Behind the Cloth Hall rises the **Sint Maartens Kathedraal**, the reproduction (but now with a spire which, though shown on early plans, was not originally built) of a 13C Gothic building destroyed in 1914 and itself a successor of a church founded and built here in c 1073; part of the early cloister survives on the N side against the reconstructed domestic buildings of the 12C abbey. Most of the cathedral's works of art were lost in 1914, but a Flemish diptych of 1525 survives on the W wall, where there is also a memorial to Abbé Camille Delaere

(1860–1930), a parish priest who in 1914, and always under fire, gallantly ministered to the wounded. The rose window above the S door (explanation near the entry by the S transept) is a memorial to King Albert, presented in 1935 by the British Army and the Royal Air Force. The S transept contains the reconstructed tomb of George Chamberlain, born at Ghent of English parents, who became Bishop of Ypres in 1628–34, and here too is a memorial to all those French soldiers who fell in Belgium in 1914–18.

The British Empire Memorial—a standard design and one of a number in churches along the 1914–18 front line—in the N transept remembers the one million dead of the Empire 'many of whom rest in Belgium'. In the E chapel hangs a graphic if naive picture of the siege by the English and rebels in 1383, and here also is the tomb of Bishop Jansenius (Cornelis Jansen, 1585–1638), the religious reformer who gave his name to Jansenism.

Jansenism was a Catholic cult based on the teachings of St. Augustine which, with its insistence that man's personal relationship to God is more important than formal worship, soon came into conflict with the Jesuits. Jansenius himself kept clear of serious trouble, becoming a teacher at Louvain and bishop here at Ypres, but after his death the Jansenists were much persecuted.

Outside the NE corner of the cathedral a Celtic cross, the *Munster Memorial*, honours the Munster Irish soldiers killed in the First World War, while to the NW, at the corner of Elverdingestraat, is **Saint George's English Memorial Church** (Reginald Blomfield, 1929), inside which the figure on the font cover is a memorial to Field Marshal the Earl of Ypres (Sir John French; 1852–1925), commander of the British Expeditionary Force in 1914–15. Virtually everything in the church, as also every part of it, is a memorial, and visitors with a special interest may refer to the guides on either wall just inside the entrance.

Just beyond the W end of the Grote Markt are the *Gedenkteken* (corner of Boterstraat), the memorial to the people of Ypres of both wars, and, in Boomgardstraat, the reconstructed *Vleeshuis*, the ground floor in origin of 1275, the upper floor of 1530, and now a youth centre. The parallel Rijselstraat (Lille Street), leading S out of the Grote Markt, soon passes (W) the **Belle Godshuis**, an almshouse in origin of about 1276 but rebuilt in the 16C and 17C and bearing a tablet to its physician founder Jean Yperman. The house is now a museum showing some paintings (including a Madonna with Donors, of 1420), 17C vestments, 17C and 18C silver, furniture and suchlike (Monday–Friday, 10.00 to 12.00, 14.00 to 16.00). Farther S, on the left, the **Hotel-Museum Merghelynck** is a reconstruction of a patrician home of 1774, magnificent contemporary period rooms being the feature of the interior (Monday–Saturday, 10.00 to 12.00, 14.00 to 17.00. Closed Holidays and second half of July). The museum is opposite the *Post Office*, in a replica of a 14C house thought once to have belonged to the Knights Templar. Beyond, on the left, the *Sint Pieterskerk* preserves Romanesque traces in the lower course of its W tower, while beyond again, off to the right in Ieperlee Straat, will be found the *Stedelijk Museum* (in what was originally an almshouse of 1277) with general material on the town's history (July and August: daily, 14.00 to 18.00. September: Saturday, Sunday 14.00 to 18.00). Rijselstraat ends at the **Rijselpoort** (the Lille Gate) with Ramparts Cemetery, two pre-Vauban flanking bastions, and vaulted chambers on either side. That on the E was once a 17C guardroom, while those on the W, used for water control, are at the point where the Ieperlee starts its now underground course through the town. Less exposed than the Menin Gate, this Lille Gate was whenever possible the choice of route out to the front.

The E end of the Grote Markt is occupied by the *Gerechtshof* (Law Courts), on the site of a 12C almshouse still standing in 1914, beside which the Menenstraat leads to the **Menin Gate**, a main entry to the town and successor to earlier entries here through the ramparts (the Antwerp Gate, and, after a visit by Napoleon in 1804, the Napoleon Gate). Opened (by Field Marshal Plumer) in its present form in July 1927 as a memorial to the armies of the British Empire and to those of their dead who have no known grave, the gate stands on the site of the chief, and always very dangerous, approach from the town to the Salient battlefields. The memorial, by Sir Reginald Blomfield, takes the form of a gateway with three entrances, above the main archway being a brooding lion by Sir W. Reid Dick. The names of nearly 55,000 men who fell within the Salient only to be listed as Missing are inscribed all over the walls and beside the steps and galleries leading to the adjacent ramparts. Every evening, at 20.00, the traffic is briefly halted and the Last Post is sounded; a simple but moving ceremony started by the Chief of Police in 1928 and, apart from 1939–45, carried out every evening since.

Remains of the **Ramparts**, with moat below—of ancient origin, but largely the work of Vauban in the 17C—line the E side of the town. These ramparts were much used by British artillery observers, and the paths along the top still command a view of the arc of ridges on which the Germans were established after the Second Battle (from left to right, Pilkem, Zonnebeke and Mesen, or Messines).

For Ypres to *Ostend*, see Rte 6.

B. The Salient and the Battles of Ypres

The 'Salient' was the name given in 1914–18 to the arc of Allied front rounding the E of Ypres, the scene of some of the costliest yet in results most barren fighting of the war, the three battles of Ypres. The Salient was established by the first battle (1914), much reduced by the second (1915), and modestly enlarged by the third (1917). The key tactical feature was the series of low ridges, from Pilkem in the N to Mesen (Messines) in the S; holding these from 1915 to 1917, the Germans were able to keep much of the Allied forward and rear areas under observation.

The text below is in five parts. The first summarises the three Battles of Ypres, and also the Battle of the Lys (the German offensive of April 1918). The next three parts suggest tours of the northern, central and southern sectors of the Salient, while the fourth describes Poperinge, the rear base for the Salient and in itself a town of some interest.

Battered concrete bunkers, eroded and overgrown trenches, traces of barbed wire, pocked ground and huge mine craters; over much of the area all these survive amid the crowding cemeteries (there are some 170) and monuments, large and modest, Allied and enemy. But today this is modern, provincial Belgium, a mainly flat and not particualy inviting land of isolated farms and neat villages, apart from surfaced roads and a motorway, and with cars instead of horses, probably not greatly different to the scene prior to 1914. Amid such surrounds it requires a constantly goaded imagination to substitute the utter devastation and desolation of 1914–18: the rubble that was once a village, the flooded trenches, the entanglements of barbed wire, the stark tortured stumps that once were trees, the constant shelling, and, above all perhaps, the mud in which men could and did drown. As more than one survivor has remembered, it was always raining. Yet, without such a picture, a tour must be largely meaningless to the modern visitor, comfortable in his car rather than struggling on foot, heavy pack on back. The photograph reproduced on page 156 will, it is hoped, provide a ready reminder, and there is also much to be gained through studying the old photographs which are perhaps the most rewarding feature of local museums, of which there are a number around the Salient (times flexible, but normally open when a reasonable number of tourists may be expected).

And a warning. With age, explosive progressively becomes less stable; it is extremely dangerous to touch virtually any kind of wartime debris, and dangerous also, particularly in woods, to stray off obvious paths. Frequently, stacks of shells and suchlike will be found beside the road, or maybe around the base of a memorial or signpost; these are not for souvenir hunters but are awaiting collection by the Belgian bomb disposal units.

The Battles of Ypres

In October 1914 the Allies aimed to strike at the German communications across Flanders. At the same time the Germans mounted their offensive, the two attacks thus meeting one another and becoming the **First Battle of Ypres** (19 October–22 November). The Allied strength was about one-third that of the Germans, but although there were withdrawals, Ypres was saved and a salient established that would last until April the following year. During the first part of the battle (till end October) the Battle of the Yser (Rte 4) was being fought to the north.

The Belgians held from the sea, up the Yser, to about Steenstraat. Here the Salient began, with the French responsible for the NE sector, and the British along a line from Zonnebeke, S past the E of Polygon Wood to Geluveld and Kruiseke, thence to the Lys opposite Frelinghien in France. On 21 October the French fell back to the canal, exposing the British left; but the line was held and on 23 October the French took over the Zonnebeke-Langemark sector. Stalemate followed for several days, although the British were forced out of Kruiseke. In the N, the Belgians opened the Yser sluices, and the Germans now concentrated on Ypres, launching their offensive on 30 October. The greater part of the Allied line held, but the British lost Zandvoorde and Hollebeke and were forced back to the Mesen-Wijtschate ridge. The next three days were critical—on 31 October Geluveld was lost, retaken, and lost; on 1 November Mesen was lost, and on 2 November the Wijtschate ridge (a disaster which gave the enemy a view over Ypres and its surrounds)—but after this the situation stabilised, and by the close of 2 November the Allied line ran (from N to S) from the canal at Steenstraat, round Langemark to Zonnebeke (French); from Zonnebeke, along the E of Polygon Wood to Hill 60 and the railway (British); from the railway to W of Mesen (French); from here to the Lys at Frelinghien (British). Both sides now reinforced—the balance remaining much the same—and the main German offensive was launched on 11 November. But there were only minor changes and by 22 November open warfare had given way to trench warfare.

Second Battle of Ypres (22 April–25 May 1915). Concentrating now against Russia, the Germans were on the defensive in the West, but

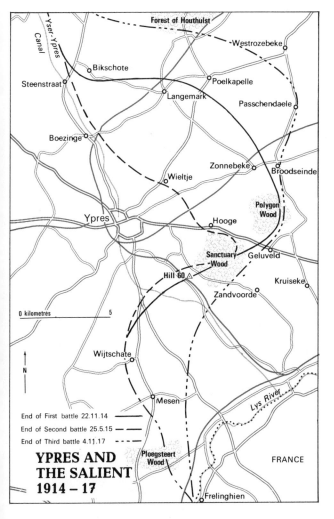

Forest of Houthulst

Westrozebeke

Yser-Ypres Canal

Bikschote

Steenstraat

Poelkapelle

Langemark

Passchendaele

Boezinge

Zonnebeke

Broodseinde

Wieltje

Polygon Wood

Ypres

Hooge

Sanctuary Wood

Geluveld

Hill 60 △

Kruiseke

Zandvoorde

0 kilometres   5

N

Wijtschate

Mesen

Lys River

End of First battle 22.11.14 ———
End of Second battle 25.5.15 — — —
End of Third battle 4.11.17 —·—·—

**YPRES AND
THE SALIENT
1914 – 17**

Ploegsteert Wood

FRANCE

Frelinghien

wished nevertheless to try out their new weapon, gas. On meteorological advice the Ypres front was chosen. At this time the Salient was as at the end of the first battle, with the French (mainly North African troops) holding from Steenstraat round Langemark to what is now N313, and the British the rest. On the British front the Canadian 1st Division held the section adjoining the French. At 17.00 on 22 April a yellowish cloud (chlorine released from cylinders) formed in front of the German trenches and drifted towards the French, who were forced to retreat behind the canal, leaving the entire British flank exposed. The Germans, taking Langemark and the Pilkem ridge, got across the canal at Steenstraat. At 04.00 on 24 April came the second gas attack, this time against the Canadians, and after two days of fierce fighting, in which 's Graventafel and Sint Juliaan were lost, the British were left with an untenable long narrow tongue pointing towards Passendale (then Passchendaele). May saw a two-stage withdrawal (with the line first through Frezenberg, but soon S and W of Wieltje), and in the heavy fighting Hill 60 was lost, but the French drove the Germans off the W bank of the canal. When the battle closed on 25 May, the base of the Allied salient had been shortened

Château Wood, Ypres, 29 October 1917

from 13km to 8km, and its maximum depth from 9km to a mere 4km. The Salient now ran from S of Boezings, S of Wieltje, through Hooge and Sancturay Wood to NW of Hill 60, thence following the original line W of Mesen to the Lys.

The Third Battle of Ypres (1917) was intended to open the way for a follow-up offensive on the German positions along the coast. The battle divides into two phases, the first being the *Battle of Mesen*, or Messines, on 7 June, the object being to secure the German salient along the Mesen-Wijtschate ridge. A combination of artillery barrage,

mines (19 huge mines, spaced between Hill 60 and Ploegsteert Wood, wrecked the German trenches), and gallantry by the Australian, New Zealand, Irish, and London regiments, brought success and by evening the whole ridge was in British hands. The *Main Offensive* opened on 22 July with a ten-days artillery barrage by 2300 guns. On 31 July, in heavy rain, the infantry attacked along a 24km front. On the left Bikschote, Sint Juliaan, and the Pilkem ridge were all taken, but in the central section by the Menen road there was no progress. A second attack on 16 August had much the same result, the left passing what once had been Langemark but the centre achieving nothing. Fresh offensives, always in heavy rain, between 30 September and 4 October gave the British (largely Australian and New Zealand divisions) the main ridge Geluveld—Polygon Wood—Broodseinde. Although this was something, it was far from enough, and the 'forest' of Houthulst with the high ground behind had to be won if the coastal campaign was to be possible. Several attacks were made, all foundering in mud, but on 4 November the Canadians fought their way across the morass to the site of Passendale (Passchendaele) village. This ended the tragic and barren Third Battle of Ypres, generally considered to have been doomed from the start by a combination of German preparedness, German use of mustard gas, and above all by mud, made worse by continuous rain and a scale of bombardment that turned the ground into an impassable quagmire.

Battle of the Lys (1918). On 9 April 1918 the Germans made their last drive to end the war, the main weight of the attack falling along the Lys and against the Salient. By 30 April, when the battle ended, all the Allied gains of 1917 had been lost and S of Ypres the Allied line no longer reached the Lys but ran through Voormezele, Vierstraat, and Loker. All was regained in the final victorious Allied offensive of August–October.

The Northern Salient

A tour of some 27km, much of it across the country which was the scene of the devastating first German gas attack in April 1915.

Ypres is left by N369, passing first Dudhallow Cemetery and then *Essex Farm Cemetery* with the tall obelisk of the 49th Division Memorial. In the grass bank to the left just behind the Cross of Sacrifice there is a group of British dugouts, in surprisingly good condition and well demonstrating how even a modest feature such as this bank could be defensively valuable. It was at a dressing station here that John McCrae, an officer with the Royal Canadian Medical Corps, wrote his poem 'In Flanders Fields', which appeared in 'Punch' on 8 December 1915. Beyond (5km from central Ypres) **Boezinge,** now bypassed, long marked the northern point of the British sector which, on the N side of the village, joined the French; the village was also, after the Second Battle, the NW corner of the much reduced Salient. Today, in the village, the past is recalled by a bunker with a German mortar on top.

A memorial of a very different kind will be found 1km E along the Langemark road beyond the railway crossing. Honouring the French 87th and 45th divisions, the memorial is made up of a calvary, a dolmen and a small menhir, all brought from Brittany, while an orientation table and map recall and explain how, during the late afternoon of 22 April 1915, the men of these divisions faced the first

German gas. The concrete posts surrounding the site represent the early wooden ones to which the barbed wire was attached before the provision of iron screw-pickets.

Steenstraat, 3 km N of Boezinge and in April 1915 near the end of the French line, is the area where the Germans, profiting from the surprise achieved through their gas, for three weeks (22 April–15 May) held a bridgehead on the W side of the canal. Here today, on the left just after N369 kinks to the right at Lizerne, stands what is generally known as the *Cross of Reconciliation*. Slim and effectively simple in dark aluminium, the cross—a replacement of a French original of 1929 destroyed by the Germans in 1942 because they objected to being called 'barbarians'—is a less controversially worded Franco-Belgian memorial to the first gas victims. During the 1915 fighting the Belgian and French lines ran close to one another in this area, a fact recalled by a number of Belgian memorials, both to units and to individuals.

N369 is now exchanged for the minor road which heads SE through Bikschote for Langemark, the whole area to the SW between this road and the canal (well served by small roads for those who wish to explore) being littered with bunkers large and small.

Langemark, though attacked as early in the war as October 1914 (German student battalions playing a large part in what was foreseen as a walkover), was not in fact taken by the Germans until April 1915 as their greenish-yellow gas cloud crept either side of the town towards the French and Canadians whose sectors met here. Retaken by the British 20th Light Division on 16 August 1917, what little was left of the town was lost again in April 1918 but regained the following September by which time the place was no more than rubble.

DIVERSIONS FROM LANGEMARK. The road due N soon passes a large heavily Teutonic war cemetery (with a Student Room recording the names of the students who lost their lives in the abortive and costly assault of October 1914), beyond reaching a stream (the Sint Jansbeek). Immediately across this, a left turn almost at once arrives at the British *34th Division Royal Artillery and Royal Engineers Memorial*, standing in front of a German bunker and remembering those 'who fought near this spot, October–November 1917'. Finally taken in September 1918, the bunker then for a while served as a British advanced dressing station. Continuing N through Velhoek, the road in 5km flanks the SW edge of *Houthulst Forest* (Belgian cemetery and several memorials), a place once somewhat surprisingly described by Napoleon as the 'key to the Netherlands'. A century later the Germans certainly considered these woods to be of key importance, overcoming stubborn Belgian and French resistance by October 1914 and using the forest for the next four years as a main rear concentration zone for the Salient campaigns.

Poelkapelle, 2km E of Langemark and for the most of the war in German hands, is visited for the memorial to Georges Guynemer (1894–1917), the best known and most dashing of France's air heroes, credited with 54 victories but eventually shot down near here on 11 September 1917. Guynemer's squadron was known as 'The Storks' and the memorial (1923), with a portrait-plaque, is movingly effective with its crippled bird retracing the direction of the airman's last flight.

On the SW edge of Langemark, on the right just before the Steenbeek, stands the *20th Light Division Monument*, an ugly grey cenotaph, today in a drab modern setting, commemorating those who freed what was left of Langemark in August 1917. After crossing the Steenbeek the road passes *Cement House Cemetery*, so called from a bunker in the nearby farm, immediately beyond reaching a crossroads, once one of the most heavily bombarded spots in this area. A left turn here (Groenestraat), followed almost at once by a right fork, soon passes *Goumier Farm*, part of which was fortified by the Germans. After frequently changing hands, Goumier was taken by 38th Welsh Division (memorial plaque) in July 1917. From here minor roads lead S to Ypres or NW to Boezinge.

The road SE out of Langemark in 2km meets a crossroads (with N313) known as Vancouver Corner beside which soars the impressive *Canadian Memorial*, a lofty shaft of granite merging into the bust of a Canadian soldier, his head lowered and his hands resting on reversed arms. Surrounded by a sombre garden in which clipped trees and low bushes represent shells and craters, the memorial is to the 18,000 Canadians on the British left who in this area withstood the first German gas attacks on 22–24 April 1915 and of whom 2000 lost their lives.

N313 is now followed SW through Sint Juliaan to reach Seaforth Cemetery, immediately beside and N of which is a German bunker known as *Cheddar Villa*. Today peacefully incorporated in a farm, this bunker, taken in July 1917, was, a month later, the target of German shelling, direct hits killing or wounding most of the members of a platoon of the 1st Buckinghamshire who were sheltering here. Beyond, at *Wieltje* in the shadow of the motorway and close to Oxford Road Cemetery, stands the dignified obelisk monument of 50th Northumberland Division, also honouring the same division's fallen of 1939–45. Passing two more cemeteries (Wieltje Farm and White House), N313 runs into Ypres.

The Central Salient

A circuit of some 30km through a region where many place names recall the desperate rallies that saved the wavering British line during the Second Battle; the costly Third Battle, with its heroism and mud; the retreat almost to the gates of Ypres in Spring 1918; and the victorious push of September 1918. These battlefields are particularly associated wth Canadian, Australian and New Zealand arms. The return to Ypres is along the notorious Menin Road (today N8), the W section representing a main link between Ypres and the front.

Ypres is left by the Menin Gate, beyond which a left fork is taken for the village of *Potijze*, with, to the N, four British war cemeteries, and, to the S, down the road signed to Menen and Zillebeke, an interesting blockhouse half hidden by a farm building; known as Hussar Farm, this strongpoint, though under constant bombardment, survived for four years as a valuable observation post. Beyond Potijze, the French flag flies over their great cemetery of *Saint Charles de Potyze* with its monument in the form of a Crucifixion and grieving women, particularly effective in sombre stone. Aeroplane Cemetery (British) is a short way beyond.

Zonnebeke, today a prosperous enough place with its neat homes either side of the through road, was among the most contested places along the curve of the Salient, an aerial photograph of October 1917 showing no more than an eerie huddle of grey rubble in a nightmare mudscape of craters and shattered tree stumps. At the war's start Zonnebeke was chosen as the base from which the Kaiser would make his triumphal entry into Ypres on 1 November 1914, but the village was stubbornly defended until May 1915. Recaptured in September 1917, it was lost again in April 1918 but finally taken again in the following September. Beyond, the hamlet of *Broodseinde* straddles a crossroads on the tactically important ridge of the same name; here a curious geometrical monument in brick is to the French who gave their lives in the defence of this crest, while a short way down the Beselare road stands the British 7th Division Monument, this division having fought here in both 1914 and 1917.

From Broodseinde this tour bears N along N303 for **Tyne Cot Cemetery*, just to the left of the road, so called because the Northumberlanders (50th Northumbrian Division) thought that an old barn here, surviving amid the defensive complex which they were assaulting, resembled typical Tyneside cottages. The complex was eventually taken by the 2nd Australian Division on 4 October 1917, lost again in April 1918 and retaken the following September. While in Allied hands the largest of the bunkers was used as an advanced dressing station, casualties of this period being buried nearby. Designed by Herbert Baker, and particularly effective on a gentle green slope, this is the largest (worldwide) of all British war cemeteries, with nearly 12,000 graves and serving also as memorial to nearly 35,000 missing. From the entrance the path ascends between the massed graves to the Cross of Sacrifice on its mound, with blockhouses to the right and left and, immediately below and forming the mound, something of the large blockhouse which was the objective of 2nd Australian Division on 4 October 1917 (plaque) and which later became the advanced dressing station (it is said that it was the suggestion of George V that the bunker be preserved and the Cross sited above it). Beyond, between the Cross and the Stone of Remembrance, the scattered graves of October 1917 to April 1918 remain as originally placed, while, beyond again, is the great wall of the Memorial to the Missing which includes, in a central apse, the names of the New Zealand missing of Broodseinde and Passchendaele (October 1917). The New Zealanders who lost their lives in the Battle of Broodseinde (4 October 1917) are also remembered on another memorial roughly 2km NW on the site of 's Graventafel crossroads which the New Zealand Division assaulted and won.

Tyne Cot looks northwards across meadows, tranquil enough today but in 1917 a scene of rain, mud and carnage as the Canadians fought their way up this valley of the Strombeek towards Passchendaele.

Continuing N, N303 passes, on the right along a grassy path, a cairn monument to the 85th Canadian Infantry Battalion (Nova Scotia Highlanders) who fought on this spot in 1917 and reaches **Passendale**, historically better known as by its earlier spelling as Passchendaele, a name frequently used to describe the whole main offensive of the Third Battle of Ypres which ended with the capture of this ridge; a name, too, which has become synonymous with mud, heroism, superhuman effort and tactical futility. Held by the Germans from early in the war, the rubble that represented Passchendaele was taken by the Canadians on 6 November 1917 and many and vivid have been the descriptions of the contrast between the bloodied morass of flood and mud of the western slope up which they had fought and the unsullied green of the fields stretching away eastwards. The principal memorial here, of course, is the Canadian *Crest Farm Memorial*, just W of the small town and well sited above the shallow valley across which those commemorated fought quagmire as much as enemy shot and shell. In the town itself a window in the N transept of the church remembers 66th Division, while tablets on the Stadhuis recall the Belgian units (Grenadiers and Carabiniers) who in September 1918 finally took Passchendaele after its reoccupation by the Germans during their April 1918 last fling. Two other tablets remind that Passchendaele did not escape World War II, being defended in 1940 by the Belgian 43rd Régiment de Ligne and liberated in 1944 by the 1st Polish Armoured Division.

Westrozebeke, 4km N, was, centuries earlier in 1382, the scene of a very different kind of battle when Charles VI of France defeated the Flemish weavers and killed their leader, Philip van Artevelde. The battle (described by Froissart) was fought on the spur of Goudberg S of the village, high ground which marked also the limit of the 1917 Allied advance.

This tour of the central Salient now returns S through Broodseinde and past the 7th Division Monument to reach (at Molenaarshoek, 1.5km S of Broodseinde) a minor road which bears SW to make an anticlockwise round of the once notorious **Polygon Wood** (until 1914 the home of the Belgian army's Polygon riding school), all or parts of which several times changed hands during 1914–18, the wood as a result being reduced to no more than a lethal wilderness of pocked ground and shattered stumps. Today, replanted, carefully tended as a State forest, and with the A19 motorway sweeping past its southwestern flank, the wood is a very different place, although bunkers (British and German), eroded traces of shell craters, some memorials, and, on the N side, two cemeteries, combine as reminders of the past. On the N of the circuit road*Polygon Wood Cemetery*, largely New Zealand, lies behind a polygonal wall, while, opposite, a glade provides the approach to *Buttes New British Cemetery*, so called because until 1870 this was a Belgian army firing range, its butts represented today by a large mound on which stands the 5th Australian Division Memorial (this division retook the wood in September 1917). The ranks of graves are spread below, beyond being the New Zealand Memorial Pavilion in which are engraved the names of all the New Zealand missing who fell in this sector between September 1917 and May 1918.

Rounding the wood this minor road crosses the motorway near what is sometimes known as Black Watch Corner (because it was here that the Royal Highlanders and Cameron Highlanders defied the Prussian Guard in November 1914) and joins the Menen-Ypres road a short 2km W of **Geluveld**, a name famous in the story of the First Battle of Ypres. Here in October 1914—when the 2nd Welsh Regiment and 1st South Wales Borderers (monument) were driven from their trenches and forced back to the château—Brigadier General FitzClarence (later VC), leading the 2nd Worcestershire Regiment (to which he had attached all the cooks, orderlies and others he could muster), relieved the Welsh and drove back the enemy, thus forcing a delay generally considered to have thwarted a breakthrough to Ypres and even the Channel ports. *Zandvoorde*, 2km S of Geluveld, is closely associated with the Household Cavalry who on 26 October 1914 had charged to hold this position. Reinforced by other units, the cavalry dug in until overwhelmed. The graceful tall monument (reached by a footpath off Komenstraat on the SE edge of the village) remembers the 1st and 2nd Lifeguards and the Royal Horse Guards 'who died fighting in France and Flanders in 1914, many of them in defence of the ridge on which this cross stands'.

Menen, 3km E of Geluveld, is an industrial border town on the Lys.—At *Dadizele*, 6km N of Menen on the Roeselare road, the church houses a miraculous Virgin, venerated since the 14C.

Returning towards Ypres from Geluveld the road passes (right) a memorial to the 2nd Worcestershire Regiment, immediately afterwards reaching the intersection once known as *Clapham Junction*. Here, complementing one another on either side of the road, stand two similar obelisk memorials: one, on the S, to 18th Division, engaged here in 1917; the other to the Gloucestershire Regiment, one of the battalions of which fought around Geluveld in 1914 and another here at Clapham Junction the following year.

Immediately beyond Clapham Junction, the recreation and safari park of *Bellewaerde*, with much for children, now spreads across the area over which the King's Royal Rifle Corps fought; their memorial stands beside the coach park. Here, too, are (S) *Hooge Crater Cemetery*, where the Stone of Remembrance stands within a symbolic crater (the actual crater from which the cemetery takes its name, the result of a British mine exploded in July 1915, is on private ground opposite), and, roughly opposite, *Hooge Château*, a name notorious in the Salient story. On 31 October 1914 the château was the headquarters of 1st and 2nd Divisions, most of the staffs of which were killed or gravely wounded by shelling just at the crucial time of the fighting at Geluveld; taken by the Germans in a gas attack of May 1915, Hooge two months later witnessed the first use by the Germans of their new flame-thrower weapon (liquid fire).

On the S, beyond Hooge and just before Birr Crossroads Cemetery is reached, a road (Canadalaan, or, for obvious reasons, Maple Avenue) angles back SE to pass *Sanctuary Wood Cemetery* (with the grave of Lieutenant 'Gilbert Talbot MC, see Poperinge below) and reach *Sanctuary Wood Trenches Museum* where trenches, scarred and long dead tree stumps and some scattered debris combine to belie this place's name. And, inside the museum building, some remarkable bioscope photographs together with many straightforward photographs of devastated Ypres and of this wood confirm that if ever this place was a sanctuary it was not for long. In fact the wood was, for a brief period in October 1914, a quietish corner and is said to owe its name to the orders given by a brigade commander that some stragglers collected here were not immediately to be sent back into the line. Soon, though, the wood became a part of the front line, fought over by both sides and notably by the Canadians, in April–August 1916, whose memorial is on Hill 62, or Mount Sorrel, just beyond the museum.

In rather over 1km W of its junction with Canadalaan, N8 reaches a crossroads (for Zillebeke S and Potijze N), an exposed spot once infamous as *Hellfire Corner*. Today the neat scene here, typical of modern Flanders, defies any effort to picture what was the hub of a flat expanse of devastation, the road lined by canvas screens which, moderately successful though they may have been in thwarting enemy observers, did nothing to deter his gunners who knew that there would always be a target behind them. In 1918 the Germans reached this spot, less than 1km distance from Ypres.

The Southern Salient

A tour of some 40km which includes the notorious Hill 60; the Messines (Mesen) Ridge, dramatic scene of the opening phase of the Third Battle; Ploegsteert ('Plugstreet') Wood; and the French area around Kemmelberg.

Ypres is left by the Rijselstraat (becoming N365), an exit which was less exposed than the Menen one and thus the more favoured approach to the front; nevertheless the road crossing just beyond the first railway soon earned the name Shrapnel Corner. Just beyond, the main N365 continues S, but this tour turns E to cross another railway and angle sharply SE to pass *Railway Dugout Burial Ground* (Transport Farm), still aptly named for there are still concrete traces in the railway embankment. *Zillebeke* lake, just to the N, has a long history. Dug in medieval days (certainly before 1300) as a reservoir and for centuries a peaceful corner, the scene was transformed in 1914 when the lake's surrounds became a morass as artillery and other units dug into its banks; but today's visitor must search if he wishes to find traces of war in this modest recreational area.

Continuing SE, and at once recrossing the railway, the road in about 2km reaches a sign to the left back across the railway to **Hill 60**, a man-made hillock (spoil from the cutting of the railway during the 19C) which, after Passchendaele, is probably the most notorious name along the length of the Salient. Bitterly disputed (the hill area changed hands some six times between 1914–18), unceasingly shelled, drenched in gas, its mixed sand and clay the scene of mining warfare of massive scale, Hill 60, which early on lost all resemblance to its original shape, was in 1930 in large part given to the Imperial War Graves Commission as a gift to the nations of the Empire, and has since as far as is possible been left to nature as a memorial. There is a parking area beside two memorials, one to the 14th Light Division, the other to the 1st Australian Tunnelling Company who in November 1916 took over responsibility for the mine shafts, the two mines here being the most northerly pair of the series stretching from the Messines Ridge the detonation of which on 7 June 1917 marked the opening of the Third Battle of Ypres. The memorial bears bullet scars to witness that Hill 60 was again fought over in the Second World War. To the left is the modern entrance with, beside it, a stone outlining the Hill 60 story. The visitor is free to wander where he will around this cratered place, but he sees of course only the surface and should remind himself that here the war below ground was waged as viciously as above and that he is walking above what are, with their countless Allied and enemy dead, catacombs of collapsed tunnels and shafts. Above ground the main features of interest are a blockhouse (German in origin but used by both sides) and the memorial to Queen Victoria's Rifles who fought here in 1915; badly damaged in the fighting of 1940, the memorial was rebuilt and now serves also as a remembrance to the victims of 1939–45.

Beside the road, just beyond the Hill 60 entrance, a café incorporates a museum, called the *Hill 60 Museum* but in fact with somewhat wider scope and, as so often the case, the photographs being perhaps the most worthwhile feature.

This tour now returns over the railway to bear right and then left for *Sint Eloi* on N365, on the way passing the adjoining Chester Farm and Spoilbank cemeteries. **Wijtschate**, 2km farther S and on the ridge (the Messines Ridge) which overlooked Ypres and was thus tactically vital, changed hands several times in bitter fighting until, in June 1917 and signalling the start of the Third Battle of Ypres, the German trenches here were blown apart by huge mines the reverberations of which were felt as far away as London. A glimpse of those days, from the German angle before the mines were exploded, is offered by a museum 2km N of Wijtschate along a minor road roughly parallel to N365. Variously named the *Museum of Peace*, Bois 40, or, using German terminology, Croonart, the museum has indoor and outdoor sections, the latter being perhaps the more interesting with the trenches and bunkers which were the advanced part of the German line from 1915–17 and, in which, it seems, Corporal Adolf Hitler was wounded in 1917 (at any rate Hitler visited here in 1940; photograph in the museum). But the star feature here is a German mine shaft, 30m to 40m deep; no entry, but with care it is possible to peer into the flooded depths. The pond by the museum entrance represents a German mine crater, as likely as not set and exploded from the shaft in the museum, and a few metres away, beside Croonaert Chapel Cemetery, a French memorial recalls the fighting here in 1914.

Spanbroekmolen, 2km SW of Wijtschate off the Kemmel road (which passes a memorial to 16th Irish Division), is the crater of one of the largest of the 19 mines exploded at 03.10 on 7 June 1917, the charge being 91,000 lbs of ammonal laid at the end of a tunnel of 517m. Long known as Lone Tree Crater, this site was acquired in 1930 by the philanthropist Lord Wakefield for Toc H and, now a deep pond (at least 25m) known as the Pool of Peace, is preserved as a shrine which for all its superficial tranquility can never hope to shed its sinister undertone.

Mesen (Messines) is 2km S of Wijtschate, on the left approaching the small town being the *London Scottish Memorial* recording that it was near here on Hallow E'en 1914 that this regiment went into action, thus earning the distinction of being the first Territorial Army battalion to engage the enemy—in a gallant though doomed charge to relieve the cavalry who had held against overwhelming odds for over 48 hours. Twinned with Featherston, New Zealand, Mesen was taken in 1917, following the detonation of the mines, by the New Zealand Division which is commemorated in two places here. The *New Zealand Memorial to the Missing* is at Messines Ridge Cemetery, immediately W of Mesen beside the Wolvergem road; and *New Zealand Park* is just to the S of the town. In this latter there are two German bunkers close to the white obelisk divisional memorial which records the capture of this ridge and an advance of 2000 yards to the objective beyond Messines. In the town there is a modest museum in the town hall, some emphasis being placed on the New Zealand Division; and the crypt of the church, all that survived the early fighting, is said to have sheltered Hitler.

Ploegsteert ('Plugstreet'), 4km S of Mesen, is best known for its wood which, today thickly regrown and private property, still stretches across the northern high ground. Descending through the wood, N365 passes between, on the right, the rotunda of the Ploegsteert Memorial to the Missing and, opposite, Hyde Park Corner (Royal Berks) Cemetery. Until April 1918 *Ploegsteert Wood* was never fully taken by the Germans and for much of the war enjoyed a reputation as a relatively quiet area. Today roads circle the wood (turn E in the village) enabling the several cemeteries around and within it to be visited. Of these perhaps the most interesting is Prowse Point (beyond the wood's northern edge and to the W of the village of Saint Yvon), named after Major (later Brigadier) Prowse who here fought with the Hampshire Regiment and Somerset Light Infantry in October 1914. Many of the graves are of members of 2nd Dublin Fusiliers and 1st Royal Warwickshire who defended this sector of the wood in the following month. The water below the Cross is part of the actual front line and a concrete shelter can be seen here.

The road NE out of Ploegsteert (the road which starts the circuit of the wood) in 10km reaches *Comines* (Komen), the principal town of an enclave of the province of Hainaut. The town stands on the Lys, here the international border, French Comines being across the river. Comines was the birthplace of Philippe de Comines (c 1445–1509), the French statesman, biographer and historian.

Roads W out of Ploegsteert, and then N, in 6km reach *Nieuwekerke* (Neuve Eglise), an important road junction lost in 1918 but only after a party of the Worcestershire Regiment had long held out in the town hall while the enemy occupied the rest of the town. **Kemmelberg** (159m), 4km farther N, was long an invaluable buttress of the Allied position, until its loss by the French in April 1918 gravely endangered Allied communications, especially along the important Ypres-Poperinge road; the hill was retaken on 31 August by British 34th Division. The visitor approaching from Nieuwekerke, Dranouter and the W first comes to the Ossuaire Francais, a pyramidical obelisk with a cock on top, covering the remains of 5294 men killed near here but of whom only 57 were identified and not all of these for certain. Beyond, at the top of a steep cobbled approach, stands the French monument to all who died in Belgium, and especially here, in 1918. An ugly column bearing a characterless Winged Victory, the monument was unveiled by General Pétain in 1932; later, lightning damaged the column and the laurel-crowned helmet which had capped it was never replaced. Farther along the road there is a look-out tower (April–September), a rebuilding and not in fact to the same design as the original. The woodland of Kemmelberg is still in part trenched and pocked, but the ground up here is soft and erosion is steadily levelling and softening the marks of the past.

At the close of the German offensive of Spring 1918, the Allied line in this area ran from Vierstraat (4km NE) to Loker (3km W), twice lost and retaken by the French, and thence to Méteren in France (8km SW of Loker). The hills along the border—*Rodeberg* (Mont Rouge) and *Zwarteberg*(Mont Noir)—form a small chain which became vital for Allied observation after the loss of Kemmelberg.

The road back to Ypres (8km from Kemmel) in 2km, just before Vierstraat, passes an American memorial, a simple white stone honouring 'the services of American Troops who fought in this vicinity Aug. 18–Sept. 4 1918'. The lake of *Dikkebus* (1km W approaching Ypres; access from N375), the result of the damming of a stream in 1320, has since that date continued to provide Ypres with water. Now also a recreation area, the lake even boasts an antiquity, the Vauban Tower of 1684, once an outlier of the town's defences but now used for water control.

Poperinge

Poperinge is 12km W of Ypres by either N308, the old road, or, just S and parallel, the faster N38. It was along these 12km of back area that five million British and other troops marched to run the gauntlet of Ypres and take their place around the Salient. One million of them returned wounded, and 300,000 fell.

Known simply as 'Pop' by the British, Poperinge, today with some 20,000 inhab. and twinned with Hythe, Kent, is a rather old-fashioned town, the centre of a district in which hops have been grown since c 1400.

Once a cloth town, Poperinge was unable to compete with Ypres and therefore in the early 15C turned to hops. That the town had an early international reputation may be assumed from three references in English literature: the hero of Chaucer's (c 1340–1400) 'Rime of Sir Topas' was born 'in Flaundres, al beyonde the sea, at Popering, in the place'; Mercutio, in Shakespeare's 'Romeo and Juliet' (1594), refers to the 'poperin pear', a variety which came to England from this district; and Sebastian, in 'The Atheist's Tragedy' by Cyril Tourneur (c 1575–1626), describes a 'poppring pear tree'. In 1436, when Philip the Good was helped by Poperinge men in his attack on English-held Calais, the English besieged Poperinge, burning down the Sint Bertinuskerk and killing 2500 of the inhabitants. Lancelot Blondeel, the painter, was born here in 1496. Occupied by the Germans in August 1914, but retaken in October, Poperinge was for long intermittently shelled and suffered a good deal of damage.

The *Sint Bertinuskerk* (dedicated to a Benedictine abbot who died c 700), in the Botermarkt, the main square, is an outstanding example of a Flemish hall-church; dating from the 15C, it succeeded the church burnt down by the English in 1436. The interior has some good woodwork, including an 18C pulpit (from the Dominican church in Bruges), two Baroque confessionals, and an 18C rood-screen. The town has two other old churches, both dating from c 1290 but with later alterations and additions: the church of *Onze Lieve Vrouw*, in Kasselstraat, has a tower of c 1400 and a 16C portal, and contains splendid choir stalls of 1752 by E. Wallijn; and the church of *Sint Jan*, in Bruggestraat, also with woodwork by Wallijn, houses a miraculous figure of Our Lady of St. John.

In Gasthuisstraat, so called from an ancient hospice founded here in 1312, No. 43 is *Talbot House* ('Toc H', from the army signallers' alphabet of the First World War). Named after Gilbert Talbot (killed at Hooge on 30 July 1915), younger brother of the senior chaplain of the 16th Division, the house, placed in the charge of the Rev. P.B. Clayton, served as club and home ('Everyman's Club') to half a million officers and men from December 1915 until the end of the war.

The Rev. P.B. Clayton CH.MC. (1885–1972) founded Toc H, a worldwide active Christian voluntary movement for all ages. Talbot House, bought by Lord Wakefield for Toc H in 1929, now serves as a centre of European reconciliation. Visitors are welcome and limited self-catering accommodation is available. The house has many interesting features and much of its contents were saved during the Second World War by local people who hid them in their homes.

Skindles, a short distance farther along the street and originally an 18C patrician home, was during the First World War in turn the advanced headquarters of Sir Douglas Haig and a British officers' club.

The *Nationaal Hopmusem* (May, June, September: Sunday and Holidays, 14.30 to 17.30. July and August: daily, same times), at 71

Gasthuisstraat, occupies the former municipal weighhouse (1866), the weighbridge, which was in use from 1866 to 1966, being part of the museum. All aspects of hop growing and use are explained and the visit ends with a taste of the regional brew.

The huge war cemetery of *Lijssenthoek*, 3km SW, shelters some 9900 Commonwealth graves, mostly of men who died of wounds in the nearby casualty clearing stations.

8   Ostend to Brussels

Total distance 116km—*15km* **Jabbeke**.—*10km***Bruges**.—*24km*
Eeklo.—*18km***Ghent**.—*26km* **Aalst**.—*23km***Brussels**.—The E40
motorway is taken as far as Jabbeke. From Bruges to Brussels N9 is
followed.

15km **Jabbeke** is known for the *Constant Permeke Museum*, occupying the house built in 1929 by this painter and sculptor (1886–1952), a leader of the Flemish Expressionists. The museum contains a large part of the artist's work, some of his best-known sculpture being in the garden (Daily except Monday, 10.00 to 12.30, 13.30 to 18.00, or 17.00 in November–March). *Klein Strand*, just NW of Jabbeke, is a recreational lake and beach where water skiing displays are given in summer.—*10km* **Bruges**, see Rte 9.

Bruges is left at the Kruispoort, the road in *4km* reaching *Male* where the abbey of Trudo occupies the site and some of the remains of a castle of the counts of Flanders; the 14–15C keep has been restored.—*3km Sijsele*, a short way N of which is *Stockmanshoeve* rural park (see end of Rte 9). The border of East Flanders is crossed before *(8km) Maldegem*.—*9km* **Eeklo** (19,000 inhab. Tourist Information: Markt), the chief town of the MEETJESLAND (land of little meadows) is an important agricultural and textiles centre (local museum in the provincial park of Het Leen, 2km S. Easter– September: daily, 10.00 to 12.00, 14.00 to 16.00). There is a large main square, and the *Stadhuis*, with a belfry, is of the early 17C. Karel Ledeganck (1805–47), a leading Flemish poet, was born here.

Kaprijke (4km NE) has an attractive small 17–18C town hall. From here the road N crosses polder country for 6km to reach **Watervliet**, just short of the Dutch border, with a 15C church, restored in 1893 when the tower was built, and again, to make good war damage, in 1973. The interior contains an altar from the workshop of Luc Fayd'herbe, a pulpit and other woodwork by Hendrik Pulincx, and a Descent from the Cross (15C), ascribed to Quinten Metsys.

18km **Ghent**, see Rte 13. After leaving Ghent the Scheldt is crossed at *(8km) Melle*, with a horticultural college, and begonia gardens on the N bank.

18km **Aalst** (78,000 inhab. Tourist Information: Grote Markt), on the canalised river Dender and today a textiles and brewing town, was once an important seat of the counts of Flanders, later becoming the provincial capital. The centre and the most attractive part of the town is the irregular GROTE MARKT, with a statue (Jan Geefs, 1856) of Dirk Martens (c 1450–1534), a humanist and the first Belgian printer who produced his first work ('Speculum Conversionis Peccatorum') here in 1473. The arcaded building on the left, now a restaurant, was originally the *Vleeshuis*, but later the meeting-place of the Barbaristes, the literary guild of St. Barbara; burnt in 1743, it was rebuilt five years later. At the NW corner stands the *Schepenhuis*, the former town hall; of the original building of c 1225 only the left and rear façades as well as something of the building's lower part survive, most of what is seen today dating from the early 15C. The *Belfry* was completed in 1466; its two statues are of a knight and a citizen, symbols of power and freedom, and the carillon has 52 bells (concerts in summer). The Flamboyant Gothic corner gallery (1474) was used for the making of proclamations; the 19C statues represent Justice; Charles V; Dirk, the last lord of Aalst (1166); Pieter Coecke (1502–50), who lived here and was one of the apostles of Renaissance art; and Cornelis de Schrijver (1482–1588), secretary of Antwerp. The *Stadhuis* (Louis Roelandt, 1831) preserves in its courtyard the façade of the Landhuis (1646), seat of the States of Flanders when Aalst was provincial capital.

The *Sint Maartenskerk*, just E of the Grote Markt, is a large Gothic building of 1480–1638, largely following the designs of Jan van der Wouwe and Herman and Domien Waghemakere (father and son), builders of the cathedral at Antwerp. Because of the wars of the 16C the church was never finished, its uncompleted state being finally accepted in 1730 by the building of a Baroque portal. The church is known for its celebrated painting (S transept) by Rubens, *St. Roch receiving from Christ the gift of healing the plague-stricken, a large and highly decorative composition in a contemporary carved wood frame which also encloses some minor works from Rubens's studio; carried off to Paris in 1794, the picture was returned in 1816, largely through the efforts of the Duc de Berri who had been a refugee in Aalst. In the next chapel is a work by De Crayer (St. Simon). The fine marble *Tabernacle (1605) is by Jérôme Duquesnoy the Elder. Of the many chapels, recalling the numerous guilds, each of which had its own, some have vault paintings, the oldest and best (1497; restored 1947) being in the easternmost. In one chapel (Sacré Coeur) is the tomb of Dirk Martens the printer; and in the first ambulatory chapel on the right there is an Adoration of the Shepherds by Otto Venius.

Just to the E of the church are the 15–17C buildings of the former hospital of *Onze Lieve Vrouw*, the restored courtyard of which, together with the surrounding rooms, now forms an attractive setting for the *Museum Oud Hospitaal* with general and local exhibits and some Roman material (Monday–Thursday, 10.00 to 12.00, 14.00 to 17.00. Saturday, 14.00 to 17.00. Sunday, 10.30 to 12.00, 14.00 to 18.00).

Pontstraat runs SE from the church, off the left side being the *Begijnhof*, with a chapel of 1787 and converted into a group of small houses, more or less on the original lines.

At *Moorsel*, 4km E, there are a 13–14C church, and, beside the road, a moated château built in 1646.

The Brabant border is crossed at (*5km* from Aalst) *Hekelgem* (11,000 inhab.), once known for its 'Zandtapijts' (sand carpets, or pictures) of which examples can still occasionally be seen.

The art, once widespread in Flemish villages, demands many weeks of meticulous work and is now rare. The 'carpet' is built up on a board divided into squares on which the artist first produces his outlines before laying down his chosen sand colours. Pictures may be originals, or reproductions of famous works.

The abbey of *Afflighem* is on the N edge of Hekelgem. Founded in the 11C, it was almost wholly destroyed in 1796, all that now survives

being a wall of the church nave and some 17C buildings, including
the entrance lodge. The site was reoccupied by Benedictines in 1869,
since when there has been extensive building, this including the large
church of 1972. In the abbey lie Godfrey of Louvain and his daughter
Adeliza (died 1151), second queen of Henry I of England.—
18km **Brussels**, see Rte 1.

9   Bruges and Damme

BRUGES is the English and French name for the Flemish town of
Brugge (119,000 inhab.), the capital of the province of West Flanders.
Virtually entirely surrounded by water following the course of the old
fortifications, the town is linked by canals to its foreport of Zeebrugge
and also to Ostend and Ghent and via Damme to Sluis in Holland. The
beauty of the 'medieval' buildings, whether original, restored, or good
modern replicas; their setting along the many small and picturesque
waterways which thread the town and are spanned by over 50 bridges
(whence Bruges derives its name); the rich historical and commercial
background; and the town's wealth of architectural and art treasures,
all combine to make Bruges one of Belgium's most popular tourist
centres.

But Bruges is not only a tourist town. Since the opening of the canal
to Zeebrugge and the development of the port (from the turn of the
19–20C) it has also regained much of its medieval prosperity and
become of increasing industrial importance. Industry, however, is
confined to the perimeter and is not allowed to intrude into old
Bruges.

Centre. Markt.

Tourist Information. *Bruges*: 11 Burg. April–September: Monday–Friday, 09.30
to 18.30. Saturday, Sunday, Holidays, 10.00 to 12.00, 14.00 to 18.30. October–
March: Monday–Saturday, 10.00 to 12.45, 14.00 to 17.45. Tel: 330711. *Province
of West Flanders*: Kasteel Tillegem, Tillegembos (SW between Bruges and the
motorway).

Post Office. Markt.

Station. On S edge of the town, 1.5km from the Markt.

Ways to see the Town. *On Foot*: Most places of immediate tourist interest are
within walking distance of the Markt and of one another, and the Tourist Office
outline guide and map suggests several walking itineraries, most based on
specific themes. In July and August, there are also daily guided walks, normally
leaving Tourist Information at 14.15.—*Horse-drawn Carriage*: March–
November: daily, 10.00 to 18.00. Departures from the Burg or (Wednesday) the
Markt. Standard round, 35 minutes—*Bicycle*: Hire addresses from Tourist
Information.—*Canal Boats*: Several embarkation stages, principally a short way
SE of the Markt by Wollestraat. March–November: daily, 10.00 to 18.00.
Duration, 35 minutes. Also boat excursions to Damme. April–September: daily,
every two hours, departures from Norweegse Kaai, reached by bus No. 4; and to
Ghent, this service operating out of Ghent and being only one-way from Bruges
(July and August: Thursday, leave Bruges 15.30, arrives Ghent 20.00).—*Coach*
and *Minibus*. Information and coach bookings through Tourist Information.

Museum Tickets. Combined tickets at considerably reduced price give access to
two groups of museums. *Central*: Groeninge, Gruuthuse, Memling (Sint Jans),
Brangwyn. *Outer*: Folklore, Guido Gezelle, Lace Centre, De Potterie, Sint
Janshuismolen.

Lace. Bruges has long been known for its lace, the work winning special acclaim
during the 17C. Although lacemakers are now rarely seen on the doorsteps,
Bruges still produces both handmade and machine made lace, and both can be

bought. The best-known Bruges designs are the flower pattern, rose lace and the witch-stitch. Visitors interested in lace should visit the Gruuthuse Museum and the Kantcentrum (Lace Centre).

History. Bruges first grew under the protection of a castle built in 865 by Baldwin Iron Arm, the first Count of Flanders, mainly for defence against Norse raiders, the town thereafter rapidly prospering owing to its situation close to the Zwin (Rte 3) which at that time penetrated as far as Damme, connected with Bruges by the Reie. In the 13C prosperity continued with the manufacture of cloth, and the annual fair at Bruges was one of the most important in Flanders. Dissentions between the francophile counts, set on protecting their privileges, and the merchants afforded a pretext for intervention by Philip the Fair of France who made a triumphal entry in 1301. Such was the luxury displayed by the citizens' wives that the Queen, Joanna of Navarre, observed that hitherto she had thought herself the only queen, but now she saw hundreds all around. French rule, however, was oppressive and in the following year the citizens, headed by Pièter de Coninck and Jan Breydel, rose in revolt, on 18 May 1302 massacring the French and putting to death all who were unable to pronounce correctly the shibboleth 'Schild en Vriend' (shield and friend). This occasion became known as the 'Bruges Matins'. Six weeks later Bruges played a prominent part in the defeat of the French nobility at the Battle of the Golden Spurs near Kortrijk. During the Burgundian period (14–15C), despite having to surrender many of its privileges to Philip the Good, Bruges reached its greatest prosperity and became the chief market of the Hanseatic League (a 14–17C association of towns, mainly N German, the principal aims of which were the suppression of piracy and the concluding of commercial treaties). As well as being famed as a banking centre, Bruges traded in fabrics from Italy and the East; furs from Russia and the Balkans; metals from Hungary, Poland and Bohemia; wool, cheese and coal from the British Isles; fruit from Spain; Arabian spices and Rhenish wines. It is recorded that as many as 150 vessels entered the port in a single day and that the population grew to over 80,000. The town's tapestry manufacturers became world-famous, illustrious artists (Jan van Eyck, Hans Memling and others) were patronised by the opulent citizens, and in 1430 Philip the Good here established his famous Order of the Golden Fleece, in part as a compliment to the skill of the Flemish weavers but at the same time as a symbol of the power and splendour of the House of Burgundy. In 1464 Bruges was the meeting-place of the first States General of the Netherlands.

Philip died in Bruges in 1467, an event which marked the beginning of a slow decline in the fortunes of the town. Many factors contributed to this, amongst them the silting of the Zwin, a general recession in the cloth industry, changing trade routes, and the transfer from Burgundian to Habsburg sovereignty. In 1488, as retaliation against infringements of its privileges, Bruges somewhat unwisely held its ruler, Archduke Maximilian, prisoner for three months, one unfortunate result being that thenceforward Maximilian favoured Antwerp, which rapidly outstripped Bruges, officially becoming the Hanseatic emporium in 1545. Bruges now became known as 'Bruges-la-Morte'; it suffered frequent attacks and sieges during the 16–18C, and did not start to recover until the digging of the Boudewijn Kanaal and the development of the port of Zeebrugge (1895–1907).

Natives and Others. Bruges ('Brugges') is frequently mentioned by Chaucer and other early English writers. Later, Wordsworth described the quiet streets, and Longfellow the Belfry. Caxton (c 1422–91) was in Bruges between some time after 1441 and 1476, becoming acting governor of the Merchant Adventurers in the Low Countries. Here he 'practised and learnt at great charge and dispense' the art of printing, later, in partnership with the Bruges printer Collaert Mansion, setting up a press and printing his 'Recuyell of the Historyes of Troye'. The exiled Charles II established his court in Bruges in 1656, being elected 'King of the Archers' Guild of St. Sebastian'; in the same year he founded the Royal Regiment of Guards, thus making Bruges the birthplace of the Grenadier Guards. Simon Stevinus (1548–1620), mathematician and expert in the use of sluices for war purposes, was born here, as was also Frans Gomeer (Gomarus; 1563–1641), the rigidly Calvinist theologian. The painter Jan van Eyck lived in what is now Gouden Handstraat and died here in 1441. Hans Memling occupied a house in the present Sint Jorisstraat (the extension of Vlamingstraat), and Frans Pourbus the

Younger lived in the parallel Jan Miraelstraat. Gerard David died in Bruges in
1523.

For *Damme*, see Section C. below. For Bruges to *Ostend*, and to *Ghent* and
Brussels, see Rte 8; to *Zeebrugge*, see Rte 3; to *Kortrijk*, see Rte 10.

A. Central and Southern Bruges

The town centre is the MARKT, a typical Flemish square with several
17C façades and dominated on the S by the ancient Halle and Belfry.
In the centre stands a monument (Paul de Vigne, 1887) to Jan Breydel
and Pieter de Coninck, the two leaders of the 'Bruges Matins' uprising
of 1302. On the E are the 19C buildings of the **Provinciaal Hof**, seat of
the provincial government, and of the **Post Office**. The N side is lined
by restaurants and cafés with terraces. Sint Amandstraat, leading off
the W side, has on one corner the *Huis Bouchoute*, a tall square house
of the late 15C which in 1656–57 was the residence in exile of Charles
II of England; across the road once stood the Craenenburg where
Maximilian was held in 1488.

The **Halle** (13C), a large block around a courtyard, has been several
times restored, mainly during the 16C. The building long served as
the main market, an activity which can more easily be pictured if it is
remembered that until the late 18C a canal ran up to this corner of the
Markt. Until 1769 laws were promulgated from the balcony above the
entrance. The **Belfry, the finest in Belgium, is the best known and
most prominent architectural feature of Bruges, since the 13C a
symbol of civic power visible across the polders from many kilometres
away. It is 83m in height and leans slightly (1.19m) to the southeast.
Succeeding a wooden tower (1240; burnt down), the two lower
storeys date from 1282–96 and the octagonal upper portion from
1482–87. The belfry may be climbed (April–September: daily, 09.30
to 12.30, 13.30 to 18.00; October–March: daily, 09.30 to 12.30, 14.00 to
17.00). The climb is one of 366 steps, the first break being at the
Treasure Room (normally viewed only through the door grille) where
the town charters were once kept; the fine vaulting dates from 1285,
and the equally fine wrought-iron, the work of Nicolaas Grootwerc,
from 1300. At the 172nd step a room is crossed which affords a vertical
view upwards, while at the 220th there is a landing with a board on
which visitors who cannot resist the urge are invited to write their
names instead of elsewhere. At No. 333 the carillon (concerts) is
reached with its huge drum and the works of the clock of 1748
(Antonius de Hondt); the clock chimes every quarter-hour. From the
top there can be a magnificent view, incised arrowed place names
indicating what can be seen.

Oude Burg runs behind the Halle, on the S side being an archway giving access
to the small Karthuizerinnenstraat, named after the Carthusian nuns whose
chapel of 1632 was much restored in 1927. Here too is a War Memorial Chapel,
set up by the town in honour of the fallen of both world wars. The crypt-like
interior contains an effigy of a soldier in white marble, and here also rest the
ashes of victims of Germany's Dachau concentration camp.

Wollestraat, beside the Halle, is the shortest way from the Markt to the canal,
the boat embarkation stages, and the Groeninge, Brangwyn and Gruuthuse
museums, for all of which see below. No. 28 Wollestraat is the house *In de Grote*

Bruges, Halle and Belfry

Mortier (1634), decorated with damaged carvings of the relief of Bruges from a siege of 1631.

Beside the Post Office, Breidelstraat leads to the BURG, the square which was the site of the original 9C fortress in the shadow of which Bruges was born. On the left on entering the square stands the **Landshuis**, a late Renaissance building of 1664 by F. van Hillewerve, formerly occupied by the próvost of the church of Sint Donatian which stood in the adjacent garden. (A Roman who became Bishop of Rheims, Donatian died in 390; his relics were brought to Bruges in the 9C.) The church, which dated from the 10C and became a cathedral in 1559, and in which the painter Jan van Eyck was buried, was demolished by the French in 1799, but a fragment of the choir has been reerected here with a small reproduction of the apse; a statue of Van Eyck stands nearby.

Opposite, forming a splendid group, are (from right to left and using English names) the Basilica of the Holy Blood, the Town Hall, the former Recorder's House, and the Law Courts.

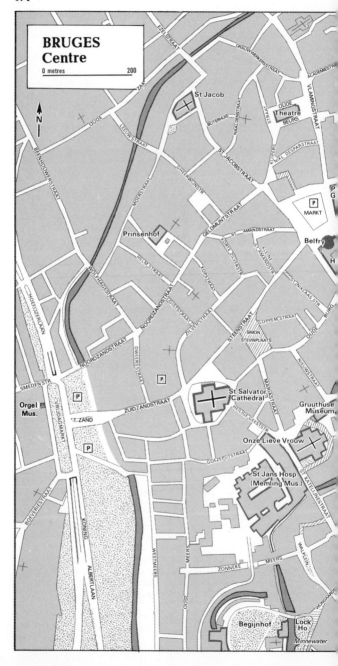

BRUGES Centre

0 metres   200

N

St Jacob

Theatre
BEURS
OUDE

VLAMINGSTRAAT
ACADEMIESTRAAT
GRAUWWERKERSSTRAAT
EZELSTRAAT
ZAK
OUDE
LEEUWSTRAAT
BOTERHUIS
NAALDENSTRAAT
SMIT
NIKL DESPARSTRAAT
ST JACOBSTRAAT
GHEERWIJNSTR
BEENHOUWERSSTRAAT
NOORSTRAAT

Prinsenhof

GELDMUNTSTRAAT
ST AMANDSTRAAT
KLEINE ST AMANDSTR
KORT ZILVERSTR
HEEM STRAAT
KORTSTRAAT

MARKT
Belfry
H

P
G

WOLHAGESTRAAT
HOEFIJZERLAAN
NOORDZANDSTRAAT
NOORDZANDSTRAAT
ZILVERSTRAAT
OOSTSTRAAT
STEENSTRAAT
ST NIKLAAS STR
LOPPEM STRAAT
OUDE
BURG
SIMON
STEVINPLAATS
NIEUWSTRAAT

DWEERSSTRAAT

SMEDEN STR
Orgel
Mus.
VRIJDAGMARKT
'T ZAND

P
P
P

ZUIDZANDSTRAAT

St Salvator
Cathedral

HEILIGE GEESTSTR
MARIASTRAAT

Gruuthuse
Museum

Onze Lieve Vrouw

GOEZEPUTSTRAAT

St Jans Hosp
(Memling Mus.)

ST KATELIJNESTRAAT
WALPLEIN

BOEVERIESTRAAT

KONING
ALBERTLAAN
WESTMEERS
MEERS
OOST
ZONNEKE
MEERS

WIJNGAARD

Begijnhof

Lock
Ho.
Minnewater

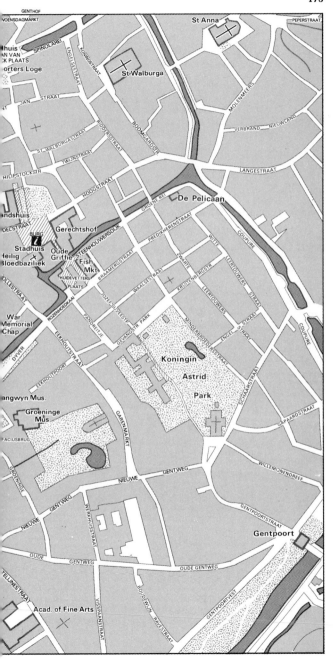

The **Heilig Bloedbaziliek** (Basilica of the Holy Blood) is of two storeys; a lower chapel of the 12C, and an upper chapel of the 15–16C reached by a staircase of 1523. The name of the building refers to some drops of the blood of Christ presented during the Second Crusade (1147) by the Patriarch of Jerusalem to Dirk of Alsace, Count of Flanders, as a reward for his bravery. The rock-crystal phial (see below) has remained intact since its arrival in Bruges. The Lower Chapel, built to house a relic of St. Basil (c 330–79) brought from the Holy Land in c 1099 by Count Robert II of Flanders (who also brought the relic of the True Cross now at Veurne), and rebuilt in 1134, is a dark, crypt-like Romanesque structure, one of the purest of its kind surviving in Flanders. It contains a 13C or 14C figure of the Virgin, protected by a part of its original iron enclosure. Above the inside of the entry to the side-chapel there is a (?) 12C relief of the baptism of Christ, or perhaps of St. Basil. The Upper Chapel, the actual Chapel of the Holy Blood, although originally Romanesque is now 15–16C Gothic with later alterations. Stained-glass windows of 1847 show portraits, based on 15C originals, of the dukes of Burgundy. The pulpit (1728) by Hendrik Pulincx, representing the globe, is carved from a single piece of oak. The sacred relic is in a silver reliquary, presented by Albert and Isabella in 1611; it is venerated every Friday 08.30 to 11.45 and 15.00 to 16.00.

The **Museum of the Holy Blood** is open April–September: daily, 09.30 to 12.00, 14.00 to 18.00. October–March: 10.00 to 12.00, 14.00 to 16.00. Closed Wednesday afternoon in October–March, 1 January, 1 November, 25 December. This is a small, single-room museum of church treasures and pictures. On the entrance wall hangs a Flemish tapestry of 1637 depicting the Translation of the body of St. Augustine, while in a case below are chasubles and old manuscripts. Along the left side of the room are two very fine shutters of a triptych (Members of the Brotherhood of the Holy Blood) by Pieter Pourbus (1556), placed either side of a reliquary of the Holy Blood (1614–17), an exquisite work in gold, silver and precious stones by Jan Crabbe of Bruges. Also a triptych (Crucifixion) attributed to Van Dyck; a Life of St. Barbara (15C) by the Master of the Barbara Legend; and, by an unknown artist, several pictures within an illustrated frame depicting the Life of the Virgin (c 1500). On the opposite wall are a triptych (Descent from the Cross, 1620) by the Master of the Holy Blood and an Adoration of the Magi by Van Dyck.

The **Stadhuis**, dating from 1376–1420, is the oldest Gothic town hall in Belgium and also one of the finest, a magnificent setting for the first meeting of the States General of the Netherlands which took place here in 1464. The façade has three graceful octagonal turrets, and the niches between the windows are occupied by statues of the counts and countesses of Flanders; originally 48 in number, the statues were destroyed by the French in 1792 and replaced during the 19C, though not all have survived. INTERIOR (Daily, 09.30 to 12.00, 14.00 to 18.00 or 17.00 in October–March. Closed 1 January and Ascension Day afternoon). On the ground floor the entrance hall has a joisted ceiling resting on four stone pillars. Off this leads a broad passage along which are some large canvases: Death of Mary of Burgundy by Camille van Camp (1878) and Rubens at the deathbed of Brueghel by Bruno van Hollebeke. The great *Gothic Hall, scene of the meeting of the first States General, is on the first floor. The superb wood ceiling, with a double row of six hanging painted arches, dates from 1385–1402; the 12 vault-keys represent scenes from the New Testament, and the 16 corbels the months and the elements. Around the walls are 12 vivid paintings by Albert and Julien Devriendt (1895) illustrating the history of Bruges. The Maritime Hall, opening off the Gothic Hall, is devoted to the harbour of Bruges and the Boudewijn canal to Zeebrugge.

To the left of the Stadhuis stands the **Oude Griffie**, the former Recorder's House, now used as part of the law courts, a richly decorated Renaissance building of 1537 by Christian Sixdeniers, with sculptures by Willem Aerts.

The **Gerechtshof** (Law Courts) was built in 1722 on the site of the palace of the Brugse Vrije, or Liberty of Bruges, an independent jurisdiction which stretched as far as Dunkirk but did not include the town of Bruges. Of the 15C palace only fragments survive, including part of the Schepenzaal, the hall in which the magistrates of the Liberty held their courts and which is now the **Brugse Vrije Museum** (April–September: daily except Monday, 10.00 to 12.30, 14.00 to 17.00. October–March: Saturday, Sunday, 14.00 to 16.00). The museum is known for its splendid Renaissance *Chimneypiece in black marble, with oak carvings, executed in 1529 by various artists working under the direction of Lancelot Blondeel. The oak statues by Guyot de Beaugrant represent Charles V (centre), Maximilian of Austria and Mary of Burgundy (right), and Ferdinand of Aragon and Isabella of Castile (left).

The road through the arch beneath the Oude Griffie leads past the site of the old south gate (plaque) and crosses the main canal through central Bruges. To the left, on Groene Rei, the extension of Steenhouwersdijk, *De Pelicaan* is a picturesque ancient almshouse beside a normally uncrowded stretch of canal. Ahead (left) is the *Vismarkt*, the fish market with a Doric colonnade of 1821, beyond which the Braambergstraat has several 17C façades. Ahead (right), filling an angle of the canal, is the attractive little Huidevettersplaats in which (Nos 11 and 12) the *Huidevettershuis* (1630 and 1716) was the house of the tanners; note the descriptive stonework above the windows.

Rozenhoedkaai, following the canal SW, soon reaches the bridge at the foot of Wollestraat, the statue on the bridge being of St. John Nepomuk, patron of bridges (from Nepomuk in Bohemia and chaplain to Wenceslas IV, John is said to have been martyred in 1393 by being thrown from a bridge into the Moldau because he refused to divulge the queen's confessional secrets). The turreted house (c 1480) in the angle of the quay is where the Holy Blood was hidden from the iconoclasts in 1578–83. The road continues as the Dyver, a pleasant quay with trees and benches, on the left, close to one another, being the Groeninge, Brangwyn and Gruuthuse museums.

The *Groeninge Museum*, reached through an archway, is open April–September: daily, 09.30 to 18.00. October–March: daily except Tuesday, 09.30 to 12.00, 14.00 to 17.00. Closed 1 January and Ascension Day afternoon. The museum houses the municipal collection of paintings, with notable Flemish Primitives, later Old Masters, and works of the 19th and 20C. The collections are larger than can be shown at any one time and some pictures are therefore rotated. The following—only a fraction of the collections—are representative examples of the works likely to be seen on a more or less chronological tour through 15 rooms of constant contrast. Room numbers indicate probable locations.

Jan van Eyck: **Madonna with St. Donatian and St. George and the

N31
Zeebrugge

DOCKS

OOSTENDSE STEENWEG

BLANKENBERGSE STEENWEG

SINT

PIETERSKAAI

KOMVEST

STEEN-KAAI

LEOPOLD II LAAN

COUPERE STR

W.R.F. STRAAT

CALBERTLAAN

SCHEEPSDALELAAN

KONINGIN ELISABETHLAAN

VLAMINGDAM

SINTE-CLARE STRAAT

Ezelpoort

KLAVERSTRAAT

LEOPOLD I LAAN

LAUWER STRAAT

VLIES LAAN

EZELSTRAAT

KAREL DE STOUTELAAN

BEVRIJDINGSLAAN

GULDEN

ST. JACOB STRAAT

VLAMINGSTRAAT

MARKT

Halle

P. PETER BENOIT LAAN

JAN BREYDELLAAN

NOORWEGER LAAN

NOORDZANDSTRAAT

Museum

GUIDO GEZELLELAAN

SMEDENSTR.

Smedenpoort

KONING ALBERTLAAN

ZANDSTRAAT

GISTELSTEENWEG

STEENWEG.

HENDRIK CONSCIENCELAAN

Begijnhof

Veurne N367

N32
Torhout

OUDDOVC?E

MAGDALENASTRAAT

STATIONSLAAN

Poedertoren

Minnewater

Station

Ostend & Brussels
E40

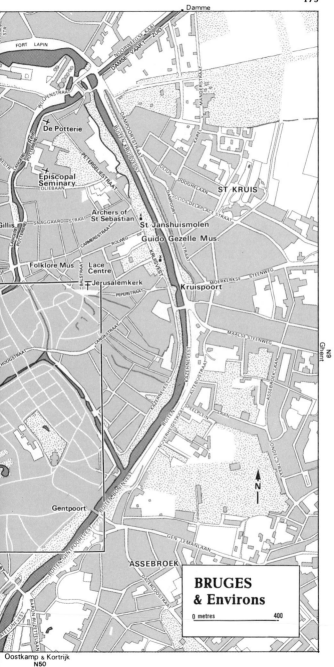

BRUGES & Environs

0 metres   400

Oostkamp & Kortrijk
N50

Bruges, the Oude Griffie

donor, Canon van der Paele (1436; a masterpiece of portraiture).
*Portrait of Margarete van Eyck (1439; the artist's wife). *Roger van
der Weyden*: Philip the Good (copy of the late 15C). St. Luke painting
the Virgin (15C copy). *Hugo van der Goes*: *Death of the Virgin.
Master of the Ursula Legend: Story of St. Ursula; wings of a triptych
from the Augustinian nunnery of Bruges. *Master of the Strauss
Madonna*: Crucifixion. *Master of the Prince's Portrait*: Portrait of
Louis of Gruuthuse (see below). *Master of the Lucia Legend*: St.
Nicholas, notable for the skilful and detailed rendering of the robe.
Hans Memling: Annunciation. *Triptych of SS. Christopher, Maurus
and Giles, with the donors Willem Moreel, burgomaster of Bruges,
and his wife (1484); Memling's earlier (1478) portrait of Moreel and

his wife hangs in the Musée d'Art Ancien in Brussels. *Gerard David* (R4): *Triptych (1508), including the Baptism of Christ, the donor Jean des Trompes and his son with St. John the Evangelist, and a portrait of the donor's first wife, Elisabeth van der Meersch, with her four daughters and St. Elizabeth of Hungary. On the back of the shutters are a Virgin and Child, and a portrait of the donor's second wife, with her daughter and St. Mary Magdalene. (This is one of the finest paintings of the last great master of the Bruges school.) Two panels (1498) illustrating the story of the Unjust Judge, as told by Herodotus.

In 1488, when Bruges held Maximilian prisoner, the town's action was opposed by Pieter Lanchals, Maximilian's treasurer, who was promptly executed. Later, by way of atonement, the magistrates of Bruges commissioned these panels. In the first, the corrupt judge, Sisamnes, is sentenced by King Cambyses to be flayed; in the second, the sentence is carried out and the skin of Sisamnes is hung on the judicial seat, now occupied by his son.

Hieronymus Bosch: *Last Judgement (R5). *Ambrosius Benson*: Rest on the Flight to Egypt. *Anon*: Two panels, Legend of St. George, with much crude detail. *Abel Grimmer*: Bearing of the Cross. *Adriaen Isenbrant*: Triptych. *Jan Provoost*: Last Judgement. Crucifixion. *Bernard van Orley*: Legend of St. Rochus. *Lancelot Blondeel*: St. Luke painting Our Lady (R6).

With Rooms 6 and 7 the scene begins to change as religion gradually cedes place to portraits, land and seascapes and historical themes. *Frans Pourbus the Younger*: Portrait of Petrus Ricardus. Portraits of Albert and Isabella. *Marcus Gheeraerts*: Portrait of Lady Anne Rushout. *Pieter Pourbus*: Several works, including a fine portrait of Rogerius de Jonghe. *Hendrik van Minderhout*: Two large harbour scenes. *Jacob van Oost the Elder*: A Bruges Family. *Jan van Goyen*: River scenes. *Adriaen Key*: Portrait of a Man.

Room 9, moving into the 18C, brings dramatic change, exemplified by *Jan Garemijn*'s astonishing Digging of the Ghent Canal with its swarm of antlike workers, while in Room 10, by way of contrast, hang *F.J. Kinsoen*'s perceptive portraits of some lovely ladies. Beyond, in Room 11, even more startling contrast is provided by a whole wall devoted to *Jean Delville*'s huge, ghostly, symbolic fantasy L'Homme-Dieu, this in turn contrasting with the down-to-earth realism of La Buée (Washerwomen) by *Leon Frederic* and sensitive portraits by *Edmond van Hove*.

Room 12 moves into a quieter world of 19C and early 20C landscapes (notably by *Emile Claus*) prior to the shock of Room 15 with the grotesque and oversize yet strongly effective beings who appear in, for instance, *G. van Woestyne*'s Last Supper, *Leon de Smet*'s Lady with a Fan, and *Constant Permeke*'s Flemish Farm and Angelus. A sculpture group by *George Minne*, Three Pious Ladies by a Grave, is in different mood. The tour ends with artists such as *René Magritte* (L'Attentat), *Paul Delvaux* (Le Lever) and several typical works by *Jan Brusselmans*.

To the W of the museum a path across a picturesque small bridge (the *Bonifaciusbrug*, so called because relics of this saint were held by the church of Onze Lieve Vrouw) leads below the Gruuthuse, with an overhanging verandah (see below) to the church of Onze Lieve Vrouw (see also below). By the bridge there is a bust of Juan Luis Vives (c 1540), the Spanish scholar and friend of Erasmus, who introduced a system of public assistance to Bruges.

The **Brangwyn Museum** (Daily except Tuesday in October–March, 09.30 to 12.00, 14.00 to 18.00 or 17.00 in October–March. Closed 1

January and Ascension Day afternoon) shows a rich collection of the paintings, drawings and etchings of Frank Brangwyn (1867–1956) who was born in Bruges and presented these works to his native town. Here, too, are a particularly attractive and interesting collection of *Views of old Bruges, together with collections of pewter, brass and porcelain.—Near the entrance arch there is a collection of carriages and sleighs, a part of the Gruuthuse museum.

The **Gruuthuse** Museum (entry times as for Brangwyn Museum above) is in the 15C patrician mansion of the same name, with an elegant interior notable for its fine chimneypieces and tiled hearths.

The name originates from 'gruit', fermented barley used in the brewing of beer, long ago stored in a building on this site. Although the wing overlooking the canal dates from 1420, the main mansion was built in c 1465–70 by Louis de Bruges, lord of Gruuthuse and lieutenant-general (for Charles the Bold) of Holland, Zeeland and Friesland. It was this grandee (see portrait in Groeninge museum) who in 1470–71 entertained England's fugitive Edward IV and his brother Richard. On regaining the throne, the grateful Edward conferred the earldom of Winchester on Louis, but the title was renounced by his son, John, in 1500.

The museum, as interesting for its interior architecture as for its contents, houses a varied collection of paintings and of domestic and applied art, with woodcarving, furniture, tapestry, glass, brass and silver. Of especial note are the 16C Flemish kitchen (Room 3); two works by Pieter Pourbus, the wings of a triptych (attributed) in Room 7 'and a double medallion in Room 8 where there is also a picture of the Battle of 's Hertogenbosch by S. Vranckx; a collection (Room 11) of musical instruments, including a musical cabinet (Polyphone, Leipzig, 1890) and a spinet of 1591; the family oratory overlooking the choir of the church of Onze Lieve Vrouw (Room 17); lace exhibits (Rooms 18–20), including a *Collection of old Flemish lace, with a magnificent altar cover, once the property of Charles V, and tools and pattern blocks; a verandah overlooking the Bonifaciusbrug; and a collection of arms and weapons and a guillotine in Room 22.

In the little square opposite the museum and the church of Onze Lieve Vrouw there is a statue of the poet Guido Gezelle.

The early Gothic **Onze Lieve Vrouwekerk** (April–September: Monday–Saturday, 10.00 to 11.30, 14.30 to 18.00 or 16.30 on Saturday. Sunday, Holidays, 14.30 to 18.00. October–March: Monday–Saturday, 10.00 to 11.30, 15.00 to 16.30 but 14.30 to 16.30 on Saturday. Sunday, Holidays, 14.30 to 16.30) traces its origins to a chapel of the 10C, this (or a successor) being burnt down in 1116. The next church has also left no trace, but the third church, started in about 1220, survives as the central part of today's building. Outer aisles were added in the 14C (N) and 15C (S). The outstanding feature is the tower (13C), with its spire, several times rebuilt, the highest in Belgium (122m); the pinnacles at the angles were added in 1872. Also noteworthy is the graceful N portal (1465), known as 'Paradis', a corruption of the French 'parvis' (small square in front of a church). The alley round the N end of the church leads to the Bonifaciusbrug (see above).

The *Interior is particularly rich in paintings and other works of art, these including a sculpture by Michelangelo. The NAVE contains statues of the Apostles (1618) and a Baroque pulpit of 1722, carved from a sketch by Jan Garemijn. SOUTH AISLE. High above the W end hangs an *Adoration of the Magi, a masterpiece of 1630 by Gerard Seghers, while, lower down and on the second pillar, there is a Virgin,

Child and St. Joseph by De Crayer. In the chapel at the E end of the S aisle, in the centre of the 18C altarpiece, the white marble *Virgin and Child is by Michelangelo. Commissioned in 1505 by a Bruges merchant and given to the church in 1514 or 1517, the group was stolen by the French in 1794 and by the Germans in 1944; the sculptor's sketch for the head of the Virgin is in the Victoria and Albert Museum in London. In the right corner of the chapel is the tomb (1560), with black marble statues, of the Sire de Haveskerke and his two wives, and on the wall a painting (1628) of Christ at the House of Simon the Pharisee by Frans Francken the Younger. A fee is charged for entry to most of the CHOIR AND AMBULATORY, the former separated from the nave by a black and white marble rood-screen of 1722. The high-altar and stalls date from 1770–79, above the latter being the painted armorial bearings of the Knights of the Golden Fleece, commemorating their eleventh chapter held here in 1468. The adjacent *Mausoleums of Charles the Bold (died 1477) and of his daughter Mary of Burgundy (1457–82) are the principal feature of the choir. That of Charles the Bold was erected in 1559–62 from the designs of Cornelis Floris of Antwerp; that of Mary of Burgundy, the finer of the two and the work of Pieter de Beckere of Brussels, dates from 1495–1502. Both mausoleums bear magnificent heraldic decoration. Charles the Bold was killed in battle at Nancy where he was later buried. In 1550 Charles V ordered that the remains be brought to Bruges, an order which was so opposed by the Nancy authorities that some doubt exists as to whether the body removed was Charles's or that of one of his knights. The transfer took several years (the body rested three years in Luxembourg), and when the remains eventually reached Bruges Charles V had abdicated and it was Philip II who ordered the construction of the mausoleum. About Mary, however, there is no doubt, and her actual tomb can be seen here, the central rear one of a group below the mausoleums. The coffin, though, with on top a box containing the heart of her son Philip the Handsome, is a replacement of the 19C when masonry collapsed during restoration work, exposing the original coffin which was then broken up and plundered by workmen. The other three adjacent tombs are those of three canons of the late 13th and early 14C. All the tombs are notable for their contemporary frescoes.

Also in the choir hangs a large arched triptych of the Crucifixion and Passion, begun by Bernard van Orley, completed by Marcus Gheeraerts in 1561, and restored by Frans Pourbus the Younger in 1589.

SOUTH AMBULATORY. Pictures here include the Disciples at Emmaus by Caravaggio and two works by Jacob van Oost the Elder. Also, two wings of a triptych with portraits of donors by Pieter Pourbus; and, at the E end, a triptych by Gerard David (centre panel, c 1520) and Pieter Pourbus (side panels of donors and children, c 1573). The Lanchals Chapel, off this ambulatory, contains a monument to Pieter Lanchals (p 181) and some frescoed c 14C tombs. Also a Last Supper by Pieter Pourbus (1562); by Adriaen Isenbrant a *Madonna of the Seven Sorrows (1518), rich in fascinating detail; and a Crucifixion (1626) by Antoon van Dyck.

Behind the high-altar there is a reliquary of St. Anthony, much invoked against plague and especially the Black Death.

In the NORTH AMBULATORY the Gothic oratory (1474) of the Gruuthuse family communicates with their mansion. Pictures include large paintings by De Crayer, Jacob van Oost the Elder, Louis de

Deyster and, at the E end, a triptych (Adoration of the Shepherds) by
Pieter Pourbus (1574).

Sint Jans Hospitaal (with the ****Memling Museum**) is immediately
SW of the Onze Lieve Vrouwekerk. The complex is open April–
September: daily, 09.00 to 12.30, 14.00 to 18.00. October–March:
daily except Wednesday, 10.00 to 12.00, 14.00 to 17.00. Closed 1
January and Ascension Day afternoon. On the outside the tympanum
of the old main porch carries 13C reliefs (Death and Coronation of the
Virgin).

On the right, just inside the entrance, a corridor leads to the 15C
Dispensary, in use until 1971 and now preserving old equipment,
including attractive pharmacy jars. An interesting painting shows the
dispensary in use at the beginning of the 19C. The room beyond, used
for meetings of the hospital board, contains two fine chests (note the
carvings of hospital scenes); a 14C Christmas cradle; and a collection
of Delft tiles depicting a series of children's games.

Opposite the dispensary is the entrance to the Hall (may be closed
for temporary exhibitions) and to the Chapel. The 13–14C Hall,
together with the adjoining smaller hall (now the museum entrance),
once formed one huge hospital ward, and a fascinating picture here
(by Jan Beerblock, 1778) shows the ward in use. At the end of the
main hall there is a copy of the 13C reliefs above the outer porch.

The Chapel, dating from the 15C and with good woodwork and
marble, now houses the ****Memling Museum**, the two principal works
being his altarpiece (Mystic Marriage of St. Catherine) and his
Reliquary of St. Ursula.   The large winged ****Altarpiece**, dedicated to
the patron saints of the hospital (St. John the Baptist and St. John the
Evangelist), was originally painted for the altar of the chapel. The
middle panel represents the Mystic Marriage of St. Catherine, while
on the inner wings are the Beheading of St. John the Baptist and the
Vision of St. John the Evangelist at Patmos; on the outer shutters are
the donors and their patron saints. Although the date is correct, the
signature 'Opus Johannis Memling, 1479' was added later.

The ****Reliquary of St. Ursula** (1489), in carved wood in the shape of
a Gothic chapel, is decorated by Memling's finest, if smallest,
paintings. It is exhibited on a revolving pedestal, and a magnifying
glass is provided on request. This engaging legend of Early Christian
times is represented with the freshness and precision of a contemporary event, the characters wearing the clothes of Memling's time and
Cologne buildings being faithfully reproduced, an indication of the
artist's personal knowledge of that town. On one end is the Virgin
with two nuns; on the other, St. Ursula sheltering ten maidens
beneath her cloak. The top is adorned by six medallions, possibly the
work of a pupil, and the sides tell the story of St. Ursula and the 11,000
virgins.

The events of the legend are placed by various sources between c 238 and 451.
Ursula, daughter of a Christian king of Britain, or perhaps Brittany ('in partibus
Britanniae'), was asked in marriage by the son of a pagan king. She consented,
on condition that he should embrace Christianity and send 11,000 virgins to
accompany her on a three-years pilgrimage to Rome. The multiplication
'thousand' is perhaps due to a misreading of an early manuscript, but it has
added much to the charm of the tale. Memling's reliquary depicts incidents of
this pilgrimage.—1st Scene: The arrival in Cologne, the picture showing the
cathedral, the church of St. Martin, and the Bayenthurm. 2nd Scene: Entry into
Basel (Basle), where the party disembark in order to cross the Alps. 3rd Scene:
Ursula is welcomed in Rome by the Pope; she receives the Sacrament and her
companions are baptised. 4th Scene: The party re-embark at Basel, accom-

panied by the Pope, who has been commanded in a vision to travel with them. 5th Scene: Returning to Cologne, the virgins are massacred by the pagans. 6th Scene: The pagan chief, moved by Ursula's beauty, offers to spare her life if she will marry him; she refuses (note the expressive gesture), and is killed by an arrow.

Other important Memling works are also exhibited here. A triptych, the *Adoration of the Magi (1479), with the donor Jan Floreins and his (?) brother on the left; the inner wings represent the Nativity and the Presentation in the Temple, and the outer shutters St. John the Baptist and St. Veronica. Diptych, Virgin with an apple, and a *Portrait of the donor Martin van Nieuwenhove at the age of twenty-three; dated 1487, this is considered one of Memling's finest portraits. Another triptych, a Pietà (1480), has St. Barbara and the donor Brother Adriaan Reyns, with St. Adrian on the inside of the leaves and the empress Helena and St. Mary of Egypt on the outside. The so-called Sibylla Zambetha, or Persian Sibyl (1480), marred by restorations, is a portrait of Maria Moreel, daughter of the burgomaster of Bruges.

The Begijnhof, reached by Katelijnestraat and Wijngaardstraat, is c 800m S of Sint Jans Hospitaal. It should be noted that in order to visit the cathedral (see below) and regain the Markt it is necessary to return past the hospital.—In Katelijnestraat Nos 8–18 (right, down an alley) are old almshouses, and No. 84, the *Academy of Fine Arts*, in part occupies a former orphanage. Other old almshouses can be seen in Nieuwe Gentweg, leading E off Katelijnestraat; these are (both right) *Meulenaer* (1613) and *St. Joseph*'s (1567).

The ***Begijnhof**, and the adjacent Wijngaardplaats and Minnewater, with the canal and ancient trees, form one of the most attractive corners of Bruges.

A begijnhof was founded here c 1235 and received a charter from Margaret of Constantinople in 1245. In 1299 Philip the Fair absolved it from dependence on the city magistrates and allowed it the title 'Béguinage princier de la Vigne' ('vigne', or 'wijn', coming from the name of a piece of land, presumably once bearing vines, on which the original enclosure had been set up). In the 16C, the begijnhof from time to time served as a place of refuge, unhappily in 1584 when peasants accidentally burnt the church (rebuilt 1605). Today the buildings are occupied by Benedictine sisters.

The gateway dates from 1776. The buildings (15C and later) surround a large courtyard planted with trees, one house by the entrance serving as a Museum in which the simple arrangements and furniture of the original community are preserved. The church has in the first N bay a Romanesque doorway of its predecessor.

The **Minnewater**, just S of the Begijnhof and now a quiet lake, was the busy inner dock of the harbour during the Middle Ages. The *Lock House*, at the N end, is a building of the 15C (restored 1893), and at the S end stands the *Poedertoren* (powder magazine) dating from 1398 and a relic of the old fortifications.

The course of the old fortifications is today followed by a ring road. Of the original seven gates, four remain. These are the *Gentpoort* (1km NE of the Minnewater); the *Smedenpoort* (on the SW edge of the town, by the start of N367); the *Ezelpoort* or Oostendepoort (NW, where N9 leaves the town); and the *Kruispoort* (E).—The Station is c 500m W of the Minnewater.

From Sint Jans Hospitaal, Heilige Geeststraat leads in 300m to the **Kathedraal Sint Salvator**, a Gothic building essentially of the 13C which replaced an earlier Romanesque church reaching back to the 9C. The base of the W tower probably dates from c 1200, the brickwork here being among the oldest in Belgium, but the Neo-Romanesque upper part is of 1844–71. The W part of the choir and

part of the transepts date from the end of the 13C; the nave and S
transept are a rebuilding after a fire of 1358; the ambulatory and
apsidal chapels are Flamboyant work (1480–1530) of Jan van der
Poele. In the garden the statues of St. Peter and St. Paul are by Pieter
Pepers (1765).

The former cathedral, dedicated to St. Donatian, was demolished by the French
in 1799 and the bishopric of Bruges was abolished by Napoleon in 1802. When
the bishopric was restored in 1834, this church was chosen as the new cathedral
and received many of the art treasures which had belonged to its predecessor.

In the NAVE the pulpit of 1778–85 is the work of Hendrik Pulincx,
while at the W end the Baroque 17C rood-screen in mixed bronze,
wood and marble is crowned by a figure of the Creator (1682) by
Quellin the Younger; until as recently as 1935 this screen stood at the
entrance to the choir, as interestingly shown in a picture in the
cathedral museum. In the S aisle hangs a Resurrection by P. Claessins
(1585), and in the N aisle, in the baptistry, a scene from the Battle of
Lepanto by Hendrik van Minderhout (c 1672). Off the NORTH TRAN-
SEPT opens the Chapel of the Shoemakers, with a screen of 1430, a
14C Crucifixion and the emblem of the guild, a boot below a crown,
on the altar, on chairs and on the doors. Across in the SOUTH
TRANSEPT hang an Adoration of the Shepherds by Jacob van Oost the
Elder and a Gobelins tapestry, while, below, a handsome bench with
carved horses and a bust of St. Eloi was once the property of the Guild
of Waggoners.

The 13C CHOIR is the oldest part of the interior, particularly
noteworthy being the stalls, commissioned in 1430 on the occasion of
the founding of the Order of the Golden Fleece; the misericords carry
small reliefs illustrating everyday life, crafts and proverbs, and the
armorial bearings above, those of the 13th Chapter of the Golden
Fleece, date from the chapter's year, 1478. The two bishops' tombs on
either side of the high-altar are by Hendrik Pulincx (1749–58), the
Resurrection on the altar is by Abraham Janssens, the brass lectern is
of 1605, and the tapestries are six out of a collecton of eight (Brussels,
1731).

Off the AMBULATORY are five apsidal chapels, described below
anticlockwise. The first, with a retable of c 1500, is dedicated to Our
Lady of Loretto whose story is told in three paintings. In the second
chapel (Our Lady of Seven Sorrows) a Mater Dolorosa (17C) holds a
plague wand used by priests ministering to the afflicted; the wand
was donated by a priest in gratitude for having been spared. There
are several features of interest in the central chapel, immediately
noteworthy being a white marble Madonna by Pieter Pepers (1776).
Other features are two paintings by Jacob van Oost the Elder of SS.
Peter and John and some fine 19C stained glass. Beyond, in the
Fourth chapel, there is a 15C wooden altarpiece with scenes from the
Passion, while the last chapel has a stained glass window, interesting
for having been made in 1903 out of glass of 1531 from a window
destroyed by iconoclasts. Beyond, though not part of the ambulatory
proper, are two adjoining small chapels one of·which was that of the
Coachbuilders whose window emblem is incorporated in the door.

The CATHEDRAL MUSEUM (Almost always closed Wednesday.
Otherwise, April–June, September: Monday–Saturday, 14.00 to
17.00; Sunday, Holidays, 15.00 to 17.00. July, August: Monday–
Saturday, 10.00 to 11.30, 14.00 to 17.00; Sunday, Holidays, 15.00 to
17.00. October–March: Monday–Saturday, 14.00 to 17.00), built as an

annexe in 1912, houses material some of which always belonged to St. Salvator's and some of which came from St. Donatian's. In the Gallery there is a group of six funerary *Brasses (1387–1555); of the six subjects, Jacob Schelewarts (died 1483) taught theology at the University of Paris and was pastor of this church, and Adriaan Bave (died 1555) was burgomaster of Bruges. Room One (note that this and Rooms 2 and 3 are little more than recesses off the gallery) contains a *Triptych by Dirk Bouts and Hugo van der Goes, the Martyrdom of St. Hippolytus. The right and centre panels, both by Bouts, show the Emperor Decius, notorious for his persecution of Christians, trying to persuade the saint to deny his faith, and Hippolytus about to be torn apart by four horses. The donors, in the left panel, are by Van der Goes. (Hippolytus, a Roman, waš a controversial early ecclesiastical writer. Although martyred in 235, he did not die by the method shown here, this portrayal arising out of confusion after his death with other characters, both actual and mythical, of similar name, these including the son of Theseus who in legend died in this way.) Room Two shows vestments dating from the 15C, reliquaries and a 17C crozier. In Room Three are the silver shrine of St. Donatian, made in 1843 but with 12th and 13C silver and ornamentation; a 13C crozier-head in Limoges enamel, depicting St. Martial (died c 250: bishop of Limoges) receiving the heart of St. Valeria, a saint of doubtful authenticity, said to have been converted by St. Martial and then to have been beheaded for her faith; and a triptych (Presentation in the Temple) by Adriaen Isenbrant. Room Four (the first real room) contains, with Room 5, tombstones of 1380, found under the floor of the church, and also a painting (Crucifixion) by an unknown Flemish master of c 1500. Room Five: Reliquary of St. Eloi by Jan Crabbe (c 1616); Eloi (or Eligius. 588–660) was a skilled metalworker who in 640 became a priest, thereafter spending much of his time evangelising in Flanders. Also in this room are a painting of the Virgin between St. Luke and St. Eloi by Lancelot Blondeel (1545), and an altarpiece (Calvary) of the Tanners' Guild, a rare example of a 14C panel painting. Room Six: Copes. Woodcarving (early 16C) of the consecration of a bishop. An interesting painting of the interior of St. Salvator's in the 17C by Cornelis Verhouven, showing the rood-screen in its original position. In Room Seven, used for meetings of the cathedral chapter, are a cloth antependium of 1642; a triptych (Last Supper) by Pieter Pourbus (1599); and another triptych by Anthony Claeissins.

Zuidzandstraat, running SW from the cathedral, has some old, if restored façades: No. 41 (1570), No. 40 (1630; note the stone carving), and No. 18 (1703). The street ends at 'T ZAND, an open space (above a large car park) which was the site of the earlier railway station, dismantled and then rebuilt at Ronse. The successor station (1931), farther S, is reached by Koning Albertlaan, a wide boulevard with gardens. Just W of 'T Zand is the *Orgel Museum* (entrance 3 Zwijnstraat. Easter–early or mid November: daily 10.00 to 18.00 or 19.00) showing music boxes, street organs and suchlike.

From the cathedral Steenstraat, leading NE, quickly reaches SIMON STEVINPLAATS with a statue of the mathematician. Between here and the Markt there are a number of good façades: No. 90 (1570); No. 40, the guild house of the shoemakers (1527); No. 25, the guild house of the masons (1621); and No. 28, 'De Lam' (1654). An alternative route back to the Markt is to take Kemelstraat NW out of Simon Stevin-plaats, this soon crossing Zilverstraat in which No. 38, dating from 1468, was the house of Juan Vasquez, secretary of Isabella of

Portugal, third wife of Philip the Good. The next street parallel to
Zilverstraat is Noordzandstraat which may be followed NE, off the W
side, roughly opposite the Hôtel du Sablon, being the narrow
approach to the picturesque *Prinsenhof*, representing the courtyard of
the 15C palace in which Philip the Handsome was born in 1478.
Noordzandstraat becomes Geldmuntstraat, off the W side of which
the vaulted *Muntpoort* (rebuilt 1961) leads to Muntplaats, the site of
the Bruges mint; here a gabled front bears a bust of Marc Houterman
(1537–77) who was organist at St. Peter's, Rome. Geldmuntstraat ends
at the attractive small Eiermarkt (cafés), adjacent to the Markt.

B. Northern and Eastern Bruges

This round, starting from the Markt and returning to it, covers some
6km, but it is practicable to use a car from Jan van Eyckplaats
onwards.

Sint Jacobstraat leaves the NW of the Markt, skirts the Eiermarkt with
its pedestrian area and cafés, and reaches the **Sint Jacobskerk**, of
which the base of the tower, the N transept and the NE chapel (once
the choir) date from c 1240; the remainder of the church was rebuilt
between 1459 and 1478. The interior contains several paintings, the
artists including Jacob van Oost the Elder, Pieter Pourbus and Louis
de Deyster. Roughly opposite the church, the narrow arched Boterhuis connects to Naaldenstraat, by the junction being a house with a
graceful 15C brick turret. Farther on in Naaldenstraat, **Hof Bladelin**,
with its turret and spire, was the home of Pieter Bladelin (died 1472),
treasurer of the Order of the Golden Fleece; the house later became
the residence of Tomaso Portinari (fl. c 1480), a Florentine banker and
agent for the Medici. Naaldenstraat ends at Grauwwerkersstraat, at
the E end of which is Vlamingstraat with, just S, a square in the centre
of which stands the municipal theatre (**Schouwburg**). Within the N
angle of Grauwwerkersstraat and Vlamingstraat, the house called
Ter Beurze, dating from 1493 and now a bank, was the mansion of the
Van der Beurze family who here welcomed merchants of all nations to
meet and exchange goods and money; variations of the family name
have since been adopted in many languages to describe a place of
commercial or financial exchange. Within the S angle of Vlamingstraat and Grauwwerkersstraat is the *Natiehuis van Genua*
(sometimes called the Saaihalle. 1399; altered 1720), the headquarters of the Genoese merchants.

From opposite Ter Beurze, Academiestraat leads NE to JAN VAN
EYCKPLAATS at the head of a canal arm which formerly continued to
the Markt. Little visited by tourists, this is the centre of one of the most
characteristic and often lively 'popular' quarters of Bruges; the statue
of Van Eyck is by Henri Pickery (1878). The **Poorters Loge**, on the S
side, was originally the meeting-place of the 'privileged' merchants,
those who lived within the walls as distinct from those outside and
under the jurisdiction of the Brugse Vrije. Dating from the 14C, except
for the slender turret rebuilt after a fire of 1775, this building was at
one time the meeting-place of an exclusive society known as the
White Bear, and the bear (1417) in a niche is honoured as the 'oldest
citizen of Bruges'. On the N side of the square are (left) the *Pynderhuis*
(1470) and (right) the *Tolhuis*, the customs house of 1477 (rebuilt

1878), now the municipal library. The tall house (*Roode Steen*) on the E at the corner of Spiegelrei and Genthof is a restored late 16C mansion.

Woensdagmarkt, a short way along Genthof, was formerly Hans Memlingplaats and still has a statue of the painter (Henri Pickery, 1871). The tall 15C turret is a relic of the *House of the Smyrna Merchants* while, just beyond, Oosterlingenplaats is named after the consular house here of the 'easterlings' or eastern merchants. The **Sint Gilliskerk**, 200m N beyond the canal, founded in 1277 and enlarged during the 15C, contains works by Jacob van Oost the Elder, Louis de Deyster and others; many painters, including Memling, Provoost, Blondeel and probably Pourbus the Elder, were buried in the church's yard. Collaert Mansionstraat, running N on the E of the church, is named after Caxton's partner, and Jan van Eyck lived in Gouden Handstraat, a short way south.

The Reie waterway, 100m E of Sint Gillis, is flanked by the roads Langerei (W) and Potterierei (E). Northwards the latter reaches (500m from the bridge) the **Groot Seminarie** (the episcopal seminary) in the buildings of the former abbey Ter Duinen, transferred here in 1627 from its original site at Koksijde and suppressed in 1796. The church, which carries on the name of the abbey, is a rebuilding of the 18C.

De Potterie, just beyond the seminary and probably on land long ago belonging to the potters' guild, is an ancient hospice founded in 1276 for aged women. The three gables are, from N to S, the front of the hospital (1529), that of the early church (1359), and that of a chapel (of Onze Lieve Vrouw) added in 1623. Visitors are admitted to the chapel and a small museum (April–September: daily, 09.00 to 12.30, 14.00 to 18.00. October–March: daily except Wednesday, 10.00 to 12.00, 14.00 to 17.00. Closed 1 January and Ascension Day afternoon). The Chapel has two aisles between which (Easter–October) are hung some notable tapestries: Virgin adoring the Child (late 15C), Madonna and two Saints (16C), and a *Series of three (late 16C) depicting miracles of Our Lady in the hospital. These stories are also illustrated in stained-glass opposite. On the right altar is the miraculous statue (early 14C) of Our Lady, and in the side-chapel the tomb (modern) of St. Idesbald (died 1167), originally buried at Ter Duinen. In the left aisle the rood-screen dates from 1644 (statues later); behind it is an Adoration of the Magi by J. van Oost the Elder, while on either side of the altar are the tombs of two burgomasters who died in 1597 and 1608. The Museum contains pictures, these including a triptych (Descent from the Cross, 1520); a portrait of a sister of the Hospice de la Madeleine (1575); and pen and ink drawings attributed to Jan van Eyck. Material here also includes a leper's clapper in carved wood (16C), a coloured relief of the Agony in the Garden, and illuminated missals.

Beyond De Potterie, Peterseliestraat bears SE, in 600m becoming Kruisvest on which stands **Sint Jansmolen**, dating from 1770 and one of three windmills along this stretch of vest (Easter. May–September: daily, 10.00 to 12.00, 13.00 to 18.00). Roughly opposite the windmill two streets run W, the northern one being Carmersstraat, with, on the corner, the **Schuttersgild Sint Sebastiaan**, the guild house (1565) of the Archers of St. Sebastian with collections of paintings and gold and silverwork and also records of the guild reaching back to 1416 (Monday, Wednesday, Friday, Saturday, 10.00 to 12.00, 14.00 to 17.00). Farther along Carmersstraat a domed chapel of 1736 belongs to an English nunnery founded in 1629. In Rolweg, also running W from the windmill, the building at the corner is the **Guido Gezellemuseum**, the birthplace of the Flemish poet (1830–99); he was chaplain to the English nunnery and is known for his translation into Flemish of Longfellow's 'Song of Hiawatha' (daily, except Tuesday in October–March, 09.30 to 12.00, 14.00 to 18.00 or 17.00 in October–March). Two blocks S, near the corner of Stijn Streuvelsstraat, the **Schuttersgild Sint Joris**, the guild house of St. George, shows paintings and bows (daily except Wednesday, 10.00 to 12.00, 14.00 to 18.00). The **Kruispoort**, a short way S along Kruisvest, a gate of 1402 but much altered, is one of the oldest buildings in Bruges.

From the Kruispoort, Peperstraat leads W to the privately owned **Jeruzalemkerk**, built originally as a chapel by the Adorne of Genoa, one of several foreign merchant families who settled in Bruges during the 13C. The chapel was followed in c 1427 by the present church, built generally to the plan of the church of the Holy Sepulchre in Jerusalem, whither the builders, the brothers Pieter and Jacob Adorne, had made a pilgrimage. The church still belongs to descendants of the family. In the interior is the black marble tomb of Anselm Adorne (died 1483) and his wife; son of Pieter Adorne, Anselm became burgomaster of Bruges and consul for Scotland, where he was murdered. The 15th and 16C stained-glass is some of the best in Bruges.

Balstraat runs N beside the church, on the W being the **Museum voor Volkskunde**, with interiors, costumes and domestic material (Daily except Tuesday in October–March, 09.30 to 12.00, 14.00 to 18.00 or 17.00 in October–March. Closed 1 January and Ascension Day afternoon). Opposite is the **Kant Centrum**, or Lace Centre, where the ancient craft of making bobbin lace is taught and demonstrated (Monday–Saturday, 10.00 to 12.00, 14.00 to 18.00 or 17.00 on Saturday. Sunday, Holidays, 14.00 to 17.00).

The **Sint Annakerk**, just W of the Jeruzalemkerk, was founded in 1496, demolished in 1581, and rebuilt between 1607–21. Guido Gezelle was christened here. The interior is rich Baroque, panelled all round, with 17C stalls, confessionals and pulpit. The rood-screen (1628), in marble and porphyry, is by Jan van Mildert, and there are paintings by Louis de Deyster, Jacob van Oost the Elder, and Jan Baptist Herregoudts (a huge Last Judgement). The **Sint Walburgakerk**, 300m W of that of St. Anna and somewhat confusingly in Sint Maartensplaats, was built in 1619–40 by Pieter Huyssens as the church of the Jesuits and was the first to be dedicated to St. Francis Xavier whose figure is on the imposing façade; it became the parish church on the suppression of the Jesuits in 1779. Among features of the interior are a marble communion-rail by H. Verbruggen (1695), a pulpit of 1667 by Artus Quellin the Younger, a marble retable of 1643, and a painting by Joseph Benoît Suvee (1783).

From the church the Markt is some 600m SW, the pleasantest route being via Koningstraat to Spinolarei, then along the water to Jan van Eyckplaats.

The **Docks** are at the N edge of the town by the start of the Boudewijn canal.

On the opposite (S) edge of the town, to the E of Koning Albertlaan leading to the Ostend–Brussels motorway, the **Boudewijn Park** is a recreational park offering, among many attractions, a Dolphinarium, a collection of snakes and reptiles and an astronomical clock (Easter–September: daily, 10.30 to 18.00).

C. Damme

Damme (10,000 inhab. Tourist Information: De Grote Sterre, 3 Jacob van Maerlantstraat) is a delightful old town on the tree-lined canal from Bruges to Sluis (Holland), near where this crosses the adjoining Schipdonk and Leopold canals in the heart of typical polder countryside. Only 7km from Bruges, and renowned for its small hotels and restaurants, Damme offers a quiet, uncrowded and, for motorists, convenient alternative to staying in Bruges itself. Boat link with Bruges in the season.

Damme was founded in the 12C by Philip of Alsace, Count of Flanders; situated on the Zwin (Rte 3), the new town was to serve as the foreport of Bruges. In 1213 it was pillaged by Philip Augustus (Philip II of France) during his war against Count Ferdinand of Flanders, but the latter's English allies burnt most of Philip's fleet in Damme harbour. The port, with a population that grew to 10,000, became sufficiently important to have its own maritime law (the 'Zeerecht van Damme'). In 1430 Philip the Good and Isabella of Portugal were married here, and in 1468 Charles the Bold and Margaret of York, sister of England's Edward IV. With the silting of the Zwin during the 15C, decline set in and Damme ceased to be of importance. The town was taken by Marlborough in 1706 and its fortifications were dismantled.—Damme is associated with Jacob van Maerlant (c 1235–1300), who lived, died, and is buried here. The 'father of Flemish poetry', he was also one of the most learned scholars of his time, being best known for his 'Spiegel Historiael', a history of the world. Local tradition, originating perhaps in the title of Maerlant's book, holds that Till Eulenspiegel (in fact a German folklore figure from the district around Hanover) also lived and died here.

The *Stadhuis* (July–September: daily, 10.00 to 12.00, 14.00 to 18.00) was built in 1464–68 on the site of a trade hall of 1241. Already Damme was losing its importance and the building had to be financed by a special tax levied on the barrels of herrings discharged here. The ground floor was used as a market, and the four shutters which can be seen today were for small shops. The statues on the façade, either side of the double stairway, include Philip of Alsace, founder of the town; the countesses Joanna and Margaret of Constantinople, the latter bearing a model of the hospital she is said to have founded; and, on the right, Charles the Bold giving a wedding ring to a somewhat bashful Margaret of York. The turret rising from the centre of the steeply pitched roof houses bells, two of which are dated 1392 and 1398. The interior contains a monumental chimneypiece, tiling, and some curious woodcarving, including a scene of a man and woman together in a bath.

A statue (1860) of Jacob van Maerlant stands in front of the Stadhuis. To the right, *De Grote Sterre* (Daily, 09.00 to 12.00, 14.00 to 18.00 or 17.00 in October–April), a patrician mansion of the 15C, during the 17C the residence of Spanish military governors, now houses Tourist Information, an art gallery and a museum largely relating to Charles de Coster (1827–79), author of a 19C version of the legend of Till Eulenspiegel. Nearby, just NE, the *Huis Sint Jan*, of 1468, is where the marriage was celebrated between Charles the Bold and Margaret of York. Beside the canal the *Zeemuseum Devaere* (March–October: daily, 09.00 to 12.00, 14.00 to 18.00) shows ship models and some interesting old maps of the Zwin.

In Kerkstraat the *Museum Sint Jans Hospitaal* (April–October: Monday, 14.00 to 17.30; Tuesday–Saturday, 10.00 to 12.00, 14.00 to 18.00; Sunday, Holidays, 11.00 to 12.00, 14.00 to 18.00. November–March: daily, 14.00 to 17.30) houses a mixed collection of furniture, liturgical material, ceramics and graveslabs. The hospital was foun-

ded in c 1249 by, it is said, Margaret of Constantinople. A short way
beyond (S) the *Onze Lieve Vrouwekerk* (Tower ascent. May–
September: daily 10.00 to 12.00, 14.30 to 17.30. Apply 37 Kerkstraat)
preserves a high square tower (c 1210–30), separated from the 14C
body of the church (mainly choir) by two ruined bays with triple
triforium. The transepts were demolished in 1725 and the central
nave abandoned. The lower part of the rood-loft (1555) serves as
vestibule. Inside there are Baroque confessionals from the cathedral
of St. Donatian in Bruges; statues of the Apostles (14C); the altar of the
Holy Cross (1636), with a cross brought up from the sea by fishermen;
and an Assumption by Jan Maes. Jacob van Maerlant was probably
buried below the tower, but his gravestone was sold during the 19C
and replaced by a plaque. Tradition holds that Till Eulenspiegel also
lies here, and a small statue stands in the garden.

Stockmanshoeve, c 5km SE of Damme (signs), is a rural recreation estate with
fishing ponds, a children's farm, enclosures with farmyard animals, aviaries, a
swimming and boating lake, restaurant, and a museum of agricultural imple-
ments and machinery (Easter—October, daily from 10.00).

10 Bruges to Kortrijk (Courtrai)

A. Via Torhout and Roeselare

Total distance 49km—*19km***Torhout**.—*12km***Roeselare**.—*18km*
Kortrijk.

Bruges (see Rte 9) can be left by the Smedenpoort, soon after which
the road (N32) runs through the woods of *Tillegem*, once the estate of
a château and now a provincial recreational park; the large moated
château, in origin of the 9C, rebuilt in the 13C and much altered in
1870, now houses the West Flanders tourism offices.—Just beyond the
Ostend-Brussels motorway, the abbey of *Zeven-Kerken*, or *Sint
Andries*, lies (W) in woods at the end of an avenue; founded in c 1100
but destroyed in 1793, this Benedictine abbey was rebuilt on its
present site in 1901. Benedictine sisters occupy a nearby nunnery. At
Loppem, 2km E, the château (April–October: daily except Monday
and Friday, c 10.00 to 12.00, 14.00 to 18.00), an outstanding example
of 19C Flemish Neo-Gothic, was built in 1858–63 by Jean Béthune.—
At (*10km* from Bruges) *Zedelgem*, to the W of the road, the church has
a 12C font of Tournai marble.—*9km* **Torhout** (17,000 inhab. Tourist
Information: 1 Markt), an industrial and agricultural centre, is the
'capital' of the Flemish HOUTLAND (Wood Land). Destroyed in both
world wars, the *Sint Pieterskerk*, with a Martyrdom of St. Sebastian by
Van Dyck, has been rebuilt to the original Romanesque plan. The
Stadhuis, dating from 1713, contains a local museum exhibiting
earthenware of a type associated with this district for several centuries (mid March–mid November: Tuesday, Saturday, 14.00 to 17.00;
Wednesday, 10.00 to 12.00, 14.00 to 17.00; Sunday, 10.00 to 12.00).

At **Wijnendale**, 3km NW of Torhout, the historic but much restored 12C château
has in part been organised as a museum with tableaux illustrating its history
(mid May–mid September: Tuesday, Wednesday, Sunday, 14.00 to 18.00). Here
in 1292 Guy de Dampierre, son of Margaret of Constantinople and Count of

Flanders, received the embassy of England's Edward I asking for the hand of his daughter for Edward's son; this so enraged Guy's suzerain, Philip the Fair, who intended that the future Edward II should marry his own daughter, that for this and other reasons Guy was imprisoned in France and forced to cede Flanders. It was while hunting in the park that Mary of Burgundy had her fatal fall from her horse (see picture in Bruges Stadhuis). In 1940 the château was the scene of the final meeting between Leopold III and his prime minister (Pierlot) and of the decision to surrender; the armistice with Germany was then signed here.

At (*7km*) *Gits* a road forks SW for Ypres (20km), passing *Westrozebeke* (p 162).—*5km* **Roeselare**(52,000 inhab. Tourist Information: Stadhuis) was the German headquarters facing the Ypres salient. The *Sint Michielskerk* (1497–1504) contains good woodwork, including an elaborately carved 18C pulpit from the Carmelite church in Bruges, while the pictures include a 'Christ Scourged' by A. Janssens, the scourgers being in the dress of the artist's day. Just S of the town, beside the road, stands the very attractive red-brick château of *Rumbeke*, dating from the 16C though some parts are earlier; the park, laid out in 1770 by F. Simoneau, is now a provincial recreational estate (Sterrebos) but the château is open only to groups. Across the road from the château there is a monument to men of the 1st Grenadier Guards who fell near here on 17 May 1940.—*8km* Izegem (26,000 inhab.) has long been, and still is, a centre of two domestic industries, brush manufacturing and footwear, both represented by museums; brushes at 2 Wolvenstraat, footwear at 9 Wijngaardstraat, both open Saturday, 10.00 to 12.00.—*10km* **Kortrijk (Courtrai)**, see Rte 11.

B. Via Oostkamp

Total distance 37km.—*5km Oostkamp.*—*23km Ingelmunster.*—*9km* **Kortrijk**.

Bruges, see Rte 9.—The road (N50) crosses the Bruges-Ghent canal, reaches (*5km*) *Oostkamp*, with an octagonal 12C church tower, and then crosses the Ostend–Brussels motorway. The Diksmuide-Tielt road (Rte 5) is met just E of (*15km*) *Koolskamp*, 3km S of which is the shoe-making town of *Aardooie* (8000 inhab.), birthplace of Victor Roelens (1856–1947), first Bishop of the Congo.—*8km Ingelmunster* (10,000 inhab.) has an 18C château which is successor to the castle where Philip the Fair was handed the keys of Bruges (p 171). A battle near here in 1580, subsequent to the Union of Arras, was one of Parma's first successes against the Protestants.—*9km***Kortrijk (Courtrai)**, see Rte 11.

11   Kortrijk (Courtrai) to Ghent

Total distance 37km.—*4km* **Harelbeke**.—*19km Petegem* (**Deinze**).— *5km* **Deurle**.—*9km* **Ghent**.

KORTRIJK (Courtrai. 77,000 inhab. Tourist Information: Schouw-burgplein) is a pleasant and lively commercial town on the Lys (Leie) which, with origins reaching back to Roman times, today successfully combines the old with the new, the latter exemplified by several particularly good pedestrian shopping streets. Though mostly Flemish-speaking, Kortrijk is only 7km from the French frontier, the border town (Mouscron or Moeskroen) being in the NW bulge of the province of Hainaut; the great French city of Lille is 14km beyond Mouscron.

Known to the Romans as Cortracum, Kortrijk was established as a town possibly during the 7C, though it was later destroyed by the Norsemen and then rebuilt in the 10C by Baldwin III of Flanders. The Lys, a chalk-free river especially suitable for flax-retting, ensured the town's prosperity as a cloth centre and by the 15C the population of the district had risen to around 200,000. It was under the walls of Kortrijk on 11 July 1302 that the Battle of the Golden Spurs was fought, the weavers of Bruges, Ghent and other Flemish towns routing an army of French knights under Robert of Artois. In 1382 Charles VI of France burnt Kortrijk after his defeat of Philip van Artevelde at Westrozebeke, and in 1488–92 the town was occupied by Charles VIII, the French on this occasion supporting Flanders against Maximilian of Austria. Taken in 1914, Kortrijk became a main German base behind the Ypres front.—The painter Roelant Savery (1576–1639) was born here, but soon moved to Utrecht.

The centre of the town is the irregularly-shaped GROTE MARK, most places of interest being to the E and north. The pedestrians-only shopping streets are just SE, while in the middle stands the 14–15C **Belfry**, all that survives of the cloth hall which was so damaged by bombing in 1944 that it was later demolished.

The **Stadhuis** (Monday–Friday, 08.30 to 13.00, 14.00 to 17.00. Also, July and August, Saturday at same times and Sunday morning), off the NW corner of the Grote Markt, dates from 1519 but has been repeatedly enlarged and restored, the last restoration being by J. Vierin and his son Luc in 1959–62. The façade statues of the counts of Flanders are modern. In the Schepenzaal, on the ground floor, are modern stained-glass windows and frescoes depicting historical events, and also a fine 16C chimneypiece with the arms of Ghent and Bruges, figures of Albert and Isabella, etc. Upstairs, in the Council Chamber, there is a still finer *Chimneypiece (1527), representing, in three rows of statuettes, the Virtues (above), the Vices (in the middle), and the punishments of Hell (below). Just W of the Stadhuis is the *Jesuit Church* of 1611, with, on the S side, a modern chapel housing a 13C ivory statuette of Our Lady of Groeninge.

The **Sint Maartenskerk**, off the SE corner of the Grote Markt, is in part of the 13C but was largely rebuilt in the 15C. The main features of the interior are a richly carved and gilded stone tabernacle of 1585 by Hendrik Maes and a triptych of 1587 by Bernard de Ryckere.

To the SE of the church the long pedestrians-only street running from SW to NE is made up of Lange Steenstraat, Steenpoort and Voorstraat. Where the latter two join, Sint Jansstraat bears SE, at the corner with Potterijstraat being the *Bagghaertshof*, a group of old almshouses with a small courtyard and a chapel of 1638.

The **Begijnhof**, immediately N of the church of Sint Maarten, was founded in 1238 by Joanna of Constantinople (statue of 1891). Since then though it has been many times destroyed and most of the small houses (one with a museum) seen today are of the 17C. The 18C chapel has a 15C flank giving on to Begijnhofstraat.

The adjacent **Onze Lieve Vrouwkerk**, although mainly of the 13C, was partly rebuilt in the 18C and again after war damage of 1944. The W exterior is curious, with arches along the pavement, and the church generally has an unusual fortified aspect. The interior contains two notable works of art. One is an alabaster *Statue of St. Catherine (1374–84) by André Beauneveu; this is in the Chapel of the Counts, founded by Louis de Male in c 1365, restored in 1963, and known for its interesting collection of portraits of all the counts of Flanders and of some of their wives. The other outstanding work (in the N transept) is the *Raising of the Cross (1631) by Van Dyck, one of this artist's last paintings before his departure for England. In the adjoining chapel there is an Adoration of the Shepherds by Louis de Deyster, another of whose works hangs in the S transept. The two chancel lecterns are by Ignace de Cock (1695), best known as a bell-caster, and Jan Lepies (1711).

From the church Guido Gezellestraat leads to the river, the bridge here being flanked by the twin squat and massive **Broeltorens**; impressive survivals of Kortrijk's ancient fortifications, the towers date from the 12C (S) and the 15C (N). To the left, across the bridge, an 18C mansion contains the **Stedelijk Museum** (Monday, Tuesday, Wednesday, Thursday, Saturday, 10.00 to 12.00, 14.00 to 18.00; Sunday, 10.00 to 13.00, 15.00 to 18.00). The exhibits include an important collection of local lace and damask; ceramic; pewter; copper and bronze; period furniture; coins; prehistoric and Roman material; and a Roelant Savery exhibition.

The *Onze Lieve Vrouwhospitaal* (400m W of the museum) was founded by Margaret of Constantinople in 1219, but almost entirely rebuilt in the 16–17C. It has a Baroque chapel, and a courtyard with some 13C fragments.

The site of the BATTLE OF THE GOLDEN SPURS is marked by a monument in Groeningelaan, 700m E of the Grote Markt. The battle was fought on 11 July 1302 between the Flemish weavers and others under Pieter de Coninck, already famed as a leader of the Bruges Matins, and an army of French knights led by Robert of Artois. The Flemish army, if it can be called such, stood facing a stream (now the

Groeningelaan), their left protected by the Lys and their right by marsh. The French chivalry, contemptuous of their low-born opponents, made two frontal attacks across the stream, but each was repelled by the Flemish pikemen, the French losing 63 nobles, including Robert of Artois, and 700 knights. It is said that after the battle 700 pairs of golden spurs were collected and displayed in the church of Onze Lieve Vrouw. The battle, the first occasion on which ordinary citizens defeated mail-clad knights, is important in medieval military and social history as marking the beginning of the end for chivalry.

Kortrijk's long association with flax is recorded at the *Nationaal Vlasmuseum* at 4 E. Sabbelaan in the SE outskirts beyond the motorway ring (March–October: daily except mornings of Tuesday, Saturday, Sunday, 09.30 to 12.30, 13.30 to 18.00). Here, in a restored 19C flax farmhouse, period rooms and a series of tableaux tell the story from cultivation through to weaving.

Kortrijk is left by the Gentsesteenweg, at the edge of the town on the N side of the road being a memorial, in the form of a moose, to Newfoundlanders who fell in Belgium in 1914–18.—*4km* **Harelbeke**, in a flax- and tobacco-growing district, has an 18C Neo-Classical church and a detached 11C Romanesque tower, part of the earlier church; badly damaged in 1940, the tower was rebuilt in 1954 and later given a carillon of 50 bells. Opposite the old town hall (1764), a statue commemorates Pierre Benoît (1834–1901), the composer, who was born here and who was active in trying to establish a distinctive Flemish style in music. At Harelbeke, Rte 12 bears southeast.—The border into East Flanders is crossed at (*8km*) *Sint Eloois-Vijve*—*11km Pettegem* (**Deinze**) straddles the Lys. From here there is a choice of roads. For the road N of the river (Deinze, and the château of Ooidonk), see Rte 5. This Rte continues S of the river to (*5km*) **Deurle**, a scattered village in woods beside the Lys which has become an elegant residential, gastronomic and art centre, this last because Deurle was popular with the painters of two successive schools who settled around the village of Sint Martens-Latem (3km NE). The first school (Symbolists, c 1905) included George Minne and Gustave van de Woestyne; the second school (Expressionists, c 1910) Constant Permeke, Gustave de Smet and Frits van den Berghe. At Deurle, works by these and other artists can be seen at three museums. The *Museum Gust de Smet* (March–November: daily except Monday, 10.00 to 12.00, 14.00 to 18.00 or 16.00 during the first half of March), at 1 Gust de Smetlaan, is the house which the artist built in 1935 and in which he lived until his death here in 1943. Virtually unchanged, the house shows many of its owner's works. The *Museum Leon de Smet* (Sunday, 10.00 to 12.00, 14.00 to 18.00. Tuesday, Wednesday, Thursday, Saturday, 14.00 to 18.00), at 18 Museumlaan, shows works by this artist, together with memorabilia and documentation; and thirdly, there is the purpose-built *Museum Mevouw J. Dhondt-Dhaenens* (March–November: Wednesday–Friday, 14.00 to 17.00 or 18.00 in May–September. Saturday, Sunday, Holidays, 10.00 to 12.00, 14.00 to 17.00), the gift, with their private collection, of Jules and Irma Dhondt-Dhaenens. Virtually every representative of 19C Flemish art has a place here. Finally, at Sint Martens-Latem itself, the *Museum Minne-Gevaert* (Wednesday–Sunday, 15.00 to 18.00), at 45 Kapitteldreef, shows works by George Minne in a house built in 1922 by his son-in-law.—*5km* **Sint Denijs-Westrem**, with Ghent's airport just N of the Ostend–Brussels motorway. At *Afsnee*, just W of the airport, there is a particularly interesting small church (Sint Jan), successor to a foundation of 945 or earlier and notable for its early 13C octagonal tower.—*4km* **Ghent**, see Rte 13.

12 Kortrijk (Courtrai) via Oudenaarde and Ronse to Brussels

Total distance 81km.—*4km* **Harelbeke**.—*15km Kerkhove*.—*9km* **Oudenaarde** or **Ronse**.—*13km* **Brakel**.—*8km Ophasselt* (with diversions N to **Zottegem** and S to **Geraardsbergen**).—*10km* **Ninove**.—*22km* **Brussels**.

For **Kortrijk** and (*4km*) **Harelbeke**, see Rte 11. At Harelbeke this Rte bears SE to reach (*2km*) *Deerlijk* where the church contains an early 16C altarpiece with scenes from the life of St. Columba.—At (*13km*) *Kerkhove* the river Scheldt (Escaut) is reached. Here there is a choice of roads, both roughly the same distance, northwards through Oudenaarde (*9km*) or southwards through Ronse (*9km*), the two roads meeting at Brakel. The two towns, 10km apart and both in the province of East Flanders, are linked by N60. Both places well merit a visit.

Oudenaarde (Fr. **Audenarde**. 28,000 inhab. Tourist Information: Stadhuis), on the Scheldt, is perhaps most associated with Marlborough's victory of 1708. Although today a busy textiles and brewing town, this aspect is little apparent in the town centre where the huge Grote Markt, the many elegant old buildings, and the open areas beside the river combine to convey an impression of calm and spaciousness.

The name means 'old earth' or 'old landing place' and it is known that there was a settlement here by Roman times. It is also known that St. Amandus preached in Pamele, the district E of the river, in 613, and that under the Treaty of Verdun (843) the settlement was split, either side of the river, between Lower Lotharingia and West Francia. In the early 11C however this whole area fell to the counts of Flanders and it was not long before a town began to grow around their castle which in 1030 was the scene of the first meeting of the States of Flanders. A charter granted in 1193 gave an impetus to trade, especially in cloth, and by the 15C Oudenaarde was famous for its tapestry, a craft which however had died out by the late 17C. Margaret of Parma, governor of the Netherlands from 1560–67, was born here in 1522, the illegitimate daughter of Charles V and his mistress Joanna van der Gheynst, who came from Nukerke (5km S). The painter Adriaen Brouwer was also born here (1605). In 1708, during the War of the Spanish Succession, Marlborough defeated the French here, the battle being fought mainly to the N and NW of the town. In 1745 (War of the Austrian Succession) the French took the town and dismantled its fortifications.

The town centre is the large GROTE MARKT, at the N end of which stands the beautiful **Stadhuis, successor to a Romanesque building burnt by a carnival mob in 1525. It was built in c 1525–36 by the Brussels architect Hendrik van Pede in Flamboyant Gothic style; the sculptured façade is supported by an arcade with a projecting porch, and in the centre rises a tower with a cupola in the shape of a crown, above which stands the gilded figure of Hanske de Krijge (Little John the Warrior) waving a banner bearing the town's arms. The fountain in front was presented by Louis XIV in 1675. At the rear extends the rectangular Romanesque *Halle* (13C with 17C alterations). The main feature of the Stadhuis interior is the carving by Paul van der Schelden, notably chimneypieces and a magnificent oak *Doorway (1531) with 28 panels; a measure of the merit of this is that reproductions are exhibited in the Louvre in Paris and in the Victoria and Albert in London. Within the Stadhuis and Halle are archives dating from 1200; tapestries; paintings, notably by Adriaen Brouwer; guild material; local archaeological finds; seals and coins, etc. (April–October: daily except Friday afternoon. Guided tours at 09.00, 10.00, 11.00, 14.00, 15.00, 16.00. No 09.00 tour on Saturday, Sunday, Holidays. Tour lasts one hour).

The *Archeologisch Museum*, showing mainly local prehistoric, Carolingian and medieval material, is at 9 Hoogstraat, the street to the NW of the Stadhuis (Thursday, 09.00 to 12.00; Saturday, Sunday, 14.00 to 18.00), while in the *Liedtskasteel* (1883), in the park of the same name some 300m NE, there is a more general regional museum (Monday–Friday, 09.00 to 12.00, 14.00 to 17.00. Sunday, 14.00 to 18.00). Hoogstraat, followed N, ends at Tacambaroplein, where a monument of 1867 remembers volunteers from Oudenaarde who fell in Mexico fighting for the ill-fated Emperor Maximilian, son-in-law of Leopold I. Also in this square are an American war memorial, a local war memorial, and a memorial to the deportees of the First World War.

The *Sint Walburgakerk*, off the SW corner of the Grote Markt, dates from two periods, the choir being of the 12–14C and the nave (Jan van Ruysbroeck) and apse of the 15–16C. The spire was burnt in 1804, since when the tower has ended in its bell-shaped lantern. The interior contains Oudenaarde tapestries; a triptych (Trinity) by the local artist Simon de Paepe; screens by Luc Fayd'herbe; and, in the choir, a monument to four Catholic priests murdered in 1572 by being thrown into the Scheldt (see also below). To the N of the church the *Hospital* (of Onze Lieve Vrouw), founded in the 12C, dates mainly from the 17th and 18C but preserves a 13–14C chapel. To the S of the church, across the road, are the *Boudewijnstoren*, a relic of the 11–13C fortifications and possibly even of the early castle, and, alongside, the early 16C *Huis van Margareta van Parma* in which Margaret may have been born.

From the SW of the Grote Markt, Burgstraat, continued by Kasteelstraat, leads to the river, at the junction of these two streets being the mellow 17C portal of the Begijnhof, founded during the 13C. The Scheldt bridge is 150m to the NE; immediately to the left across the bridge, the name 'Bourgondiestraat' recalls that here stood the Burgundian castle built in 1385 by Philip the Bold. Louis XI of France took refuge in this castle during his exile in c 1460, and it was from the castle windows in 1572 that the Protestants threw the four Catholic priests whose monument is in the church of Sint Walburga. The *Huis de Lalaing* (c 1717), at 9 Bourgondiestraat close to the law courts, has a tapestry centre (restorations) and also shows works by local artists (Monday–Friday, 09.00 to 11.30, 14.00 to 16.00 or later).

To the SW, on this side of the Scheldt, stands the *Onze Lieve Vrouwekerk* (of Pamele, the ancient name of this district), a Scheldt Gothic building started in 1234 and largely completed in only four years; the N transept is 14C and there are two chapels of the 16C. The church was founded and largely designed by Arnulf de Binche, a monk and the first master-builder in Belgium to be known by name (plaque in Latin on the outside wall of the choir). Inside the church, where some of the pillars and walls have taken alarming angles, there are paintings by Simon de Paepe and Jan Snellinck, and also the tombs of two lords of Pamele and their wives (1504 and 1616).

The NE suburb of **Ename**, an early fortress of the German emperors and until the 11C a prosperous trading centre, was taken by Count Baldwin IV in 1002 and its

castle demolished by Baldwin V in 1047, much of the town's trading activity then
moving to Oudenaarde.

Ronse (Renaix. 25,000 inhab. Tourist Information: Stadhuis, Grote
Markt), a pleasant place mainly concerned with textiles, lies along the
line of hills sometimes known as the Flemish Ardennes. The road from
the Scheldt (from Kerkhove) passes between two of the higher points,
Kluisberg (S 140m) and *Hotondberg* (N 150m), the latter with an
orientation table. The *Mont de l'Enclus* (S 141m) is another high point
offering an extensive view. Ronse is just within East Flanders, but the
Hainaut province border is barely 1km away and the town is
bilingual.

In the MARKT stands an *Obelisk*, erected in 1815 and originally
surmounted by the initial W for William I of the United Kingdom of the
Netherlands. The W was removed during the revolution of 1830 (it is
now in the museum) and later replaced by the Habsburg eagle and
the arms of the town. The *Stadhuis* (Frank Blockx), also on the Markt,
is a 1953 reconstruction in the 16C Spanish style. Out of the N of the
Markt, Hospitaalstraat leads into Priesterstraat, at the end of which is
the *Sint Hermeskerk*, a late Gothic building of the 15–16C with a high
W tower. Hermes was a Roman martyr of c 270 who was known as an
exorcist; in c 855 his relics were given by Pope Leo IV to Lothair (of
Lower Lotharingia) who in turn gave them to Ronse where they
became an objective of pilgrimage and accepted as a cure for lunacy.
Today the embroidered 17C reliquary of the saint, shown as an
equestrian figure leading a chained demon, is in the S choir chapel; a
statue with the same theme stands above, and in a niche opposite the
altar the iron rings in an old bench were used for securing the
demented pending exorcism. A main feature of the church is the large
Romanesque crypt; dating from 1089, it was restored in 1267,
enlarged and again restored in 1518, and is still used for worship
(Daily except Tuesday and Wednesday, 09.00 to 12.30, 14.30 to 18.00).

Outside the church, beside the N wall, can be seen part of the
foundations of the church of *Sint Pieter*, built in c 1100, enlarged in 1510
and demolished in 1843; hedges trace out the lines of the cloister.

Adjacent, beside the pleasant Bruul Park, are the town's two
museums. The *Stedelijk Museum* (Folklore and regional history.
Daily except Tuesday and Wednesday, 09.00 to 12.30, 14.30 to 18.00),
occupying former canon's houses of the second half of the 18C, offers
period rooms with pictures by local artists; a room devoted to
distinguished citizens of Ronse and its district; a room with guilds
material; some prehistoric archaeological material; a Folklore
section; and instructive glimpses of old crafts (weaving, basket
making, shuttle making, clogs, printing, the local inn and suchlike).
Alongside is the *Textiel Museum* (same times) providing a survey of
the local textiles industry from 1800 to 1950.

The *Station*, in the S of the town, is interesting for having been
originally at Bruges, whence it was transferred brick by brick and
rebuilt here. In front stands the figure of 'Bonmos', symbol of the local
'Fools' Monday' (Saturday after Epiphany) carnival.

13km **Brakel** is where the roads from Oudenaarde and Ronse
meet.—*8km Ophasselt*, from where diversions of interest may be
made both N and south.

NORTH. **Zottegem**, 7km NW of Ophasselt, is an industrial town
(25,000 inhab.) which was once a fief of the counts of Egmont; in the
vault below the church are buried Lamoral, the patriot victim of Alva,

his wife and his two sons. What is left of the family château is largely rebuilding of the 19C.—The château of *Leeuwergem* (groups only; by appointment), 2km NE of Zottegem, was built in 1724 as successor to a 12C castle.

SOUTH. **Geraardsbergen** (**Grammont**. 30,000 inhab. Tourist Information: Stadhuis), 5km S of Ophasselt, is an ancient small town lying below the *Oudeberg* (113m), the steep slope of which (the 'Mur de Grammont') is well known in cycle-racing circles. The *Stadhuis* is in origin 14C, but of this period little survives and today's building is mainly 18C. Outside are the 15C *Marbol* (market cross) and a copy of *Manneken-Pis*, presented by the city of Brussels in 1745. The much-altered but in origin 15C *Sint Bartholomeuskerk* has attached to it a chapel, formerly a separate building, the lower part of which is of the 13C. Inside the church there is marble work of 1770 by Pieter Pepers and also a painting (Martyrdom of St. Bartholomew) by De Crayer. Signs ('Tourist Centre') from the Markt lead N to the former abbey of *Sint Adriaan* on the slope of the Oudeberg. The grounds have been converted into public gardens and a children's playground, while the buildings contain a museum (Easter–October: Monday–Friday, 08.30 to 12.00, 13.30 to 17.00. Saturday, Sunday, Holidays, 14.00 to 18.00) with local material, including portraits of abbots.

10km (from Ophasselt) **Ninove**(33,000 inhab.). Here the *Onze Lieve Vrouwekerk* is all that survives of the abbey of SS. Cornelius and Cyprian, founded in 1137, disestablished in 1796, its domestic buildings demolished in 1822. In Baroque style, the church dates from 1660–1723, with a tower which was added in 1844; it is known for the richness of its Baroque interior, most of the work being by the three best sculptors of the day: Theodoor Verhaeghen, J.B. van der Haeghen and Jacques Bergé. In the street called Vestbaan, c 200m SE of the church, the *Koepoort* is the town's only surviving 14C gate.

The road crosses into the province of Brabant to reach (*6km*) the village of *Onze Lieve Vrouw Lombeek*, just S of the road, where the 13–14C church is known for its superb *Retable of the Virgin.—6km* **Schepdaal**where the *Musée du Tram* (or *Musée Vicinal*. April–October: Sunday, Holidays, 14.00 to 18.00; in July and August, also Saturday) records the story of the tramways and light railways of Belgium; located in a typical country tram depot of 1888, the museum shows around 30 vehicles.

The château of **Gaasbeek** is 5km south. First built in the 13C, the place was destroyed by the citizens of Brussels after the murder of Everard 't Serclaes in 1387. Rebuilt, it lasted until 1545 when it was converted from castle to château; there were further additions and restorations during the 18th and 19C, and in 1921 Gaasbeek became state property and a museum. The interior contains notable tapestries (Brussels, 16th and 17C. Tournai, 15C. English, 17C); furniture; ceramic of the 15C and 16C; a large variety of valuable objets·d'art; and pictures, outstanding among which are a Tower of Babel by Martin van Valekenborgh, which once belonged to Rubens, and a portrait of the Countess of Dorset by Van Dyck (April–October: daily, except Monday and Friday, 10.00 to 17.00. In July and August also open Monday).

10km **Brussels**, see Rte 1.

13 Ghent

GHENT (235,000 inhab.) is the English name for the Flemish town of **Gent**(Fr. *Gand*), the capital of the province of East Flanders. Although a major industrial complex served by one of Europe's largest inland ports, Ghent is also a leading tourist town, notable for its historical background as principal seat of the counts of Flanders as also for its museums, its medieval quarters, its massive castle, and its splendid cathedral within which is the Van Eyck masterpiece, the 'Adoration of the Mystic Lamb'. The town sprawls across waterways, notably the rivers Lieve and Lys (Leie) in the centre and the Scheldt to the south. The first two, in many places forming islands, do much to enhance the attraction of the town's medieval aspects.

Ghent claims also the title of 'City of Flowers', surrounded as it is by nurseries, devoted largely to azaleas, rhododendrons and begonias; the internationally known 'Floralies' pageant is staged here every five years (1990).

Centre. Sint Baafskathedraal—Koornmarkt.

Tourist Information. *Ghent*: Stadhuis (crypt). April–October: daily, 09.00 to 20.00 or 21.00 on Friday and Saturday. November–March: daily 09.00 to 12.00, 14.00 to 17.00. *Province of East Flanders*: 64 Koningin Maria Hendrikaplein (opposite Sint Pieters station).

Post Office. Koornmarkt.

Stations. *Sint Pieters*, in the SW of the town c 2.5km from the centre, for all main-line services. Public transport connects with the centre, passing close to Bijloke and Fine Arts (Schone Kunsten) museums. *Dampoort*, in the N of the town, c 1.5km from the centre, for local services to Eeklo, Zelzate, Antwerp.

Ways to see the Town. *On Foot*. Guided walks. April–September except July: Saturday, Sunday, Holidays, at 14.30 from Tourist Information. Duration at least two hours.—*Horse-drawn Carriage*. April–September: from Sint Baafsplein. Standard tour c 35 minutes.—*Public Transport*. Free, using Tourist Card.—*Boat*. Inner town waterways tours from Koornlei and Graslei. Frequent departures roughly Easter–October. Duration c 35 minutes. Also Lys (Leie) excursions from Recollettenlei (5 hours, May–September); and Bruges, also from Recollettenlei (11 hours including two in Bruges, July and August).—*Private Car*. Not generally practicable, though it is worth noting that there is parking at both the Museum voor Schone Kunsten (Fine Arts) and the Bijloke Museum.

Horticulture. The principal horticultural districts, with begonias at their best July–September, are *De Pinte* (8km SW); *Merelbeke* (5km S); *Lochristi* (8km NE); and *Laarne* (8km SE, with a château).

History. The two 7C abbeys of St. Baaf and St. Pieter, the later buildings of both of which still survive, were probably the nucleus of the first settlement here, this growing into a riverside village round the castle built by Baldwin Iron Arm c 867, at the confluence of the Lieve and the Lys, for defence against the raiding Norsemen. Thus Ghent became the seat of the counts of Flanders. During the 11C and 12C the counts' castle was enlarged and strengthened, and during the 13C much land was reclaimed and the Ghent to Bruges canal dug. The cloth industry early became important and by the end of the 13C Ghent was larger than Paris. It was also during the 13C that the enmity between the nobles, generally loyal to their suzerain, the French king, and the wealthy and ambitious citizens came to a head. The town had been granted charters by the counts in c 1180, 1191, and in 1212, this last introducing the election of magistrates, hitherto nominated. Despite these charters, prosperity brought increasing assertion of independence and in 1302 a contingent from Ghent, led by Jan Borluut, played its part in the Battle of the Golden Spurs. In 1338 (at the start of the Hundred Years War, when the count sided with France against England, this endangering the cloth trade) Jacob van Artevelde (1287–1345), a noble who supported the merchants, made himself master of the town, entering into an alliance with England's Edward III, whose third son, John of Gaunt (Ghent), was born here (in the abbey of Sint Baaf) in 1340. Both Ghent and the wool-growers of England prospered, but in 1345 Van Artevelde was murdered by guildsmen who mistrusted his ambition. His son Philip (1340–82) took his father's place in 1381 and inflicted a severe defeat on the pro-French Count Louis de Male; however, the following year Charles VI of France came to his vassal's assistance, crushing the rebels and killing Van Artevelde at Westrozebeke. Two years later (1384) Louis de Male died, and, because of the marriage between his daughter and heiress and Philip of Burgundy, Flanders ceased to exist as a separate state and the Burgundian period began.

Under the Burgundians the town again revolted, but after five years of struggle (1448–53) was subdued and subjected (by Philip the Good) to a humiliating limitation of privileges. However, on the death of Philip's son (Charles the Bold) in 1477, the citizens held Charles' daughter Mary virtually prisoner, forcing her to sign the Great Privilege which conferred a liberal constitution. On Mary's death, Flanders passed to her widower, Maximilian of Austria, who subdued the towns, his grandson, Charles V, being born in Ghent in 1500. By this time the cloth industry had been ruined by English competition, but, helped by the growing prosperity of Antwerp, Ghent found a new source of wealth in the export of grain from France via the Lys and Scheldt, the boatmen replacing the clothworkers as the leading guild. The canal to Terneuzen was first dug in 1547, and, thanks to this forwarding and carrying trade, and to a revival of the tapestry industry, Ghent continued to flourish in the 16C, when Bruges and Ypres were already in decay.

Ghent supported Charles V (Charles Quint) at the opening of his reign, but later refused to pay taxes for his military adventures in France. Charles's reaction (1540) was swift and effective. He crushed the rising, abolished the town's privileges, filled in the moat, and built a new citadel (on the site of the abbey of Sint Baaf) at the town's expense. During the succeeding years Ghent, like other towns, was involved in the religious disturbances. In 1561 the bishopric was established by Philip II, while the consequent excesses by the Calvinist iconoclasts in 1566 were soon punished with ferocity by Alva. In 1576, on the death of Requesens (Alva's successor as governor), William of Orange marched into Flanders and occupied Ghent, the Pacification of Ghent (trying to secure religious freedom and the withdrawal of Spanish soldiery from the Netherlands) being signed in November. This period lasted under ten years, and by 1585 Philip II's governor, Parma, had reconquered Ghent and most of what makes up today's Belgium. The United Provinces were, however, able to close the Scheldt (until the French occupation of all the Netherlands in 1794), and in consequence Ghent went into commercial decline.

In 1814 Ghent was the scene of the signing of the treaty which ended the Anglo-USA war of 1812–14, and in 1815 the fugitive Louis XVIII, accompanied by Chateaubriand and other royalists, took refuge here during the 'Hundred Days'. The town shared in the industrial growth of the 19C, dating its modern prosperity from the introduction of cotton-spinning in 1799; this it owes to Lieven Bauwens (1769–1822), a local tanner, who smuggled machinery and workmen out of England and set up the first Belgian cotton-mill in the buildings of the recently dissolved abbey of Drongen. A great boost to prosperity was given in 1822–27 when the 16C canal to Terneuzen (in Holland) on the Scheldt estuary was replaced by a large canal capable of taking sea-going vessels, this also giving Ghent a large new maritime port.

Natives and Others. The best known native is probably John of Gaunt (Ghent). Others named after the town were the theologian Henry of Ghent ('Doctor Solemnis'; c 1217–93) and the painter Justus van Gent. The brothers Jan and Hubert van Eyck rank as the greatest of the many painters who worked here. Distinguished natives include Lucas de Heere (1534–84), painter and poet; Daniel Heinsius (1580–1655), one of the leading scholars of the Dutch Renaissance, and Maurice Maeterlinck (1862–1949), author and winner in 1911 of the Nobel prize for literature. Two saints are also associated with Ghent. St. Amand (c 584–c 675) was a Flemish monk who founded several monasteries, including two in Ghent and one near Tournai. St. Baaf (or Bavo, or Bavon, died c 655), a native of Brabant, was converted by St. Amand and ended his days as a hermit in Ghent.

Ghent is described in four parts: A. Central Ghent, which includes the Cathedral, the Belfry, the Castle of the Counts, and the medieval district; B. Southern Ghent, with the Bijloke and Schone Kunsten (Fine Arts) museums; C. Eastern Ghent, with the Klein Begijnhof and the ruined Abbey of Sint Baaf; and D. the Port of Ghent and the Terneuzen canal.

A. Central Ghent

The round described below covers a distance of rather over 2km, or 4km if the extension N and W of 's Gravensteen is included.

**Sint Baafskathedraal, one of the most splendid churches in Belgium, is celebrated for its works of art, notably the famous Van Eyck 'Adoration of the Mystic Lamb'. (*Cathedral*, '*Mystic Lamb*' and *Crypt*: April–September: Monday–Saturday, 09.30 to 12.00, 14.00 to 18.00. Sunday and Holidays, 13.00 to 18.00. October–March: Monday–Saturday, 10.30 to 12.00, 14.30 to 16.00. Sunday and Holidays, 14.00 to 17.00. Fee for 'Mystic Lamb' and Crypt.)

It is known that a chapel dedicated to St. John the Baptist stood here in 941, and that during the 12C this gave way to a Romanesque church. Towards the end of the 13C this in turn began to give way to today's Gothic church, only the central part of the Romanesque crypt surviving. The choir dates mainly from c 1290–1310; the transepts, nave and aisles, started during the 15C, were completed by c 1550; the W tower (82m) rose between c 1460 and 1554. The seventh chapter of the Order of the Golden Fleece was held here in 1445 by Philip the Good, and the twenty-third by Philip II in 1559. Charles V was baptised here in 1500. In 1540, as part of his reprisals for the town's revolt, Charles demolished much of the abbey of St. Baaf to make way for a fortress, the abbey chapter then being transferred to this church, the dedication of which to St. John was at the same time changed to St. Baaf. In 1561 Philip II declared Ghent a bishopric. Iconoclasts did much damage in 1566 and 1576, and after the latter occasion the cathedral was used for Protestant worship for nearly ten years.

The beautifully proportioned interior is remarkable for the richness and variety of its decoration; noticeable also is the difference between the 13–14C choir, with its grey-blue Tournai stone, and the 16C white stone remainder of the church.—In the NAVE the carved oak and marble pulpit (1745) is by Laurent Delvaux; the aisles show paintings by Gaspard de Crayer and Abraham Janssens; and in the N transept hang works by Theodoor Rombouts and Michiel Coxie.—The CHOIR is embellished with sumptuous marble screens, the gift of Bishop Triest (died 1657), who did much to restore the church after the destruction by the iconoclasts and whose tomb, by Duquesnoy the Younger, on the N side, is the finest of the four episcopal monuments that flank the high-altar. The tomb of Bishop Allamont (died 1673) is by Jean Del Cour. In front are four copper candlesticks, by Benedetto da Rovezzano, bearing the arms of England's Henry VIII, for whose tomb at Windsor they were originally executed, and of Bishop Triest, who presented them to the church after they had been sold by Cromwell. On the altar the statue of St. Baaf is by Hendrik Verbruggen (1719).

The AMBULATORY, with its many chapels, is described from the S transept, in which are the hatchments of the Knights of the Golden Fleece. Some of the chapels contain notable works of art. 1st Chapel: *Christ among the doctors, a masterpiece by Frans Pourbus the Elder, in which are included portraits of Charles V, Philip II, the Duke of Alva, Viglius ab Aytta (died 1577, chief secretary of Charles V and Philip II), and Jansenius (died 1576), first bishop of Ghent. On the wings are the Circumcision and the Baptism of Christ, and on the exterior another portrait of Viglius, whose tomb is opposite. 2nd Chapel: Martyrdom of St. Barbara by Gaspard de Crayer. 4th Chapel: Tombs of bishops. 6th Chapel: It was to this chapel, in 1422, that Joos Vydt presented the painting The Adoration˚ of the Mystic Lamb,

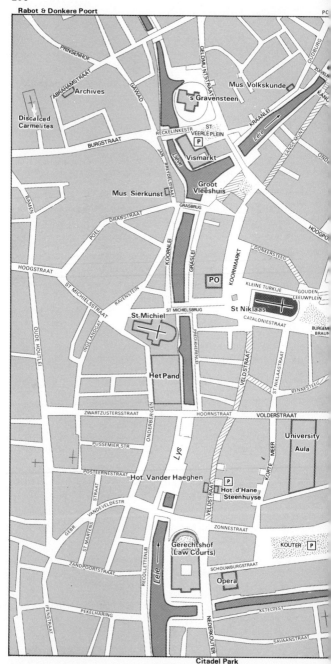

Library
(Baudelo)

BAUDELOOSTRAAT

OTTOGRACHT

STRAAT

BIBLIOTHEEK

BAUDELOO KAAI

REKE

HAMHAM

STEENDAM

Vrijdagmarkt
P

St Jacob

Toreken

VLASMARKT

KAMMERSTRAAT

NIEUWPOORT

RAAT

BORLUUTSTRAAT

KONINGSTRAAT

Royal Flemish Acad.

VOLMOLENSTRAAT

ZANDBERG

BAASTEEG

ST JACOBS NIEUWSTRAAT

GILDESTRAAT

dhuis

BOTERMARKT

St Jorishof

NEDERPOLDER

KWAADHAM

Abb. St Baaf & Dampoort Sta.

th
l

BEER STRAAT

KAPEL

Theatre

ST BAAFSPLEIN
P

St Baaf

REEP

KEIZER

fry

HENEGOUENENST

LIMBURGSTRAAT

Geraard
Duivelsteen

SEMINARIESTRAAT

KAREL

ORANJIBERG

GOUVERNEMENTSTRAAT

L. BAUWENSPLEIN

WINKELSTRAAT

BOOMGAARDSTR

ELEGRADOS IKKAY

STRAAT

JODENSTRAAT

TOJSTRAAT

LANGE

VLAANDERENSTRAAT

BRABANTDAM

BURG
LIPPENSPLEIN

BRABANTDAM

ABEEL

N

WAJDOORISTRAAT

KUIPERSKAAI

STATION
STR

GHENT
Centre

0 metres   100

PRES
WILSON
PLEIN

Koning Albert Park

which he had commissioned from the Van Eyck brothers. For reasons of space and security the masterpiece is now (though perhaps temporarily) shown in a special room at the W end of the N aisle (see below). 7th Chapel. Bronze doors of 1633. Pietà by Gerard Honthorst. 9th Chapel. Glorification of the Virgin by Niklaas de Liemakere. 10th Chapel. *St. Baaf entering the Abbey of St. Amand (or, The Conversion of St. Baaf) by Rubens (1624). The saint has distributed his belongings among the poor; his wife, with two followers, is seen on the left. The bearded head is a portrait of Rubens. Also in this chapel are Raising of Lazarus, by Otto Venius, and an alabaster tomb of Bishop Damant (died 1609). 11th Chapel: Martyrdom of St. Livinius, by Gerard Seghers. Last Chapel: Seven Works of Mercy, by Michiel Coxie.

The large CRYPT was begun c 1150 and extended laterally when the present choir was built (c 1300); the crown of five chapels to the E was added c 1400. The mural paintings (discovered in 1936) are of 1480–1540. Of the 26 bishops of Ghent, all bar five are buried here. The chapels contain tombs of patrician families, the oldest being the monument of Margaret de Gistel (died 1431), in the SE chapel.—Part of the Treasury is displayed in the crypt in summer, this including reliquaries, vestments, documents, illuminated manuscripts, and a particularly good display of lace (catalogue available). Among the pictures are triptychs by Frans Francken the Elder and Justus van Gent, and also the Story of St. Andrew, in a series of 14 paintings by Frans Pourbus the Elder.

The **ADORATION OF THE MYSTIC LAMB, a polyptych altarpiece ranking as chief among the masterpieces of the Early Flemish School, is renowned for the delicacy and integrity of its crowded detail.

The work was painted for Joos Vydt, a rich patrician, who presented it to one of the choir ambulatory chapels (see above) in 1432. The orthodox view is that it was designed and partly painted by Hubert van Eyck, and finished by his brother Jan van Eyck; but doubt has been cast on the existence of Hubert, by whom there are no known signed paintings. The work has survived many adventures. Philip II coveted it, and in 1566 it narrowly escaped destruction by Calvinist iconoclasts. During the 18C, the prudish Joseph II took exception to the naked Adam and Eve, placing them in the museum in Brussels and substituting the clothed versions which may now be seen at the W end of the nave. During the French Revolution the picture was removed to Paris, whence it returned in 1815. The outer wings were then sold to the Berlin Museum, their place being taken by 16C copies by Michiel Coxie. The wings were restored under the Treaty of Versailles (1919). In 1934 the panel with the Just Judges was stolen. It has never been found, and in 1941 was replaced by a copy made then by Jef Vanderveken; so good is this, but so anxious was the painter that his work should never be thought to be part of the original, that he included the features of Leopold III. Soon afterwards the painting was removed by the Germans, spending the remainder of the war in an Austrian salt mine. Returned after the war, it was replaced in its chapel, remaining there until moved to its present home.

The central theme is the Mystic Lamb, adored by angels, redeeming the world from original sin. In the foreground, on either side of the Fountain of Life, are patriarchs and prophets (left) and apostles and confessors (right); in the background are processions of bishops and virgins. The landscape is clear and accurate, and botanists have identified over 40 of the plants. The wings represent (left) knights and just judges (the latter a copy, see above), and (right) hermits and pilgrims moving towards the scene of sacrifice; these groups abound in contemporary portraits. On the wings are also the towers of New Jerusalem (said to be in fact those of Bruges, Utrecht, Cologne, and

Maastricht). In the upper portion is Christ in Majesty between the Virgin and St. John the Baptist, with angels, singers, and musicians on the wings; on the outer wings, Adam and Eve with Cain and Abel above them. On the back of the shutters are portraits of the donor and his wife, an Annunciation, and statues of prophets and sibyls. Some of these may have been the work of pupils.

Just E of the cathedral, beside an arm of the Scheldt, stands the **Gerard Duivelsteen** (reopened after long term restoration; times from Tourist Information); dating from 1245 and with a fine Romanesque undercroft, this is a good example of one of the private fortresses built by the nobles of this period. In later years the building was used as an armoury, a school, a seminary, a mental hospital, a prison, an orphanage, a fire station, and, recently, for archives. Adjacent there are monuments to Jan and Hubert van Eyck (George Verbanck, 1913) and to Lieven Bauwens (P.P. de Vigne-Quyo, 1885).

The open space immediately W of the cathedral is SINT BAAFS-PLEIN, with a statue by Isidoor de Rudder of Jan Frans Willems (1793–1846), father of the Flemish nationalist movement. To the N the little Biezerkapelstraat leads to some attractive old houses (p 210). Also on the N side stands the *Nederlandse Schouwburg* (Netherlands Theatre), built in Renaissance style in 1899. The W side of the square is occupied by the Lakenhalle and Belfry. Though these now stand clear, this has been so only since the beginning of this century, and historically they should be pictured hemmed close in by crowded narrow streets.

The **Lakenhalle** (Cloth Hall), dating from 1425, has a vaulted undercroft today serving as a restaurant. The large hall on the first floor is generally used for an audio-visual presentation on Ghent and its past, the presentation lasting about 20 minutes and being in four languages (Flemish, French, English and German) in rotation throughout the day.

The **Belfort** (Belfry. Guided visits only. May–October: Monday–Thursday, 10.30 for English or French) was built between 1321 and 1380, but has several times been modified. The spire, restored to its original form in 1913, is topped by a dragon in gilded copper, made in Ghent in 1378 though legend insists that it was carried off by the men of Ghent from Bruges whither it had been brought from Const-antinople during the Fourth Crusade. Built on to the Belfry is the former lock-up and gaoler's house ('t Kindt, 1741), popularly known as the 'Mammelokker' (suckling) from the relief on the façade. In the vaulted ground floor room, which from 1402–1550 housed the iron chest in which were held the charters of the privileges of Ghent, can be seen the sole survivor of the four stone armed figures of 1338 that once stood at the belfry's corners. Other rooms contain general material on the belfry and its history, while above are the 52 bells, 37 of which were cast in 1660 by Pieter Hemony of Zutphen. Most of the others are 18C, but the largest (6050 kg; 1948) replaces one (called 'Roelant'), cast in 1318, and its successor 'Triomfante' (Hemony, 1660). The original 'Roelant' was once taken down by order of Charles V after being convicted of 'having played a very turbulent part with its tongue' during the uprising against him. 'Triomfante' cracked in 1914 and now stands in Burgemeester Braunplein, immediately W of the belfry. Nearby stands also a fountain with kneeling figures ('Youth', 1892) by George Minne.

The **Stadhuis** (guided visits only; May–October: Monday–Thursday, afternoons), occupying the corner of Botermarkt and

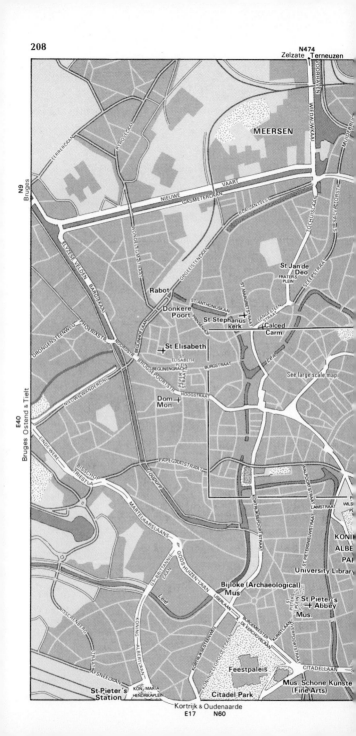

MEERSEN

N474
Zelzate Terneuzen

N9
Bruges

E40
Bruges Ostend & Tielt

Rabot

Donkere
Poort

St Jan de
Deo
FRATERS
PLEIN

St Stephanus
Kerk

Calced
Carm

St Elisabeth

Dom
Mon

BURGSTRAAT

See large scale map.

PAPEGAAISTRAAT

Bijloke (Archaeological)
Mus

KONI
ALBE
PAR
University Library

St Pieter's
Abbey
Mus

Feestpaleis

Citadel Park

Mus Schone Kunste
(Fine Arts)

CITADELLAAN

St-Pieter's
Station

KON. MARIA
HENDRIKAPLEIN

Kortrijk & Oudenaarde
E17   N60

GHENT
& Environs

0 metres   600

R4
Zelzate Terneuzen
GROOTDOK

BELLEVUE

GRONDWETLAAN
STEENWEG

N

N70
Antwerp

AFRIKALAAN
TOONVAARDOLAAN

GENTSTRAAT
ANTWERPSE

V. BRAECKMANLAAN

HANDELSDOK
STAPELPLEIN

KOOPVAARDIJLAAN
ACHTERDOK
DOK ZUID

Groot
Begijnhof

SINT-AMANDSBERG

DAMPOORTSTR

ANTWERPEN
PLEIN
Dampoort
Sta.

KASTEELLAAN

DENDERMONDSE STEENWEG

Abb. St Baaf

DRILOKESTRAAT

DENDERMONDSE STEENWEG

HEIRNISLAAN

LOUSBERGKAAI

KASTEELLAAN

VISSERIJ
PLUGGENSTRAAT

Klein Begijnhof

VIOLETTENSTRAAT

KERKSTRAAT

VLAAMSEKAAI
Scheldt

BRUSSELSEPOORTSTR

OUDE BRUSSELSEWEG

KEIZERSVEST

E3

SLAAN

LEDEBERG

BRUSSELSE STEENWEG

ijk & Antwerp   Ostend & Brussels
E17   E40

Aalst
N9

Hoogstraat 100m N of the belfry, first came to this site in 1321 when the aldermen had to move from their previous room, razed to make way for the belfry. Of this 14C building all that survives are two vaulted rooms in the basement. Today's building comprises two distinct parts. The N front, facing Hoogpoort and rounding the corner into Botermarkt, is a rich example of Flamboyant Gothic (1518–c 1560) by Rombout Keldermans and Domien de Waghemakere, while the E façade of c 1581, in a soberer style, reflects the Calvinist regime of that period. The sections facing the Stadhuissteeg and the Poelje-markt were added during the 17th and 18C.

The interior includes several fine halls. The *Pacificatiezaal*, with painted arms of the governors of Flanders and a curious 'maze' paving, was where the Pacification of Ghent was signed in 1576. The *Trouwzaal* (Marriage Room) was formerly the chapel, and there is also the *Troonzaal* (Throne Room), a Gothic hall in which hang a number of historical pictures. The *Collaciezaal* (or Armoury), first the meeting-place of the 'Collace' (representatives of the tradesmen) and later used for the storage of weapons, dates from 1482.

There are several attractive old houses quite close to the Stadhuis. In Hoogpoort, No. 33 was the *Goldsmiths' Hall* (15C), while across Botermarkt on the corner with Nederpolder, *Sint Jorishof* (1477), now a hotel, was once the home of the Guild of Crossbowmen; it was here that Mary of Burgundy was compelled to sign the Great Privilege. Beyond, in Nederpolder, are (right) two fine 15C gabled houses, *Grote Moor* and *Zwarte Moor*, immediately followed by a group of three houses once belonging to the Van der Sikkelen family. These are *Grote Sikkel* (14C double gable), now the Academy of Music, and, the other side of Biezerkapelstraat, *Kleine Sikkel*, a Romanesque building of the 13C with the family arms above the old door. In a little courtyard off Biezerkapelstraat, *Achter Sikkel* (14–15C) forms the rear part of Grote Sikkel. Opposite the Kleine Sikkel stands the 18C *Hôtel Van der Meersch*, with a 16C corner wing. ZANDBERG, just N of Nederpolder, is a pleasant square surrounded by 18C houses and with in its centre a pump of 1810.

The **Sint Niklaaskerk**, just W of the belfry, is the Scheldt Gothic successor of an 11C Romanesque church which stood here until c 1200. Of the present church's early 13C structure there survive only the base of the tower and the nave walls, while the Baroque W porch is of 1681. The transepts and the W part of the choir were built after 1230; the tower, which served as Ghent's first belfry, was completed in c 1300, and the apse is of 1432.

Albrecht Dürer lodged in 1521 at the *Rode Hoed* (12–16C; once the house of the grocers' guild) in Kleine Turkije, N of the church. The house *De Fonteyne* (1539), at the corner of Gouden Leeuwplein and with a fine Renaissance façade, the oldest of its kind in Ghent, was the home of a chamber of rhetoric.—For Ghent S of Sint Niklaas, see B.

The W front of Sint Niklaas faces the KOORNMARKT, a large and lively rectangle which was the medieval corn market and has ever since remained in many respects the centre of Ghent. It preserves some Renaissance houses on the W side, others of which were demolished in 1906 to make room for the imposing *Post Office*, while on the E side is the *Borluutsteen*, the 13–15C mansion of the family which gave Ghent its leader at the Battle of the Golden Spurs.

South west of the Koornmarkt, the Lys is crossed by the *****Sint Michielsbrug**, offering (especially N) Ghent's most famous view (see below), and with (S) the **Sint Michielskerk**, begun in Flamboyant Gothic style in 1440 and completed, less its tower, in 1648; since the 15C no less than six plans for a lofty tower were submitted, but all were for various reasons rejected and the tower remains incomplete. The church interior contains a Crucifixion by Van Dyck, and also works by, amongst others, Gaspard de Crayer, Otto Venius and Jean-Baptiste de Champaigne.

See B., Southern Ghent, for De Pand immediately S of the church. See p 213 for the Dominican Monastery, c 350m west.

From Sint Michielsbrug the view to the N, along the length of the old port, includes in the foreground the superb old guild and other houses beside the Graslei (E) and the mainly 17–19C houses along the Koornlei (W). Either bank may be followed, but the Koornlei is recommended as offering the better view across the water. In Koornlei the best house is the *Huis der Onvrije Schippers* (1740), marked by a gilded boat, while No. 24, now restored to a 17C appearance, was originally a Romanesque building of c 1200.

From S to N the following houses line the *Graslei. The *Gildehuis der Vrije Schippers*, built in 1500–31 by C. van den Berghe. The *Gildehuis der Graanmeters* (1698), the second House of the Grain Weighers. The tiny *Tolhuisje* (1682), the customs house. The *Spijker* or *Koornstapelhuis*, the public grain warehouse, used for the storage of grain held as customs duty payment in kind; a plain Romanesque building c 1200, this is the oldest along Graslei. The *Korenmetershuis* (16C), the first House of the Grain Weighers. The *Gildehuis van de Metsers* (1526), the House of the Masons.

Koornlei ends at the Grasbrug, to the S of the junction of the Lieve and Lys, across the bridge and left being the **Groot Vleeshuis** (1406–10), the medieval meat market with its many little gables and, against the S side, the small annexes at which the poor were given offal. The **Museum voor Sierkunst** (Decorative Arts. Daily except Monday, 09.00 to 12.30. 13.30 to 17.30. Closed 1 and 2 January, 25 and 26 December), at 5 Jan Breydelstraat opposite the W end of Grasbrug and occupying the former mansion (1754) of the De Coninck family, exhibits good collections of period furniture, ceramics, woodcarving, etc. Farther on (100m), near the corner of Burgstraat and Gawad, there are some 16–17C façades, notably the *Huis der Gekroonde Hoofden* (House of the Crowned Heads), bearing heads of the counts of Flanders down to Philip II. From here Reckelingestraat leads E into SINT VEERLEPLEIN with (S) the portal of the **Vismarkt** (Fish Market) originally built by Artus Quellin the Younger in 1689; destroyed by fire in 1872, a rebuilt and enlarged market absorbed the site of the Hospice Wenemaer, a foundation of the 15C. Early fronts of the fish and meat markets, bearing appropriate tile pictures, are round the corner in Reckelingestraat. The house on the left of the fish market occupies a transept of a former church (mostly demolished in 1578) dedicated to St. Veerle, an 8C virgin martyr of Ghent. Around the square, especially on the SE corner by Kraanlei, there are several old houses, some with interesting carving. Until the late 18C Sint Veerleplein was frequently chosen as the site for executions.

's Gravensteen, the Castle of the Counts, is a magnificent feudal fortress, a tour of which is essential to any appreciation of the early days of Ghent. The most important parts are well identified in English. (Daily, 09.00 to 18.00 or 16.00 in October–March. Closed 1 and 2 January, 25 and 26 December.) Squeamish visitors are warned that

Ghent, 's Gravensteen (Castle of the Counts)

several rooms are devoted to the subject of torture, with displays of instruments accompanied by horrific and specific illustrations.

It was here, within the confluence of the Lieve and the Lys, that c 867 Baldwin Iron Arm built his castle, parts of which survive in the cellars of the keep. This castle was for defence against the Norsemen; its successor, begun in 1180 by Philip of Alsace, was for the express purpose of overawing the unruly citizens of the fast-growing town. It was stormed by these same citizens in 1302, at the time of the Battle of the Golden Spurs, and again in 1338 by Jacob van Artevelde. From 1349 until the end of the 18C the castle was used only for special ceremonies, as a prison, mint, and law court; and from 1797 to 1887 it was occupied as a factory. Major restoration was carried out between 1894 and 1913.

From the gatehouse visitors ascend half-left to a walk along the outer wall, crossing the gatehouse (noting the holes down which boiling oil could be poured on to attackers) and continuing along a further length of wall (where loos perched high above the water are a feature) to reach the Count's Residence to the N of the keep. On the ground floor the vaulted Audience Chamber was for some 300 years the meeting-place of the Council of Flanders. Above are a group of rooms, once used by the counts and their countesses but today showing instruments of torture. Beyond is the Upper Hall (in which the torture theme continues), out of which a winding stair climbs to the roof, commanding views across the town. The tour descends back to the Upper Hall, off which what was once a large window frame opens on to what was probably the top of the chapel, before descending further to the Great Hall, scene in 1445 of a great banquet of the Order of the Golden Fleece presided over by Philip the Good. After the above main tour, various cellar areas may be visited. One (below the keep) shows fragments of the 9C castle and also two grim oubliettes; another cellar was used as a stable until the 14C and then as a torture room; and a third contains the refuse pit, cesspit and, virtually alongside, the fresh-water well.

NORTH AND WEST OF 'S GRAVENSTEEN. A varied and interesting

round of some 2km may be followed through the old, historic, and often picturesque district N and W of 's Gravensteen. Geldmuntstraat, the name recalling that a part of the counts' mint was established here during the 14C, is continued by Sint Margrietstraat on the W of which, on the corner with Academiestraat, stands the **Sint Stephanuskerk**, founded in 1606 and rebuilt in 1838 after a fire; there is a good Baroque portal and the interior contains altar paintings by Gaspard de Crayer and Baroque furnishing formerly in the church of the *Calced Carmelites*. This latter (14–16C) is a short way to the SE within the angle of Lange Steenstraat and Vrouwebroerstraat, this also being the site of the Carmelite house founded in 1285, an octagonal tower of which survives in a corner of the first courtyard; the church now belongs to the town and the rest of the complex to the provincial government. On Academiestraat (No. 1) are the mainly 17C buildings of the *Augustinian Monastery* founded in 1296. Beyond, Academiestraat reaches Sint Antoniuskaai along the N bank of the Lieve, here, among other old houses, being **Sint Antoniushof Godshuis**, a building of 1641 which was once the house of the shooting guild of St. Anthony and in 1805 became an almshouse; note the cartridges and crossed arquebuses. The river may be crossed at the next bridge, from which there is a view (NW) to the **Rabot**, a fortified sluice of 1491. The **Donkere Poort** (Dark Gate), just across the bridge, a vaulted archway between two turrets, is a relic of the palace (Prinsenhof) of 1353 in which Charles V was born in 1500. A plaque on the inner side depicts the palace as it was in the 16C, and its existence is also recalled by the name (Prinsenhof) of the street which leads SE from here. At this street's far end, at 13 Abrahamstraat (W), the *City Archives* have since 1932 been housed in the former public pawnshop, founded in 1621 and built by Wenceslas Coeberger; note the inscription about lending to the poor. At 13 Gawad, by the corner with Abrahamstraat, is the *Museum of Industrial Archaeology and Textiles* (Monday–Friday, 09.00 to 12.30); arrangements can be made here for an industrial-archaeological tour through Ghent. Burgstraat, immediately S, may now be followed W passing on the right (No. 46) the mainly 17C buildings of the *Monastery of the Discalced Carmelites* (a 17C foundation) with a church of 1712 containing three Baroque altars and, in the garden, a fragment of the Prinsenhof palace.

A short way beyond the W end of Burgstraat is SINT ELISABETHPLEIN, off the square being the **Sint Elisabeth Begijnhof**, a foundation of the 13C of which some 16C and 17C houses survive; the begijnhof's 16C portal was removed during the 19C and now forms the entrance to the Bijloke Museum, and the church dates from the 15C with transepts of two centuries later. Eastwards Burgstraat returns to 's Gravensteen, but visitors wishing to see another religious house may follow Peperstraat S from Elisabethplein to reach (200m) the *Dominican Monastery* (41 Hoogstraat), once a medieval leper house, rebuilt in the 17C as a convent and school and in 1845 taken over by the Dominicans.

From Sint Veerleplein, Kraanlei beside the Lys has elegant and picturesque houses both along itself and across the water. Here (No. 65) the ***Museum voor Volkskunde** (Folklore), occupying delightful and beautifully restored 14C almshouses, is outstanding among its kind (April–October: daily, 09.00 to 12.30, 13.30 to 17.30. November–March: daily except Monday, 10.00 to 12.00; 13.30 to 17.00. Closed 1 January, 25 December).

The almshouses (*Hospitaal der Kindren Alyns*) owed their existence to a quarrel between two Ghent families, the Ryms and the Alyns, culminating in the assassination by the Ryms of the two leading Alyns. The Ryms were sentenced (1354) to have their houses razed and (1362) to provide an annuity for a hospice, and at the same time, in a gesture of reconciliation, the surviving Alyns offered their house in the Kraanlei. A chapel was built in 1363; more houses were added in 1519 by the then guardian, Lieven van Pottelsberghe, whose portrait hangs in the Museum of Fine Arts: a new chapel was built in 1543–47; and, after acquisition (1940) by the town of Ghent, the almshouses were thoroughly restored as a home for the Folklore Museum.

The main theme of the museum is to recall (often by replica shops, etc.) the life of the people of Ghent, and particularly its craftsmen, during the 19C. A condensed guide is available in English. Some of the principal attractions are listed below.—Games and toys, including a hobby-horse made by the sculptor Laurent Delvaux for his grandchildren. A grocery. A cooper's workshop. A cobbler at work, with an interesting water-filled glass bowl for concentrating light. Puppet theatre (with a show, usually Saturday afternoon). An inn of c 1900. Clog-maker. Fashion and clothing. Printing. The chapel and sacristy, with in the latter a painting of the Ryms murdering the Alyns. Baker. Barber's saloon of c 1900. An exhibition of means of lighting. Chemist, and apothecary's laboratory. Lace. A typical almsman's room.

Just beyond the museum two 17C carved façades are worth noting, No. 77 with the Seven Acts of Charity and No. 79 with the five senses, a flying deer, the virtues, a flute player, etc. Zuivelbrug crosses to Groot Kanonplein in which stands the 15C iron mortar '*Dulle Griet*' (Mad Meg), once used by Ghent in an attack on Oudenaarde. The adjacent VRIJDAGMARKT, once the focus of the town's political and civil life and a meeting- and brawling-place of the guilds, is now the scene of a busy Friday market. The bronze statue of Jacob van Artevelde, whose uprising of 1338 probably started here, is by De Vigne-Quyo (1863), and the *Toreken* (1460), at the SE corner, with a slim turret, was the House of the Tanners. The **Sint Jacobskerk**, begun in the 12C, to which period belong the two Romanesque W towers and the lower part of the steeple above the crossing, was finished between the 13C and 15C. Kammerstraat leads SE out of the Vrijdagmarkt: No. 18 was where the painter De Crayer died in 1669, and at the end of the street, in Koningstraat, the façade of the *Royal Flemish Academy* is by 't Kindt (1746).

Just N of the church of Sint Jacob the 17C buildings of the Cistercian former abbey of *Baudelo* (originally only a refuge but in the 17C enlarged to full abbey) now house a school and library; Mozart is said to have played on the Hemony carillon in the turret. Farther NW (600m, beyond the river) is FRATERSPLEIN, with a statue of Pieter van Gent (1486–1572), known for his educational work in Mexico; the statue (1976) is a replica of one in Mexico City. On the N side of the square the convent of *Sint Jan de Deo*, formerly a Carthusian house, contains the *Museum Meerhem* (Sunday, 14.00 to 17.00) showing documentation on local history reaching back over five centuries.

From the church of Sint Jacob, Borluutstraat reaches the Stadhuis in 300m.

B. Southern Ghent

Southern Ghent is visited mainly for the Bijloke (or Archaeological) Museum and the Museum voor Schone Kunsten (Fine Arts). The former is a short way NW of

CITADEL PARK; the latter at the park's E corner. This area can be reached by public transport from the Koornmarkt, or on foot or by car along Veldstraat and its continuations to the crossing of Kortrijkse Poortstraat and Ijserlaan with Burgemeester K. van Kerchovelaan. This point, close to both museums, is about 1.5km from Koornmarkt. Parking is possible near both museums.—An alternative and quieter approach on foot, starting from Sint Michielsbrug, is first to follow the E bank of the river (Predikherenlei), with generally 16C to 19C façades and, across the water, **Het Pand**, the site of an ancient hospice where the Dominicans built a monastery in the 13–14C; the buildings now form a part of Ghent university. Beyond Het Pand the W bank is followed to cross (in c 700m from Sint Michielsbrug) the *Coupure* canal and then pass various scientific institutions of the university before reaching the Bijloke Museum.

Veldstraat leads S out of Koornmarkt, the first building of interest being on the corner of Volderstraat; now a shop, this was formerly the *Hôtel Schamp*, used as the residence of John Quincy Adams and his staff during the negotiations before the signing of the Treaty of Ghent (plaque). Just beyond, on the same side, the former *Hôtel d' Hane-Steenhuyse*, an 18C mansion with a Rococo façade, was the residence of Louis XVIII of France during the 'Hundred Days'; today the house is used for exhibitions on urban renovation and expansion. Opposite, No. 82 is the **Hôtel Vander Haeghen**, another 18C mansion which now serves as a centre for various exhibitions and houses documentation and other material on Maurice Maeterlinck (1862–1949), winner of the Nobel prize for literature in 1911, and also a collection of the graphic work of the Ghent artist Victor Stuyvaert (1897–1924). The *University Aula* (university founded in 1816), 100m E along Volderstraat, occupies a porticoed building of 1826 by Louis Roelandt, adjacent being the gateway (1642) of the former Jesuit college. The university's **Museum Wetenschap en Techniek** (Science and Technology. Monday and Wednesday, 14.00 to 17.00), illustrating the work of various early scientists and inventors, is at 9 Korte Meer, the road flanking the W side of the university.

Korte Meer continues S into the large open space known as the KOUTER (ploughed field) with many trees, from early times a popular focus for purposes as varied as political demonstrations, archery contests, military parades, and markets, these last including a flower market held here from 1772 until the present day. The **Koninklijke Opera** (opera October–mid June), off the SW in Schouwburgstraat, was built by Louis Roelandt in 1836–48; No. 29 is the *Handelsbeurs*, the commercial exchange occupying the former Guard House (1738); and, on the N side, the 18C *Hôtel Falignan* (Bernard de Wilde) is now a club. To the W the *Gerechtshof* (Law Courts. Louis Roelandt, 1836–46) stands at the junction of Schouwburgstraat and Veldstraat, in front being a statue (Julien Dillens, 1886) of Hippolyte Metdepenningen (1799–1881), a prominent lawyer and political figure.

Veldstraat becomes first Nederkouter and then the Kortrijkse Poortstraat to reach a crossroads, with the Bijloke Museum (right) and the Museum voor Schone Kunsten (left, 500m). Ahead the Kortrijkse Steenweg continues to (900m) **Sint Pieters Station**. Approaching the Bijloke Museum, in a garden by the corner of Bijlokekaai, a statue (G. de Vreeze, 1952) commemorates Jan Palfijn (1650–1730), a surgeon credited with the invention of forceps.

The ***Bijloke Museum** (rather misleadingly also called the Archaeological Museum) occupies the very attractive 14–17C former domestic buildings of the abbey of Bijloke. (Daily except Monday, 09.00 to 12.30, 13.30 to 17.30. Closed 1 and 2 January, 25 and 26 December.)

The abbey, for nuns, was founded on this site as a hospice and hospital in 1228, the nucleus being a group of nuns who came from the Cistercian nunnery of Nieuwenbosse, 3km SE of Ghent. The abbey suffered severely under the anti-monastic troubles of the 16C, and in 1579, during the Calvinist years, the construction of new ramparts led to the demolition of many of the abbey buildings, though the refectory and dormitory survived. The nuns returned in 1585 when Parma reoccupied Ghent, and the 17C was generally one of rebuilding. Expelled again in 1797, the nuns finally returned in 1801, since then occupying mainly 17C buildings. The hospital survived the various troubles, today being a part of the municipal hospital, incorporating parts of the abbey and still served by nuns.

The museum houses varied material generally relative to the past of Flanders and of Ghent. Entrance is through the portal (1660) of the former Sint Elisabeth Begijnhof, removed from its original site and set up here in c 1874. Immediately on the right are two rooms and a passage, the first room (17C) being the Room of the Governors of the Poor House with a chimneypiece and panelling by Norbert Sauvage, and, over the chimneypiece, an allegorical picture by Joos van Cleef of the founding of the Poor House. In the passage hang some interesting original plans of 1518 for the Stadhuis and also 17C woodcarvings (the Four Seasons) by Laurent van der Meulen. The second room, known as the Room of the Abbots of Baudelo, exhibits late 17C and early 18C Brussels tapestries.

The COURTYARD is now crossed, here being (left to right) the 17C House of the Abbess, the 14C refectory and dormitory, and part of an 18C façade. The entrance beyond is into a corridor, in a room off which is a collection of wood carving from demolished old Ghent houses. From the end of the corridor stairs ascend from the cloister up to the *REFECTORY, a superbly proportioned hall with a high wooden vault, and, in the centre, the *Monument of Hugo II, castellan of Ghent (died 1232), found in 1948 in the ruins of the abbey of Nieuwenbosse. On the hall's entrance wall is a 14C *Mural of the Last Supper, with the coronation of the Virgin above, while, on the fireplace wall, there are representations of St. John the Baptist and St. Christopher. The other exhibits are mainly ecclesiastical, of particular note being engraved liturgical dishes dated to the late 12C and found in the Scheldt. The tour now makes a circuit of the UPPER CLOISTER, the material around which covers many themes, these including medieval ceramic; Delft tile walls (with a Crucifixion); porcelain and glass; dress of the 18th and 19C; weapons and armour; brass, pewter and ironwork, notably a collection of intricate locks and keys and the large *Brass of Leonard Betten (died 1667), Abbot of Sint Truiden. The DORMITORY, another fine hall, which opens off the upper cloister SE corner, is largely devoted to the guilds but has as its centre-piece a large model of a 17C man-of-war.

A clockwise tour is normally made of the LOWER CLOISTER, starting along the S walk in which can be seen the 16C lavatorium. In the W walk hangs a fascinating Panorama of Ghent in 1534 (but this picture tends to change position), and off this walk opens a large hall, the stucco ceiling (1715) of which was earlier in the refectory but removed when the latter was restored to its original state. Off the N walk open three more rooms, all large, dignified and with gilt hangings and all largely concerned with the shooting guilds. In the first (the westernmost) there are guild chairs and historical pictures; in the second, with a small cannon, the large painting is of a meeting of the Guild of St. Anthony; and in the third there are more guild chairs. In the E walk the most notable feature is a painting, Coronation of Christ, by Dirk Bouts.

From the SW corner of the cloister a passage leads to the 17C HOUSE OF THE ABBESS with a series of rooms containing furnishings from old Ghent houses, abbeys and hospices. The kitchen is interesting with its contemporary utensils, and in the last room there is a fine chimneypiece by Norbert Sauvage, the painting showing aldermen meting out justice.

From the Bijloke Museum, Ijserlaan, becoming Karel van Kerchovelaan, ascends SE along the flank of Citadel Park (see below). Karel van Kerchove was burgomaster of Ghent between 1857–81, a period during which much modernisation took place, and he is remembered by a fountain of 1898 (by Hippolyte Leroy) at the NW end of the street bearing his name.

At its SE end Karel van Kerchovelaan reaches (right, just in the park) the *Museum voor Schone Kunsten** (Daily except Monday, 09.00 to 12.30, 13.30 to 17.30. Closed 1 and 2 January, 25 and 26 December), occupying a building of 1902, arranged as two series of rooms (Rooms 1 to 15 and Rooms A to L) showing works spanning from the Flemish Primitives up to the 19th and 20C, these last two centuries starting at Room 13 and continuing through to Room L.

In the case of most rooms of the earlier periods excellent multilingual carry-round, self-guide boards are provided. Some representative works are selected below.

Beyond the entrance comes a Hall hung with Brussels tapestry—ROOM 1. All works *Anon.*, especially notable being an Annunciation, using gold to an extent unusual at this period. ROOM 2. *Hieronymus Bosch*: *Bearing of the Cross, one of this artist's last works, notable for the grotesque faces. St. Jerome at prayer. *Adriaen Isenbrant*: Madonna and Child, an attractively gentle rendering. *Gheeraert Hoorenbaut*: *Triptych of St. Anne, with the family of the Virgin, and Portraits of Lieven van Pottelsberghe (died 1531) and his wife (died 1523) as donors. Lieven van Pottelsberghe became in c 1515 guardian of the Hospitaal der Kindren Alyns, now the Folklore Museum. *Christian Engerbrechtsz*: Pietà, from the destroyed Ghent Dominican church. ROOM 3 shows medieval sculpture, including two 14C bas reliefs (Baptism of Christ. Coronation of Mary), both Nottingham work. ROOM 4. *Frans Pourbus the Elder*: Portrait of a Young Woman, this artist's last known signed and dated work. *Marten van Heemskerk*: Calvary. *Frans Francken the Younger*: Calvary, a work in an unusual dark and restrained style with the emphasis strongly on sorrow rather than historical drama. ROOM 5 shows very large canvases, these including Rest on the Flight to Egypt by *Jacob Jordaens*; Judgement of Solomon and other works by *Gaspàrd de Crayer*; *Crown of Thorns and Annunciation by *Jan Janssens*; and *Stigmata of St. Francis of Assisi by *P. P. Rubens*. ROOM 6. *Theodoor Rombouts*: Allegory of the Five Senses. At the Dentist. *Philippe de Champaigne*: Portrait of Pierre Camus. *Daniel Seghers*: Wreath of Flowers, without a religious centre, a picture which may be compared with (in ROOM 7) another Wreath of Flowers by the same artist, this one with a religious centre by *Cornelis Schut*. *Jacob*

Jordaens: Several works, including two studies for a head. *Gaspard de Crayer*: Head of a Young Man, for this artist an unusually small and restrained work. *P.P. Rubens*: Scourging, the sketch of the painting now hanging in Antwerp's Sint Paulus church. *Antoon van Dyck*: Jupiter and Antiope. *Cornelis de Vos*: Family Group.

In ROOM 8 interest focuses on *The Village Lawyer by *Pieter Brueghel the Younger*, an original work by an artist better known for his copies of his father's paintings (of which there are examples here); this is a fascinating genre scene of contemporary bureaucracy and illustrating also the extent of payment in kind. Also in this room are Landscapes by *Roelant Savery*, and the Scourges of Mankind by *Kerstiaen de Keuninck*, an artist who was unknown until 1902 when this work was discovered in the museum's storeroom. ROOM 9. *Willem van de Velde the Younger*: Marine scenes. *Paul de Vos*: Buffalo attacked by Dogs. *Andries van Eertvelt*: Ships in Distress, a theatrically stormy scene. ROOM 10. *P. de Keyser*: Portrait of a Man. *Willem Claesz Heda*: Several examples of Still-life. *Jan de Bray*: Portrait of a Young Woman. ROOM 11. *Frans Hals*: Portrait of a Woman (1640). *Aelbert Cuyp*: Cock and Hens. *Govert Flinck*: Portrait of a Woman. *Nicolas Maes*: Portrait of a Woman. *Jan van Goyen*: Landscape (1648) ROOM 12 shows foreign schools, artists including Tintoretto (Portrait of a Sculptor) and *Alessandro Magnasco* (Monks at Prayer).

With ROOM 13 the tour of the gallery reaches the 19th and 20C, works of these centuries being shown in ROOMS 14 and 15 (the latter not so much a room as a semicircle of divisions around ROOM 14) and in ROOMS A to L. The arrangement of these rooms is less settled than is the case with the earlier periods and they are also more likely to be disturbed by temporary exhibitions. Following, however, is a selection from the many works. *Henri Evenepoel*: *The Spaniard in Paris. *Emile Claus*: Typical soft landscapes, including Winter Scene and Cows swimming across the Lys. *Jan Verhas*: *The Master-Painter, a delicious study of childen around a table. *H. Remaeker*: The Painter. *Gustave de Smet*: Village Fair. *Edgard Tytgat*: The Painter's Studio (1934). *Jan Brusselmans*: Nude. *Rik Wouters*: Woman Seated (1915). *Gustave van der Woestyne*: Young Peasant Woman (1913). *George Minne*: (Sculptures). Boy kneeling. Man weeping over his dead Dog. Kneeling Man and Woman. *Constantin Meunier*: (Sculpture). The Prodigal Son. *James Ensor*: Several typical works. *Théo Rysselberghe*: *The Poet E. Verhaeren reading to his Friends.

The Department of Contemporary Art shows visual art forms of the 20C, the emphasis being on the period after 1945, with movements such as Jeune Peinture Belge, Cobra, Lyric Abstract, Pop Art, Minimal Art and Conceptual Art.

CITADEL PARK, laid out in 1871 on the site of a fort raised by the Duke of Wellington, surrounds the **Feestpaleis**, used for exhibitions and fairs and for the five-yearly 'Floralies' (1990). Oswald van Kerchove (1844–1906), son of Karel van Kerchove mentioned above, a distinguished botanist and horticulturalist who played a leading part in establishing the 'Floralies', is commemorated by a nearby statue (G. van den Meersche, 1923). Two other memorials, both in the E part of the park, may be mentioned: one (Yvonne Serruys, 1926), near the large lake, honours Emile Claus, the painter and leader of Flemish Impressionism; the other (Julius van Biesbroeck, 1926), close to the Museum voor Schone Kunsten, is to Edmond van Beveren (1852–94), prominent in the Ghent Socialist movement. The university's **Botanic**

Garden, with over 7500 species, is off the SE of Citadel Park (Monday–Thursday, 14.00 to 17.00. Saturday, Sunday, Holidays, 09.00 to 12.00).

Kunstlaan or Overpoortstraat, both from the N side of Citadel Park, in c 400m reach the large, open SINT PIETERSPLEIN, bounded on the E by the buildings of the former abbey of **Sint Pieter**. Founded by St. Amand as early as the 7C, the abbey suffered the usual vicissitudes of the later centuries and a rebuilding started in 1584 was not completed until the 18C. Today the N wing, which includes the chapter-house, has been converted into an *Arts and Culture Centre*, while off the courtyard and occupying the former hospital and reception wing is the **Schoolmuseum Michiel Thiery** (daily, 09.00 to 12.15, 13.30 to 17.15. Closed Friday afternoon and Holidays), a museum of wide scope, based on models and embracing natural history, geography, the evolution of man and even the history of the computer. Beyond the courtyard some of the old abbey buildings have in part been excavated. The **Sint Pieterskerk**, designed by Pieter Huyssens and with a fine dome, is a Baroque achievement of 1629–1719. Inside are a wrought-iron choir screen (1748), paintings by Niklaas de Liemakere and Theodoor van Thulden, and the porphyry cenotaph of Isabel of Austria (1501–26), sister of Charles V and queen of Christian II of Denmark, whose remains were removed to Odense in Denmark in 1883.

Sint Pieternieuwstraat leads N, passing the library and various scientific departments of the university and becoming Walpoortstraat which, frequently changing name, continues N back to the town centre. From near the start of Walpoortstraat, Lamstraat bears E across an arm of the Scheldt for President Wilsonplein (see C. below).

C. Eastern Ghent

The main places of interest in Eastern Ghent are the Klein Begijnhof and the Abbey of Sint Baaf. The round described below is one of c 3km; it is practicable by car, parking normally being possible near both sites.

Limburgstraat runs SE from the cathedral, passing the Geraard Duivelsteen and the Van Eyck and Lieven Bauwens monuments, to become the broad Vlaanderenstraat and reach President Wilsonplein. In front extends the KONING ALBERT PARK, with, at this end an exhibition building and, in the park, an equestrian memorial to King Albert (J.A. de Bondt, the pedestal; Domien Ingels, statue. 1937). In a triangular garden near the park's SW corner will be found the Congo Star (1936) or the Memorial of the Colonials.

Twee Bruggenstraat (from the NE of the park) crosses Lange Violettenstraat, to the S down which is the **Klein Begijnhof** founded in 1234 by the sisters Margaret and Joanna of Constantinople. Today's buildings (17–19C) surround a peaceful enclosure, often with grazing cattle or sheep. The Baroque church here dates from 1658–1720, the façade being the later part. Inside are a curious polyptych, the Fountain of Life by Lucas Hoorenbaut, and also altarpieces by De Crayer and Niklaas de Liemakere.

Twee Bruggenstraat ends at the Nieuwe Bosbrug and the Lousbergsbrug, adjacent bridges across parallel channels of the Lys. From the latter, Lousbergskaai followed N for 500m reaches the historic ruined **Abdij Sint Baaf** (Daily except Monday, 09.00 to 12.30, 13.30 to 17.30. Closed 1 and 2 January, 25 and 26 December).

This Benedictine abbey was founded by St. Amand during the 7C, laid waste by the Vikings in the 9C and rebuilt by the then Count of Flanders in the 10C, thereafter flourishing, especially during the 12C and 13C. In 1340, during Jacob van Artevelde's alliance with England's Edward III, the latter visited Ghent, his queen, Philippa of Hainaut, giving birth here in the abbey to John of Gaunt. In 1369 the abbey saw the marriage of Philip the Bold of Burgundy to Margaret, heiress of Louis de Male, an alliance which marked the beginning of the Burgundian period for Flanders. In 1540, on crushing the Ghent revolt, Charles V built a fortress here, destroying the abbey church and using the domestic buildings as barracks, armouries and suchlike. This fortress was demolished during the 19C, the abbey remains then becoming a Lapidary Museum (the *Museum voor Stenen Voorwerpen*).

The E wall of the Gothic Cloister, partly restored, has vaulting of 1495; on the left is the small octagonal Lavatorium (12C but since altered), while opposite is the 13C Chapter-House, with Romanesque bays and two ancient curiously shaped tombs, one even with a head-rest. Beyond, the Old Refectory (12C or earlier) was used since the 13C as a store. From the N walk of the cloister, steps ascend to the large 13C Refectory, with a 16C wood ceiling. From 1589 until the close of the 18C this great hall served as the chapel, then from 1834 to 1882 as local parish church; today it houses a collection of stonework which includes a Romanesque font, a 12C double-tympanum from the destroyed abbey church, and several ancient graveslabs including one said to be that of Hubert van Eyck.

Dampoort Station (400m NE of the abbey) is at the S end of Achterdok and Handelsdok (see D.). The Neo-Gothic **Groot Begijnhof**, some 400m E of the station, was built in 1872 as an extension of the Sint Elisabeth Begijnhof; there are two gateways, the one on the Ghent side having a statue of the saint and the other bearing the arms of the Arenberg family, responsible for buying the land. The museum (at No. 64) provides a survey of begijnhof life (April–October: Wednesday–Saturday, Holidays, 10.00 to 11.00, 14.00 to 18.00).

From the Abdij Sint Baaf, the cathedral is c 700m to the west.

D. The Port of Ghent and the Terneuzen Canal

Ghent has long been a port, first by means of the 13C canal to Bruges and thence to the sea by way of the Zwin, then from 1547 also using the new canal to the Scheldt estuary at Terneuzen, now in Holland. In these early times the port was along the waterways within the town, notably beside Graslei and Koornlei. The Scheldt was closed from 1648 to 1795, but in 1827 the Terneuzen canal (30km) was opened to sea-going vessels, this making possible Ghent's great maritime port. In 1968 a new lock at Terneuzen opened the canal to ships of 60,000 tons deadweight, and plans now include a 125,000 tons facility. Much of the port area is served by public roads, offering views of the ships and barges, and a drive along the road which follows the W bank of the canal, both sides of which are fast becoming one vast industrial zone, is not without interest.

The southern arm of the port (*Achterdok* and *Handelsdok*) starts close to Dampoort station. From here the W side of the basin can be followed for 1.5km to Muidebrug, across which lies the main port area with the Grootdok and its three arms and, beyond, the Sifferdok for larger ships.

Here a diversion may be made eastwards into the suburb of **Oostakker** in which is the *Basiliek Onze Lieve Vrouw van Lourdes*, dedicated in 1877 and built to plans by Baron Jean Béthune who was responsible also for much of the painted symbolic decoration of the interior. In the gardens of the adjacent complex there is a grotto with a figure of Our Lady of Lourdes.—On Gefusilleerdenstraat, between Oostakker and the main road to Antwerp, the *Monument der Onthoofden* honours 56 members of the Resistance executed here; dedicated in 1951, the site includes memorial crosses and also statues by George Vindevogel.

From Muidebrug, Sassekaai bears briefly S to Neuseplein, just beyond which Nieuwe Tolhuisbrug crosses a canal. Wiedauwkaai, passing (right) the *Tolhuis* (Customs), then heads N beside *Voorhaven*, at the end of which (just under 3km from Nieuwe Tolhuisbrug) is the entrance to *Grootdok* at what is officially the start of the canal. To the W in **Wondelgem** the church is an imposing Baroque building of 1687.

The road briefly leaves the water before crossing the *Ringvaart* (ring canal); the entrance to *Sifferdok* is opposite, some 500m farther. The road continues as Wondelgemkaai and Langerbruggekaai, across the water being (2.5km from the Ringvaart) the *Petroleumdok*, surrounded by oil tanks. After a further 3.5km the site of he projected *Kluizendok* is reached; this, 400m wide, will extend nearly 2km NW towards Ertvelde. Across the canal, the *Rodenhuizedok*, 1km in length, is the planned starting-point of the projected 125,000 tons canal which will loop E of Wachtebeke and Zelzate. The road continues beside the canal, passing *Rieme* where a memorial marks the execution site of a group of Resistance fighters, and then above a main road led below the canal by a tunnel, to reach **Zelzate** (19km from Ghent-Dampoort), a modern industrial town (13,000 inhab.) on the Dutch border. For **Terneuzen**, on the Scheldt 15km farther, and for the Dutch district of Zeeland Flanders, see 'Blue Guide Holland'.

From Ghent to *De Panne*, see Rte 5; to *Bruges* and *Ostend*, and to *Brussels*, see Rte 8; to *Kortrijk*, see Rte 11; to *Antwerp*, see Rte 14.

14 Ghent to Antwerp

A. Via Sint Niklaas and Temse

Total distance 58km.—*20km* **Lokeren.**—*13km* **Sint Niklaas.**—*7km* **Temse.**—*18km* **Antwerp.**—This road traverses the WAASLAND, today one of the most productive agricultural districts of Europe but until about the 12C a virtually uninhabitable tract of swamp and undrained forest. The development of the district started when it came under the sway of the counts of Flanders. Gradually hermit settlements became larger religious communities who cleared the land and built the first dykes; peat-cutting grew as an industry, and a network of small waterways was dug to serve both for drainage and for transporting the peat; sheep were introduced to supply the wool demands of Ghent; villages and towns sprang up. Although the reclaimed land was largely of sand and clay, it was increasingly made fertile by the addition of rich soil and the spread of scientific farming.

Ghent (Rte 13) is left by N70 through the suburb of *Sint Amandsberg*, here being the Groot Begijnhof, for which, as also for *Oostakker* 3km N, also see Rte 13.—*9km Lochristi* is a flower-growing centre, mainly concerned with begonias (festival during last weekend of August).—

5km Zeveneken is 4km S of *Domein Puyenbroeck*, a provincial park in typical Waasland scenery, offering swimming, boating, riding, a zoological garden and a mill museum (Daily from 09.00. Closed 1 January, Easter Sunday, 1 November, 25 December. Mill open May–August: daily, 10.00 to 12.00, 13.00 to 18.00. March, April, October: Sunday, 14.00 to 17.00).—*6km* **Lokeren** (33,000 inhab. Tourist Information: 1 Torensstraat), a pleasant town on the small river Durme and after Sint Niklaas the most important centre in the Waasland, has several 17–18C buildings, including the town hall; a local museum at 3 Grote Kaai; and a church (Sint Laurentius, 1721) with a pulpit of 1736 by Thoedoor Verhaeghen. At *Daknam*, 2km NW, the church dates from the 11th and 12C.

13km **Sint Niklaas** (68,000 inhab. Tourist Information: 45 Grote Markt), the chief town of the Waasland, has the largest market square in Belgium. Here the *Sint Niklaaskerk* dates in part from 1262 but is mainly 16th and 17C. Above the altar the Descent from the Cross is by Pieter Thys, adjacent being statues of SS. Peter and Paul by Luc Fayd'herbe. There is also a church museum, normally, however, only opened to groups and by prior arrangement. On the other side of the square, the *Stadhuis*, with a tower and carillon (frequent concerts) is a pleasingly proportioned and symmetrical 19C rebuilding of a 17C predecessor; behind, another church (Neo-Byzantine, 1844) is strikingly crowned by a golden Virgin. To the SE of the Grote Markt, the *Walburghof* (1550), the former castle, stands within what is now a municipal park. The *Stedelijk Museum* (Sunday, 10.00 to 13.00, 15.00 to 18.00. Wednesday, Saturday, 14.00 to 17.00), at 49 Zamenstraat, 400m NE of the Grote Markt, is devoted to local archaeology and history and includes atlases, maps and globes (terrestrial and celestial) made by Mercator who was born at Rupelmonde (see below) in 1512; there is also an art gallery with works spanning the 17–20C, among the artists being Rubens (attributed), James Ensor, Henri de Braekeleer, Henri Evenepoel and Louis Artan.

The direct road to Antwerp (N70) continues NE through *Beveren* where the 15C church contains Baroque furnishings, and gold- and silverware. A more interesting road bears SE for (*7km*) **Temse** (23,000 inhab.), an industrial and shipbuilding town on the Scheldt long associated with St. Amelberga (procession on Whit Tuesday), niece of Pepin of Landen, who here escaped an importunate suitor by crossing the river on the back of a giant sturgeon. The town has two small museums, the municipal museum at 16 Kasteelstraat (Saturday, 14.00 to 19.00. Sunday, 10.00 to 12.00, 14.00 to 19.00) and a museum of heraldry at 74 Kasteelstraat (Sunday, Wednesday, 14.00 to 17.00).

South of the Temse bridge, in the province of Antwerp, there is a curious lost district of marshland enclosed by the Scheldt and the Oude Scheldt, a channel abandoned by the river during the 13C. There is a regional museum (the *Zilverreiger*: Easter–October: daily except Monday, 14.00 to 18.00) in the picturesque village of **Weert**.—**Bornem** (11,000 inhab.), a centre of asparagus growing and basket weaving, was important during the Peasants' Revolt of 1798 against the anti-clerical French (monument). The church preserves a 12C choir and tower-base and the 10–11C crypt of a Benedictine priory church.

5km **Rupelmonde**, opposite where the Rupel flows into the Scheldt, was the birthplace of the cartographer Mercator (Gerhard Kremer, 1512–94) at 54 Kloosterstraat; his statue (1871) stands in the square. By the waterfront, with something of the atmosphere of a fishing village, a ruined tower is all that is left of the town's once powerful castle which in the 13C protected an important regional market.—At

(*2km*) *Bazel* the church stands within a pleasant close with some old façades. The adjacent château, now a restaurant, is best seen from the rear across its lake and moat.—*3km Kruibeke* has a church of c 1300 which is exceptionally rich in Baroque woodwork (1711–45) by the Kerrickx family, father and son, and others.—Just N, the road crosses into the province of Antwerp, looping round one of the city's great outer forts, then joins the motorway to cross the Scheldt by the J.F. Kennedytunnel.—*8km* (from Kruibeke) **Antwerp**, see Rte 16.

B. Via Dendermonde

Total distance 69km.—*12km* **Laarne**.—*20km* **Dendermonde**.—*10km* **Sint Amands**.—*10km* **Fort Breendonk**.—*17km* **Antwerp**.

Ghent (see Rte 13) is left by the Dendermondse Steenweg in the S part of the suburb of Sint Amandsberg.—*12km* **Laarne**, known for its moated *Château* (Daily except Monday, 10.00 to 12.00, 14.00 to 18.00. Closed 24 December–31 January). Of the original 12C castle only the cellars and perhaps the chapel survive, the building seen today being mainly 13–14C with 16–17C additions and alterations. The interior houses some outstanding 16C Brussels tapestry, beautifully depicting domestic life in a noble household, and also a notable collection of 15–18C silver.—*7km Overmere* was the scene of the first incident of the Peasants' Revolt of 1798 against the anti-clerical policy of the occupying French, an occasion remembered by a monument and the *Boerenkrijgmuseum* at 2 Baron Tibbautstraat (Monday–Friday, 08.30 to 12.00, 13.00 to 16.00; Sunday, 14.00 to 16.00). A short way E, *Donkmeer* is the largest lake in Flanders. An abandoned arm of the Scheldt, the lake was formed during the 16C by the flooding of peat diggings; today the attractions include boating, fishing, an animal park and a duck decoy.

13km **Dendermonde** (42,000 inhab. Tourist Information: Stadhuis), at the confluence of the Dender with the Scheldt and both interesting and picturesque for the way in which barge traffic passes virtually through the town centre, is visited mainly for the two works by Antoon van Dyck which hang in the church.

The town's strategic situation has brought it turbulent times. Incorporated in the county of Flanders in the 13C, Dendermonde was the first town to be taken by Maximilian (1484) in his reconquest. Louis XIV was repulsed in 1667, when the inhabitants flooded the whole district, but Marlborough took the town in 1706. It was occupied by the Dutch under the Barrier Treaty of 1713, and in 1914 was largely destroyed by the Germans.

The *Stadhuis* is on the E side of the Grote Markt. Built in the 14C and 16C and formerly the cloth hall, all that survived 1914 were the belfry and the outer walls; it was restored to its original form in 1921–26. On the N is the *Vleeshalle* (1460), with an octagonal turret, now housing the local museum (May–October: Saturday, Sunday, Holidays, 10.00 to 18.00), while just off the square stands the huge *Justitiepaleis* of 1924. Off Brusselsestraat, beyond the Dender, the *Begijnhof*, reached by a narrow street, forms a triangle enclosed by largely 17C houses; founded in 1233, the community settled in this site in 1288; the church is a rebuilding of the 1920s on the original foundations. Farther on, near the station, there survive two gateways of the 17C ramparts.

From behind the Vleeshalle the wide Kerkstraat leads W to the *Onze Lieve Vrouwekerk*, with an octagonal central tower; successor to an earlier church and chapel, today's Gothic church is mainly of the 14–15C. The tower was badly damaged when Dendermonde was attacked by Ghent in 1379, the story being that six cartloads of stones were removed and used as ammunition; rebuilding was not completed until c 1468, in which year Margaret of York, wife of Charles the Bold, visited here. The church is known for its two major works by Van Dyck, *Crucifixion (baptistry) and *Adoration of the Shepherds (N aisle). Also in the baptistry is a 12C font in Tournai marble, bearing on one side a Last Supper. In the N ambulatory there is a Donor adoring the Virgin by De Crayer, while the N transept and choir contain early 15C murals.

10km **Sint Amands** (7000 inhab.), 2km N of the road and in the province of Antwerp, is a straggling small town with a pleasant open area beside the Scheldt where there is a tomb-memorial of the poet Emile Verhaeren (died 1916) who was born in 1855 at No. 69 in the street bearing his name. Near the memorial stands a modern sculpture, the Ferryman, by M. Macken. There are two museums, the Verhaeren Museum at 22 Kade (March–June; mid September–October: Saturday, Sunday, 12.00 to 19.00. July–mid September: daily, except Monday and Friday, 12.00 to 19.00) and a mill museum at 7 Emile Verhaerenstraat.—*10km* **Fort Breendonk**. For the fort, and from here to (*17km*) **Antwerp**, see Rte 15A.

15 Brussels to Antwerp

The fastest approach to Antwerp is the motorway (A1/E19) which skirts the W side of Mechelen, see Rte 15B below.

A. Via Boom

Total distance 45km.—*11km* **Meise** (for **Grimbergen**).—*5km* **Fort Breendonk**.—*4km* **Boom**.—*15km* **Antwerp**.

Brussels (see Rte 1) may be left by a choice of roads, the easiest from the centre being either through Laeken or the road along the NE flank of the Domaine Royal; these meet at the Pavillon Chinois, and the Atomium is soon seen to the left, after which the outer ring motorway is crossed.—*11km* **Meise**, with, immediately W of the road, the *Plantentuin*, the national botanic gardens with superb trees and beautiful sweeps of green. The Palais des Plantes (1966) comprises several large hothouses, including one devoted to tropical water plants, and the 18C Orangery now serves as a restaurant and lakeside café. The gardens are within the estate of Bouchout, the castle of which (13C, but much altered during the 17C) became the residence of the widowed Empress Charlotte of Mexico who, never fully recovering her reason after her experiences, died here in 1927. (Gardens: daily, 09.00 to sunset. Palais des Plantes: Monday–Thursday, 13.00 to 16.00. Also Sunday and Holidays from Easter–October, 14.00 to 18.00. Castle not open.) **Grimbergen**, 3km SE of Meise, is known for its huge Baroque *Abbey Church of Sint Servaas*.

The abbey founded here in 1128 was destroyed in 1579 and it was only in the following century that the monks returned, Brother Gilbert van Zinnik then beginning work on today's church in 1660. The interior is notable for a towering high-altar by Frans Langhermans (1701); the monument of Philippe-François, lord of Grimbergen (died 1704) by Theodoor Verhaeghen; and the four confessionals, the transept altars and the pulpit by Hendrik Verbruggen, though the pulpit may be by Verhaeghen. The sacristy is a Rococo achievement of 1763, and between it and the church some Romanesque arches have survived. On the NW edge of Grimbergen, beside the Meise road, a curious monument honours Frans Hemerijckx (1902–69), a worker among lepers.

2km (from Meise) *Wolvertem* has a church with Baroque confessionals and a pulpit in similar style vividly depicting the story of St. Hubert.—Beyond *Londerzeel* the road crosses into the province of Antwerp, after which (*13km*) **Fort Breendonk** is reached, Rte 14B from Ghent and Dendermonde joining here. The fort (April–September: daily, 09.00 to 17.00. October–March: daily, 10.00 to 16.00. Closed 1 January and 25 December), built in 1906–14 as an outlying defence of Antwerp, was used by the Germans during the Second World War as a concentration and reprisals camp and is today maintained as a memorial museum (cells, execution site, torture room, etc.). The resistance monument by the fort entrance is by S. Jankevitsj (1954). At **Willebroek**, just E of the fort, the church has a 12C Romanesque tower, and an inn (Het Gulden Vlies, at the bridge) was in 1567 used for a meeting between William the Silent and Count Egmont. The small town straddles the canal of the same name which links Brussels with the river Rupel; first authorised by Mary of Burgundy in 1477, the project was bitterly opposed by Mechelen which would have been by-passed, thus losing toll rights, and the canal was not opened until 1561.

4km The Brussels-Scheldt canal and the river Rupel are crossed (bridge or tunnel), immediately beyond being **Boom** (15,000 inhab.), the most important brickmaking centre in Belgium (museum at 196 Noeveren. Monday–Friday, 09.00 to 17.00).—The main road continues N, reaching central **Antwerp** (Rte 16) in *15km*. An alternative from Boom is to take the busy and industrialised road closer to the Scheldt. At *Hemiksem* something survives (mainly 18C) of the former abbey of Sint Bernard (1246), which gave hospitality in 1338 to England's Edward III and the monks of which were the founders in the 13C of the local brick industry. From Hemiksem, Antwerp is approached through the industrial suburb of *Hoboken*, the town hall of which occupies a mansion of 1745 built by the younger Baurscheit.

B. Via Mechelen

The fastest road to Mechelen and Antwerp is the motorway. There are though several places of interest between Brussels and Mechelen, and over this stretch this Route therefore follows smaller roads. Beyond Mechelen it is assumed that most visitors will wish to take the motorway; attention is however drawn to points of interest on either side.

Total distance 46km.—*12km* **Vilvoorde**.—*12km* **Mechelen**.—*22km* **Antwerp**.

From **Brussels** (Rte 1) there is a choice of roads to Vilvoorde. One, not without industrial interest, is to follow the N side of the canal and basins extending NE from Place Sainctelette; this road, starting as the Avenue du Port, becomes the Chaussée de Vilvoorde (Vilvoordsesteenweg) which skirts the SE side of the Domaine Royal, passes below the outer ring motorway, and then crosses the canal into Vilvoorde. Another choice is to take the airport and motorway road from Place Général Meiser, branching off to visit such places as *Evere, Diegem* and *Zaventem*, for all of which see Rte 1 F.

12km **Vilvoorde** (32,000 inhab.), an industrial town on the Willebroek canal, has a 14–15C church with an unusually broad yet well-proportioned interior. The Baroque choir stalls (1663), amongst the best in Belgium, are from the former abbey of Groenendael, and the pulpit (1665) by Artus Quellin the Younger comes from the church of Sint Joris in Antwerp. Among the church's many pictures are works attributed to P.J. Verhaghen and Michiel Coxie. At one time Vilvoorde was notorious for its castle and prison, among the victims being William Tyndale, arrested as a heretic in Antwerp in 1535, imprisoned here and burnt, and also Antonie van Straelen (1521–68), the burgomaster of Antwerp who supported William of Orange and was executed here.

The direct road to Mechelen (N1. 12km) continues N out of Vilvoorde, but this Route follows a more interesting choice to the E, crossing the motorway and reaching the NW side of Brussels (Zaventem) airport. Here the road bears NE for a crossroads at **Steenokkerzeel** in which is the château of *Ham*; badly damaged in 1942 and shorn of its turrets, this was once the home of Charles de Lannoy to whom France's Francis I surrendered at Pavia in 1525.— The road N from the crossroads soon reaches **Perk**, the home of Hélène Fourment, Rubens's second wife, and of David Teniers the Younger who bought her house in 1663. The attractive *Gemeentehuis* (1652) appears in some of the artist's paintings. On the SE of the village stands the large, turreted *Château Ribaucourt* (17–19C).— *Elewijt*, 4km N, is 2km E of *Het Steen* (or *Rubenssteen*), well seen from the road. First mentioned in 1304, this château was bought by Rubens in 1635 and sold on the death of Hélène Fourment in 1681; it was much restored in 1875 and 1918. *Hofstade*, 4km N of Elewijt, is a recreation park with swimming, boating, etc. **Planckendael** (Summer, 08.30 to 18.30. Winter, 10.00 to 17.00), a short way N of Hofstade and reached off the Leuven-Mechelen road, is the breeding park of the Antwerp zoo; many animals and birds can be seen here in beautiful, open surroundings.

12km (from Vilvoorde) **MECHELEN** (Fr. *Malines*. 76,000 inhab.), in the province of Antwerp and strongly Flemish in character, is an attractive and ancient place on the Dijle with much to offer the visitor. It is particularly noted for its cathedral's massive tower, nearly 100m in height. Long famous for lace and tapestry, Mechelen is also the ecclesiastical capital of Belgium, and known too for its carillon school and carillon concerts.

Tourist Information: Stadhuis, Grote Markt.

History. In the early centuries a settlement grew among the marshes beside the Dijle and in 756 St. Rombout is said to have come here from England or Ireland, converting the people, founding an abbey, and suffering martyrdom in 775. At the beginning of the 11C the settlement became a fief of the prince-bishopric of Liège, but in 1213 this sovereignty was delegated to the locally powerful Berthoud family. Despite disputes over ownership the settlement grew into a town the citizens of which were granted charters in 1301 and 1305, enjoying a large measure of freedom until c 1333 when the place was acquired by Louis de Male, Count of Flanders, on whose death Mechelen, with the rest of Flanders, passed to the dukes of Burgundy. Much of the town was destroyed in a fire of 1342. In 1452 work started on the cathedral's great tower. In 1473 Charles the Bold founded the Grand Council as sovereign tribunal for the Netherlands, with its seat at Mechelen, and after his death his widow Margaret of York, sister of Edward IV of England, settled here. When, in 1506, Margaret of Austria was appointed governor of the Netherlands (as regent for the infant Charles V), she chose Mechelen as her capital, forming a brilliant court frequented by artists and scholars. Among these were the painters Jan Mostaert, Jan Gossaert and Bernard van Orley, the humanist Hieronymus van Busleyden, the architect Rombout Keldermans, the German artist Albrecht Dürer, and many others. But the town's period of brilliance was a short one, and after Margaret's death in 1530 the capital soon transferred to Brussels. Nevertheless Mechelen was made an archbishopric in 1559, the first archbishop (Granvelle, Philip II's French adviser) being created Primate of Belgium, a title ever since retained by his successors. A brief Calvinist interlude led to the sack of the town by Alva in 1572, but after this Mechelen thrived again, during the 17–18C becoming known for its lace and its Baroque woodwork, and during the 19C for its tapestry.

In 1914 the town was bombarded three times before being occupied, and Belgian resistance to the Germans was much encouraged by Cardinal Mercier's pastoral letter 'Patriotism and Endurance'. At the close of the Second World War damage was caused both by bombing and by German V weapons.

Mechelen was the birthplace of the painters Michiel Coxie (1499) and Frans Hals (1580).

The description below starts at the GROTE MARKT, then travels roughly clockwise round the district to its N, a round of some 2.5km. A description of the area S of the Grote Markt then follows.

In the centre of the Grote Markt stands a statue (1849) of Margaret of Austria, surrounded by a paving circle equal in size to the clock dial once on the cathedral tower. The E side of the square is filled by the **Stadhuis**, made up of two distinct buildings. That on the right is the former Lakenhalle begun in 1320 and originally modelled on that at Bruges; it was badly damaged by the great fire of 1342, the tower was never completed, and the octagonal turrets are of the 16C. In 1526 the N wing was demolished to make way for a new building to serve as the meeting-place of the Grand Council; designed by Rombout Keldermans, work on this building started in the same year but ceased in 1534, one casualty of the death of Margaret of Austria and the move of the court to Brussels. Thereafter the site was used for various purposes, but more often neglected, a fake façade being set up for formal occasions. Only in 1911 did the town take over the site and build to Keldermans's original plans. In a niche, and looking rather sour, sits Charles V, while through the arch of the Lakenhalle there is a courtyard in the centre of which is a modern sculpture, 'Mother' by Ernest Wijnants.

On the W side of the square the *Post Office* occupies an 18C house, on 13C foundations, which until 1911 served as town hall. Just S of here the **Schepenhuis**, a building of 1374, was the seat of the Grand Council from 1474 to 1618; later used as town hall, theatre and museum, today the building houses the town archives.

*Sint Romboutskathedraal is justly renowned for its great tower, but the interior of the church also merits a visit for its furnishings and paintings by several well-known artists.

In c 1217 work started on the draining of the marsh and then the construction of a church, parts of which survive in the crossing and transepts, the central nave and the lower courses of the choir. This church was dedicated in 1312 but was soon badly damaged in the fire of 1342. Rebuilding included the triforium and the enlargement of the choir with its ambulatory and chapels. The chapels off the N aisle date from 1498–1502 and the church was completed during the 16C.

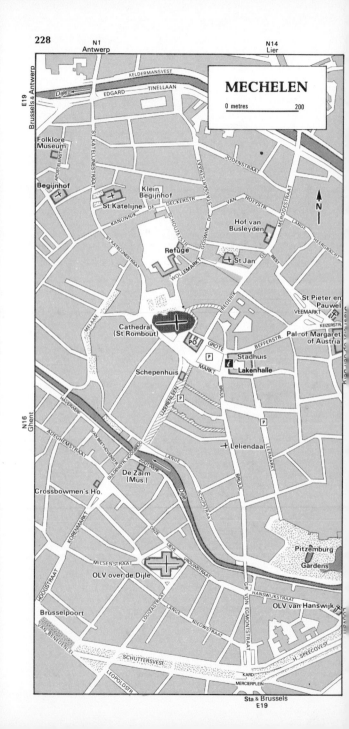

N1
Antwerp

N14
Lier

KELDERMANSVEST

EDGARD TINELLAAN

Dijle

E19
Brussels & Antwerp

MECHELEN

0 metres   200

ST KATELIJNESTRAAT

JODENSTRAAT

Folklore
Museum

APOSTELENSTRAAT

Begijnhof

St Katelijne

Klein
Begijnhof

DE BECKERSTR

VAN HOEYSTR

MERODESTRAAT

N

KANUNNIK

DE SCHOUTETSTR

GOSWIN DE STASSARTSTRAAT

Hof van
Busleyden

LANGE HEERGRACHT

ST KATELIJNESTRAAT

Refuge

WOLLEMARKT

St Jan

DE BEST

St Pieter en
Pauwel

VEEMARKT

KEIZERSTR

MELAAN

FREDERIK

Cathedral
(St Rombout)

PO

GROTE

BEFFERSTR

Pal. of Margaret
of Austria

MARKT

i

Stadhuis
Lakenhalle

Schepenhuis

P

P

IJZERENLEEN

BRUUL

HAVERWERF

VAN BEETHOVENSTR

ADEGHEMSTRAAT

N16
Ghent

GULDENSTR

P

Leliendaal

LEERMARKT

P

K HOOGBRUG

LANGE

ZOUTWERF

BRUUL

De Zalm
(Mus.)

Crossbowmen's Ho.

KORENMARKT

Dijle

SCHIPSTRAAT

ONZE LIEVE VROUWSTRAAT

Pitzemburg
Gardens

HOOGSTRAAT

MILSENSTRAAT

OLV over de Dijle

LANGE NIEUWSTRAAT

LOUIZASTRAAT

GR VON EGMONTSTRAAT

HANSWIJKSTRAAT

OLV van Hanswijk

Brusselpoort

VAN BENEDENLEI

SCHUTTERSVEST

LEOPOLDSTR

H. SPEECOVEST

KARD
MERCIERPLEIN

Sta & Brussels
E19

The TOWER was started in 1452, probably to the design of Wouter Coolman (died 1468) or Jan Keldermans who had died in 1445. The original plan for a height, with a spire, of 167m was abandoned (a model of this project can be seen in the cathedral and there are also plans in the Hof van Busleyden) and, under the direction of the Keldermans family, the tower reached its present height of 97m in 1546. The tower may be climbed, the 504 steps passing the two carillons, both with 49 bells; one dates from the 15C onwards and the other was installed in 1981. Carillon concerts are given in June–mid September: Monday, 20.30 to 21.30, with a guided visit to the tower at 19.00.

The statues of the Apostles in the nave are of the 17C. At the most western but one of the chapels off the N aisle there is a *Baroque Communion Bench attributed to Artus Quellin the Younger, while within the chapel can be seen a Circumcision by Michiel Coxie (1580) and also the mausoleum (Louis Jehotte, 1837) of Archbishop de Méan (died 1831) who piloted the see through the troubles of the French Revolution. Note also the chapel's elaborate vault. In the next chapel there is a figure (Christ Suffering, 1688) by the local sculptor Niklaas van der Veken, and in the next again a Virgin which has been venerated here since the 16C. The eastern N aisle chapel is the tomb-memorial of Cardinal Mercier (died 1926). A plaque, presented by representatives of the Church of England in 1966, honours Mercier and others who took part in the interdenominational Malines Conversations (1921–26) aimed at furthering union between the Churches. In the N transept the altar (Frans Langhermans, 1699) carries an Adoration of the Shepherds by Jan Erasmus Quellin, while opposite there is an interesting picture of the lively scene in the cathedral in 1755. In the S transept the altar (Jan van der Steen, 1700) includes a *Crucifixion by Antoon van Dyck (1627), regarded as one of the artist's most expressive works. Also in the transepts are eight statues of saints by Luc Fayd'herbe, Theodoor Verhaeghen and Pieter Valckx.

In the choir the spectacular high altar is by Luc Fayd'herbe, and there is a Mater Dolorosa by the same sculptor above a door near the northern entry to the ambulatory. Farther into the ambulatory is the tomb of the Berthoud family, lords of Mechelen during the 13–14C, opposite being a triptych (Martyrdom of St. George) by Coxie, while there is another work by Coxie (Martyrdom of St. Sebastian) in the S ambulatory. The ambulatory chapels are described clockwise. 1. Triptych by Jean le Sayve the Elder (1607). Virgin and Child surrounded by Saints by Gaspard de Crayer (1649). 2. Funerary monuments and slabs (17–19C). 3. Graveslab of Igramus van Achelen (died 1604), president of the Grand Council. 4. Graveslab of Arnould de Mérode (died 1553) and of his wife. 5. Chapel of the Holy Sacrament. 7. A chapel dedicated to priests of the see who fell during the First World War. St. Francis adoring the Madonna by De Crayer. 8. Known as the Chapel of the Relics, with a reliquary of the Martyrs of Gorcum (Gorinchem, near Dordrecht in Holland), 19 monks, priests and others cruelly killed by Calvinists in 1572 and all canonised in 1867. Hatchments of the Knights of the Golden Fleece present at the chapter held here in 1491. 9. St. Luke painting the Virgin by Abraham Janssens.

At No. 5 Minderbroedersgang, immediately W of the cathedral, the *Ernest Wijnants Museum* is devoted to the sculptor of this name (Easter–first Sunday in October: Saturday, Sunday, Holidays, 10.00 to 12.00, 14.00 to 17.00. Also open Monday in July and August).

From the cathedral Sint Katelijnestraat curves NW to reach in c 400m (right) the church of Sint Katelijne (left), the church of the Begijnhof, and, just N of the latter, the Museum voor Folklore. The **Sint Katelijnekerk**, of the mid 14C but with a portal of the 15C, contains *Confessionals by Niklaas van der Veken (1700), a statue (at the choir entrance) of St. Catherine by Piérard de Lyon (1716), and stalls with 18C reliefs by Pieter Valckx, the character achieved in the exquisitely carved faces deserving attention. The Baroque **Begijnhofkerk** was built in 1629–47 by Jacob Franckaert and is associated with Luc Fayd'herbe, responsible for the statue of St. Catherine above the porch and for that of God the Father at the top of the façade. The interior contains sculpture and paintings by Fayd'herbe, Jan van der Steen, Jerome Duquesnoy the Younger, De Crayer, Jan Erasmus Quellin and Cornelis Cels. The **Museum voor Folklore** (Easter–first Sunday in October: Saturday, Sunday, Holidays, 10.00 to 12.00, 14.00 to 17.00; also Monday in July and August), due N of the Begijnhof church at 17 Twaalf Apostelenstraat, features an old pharmacy and an inn.

The KLEIN BEGIJNHOF, still with some small houses and alleys, is just E of the church of Sint Katelijne.

The story of the Mechelen Begijnhof is little documented and rather confused, but it seems to have formed during the 13C and to have become an autonomous parish to the N of the town by c 1295. Some of the older members, however, chose to settle in the area now known (since 1562) as the Klein Begijnhof. The Begijnhof proper was frequently attacked and pillaged, notably by Calvinists in 1580–85, and in 1595 a new close was obtained within the town. This, known as the Groot Begijnhof, and also with small houses and streets, is to the W of the Begijnhof church.

Immediately to the S of the Klein Begijnhof, between Kanunnik de Deckerstraat and Schoutetstraat, are the _Refuge of the Abbey of Tongerlo_ (1483) and the _Refuge of the Abbey of St. Truiden_ (c 1500). The latter, in a particularly attractive setting by a pool surviving from a now covered branch of the Dijle, is best seen from Wollemarkt, the SW extension of Goswin de Stassartstraat. Opposite this view-point leads to the little Klapgat leads to the 15C **Sint Janskerk**, noted for a *Triptych by Rubens (1619) with, in the centre, the Adoration of the Magi in which the artist's first wife is a model for the Virgin. Also in this church are (W end) benches and organ case carved by Pieter Valckx; pulpit and two benches by the transept pillars by Theodoor Verhaeghen and pupils; and a painting of the Disciples at Emmaus by G.J. Herreyns.

To the NE of the church and next door to one another are the Carillon School and the Hof van Busleyden.

The _Carillon School (Koninklijke Beiaardschool 'Jef Denyn')_ is named after Mechelen's distinguished master-carilloneur (1862–1941) on whose sixtieth birthday the school was founded. Students come from all over the world. The **Carillon Museum**, with bells, carillons and documentation, is on the S side of the main entrance to the Hof van Busleyden (opening usually as for Hof van Busleyden).

The **Hof van Busleyden** (1503–17), the home of Hieronymus van Busleyden (c 1470–1517), now houses the municipal museum. Quite apart from the interest of its contents, the house is well worth visiting as an old and gracious mansion with a fine courtyard. It is open daily except Tuesday, 10.00 to 12.00, 14.00 to 17.00, or to 16.00 October to Easter.

Hieronymus van Busleyden, member of a noble Luxembourg family, studied at Louvain and Bologna, becoming a Doctor of Law and so impressing Philip the Handsome that he was appointed counsellor to the Grand Council. A friend of

Mechelen, Refuge of the Abbey of Sint Truiden

Thomas More and Erasmus, he helped the latter found his Collegium Trilingue (Latin, Greek and Hebrew) at Louvain. He was a member of the brilliant and scholarly circle around Margaret of Austria, and died on the way to Spain while on a mission for Charles V.—The mansion was probably to the plans of Antoon Keldermans and built by his son Rombout. In 1619 Wenceslas Coeberger opened a municipal pawnshop here, and the building continued to be in part used for this purpose until the First World War.

The museum collections are mixed but not without interest and there are also some good pictures. In the Entrance Hall and adjacent room there is sculpture (including pieces by *Luc Fayd'herbe*), stonework from old Mechelen and some Gallo-Roman material. Room 6 shows an interesting plan of Mechelen in 1574, and in Room 8, with a curious candelabra designed for oil lighting, the paintings include a Landscape by *David Vinckeboons* and other paintings. In Room 10 pride of place is given to a Crucifixion by *Rubens*. Room 11 is devoted to the Grand Council, with some interesting pictures of the Council in session. Room 12, once Van Busleyden's small dining room, contains murals, in origin attributed to *Bernard van Orley* or *Michiel Coxie*.— Upstairs, to the right, Rooms 14 to 20 are for the most part devoted to 19th and 20C art, notable being sculpture by *Rik Wouters* and a Virgin and Christ painted by *A. Servaes*. Room 17, though, is that of the halberdiers and arquebusiers, with a number of group and individual portraits.—Upstairs, to the left, first comes Room 21 showing the interesting and ambitious plans for the originally proposed 167m-high cathedral tower and spire. Room 21 is also the home, in a glass case, of 'Op Signor', a grotesque wooden doll of 1647 which is the mascot of Mechelen; the name derives from 'señor', long given in mockery to the men of Antwerp. Room 22 contains Mechelen alabasters (16C); wooden statuary (14C); and pictures by *Joos de Momper, Gaspard de Crayer, Frans Snyders* and others. In Room 23 there is a sculpture by *Luc Fayd'herbe*, and also pictures by, amongst others, *Frans Pourbus the Elder* (attributed) and *Jacques Carabain*. In Room 26 can be seen a portrait of Luc Fayd'herbe, in Room 25 the pictures are mostly of the 19C, and in Room 26 the pictures include a portrait of the Abbot of Tongerlo by *Jan Erasmus Quellin*, an Adoration of the Shepherds by *Pieter Coecke*, and a Crucifixion by *Michiel Coxie*. Room 27 shows 17C globes and 19C portraits, and Room 28 historical pictures, including two of the attack on Mechelen in 1580 by the Sea Beggars and one of the surrender to Alva in 1572.

From opposite the Carillon School, the street known as Biest leads to the triangular VEEMARKT with the **Sint Pieter en Sint Pauwelkerk**. Built in the Jesuit style (1670–77), the church contains paintings by Jan Erasmus Quellin and others depicting the life of St. Francis Xavier and also a pulpit (Hendrik Verbruggen, 1700) symbolising the saint's missionary work. The **Palace of Margaret of Austria**, roughly opposite on Keizerstraat, became the seat of the Grand Council in 1618–1794 and today serves as law courts. The Renaissance front, among the first of its kind in the Netherlands, is by Guyot de Beaugrant, while the oldest part of the building, in the courtyard (1507–17), is by Rombout Keldermans. The **Schouwburg** (municipal theatre), opposite, also known as the Keizershof and in part of the 15C, was the palace of Margaret of York.

To the NE, 300m away by way of Keizerstraat and near the Nekkerspoel station, the *Centrum voor Speelgoed* (Toy Museum. Daily except Monday, 14.00 to 17.00) is essentially a museum of life as seen through the eyes of children.

From the Schouwburg the return to the Grote Markt is due W along Befferstraat (350m).

SOUTHERN MECHELEN is best visited by following Ijzerenleen SW from the Grote Markt, the round, excluding the diversion to the

Brusselpoort, covering c 2.5km. Ijzerenleen (the name deriving from the iron railings of 1531 which here bordered a canal covered over during the 17C) ends at **Hoogbrug**, dating from 1298 and even then successor to a wooden bridge which was the town's first; rebuilt in 1595 the bridge has irregular arches and traces of guard towers.

To the right across the river, on Haverwerf (Oats Wharf) beyond a brewery, there are three 16–17C façades, one being of wood. Van Beethovenstraat, running through the brewery, is named after the composer's grandfather (1712–73) who was born here.

Continuing SW from the Hoogbrug, Guldenstraat leads into Korenmarkt, with the *House of the Crossbowmen* on the right. Beyond, at the end of Hoogstraat (500m from Hoogbrug) stands the solid **Brusselpoort**, the only survivor of Mechelen's original 12 gates; built in c 1300 the gate has 17C additions.

On the picturesque Zoutwerf (Salt Wharf), to the left across the Hoogbrug, **De Zalm** (Salmon) is a house with a façade of 1530. Built for the Guild of Fishmongers, the house is now a small, mixed museum, with some rooms devoted to lace and, upstairs, metalwork, including some intricate old locks (Daily except Friday, 10.00 to 12.00, 14.00 to 17.00). To the S (c 250m) is the church of **Onze Lieve Vrouw over de Dijle**, with a nave and tower built during the 15C although the church was not completed until well into the 17C by Jacob Franckaert who was at the same time working on the Begijnhof church; damaged by artillery in 1914, by air raids in 1944, and by a V weapon in 1945, the church was restored by J. Lauwers in 1962–68. Inside, in the S transept, hangs the *Miraculous draught of Fishes, a triptych painted by Rubens in 1618 for the Guild of Fishmongers, while above the high-altar there is a Last Supper by Jan Erasmus Quellin.

Onze Lieve Vrouwstraat leads SE from the church, soon reaching a small open space known as VIJFHOEK.

To the S, Graaf van Egmontstraat leads to Kardinaal Mercierplein and, beyond, the station.
To the N across the river, Bruul returns in 600m to the Grote Markt, on the way passing the Jesuit church of **Leliendaal** (Luc Fayd'herbe, 1662).

Hanswijkstraat, E out of Vijfhoek, reaches the church of **Onze Lieve Vrouw van Hanswijk**, built in 1663–78 to plans by Fayd'herbe and containing statues and reliefs by Fayd'herbe and a pulpit by Verhaeghen. Just beyond the church there is an old fulling mill beside the river. Here the river can be crossed to the **Kruidtuin**, or Pitzemburg Garden, with a statue to Rembrecht Dodoens (1517–85), a botanist native of Mechelen. From the NW corner of the garden Leermarkt returns in 400m to the Grote Markt.

From Mechelen the motorway reaches **Antwerp** (Rte 16) in *22km*. Places of interest to either side of the motorway are noted below.

WEST OF THE MOTORWAY. **Heindonk**, S of the Rupel, has a town hall of 1550. **Rumst**, within the N angle of the confluence of the Rupel and the Nete, is an important horticultural centre. At **Reet**, 3km NW of Rumst, the church has a 15C tower and the Hof van Reet is a château of the 17C.

EAST OF THE MOTORWAY. **Duffel**, on the Nete, was during the 16C known for its manufacture of woollen garments (hence 'duffle coat', etc.). The town was the birthplace of Kilianus (Cornelis Kiel, 1528–1607), founder of Dutch philology and associate of Christopher Plantin. The castle of Ter Elst is of the 16C. **Kontich** traces its origins to Gallo-Roman times, from which period there is a 'fountain' in the municipal park. The *Sint Maartenskerk* has a 12C Romanesque tower, and there is a small museum at 32 Molenstraat. At **Hove**, 3km NE of Kontich, the *Urania Observatory* is open on Tuesday and Friday at 20.00. At **Edegem**, with a Grotto of Our Lady of Lourdes, the château of Ter Linden dates from 1760.

16 Antwerp

ANTWERP (Flem. **Antwerpen**. Fr *Anvers*. 500,000 inhab.), the chief
city of Flemish Belgium and capital of the province of the same name,
is not only a great city, port and expanding industrial complex but
also one of Belgium's principal tourist centres, known for its historic
old quarters; for its cathedral famed for its collection of religious
works by Rubens; for its numerous and diverse churches, museums
(including Rubens's house) and art galleries; for its lively cafés and
restaurants; and for its waterfront and port, most of which is readily
accessible.

On the right bank of the broad Scheldt and one of Europe's leading
ports, Antwerp is some 90km from the sea, the greater part of the
passage being through Dutch waters which begin a short distance
beyond the limits of the port area; a geographic fact which for
centuries has had a decisive influence on the city's fortunes. The
main city lies within a semicircle of boulevards (Italielei, Britselei,
etc.), nearly 4km long, laid out in 1859 along the course of the former
ramparts. An outer ring of replacement fortifications, about 30km in
circumference, proved ineffective in 1914 and though something can
still be seen of the great star-shaped forts these defences are fast
being swamped by the city's modern spread.

LEFT BANK. The land enclosed by the sharp curve of the Scheldt
opposite Antwerp, once site of a great moated redoubt but now
largely covered by modern residential and office development, is of
little tourist interest. By the exit from the Sint Annatunnel there is a
garden with anchors, buoys and suchlike, while, farther N beyond
the yacht basin, *Sint Annastrand* is a popular waterside area and
beach.—The districts along this left bank of the Scheldt are becoming increasingly industrialised. *Kallo*, 8km from Antwerp's Waaslandtunnel, was where in 1584 Parma built a long barrage into the
river in order to block the port, then under siege, and the star-shaped
fort to the N is the most NW of those built during the 19th and 20C.
Doel, a polder village 8km farther N and close to the Dutch border,
has a picturesque port and an old stone windmill. To the N there is a
nuclear power station.

City Centre. The main central axis extends from the Grote Markt along the
Meir to the Centraal Station.

Tourist Information. *City*: 9 Gildekamer, just off the SW corner of the Grote
Markt. Monday–Friday, 08.30 to 18.00; Saturday, Sunday, Holidays, 09.00 to
17.00. Tel: 232 01 03. It should be noted that a move is planned for 1990–91
across to the corner of the Grote Markt and Wisselstraat. There is also an office
on Koningin Astridplein in front of the Centraal Station. Monday–Friday, 08.30
to 20.00; Saturday, 09.00 to 19.00; Sunday, Holidays, 09.00 to 17.00.—*Province
of Antwerp*: 11 Karl Oomsstraat.

How to see the City. Although much of interest is reasonably close to the Grote
Markt, Antwerp is a large city and there is much that is farther afield and thus a
good deal of walking must be expected. *Guides*. Tourist Information will
arrange individual guided visits, these including some of the museums, the city
and the port. Two hours minimum. *Coach*. Normally from Grote Markt.
Information and tickets from Tourist Information. *Public Transport*. Basically a
tram system, in part becoming Metro. Map from Tourist Information. *Horse-
drawn Carriage*. Grote Markt. Easter–September: About 12.00 to 18.00. *Boat*.
See below. *Private Car*. Antwerp is reasonably well provided with parking
facilities and (with a navigating passenger) it is practicable to use a car, at least
for sites outside the immediate centre.

Stations. *Centraal*, E of the ring boulevards, for most main line services.
Berchem, to the S, for many international expresses.

Airport. Deurne, 5km E of centre.

Scheldt Tunnels. In the S the *J.F. Kennedytunnel* is for the A14/E17 motorway to Ghent. The *Sint Annatunnel* (500m), a short distance upstream from the Steen, is for pedestrians and cyclists. *Waaslandtunnel* (entrance in Tunnelplaats, off Italielei) is for motor traffic only. A fourth tunnel, for the Metro and near the Sint Annatunnel, is planned for c 1989.

Post Office. Main office, 42 Groenplaats. Also many others, including 12 Pelikaanstraat near the Centraal Station. Most offices open Monday–Friday, 09.00 to 17.00.

Telegraph and Telephone. Main office, 1 Jezusstraat (Daily 08.00 to 20.00). Also Centraal Station (Monday–Friday, 09.00 to 17.00).

Diamonds. Lodewijk van Bercken, a native of Bruges but living in Antwerp, in 1476 developed the art of diamond polishing. Since his time diamond handling has become an important industry both of Antwerp province and of the city. Something of the background of this industry may be seen at the Provinciaal Diamantmuseum at 28 Jezusstraat.

Boat Excursions. The operating company is Flandria on Steenplein. Tel: 233 74 22. The principal excursions are the local Scheldt cruise (50 minutes); an extended Scheldt cruise (1½ hours); and the round of the port (2½ hours). Day excusions may include Ostend and, in Holland, Flushing (Vlissingen), Zierikzee, Middelburg, Veere, Willemstad and Rotterdam.

History. Legend associated the origin of the city with the activities of a giant, Druon Antigonus, who exacted tribute from Scheldt shipping, severing the hands of all who failed to pay. Hence the severed hands in the city arms, and hence also perhaps the origin of the name ('hand werp', meaning 'hand throw'). Antigonus was finally vanquished by Silvius Brabo, a youthful relative of Julius Caesar, who, adapting his own name, became first duke of Brabant. A more probable if less colourful derivation of the city's name is from 'Aen de werpen', meaning either 'at the cast' (of the anchor) or simply 'at the wharf'. Historically, it is known that there was a settlement here in the 2C, and the first church is said to have been built by St. Amand in 660. Benedictine monks from Ireland may have undertaken the draining of the polders.

In the 9C, the Norsemen built a fortress here, parts of which have been traced in the Steen. The first town walls date from the 11C, when the margravate (border countship) of Antwerp was held by the counts of Ardennes and Bouillon, one of whom was the famous Godfrey de Bouillon, leader of the First Crusade. In the 13C, the town passed to the dukes of Brabant, of whom John II (died 1312) was the husband of Margaret, daughter of Edward I of England. In 1338–40, when Ghent's Jacob van Artevelde allied the Flemish towns to England's Edward III, the latter held court at the abbey of St. Bernard, near Hemiksem, and here was born his second son, Lionel, later Duke of Clarence. Soon afterwards (1357) Louis de Male invaded Brabant and acquired Antwerp for the counts of Flanders, and it was as a part of Flanders that it passed to Burgundy. In the 15C, Antwerp rapidly rose in importance, at the expense of Bruges, then in full decline, and, while the Zwin was silting up, the Scheldt had been considerably widened by flooding in Zeeland. Thus Antwerp became the chief port of the Netherlands, and by the beginning of the 16C a thousand foreign business houses were established here. The Antwerp Guild of St. Luke, founded in 1454 by Philip the Good for the encouragement of painting, may be regarded as a foundation of the Flemish School; the guild was host to Albrecht Dürer during his stay in Antwerp (1520–21).

This prosperity could not survive the reign of Philip II and the rule of the Spaniards. The city was rent by religious dissensions and in the Calvinist 'iconoclastic fury' of 1566 the cathedral was pillaged. Ten years later came the 'Spanish fury', when Antwerp was sacked by Alva's mutinous soldiery. The following year (1577), with William of Orange in Flanders, Antwerp threw off the Spanish yoke and for eight years the open practice of Catholicism was forbidden. But 1580 saw the beginning of Parma's campaign of reconquest for Spain, and in 1585, after withstanding a two-years siege under Marnix van St. Aldegonde, the city capitulated, giving Parma his last real success. This meant that Antwerp was destined to belong to Belgium rather than Holland, while from now on the United Provinces, an ever-present threat to the vital Scheldt, ruled most of the lands to the north.

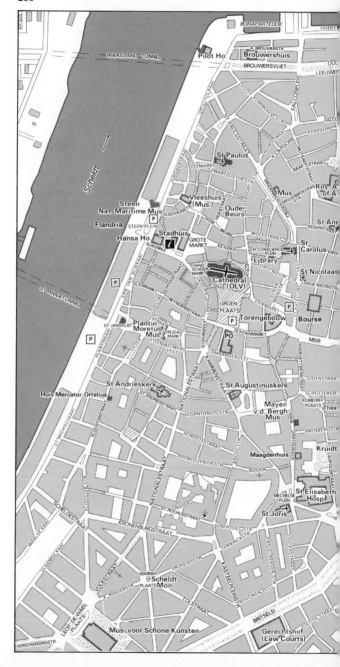

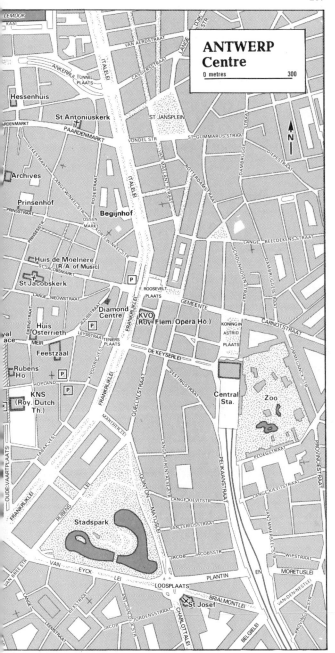

The reign of the 'archdukes', who made their state entry on 20 December 1599, inaugurated a brief peaceful interlude during which Antwerp regained something of its pristine glory. With Rubens as their leader, the painters of this period included David Teniers the Elder, David Teniers the Younger, and Jacob Jordaens, while at about the same time a literary circle revolving round Balthasar Moretus included G.C. Gevaerts, or Gevartius, poet and secretary of the city, and also the poetesses Anna and Maria Visscher. Throughout this period, though, there was increasing pressure from the United Provinces, culminating in the signing of the Treaty of Münster (1648), under which Spain had to agree to the closing of the Scheldt. For Antwerp this meant 150 years of ruin, accompanied by all the vicissitudes of the Spanish decline and the many wars that filled these years.

By the close of the 18C, and now in the hands of the French, the city, with a population of only 40,000, had reached the lowest point of its fortunes. It owes its revival to Napoleon, who not only reopened the Scheldt but also constructed docks and a naval harbour, 'a pistol aimed at the heart of England'. There followed the years (1815–30) of the United Kingdom of the Netherlands, ended by the Belgian revolution during which Antwerp was bombarded by the Dutch, whose garrison held out until forced to surrender in 1832 by Marshal Gérard, leading a French force assisting the first Belgian king, Leopold I.

The modern prosperity of Antwerp, and the growth of today's port, dates from 1862, when the right to levy dues on Scheldt shipping, granted to Holland in 1839, was redeemed by the payment by Belgium of a large compensation.

Antwerp played an important part at the beginning of the First World War, the government arriving from Brussels on 17 August 1914 and the city coming under German siege on 28 September. The forts, vaunted as the last word in modern defence, were rapidly silenced. On 4 October the British First Lord of the Admiralty, Mr Winston Churchill, arrived with Royal Marines and Royal Navy reinforcements, but two days later the Germans pushed within bombardment range of the city itself, the government sailed for Ostend, and Antwerp surrendered on 10 October. Many of the population fled to Holland, and some 2500 British troops were forced across the border into internment. During the Second World War Antwerp was early abandoned, but towards the end, retaken by the Allies, it suffered severely under V1 and V2 attack.

Routes from Antwerp. To *Holland*, see Rte 17; to *Turnhout* and *Maaseik*, see Rte 18; to *Genk*, see Rte 19; to *Hasselt* and *Maastricht*, see Rte 20; to *Ghent*, see Rte 14; to *Brussels*, see Rte 15.

Antwerp is described below by four districts: A. Central Antwerp; B. South-West of the Centre; C. South-East of the Centre; and D. The Docks and Beyond (Havenroute). Three principal museums are described as individual sections: E. Plantin-Moretus; F. Rubens's House; and G. Schone Kunsten.

A. Central Antwerp

The tourist heart of Antwerp is the GROTE MARKT, from where many places of interest are within walking distance. These include the Stadhuis; the Cathedral; the Volkskunde Museum (folklore and ethnology); the Plantin-Moretus Museum (printing; art treasures); the waterfront, with the Steen fort housing the Maritime Museum; and the Vleeshuis, the ancient Butchers' Hall with its museum of applied art. Rather farther afield are (N) the Sint Pauluskerk and the Brouwershuis, (E) Rubens's House, and (S) the Mayer van den Bergh and Maagdenhuis collections.

The central feature of the GROTE MARKT is the **Brabo Fountain** (1887) by Jef Lambeaux, with a figure of Silvius Brabo in the act of throwing the hand of the giant Antigonus into the Scheldt. Around the square there are a number of old or restored houses, many now with restaurants or cafés. The Stadhuis apart, the most noteworthy buildings are, on the N side, *In den Engel* (No. 3, 1579); the *Coopers' House* (No. 5, 1579); the *Oude* and the *Jonge Handboog* (Nos 7 and 9,

1582 and c 1500), belonging respectively to two guilds of crossbow-men; the *Mercers' House* (No. 17, c 1515). On the SE side No. 38 was the *Drapers' House* (1615) and No. 40 the *Carpenters' House*, both these houses bearing trade carving.

The **Stadhuis** (Monday, 09.00 to 12.00; Tuesday–Thursday, 09.00 to 15.00; Friday, 12.00 to 15.00; Saturday, 09.00 to 16.00. Closed during official receptions), filling the W side of the Grote Markt, was built in Renaissance style in 1561–65 by Cornelis Floris, possibly working to plans by the Florentine Nicolo Scarini. Ten years later, during the 'Spanish fury', the building was in part destroyed by rioting Spanish soldiery, largely because it housed the city's armoury; it was rebuilt immediately afterwards. The long façade bears in the centre a statue of the Virgin, below which are the arms (left to right) of Brabant, Philip II, and the margravate of Antwerp, while between stand figures of Justice and Wisdom. Inside, a stairway ascends to the Landing, a part of the building which until covered during the 19C was an open court with the city's guns. Paintings here of 1899 show scenes from the 16C history of Antwerp, those on the W depicting economic prosperity, those on the other side the arts. The Grote Leyszaal contains four large historical paintings by Hendrik Leys, who died in 1869 before completing the planned six. Other pictures (1855) by the same artist, once in his house, now hang in the Kleine Leyszaal. In the Trouwzaal, the Wedding Room, the 16C chimneypiece has caryatids by Cornelis Floris, and the murals (Victor Lagye, 1886) depict Belgian wedding ceremonies throughout the centuries. In the Militia Room, once the scene of the conscription ballot, there is a picture showing Antwerp's earlier town hall (1406). The Raadzaal (Council Chamber) has ceiling panels by Jacob de Roore; painted in c 1715 they reflect in allegory the city's reaction to the Barrier Treaty under which Belgium was forced to accept Dutch garrisons. The Burgemeesterzaal, generally in the style of 1885, contains a 16C chimneypiece by Pieter Coecke.

Behind the Stadhuis runs the short Gildekamerstraat, in 1954 attractively rebuilt in the old style. No. 4, perhaps originally by Cornelis Floris, is striking, while Nos 2–4 now house the **Volkskundemuseum**, in the process of major reorganisation and due to open in c 1989 as an important two-part museum, one devoted to the Antwerp region (archaeology, custom, crafts, guilds, etc.) and the other a museum of worldwide ethnology (probably daily except Monday, 10.00 to 17.00. Open Monday if Holiday. Closed 1 and 2 January, 1 May, Ascension, 1 November, 25 and 26 December).

At the S end of the Stadhuis stands Constantin Meunier's figure, 'The Docker'. From here the short Suikerrui soon reaches the Scheldt, on the quay corner being the **Hansahuis** decorated with female figures by Jef Lambeaux. (Under a long-term redevelopment plan for the N side of Suikerrui, Tourist Information will move in 1989–90 to the corner of Grote Markt and Wisselstraat, the present premises then becoming part of the large new museum mentioned just above.)

To the immediate S of Suikerrui, Nos 11–13 Hoogstraat occupy the site of the birthplace (1593) of the painter Jacob Jordaens, while just beyond (left) No. 4 Reyndersstraat is the house he built in 1641 and in which he lived until his death in 1678. Heilig Geeststraat, the next street parallel to Reyndersstraat, runs into the VRIJDAGMARKT, scene of a second-hand market on Wednesday and Friday mornings. The W side is occupied by the **Plantin-Moretus Museum, see E. The adjacent *Prentenkabinet* (Print Room) contains a valuable collection of prints and engravings, especially by Antwerp masters; admission is normally only for study purposes. The **Sint Annatunnel** beneath the Scheldt, built in 1933 for cyclists and pedestrians, starts from Sint Jansvliet, an open space just W of the Vrijdagmarkt.

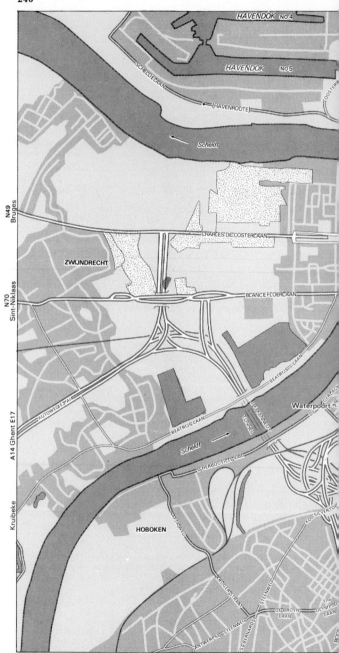

HAVENDOK No 4

HAVENDOK No 5

SCHELDE KAAI

(HAVENROUTE)

OOSTER

Scheldt

N49
Bruges

CHARLES DE COSTERLAAN

ZWIJNDRECHT

N70
Sint-Niklaas

BLANCEFLOERLAAN

BEATRIJS LAAN

Waterpoort

DE CLERC PL

A14 Ghent E17

AUTOWEG E17

J.F. KENNEDY

TUNNEL

BEATRIJS LAAN

Scheldt

KOG SILVER TOP

Kruibeke

SCHERBOOQUILLE KAAI

HOBOKEN

KRIJGSBAAN

ANTWERPSE STEENWEG

ST BERNARDSE STEENWEG

DE BRUYN LAAN

Ville
OLYMPIA
LAAN

Brusse
N17

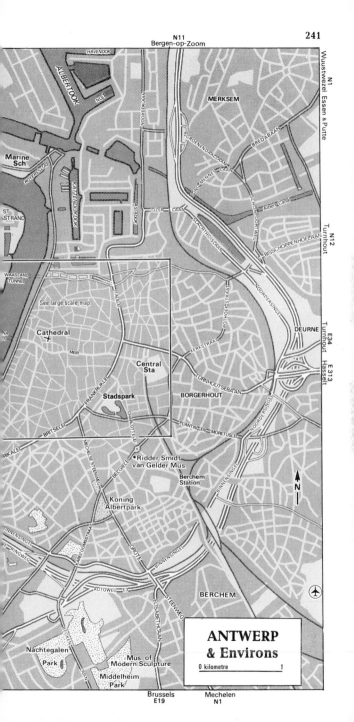

ANTWERP
& Environs

0 kilometre   1

The QUAYS, started by Napoleon, completed between 1880 and 1885, but today decreasingly used as the main port downstream expands, stretch for some 5km from SW of the J.F. Kennedytunnel up .to beyond the Waaslandtunnel. They took the place of the crowded, casual old waterfront and to build them the river bank was straightened, some 800 houses were demolished, and a pier which carried the town crane was removed. Near the foot of Suikerrui are the Steen fortress and the wharf used by the 'Flandria' excursion boats, and from here in either direction extend open warehouses notable for their ironwork pediments and carrying pedestrian terraces.

The **Steen** has foundations as old as the 9C when a fortress was built here to defend the frontier established by the Treaty of Verdun, but the oldest section of visible wall dates from c 1250 at which time the building served as a prison which became especially notorious during Alva's rule. Restored under Charles V in 1520 (by Domien de Waghemakere and Rombout Keldermans), the Steen was rebuilt in 1890 and received further attention in 1953, but what is seen today represents only the gatehouse and front section of the original castle. Outside the entrance stands the figure known as 'Lange Wapper' (A. Poels, 1963). In medieval times the canal from Herentals (used for bringing clean water for brewing) ran under a bridge on which the brewers constructed a large wooden fork with a long beam (wapper) used to lift the barrels of water. When this landmark, known as the 'Lange Wapper', disappeared, contemporary imagination soon replaced it with a similarly shaped folklore figure notorious for his tricks, one of which was to grow at will and peer through windows.

Today the Steen houses the **National Maritime Museum** (Daily 10.00 to 17.00, but closed 1 and 2 January, 1 May, Ascension Day, 1 and 2 November, 25 and 26 December). The museum, in a series of small rooms (linked by narrow passages and some steep stairs) and especially notable for its many superb ship models, is organised as twelve sections as follows. 1. The Waterfront, arts and crafts. 2. The Waterfront, ship models. 3. The Waterfront, religion and superstition. Noteworthy here are a votive ship of c 1757 and a graveslab bearing a caravel. 4. The Waterfront, the people. 5. Inland navigation, with two attractive and interesting pictures of old Antwerp by Jan.Ruyten. 6. Fishing, with models explaining methods of netting. 7. A room with a variety of ship models. 8. Shipbuilding, here being a particularly good *Diorama of an Antwerp shipyard of c 1850. 9. History of shipping from early times to the close of the 18C, this section and No. 10 containing some of the finest and largest models; also fragments of a 2C boat found in 1899 during the digging of the Bruges–Zeebrugge canal. Pictures by Willem van de Velde the Younger (Salute to an Amsterdam ship). 10. History of shipping (19th and 20C), the models here ranging from Napoleon's state barge to more or less modern ships. 11. New acquisitions. 12. Council chamber, with paintings by Bonaventure Peeters and J.B. de Bonnecroy which vividly bring to life old Antwerp and its waterfront. Behind the Steen there is an open-air section of the museum with a lighter (the 'Lauranda', 1928) which can be walked through (exhibitions). Here too there is a large shed showing barges, lighters and other craft, and here also a plaque honours the 1st Canadian Army, which, with British and Polish units, liberated the Scheldt estuary in Autumn 1944 and thus reopened the port of Antwerp.

Just across the road from the Steen the short Vleeshuisstraat runs E through a cut in the old wall to the *Vleeshuis, a large gabled and turreted building erected by Herman de Waghemakere in 1503 for the Butchers' Guild and today housing a museum (Daily except Monday, 10.00 to 17.00, but open Easter Monday, Whit Monday, and the Monday following the second Sunday in August. Closed 1 and 2 January, 1 May, Ascension Day, 1 November, 25 and 26 December). The museum collections are rich and varied, some emphasis being placed on musical instruments, and the building is also well worth visiting for its magnificent halls and elegant rooms. The Ground Floor Hall, vaulted in brick from a central row of six columns and used for the sale of meat until the 1840s, now shows metalwork, arms and armour; 16–18C sculpture and woodcarving, notably an oak pulpit and a Brabant altarpiece (1514); an embroidered cope of 1525; several magnificent chests; and 16C murals from an old Antwerp house now in the museum at Bokrijk. A long steep spiral stair climbs to the First Floor (another great hall), at the top of the stairs being a small picture-tiled kitchen with a huge pump. Adjacent, but around the corner, there is a small room with leather wall hangings and, adjacent again, is the Council Chamber of the Butchers, its walls covered by gilt-leather and tapestry. Beyond, around the hall, are gold, silver and jewellery; some musical instruments; and furniture, including a chest of the 14C. Among the several pictures on this floor, note a Spanish Fury (Anon., 1576, and thus possibly the work of an eye-witness), filled with lurid and bloody detail and including (bottom left corner) an incipient rape in which the victim's reaction provides almost comical relief amid the gore.

Another steep stair spirals up to the Second Floor, with a small Egyptian section and the main collection of musical instruments. In the spacious, brick-vaulted Basement, a Lapidarium houses old stonework from Antwerp churches and other buildings.

Burchtgracht, running N from the Vleeshuis, was once the moat of the 'burcht', or castle (the Steen).

The immediate surrounds of the Vleeshuis have been pleasingly redeveloped in the old style. Just to the E, beyond a small housing complex, the street called Oude Beurs leads eastwards, at this street's W end behind a modern building incorporating a Baroque portal being a house with a turret; known as *De Spieghel*, it was here that Thomas More stayed in 1515, meeting Erasmus and his friend Peter Giles (Aegidius) and sketching out 'Utopia'. It was also in this street that William Tyndale, translator into English of the New Testament, lived as a refugee in 1534–35 before being burnt at the stake at Vilvoorde. No. 15, in adjacent Hofstraat, is the actual Oude Beurs (Old Exchange), in origin of 1515, and the painter Adam van Noort lived in a house which once stood opposite.

To the North of the Steen and Vleeshuis

To the N of the Steen and the Vleeshuis are (200m) the church of Sint Paulus, with works by Rubens and others, and the Brouwershuis (300m farther). To the N again begin the docks (see D.).

The *Sint Pauluskerk (May–September: daily except Sunday and Monday, 09.00 to 12.00, 14.00 to 17.00. October–April: daily, 09.00 to 12.00. Entrance 20 Sint Paulustraat) stands on the site of a church built for the Dominicans in 1276. The present church, one of the last in Gothic style, was begun in 1517, though not consecrated until 1571. Seven years later the Dominicans were expelled by the Calvinists, the transepts and choir then being largely demolished and their stones later used to ballast the fireships used in 1584 against Parma's Scheldt barrage at Kallo. On their return the Dominicans completed rebuilding by 1639, only to have the tower destroyed by fire in 1679; it was then rebuilt in Baroque style. Badly damaged by Dutch bombardment in 1830, the church was again severely damaged, this time by fire, in 1968.

Today this church is a surprising place, filled with works of art by a galaxy of names, not least, so far as sculpture and carving are concerned, Pieter Verbruggen the Elder. There are also three works by Rubens.

On entering, the first thing that strikes the visitor is the rich glow of the row of paintings along the wall of the NAVE N Aisle, these being the Fifteen Mysteries of the Rosary, all panels painted between 1617–19. Among the artists are Frans Francken the Younger (Visitation); Cornelis de Vos (Nativity. Presentation at the Temple); David Teniers the Elder (Gethsemane); Antoon Van Dyck (Bearing of the Cross); Jacob Jordaens (Crucifixion); and Pieter Paul Rubens (Scourging, the sketch for which can be seen in the Museum Voor Schone Kunsten in Ghent). In the Central Nave the statues of the apostles are attributed to Michiel van der Voort and the organ carving to Pieter Verbruggen the Elder, while the 'Soeten Naem' marble of 1644 is the work of Artus Quellin the Elder. In the Nave S Aisle the five confessionals are attributed to Pieter Verbruggen the Elder.

Moving to the SOUTH TRANSEPT, Verbruggen created the two altars (both 1654) and also probably the communion bench of 1655. Above one altar hangs The Dispute on the Nature of the Holy Sacrament, painted by Rubens in c 1609 and superbly restored in 1973; above the other altar a Pietà by Gaspard de Crayer (c 1654). Also in this transept, the Walk to Emmaus by Erasmus Quellin. In the NORTH TRANSEPT the outstanding picture is Rubens's Adoration of the Shepherds, painted in c 1609, badly damaged by the fire of 1968 and returned, restored, in 1972. Other canvases here are a copy of Caravaggio's Madonna of the Rosary (the original, removed by the Emperor Joseph II in 1781, is now in Vienna's Kunsthistorisches Museum) and Our Lady and St. Dominic by Gaspard de Crayer, while equally noteworthy is Artus Quellin the Younger's marble figure of Rose of Lima.

In the CHOIR the high-altar is in part the work of Pieter Verbruggen the Elder. Once, this framed Rubens's Vision of St. Dominic (now in the Musée des Beaux Arts at Lyon), replaced by the Descent from the Cross by Cornelis Cels (1807). Also noteworthy are the stalls, decorated with the arms of donors, attributed to Verbruggen; and the eight statues of Dominican saints, four of which are by Verbruggen (Catherine of Siena. Raymond of Pennafort. Vincentius Ferraro. Anthony of Florence), while Hyacinthus is by Artus Quellin the Elder and Peter of Verona by J.P. Baurscheit the Elder.

The CHAPEL OF LEPANTO (not always open) is so called from the four paintings (Jan Peeters, 1668) of the Battle of Lepanto. Here, in 1571, the Christian League, under Don John of Austria, defeated the Turks and released some 15,000 Christian slaves; this was also the last major sea battle in which oar-driven ships were used by both sides. The battle has always been of special importance to Dominicans since

the Christian fleet sailed under the protection of Our Lady of the
Rosary and all its chaplains were Dominican friars. Another picture in
this chapel, Christ Mocked, is attributed to Otto Venius.—In the
grounds there is a MOUNT CALVARY, with a grotto and 36 statues
commemorating the suffering of Christ, the story of Mary Magdalene
and some of the penitents of the Holy Land; the whole dates from
1697–1747, the statues having been contributed by well-kown local
sculptors.

The **Brouwershuis** (Daily except Monday, 10.00 to 17.00, but open
Easter Monday, Whit Monday and the Monday following the second
Sunday in August. Closed 1 and 2 January, 1 May, Ascension, 1
November, 25 and 26 December), at 20 Adriaan Brouwerstraat, a road
branching E off the quay just short of the docks and 500m N of the
Steen, was formerly the Waterhuis, built in 1554 by Gilbert van
Schoonbeke as part of a system for supplying Antwerp's breweries
with clean water brought by barge along canals from Herentals (28km
E). The street behind (Brouwersvliet) was at that time, and until the
late 19C, a canal lined with breweries. The clean water was discharged into a cistern from which it was raised by bucket-chain, at first
powered by horses but later by an engine. On the ground floor, the
stable is beyond the hall. The bucket-chain is behind a trap-door in
the wall by the entrance to the court, in which can be seen the
mechanism, and the cistern is beyond and below. Steps lead up to a
landing on which there is a painting of Vulcan's Forge by the Venetian
Antonio Pellegrini and a tile-picture of 1680, installed here in 1932.
Off the landing are the Laboratory and the Council Room, the latter
with a fireplace of c 1660 and Mechelen leather hangings. Notable are
the Four Seasons by Pellegrini and the chandelier of 16C Antwerp
glasswork, while above a cabinet of 1625 are the Brewers' insignia in
carved wood.

Off the SE corner of the Grote Markt and below the W façade of the
cathedral the attractive small HANDSCHOENMARKT, today with cafés
and restaurants, was once the glove market. It is surrounded by old
houses, one of which (No. 13) was the birthplace in 1610 of the painter
David Teniers the Younger. Here also stands a stone well with a
graceful ironwork canopy ascribed to Quinten Metsys (c 1495). The
story goes that Metsys started life as a smith but exchanged the anvil
for the brush because of his passion for a painter's daughter; hence
the inscription on a tablet beside the cathedral door 'Connubialis
Amor de Mulcibre fecit Apellem' ('Twas love connubial taught the
smith to paint'). The figure with a glove on the well canopy represents
Silvius Brabo. At the SW corner of the cathedral façade there is a lively
monument (by Jef Lambeaux) to Jan Appelmans, the man who with
his son and others planned and built the cathedral.

The ****Cathedral** (Onze Lieve Vrouw), the largest Gothic church in
Belgium but hemmed in by buildings and not seen as a whole, is
famous for its paintings by Rubens and others. Major restoration
started in 1965 and will not be completed until the 1990s. However,
much of the exterior, including the tower, has been finished as has
also the nave, though it will be some time before visitors can see the
choir, with its ambulatory chapels. The restoration programme
includes also the restoration of some of the paintings. Meanwhile, the
major works are shown as may be convenient both in the nave and in
an Art Room (not always open). The cathedral is normally open

April–mid October: Monday–Friday, 12.00 to 17.00; Saturday, 12.00 to 15.00; Sunday and Holidays, 13.00 to 16.00. Mid October–March: Monday to Friday, 12.00 to 16.00; Saturday, 12.00 to 15.00; Sunday and Holidays, 13.00 to 16.00.

History and Structure. An ancient chapel was superseded during the 12C by a Romanesque church, parts of which are now being revealed. The present cathedral was built between 1352 and c 1525, the first portion being the choir which seems to have been finished early in the 15C. The general cathedral plan can probably be ascribed to Jan Appelmans, whose son Pieter (died 1434) took over the direction of the work. By 1425 work had begun on a new W front, the Romanesque nave then being demolished and work started on the Gothic nave, much of this the work of Herman de Waghemakere. The superb tower (123m), erected in 1431 as far as the gallery beneath the clock, was completed by c 1521 by Domien de Waghemakere. In 1519 Charles V commissioned a new choir, as large as the entire existing church, but although he laid the foundation stone in 1521 the project was abandoned. Twelve years later (1533) the church was badly damaged by fire; in 1566 there was more damage, this time by Calvinist iconoclasts, and in 1794 most of the art treasures were removed by the French who closed the building. Reopened in 1802, the cathedral received back some of its treasures, as well as material from other churches.

Besides the carillon of 47 bells, the cathedral has several other bells, the largest of which dates from 1507 and is named 'Carolus', for Charles V who stood sponsor at its 'baptism'.

PAINTINGS. *Rubens*: 1. **Raising of the Cross, a triptych, painted in 1610 and the artist's first major work after his return from Italy. The central panel depicts the Nailing to the Cross, the right shutter a group of Roman soldiers with the two thieves in the background, and the left shutter disciples and holy women (note the superbly portrayed old woman in the centre). On the outside of the shutters are (left) St. Eligius and St. Walburga, and (right) St. Catherine and St. Amand. Originally there was also an upper panel (God and two Angels) and a predella. Rubens seems to have borrowed the idea for this work from Tintoretto's great Calvary in the Scuola di San Rocco at Venice. 2. **Descent from the Cross, a triptych painted in 1611–14 for the altar of the Guild of Arquebusiers. The central panel is perfect in composition and in its restrained style reflects the lessons, the artist had learnt during his stay in Italy. Van Dyck is said to have contributed to this work as restorer of damage it suffered in Rubens's studio, to him being attributed the cheek and chin of the Virgin and the arm of St. Mary Magdalene. On the inside of the shutters are the Visitation and the Presentation in the Temple; on the outside, St. Christopher and the Hermit. 3. *Assumption, painted in 1626 and one of the finest of the artist's six versions of this subject (on the high-altar). 4. Resurrection, with John the Baptist and St. Catherine on the wings.

Paintings by other artists include the following. *Jacob de Backer*: Triptych, Last Judgement, with Christopher Plantin, his son and St. Christopher on the left wing, and his wife, his daughter and St. John on the right (properly hangs above the tomb of Christopher Plantin in the fourth choir ambulatory chapel). *Ambroos Francken*: Descent of the Holy Spirit. *Frans Francken the Elder*: The Fifteen Wounds (attributed). Jesus in the Temple, with, it is said, portraits of Luther, Calvin and others. *G.J. Herreyns*: Portraits of Christopher Plantin and Jan Moretus. Men of Emmaus. *Leonardo da Vinci* (?): Head of Christ, painted on marble. *Adam van Noort*: The Miraculous Draught of Fishes. *Cornelis Schut*: Ascension. *Otto Venius*: Last Supper. Entombment. Raising of Lazarus. *Cornelis de Vos*: Triptych, Pietà, with donors. *Martin de Vos*: Marriage at Cana. Pietà.

OTHER WORKS OF ART. NAVE. The nave has six aisles, separated by as many rows of pillars which rise without capitals to the vaulting which dates from 1614. For ease of identification, some items of particular note are listed below under four sectors: SW, NW, NE, SE.—In the SW. *Artus Quellin the Younger*: Carved memorial of Bishop Capello (1676). Marble statue of Jonathan (1650–60). Marble of Our Lady of the Immaculate Conception. *Abraham van Diepenbeek*: Glass of 1635, The Four Almoners (a remnant of a window destroyed in 1794). *J.B. Capronnier*: Glass of SS. Peter and Paul (1867).—In the NW. *Artus Quellin the Younger*: Statue of Gideon. *Pieter Scheemaeckers*: Memorial to the Kuerkinckx family.—In the NE. *Artus Quellin the Younger*: Altar of Our Lady. Pietà.—In the SE. *Hendrik Verbruggen*: White marble communion table (1687). *M. van der Voort*: Pulpit of 1713, made for the abbey of Hemiksem. *Nic Rombouts*: Glass, Last Supper (1503).—CHOIR AMBULATORY CHAPELS (S to N, but some of these items are temporarily in the nave). No. 2. Monument of the printer Jan Moretus (died 1601) and his wife. No. 3. Tomb of Bishop Capello (died 1676) by *Artus Quellin the Younger*. No. 4. Tomb of Christopher Plantin) (died 1589). No. 6. A polychrome Mater Dolorosa by *Artus Quellin the Younger*. The sculpture of Christ in the Tomb, in a niche on the left, dates from the 15C. This chapel is at the back of the high-altar, with here the tomb of Isabella of Bourbon (died 1465), second wife of Charles the Bold. No. 9. Here, and beyond, the statues on the confessionals are by *Hendrik Verbruggen*. In the last chapel (of St. Anthony), on the left of the outer altar, there is a notable window of 1503, with the kneeling figures of Henry VII of England and his wife, set up to commemorate the commercial treaty between him and Philip the Fair. Opposite the inner altar the altarpiece of St. Michael and the Dragon, on a gold background, is 15C Spanish.

Immediately to the S of the cathedral the GROENPLAATS, once the town graveyard, is now a spacious open area reserved for pedestrians with, in the centre, a bronze statue of Rubens (Willem Geefs, 1843). The Post Office is on the S side, and below the square there is an underground station and concourse.

A number of places of interest, notably the Fine Arts museum, lie S of Groenplaats to either side of Nationalestraat and its extension Volkstraat. The distance from Groenplaats to the museum is well over 1km. This part of the city is described under B. South-West of the Centre.

Schoenmarkt, once the shoe market, leads E out of Groenplaats, passing (right) the former provincial government buildings, once the 18C episcopal palace, and reaching (left) the *Torengebouw* (1930), Europe's first 'skyscraper'. This stands at the W end of the MEIR, once a swamp but now a wide and busy principal thoroughfare. This description of Central Antwerp now divides into three: Along the Meir and South and North of the Meir.

Along the Meir

The short Twaalfmaandenstraat (Twelve Months), where Plantin printed his first book in 1555, reaches the **Beurs** (Monday–Friday, 07.30 to 17.00), rebuilt in 1872 by J. Schadde in the style of its predecessor designed by Domien de Waghemakere in 1531 and destroyed by fire; this early building served as a model for other European exchanges, including Gresham's in London. The large hall has a ceiling decorated with the arms of the seafaring nations. Farther E along the Meir (250m from the Torengebouw) the former **Royal**

Palace occupies the corner of the Meir and Wapper; built in 18C Rococo style, the building now serves as an international cultural centre. Wapper is a pleasant, open rectangular pedestrian area (fountain, benches) on the E side of which stands the ****Rubens House**, see F.

Continuing E the Meir reaches (No. 85, 200m from the Wapper, N) the *Huis Osterrieth*, a Rococo 18C patrician mansion by J.P. Baurscheit the Younger, while, opposite, the *Feestzaal* of 1907 is by A. van Mechelen.

Jezusstraat bears NE from the end of the Meir. Here at Nos 28–30 is the **Provinciaal Diamantmuseum (Diamond Centre**. Daily except Monday and Tuesday, 10.00 to 17.00. Demonstrations on request Saturday, 14.00 to 17.00. Closed 1 and 2 January, 25 and 26 December), with beautifully displayed exhibits, all well explained in English and covering such aspects of the diamond world as history, geology, mining, cutting and polishing, tools, and the industrial diamond and its uses. In the same building the exhibition hall of the **Veiligheidsinstituut** (Safety Institute. Daily 10.00 to 16.00. Closed 1 and 2 January, 25 and 26 December) may be visited. The exhibition, the general theme of which is safety at work, on the road and at home, is spacious and imaginative, but the often very technical explanations are in Flemish only.

A monument to Lodewijk van Bercken (F. Joris, 1906), who in 1476 established in Antwerp the tradition of diamond polishing, stands at the junction of Jezusstraat and Leysstraat, the latter linking the E end of the Meir with Teniersplaats, the E side of which is the ring boulevard, here Frankrijklei. Across the boulevard stands the **KVO (Royal Flemish Opera)**, built by Van Mechelen in 1907. Franklin Rooseveltplaats, just beyond, is a busy bus terminal. From Teniersplaats the broad De Keyserlei continues E to reach the main railway station and the zoo, for both of which see C. South-East of the Centre.

South of the Meir

From the Meir's W end Huidevettersstraat (Tanners Street), leading S, in 250m reaches Lange Gasthuisstraat a short way down which at No. 19 is the ***Mayer van den Bergh Museum** (Daily except Monday, 10.00 to 17.00, but open Easter Monday, Whit Monday, and the Monday following the second Sunday in August. Closed 1 and 2 January, 1 May, Ascension Day, 1 November, 25 and 26 December), a connoisseur's exquisite collections, principally of medieval, late Gothic and Renaissance art.

Emil Mayer (1824–79), born in Cologne, settled in Antwerp in 1849, becoming a wealthy businessman and in 1857 marrying Henriette van den Bergh, daughter of an equally prosperous local family. Their son, Fritz Mayer van den Bergh (1858–1901), devoted his life to the study and collection of art treasures, these embracing not only works by great names but also those by lesser known artists who appealed to the collector's taste. Henriette Mayer van den Bergh was a constant artistic and financial support and on her son's death she established this museum, commissioning this building which, although 16C in appearance, could at the same time incorporate the most modern display methods then known. On Henriette's death in 1920, administration of the museum passed to a trust.

The large and diverse collections embrace paintings, furniture, metalwork, sculpture, tapestry, ceramics, objets d'art, etc., and no more than an indication of the museum's scope is attempted through the representative items mentioned below. Among the many outstanding pictures, perhaps the most important is Pieter Brueghel the Elder's 'Dulle Griet'. Most of the rooms contain fine furniture and chimneypieces, and into the windows of several have been inserted small 15C and 16C stained-glass panels or medallions.

GROUND FLOOR PASSAGE. Bruges and Oudenaarde tapestry (16th and 17C). Portrait of Henriette Mayer van den Bergh.—ROOM 1. Portrait groups (all 17C) by *Jan Rotius, Christiaen van Couwenbergh* and *Jan Mytens*.—ROOM 2. Small works by *Jan Brueghel, Hans Bol, Frans Hals* and *Gillis van Coninxloo*. Also works by *Daniel Seghers, Adriaen van Ostade, Jacob Jordaens, David Teniers the Younger* and *Gérard de Lairesse*.—ROOM 3. Two stone columns bearing female figures (early examples of French 12C Gothic sculpture). A Mechelen portable altar of c 1500. A polychromed stone Virgin and Child of c 1380—ROOM 4. *Calvary Triptych by *Quinten Metsys*. An embroidered St. Mary Magdalene (15C).—STAIRS. Oudenaarde and Bruges tapestry (16th and 17C). Portrait of Fritz Mayer van den Bergh.—In ROOM 5 the theme is still-life, with works by *Willem Heda, Roelof Koets* and others.—ROOM 6. The outstanding piece here is the *Polychromed wood group (St. John resting on the breast of Jesus) by *Heinrich of Constance* (c 1300). Also in this room are three small panels of a polyptych (remainder in Baltimore, USA) dating to around 1400 and one of the earliest examples of Netherlands panel painting; a painted spire-retable of c 1400; and *Small Ivories (Baptism of Jesus, 8–9C. Miracles of Jesus, 9–10C. Birth of Jesus, 11C).—ROOM 7 is generally devoted to Renaissance works. Peasant Interior by *Pieter Aertsen* (1556). Landscape by *Herri met de Bles* (1550). Triptych by *Ambrosius Benson*. Adoration by *Adriaen Isenbrant*. St. Christopher by *Jan Mostaert*.—ROOM 8. Small sculptures (13–15C) in a row of cases arranged chronologically. Against the balustrade, a case with portrait medallions, including one of Christina Metsys by *Quinten Metsys*, one of the earliest Netherlands examples of this kind of work. Small retable (c 1490) of the Passion.—In ROOM 9 hangs what is generally accepted to be the museum's most important painting, **Dulle Griet (or Mad Meg) by *Pieter Brueghel the Elder*, a wild and disturbing composition about the meaning of which even Karel van Mander remains vague though it is generally accepted as being an allegory of madness and vice. Alongside, and also by Brueghel, hang The Twelve Proverbs, painted on wooden plates, while by *Pieter Brueghel the Younger* there is a copy of his father's Census at Bethlehem.—ROOM 10, the Library. Portraits by *Adriaen Key* (1589), *Jan Rotius* (1659) and *Jan Mytens* (1658). A collection of plaquettes by the German *Peter Flötner* (c 1535).—ROOMS 11 and 12 were designed to accept 18C panelling, etc., from a house in Tournai. They exhibit porcelain and also portraits by the 18C French artists *Nicolas de Largillière* and *Louis Tocqué*.

Farther S along Lange Gasthuisstraat, No. 33 is the **Maagdenhuis** (Daily except Tuesday and Holidays, 10.00 to 17.00), formerly a girls' orphanage. The building is of two periods, the entrance and chapel dating from 1564 and the remainder completed in 1636. Above the entrance the delightful carvings recall the building's first paupers, and in the pleasant courtyard stands a 17C wooden figure of one of the orphans ('Houten Klara').

The Museum is in two sections either side of the entrance passage, to the right being the former chapel and to the left a series of six rooms. The museum—which combines interesting historical and orphanage material (in the chapel) with an important collection of Old

Masters including Rubens and Van Dyck—provides a catalogue in English, and as all the exhibits are clearly numbered or, occasionally, lettered, it is easy enough to identify anything which particularly strikes. Special attention may be drawn to the following. CHAPEL. 46 and 47: Porridge bowls, Antwerp and possibly Frisian, 16C and 17C. 50: Bull of Pope Honorious III (1226). 51 to 53: Seals, No. 51 being the oldest known Antwerp seal (1232). 49: Certificate of Election of Charles V as Holy Roman Emperor (1519), with five of the original seven seals. 26: Panel of the Last Supper by Lambert Lombard (16C). 24: The Last Supper by Pieter Pourbus. Also a most interesting cabinet containing items A to F, A being caps and coats worn by foundlings in 1860; C, 19C foundling tokens for bread and peat; D, the token of a child, later reclaimed by his mother in 1811; F, collar, shawl and caps of 1860.—ROOMS. In the first (ticket desk) room, note the Portrait of an Old Lady at a Crucifix by Cornelis de Vos; in the room to the right paintings by Rubens and Jacob de Backer; in the room to the left a portrait by Frans Floris; in the room beyond, a work by David Teniers the Younger. Along the passage are a Virgin (Anon.), St. Ambrose by A. Bloemaert, and *Orphan Girl at Work by Cornelis de Vos. The remaining two rooms are particularly rewarding. To the right at the end of the passage, Men of Emmaus by Theodoor Rombouts; *St. Jerome by Van Dyck; and Descent from the Cross by Jacob Jordaens. To the left off the end of the passage, *Last Judgement, the Seven Works of Mercy, the Seven Capital Sins by an unknown Antwerp Master (1490–1500). This is a work rewarding study of its detail; note how the presence of Christ identifies the Mercies, that of the Devil the Sins.

Farther S down Lange Gasthuisstraat the Sint Elisabeth Gasthuis, a hospital, is the oldest such foundation in Antwerp, founded in perhaps 1204 but within the city walls. Soon (by 1238), needing to expand, the hospital moved outside to a meadow which was later to become known as (today's) Gasthuisstraat. The Maagdenhuis entry ticket admits to the hospital's chapel, in part (the nave) 15C. As in the case of the Maagdenhuis, a comprehensive guide in English indentifies the chapel's features and contents, among the highlights being the altar surround by Artus Quellin the Younger and the pulpit by Erasmus Quellin.

In Mechelseplein, at the end of Gasthuisstraat (600m from the Meir), the **Sint Joriskerk** (1853) embodies fragments of its 14C predecessor in which Jan Brueghel and Jan and Pieter Appelmans were buried. From here Sint Jorispoort connects E to the Leopoldplaats with a statue of Leopold I by Willem Geefs (1867). Leopoldstraat, leading back N, passes the small **Kruidtuin** (Botanic Garden) and reaches the Komedieplaats in which stands the **KNS (Royal Dutch Theatre)** built by Bruno Bourla in 1834. Rubens's House and the Meir are now some 150m to the north.

North of the Meir

The district (c 1km by 1km) N of the Meir and W of Italielei offers a number of old houses and some interesting churches. There is a wide choice of walks but the one outlined below, starting from Hendrik Conscienceplein (150m NW of the Beurs), embraces most places of interest.

HENDRIK CONSCIENCEPLEIN, a quiet small 17C square reserved for pedestrians, is named after the prolific Flemish novelist (1812–83), known in particular for his historical work 'The Lion of Flanders'. His statue (F. Joris, 1883) stands in the square, the S side of which is occupied by the 17C former Jesuit House, now a municipal library, and the E side by the church of **Sint Carolus Borromeus**, a Baroque basilica built in 1615–25 by the Jesuit architect Pieter Huyssens (Monday–Friday except Tuesday, 07.30 to 13.00, Saturday, 07.30 to 12.00, 15.00 to 18.15). The superb W front is said to have been designed by Rubens, who also painted the ceilings of the former nave and aisles, but in 1718 the church was struck by lightning, all that survived the consequent fire being the choir, two chapels, the portal and the tower. Reconstruction in the following year was entrusted to Jan Baurscheit the Elder who, with Michiel van der Voort, was also responsible for much of the interior woodwork. The Lady Chapel, which survived the fire, is lined with the coloured marble that was a main feature of the earlier church.

From Hendrik Conscienceplein three parallel streets, with several connecting streets, run east. At the nearer end of KEIZERSTRAAT, the northernmost of the three, are the adjacent (Nos 9 and 10) 17C *Huis Delbeke* and 16C patrician **Huis Rockox**, this latter between 1603–40 the home of Nicolaas Rockox, burgomaster of Antwerp and friend of Rubens (see portrait on a triptych by Rubens in the Museum voor Schone Kunsten). Huis Rockox, with works by Rubens, tapestries, fine furniture, etc. is open daily except Monday, 10.00 to 17.00, but open Easter Monday, Whit Monday, and the Monday following the second Sunday in August. It is closed 1 and 2 January, 1 May, Ascension, 1 November, 25 and 26 December. Farther along this street, on the N side, the 16C *Sint Annakapel* has a Baroque doorway of 1624. KIPDORP, the central of the three parallel streets, becomes Sint Jacobsmarkt, near the junction being Sint Jacobskerk (see below). The southern of the three streets is LANGE NIEUWSTRAAT, at this street's W end being the *Sint Nicolaaskapel* (15C; no adm.). The house which is now No. 43 belonged to Sir Thomas Gresham, an English merchant who lived in Antwerp during c 1555–67 and acted as financial agent for four Tudor sovereigns; by clever if dubious means he so raised the value of the pound on the Antwerp exchange that England's debts were paid off. No.31 is the so-called **Chapelle de Bourgogne** (Burgundian Chapel), built in 1496 by Domien de Waghemakere for Jan van Immerseel, margrave of Antwerp; the name derives from the heraldic paintings of the historic Burgundian marriages.

---

*Sint Jacobskerk (April–October: Monday–Saturday, 14.00 to 17.00. November–March: 09.00 to 12.00. Entry from Lange Nieuwstraat), begun in 1491 by Herman and continued after 1503 by Domien de Waghemakere, was not completed until 1656. As the patrician church of Antwerp—with the burial vaults, private chapels and altars of many of the leading families, including the Rubens—the church became richly endowed with paintings and sculptures. After a serious fire in 1967 the paintings were removed to the Museum voor Schone Kunsten for safekeeping and restoration, but now the church has been fully repaired and serves as an outstanding museum showing a wealth of important paintings, together with plate, vestments, small statuary and suchlike. The paintings and sculptures apart, the chief attraction for visitors is the Rubens Chapel.

The church is normally entered at the S transept, from where the description below runs anticlockwise. SOUTH TRANSEPT. Among the paintings here are works by *Gaspard de Crayer, Bernard van Orley* and *Jan Metsys*, but the most notable feature of this part of the church is a richly sculpted marble communion rail of 1696 by *Hendrik Verbruggen* and *Willem Kerrickx* (Chapel of the Holy Sacrament). The altar of 1670 is by Pieter Verbruggen the Elder.—In the CHOIR the stalls, with the arms of benefactors, are by the *Quellins*, while the

magnificent high-altar (1685) with a figure of St. James, the gift of the
prosperous art dealer Hendrik Hillewerve, is the achievement of
Artus Quellin the Younger with decorative detail by *Willem
Kerrickx.*—Seven chapels radiate off the AMBULATORY, the 1st
(Trinity) once being the chapel of the doctors. Here hang a Trinity by
Hendrik van Balen, based on a similar work by Rubens, and a St. Peter
by *Jacob Jordaens*. The 2nd chapel is dedicated to St. Ivo (1253–
1303), a priest from Brittany who became the patron of lawyers.
Opposite the altar are two wings of a triptych by *Otto Venius*, the
central panel of which is in the chapel of St. Job off the S nave aisle.
The 3rd chapel (Resurrection) is that of the powerful merchant family
of Le Candele-Vincque. Directly behind the high-altar, the 4th chapel
is the Rubens Chapel with the vault in which the artist and his family
lie. The altar here is the work of *Cornelis van Mildert*, though the
figures of the sorrowing (heart-pierced) mother and the two angels
above are by *Luc Fayd'herbe.* The most striking feature of the altar is
the **Painting of the Virgin, Child and Saints, intended by *Rubens* for
this position and one of his greatest works; it is generally accepted
that St. George is a self-portrait, that Our Lady has the features of the
artist's first wife, the Infant those of his son, Mary Magdalene those of
his second wife, and St. Jerome those of his father. The artist's
tombstone in the chapel pavement shows his armorial bearings, and
the long Latin inscription gives a summary of Rubens's life and also
records restoration work of 1775. The next and 5th chapel is dedicated
to St. Carolus Borromeus (1538–84), and it is of interest that this
Catholic cardinal, archbishop of Milan and uncompromising leader of
the Counter-Reformation, should here be portrayed (1655) by the
Protestant *Jacob Jordaens*; the picture shows the saint pleading with
the Virgin on behalf of those stricken by the plague in Milan in 1576.
This chapel was the gift of Jacob Antoon Carenna, whose graveslab is
on the floor outside. The 6th chapel is that of St. Peter and St. Paul and
the 7th that of the Visitation, the latter a gift (1640) by Bento
Rodriguez, consul of Portugal, and others. The altar painting is by
Viktor Wolfvoet who here gives Mary the features of Rubens's second
wife. Nearby in the ambulatory there are 17C confessionals, with (left)
a Virgin and Child surrounded by Flowers by *Ambroos Brueghel* (son
of Jan) and (right) an Adoration of the Shepherds by *Hendrik van
Balen.*

NORTH TRANSEPT. At the ambulatory entrance the marble Apostles
(John and Paul) are by *Michiel van der Voort*, who also sculpted the
epitaph in the Chapel of Our Lady to the nobleman Michiel Peeters
and his wife. Also in this chapel are an altar by *S. van den Eynde*
(1664); by *Artus Quellin the Elder*, a Pietà (left of the altar) and a
Joseph and Infant (right central pillar); and, by *Artus Quellin the
Younger*, the stalls and the memorial to Jan de Gaverelle (1579–1645),
admiral, statesman and priest. The stained glass (Annunciation) here
is by *Jan de la Baer*. High above the church's N door hang three
paintings—Annunciation by *Gerard van Honthorst*, Jesus in the
Temple by *Robert van Audenaerde*, and Adoration of the Magi by
Gerard Seghers—while on the W wall of the transept are an
Ascension of the Virgin by *Pieter Thys* and an Adoration of the
Shepherds by *Erasmus Quellin.*

NAVE. NORTH AISLE. Here there are six chapels, the 1st, that of the
Holy Cross (sometimes called the Robyns Chapel after its founder),
known for the masterpiece and last work of *Wenceslas Coeberger*,
*Constantine the Great kneeling before the Cross held by St. Helena;

the features are those of Joos Robyns and of his wife. The 2nd chapel (All Saints, or St. Hubert) was in succession that of the peat and the coal carriers, the latter dedicating an altar here in 1520; a triptych of 1608 is by *Ambroos Francken* and the 16C window here (Last Supper) is the oldest in the church. In the 3rd chapel (St. Dimpna) rest members of the Rockox family, portrayed on the panels of the triptych by *Jan Sanders* opposite the altar, while in the 4th (Three Kings), the chapel of the woodworkers, there is an altar-triptych by *Hendrik van Balen* (Adoration of the Magi), painter also of the two small panels immediately below. The 5th chapel (Holy Name) commemorates the philanthropist Cornelis Lantschot (died 1656) with a graveslab, a carved wall-epitaph by *S. van den Eynde*, and, above, a portrait by *Abraham van Diepenbeek*. The last chapel of this N aisle, that of St. Gertrude, is notable for a macabre memorial by *Pieter Scheemaeck-ers* showing the last hour of Francesco Marcos del Pico (died 1693), Spanish governor of Antwerp. Note also the bronze balusters here, one of them donated by Rubens.

Off the NAVE SOUTH AISLE there are again six chapels, the 1st (from the W end; Our Lady, Presentation) housing a St. George and the Dragon by *Van Dyck*. In the nave close to this chapel the tomb of *Hendrik van Balen* and of his wife is at the foot of a pillar on which, forming part of a stone memorial, hangs a Resurrection by this artist; the portraits above are also by Van Balen. The 2nd chapel is dedicated to St. Anthony, portrayed here by *Martin de Vos* who used his wife as model for the temptress, and here also hangs a Madonna by *Guido Reni*. St. Roch, who gave his life caring for the plague-stricken in Italy in c 1337, is the patron of the 3rd chapel; the altar here with its figure of the saint, one of the finest sculptures in the church, is by *Artus Quellin the Elder* while in the altar picture the saint is a self-portrait by *Erasmus Quellin*. The 4th chapel belonged to the Guild of Musicians of whom St. Job, to whom the chapel is dedicated, was patron. The altar picture here by *Otto Venius* is the central piece of a triptych the wings of which are in the chapel of St. Ivo off the choir ambulatory. In the 5th chapel (St. Ann) the altar painting is by *Frans Floris*, and in the 6th (John the Baptist) there is an altar painting by *Michiel Coxie*, a triptych of which the central panel (Martyrdom of St. James) is by *Martin de Vos*.

To the N of the church, in Sint Jacobsmarkt, the Royal Academy of Music occupies the 16C *Huis de Moelnere*, a short way NE of which is the small OSSENMARKT, just off which No. 39 Rodestraat is the doorway to the 15–16C **Begijnhof**. From Ossenmarkt, Pieter van Hobokenstraat leading W becomes Prinsstraat in which No. 13 is the dignified **Prinsenhof** (or **Huis van Liere**), a large 16C building with a 17C façade. Occupied by Charles V in 1520 and by English merchants from 1558 until the closing of the Scheldt in 1648, the Prinsenhof was used until 1773 by the Jesuits; repurchased by them in 1929, it now houses faculties of the St. Ignatius University. Venusstraat, heading N, passes the *Archives* (No. 11; in the rebuilt 17C former municipal pawnbroker's building) and reaches PAARDENMARKT, once site of the horse market. At this street's E end, opposite the 19C **Sint Anto-niuskerk**, Nos 92 and 94 were 16C charitable institutions, the former being an asylum and the latter an orphanage. The parallel street immediately N of the W section of Paardenmarkt is Falconrui, at this street's E end (in Hessenplein) being the solid **Hessenhuis**, built in

1562 by Cornelis Floris and once the house of the German merchants. No. 47 Falconrui was the *Lantschot Hospice* (17C, with a good doorway) and No. 33 was the 16C *Van der Biest Hospice*. At the W end of the street is the *International Seamen's House*. Mutsaertstraat, running SE from here, soon crosses Raapstraat in which No. 27 is the 16C **Huis de Raap** with one of the oldest façades in Antwerp. At the S end of Mutsaertstraat are (E) the **Academie voor Schone Kunsten** (Academy of Fine Arts), occupying a part 15C former Franciscan house, and (W at 22 Minderbroedersstraat) the **Museum voor het Vlaamse Cultuurleven** (Flemish Culture), mainly comprising documents, books and pictures.

B. South-West of the Centre

The principal place of interest in this part of the town is the Museum voor Schone Kunsten, Antwerp's famed art gallery. This is rather over 1.5km S of the Grote Markt.

Nationalestraat leads S out of Groenplaats and soon crosses Kammenstraat in which is (E) the 17C Baroque **Sint Augustinuskerk**. The church is under long-term restoration and pending reopening some of its more important paintings may be shown in the Museum voor Schone Kunsten. In Sint Andriesstraat, off the W side of Nationalestraat, the **Sint Andrieskerk** (open to groups only who must make advance arrangements) was built in 1514–29 and enlarged during the 18C; the church houses pictures by Gerard Seghers, Erasmus Quellin and Otto Venius.

To the W of this church (200m; at 11–17 Kloosterstraat) is the *Huis Mercator-Ortelius*, in origin of 1619 but rebuilt. Rubens lived in this street in c 1610–17, lodging with the Brant family, one of whom, Isabella, became his first wife. Ortelius (A. Wortels. died 1592), the geographer, had a house here at No. 43.

Farther S off Nationalestraat, in Sint Rochusstraat (E), is the 17C former Capucin Chapel. Nationalestraat becomes Volkstraat, and just SE of this point the MARNIXPLAATS contains the towering and elaborate **Scheldt Monument** (J.J. Winders, 1883), erected by the town to celebrate Belgium's redemption in 1862 of Holland's right to levy dues on Scheldt shipping. Volkstraat soon reaches LEOPOLD DE WAELPLAATS (named after the burgomaster of 1876 who negotiated the purchase of the Plantin-Moretus Museum) in which stands the ****Museum voor Schone Kunsten**, see G. Opposite the museum, Verschansingstraat runs SW to GILLISPLAATS in which stands the **Waterpoort**, a reconstruction of 1883 of a gateway set up in 1624 in honour of Philip IV with sculpture of Father Scheldt and the arms of Spain by H. van den Eynde; originally farther N, at the foot of Vlasmarkt, the gate was moved to its present position when the Sint Anna tunnel was built.

At the rear of the Museum voor Schone Kunsten runs Amerikalei, a section of the ring boulevards. To the NE, where the boulevard becomes Britselei, the *Gerechtshof* (Law Courts) was built by J. and F. Baekelmans in 1871–77. Farther N, where Britselei becomes Frankrijklei, the *National Bank* is by A. Beyaert (1879).

C. South-East of the Centre

This description starts at the Centraal Station. Places of principal interest are the Zoo, adjacent to the station, and the exquisite Ridder Smidt van Gelder Museum, about 1km south. Middelheim Park with its open-air Museum of Modern Sculpture is some 4km S of the Centraal Station. There are good public transport services.

Centraal Station (L. Delacenserie, 1905) is 400m E of the ring boulevard (Frankrijklei). To the N the high Neo-Renaissance façade forms one side of KONINGIN ASTRIDPLEIN while from the station's W side the broad De Keyserlei crosses the busy Frankrijklei to reach the E end of the Meir. This area N and W of the station is one of hotels, cafés, restaurants and bars.

The **Zoo** (**Dierentuin**), one of the best known in Europe, is open daily from 08.30 but has seasonal closing times, generally 18.30 in summer and 17.00 in winter. It includes a dolphinarium, a planetarium, a museum of natural history, an aquarium, a 'nocturama' for animals preferring darkness, and a 'baby zoo' with small domesticated animals and a children's playground. For the Zoo's breeding park at Planckendael near Mechelen, see Rte 15B.

The triangular **Stadspark**, 400m SW of the station, was laid out on the site of a bastion of the old fortifications the moat of which has been converted to an ornamental lake. Sculpture in the park includes a war memorial (E. Deckers, 1935), a group, Mother and Child (George Minne, 1938) in memory of Queen Astrid, and a fountain-figure by Slojadinovic, 1954. Loosplaats, at the SE corner, is named after a burgomaster of 1848–62, and from here Charlottalei in 350m reaches the ***Ridder Smidt van Gelder Museum** (91 Belgielei. Daily except Monday, 10.00 to 17.00, but open Easter Monday, Whit Monday, and the Monday following the second Sunday in August. Closed 1 and 2 January, 1 May, Ascension, 1 November, 25 and 26 December). The museum houses the exquisite collections of Pieter Smidt van Gelder (1878–1956) which, together with his 18C mansion, he presented to the city in 1949. Including furniture, tapestry, porcelain, jewellery, objets d'art, and many paintings by old masters, the collections are arranged less as a formal museum than as the personal treasures of a wealthy connoisseur. Behind the house there is an attractive formal garden.

Belgielei, followed SW, ends at the **Koning Albertpark**; once the site of the gallows, the park was laid out by the Marquis d'Herbouville, prefect of Antwerp under Napoleon. Near the SW corner (22 Koningin Elisabethlei) is the high-rise block housing the Antwerp provincial administration, though the tourist information office is at 11 Karel Oomsstraat, a short way S across the intersection of the main roads. To the SE of the park is the suburb of BERCHEM, with the international lines railway station, while to the SW begins Jan van Rijswijklaan, the road to Boom and Brussels; along here after some 2km a Cromwell tank commemorates the liberation of Antwerp.

Karel Oomsstraat, running S from the Koning Albertpark, crosses the railway and motorway to become Beukenlaan which traverses **Nachtegalenpark** (Nightingale), laid out in the 18C by the Frenchman Barnabé Guimard and embracing three estates: *Vogelenzang* (Birds' Song), with an aviary, animal enclosure and an educational garden; *Den Brandt*, with an 18C mansion; and *Middelheim*. Since 1950 this last has in part been arranged as a **Museum of Modern Sculpture** with the exhibits spaced around the lawns amid fine trees.

Among the many artists represented are Rodin, Rik Wouters, Ossip Zadkine, Meunier and Henry Moore. (Open 10.00. Closes November–mid February, 17.00. Mid February–mid March and October, 18.00. Mid March–mid April and September, 19.00. Mid April–end May and August, 20.00. June and July, 21.00.)

D. The Docks and Beyond

A visit to the vast and still expanding area of the docks is not only of much interest but also essential to any proper appreciation of Antwerp's commercial status. The docks may be visited by 'Flandria' boat excursion, by bus, though these normally only run as far as Van Cauwelaertsluis and Leopolddok, or by car. The car circuit (HAVENROUTE, marked by hexagonal signs) outlined below starts at the Steen and covers a distance of some 60km; a shorter round, using the Frans Tijmanstunnel, is c 35km, while a yet shorter route of about 12km cuts across the base of Nos 5 and 4 Havendoks and Leopolddok.

From the Steen the quays are followed N as far as the *Pilot House* (1894), serving both the Belgian and the Dutch pilotage services, roughly opposite being the Brouwershuis. From here the Havenroute continues N passing *Bonapartedok* to the right; this, and *Willemdok* immediately to its E, both constructed on Napoleon's orders in 1804–13, are Antwerp's two oldest docks. *Kattendijkdok*, running N from Willemdok and containing municipal drydocks, dates from 1860–81 and is the largest of the older docks. The route now crosses in turn *Kattendijksluis* and then *Royerssluis* ('sluis' = lock), the latter (1907) the first large sea lock, bearing left to pass the **Hogere Zeevaartschool** (High Merchant Marine School) and then right along the stretch known as Noord Kasteel, once site of one of the city's northern fortresses and in the future possibly to be bisected by the Boerinnesluis for inland and coastal traffic. Scheldelaan is now followed past petro-chemical installations, an alternative being a more inland road along the S side of *No. 5 Havendok* (timber).

Just before reaching the petro-chemical installations, the road N (Oosterweel-steenweg) may be followed past the ends of Nos 5 and 4 Havendoks and the Leopolddok to meet the last section of the complete Havenroute round.

Pylons carry electricity cables across the river, on the far bank of which can be seen the huge industrial complex made up of such firms as Polysar, Union Carbide and BP Chemicals. Following a curve of the river, the Havenroute now bears NE, passing on the right the small *Industriedok* (ship repairs; not easily seen) and on the left the Esso installations.

The **Petroleumbrug** separates Marshalldok (left) from the water (right) off which open several docks, including *Hansadok*, taking the largest ships, and *Kanaaldok* which extends some 9km north-west. *Marshalldok*, built with Marshall Aid funds in 1951, is surrounded by petro-chemical installations, on its NW side being SIBP (Société Industrielle Belge des Pétroles), Belgium's largest refinery. Beyond Petroleumbrug, on the right, are large jetties for super-tankers and soon afterwards Havenroute crosses the parallel and adjacent **Van Cauwelaertsluis** (1928) and **Boudewijnsluis** (1955), the latter, until the opening of the Zandvlietsluis (see below), Antwerp's largest lock. From here there is a good view E across the main complex of docks, with (N to S) Churchilldok, No. 6 Havendok and Hansadok. Facing the administrative buildings stands the figure of the Universal Worker

(F. Libonati, 1962). Beyond the locks the road curves NW to skirt the huge Bayer Chemicals plant and reach a road junction by a windmill; the latter, dating from 1745, once stood farther E on land now submerged by Kanaaldok. To the right the **Frans Tijsmanstunnel** or the **Lillobrug** cross Kanaaldok, offering a short cut to the latter part of the Havenroute.

Lillo, to the left beside the Scheldt and all that is left of a much larger village which stretched across to where Kanaaldok now runs, is a picturesque spot with a *Polder Museum* devoted to the life and folklore of the now fast-disappearing Antwerp polders (April–September, Sunday and Holidays, 14.00 to 18.00). The Havenroute continues N past more petro-chemical installations to reach **Zand-vlietsluis** with a figure by Ossip Zadkine. Opened in 1967, this lock, 500m long and 57m wide, allows access to the port by ships of up to 100,000 dwt. The lock is crossed either by the great drawbridge, or over the gates, after which the road rounds BASF (Badische Anilin und Sodafabrik) to run only a few metres from the Dutch border and beside the Scheldt-Rhine canal (1975) which shortens the distance between Antwerp and the Rhine by some 40km. Crossing the entrance to Kanaaldok and then bearing S, the Havenroute runs through **Zandvliet** and **Berendrecht** which although now incorporated into the administrative district of Antwerp try to remain quiet polder villages, contrasting strangely with the surrounding development and industry; the latter even boasts a heronry between the village and Kanaaldok (mid February to end June).

The road continues S across an area of dock development to reach the intersection of roads at the E end of the Tijsmanstunnel, with a link to the motorway back to the city. Havenroute, forking right off the tunnel approach and passing below that to the bridge, passes a German Second World War concrete landing-ship (Quay 526), now a church and bar, then, as Noorderlaan, runs between the Antwerp North marshalling yards (Vormingstation) and the General Motors complex, the latter on land which until 1962 was the polder village of Oorderen (alternatively there is a road W and S of General Motors).

A round may now be made of the areas separating Churchilldok, No. 6 Havendok and Hansadok. *Churchilldok*, lying S of General Motors, was opened in 1967 for container traffic and the church tower seen here is all that survives of the village of Wilmarsdonk which was evacuated in 1962. The small *Graandok*, between the entrances of Churchilldok and *No. 6 Havendok* (1964), is used by barges and coastal vessels ready to carry grain offloaded from sea-going vessels berthed at the special pier, with grain elevators, at the rear of Graandok. The Havenroute skirts the SW side of No. 6 Havendok, then rounding the tip of the promontory (with a view across to Van Cauwelaertsluis and Boudewijnsluis) to continue along the NE side of Hansadok with the great loading bridges used in the handling of ores. Noorderlaan, rejoined near the **Nieuw Entrepotcomplex** (bonded warehouses) and Ford Tractors, is now followed E with *Albertdok* to the right; from W to E the principal activities here are timber, fruit and nitrates, while between *Nos 3* and *2 Havendoks* can be seen the network of pipes for potassium. The road now curves S, crosses the *Albert Kanaal* and reaches the city at Noorderplaats.

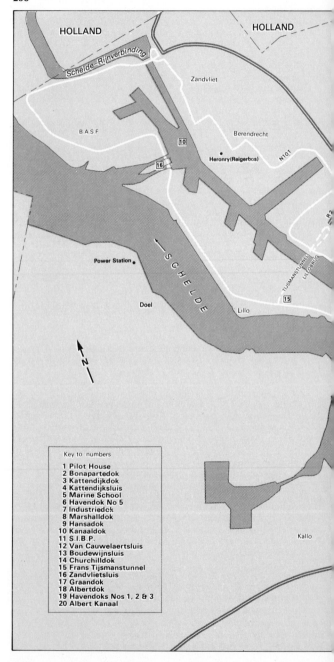

Key to numbers

1 Pilot House
2 Bonapartedok
3 Kattendijkdok
4 Kattendijksluis
5 Marine School
6 Havendok No 5
7 Industriedck
8 Marshalldok
9 Hansadok
10 Kanaaldok
11 S.I.B.P.
12 Van Cauwelaertsluis
13 Boudewijnsluis
14 Churchilldok
15 Frans Tijsmanstunnel
16 Zandvlietsluis
17 Graandok
18 Albertdok
19 Havendoks Nos 1, 2 & 3
20 Albert Kanaal

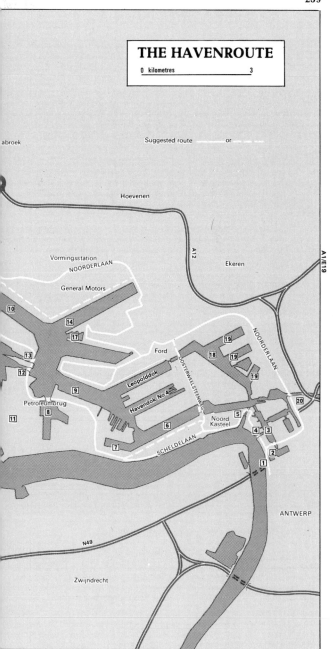

THE HAVENROUTE

0   kilometres   3

Suggested route   ——— or – – –

abroek

Hoevenen

A12

Ekeren

A1/E19

Vormingsstation
NOORDERLAAN

General Motors

NOORDERLAAN

10

14

17

Ford

19

18

19

13

OOSTERWEEL STEENWEG

19

12

9

Leopolddok

Havendok No 4

20

Petroleumbrug

8

6

Noord
Kasteel

5

11

4 3

7

2

SCHELDELAAN

1

ANTWERP

N49

Zwijndrecht

A14/E17

E. Plantin-Moretus Museum

The ****Plantin-Moretus Museum**, occupying the house and work-shops of the famous printer Christopher Plantin and his successors, and with much of the old equipment still in situ, affords a unique picture of the domestic and business environment of a rich master-printer of the 16C. It also contains many art treasures, including several works by Rubens. The exhibits are well labelled and explained in English, and an excellent descriptive catalogue in English is also available. (Daily 10.00 to 17.00. Closed 1 and 2 January, 1 May, Ascension, 1 November, 25 and 26 December.)

The Family. *Christopher Plantin* was born probably in 1520 near Tours in France. He was apprenticed to the French printer Robert Macé in Caen (Normandy), and during this time married Jeanne Rivière. In 1549 he came to Antwerp, of which he officially became a citizen the following year. At first he worked as a bookbinder, but, after being assaulted in the Meir by ruffians in 1555, he had to give up manual work and changed to the trade of printer. He made his name four years later with his sumptuous book on the funeral ceremonies of Charles V, and in 1572 appeared his famous 'Biblia Polyglotta' in five languages, with many detailed appendices. Already in 1570 he had received the title of Prototypus Regis from Philip II, this assuring him and his successors the lucrative monopoly of printing liturgical books for the Spanish empire. During the Calvinist years he remained a Catholic, but nevertheless ingratiated himself with William of Orange, even becoming official printer to the city. In 1583–85 Plantin lived in Holland and Germany, returning to Antwerp at the time of Parma's successes, and dying in 1589.—On Plantin's death the business passed to his son-in-law Jan Moerentorf, or *Moretus*, who proved as professional as his predecessor and won international repute. Moretus died in 1610, being succeeded by his son *Balthasar*, who ran the business until his death in 1641. In many ways the most brilliant member of the family, Balthasar was also an intimate of Rubens. The firm continued in the family, relying to a large extent on the monopoly for liturgical books which received a boost from the demands from Spain's colonial territories. Gradually, though, the monopoly lapsed, and in 1867 *Edward Moretus-Plantin* gave up printing.

The Building. It was only in 1576 that Christopher Plantin moved to this house, giving it the name of his previous house, the Golden Compasses. This badge, and that of Moretus (a star), are both still in evidence throughout the building. At this time the house faced Hoogstraat and was backed by a large garden, the only access to Vrijdagmarkt being by a narrow passage. Plantin made many changes, the main ones being the construction of houses along Heilig Geeststraat and of the printing workshop (1579) in the S part of the garden, where it still stands today. He also obtained permission to cover a part of the canal which ran along the S side of his property, there building the small Renaissance-style house which, after three centuries as a store, has now become the museum caretaker's house. Balthasar made many improvements, notably giving the inner court its present delightful aspect, but it was not until the 18C that the several small houses which stood immediately E of the Plantin-Moretus house were acquired by the family and demolished. The existing façade then took their place and the Plantin-Moretus house, no longer relying on the narrow passage, finally faced Vrijdagmarkt. The bas-relief above the door, by *Artus Quellin the Elder*, was originally on the Hoogstraat façade. In 1945 considerable damage was caused by a German V weapon which exploded in Vrijdagmarkt.

The Museum. Over the centuries the family had collected art treasures of many kinds, including several works by Rubens, a result of the friendship between the artist and Balthasar. When printing ceased in 1867, the city of Antwerp determined to acquire the property and its contents, this, with some government help and thanks to the generous attitude of Edward Moretus-Plantin, being achieved in 1876. The museum opened the following year. Successive curators added to the collections. During the Second World War the collections were stored in the château of Lavaux Ste Anne near Rochefort. In 1944, because of the danger of fighting in the Ardennes, they were returned to Antwerp, on the way suffering some damage through an Allied air attack and later again being damaged by the V weapon of 1945.

ENTRANCE. Near the entrance stand busts of Edward Moretus-Plantin and of Burgomaster Wael, who together negotiated the sale of 1876. Off the vestibule an 18C room has been arranged as a memorial to the poet Emile Verhaeren.—ROOM 1. Rare 16C Flemish tapestries. Above the chimneypiece, an old copy of Rubens's Lion Hunt, the original of which is in the Munich Pinakothek.—ROOM 2. Portraits of the Plantin family and their friends, ten being by *Rubens* and two (Balthasar and Gevartius) by *T.W. Bosschaert*. Two 17C cabinets. Silver-gilt clock, in the shape of a bell-tower, traditionally a gift to the family by the 'archdukes'.—ROOM 3. Paintings by *Seghers, L. van Noort, Erasmus Quellin* and *Van Helmont*. The cases contain ancient and rare manuscripts: Around the walls, Sedulius' Carmen Paschale (9C), with Prosperus' Epigrammata; Boethius' De Consolatione (9C); a German illustrated manual on firearms (16C); *Froissart's Chronicles, three volumes (15C); Book of Hours, in Flemish (15–16C); Book of Hours, in Latin (1508); *Latin Bible (1401), in two volumes, printed in Bohemia and belonging to King Wenceslas. Under the windows: A selection of the drawings, title-pages, and vignettes by masters who worked for the Plantin firm (*Martin de Vos, Adam van Noort, Van der Horst, Jan de Cock, Richard van Orley, Pieter de Joode*, and others).

One side of the COURTYARD is covered by a vine planted in 1640. From here can be seen the S and W façades, the oldest parts of the Plantin house. A pump of bluestone (17C) occupies the centre of the gallery. The marble busts of Plantin, Jan Moretus the Younger, and of Justus Lipsius are copies, the originals being in the museum; that of Jan Moretus the Elder is an original (1621) by *Jan van Mildert*.

THE SHOP (R.4) faced Heilig Geeststraat, whence it was entered by a small flight of steps. It contains the index of forbidden books, published by Plantin in 1569, and also the price-list of school and prayer books, as authorised by the city authorities. On the counter stands the money-balance, essential in an age of widespread coin clipping and debasing.—OFFICE (R.5). Above the door, a portrait of Jan Moretus. Cashier's desk and seat.—DRAWING ROOM (R.6). Oudenaarde tapestries (17C). Typical 17C patrician furniture. Portraits of Christopher Plantin and his wife.—ROOM 7 illustrates the processes involved in the making of a book (c 1450–18C).—ROOM 8 is the kitchen; earlier this room was used for weighing paper.—The PROOF READERS' ROOM (R.9) dates from 1637, the doorway being carved by *Paul Dirickx*. The picture, The Proof Reader, is probably by *Pieter van der Borcht*, and is generally thought to represent Cornelis Kiel (Kilianus), the founder of Dutch philology.—OFFICE (R.10). This is the beginning of the oldest part of the house, the part known to Plantin. The room is very much an office, with its desk, safe, money-balance, and barred windows. The walls are hung with gilded Mechelen leather, and the painting of Christ and the woman of Samaria is by *Erasmus Quellin*.—The JUSTUS LIPSIUS ROOM (R.11), where Lipsius, an intimate friend of the family, used to work, is hung with rare 16C Spanish leather. The picture, Lipsius and his Pupils, is a copy of a work by Rubens, now in the Pitti Gallery in Florence; one of the pupils is Rubens's brother, and in the background Rubens himself is seen. The portrait of Seneca, a man much admired by Lipsius, is by *Rubens*.—ROOM 12 contains books, documents, etc., relating to Lipsius, and portraits of savants. The bust (by *Jan van Mildert*, 1621) is the original of the copy in the courtyard. That of Plantin, also by *Van Mildert*, is in the passage which leads to the TYPE ROOM (R.13), with cases for type, and spare letters in their original packing.—The

PRINTING ROOM (R.14), the heart of the business, has been arranged as it was in 1576. Of the seven presses, two date from Plantin's time, the remainder being 17C and 18C.

The next two rooms, on the first floor, are in the 18C front of the house. ROOM 15 contains a leather relief depicting Christ before Caiaphas, by *Justin* (thought to be *Justin Mathieu*, 1796–1864), and a case with specimens of 16C Plantin productions. Also a portrait of Plantin, by an unknown 16C master, which was used by Rubens in painting the portrait in Room 2.—ROOM 16. Cases illustrating Plantin's life and work. *Biblia Polyglotta, the famous Bible, of which a dozen copies only were printed on vellum for Philip II. Pictures include Landscape, by *L. van Uden*; Balthasar Moretus on his deathbed, by *T.W. Bosschaert*; and portraits of later members of the family. An 18C Boulle cabinet and clock.

The remainder of the museum is in the 17C part of the house. The SMALL LIBRARY (R.17) and the MORETUS ROOM (R.18) exhibit works printed by Plantin's successors. Here too are forgeries, and the first known representation of a potato plant (1588). The bust of Jan Moretus the Younger, formerly in the court, is by *Artus Quellin* (1644).—RUBENS ROOM (R.19). Sketches and engravings by *Rubens*, who worked for Plantin as illustrator; also portraits, probably by the artist's studio. Receipts signed by Rubens. The chimneypiece and doorway are by *Paul Dirickx* (1622 and 1640).—ROOM 20. Works by other Antwerp printers. Portraits of savants, whose works were published in Antwerp.—The DRAWING ROOM (R.21) is hung with gilt leather. The chimneypiece is by *Dirickx* (1638), and the landscape above it by *Pieter Verdussen* (17C). Here too is a harpsichord (by J.J. Coenen, 1734), combining a clavecin and a virginal.—ROOM 22 holds the licences granted to the Plantin press by Belgian and foreign sovereigns, and various other records.—The GEOGRAPHICAL ROOM (R.23) recalls the supremacy of the Netherlands in this field during the 16–18C. Here can be seen 16C atlases by *Gemma-Frisius, Mercator*, and *Ortelius*. Specially noteworthy also are a great plan of Antwerp by *Virgilius Boloniensis* and *Cornelis Grapheus* (1565); a map of Flanders by *Mercator*, a world globe and a celestial globe by *A.F. van Langeren* (17C).—ROOM 24 illustrates printing outside Antwerp, by centuries and by countries, the outstanding exhibit being the 36–line *Gutenberg Bible. A large copper engraving (Charles V and Pope Clement VII at Bologna, 1530) is by *Niklaas Hogenberg*.—In ROOM 25 there is a portrait of Edward Moretus-Plantin, by *Joseph Delin* (1879).—ROOM 26, hung with Mechelen leather, is a typical rich man's 17C bedroom.—ILLUSTRATIONS ROOM (R.27). Here are exhibited the best of the c 15,000 woodcuts and 3000 copperplates in the collection. Plantin at first used mainly woodblocks, later changing to copperplate engraving and being a pioneer in this latter technique.

Beyond the Alcove (R. 28) and Room 25, a stair ascends to the TYPE FOUNDRY (ROOMS 29 and 30), the first being a workroom and the second the foundry proper. Note the stone floor, reducing the fire risk. Also the large collection of stamps and matrices, bought by Plantin from various specialists, mainly French.—Downstairs is the LIBRARY (ROOMS 31 and 32), established by Balthasar in 1640. The larger room for a long time served as a private chapel, where Mass was attended by the whole staff, and the painting (Crucifixion, attributed to *Pieter Thys*) served as altarpiece.—The MAX HORN ROOM (R.33) contains the collection of rare bindings and valuable books, bequeathed by the bibliophile Max Horn (1882–1953). The treasure of the collection (in

Case No. 1) is the 13C stamped binding (the oldest known) made for, or by, an Antwerp cleric, Wouter van Duffel. Here too is another huge engraving of Charles V and Pope Clement VII at Bologna, this one by the Liège artist *Robert Péril.*

F. The Rubens House

The ****Rubens House**, a large patrician mansion which includes the artist's studio, was built for Rubens between 1610 and 1617 on land which he bought shortly after his first marriage. It is visited as a house of the period, for its association with Rubens, and for its many paintings by Rubens and others. (Daily, 10.00 to 17.00. Closed 1 and 2 January, 1 May, Ascension, 1 November, 25 and 26 December.)

The painter's son was born here in 1618, but his daughter died here in 1624 and, two years later, his first wife, Isabella Brant. In 1630 he brought his second wife, Hélène Fourment, here. During these years the house became a meeting-place for the noble and cultured society of Flanders, among the visitors being the 'archduke' Isabella, Marie de Medicis, and George Villiers, Duke of Buckingham. Artists often here included Van Dyck, Snyders, Luc Fayd'herbe and others, many of these from time to time working in the studio. Rubens died in 1640, and from 1649 to 1660 the house was occupied by William Cavendish, later Duke of Newcastle, whose riding school in the garden was attended by Charles II. Under later owners the mansion fell into disrepair and its contents were dispersed. Efforts to secure the house for the city, starting as early as 1762, were at last successful in 1937; though little of the original remained beyond the framework of the building, it was skilfully restored by E. van Averbeke, furnished in the style of Rubens's time, and opened as a museum in 1946.

The typically Flemish patrician house is on the left, the Italianate Baroque studio to the right. Under present arrangements, visitors enter through the latter, the ticket desk being in the ANTECHAMBER (notable for its gold-leather wall hangings), adjacent to which is the GREAT STUDIO, showing works by Rubens and others and with a special high narrow door through which the large canvases were moved out of the house. From here, visitors cross the entrance court, separated from the garden by a Baroque portico, a virtually intact survival which appears in various paintings by Rubens, Van Dyck and others; but the statues on top are modern replacements (Edward Deckers, 1939) of earlier figures of Mercury and Minerva.

Next comes the house, the rooms being described below in the order normally visited, though both this and also the arrangement of the pictures and other exhibits is sometimes changed. As noted above, the exhibits (gifts, purchases, etc.) are generally contemporary to Rubens, but, with a few exceptions, the visitor is not seeing Rubens's personal collections.

The PARLOUR, or anteroom to which visitors were first shown, contains a Presentation in the Temple by *Jordaens* and an Adoration of the Magi by *Van Noort*, also of interest here, and much consulted during the restoration of 1938–46, being enlargements from prints of 1684 and 1692 showing the house and studio as they appeared at these dates. The tiled KITCHEN and the SERVING ROOM with its elaborately carved linen press are followed by the DINING ROOM in which there are a number of good paintings of which the most notable is a *Self-portrait by *Rubens* probably dating from 1625–28. Other pictures are a flower-painting by *Daniel Seghers* and a still-life by *Frans Snyders*, while there is also a bronze relief on lapis lazuli by *François Duquesnoy*. In the vestibule, over the entrance to the

Antwerp, the Baroque Portico of the Rubens House

ART GALLERY, there is a 17C Madonna in stone. It was in this gallery that Rubens displayed the best pictures chosen from his large personal collection which at the time of his death, when the collection was dispersed, added up to some 300 paintings. Today the room is once again used as a picture gallery. *Aertgen van Leyden*: Christmas Night. *Lucas van Uden*: Landscape with a Rainbow. *Rubens*: Sketches: Adoration of the Shepherds, St. Adrianus. *Frans Francken the Younger*: Corner of a studio, 1618. *Hendrik van Balen* (attributed): The Israelites in the Desert. *Willem van Haecht*: The Gallery of Cornelis van der Geest. This, one of the most interesting pictures in the house, depicts a visit by Albert and Isabella to the collection—among the most distinguished of its time—of a wealthy merchant who was a friend of Rubens. Van der Geest is seen pointing out a picture by Quinten Metsys to his visitors, and Rubens and Dürer are among other artists whose works are shown. Among other items of interest in the Art Gallery are a small ivory group of Adam and Eve made in 1627 by *Jörg Petel* and possibly belonging to Ruben's collection, and a book called 'Palazzi di Genova' published by Rubens in 1622 and intended for use by architects. Off the Art Gallery there is a small Sculpture Gallery, reminding that Rubens owned a much-admired collection which he started during his time in Italy. Among sculptures here today are two busts (Satyr. Pan) attributed to *Luc Fayd'herbe*, and also one entitled Seneca, but more probably

Aristophanes, which may well have belonged to Rubens.

Upstairs in the LARGE BEDROOM, the room in which Rubens died, hang a portrait of Nicolaas Rockox attributed to *Otto Venius* and a Martyrdom of St. Marcus and St. Marcellinus by *Veronese*. Also worth noting are a rock-crystal necklace in a gold setting, thought to have belonged to Hélène Fourment; a 17C ebony cabinet with ivory and tortoise-shell; and a gold chain with a medallion of Christian IV of Denmark which was a presentation to Rubens. In the SMALL BEDROOM a portrait of Hélène Fourment is attributed to *Jan van Boeckhorst*. The LINEN ROOM contains an early 17C five-door Antwerp cupboard and also two pictures by *Jordaens* (Moses and his Ethiopian Wife. Mercury kills Argus), while the most interesting feature of the CORNER BEDROOM is Rubens's chair as Dean of the Guild of St. Luke; his name with the date is worked into the gilt leather on the back. LIVING ROOM. *Adam van Noort*: Sermon of John the Baptist. *Pieter Snayers*: View of Antwerp. *Jacob Claesz*: Portraits (1530) of Rubens's grandparents.

Adjacent to the LANDING, with Brussels tapestry and a Descent from the Cross by *Jordaens*, is the PUPILS' STUDIO, now used for special exhibitions but otherwise possibly not open. From the landing a carved staircase, a reconstruction of an original of 1617, descends past a gallery overlooking the Great Studio to the tour's starting point in the Antechamber.

The GARDEN has been laid out to conform to old prints of gardens of the time and to a painting by Rubens now in Munich. The pavilion, designed by Rubens as a form of temple to the protectors of the land, contains a Hercules (protector of the soil) attributed to *Luc Fayd-'herbe*, a Bacchus, and, taking the place once occupied by Ceres, a modern Venus by *Willy Kreitz*. An oval monument commemorates Rubens's brother and son (both Philip), while the tombstone of the former, brought here from the now destroyed abbey of Sint Michiel, rests against the wall.

G. Museum voor Schone Kunsten

The ****Museum voor Schone Kunsten (Fine Arts Gallery)**, in a large and well-lit building of 1878–90 by J.J. Winders and F. van Dyck, houses important collections both of Old Masters and of modern works. It is open from 10.00 to 17.00, excepting Monday, 1 January, 1 May, Ascension, 1 November and 25 December.

The museum comprises a hall and two floors, the upper being devoted to Old Masters (14–17C) and the ground floor to modern art (19th and 20C). Also sometimes exhibited are paintings which are owned by churches closed for restoration or other reasons; such paintings, many of which have been restored here, are held only temporarily and are therefore not included below.

The sculpture in the HALL includes busts of two governors of the Spanish Netherlands by *Artus Quellin the Elder* and *Willem Kerrickx*, and here too are interesting murals by *Nicaise de Keyser* illustrating the history of the Flemish school; small key pictures are beside the stairway.

Upper Floor. Old Masters.

The rooms are lettered A to T, with the Primitives in S, Q, N and O running horizontally across the top of the stairway, and the Rubens rooms (I and J) leading off centrally at right angles from these. The text below covers first the Primitives, next Rubens, and then the remaining rooms in clockwise order. Out of a large and rich collection only a few selected pictures can be mentioned here, and the caution must also be given that the allocation of pictures to rooms is occasionally changed.

PRIMITIVES (ROOMS S, Q, N, O). *Gerard David*: The side panels of a triptych (1480–85), the central section of which (Crucifixion) is in the National Gallery in London. The left panel depicts Pilate and Caiaphas, the right Mary with St. John at Golgotha. *Hans Memling*: Portrait (c 1478) generally accepted to be of Giovanni de Candida, a courtier to Mary of Burgundy. Christ among Angels singing and playing Instruments. *Jean Fouquet*: Madonna and Child surrounded by Angels. The picture is notable for the contrast between the unnaturally pale and bare-breasted Madonna and the equally unnatural, strangely coloured angels. *Simone Martini*: Panels of uncertain date showing the Annunciation, the Crucifixion, and the Descent from the Cross. *Master of St. Veronica*: Man of Sorrows between Our Lady and St. Catherine, the latter with her wheel and sword. *Anon.* (possibly studio of Roger van der Weyden): Portrait of Jan Zonder Vrees (John the Fearless, son of Philip the Bold). The subject is known to have been murdered in 1419 and this picture of c 1450 is perhaps a copy or modernised interpretation of an earlier portrait. *Jan van Eyck*: St. Barbara (1437). The saint's father, a wealthy heathen, imprisoned his beautiful daughter in a tower in order to protect her from her many suitors; here she became converted to Christianity, whereupon her father first put her to torture and then beheaded her when she remained steadfast. Van Eyck shows the saint here with prayer-book and palm, symbols of her belief and suffering, while on the tower can be seen the triple-lancet window which the saint had installed as symbol of the Trinity but which raised the suspicions of her father. Madonna at the Fountain (1439). *Roger van der Weyden*: Triptych, Altar of the Sacrament. Portrait of Philippe de Croy, a nobleman at the time of Philip the Good and Charles the Bold. The panel is thought to be the right side of a diptych, the left side of which, with a Madonna and Child, is in the Huntington Collection in New York. *Antonello da Messina*; Crucifixion, with Mary and St. John the Evangelist (1475). The artist is known to have admired Flemish painting and this work is important for showing both Flemish detail and Italian scope. *Albert Bouts*: Adoration of the Shepherds. *Master of the St. Magdalene Legend*: The Holy Family; a charming, wholly natural domestic scene.

PIETER PAUL RUBENS (ROOMS I, J). The works seen here are for the most part altarpieces commissioned for various Antwerp churches. l. Triptych of the Incredulity of St. Thomas (1613–15), commissioned by Rubens's patron Nicolaas Rockox, he and his wife appearing as donors on the side panels. 2. Triptych, Christ on the Straw (1618). 3. The Prodigal Son (1618), a picture in which the animals arouse more interest than the two humans. 4. The Last Communion of St. Francis (1619). 5. Christ Crucified between the two Thieves (also known as The Lance). Commissioned in 1619 by Nicolaas Rockox, this painting well shows the artist's masterly portrayal of anatomy. 6. The Education of Mary (c 1625), a most unconventional portrayal of Mary as a young girl with her parents. 7. Portrait of Gaspard Gevartius (1593–1666), municipal official, poet and historian. Gevartius is shown beside a bust of Marcus Aurelius on whom he had written a commentary. 8. St. Theresa of Avila obtaining the delivery of Bernardino de Mendoza from Purgatory (c 1634). Bernardino, a wealthy nobleman who had given property to Theresa for a new nunnery, died suddenly and unshriven. Theresa then interceded successfully with Christ who is here shown instructing an angel to help Bernardino from the flames. 9. Virgin with a Parrot (c 1614). 10. The Triumphal car of Kallo. In 1638 the Infante Ferdinand defeated the United Provinces at Kallo, just across the river from Antwerp, and the authorities commissioned Rubens to produce a design for the consequent celebrations. The artist's feeling for symbolism and allegory is well illustrated by this sketch.

OTHER ROOMS (clockwise). ROOM T. *Jan Brueghel*: Visit to the Farm, probably a copy of a (now disappeared) grisaille by his father. Riverside Landscape. *Pieter Brueghel the Younger*: Several works. *Pieter Brueghel the Third*: Slaughter of the Innocents. *Jacob Grimmer*: View of the Kiel, a picture interesting for its animated foreground and for the view of fortified Antwerp in the right distance (1578). View of the Scheldt. *Abel Grimmer*: Four Seasons. ROOM R. *Quinten Metsys*: Triptych, Lamentation, with on the left wing Herod, Salome and John the Baptist, and on the right a Martyrdom of John the Evangelist. Dated to 1511 this triptych was commissioned for an altar in the cathedral. St. Mary Magdalene. Diptych, Saviour of the World and Mary at Prayer (c 1505). *Portrait of Pieter Gilles. *Joachim Patinir*: Flight into Egypt. The strange mixed landscape with high rock, a pastoral farm, and sea or lake commands more interest than the fleeing family. *Master of the Antwerp Adoration*: Adoration of the Magi (early 16C). *Anon.*: Sculpture of Christ Crucified (c 1500). *Lucas van Valkenborgh*: View of Huy (c 1570). ROOM L. *Lucas Cranach the Elder*: Caritas. Adam and Eve. Eve. *Lucas Cranach the Younger*: Portrait of a Man. *Jean Clouet*: Portrait of the Dauphin, son of François I to whom Clouet became court painter in 1518. *Jan Metsys*: Judith, a favourite subject with this artist. *Pieter Pourbus*: Several portraits, notably one of Olivier van Nieulant, alderman and recorder of Bruges. *Anon* (mid 16C): Portrait of a Young Man. *Bernard van Orley*: Head of a Woman. *Corneille de Lyon*: Portraits of a Young Nobleman and of a Young Man. ROOM K. *Titian*: Jacopo Pesaro introduced to St. Peter by Pope Alexander VI. Pesaro was commander of the papal fleet which defeated the Turks in 1502 and the picture (c 1502–10) is clearly associated with this. *Frans Francken the Younger*: The Gallery of Sebastian Leerse, a wealthy Antwerp merchant shown here with his second wife and his son. Among the pictures shown are a Susanna and the Elders by (?) Jan Metsys, a Mountain Landscape by Joos de Momper, and a Marine Scene by Bonaventure Peeters. Also in this room are a number of works by *Antoon van Dyck* and *Jordaens*. ROOM M. *Cornelis de Vos*: Several family and individual portraits. *Jan Brueghel*: Flowers in a Vase. Travellers attacked; in conjunction with *Sebastian Vranckx* by whom is also here Plundering of a Hamlet, as also another Travellers Attacked.

ROOM G is devoted to animals, still-life and landscapes. *Paul de Vos*: Partridge shooting. *Jan Fyt* and *Frans Snyders*: Several works. *Jan Siberechts*: An attractive series of four pictures showing peasants and carts crossing water. ROOM GA. *Abraham Janssens*: Peace. *Theodoor Rombouts*: Lute Player. Game of Cards. *David Teniers the Younger*: View of Valenciennes. ROOM F is principally for the work of *Jacob Jordaens*, notably Adoration of the Shepherds (c 1650) and runs of the Antwerp Gasthuis, a striking portrayal of charity and poverty. ROOM H, also, contains several works by *Jordaens*, amongst these Day and Night, with a remarkable candlelight effect, and As the Old sing the Young play Pipes (1638), a genre piece of a family concert in which the old man is Jordaens's teacher and father-in-law Adam van Noort. Also in this room hang a number of paintings by *Van Dyck*, including portraits, a Descent from the Cross, and an Entombment. ROOM E. *Frans Hals*: Fisher boy. Portrait (1650–52) of Stephanus Geraerdts, an alderman of Haarlem. *Rembrandt*: Portrait of Eleazor Swalmus. *Meindert Hobbema, Jan van Goyen, Salomon van Ruysdael* and *Jacob van Ruisdael*: Landscapes. *Jan Steen*: Howelijksfeest. *Adriaen van Ostade*: The Smokers.

ROOM D. *Lucas van Uden*: Landscape with a Rainbow. *Otto Venius*: St. Luke and St. Paul before the governor of Caesarea. *Jacob de Backer:* Last Judgement. ROOM B. *Joachim Beuckelaer*: The Fish Market. The Vegetable Market (1567). *Marinus van Reymerswael*: Several works. ROOM C. *Adriaen Brouwer*: Card Players. Kermesse. *David Teniers the Younger*: Several works including a weird Temptation of St. Anthony. *Sebastian Vranckx*: Landscape with an attack on Travellers. *Joos van Craesbeeck*: Several works, notably At 't Wapen van Antwerp. *Roelant Savery*: Paradise of the Birds. *Gonzales Coques*: Five delightful pictures of the Five Senses. ROOM A. *Frans Pourbus the Elder*: Portrait of a Woman. *Frans Pourbus the Younger*: Portrait of Nicolaas van Hellincx. *Lambert van Noort*: Adoration of the Shepherds. ROOM P. *Frans Floris*: Several works, notably Fall of the Rebel Angels (1554), the central section of a triptych commissioned for an altar in the cathedral; badly damaged during the iconoclastic fury of 1566, it also then lost its wings. *Paul Bril*: Landscape. *Tobias Verhaecht*: Tower of Babel.

Ground Floor. Modern Art.

The museum's collection of works of the 19th and 20C is very large (the catalogue, with particulars of several artists to each page, has over 500 pages) and only a fraction can be shown at the same time. The rooms are numbered 1 to 29. Temporary exhibitions are mounted generally in Rooms 16–18, but also not infrequently take over other sections of this floor. For this reason, and also because pictures are from time to time rotated, the arrangement can vary considerably. Only a few representative artists are mentioned below.

ROOMS 29 to 24, along the S flank, are devoted to 19C and early 20C Romanticism, Realism and Impressionism, ranging from *Alfred Stevens*'s seemingly innocent young women, through the Carnival world of *James Ensor* to the scenes of hardship and poverty so strongly recorded by *Charles de Groux*. Among many other artists hanging in these rooms are *George Hendrik Breitner, Henri de Braekeleer, Hendrik Leys* (a self-portrait and one of his wife), *Leon Frederic* (Two Peasant Children), *Louis Artan* (several typical marine scenes), and *Emile Claus* (Flax Field in Flanders).

The central section of this floor is arranged as two halls (N and S) each with three divisions. In the NORTH HALL (Rooms 13, 14, 15) the artists include *Gustave de Smet, Edgard Tytgat, Jean Brusselmans, Albert Servaes, Gustave van Woestyne, F. van den Berghe* and *Constant Permeke*. In the SOUTH HALL (Rooms 19, 20, 21) may be works by *Rik Wouters* (pictures and sculpture), *Jacob Smits* and *James Ensor*.

ROOMS 4 to 10, along the N flank of the building, bring an abrupt change of mood, with Abstract Art and Surrealism, this challenging series epitomised by *Karel Appel* in Room 9, represented by Man Flying and Animal and Child against a Blue Background; in Room 10, by *Paul Delvaux*'s spooky ladies (De Roze Strikken); and by *René Magritte*, with The Storm Cape, The Wreck, and his macabre theatrical assemblage, Madame Recamier.

17 North Between Antwerp and Holland

In addition to the A1/E19 motorway three principal roads lead N from Antwerp into Holland, all crossing the woods and heath which mark the western edge of the KEMPEN (p 133). See also 'Blue Guide Holland'.

ANTWERP TO WUUSTWEZEL (for **Breda**). 29km to the border.—*10km* **Brasschaat** (31,500 inhab.) is known for its sports and recreational park and facilities.—*14km* **Wuustwezel** (9000 inhab.) is the centre for a district popular with walkers. At *Brecht*, 5km SE beyond the motorway, there is a Kempen museum, while 2km farther E at *Sint Lenaarts* three statues above the porch of the 15–16C church are by Cornelis Floris.—The frontier is *5km* N of Wuustwezel.

ANTWERP TO ESSEN (for **Roosendaal**). 30km to the border.—The Wuustwezel road is followed as far as (*13km) Maria ter Heide* where a fork NW is taken.—*7km* **Kalmthout** (15,000 inhab.) is known for the *Kalmthoutse Heide*, a large nature reserve of mixed dunes, heath, marsh and pine woods with many miles of waymarked walking, cycling and riding tracks. The Arboretum is open March–mid November: Monday–Friday, 09.00 to 17.00; Saturday, Sunday, Holidays, 10.00 to 17.00. There is also the Apicultura Bee Museum (51A Heikantstraat. July and August: daily, 14.00 to 17.00. Open at same times Sunday only early April to mid October).—*10km* **Essen** (12,000 inhab.) the border town, boasts four small museums. In the Gemeentehuis there is the Museum Gerard Meeusen (on request during normal working hours), with local material, while at Kiekenhoeve (54 Moerkantsebaan. Daily, but closed Monday in April–June and September–October, and Monday and Tuesday in November–March), until 1767 a chicken farm of the abbey of Tongerlo, there are agricultural vehichles. In the park of Wildertse Duintjes there is a forest museum explaining the flora and fauna of Kempen, and in Sint Janstraat, in a windmill, there is a bakery museum.

ANTWERP TO PUTTE (for **Bergen op Zoom**). 17km to the border.— *17km* **Putte** comprises two villages, one each side of the border. The grave of the painter Jacob Jordaens, who as a Protestant could not be buried in Antwerp, is in the Dutch village. *Stabroek*, 3km SW and still a polder village, was the home of the Plantin-Moretus family.

18 Antwerp to Turnhout and Maaseik

Total distance 112km.—*26km* **Oostmalle**.—*14km* **Turnhout**.—*12km* **Retie**.—*19km* **Mol**.—*13km* **Leopoldsburg**.—*7km* **Hechtel**.—*16km* **Bree**.—*15km* **Maaseik**.

This Rte traverses the northern part of the KEMPEN (p 133). For places lying between this Rte and Rte 20, see Rte 19.

Antwerp (Rte 16) is left through the suburb of **Deurne**, the road (Turnhoutsebaan, N12) skirting the N side of the large recreational park of *Rivierenhof*, near the SW corner of which, at 160 Hoofdvunderlei, is the *Museum Het Sterckshof* in the château of the same name, in origin of the 14C but rebuilt in 1525 and restored in 1934. The collections include period rooms; silver, copper, pewter, iron and glassware; calico prints; coins, medals, weights and measures (Palm Sunday–October: daily except Monday and Friday, 10.00 to 17.00). Antwerp's airport is some 3km to the south.—The road continues across the Albert Canal and through the residential district of Schilde, later passing (just before *Westmalle*) a Trappist abbey founded in 1791 and with a church of 1836.—At (*26km*) **Oostmalle**, by the road junction, the modern *Sint Laurentiuskerk* stands beneath the tower of its predecessor of 1683. In the interestingly shaped interior of the former hangs a striking ironwork Christ Crowned.—For *Sint Lenaarts* and *Brecht*, 6km and 9km NW, see Rte 17.

DIVERSION TO HOOGSTRATEN AND MEERLE (N 20km).—*11km* **Hoogstraten** is known for its **Sint Katharinakerk*, built in 1524–46 to plans by Rombout Keldermans. The main external feature is the lofty tower (105m) which with much of the rest of the church was rebuilt after war damage in 1944. Inside, the handsome marble and alabaster mausoleum (1529) of the founders, Count Antoine de Lalaing (died 1540) and his wife Elisabeth of Culemberg (died 1555), is probably by Jean Mone; it is surrounded by 16C stained-glass windows showing amongst others Charles V, Margaret of Austria and members of the Lalaing line. The pulpit is by Theodoor Verhaeghen. The *Stadhuis*, adjoining the church, is a rebuilding of a 16C predecessor by Rombout Keldermans blown up by the retreating Germans in 1944. The *Begijnhof*, a short way N of the church and founded in the 14C, was largely destroyed by fire in 1506 and the buildings seen today are of the 17th and 18C, the Baroque church dating from 1687. At *Minderhout*, just N of Hoogstraten, the road crosses the little river Mark and virtually touches the Dutch border (E).—At (*9km*) *Meerle* the tower and central nave of the church in part date back to the 13C. The Dutch border is 3km farther N, or 3km SE, the latter small road leading in 10km to the curious Belgian enclave of *Baarle-Hertog* (see below), from where the main Rte 18 can be rejoined by taking the road S direct to Turnhout.

Beyond Oostmalle N12 continues through *Vlimmeren*, where the church, apart from the tower, is 14C, and *Vosselaar*, with a church housing a 13C wooden figure of Our Lady Comforter of the Afflicted.
     14km **Turnhout** (38,000 inhab. Tourist Information: 1 Grote Markt) is a lively industrial town known for the manufacture of playing cards.

From the 14C to the 16C Turnhout belonged to Brabant. Charles V then gave the town to his sister Mary of Hungary, and after the Treaty of Münster in 1648 it became for a while an appanage first of the House of Orange and then until 1753 of Brandenburg. It was at Turnhout in 1789 during the Brabançon Revolt that the Belgians defeated the Austrians, paving the way for the brief United States of Belgium.

In the GROTE MARKT stands the *Sint Pieterskerk*, first built in the 12C as successor to wooden chapels dating back to the 8C. Of this early structure all that survives is the lower part of the tower, while the apse is of 1486. Additions and alterations date through to the 18C. Inside there are Baroque stalls, confessionals by J.P. Baurscheit the Younger, and a pulpit (H. Peeters, 19C) vividly depicting the Miraculous Draught of Fishes. The road leading N out of the Grote Markt soon passes (left) the *Kasteel*; in origin of c 1110 and later the residence of the dukes of Brabant and of Mary of Hungary, this castle was rebuilt during the 17C for Prince Frederick Henry of Orange-Nassau. The *Museum van de Speelkaart* (playing cards) is in a 16C house on the opposite side of the street a little farther N (28 Begijnenstraat. Wednesday, Friday, 14.00 to 17.00; Sunday, 10.00 to 12.00, 14.00 to 17.00. In June–August, also Tuesday and Thursday, 14.00 to 17.00). A short way beyond, off the W side of the road, is the *Begijnhof*, first mentioned in 1372 but completely rebuilt during the 17C; the church is of 1665 and one of the houses serves as a museum (Sunday, 15.00 to 17.00; Wednesday, Friday, 14.00 to 17.00). Herentalsstraat leads S out of the Grote Markt; off this, after some 500m, Mermansstraat bears E, at No. 27 being the *Museum Taxandria* of local archaeology, history and industry (Wednesday, Friday, Sunday, 14.00 to 17.00. In July and August, also Tuesday–Sunday, 14.00 to 17.00).

From Turnhout a visit can be made to **Baarle-Hertog** (12km N), a geographic and political curiosity where Belgian enclaves (Baarle-Hertog) are mixed in with the Dutch village of Baarle-Nassau, a state of affairs which originated in 1479 when, for lordship inheritance reasons, the village of Baarle was divided into two, these eventually splitting politically between North Brabant (now Dutch) and South Brabant (now Belgian). Some strange situations have thus arisen: e.g. the market square is Dutch, except for one tavern, while the old church is Belgian; and there are two town halls, police stations, schools, post offices, etc.—This unique situation saved Baarle-Hertog from German occupation during the First World War. In October 1915 the Belgians established a radio station here and, in spite of a barbed-wire fence built around the commune by the neutral Dutch, made the village an important focus of Allied espionage.

Beyond Turnhout the main road (N18) bears SE, soon passing *Oud-Turnhout*, with a Last Supper (1698) by Jan Erasmus Quellin in the church, and then crossing the A21/E34 motorway.—*12km* **Retie**, with a Tree of Justice in front of the church, is the centre of a district of woods, heath and dunes. A large estate here was sold by the Crown in 1950, a part of this now being *Prinsenpark*, a nature reserve of 165ha (walks, picnic areas) some 5km along the road to Geel.

The Premonstratensian abbey of **Postel** is in wooded and marshy country 7km NE of Retie. Founded in 1140 by monks from Floreffe as a hospice for pilgrims, it became an abbey in 1621, was suppressed in 1797, and reopened in 1847. The courtyard beyond the 17C gateway is architecturally rather spoilt by a modern 'Contact Centre'. The Romanesque church, dating from c 1190 and built of tufa from the Eifel in Germany, was much altered in the 16–17C, but there survives a beautifully decorated 13C doorway by the side of the cloister. The domestic buildings date from 1631, with additions of 1713 and 1743, and the library is known for its rich collection of incunabula, 16C books, etchings, old atlases, etc. The belfry of 1610 contains a carillon of 1947 with 40 bells.

Beyond (*4km*) *Dessel* the road crosses the Kempisch Kanaal, dug in 1845, beside which (3km W) there is a research complex for the peaceful use of nuclear power, a part of which is used by Euratom.—*5km* **Mol** (29,500 inhab. Tourist Information: 22 Markt) is a straggling community amid typical Kempen surrounds. The *Sint Pieter en Pauwelkerk*, rebuilt in 1852, has a tower of 1492 with a carillon of 49 bells and a museum of religious art (April–September: Tuesday, 11.00; Saturday, 15.00. In July and August, also Sunday at 15.00). Inside the church, which preserves as a relic a thorn from Christ's crown, are two statues (transept pillars) attributed to Artus Quellin the Elder and also a painting by G.J. Herreyns. Alongside the church a monument commemorates the Peasants' Revolt of 1798, and in the square there is also part of an old pillory. *Achterbos-Sluis*, just N of Mol, was a favourite spot with the Kempen painter Jacob Smits (died here 1928) on whom there is a small museum at Sluis (Oude Pastorie. Saturday and Sunday, and daily except Monday during school holiday periods, 14.00 to 18.00). *Zilvermeer*, 5km NE of Mol, is a provincial park with two large lakes (camping, swimming, boating, natural history museum).—*4km Balen*, 3km NE of which *Keiheuvel* is an area of dunes and scrub popular for many recreational purposes including gliding. The hamlet of *Scheps*, 2km S, was the birthplace in the 8C of St. Odrade who performed miracles and is invoked to bring fair weather.—*9km* **Leopoldsburg** (10,000 inhab.), just in the province of Limburg, serves as garrison town for the military establishments at *Beverlo* (4km S) founded in 1850 by Leopold I (museum in the former military hospital, Hechtelsesteenweg). At *Oostham*, 6km W, the church tower is a rebuilding after war damage of an 11C predecessor; note the masonry in herringbone pattern.

7km **Hechtel**, at an important crossroads (N73 and N715), is also the centre of a large district of dunes, heath and woodland. *In de Brand* (NW) and *Begijnenvijver* (SE) are two nearby nature areas, and at *Eksel*, 3km NE, a museum describes the flora and fauna of the Kempen (June–August: Wednesday, Saturday, Sunday, 13.30 to 14.30, 16.30 to 17.30).

The road leading N from the Hechtel crossroads (N715) skirts the *Park der Lage Kempen* (W), with way-marked walks and picnic areas. After 10km another main crossroads is reached (with N71), just W of which there is a Polish war cemetery. To the W (4km) the small town of **Lommel**, although industrial (lead and zinc), is nevertheless set in typical Kempen surrounds; the town's *Sint Pieterskerk* has a tower of 1388 and there are two museums, the district (Streek) museum at 14 Markt and a prehistoric collection at the Eymardininstituut at *Kattenbos* to the south. The Kattenbos woods and heath, with a restored windmill of 1805 and a large German war cemetery, are a popular nature reserve area.—To the E of the crossroads lie *Overpelt* and *Neerpelt*, both zinc towns in a fast expanding industrial zone. **Achel**, 5km NE of Neerpelt, is a pleasanter place, with a 15C church and (2km NE; signs) a 13–14C tower known as *De Tomp*.

For N715 S from Hechtel, see Rte 19.

6km Peer has a town hall of 1637.—At (*10km*) **Bree** (8000 inhab. Tourist Information: 3 Cobbestraat) there are two museums, the local museum in the Oud Gemeentehuis, with a model of the town as it was in 1700, and a war museum at 85 Kanaallaan. The Gothic *Sint Michielskerk*, dating from 1452 but enlarged in 1901, is successor to a Romanesque church, itself successor to a 7C chapel.

Bree was the main town of a district which in the 14–16C grew prosperous from wool. Its own church, and those in many of the surrounding villages, are reminders of that prosperity and architecturally represent a style known as Limburg Gothic. Generally the walls are of local marl, as is also the vaulting with diagonal ribbing, while other parts are in bluestone. Many contain old statues of saints. The best of these churches is that at *Neeroeteren* (9km SE; see below). Others are (distances from Bree): *Gerdingen* (1km NW); *Beek* (2km N); *Opitter* (4km SE); *Gruitrode* and *Neerglabbeek* (5.5km S); *Opglabbeek* (11km S).

Beyond Bree the main road continues E, but this Route bears SE on N721 through *Opitter* (see above).—The *Church at (*9km*) **Neeroeteren**, the best of the Limburg Gothic group mentioned above, was built in the 15C and has since been little altered except for the addition of the tower in 1719. The church houses an outstanding collection of early 16C statues, including St. Lambert (patron), St. James and St. Christopher, while the Marianum is one of the only two in Belgium, the other being at Zoutleeuw.

6km **Maaseik** (21,000 inhab. Tourist Information: 45 Markt) is a pleasant small place on the Maas, here forming the border with Holland. The Markt, with its lime trees and several 17–18C houses, is particularly attractive, and a monument here of 1864 commemorates Jan and Hubert van Eyck, reputedly born at Maaseik, the former in c 1390 and the latter, if he ever existed, perhaps 20 years earlier. Also in the Markt are an 18C pharmacy, with contemporary furniture and equipment and now serving as a local museum (of the pharmacy itself, of local archaeology and of baking. Daily except Monday, 09.00 to 12.00, 14.00 to 17.00), and the 19C *Stadhuis* in which there hangs a copy of the Van Eycks' Mystic Lamb (see Rte 13). The streets off the Markt, notably Bosstraat, also have 17–18C façades. The *Katharinakerk* is noted for its treasury (normally opened on request) which contains an evangelistery of the early 8C (the Codex Eyckensis, the oldest book in Belgium), believed to have once belonged to the two pious ladies who in c 750 founded a Benedictine convent at *Aldeneik* (1.5km E), where an ancient church still survives. A stone church built in 870 was restored in the 11C, and additions were made in the 13C by which time the nuns had been replaced by monks. More restoration and alterations followed during the 19C. Today the central part of the Romanesque nave, with some 13C frescoes, is of the 11th or 12C; the W part of the church is early 13C and the choir late 13C; and the Neo-Romanesque aisles and the tower are of the 19C.

19 Antwerp to Genk

Motorway distance 81km.—*20km* **Grobbendonk** and **Herentals**.—*14km* **Geel** (also **Tongerlo** and **Westerlo**).—*14km* **Tessenderlo**.—*7km* **Paal**.—*17km* **Houthalen**.—*9km* **Genk**.

This Rte uses the A13/E313 and A2/E314 motorways, crossing the central and southern KEMPEN and offering a convenient way of reaching a number of places of interest lying between Rtes 18 and 20. Main distances are those between the points at which the motorway is left.

Antwerp, see Rte 16.—*7km* Motorway A21/E34 bears NE for Eindhoven in Holland.—*13km* **Grobbendonk**, just N of the motorway, is a large village best known for its *Diamond Museum*, covering mining, cutting and polishing, and industrial and decorative use (Monday–Friday, 09.00 to 16.30; Saturday, 10.00 to 13.30; Sunday, 10.00 to 12.00, 14.00 to 16.00. Closed 1 January, 30 and 31 December). At *Vorselaar*, 2.5km NE and with a pillory of 1759, an avenue of limes leads to an imposing moated château (no adm., but well seen from outside) which in the 13C belonged to the Van Rotselaar family, chief stewards of the dukes of Brabant, but was rebuilt in Neo-Gothic style during the 19C. **Herentals** (24,000 inhab.), 6km E of Grobbendonk, has since the 14C been the chief town of the Kempen and it was from here that fresh water was sent by barge to Antwerp for use by the city's breweries. The *Sint Waldetrudiskerk*, dating in part from the 14C, contains an early 16C retable by Pasquier Borremans and paintings by Frans Francken the Elder. The *Stadhuis*, once the cloth hall and with a belfry of 1590, was first built in about 1400 but was burnt down in 1512, rebuilt two years later and given major restoration in 1880; it houses a collection of casts and sculptures by Charles Fraikin who was born here in 1817 (June–August: daily, 10.00 to 12.00, 14.00 to 17.00). In the northern part of the town the *Begijnhof* is the 17–18C successor of one founded in c 1266, though on a different site, and destroyed by Calvinists in 1578; its church dates from 1595–1614 and it is of interest that the horizontal courses of white stone were brought from the previous begijnhof. Two of the town's old gates survive, the *Zandpoort* (14C), on the road to Lier, and the *Bovenpoort* (1402) on the road to Geel.

14km **Geel** (31,000 inhab. Tourist Information: Stadhuis), 5km N of the motorway, is known worldwide for its system for the treatment of the insane, patients being boarded out among the townspeople and in nearby villages and thus enjoying domestic comfort, a measure of freedom, personal care, and opportunities for useful occupation. This humane and successful system, under official and medical supervision since about 1850, originated as far back as the 13C from a pilgrimage to the shrine of St. Dimpna, patroness of the insane, an Irish princess who fled to Geel to escape her crazed and incestuous father. She and her confessor (St. Gerebernus) were sadly nevertheless caught and executed, reputedly on the site where the **Sint Dimpnakerk* now stands. Built in 1344–1492 (tower 16C) the church contains the reliquaries of the two saints as well as other treasures. The **Mausoleum of Jean III, Count of Mérode, and of his wife Anne de Ghistelles (1554) is by Cornelis Floris and there are also several superb **Retables*: one, of the Passion, is ascribed to Goswin van der Weyden (c 1490); another, of 1513 and telling the story of St. Dimpna, is by Jan van Waver; while a third, depicting the Apostles, is a sandstone carving of 1350. The 'Sieckencamere' (sick room) is where the mentally afflicted pilgrims observed their novena. Close to the church, in a 15C chapel at 1 Gasthuisstraat, the *Sint Dimpna en Gasthuismuseum* of local history includes a special St. Dimpna section (mid May–September: Sunday, Wednesday, Thursday 14.00 to 17.30). *Sint Amandskerk*, near the Markt, was built in 1490–1531 and has one of the best Baroque interiors in Belgium. The high-altar is by Pieter Verhaghen, and Pieter Valckx and W. Kerrickx also did much of the carved work here.

From Geel N19 leads S across the motorway to (9km from Geel) the walled and moated Premonstratensian **Tongerlo Abbey*, founded in 1130 in the then desolate and barren Kempen and soon becoming one of the pioneers of local agriculture; dissolved in 1796, it reopened in 1840 and is now again thriving. The approach is along a stately drive of limes, 300 years old, at the end of which two Romanesque arches (12–14C) admit to the large inner court around which the buildings are clearly marked with their names, dates and other information. To the right is the Prelaatshuis (Willem Ignatius Kerrickx, 1726), with a pleasing façade, the door of which serves as approach to the **Da Vinci Museum* (May–September: daily except Friday, 14.00 to 17.00), reached across a garden on the left of which is the Guest House (1547) with an elegant turret of 1479. The museum (1956) is a small theatre housing a copy of Da Vinci's Last Supper, painted in 1506–07 by the artist's pupil Andrea del Solario, reputedly by order of Pope Clement VII for Henry VIII of England. Bought by the abbey in 1545, this copy aroused the admiration of both Rubens and Van Dyck. The painting is beautifully lit, well positioned for study, and explained by a commentary in English. **Westerlo** (20,000 inhab.), 2km S of the abbey and pleasantly situated on the Grote Nete, is a popular centre for walkers and cyclists, especially within the large municipal recreation area. There are two châteaux, one of which, the *Kasteel van Gravin J. de Mérode*, a Neo-Gothic building of 1911, now serves as a municipal and cultural centre. The other, the *Kasteel de Mérode*, dates in part from c 1300 but shows styles covering from the 14C to the 19C.

At (*14km*) **Tessenderlo** (14,000 inhab.), 3km S of the motorway and just in the province of Limburg, the 14–15C *Sint Martinuskerk* is known for its rood-screen of c 1500 depicting the life of Christ.—*7km Paal* stands at the crossing of the motorway and N29 from Diest (Rte 20) to Leopoldsburg (Rte 18). **Beringen**, 2km E, is a small former colliery town (mine visit and museum) whose *Sint Theodardskerk* (the 'Miners' Cathedral', 1939–43) has a detached tower, so built because of the danger of subsidence; Theodard was a 7C bishop of Liège.

Continuing SE the motorway in *5km* reaches the junction with motorway A2/E314 along which this Rte bears due E, with, immediately S though not seen from the motorway, the motor trials and racing track of *Terlaemen-Zolder*.—Near (*12km*) **Houthalen**, 2km N of the motorway, there are three recreation areas: the provincial park of *Molenheide*, 5km N, with walks and an animal enclosure; *Hengelhoef*, 5km NE with accommodation, aviary, animal enclosure, bird sanctuary and many sports facilities; and *Domein Kelchterhoef*, 6km E, with similar facilities. To the S of the motorway (c 8km) is the large **Bokrijk Provinciaal Domein* (see Rte 20), with the Province of Limburg Tourist Information Office.—*9km* **Genk** (61,000 inhab.), 3km S of the motorway, is an expanding industrial town largely surrounded, especially to the S and E, by typical Kempen country of wood and heath, many parts of which are designated nature reserves. The *Villa van Doren*, at 21 H. Decleenestraat, houses a local museum and also works by Emile van Doren, the 19C landscape artist who lived here (Wednesday, Saturday, Sunday, 10.00 to 12.00, 15.00 to 18.00). The *Zwartberg Limburg Zoo*, 3km N of the motorway and due N of Genk, was formed in 1970 and shows a good collection of animals in the setting of a park (Easter–mid November, 09.00 to 19.00).

The motorway continues E through Kempen country, in 19km reaching the Dutch border and the Maas.

20 Antwerp to Hasselt and Maastricht (Holland)

Total distance 100km.—*14km* **Lier**.—*12km* **Heist-op-den-Berg**.—*14km* **Aarschot**.—*10km* **Scherpenheuvel**.—*5km* **Diest**.—*21km* **Hasselt**.—*13km* **Bilzen**.—*11km* **Maastricht** (Holland).

Antwerp (see Rte 16) is left by the Grote Steenweg past the southern suburb of *Berchem*, after which the road (Liersesteenweg, N10) bears E past Mortsel to reach *Boechout*, birthplace of J.F. Willems.

14km **Lier** (31,000 inhab. Tourist Information: Stadhuis), at the confluence of the Grote and Kleine Nete, is a delightful and compact town offering much of interest. Sections of the 14C ramparts have been arranged as walks.

Founded during the 8C, and associated with St. Gummarus (717–74), a courtier to King Pepin who became a hermit here to escape from his spendthrift and nagging wife, Lier received official town status from Duke Henry of Brabant in 1212. Philip the Handsome and Joanna of Castile were married here in 1496, and in 1523 Christian II of Denmark and his queen (Isabel of Austria, sister of Charles V) came to live here after their flight from Denmark. During the 19th and 20C the town was the home of the worker in iron L. van Boeckel (1857–1944), of the writer Felix Timmermans (1886–1947), of the painter Baron Isidore Opsomer (1878–1967) and of the clockmaker L. Zimmer (1888–1970).

In the GROTE MARKT some modern and undistinguished architecture is mixed in with older façades, one of which, the *Vleeshuis*, dates back to 1418. The *Stadhuis* of 1740, successor to a medieval cloth hall, is a Rococo building the preliminary plans for which were drawn by J.P. Baurscheit the Younger; it is remarkable for having over 3500 small window panes. Main features of the interior are the Rococo staircase of 1775 and a clock by Zimmer. The attached Belfry of 1369 formed part of the medieval combined cloth hall and town meeting-place.

The *Museum Wuyts van Campen-Baron Caroly*, just W of the Grote Markt at 14 Florent van Cauwenberghstraat, houses the distinguished collections bequeathed by the former family in 1886 and by Baron G. Caroly in 1935 (Easter–October: daily except Wednesday and Friday, 10.00 to 12.00, 13.30 to 17.30. Other months: Sunday, 10.00 to 12.00, 13.30 to 16.30). Works normally on exhibition include the following. Bernard van Orley (Madonna with Child and Angel). David Teniers the Elder (Seven works of Mercy. The Alchemist). Pieter Brueghel the Younger (St. John. Flemish Proverbs). Jan Brueghel (Madonna and Child). Frans Floris (The Van Berchem Family). Antoon van Dyck (St. Sebastian. Portrait of a Nobleman). Pieter Paul Rubens (St. Theresa). David Teniers the Younger (Jealous Wife. The Village of Perk). Jan Steen (Brawling Peasants). Murillo (Bacchus).

Eikelstraat leads SW out of the Grote Markt through the *Eikelpoort*, a remnant of the early walls dating from c 1375 but altered in 1727; long used as a prison, this gate is also known as the Prisoners' Gate. The Eikelpoort occupies the NW end of ZIMMERPLEIN (under water until the end of the 19C), at the opposite end of which stands the *Zimmertoren*, another section of the ramparts, now housing two unique clocks and the Astronomic Studio, all by Louis Zimmer (Daily, 09.00 to 12.00, 14.00 to 19.00 or to 16.00 in winter).

The *Centenary Clock* (1930–31), on the tower, has a central dial surrounded by 12 smaller dials. At 12.00 the phases of the moon. 1, the 19-year metonic cycle covering all the changes of the moon. 2, the equation of time in relation to Greenwich Mean Time. 3, the zodiac. 4, the solar cycle of 28 years is shown on the inner calibration; the outer shows the dominical letter. 5, the days of the week. 6, the globe. 7, the months, with their various features (Ice, Duck, Fish, Fool, Flower, Shearing, Hay, Harvest, Fruit, Wine, Butchering, Rest). 8, the calendar. 9, the seasons, pictorially represented. 10, the tides at Lier, indicated by the sizes of ships. 11, the ages of the moon.—Daily at noon figures appear representing the first century of Belgian independence (the national arms; three kings; the arms of Lier; the burgomasters).

The *Astronomic Studio* is on the first floor of the tower. Here there are 57 dials recording, by groups, the subdivisions of time; the tides; the planetary system; astronomical calculations; rotation of the sun and planets; the phases of the moon and the tides; astronomical phenomena; constellations of the northern hemisphere.—The combined mechanism of the Centenary Clock and the Astronomic Studio is seen on the second floor.

Lier, the Zimmertoren

Nearby is the astronomical *Wonder Clock*, which was a feature of the World Fairs of Brussels (1935) and New York (1939). It comprises 14 automata, and three large dials, each surmounting a panel of thirty small dials.

The small garden contains ironwork by Van Boeckel.

The *Begijnhof*, one of the most extensive in Belgium, lies to the SW of

Zimmerplein; although founded in c 1200 on its present site, the buildings seen today are mainly of the late 17C. The Baroque chapel (1664–1767) contains an antependium the design of which is attributed to Rubens and the embroidery to his daughter; also a tabernacle by Willem Ignatius Kerrickx and sculpture by Artus Quellin the Younger.

Close to the Zimmertoren the Kleine Nete can be crossed by a small bridge, just beyond which is the *Timmermans-Opsomerhuis* (Easter–October: daily except Wednesday and Friday, 10.00 to 12.00, 13.30 to 17.30. Other months: Sunday, 10.00 to 12.00, 13.30 to 16.30), containing material not only on Timmermans and Opsomer, who is represented by several portraits and other pictures, but also on Van Boeckel whose forge is shown together with examples of his work. The Werft (wharf), once the waterside commercial quarter, follows the river northwards, across the water being the *Fortuin*, a medieval granary which is now a restaurant.

At the next bridge Rechtestraat leads E to the *Sint Gummaruskerk, built in Flamboyant style in 1425–1540. The base of the tower is rather older (14C), but the upper octagonal part is an 18C replacement. The interior merits a visit for its many art treasures and in particular for its *Stained-glass which, restored after war damage in 1914, is some of the oldest and best in Belgium and ranges from the 15C to modern times. Especially notable are the Crowning of the Virgin (15C) in the S aisle; a window made by Rombout Keldermans in 1475 (choir, left, first row); and a group of five high windows above the altar, three of which were presented by the Emperor Maximilian when he visited Lier in 1516. The rood-loft, showing the Stations of the Cross, is of 1534, and the pulpit and altar are by Artus Quellin the Elder. In the first ambulatory chapel (left) there is a triptych of which the wings depicting St. Clare and St. Francis are by Rubens, while in the fourth chapel another triptych of c 1516 is attributed to Goswin van der Weyden. The chapels also contain works by Otto Venius, Martin de Vos, Michiel Coxie and Frans Francken the Elder.

Immediately N of the church the *Sint Pieterskapel* dates from 1225 but was largely rebuilt after war damage in 1914. The *Jesuitenkerk*, a short way SE in Berlaarsestraat and with a fine Baroque façade, was built in 1749–54.

12km **Heist-op-den-Berg** stands on a hill (45m) which is the highest natural point in the province of Antwerp. The *Sint Lambertuskerk* (1587) contains a marble Madonna by Artus Quellin the Younger, and in the pleasant close a house called *Die Zwaene* is the local museum (Easter–September: Saturday, 14.00 to 18.00. Sunday, 10.00 to 12.00, 14.00 to 18.00). Nearby (signs) there is an observation tower.

14km **Aarschot** (13,000 inhab.), in the province of Brabant and standing on the Demer at an important crossroads, is both an agricultural and light industry centre.

The town is of ancient origin, tradition maintaining that the name derives from the fact that the Romans kept their eagles (standards) here; alternatively that Julius Caesar shot an eagle here. Prosperity came with the cloth trade in the 13C, but later Aarschot lived through violent times. In 1489 it was sacked by Maximilian of Austria, afterwards suffering during the wars of Charles the Bold, and in the 16C it was several times pillaged and burnt by the Spanish. In 1782 Joseph II razed the fortifications, this inciting many of the inhabitants to support the Brabançon Revolt a few years later. In 1914 Aarschot experienced German brutality, 400 houses being burnt and 149 citizens, including the burgomaster, murdered.

The *Orleanstoren*, a relic of the 13C walls on the hill above the town, offers a good view. Near the river the Gothic *Onze Lieve Vrouwekerk* has a 13–14C choir, a 15C nave and a tower 85m high. The interesting interior, with paintings by De Crayer and Verhaghen and a chandelier by Quinten Metsys, is best known for the lively *Misericords on the choir-stalls (Jan Borchman, 1500) and for a naive and weird painting, the *Mystic Winepress, by an unknown Flemish artist of c 1525.

The theme is that Christ, on the 'press' of the Cross, shed his blood for our redemption. The lower part comprises the seven Sacraments, while the upper part likens the Holy Blood to wine. To the left the Apostles are working, with Peter pressing the grapes. The four evangelists then take the juice to the church, and the barrels are closed by pope, emperor, cardinals and bishops, then taken to the cellars. Priests offer wine to the faithful, who make confession and hear Mass.

Immediately W of the church there is a large Renaissance mansion, once a burgomaster's house, and beyond this again is the *Begijnhof*, founded in the 13C but largely destroyed by the two World Wars and by later town extensions. A part has been restored in 17–18C style and now includes municipal offices, old people's housing, and the municipal *Museum* (Monday–Saturday, except Tuesday afternoon, 08.30 to 12.00, 14.00 to 17.00; Sunday, 10.00 to 12.00). Opposite the museum entrance a small memorial (the Lacemaker) recalls a now lost local skill, and beyond, straddling the river, are *'s Hertogenmolens*, the 13–16C brick ducal mills.

The mellow and attractive château of **Horst** (Easter–September: daily, 14.00 to 23.00. October–Easter: Sunday, 14.00 to 21.00), surrounded by water, is at Sint Pieters-Rode, 6km S of Aarschot. Of the early medieval castle (13–15C) only tower and keep remain, but the rest of the building (15–17C) has been unaltered since the 17C, when the place was last inhabited, and Horst thus stands as an unspoilt example of a seignural home of that period. Despite not being occupied, the château has been well maintained, the main feature of the interior being the scenes from Ovid's 'Metamorphoses' (Jan Hansche, late 17C) which decorate the ceiling of the hall.

To the W and SW of Aarschot are **Tremelo** (7km) and **Rotselaar** (10km). The former was the birthplace in 1840 of Father Damien, the missionary who devoted his life to the leper outcasts on the Hawaiian island of Molokai and who died of the disease there in 1889; in 1936 his body was brought to the chapel of St. Antonius in Louvain. The house in which he was born is now a museum (10.00 to 12.00, 14.00 to 18.00. Closed Sunday morning and Monday).—At Rotselaar there is a high fortified tower of unknown date but thought to have been rebuilt during the 15C.

10km **Scherpenheuvel** (20,500 inhab.) is the scene of Belgium's most important annual pilgrimage (Sunday after All Saints).

In about the year 1514 a shepherd found near here a statue of the Virgin and Child attached to an oak. On trying to remove it he became fixed to the ground, and his pious master, who had come to look for him, understood this to mean that Our Lady wished to be honoured in this place and built a chapel. In 1578 Parma prayed here before investing Zichem (3km N), but two years later the statue was destroyed by iconoclasts. In 1601 Albert and Isabella vowed to make a pilgrimage to Scherpenheuvel if their commander Spinola eventually forced the United Provinces forces to retreat. Spinola took Ostend, and in 1607 Archduke Albert had the town built in the shape of a seven-pointed star.

The circular *Basilica*, completed by Wenceslaus Coeberger, the court architect, in 1627, is copied from St. Peter's in Rome, the seven windows in the lantern turret symbolising the seven Sacraments.

Inside, a copy of the original miraculous statue is above the high-altar and there are numerous gifts by pilgrims, including notably a brass font of 1610 from Albert and Isabella; six paintings by Theodoor van Loon from Isabella; and an Assumption attributed to Martin de Vos.

Zichem, 3km N, is an old town with a church of c 1300 containing stained-glass of 1387, while by the river the Maagdentoren is a remnant of the 14C ramparts. The town was the birthplace in 1885 of the writer Ernest Claes (museum).—The Premonstratensian **Averbode Abbey**, 4km farther N, stands at the junction of the provinces of Antwerp, Brabant and Limburg. Founded in 1134, the abbey was disestablished at the time of the French Revolution but reopened in 1833. A 14C gatehouse gives access to the inner court in which are the vaulted 17C cloisters and the 18C (rebuilt) abbot's house, but most of the domestic buildings are reconstructions following a serious fire in 1942. The large Baroque church (D. van der Ende, 1664–72) has a choir which is longer than its nave.

5km **Diest** (21,000 inhab.) is an ancient and attractive walled town offering much of interest and many picturesque corners. The irregular GROTE MARKT is surrounded by 17th and 18C buildings, one of these being the *Stadhuis* (Willem Ignatius Kerrickx, 1735), built as replacement to a group of much earlier buildings the several vaulted cellars of which now attractively house the beautifully arranged *Stedelijk Museum* (April–October: Monday–Saturday, 10.00 to 12.00, 13.00 to 17.00; Sunday, Holidays, 10.00 to 12.00. November–March: Sunday, 10.00 to 12.00, 14.00 to 17.00). The surviving cellars are the Gothic cellar of the fomer aldermen's house (c 1320) and the Romanesque cellar (13C), still with its original well, of the house of the lords of Diest. Of particular interest in the museum are a collection of silver (c 1600); a small frame-reliquary crammed with saintly relics, each meticulously labelled; a marble virgin of 1345, a replica of an original in the Metropolitan Museum of Art, New York; pictures by Theodoor van Loon; and a dramatic *Last Judgement by an unknown artist (c 1420–50). The adjacent *Sint Sulpitiuskerk* was long in building (1321–1534), the colours of the stone revealing the successive stages of construction. Excavations have revealed the remains of two former churches, the older of the 11C, and tradition holds that a wooden chapel stood here as early as the 7C, this also perhaps dedicated to St. Sulpitius, a bishop (died 647) famed for his care for the poor and the oppressed. The interior contains choir stalls of 1491 with lively misericords; 15–16C stained glass; a 13C Sedes Sapientiae; the tomb of Philip of Nassau (died 1618), son of William the Silent and lord of Diest; and a fine treasury.

Beside the road, just W of the church, stands 'Holle Griet', a 15C bombard, and here also is the *Halle*, the 14C Cloth Hall, best seen from its E end. East of here is the oldest part of Diest, the corner of Ketelstraat and Guido Gezellestraat providing typical views, with in the latter street the fine 17C Baroque façade of the *Sint Barbarakerk*. In the E part of the town WARANDE STADSPARK, once a hunting ground of the princes of Orange, has a cemetery at its SE corner in which are the ruins of a 14C church.

The abbeys of Tongerlo and Averbode both had refuges within the walls of Diest, these still surviving to the N of the Grote Markt between Demerstraat and Refugiestraat; that of Tongerlo (16C) can be seen E off Demerstraat, while that of Averbode (15C) is in the N part of Refugiestraat, near where it joins Demerstraat. Koning Albert-straat leads NE out of the Grote Markt to reach (500m) Begijnenstraat, at the beginning of which the *Onze Lieve Vrouwekerk* dating from the 13C is successor to an even earlier chapel. Near the far end of this street a Baroque portal of 1671 marks the entrance to the *Begijnhof*.

Founded in 1252, much reconstruction was started in 1538–75 by the then pastor, Nicolaas van Esch, and today's houses, occupying four streets, are mainly of this period and later. The 14C Gothic church has a restored Rococo interior.

On the N edge of the town, reached from the Onze Lieve Vrouwekerk by Schaffensestraat, the *Schaffensepoort* is a narrow fortified way across two arms of the river Demer and successive lines of ramparts.

Diest is left by the Hasseltsestraat (N2) and in 2km the border is crossed into the province of Limburg.—*5km* **Halen** has a pleasant square with 18th and 19C houses. A monument commemorates a victorious charge by the Belgian cavalry in August 1914, and to the right of the eastern exit from the village an attractive old mansion and bridge can be seen. In the church of the adjoining village of *Donk* there is a 16C statue of a recumbent Virgin, invoked to cure sterility.—*4km* **Herk-de-Stad** was the birthplace in 1872 of Pauline Jeuris, a missionary martyred in China in 1900 and beatified in 1946 as the Blessed Amandina (museum), and (*4km*) **Spalbeek** was that of Hendrik van Veldeke (12C), the first Netherlands troubadour. An old chapel here, to the N of the road by the railway crossing, has a 12C choir of unusual horseshoe shape and also 14C murals.—*6km* **Kuringen** is best known as the site of the abbey of Herkenrode, for Cistercian nuns, founded in 1182 and disestablished in 1797 when its treasures were dispersed. Some of the beautiful stained-glass is now in Lichfield Cathedral, and other treasures, including a Miraculous Host, are at Hasselt (see below); the buildings seen today are of the 16–18C.

2km **Hasselt** (64,000 inhab. Tourist Information: Stadhuis, 3 Lombaardstraat) is the capital of the province of Limburg.

In the 8–9C only one of a group of villages, Hasselt received a charter as a town in 1200. In 1798 the capture here of the guerilla leader Emmanuel Rollier put an end to the Peasants' Revolt, and in 1831 the Belgians were defeated here by the Dutch, although this proved only a temporary setback in the fight for independence. The town was made a bishopric in 1967.

In the GROTE MARKT a house called from its sign Het Sweert, now a chemist shop, is a good example of 17C Mosan architecture. The *Sint Quintinus Kathedraal*, opposite and dedicated to a (?) Roman who became a missionary in Gaul and was martyred in 287, has a 13C tower standing on an 11C base but with an 18C spire. In 1292 work started on the nave, transepts and choir, chapels being added in the 14–15C, the ambulatory and its chapels during the 16C, and various Neo-Gothic features during the 19C. The cathedral is associated with a monstrance of 1297 sheltering the Miraculous Host of Herkenrode (see above; may be in the Stadsmuseum, see below) which in 1317 started to bleed when subjected to sacrilege. *Onze Lieve Vrouwekerk*, just W of the Grote Markt and rebuilt in the style of 1728 after bomb damage in 1944, also houses treasures once belonging to Herkenrode, these including the high-altar by Jean Del Cour and a miraculous 14C Virgin, 'Virga Jesse'. Also here are other sculptures by Del Cour; monuments to two abbesses of Herkenrode; the cenotaph of Anne-Catherine de Lamboy (died 1675) by Artus Quellin the Younger, and that of Barbara de Rivière (died 1714) by Laurent Delvaux. The *Begijnhof*, 250m NE of the Grote Markt by Zuivelmarkt, dates from 1707.

The *Stadsmuseum* (Daily except Monday, 14.00 to 18.00. Closed

Diest, a view of the Begijnhof

January), at 73 Thonissenlaan, the northern inner ring road, covers both Hasselt and its district, while in Witte Nonnenstraat the *Nationaal Jenevermuseum* (same times) is devoted to this popular drink.

The Provincial Estate of **Bokrijk* (April or Easter–October: daily, 10.00 to 18.00) is 7km NE of Hasselt and reached from the Genk to Hasselt road (N75). The name, of medieval origin, means Beech Estate, and until 1797 Bokrijk belonged to the abbey of Herkenrode. After over a century of private ownership, the estate was acquired in 1938 by the Province of Limburg and has since become one of Belgium's most popular places of its kind, offering a park, rose garden, extensive children's play area, arboretum (with some 3000 species and a natural history museum), deer reserve and an excellent open air museum. This museum, the *Openlucht Museum* (times as above), opened in 1958 and expanding ever since, shows authentic buildings—farms, homes, industrial premises and suchlike, all with contemporary interiors—spanning from the 15C to the close of the 19C and covering the whole of Flemish Belgium, generally arranged by districts; Kempen and Haspengouw around village squares, West and East Flanders,

Brabant and Maasland. There is also (under development) an imaginative Urban Section, offering a survey of Flemish municipal architecture and with interiors illustrating contemporary daily life. A very detailed, illustrated guide in English, with over 100 entries is available.—A 'motor-train' regularly tours the estate (duration 30 minutes) and there are several cafés and restaurants. Tourist Information for the Province of Limburg has its offices here. For a similar, though more recently started, museum devoted to Walloon Belgium, see Rte 36, Musée de la Vie Rurale en Wallonie.

At *Kortessem*, 9km SE of Hasselt on the Tongeren road, a place mentioned as early as 741, the Sint Pieterskerk dates in part from 1040.

13km **Bilzen** has a town hall of 1685. The attractive château of *Oude Biezen* (*Alden Biesen*), 3km S, was founded in 1220 as a commandery of the Order of the Teutonic Knights who remained in Belgium until 1798. Badly damaged by fire in 1971, the 16–17C château has been restored and now serves as a Flemish cultural centre.—*11km* **Maastricht** is beyond the Albert Canal which marks the border with Holland. Lying along the Maas and one of the oldest fortified towns in Holland, Maastricht is an attractive, lively and interesting place, offering picturesque streets and small squares, two magnificent churches both with notable treasures, extensive lengths of town wall, and, deep in the nearby Sint Pietersberg, some well-known caves. For detail see 'Blue Guide Holland'.

21 Brussels to Liège

Two roads are described. The first (N2, N3, N79, N20) is through the interesting towns of Louvain (Leuven), Tienen, Zoutleeuw, Sint Truiden and Tongeren. The alternative, with many changes of number, chooses quieter more southerly roads across mainly French-speaking country. The A3/E40 motorway runs between the two routes, enabling places along either to be chosen.

A. Via Louvain (Leuven), Tienen, Sint Truiden and Tongeren

Total distance 100km.—*23km* **Louvain (Leuven)**.—*18km* **Tienen**.—*14km* **Zoutleeuw**.—*8km* **Sint Truiden**.—*11km* **Borgloon**.—*9km* **Tongeren**.—*17km* **Liège (Luik)**.

In addition to the motorway there is a choice of two roads from Brussels to Louvain (Leuven). The main road (N2) leaves **Brussels** (see Rte 1) by the Chaussée de Louvain, passing to the S of the national airport, for places close to which (*Evere, Diegem, Zaventem* and *Steenokkerseel*) see Rtes 1 F. and 15B; grapes from the hothouse district to the S which centres on Duisberg are often on sale beside this road. The other choice is via **Tervuren** (Rte 1 G.). Approaching Louvain along this latter road, *Leefdaal* (S, 6km from Tervuren) has a château rebuilt after 1626 but which preserves the two pepperpot towers which marked the drawbridge of its predecessor. At *Vrone*, 1.5km NE of Leefdaal, the chapel is a Romanesque building which is probably mainly of the 12C although parts (choir and tower) may be as old as c 1000, and at *Bertem*, a short distance beyond, there is an 11C church with a fortified tower.

23km **LOUVAIN** (85,000 inhab. Tourist Information: Stadhuis) is the English and French name for the ancient Flemish town of **Leuven**, famous for its history and as a bastion of Flemish Catholicism as also for its architecture (notably the Sint Pieterskerk and the Stadhuis) and its university.

History. Local tradition traces the origin of Louvain to a camp established by Julius Caesar, but the first written mention of the place is in a 9C chronicle, by which time this district had been occupied by the Norsemen. These were defeated at the end of the 9C by Arnold of Carinthia who built a castle around which a town began to grow. (The site of this castle, with traces of its successors, is the Keizerberg on the N edge of the town.) The first Count of Louvain was Lambert who in c 1000 built the first church on the site where that of Sint Pieter now stands. Count Henry II annexed the countship of Brussels and in 1190 assumed the title of Duke of Brabant, Louvain then becoming the capital of this county and in the 13C, like other Flemish towns, flourishing through the cloth trade and achieving a population of over 50,000. The 14C, with the usual conflicts between the nobles and the citizens, was a key period in Louvain's history. In 1338 England's Edward III, allied with Jacob van Artevelde of Ghent, wintered in the castle; in 1356, when Wenceslas of Luxembourg through marriage became ruler of Brabant, he was forced to sign the 'Joyeuse Entrée' declaration, this almost at once leading to increasing bitterness between the citizens (favoured by the declaration) and the nobles; in 1360 the man of the people Pieter Courtercel briefly became master of the town; in 1379 the citizens threw seventeen nobles from the windows of the Stadhuis on to the guildsmen's pikes below, this act bringing savage vengeance from Wenceslas who favoured the nobles and to whom in 1383 the citizens finally submitted. As a result thousands of weavers emigrated to England, the prosperity of the town went into rapid decline, and, when the ducal residence was removed to Vilvoorde, Brussels took over as the chief town of Brabant. Distinction returned in the following century with the foundation in 1425 of the university that was to become a renowned seat of Flemish and theological learning, and over the following centuries the history of Louvain is largely that of this university (see below). In 1466 Quinten Metsys was born here and in c 1507 Charles V lived in the castle where he was educated by Adrian Florisz, later Pope Adrian VI.

In 1914 the Germans occupied Louvain on 19 August, but a Belgian counter-attack six days later reached Herent, 3km north-west. The Germans then panicked and an outburst of firing degenerated into arson and massacre in which the famous university library and the Sint Pieterskerk were gutted. Two days afterwards the civilian population was evacuated; on their return they found the town sacked and over 1500 houses burnt down. There was similar destruction in the suburbs. During the Second World War the university library and the church were again both damaged.

The **University** of Louvain, founded in 1425 by Pope Martin V and Duke John IV of Brabant, had already become one of the leading universities of Europe by the early 16C when it boasted over 6000 students and 52 colleges. In 1517 Erasmus founded here (with the aid of a bequest from H. van Busleyden, see p 230) his 'Collegium Trilingue' for the study of Hebrew, Greek and Latin. But his dream of a liberal Catholic education was shattered by the rise of Luther in Germany; the conservative authorities took fright, strict orthodoxy was enforced, even to the establishment by Charles V of an official inquisition, and Erasmus was driven away to Switzerland in 1521, never to return to his native land. Mercator learnt his geography here, founding and running an institute of cartography until hounded out of the country in 1544. The university was suppressed by the French in 1797, and the foundation in its place of the 'Collège Philosophique' by William I of Holland in 1817 was bitterly resented by the Belgian clergy who in 1833 started a Catholic university at Mechelen, this two years later being transferred to Louvain. Controversy raged, particularly during the present century about language; whether teaching should be in both Flemish and French. This controversy was briefly silenced in 1962 by a statement from the Primate affirming again that Louvain would remain a Catholic university and that teaching would continue in both languages. But dispute and violence persisted, and in 1970 the decision was taken to form a French-speaking university at Louvain-la-Neuve (28km S; see Rte 27).—Adrian Florisz (Pope Adrian VI), Jansenius and Justus Lipsius were all teachers here. Among the students during the 19C and 20C were Father Damien, Cardinal Mercier and Emile Verhaeren.

All the main roads into Louvain converge at the GROTE MARKT on which are the Sint Pieterskerk and the Stadhuis.

*__Sint Pieterskerk__ (Tuesday–Saturday, 10.00 to 12.00, 14.00 to 17.00. Sunday and Holidays in Easter–September, 14.00 to 17.00) is successor to two earlier Romanesque churches, one of c 1000 destroyed by lightning in 1176, the second burnt in 1373; the ancient crypt, filled in during the 15C, was revealed as a result of the bomb damage of 1944. Today's late-Gothic building was begun in c 1425 by Sulpicius van der Vorst of Diest, continued on his death in 1439 by Jan Keldermans of Mechelen who completed the S aisle and part of the nave, and in 1445 by Mathys de Layens, believed to have built the central nave and N aisle. When the church was completed in c 1497, the towers of the W façade were still those of the earlier Romanesque church. These were now pulled down and in 1507 work started on new Gothic towers to a grandiose design by Joos Metsys (brother of Quinten) which envisaged a central spire 168m in height. Sadly the foundations proved too weak and in 1612–30 the still uncompleted towers were reduced to the level of the roof. In 1914 most of the nave was burnt out, and in 1944 the choir suffered the bomb damage which, at least, exposed the ancient crypt.

The interior, lit by 90 windows with Flamboyant tracery, contains many treasures, the greater number of which are around the ambulatory which is now arranged as a museum of religious art. In the Nave the most striking feature is the elaborate *Pulpit of 1742. The work of Jacques Bergé and originally at Ninove, the theme is St. Norbert struck off his horse by lightning; note the detail with beavers, birds, a frog and a cock crowing. Also noteworthy are the rood-loft of 1490; in the S Transept Joos Metsys's stone model for his ambitious W tower; and, in the Baptistry, the crane of the font cover, ascribed to Quinten Metsys. The main features of the Choir are a tall Gothic stone *Tabernacle of 1450 by Mathys de Layens and a Renaissance screen of 1568 by Jan Veldener.

The Ambulatory (with to some extent the Choir) is now a _Museum of Religious Art_, described below anticlockwise, though it should be noted that items may well be changed around because of restoration or, more frequently, temporary exhibitions. CHAPEL 1 houses the *Funerary Monument of Duke Henry I of Brabant, Count of Louvain; dated 1235 this is the oldest monument of its kind in Belgium. CHAPEL 2, once that of the Guild of St. Sebastian, shows a 12C head of Christ. CHAPEL 3 once housed a famous Descent from the Cross by Roger van der Weyden; the picture is now in the Escorial in Spain, but a reduced copy can be seen in Chapel 12. On the altar, Ecce Homo by Gerard Seghers. CHAPEL 5. Triptych of 1593 of the Martyrdom of St. Dorothea by Joost van den Baeren. CHAPEL 6. A bas-relief Crucifixion of 1520. CHAPEL 7. Triptych by Joost van den Baeren. CHAPEL 8 is the Chapel of St. (Proud) Margaret, or Blessed Margaret of Louvain (died 1225). As a servant at an inn she witnessed the murder of her master and mistress by bandits; these carried her off and when she refused to wed one of them, she was murdered and her body thrown into the river. Much of this can be seen on the reliquary shrine, but her story, or at any rate its latter part, is told more clearly in CHAPEL 9 in a series of paintings by Pieter Verhaghen—the murder; Margaret's body in the river; Margaret taken out of the river; taken to St. Pieterskerk; Believers praying at her grave. CHAPEL 10. Disciples at Emmaus by Erasmus Quellin. Martyrdom of St. Ursula by Theodoor van Thulden. CHAPEL 11. *Triptych by Dirk Bouts, Martyrdom of St. Erasmus, a

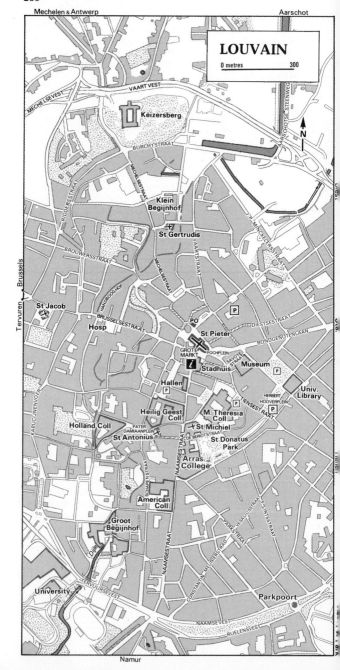

Mechelen & Antwerp   Aarschot

LOUVAIN

0 metres   300

N

Keizersberg

VAART VEST

MECHELSEVEST

BURCHTSTRAAT

AARSCHOTSE STEENWEG

Klein Begijnhof

St Gertrudis

RIDDERSTRAAT

MECHELSESTRAAT

VAARTSTRAAT

BROUWERSSTRAAT

J. P. MINCKELEERSSTRAAT

Tervuren — Brussels

St Jacob

HANEGBROOGHOF

BRUSSELSESTRAAT

Hosp

PO

P

St Pieter

DIESTSESTRAAT

BONDGENOTENLAAN

GROTE MARKT

FOCHPLEIN

SAVOYE STRAAT

Stadhuis

Museum

P

Hallen

P

HERBERT HOOVERPLEIN

Univ. Library

TIENSESTRAAT

P

Heilig Geest Coll

M. Theresia Coll

Holland Coll

PATER DAMIAANPLEIN

St Antonius

St Michiel

DE BERIOTSTRAAT

St Donatus Park

KAPUCIJNENVOER

NAAMSESTRAAT

Arras College

SCHAPENSTRAAT

American Coll.

Groot Begijnhof

PARIJSTRAAT

VLAMINGENSTRAAT

TIENTSTRAAT

Dijle

University

TERVUURSEVEST

NAAMSESTRAAT

CONSTANTIN MEUNIERSTRAAT

Parkpoort

NAAMSEVEST

RUELENSVEST

Namur

early bishop of Antioch and patron of mariners. CHAPEL 12. A reduction of 1463 of Roger van der Weyden's Descent from the Cross, now in the Escorial in Spain.

CHAPEL 14. *Triptych of the Last Supper by Dirk Bouts (c 1464); the Last Supper is shown as taking place in a Gothic hall, and it may well be that the view through the window on the left is of 15C Louvain's Grote Markt, with the Staduis still under construction. CHAPEL 15 houses the tombs of Matilda of Flanders, wife of Duke Henry I of Brabant, and of their daughter Mary, wife of Emperor Otto IV of Germany.

The Crypt, probably the mausoleum of the 12C Counts of Louvain, was architecturally the eastern extension of the early Romanesque churches. Filled in when the Gothic church was built in the 15C, it was lost until revealed by the bombing of 1944. The crypt now shows vestments, reliquaries, plate, religious sculpture and, on the pillars, some (possibly 11C) scratchings.

The ***Stadhuis**, a lavishly decorated Flamboyant Gothic achievement of 1448–63 by Mathys de Layens, ranks as one of Belgium's most noteworthy buildings. The façade, almost as high as it is long, presents three storeys of Gothic windows, the whole being continued skywards by a steep roof of dormers and six graceful turrets. Between the windows there are niches, the bases of which are carved with biblical subjects of medieval grotesqueness and freedom. The niches themselves (they total 230 large and 52 small ones) were long empty, until filled with 236 statues when the exterior of the building was restored between 1828 and 1850; these represent eminent citizens, artists, savants, royalty and nobility, religious personalities, municipal institutions, municipal privileges, virtues, vices, etc. Guided tours (Easter–September: Monday–Saturday, 11.00 and 15.00; Sunday, Holidays, 15.00; October–Easter: Monday–Friday, 11.00 and 15.00) can be made through the imposing and richly decorated interior, where sculptures and paintings can be seen by artists such as Constantin Meunier, Jef Lambeaux, P.J. Verhaghen, Gaspard de Crayer and Antoon Sallaert. In the cellars, with a separate street entrance, there is a **Brasserie Museum** (Tuesday–Saturday, 10.00 to 12.00, 14.00 to 17.00).

EAST OF THE GROTE MARKT. Immediately E of the Sint Pieterskerk is the Fochplein in which stands an amusing small fountain, the gift of the university to the town in celebration of 550 years of association (1425–1975). On the S a bank occupies a reproduction (1921) of the **Tafelronde** (Round Table), the 15C house of the guilds. Just E again in Savoyestraat, the *Museum Vanderkelen Mertens (Tuesday–Saturday, 10.00 to 12.00, 14.00 to 17.00; also Sunday and Holidays between Easter and September, 14.00 to 17.00) occupies the site of the Savoy College, founded in 1545 to house indigent students from Savoy. The portal of 1650 survives, but the building proper is mainly enlargement and restoration of the 17C and 18C. After the French Revolution this became the mansion of the Vanderkelen Mertens family who in 1918 gave it to the town for use as municipal museum. The collections, from time to time rotated and rearranged, include paintings, sculpture (wood and stone), Gothic and Renaissance furniture, metalwork, porcelain, tapestry, etc.

On the Ground Floor (generally 15C and 16C) there are mainly religious works a great many of which, both sculpture and paintings, are by unknown masters. Among named artists are *Pieter Coecke, Jan van Rillaer, Jan Rombouts* (wing of a diptych, the only known (work by this artist), *Quinten Metsys* (*Mourning over Christ, a picture with most striking lighting), *Michiel Coxie* (triptych), *Pieter Aertsen* (The Samaritan Woman), and, by an unknown artist c 1500, a circular calendrical work of fascinating detail. The Upper Floor is devoted principally to pictures of the 17C, e.g. *Michiel Mierevelt*: Several portraits. *Frans Francken the Elder*: Ulysses and Achilles. *Frans Francken the Younger*: Crucifixion (four versions). *David Vinckeboons*: Landscapes. Allegorical Fight (a strange phantasy). *Benjamin Cuyp*: Riders resting. *Wolfgang de Smet*: Interior of the Sint Pieterskerk. *Cornelis de Vos*: Two side panels of a triptych. *P.J. Verhaghen*: Several works, including an Adoration of the Magi.

Tiensestraat leads SE to Herbert Hooverplein (left), at the farther end of which rises the **University Library**, successor to that destroyed by the Germans in 1914. Today's library, in Flemish Renaissance style with a high, graceful belfry, was designed by Whitney Warren, built largely with American aid and opened in July 1928. The tower is 85m high and the carillon commemorates American engineers who lost their lives in the First World War.

The former and famous library, which was in the Hallen in Naamsestraat, was composed of 500 manuscripts, 1000 incunabula (many printed at Louvain), and over 250,000 printed books, in which theology was especially well represented; a feature of the library was its collection of Irish manuscripts and literature. The Treaty of Versailles provided that Germany should make reparation by furnishing material of equal value to that destroyed. Large contributions of books were made also by Great Britain (on the initiative of the John Rylands Library, Manchester) and by the United States. The names of institutions that contributed to the rebuilding are inscribed on the walls.

SOUTH OF THE GROTE MARKT. Naamsestraat leads S, passing the Stadhuis and (right) the *Hallen*, a Gothic building put up by the Clothworkers' Guild in 1317–45 and assigned in 1629 to the **University**, which added a Baroque upper storey to house its library. Largely destroyed in 1914, the Hallen was rebuilt and now serves as the administrative centre of the university; the rear façade of the building dates from 1723. Farther S along Naamsestraat are (right) *Heilig Geest College* (for diocesan clergy), rebuilt after air raid damage in 1944, and (left) the **Sint Michielskerk** (June–September: Thursday, 10.00 to 12.00, 14.00 to 17.00), a handsome Jesuit church built by Father Willem Hessius in 1650–66. Badly damaged in 1944, and rebuilt 1947–50, the church still has a splendid Baroque façade and contains outstanding 17–18C woodwork. Behind the church (in Sint Michielsstraat) are the 18C buildings of *Maria Theresia College*, with the university assembly hall, and of *Pope Adrian VI College*, founded by Adrian. South of the church of Sint Michiel, De Beriotstraat leads E to *Sint Donatus Park*, in which are remains of the 12–15C ramparts. At the N corner of De Beriotstraat and Naamsestraat *King's College* (18C) was founded in 1579 by Philip II. The building at the S corner is the *Premonstratensian College* (18C), founded in the 16C by the abbeys of Parc, Ninove, Grimbergen, and Averbode, next to this being *Arras College* (18C), founded in 1508 by a bishop of Arras, and the *Van 't Sestich Huis* (15C). Opposite is *Van Dale College* (16C), now a school. Beyond, on the W side of Naamsestraat at the corner of Karmelietenberg, is the *American College* (1857), occupying the mid-16C refuge of the abbey of Aulne.

Karmelietenberg descends to the *Groot Begijnhof, beside the river Dijle, founded in the 13C and becoming one of the largest in Belgium. The buildings seen today cover the 14–18C. In 1961 the area was

Louvain, the Stadhuis

acquired by the university, beautifully restored, and converted into a mainly residential university quarter. The church is of 1305; but the two side aisles of the triple nave are more recent.

Schapenstraat, leading N from the Begijnhof, reaches Pater Damiaanplein, where in the *Sint Antonius Kapel* is the grave of Father Damien (died 1889), whose body was brought here from Molokai in 1936. Opposite (W) is the former *Hollands College* (18C), now a school. Jansenius was master here from 1618 to 1636; a tower

(1616) in the gardens, used by him as a retreat, rests on remains of the 12C town walls.

WEST OF THE GROTE MARKT. Brusselsestraat, with a few old houses, runs W out of Grote Markt and crosses an arm of the river. Beyond, on the left, No. 65 opens to a court with the brick buildings of the Augustinian nunnery. The modern hospital next door preserves beside the street the 13C doorway of its former chapel, and, alongside, a Renaissance portal. Opposite the hospital, the *Handbooghof*, a garden beside the Dijle, contains remains of the 12C town walls. Farther on (700m from the Grote Markt) the *Sint Jacobskerk* dates from the 13–15C, but has an 18C choir. Outside the church stands a statue of Father Damien, by Constantin Meunier.

NORTH OF THE GROTE MARKT are the post office and the telephone building, whence Mechelsestraat continues N to cross an arm of the Dijle. Beyond the river (600m from the Grote Markt) is the 13–15C **Sint Gertrudiskerk** (June–September: Thursday, 10.00 to 12.00, 14.00 to 17.00), once the church of an abbey suppressed at the time of the French Revolution. The choir dates from 1298–1310, the naves from 1327–80, and the church was completed in 1453, although some parts were added later. The best feature is the spire (71m), by Jan van Ruysbroeck (1453), but largely rebuilt 1840–48. The interior contains 16C choir-stalls, smashed in an air raid in 1944 but skilfully restored by Jan van Uitvanck; they bear interesting *Misericords. The **Klein Begijnhof** is just N of the church. Originating as an infirmary c 1275, it flourished until suppressed in 1796; today it consists of a single street of 17C and 18C houses. At the end of Mechelsestraat, beyond a large brewery, rises the **Keizersberg**, with a modern Benedictine abbey and traces of the castle of the dukes of Brabant. The **Museum Humbeeck-Piron** (Daily except Tuesday, 10.00 to 18.00), at 108 Mechelsevest, is mainly devoted to the pictures of Pierre van Humbeeck and his wife Marie Piron. Of two other sections, one exhibits painting, porcelain and furniture collected by the couple, and the other displays material on the religious orders.

ENVIRONS OF LOUVAIN. The Premonstratensian abbey of **Park** is beyond the Parkpoort on the SE edge of the town (2km from the Grote Markt). Founded in 1129 by Godefroy I of Brabant, and suppressed in 1797, the abbey was reoccupied in 1836, since when it has flourished. Over the centuries Park grew to resemble a fort, with walls and gates; today's buildings are largely of the 17th and 18C. A road traverses the complex, passing through impressive gateways of 1722 and crossing the mellow farm courtyard. The farm with its barn is late 17C while the cloister is part 16C (E wing) and part 17C. The church, basically 13C Romanesque, was refaced in Baroque style in 1729; it contains paintings by Erasmus Quellin and Pierre Joseph Verhaghen. The library and refectory (normally open Sunday, 16.00), both Baroque, have ceilings decorated with reliefs of 1672–79 by Jan Hansche.—The château of **Arenberg**, on the S edge of the town and the W bank of the Dijle (1.5km from the Grote Markt), was built in 1511 by Guillaume de Croy but has since been much altered. Presented in 1921 to the university by the Duke of Arenberg, the park now contains several university buildings.—At **Kessel-Lo** (3km NE of the Grote Markt, just N of N2) is all that survives of the abbey of Vlierbeek, founded in 1125 and suppressed in 1796; the church (1776–83), now a parish church, was designed by Laurent Dewez.

18km **Tienen** (Fr. **Tirlemont**. 33,000 inhab. Tourist Information: 4 Grote Markt), an ancient and pleasant town at the centre of a beet district, is known for its sugar refinery (established in the 19C), the wrapped cubes from which soon become familiar to anyone travelling in Belgium; the refinery is on the E edge of the town on the right of the Liège road. Of Roman origin, Tienen was given town status in 1194. It was sacked by French and Dutch troops in 1635, and the ring round the N follows the course of the fourth and last fortifications (16–17C).

On the E side of the huge GROTE MARKT, second in size only to that of Sint Niklaas, stands the *Onze Lieve Vrouw ten Poel Kerk* (Our Lady of the Pool), built in 1345–1460, but with later additions, as successor to a 13C chapel which was a place of pilgrimage because of the cures achieved by a spring here which however dried up in the 18C. Curious for having no nave, the church owes its construction to several architects, the better known being Sulpicius van der Vorst, Jan Keldermans and Mathys de Layens. The portal (1360), with small figures decorating the pedestals of the statueless niches, leads direct to the transepts. Above the high-altar the statue of the Virgin (Walter Paris, 1365) originally stood above the W portal where there is now a

Louvain, Library of the Abbey of Park

copy. On the S side of the Grote Markt is the *Stadhuis* (1836), opposite
which a stone star marks the site of the pillory and guillotine. The
Gerechtshof (1846), on the N side of the square, occupies the site of the
medieval cloth hall; and in the NE corner there are two memorials, one
(by Jef Lambeaux) to the volunteers of 1830, the other to all who lost
their lives in 1830–31 and the two world wars. The *Museum Het
Torentje*, also on the Grote Markt and reached through the courtyard of
the Gerechtshof, contains mixed material which includes Gallo-
Roman coins, Romanesque fonts, and some sculpture of which one
example, a St. Martin, may be from the studio of Jan Borman
(Monday–Friday, 08.30 to 12.30, 13.30 to 17.00. Also, between Easter
and Christmas, Saturday, Sunday, Holidays, 14.00 to 18.00).

Peperstraat and the Wolmarkt, the latter with a group of 17C houses
replacing predecessors burnt by the Dutch in 1635, lead S up the hill
(the Celtic 'dunen' to which the town traces its name) on which stands
the *Sint Germanuskerk*. Of 9C origin, the church was several times
rebuilt; in the 12C (parts of the choir, the W façade and the main tower);
in c 1535 by P. van Wijenhoven, architect to Charles V; and in 1635 after
the sacking of the town. Inside, a 15C copper pelican lectern and some
theatrical 16–17C sculptures (e.g. SE chapel) are noteworthy. From the
Wolmarkt, Grote Bergstraat drops S to the Begijnhof, most of which
was destroyed by air raids of 1944 although the early street plan
survives with a few old cottages among the new ones.

At **Opheylissem**, 7km SE of Tienen on the Hannut road, the imposing 18C
buildings (by Laurent Dewez) of a Premonstratensian abbey are now used by the
provincial government.—At **Oplinter**, 4km NE of Tienen, the 14–16C church
houses a polychrome Christ, a relic from a Cistercian abbey some buildings of
which survive as the farm which the abbey became during the 19C.

The main road (N3) continues E out of Tienen, passing (right) the sugar
refinery, opposite which Pastoriestraat leads to the cemetery chapel of
Sint Pieter, Grimde (11C tower and nave), arranged as a necropolis for
140 Belgian soldiers who fell near here on 18 August 1914. Farther
along N3 (right, short path c 800m beyond the refinery) there are three
large *Gallo-Roman Tumuli* (c 2C).—At (*3km* from Tienen) **Hakendover** the 13–16C church, with a Romanesque tower, is known for its
oak *Retable of 1430 telling the legend behind the building of this
church. Some pious virgins, wishing to build a church near Tienen,
found their work pulled down each night. However a vision of angels
indicated this site, the virgins then building successfully, using twelve
labourers while the Saviour (hence the dedication of the church,
Salvator) helped as a thirteenth.

11km **Zoutleeuw** (Fr. **Léau**. 8000 inhab.) is a small town 4km N of the
main road. At its most prosperous during the 13–14C, the place's
subsequent commercial decline was sealed in the 18C when it was
bypassed by the Brussels to Liège road. Today Zoutleeuw is best
known for the great **Collection of religious art treasures to be found in
its *Sint Leonarduskerk* (Mid April–October: daily except Tuesday,
14.00 to 17.00. Apply 2 Markt), the only important Belgian church to
escape both the iconoclasts of the 16C and the troubles of the French
Revolution. The tower, W front and apse are of the 13C, the nave of the
14C, and during the 16C extensions were made to the chapels. The
church's treasures (retables, triptychs, church furniture, vestments,
some of these last being behind curtains in the chapels) are all clearly
described in English. Particular attention is drawn to the following—
NAVE. High up hangs a *Marianum, a Virgin in a garland of roses, of
wrought and painted iron (1533), one of the only two in Belgium, the

other being at Neeroeteren. CHOIR. The magnificent six-branched
*Candelabrum is the work of Renier van Thienen (1483); it is
surmounted by a Crucifix and statuettes of the Virgin, St. John and St.
Mary Magdalene, remarkable for drapery, attitude and expression.
The huge wooden Cross hanging in the choir arch is by Willem van
Goelen (1453). The AMBULATORY houses a series of statuettes
(12–18C), including a Sedes Sapientiae (12C) and St. Mary Magdalene
(16C). NORTH TRANSEPT. In the chapel (Holy Sacrament) the stone
**Tabernacle was made by Cornelis Floris in 1550–52 for Marten van
Wilre, lord of Oplinter; the spire, 18m high and in several tiers, bears
numerous groups of figures. The tomb of Van Wilre (died 1558) and of
his wife (died 1554) is also by Floris. To the left of the altar the triptych
(Baptism of Christ) is probably by Frans Floris, brother of Cornelis.
SOUTH TRANSEPT. The chapel, with murals of 1490 the Last
Judgement, is dedicated to St. Leonard and contains an altarpiece by
Arnold de Maeler (1478) depicting the life of the saint. A statue here of
St. Leonard, painted and studded with stones, dates back to c 1300.

Among other old buildings the *Stadhuis* (1539), built to plans by
Rombout Keldermans, and the *Hallen* (1316–20) next door recall the
town's early prosperity.

Neerwinden, 4km S of N3 opposite Zoutleeuw, has been the site of two battles: in
1693 the Grand Alliance under William III of England was defeated here by
Marshal Luxembourg, and in 1793 the Austrians defeated the French under
Dumouriez.—Landen (14,000 inhab.), 3km SE of Neerwinden, was the home of
Pepin, founder of the Carolingian dynasty; he died here, and before being
removed to Nivelles his body lay beneath a hill which still bears his name.

8km **Sint Truiden** (Fr. **Saint Trond**. 36,000 inhab. Tourist Information:
Stadhuis), an ancient place just in the province of Limburg, is named
after St. Trudo who founded an abbey here in c 655 and performed
many miracles. The town is the chief centre of the district of
Haspengouw (Fr. Hesbaye) whence originated the Pepin family and
the Carolingian dynasty. The large GROTE MARKT offers a good view
(best from the S side) of Sint Truiden's three towers, these being from
W to E the former Abbey, the Stadhuis belfry, and the Onze Lieve
Vrouwekerk. The *Stadhuis* is of the 18C but has attached to it the
Spanish-style *Belfry*, dating from 1606 when its predecessor was
blown down but standing on the earlier 12–13C base (not visible). The
Perron, at the foot of the belfry, is in origin of 1361, and it is interesting
that Sint Truiden, because it once belonged to the prince-bishopric of
Liège, has both the Flemish (belfry) and the Walloon (perron) symbols
of liberty. The *Onze Lieve Vrouwekerk*, a foundation of 1058 the first
church of which was destroyed by fire in 1186, is a Gothic 14–16C
building, the tower of which, rebuilt many times, finally collapsed in
1668 and was last reerected in 1854 by Louis Roelandt. The church
houses a reliquary of St. Trudo. The story of the *Abbey*, now serving as
a seminary, is told in a delightful carving above its entrance; every
time Trudo built something it was pulled down by an interfering
woman, so he prayed for help and the woman was struck paralysed.
This early abbey became a powerful Benedictine house, but its
buildings were much damaged at the time of the French Revolution.
Features noteworthy today are the 11C tower (new spire in the 18C)
with at its base a gateway of 1655, and the main gatehouse of 1779
giving access to the courtyard.

There are also places of interest off the S side of the Grote Markt, on
Naamsestraat (No. 5) being the *Museum Hedendaagse Kantwerken*,
showing modern lacework of the Ursuline Sisters (Easter–September:

Sunday and Holidays, 10.00 to 12.00, 14.00 to 18.00), while to the SE the Neo-Classical *Minderbroederskerk*, built in 1731, is interesting for the fifty pillars which alone support the roof. The *Sint Franciscus-museum*, at 5 Minderbroedersstraat, contains collections of medieval statuary and pictures, including an etching by Rembrandt and works attributed to Rubens and Cranach (April–October: Tuesday, Wednesday, 14.00 to 18.00. Appointment advised). To the SE, by the junction of the roads to Tongeren and Liège, is the *Brustempoort*, the undercroft of a gateway of the 15C ramparts (Easter–September: Sunday and Holidays, 13.30 to 17.30). Farther S, on Naamsesteenweg, the *Sint Pieterskerk*, a notable Romanesque building of the late 12C, contains the tomb of Wirik, an abbot of c 1180.

The *Begijnhof* is on the NE edge of the town, beyond the large cattle market on the road to Hasselt. Founded in 1258, it remains a peaceful enclosure surrounded today by 17–18C small houses with, in the centre, a 13C church known for its 13–17C murals (April–October: Tuesday–Friday, 10.00 to 12.00, 13.30 to 17.00; Saturday, Sunday, 13.30 to 17.00). Nearby, the *Festraets Studio* exhibits, amongst other things, a remarkable astronomical clock, the achievement of Kamile Festraets (1904–74). (Easter–June and September–October: Sunday and Holidays, 09.45 to 11.45, 13.45 to 16.45. July and August: daily at 10.45 and at 15.45.)

At **Kortenbos**, 5km NE of Sint Truiden, the Baroque *Onze Lieve Vrouwebasiliek* is said to owe its origin to a wealthy widow who owned land here which was constantly menaced by a band of brigands; in 1636, as a deterrent, she placed a figure of the Virgin in a hollow oak, an act of faith which seems to have been successful since by 1641 plans had been agreed for a church to take the place of the chapel which now sheltered the Virgin. The basilica (1641–c 1665, with later additions) contains Baroque furnishings and paintings by Gaspard de Crayer and A. van Diepenbeek.

TO LIEGE DIRECT.—*2km Brustem*, today with a large military airfield, was in 1467 the scene of a victory by Charles the Bold when suppressing Liège.—*10km* the border into the province of Liège is crossed. *Waremme*, 5km SW, is signposted Borgworm in Flemish. *Oreye* is the first French-speaking town and, 4km farther, the road from Tongeren to the Meuse (Maas), once an important Roman road, is crossed. *Othée*, 3km NE, was where in 1408 John the Fearless crushed the men of Liège.—*13km*. By the N side of the road, just before the motorway crossing, are the ruins of **Fort Loncin**, with a large memorial. Here in August 1914 a Belgian force under General Leman held out to the last against the Germans; the general was later found unconscious beneath the ruins, and his sword was returned to him by the German commander. Across the road a memorial commemorates the members of a Royal Air Force crew who died here in July 1943.—*6km* **Liège**, see Rte 34.

TO LIEGE VIA TONGEREN is only 6km longer than the direct road.—At (*3km*) **Zepperen** the interior of the *Sint Genovevakerk* (15C but with a Romanesque tower) is decorated with fascinating naive 15C *Murals depicting a Last Supper and the lives of St. Christopher and St. Genevieve. (Genevieve, c 422–c 500, patron of Paris, is said to have diverted Attila away from the city through fasting and prayer, and to have successfully led a foray in search of food when Paris was besieged by the Franks.) Adjacent to the church a mansion of 1655 belonged to the provost of Sint Servaas at Maastricht (Holland) to whom Zepperen was formerly subject.—At (*2km*) *Rijkel* there is a large château of c 1600, but with later additions.—*6km* **Borgloon**, now a fruit-growing centre, was in the 11C the chief town of the county of Looz (still the French name for the place), later absorbed by Limburg. In the entrance to the *Stadhuis* of 1680 the old stocks are preserved. The *Sint Odulfuskerk*, containing some 15C murals and dedicated to a native of Brabant (died c 855) who evangelised in Frisia, dates in part from the 11C but was largely rebuilt in 1139; the tower is of 1406 and Neo-Romanesque additions were made to the nave in 1900. *Klooster Marienlof*, the Cistercian convent of *Kolen* (*Kerniel*, 2km N), owns a reliquary of St. Odile, traditionally of St. Ursula's 11,000 virgins; dated 1292 it is among the oldest examples in Belgium of painting on wood, but it was seriously damaged during the 19C by a carpenter who tried to force it into a niche. Also to be seen here are a 12C Romanesque choir stall, the oldest of its kind in Belgium, paintings by M. Aubé, and 18C furnishings (Monday–Friday, 10.00 to 11.30, 15.00 to 18.00).

9km **Tongeren** (Fr. **Tongres**. 29,500 inhab. Tourist Information: Stadhuis), tracing its story back to Roman times, is the oldest town in Belgium and preserves important remains of its past, particularly Roman.

History. Tongeren originated as a Roman camp, known as Aduatuca Tongrorum, on the road from Bavai to Cologne. It lay in the territory of the Eburones and the Tungri, and it was Ambiorix, a chief of the former tribe, who defeated the Romans here in 54 BC. By the 1C a settlement had developed, protected by walls 4.5km in length (parts of which survive) and thus larger in area than today's town. This settlement was destroyed by the Franks in c 300, the Romans then building a less extensive wall, 2700m in length, of which only the foundations of a tower remain. Early becoming Christian, Tongeren was the first bishopric in Belgium, the see being established by St. Maternus of Cologne; however the first bishop, St. Servatius, transferred his see in 382 to Maastricht, and in 720 St. Hubert moved it again to Liège. The town was ravaged by the Norsemen in the 9C, but during the Middle Ages became a prosperous dependency of the prince-bishopric of Liège, in the 13–14C receiving its third surround of walls. In 1677 Tongeren was largely burnt by the soldiers of Louis XIV.

A statue of Ambiorix stands in the GROTE MARKT, on the SE side of which is the *Stadhuis* (1737–54) with Tourist Information and the *Stedelijk Museum* (10.00 to 12.00, 14.00 to 16.00) with exhibits covering the town's history, religious material (note a wooden Pietà of the 14C), and some paintings. Just to the E the foundations and lower courses of a *Roman Rampart Tower* (4C; all that is left of the second, shorter Roman wall) have been excavated (for entry, apply Gallo-Roman Museum).

The *Onze Lieve Vrouwebasiliek* claims to be the first church N of the Alps to be dedicated to Our Lady (c 350). Although a little from the 11th and 12C survives, the present Gothic building dates from 1240 (nave and S transept), the remainder being 14–16C, although the N portal of 1532 retains traces of the 13C building. In the Choir there are four stained-glass windows of 1550; an elaborately carved retable (16C) showing scenes from the life of Our Lady; and, all by Jehans Josès of Dinant, a paschal candlestick (1372), a lectern (1375) and four candelabra (1392; in transepts in front of the choir). In the N Transept, a walnut statue of Our Lady of Tongeren is dated 1479. Along the N Aisle the first chapel houses a Man of Sorrows (15C), the last a Pietà of 1400, and the NW porch a curious old tree-stump alms box and a Madonna and Child of 1280. The organ dates from 1753, below the loft being a brass door of 1711 by Christian Schwertfeger. Along the S Aisle, the first (westernmost) chapel contains a 16C altar, and the fifth is dedicated to St. Lutgart, a pious lady born in Tongeren in 1182 who became known for her visions. At the E end of the S aisle a vestibule, with an 11C *Crucifix, admits to the Treasury and the *Cloister. This latter is in two parts, one walk (with small columns, each with a different capital) being 12C and the remainder 13–14C; the lintel of the garden doorway is late 11C and the two Gothic chapels are both 15C. The *Treasury (May–September: daily, 09.00 to 12.00, 14.00 to 17.00) is one of the richest in Belgium.

The *Gallo-Roman Museum* (daily, except Monday, and Sunday morning, 09.00 to 12.00, 14.00 to 17.00), to the E of the basilica, houses imaginatively arranged collections, largely of local material, and several excellent models. The first room is devoted to prehistory, of particular interest being reconstructions of a Neolithic stone-throwing device and of an Iron Age loom. The second room, concerned with the late Iron Age and the early Roman period, exhibits coins and a map of northern Gaul at the time of Augustus (63 BC to AD 14). In the third room are a distance marker stone, a copy of the Tabula Peutingeriana (a medieval copy of a Roman world road map of the second half of the 4C), glass, and a frame of coins well set out both by emperors and by metals. A corner is rounded to reach the fourth and fifth rooms in which are ceramic and ironwork. A spiral staircase descends to two further rooms, the upper devoted largely to Roman tumuli (with a good model) while the lower shows coins.

In the SE of the town (500m from the Grote Markt) the *Moerenpoort* (1379), with a small museum of local military history (May–September: Saturday, Sunday, Holidays, 10.00 to 16.00), is one of the medieval gates. On either side lengths of the 13C ramparts survive, the section to the N along Leopoldwal being on a 2C Roman base; there is another length along the N edge of the town. The *Begijnhof*, just W of the Moerenpoort, preserves some small 17–18C houses and a church of 1294, altered during the 16C.

On the NW outskirts of the town, beyond the ring road, the Hasseltse Steenweg is crossed by a good length of 1–2C Roman wall, especially to the S along Legionenlaan; there is another section farther SW on the approach to the *Beukenberg*, a Roman raised walk of the 2C. Near here the 17C château of *Betho* has a 13C keep.

17km **Liège**, see Rte 34.

B. Via Louvain, Jodoigne and Hannut

Total distance 105km.—*23km* **Louvain (Leuven)**.—*26km* **Jodoigne**.—*8km* **Jauche**.—*10km* **Hannut**.—*38km* **Liège**.

For **Brussels** (Rte 1) to (*23km*) **Louvain (Leuven)**, see above.—Louvain is left by the Namur road (N25) which crosses the motorway before traversing the forest of Meerdaal.—*12km Hamme-Mille* is in French-speaking Brabant. The road skirts the S side of the airfield of *Beauvechain* after which N91 continues S for Namur while this Rte bears E along N240. *Gobertange*, just N of the road, gives its name to the white stone used in many local buildings as also in the town halls of Brussels and Louvain, the cathedral in Brussels etc.—*14km* **Jodoigne** (Flem. **Geldenaken**) was already a market centre in Roman times when the place was known as Geldonia. In the Middle Ages it became a fortress covering the road to Louvain and as such was frequently attacked, the funnel-shaped Grand-Place being so designed for defensive purposes. Here the *Hôtel de Ville*, standing on the site of the 13C cornmarket, dates from 1733 and the *Chapelle Notre-Dame du*

Marché from the 14C. The mixed Romanesque and Gothic *Eglise Saint Ménard*, dedicated to a Frankish nobleman of c 470–c 560 who became Bishop of Tournai and was invoked for determining the weather and for the relief of toothache, is the oldest building in Jodoigne, having been built in the 12C on the site of a 7C chapel; burnt in 1568 and 1578 by the soldiers of William of Orange, it was restored in 1606; it became a Temple of Reason at the time of the French Revolution but served again as a church from 1802. The interior houses a chalice, part of which is ascribed to Hugo d'Oignies, a painting (Virgin and Child) by Cornelis Schut, and a triptych ascribed to Otto Venius.

Just S of *Glimes*, 6km S of Jodoigne, stands one of the largest tumuli in Belgium, 12m high and 50m in diameter.

8km **Jauche**, 4km NE of which is the Romanesque church of **Orp-le-Grand**, dating mainly from the end of the 12C but much destroyed by fires in 1356, 1485, 1637, and, as the result of German attack, in 1940; this last destruction revealed the foundations of two earlier churches, the first of the 8C or 9C, and also a large crypt. At Orp-le-Grand there is also a small museum in the Maison Communale showing mainly jewellery and weapons of Neolithic to Merovingian times (Mid March–mid October: Sunday, Holidays, 10.00 to 12.00, 14.00 to 17.00). At *Foix-les-Caves*, 3km S of Jauche, there are underground quarries, perhaps of Roman or even earlier origin; some may be visited and some are used for growing mushrooms. The village of **Ramillies**, 3km farther S, is where on Whitsunday 1706 the Allies under Marlborough defeated the French under Villeroi.

The armies were evenly matched. The French, facing NE, occupied a line through Autréglise-Offus-Ramillies-Francqnée-Taviers, their flanks being protected by small, marshy streams. Marlborough made a feint against the French left, then concentrated against Ramillies while his Dutch troops attacked Francqnée and Taviers. Both attacks were successful, though Marlborough himself was for a while unhorsed, and the French retired in disorder on Louvain. The Allied casualties, mainly Dutch, were some 5000 while the French lost 15,000.

At (*10km*) **Hannut** (11,000 inhab.), in the province of Liège, the church has a striking, large 14C statue of St. Christopher.—*14km* **Waremme** (Flem. **Borgworm**), 3km N of N637, is centre for a sugar-beet district. The road crosses the Roman road from Tongeren to the Meuse (now N614), skirts the N side of Liège's airfield of *Bierset* (air tours of Liège and Walloon Brabant), then crosses the E42 motorway.—*24km* **Liège**, see Rte 34.

SOUTH BELGIUM

(Provinces of Hainaut, southern Brabant, Namur, Liège and Luxembourg)

South Belgium, apart from the small German-speaking district of the Cantons de l'Est, is 'French' or Walloon Belgium. The language is French, and the people's origins go back to the Wala, the name given to the Romanised early Celtic inhabitants. While not without interesting towns and some fine buildings, mainly churches and especially in Hainaut and Brabant, these are neither as numerous nor as splendid as in the North, and on the whole South Belgium is visited for the scenery of the Ardennes. Throughout much of southern Belgium will be found historic and often impressive castles, and also great abbeys, both ruined and flourishing.

South Belgium divides roughly into two: in the NW the provinces of

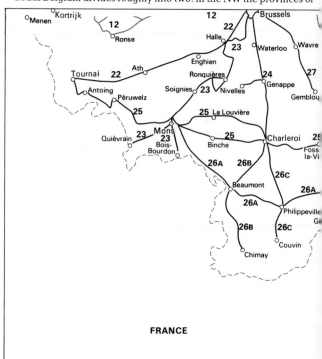

Hainaut and southern Brabant, and in the S and E the Ardennes, spreading across the other three provinces.

Hainaut and southern Brabant

Scenically the provinces of Hainaut and southern Brabant are rolling agricultural country. There are mining and industrial districts around Mons and Charleroi, and the BOTTE DU HAINAUT (chief town, *Chimay*) drops away S as a little populated, wooded extension.

The chief towns of **Hainaut** are *Tournai*, a Roman town and Frankish capital, visited for its magnificent Romanesque and early Gothic cathedral, generally held to be the finest in Belgium, and for its fine art gallery; *Mons*, with its memories of the First World War, and also with an outstanding church; *Soignies*, known for its ancient Romanesque church; and *Charleroi*, centre of mining and industry and offering an unusual and beautiful museum of glass as well as an outstanding municipal art gallery. Hainaut is crossed by an important canal system, linking Charleroi to Brussels; the great Sloping Lock at *Ronquières* attracts many visitors.

The province of **Brabant** comprises Flemish northern Brabant, the city of Brussels; and southern Brabant, this last, with *Nivelles* as its

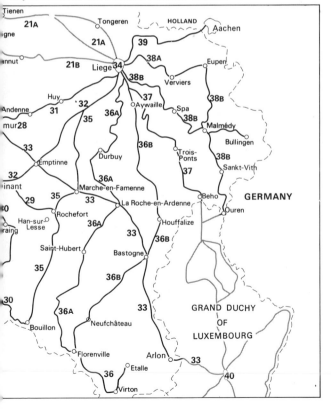

principal town, known as the 'Roman Pays'. For many tourists the main
objective in southern Brabant is the battlefield of *Waterloo*, together
with places such as *Quatre-Bras* and *Ligny* (just in Namur), famous
scenes of the preliminary fighting. (Waterloo is described at the end of
Rte 1; the preliminary battles under Rte 24.)

The Ardennes

The **Ardennes** (the Roman Arduenna Silva, and still often called the
Forest of the Ardennes) cover much of the provinces of Namur, Liège,
and Luxembourg, stretching S from the Meuse between Namur and
Liège and E of the latter city, and spilling over into Germany, the
Grand-Duchy of Luxembourg, and France. Apart from the German-
speaking Cantons de l'Est, the region is inhabited by the true
Walloons, whose name is now loosely used for the whole of French-
speaking Belgium. The landscape is one of forest, heath, and wooded
and agricultural upland, cut by a number of steep, winding, and mostly
narrow valleys. The extensive forests apart, it is these valleys that
provide the main scenic attraction, and the visitor who simply drives
across the upland may well be disappointed. Walking is a popular
activity, and most towns provide special guides and maps describing
signed tracks to local points of interest.

   Five touring areas are suggested below, largely though not entirely
on scenic grounds. The MEUSE VALLEY is best between *Namur* and the
popular resort of *Dinant*, thence continuing to the French frontier; in
summer it is possible to travel this whole stretch by boat, and a boat
excursion can also be made down the Lesse (S of Dinant). Between
Namur and Liège the valley, part industrialised, is not outstanding;
however *Liège*, a historic and lively city with good museums and art
galleries, merits a visit, as do also the smaller towns of *Namur* and
Huy.—The German-speaking CANTONS DE L'EST (*Eupen, Malmédy,
St. Vith*) are in large part a region of high forest, moor, and lakes, these
last usually reservoirs above large dams. In the highest part, the
Hautes Fagnes, the *Signal de Botrange* is the highest place in Belgium
(694m).—The winding OURTHE VALLEY can be ascended from Liège to
La Roche, a beautifully situated small town in the heart of the
Ardennes. From here Rte 36A crosses forest, followed by a lovely
descent from *Bertrix* to the Semois.—The deep, wooded SEMOIS VAL-
LEY winds along the French frontier, particularly beautiful stretches
being either side of the historic fortress of *Bouillon*, and, further E, near
Florenville (boat excursion).—Another popular Ardennes centre is
HAN-SUR-LESSE, surrounded by forests and famous for its grottoes.

Grottoes. The Ardennes are known for grottoes, many of which have revealed
evidence of occupation by prehistoric man. Several can be visited. The largest
and most popular is at *Han-sur-Lesse*, a visit to which includes a boat ride.
Remouchamps is also popular, with a 1km-long boat trip. Among others are
Goyet (with prehistoric scenes), *Rochefort*, and two at *Dinant*.
   The legendary **Quatre Fils Aymon**, associated with several Ardennes castles,
were Renaud, Guichard, Alard, and Richard, sons of Aymon of Dordogne, a vassal
of Charlemagne. The emperor knighted the brothers and presented them with
the fabulous horse Bayard, on whose back all rode at once. Later the brothers
were outlawed, and the romantic adventures and perilous feats that were
achieved in the subsequent pursuit by Charlemagne are chronicled in a 13C
poem, one of the most popular romances of the Charlemagne cycle. William
Caxton printed 'The Foure Sonnes of Aymon'; and Renaud (as Rinaldo) and the
others figure also in the poems of Tasso, Boiardo, and Ariosto.
   The **Wild Boar of the Ardennes** was the name given to a historic figure, William
de la Marck (1446–85). A nobleman, he was banished from Liège for murdering

the bishop's secretary, thereafter leading the life of a robber chieftain, with strongholds at *Amblève, Franchimont, Aigremont, Logne*, etc. In 1482 he took Liège and slew the bishop. However, the latter's successor invited him to a feast, seized him, and had him executed.

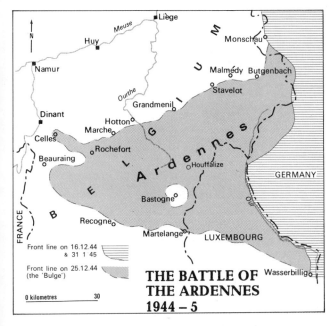

THE BATTLE OF THE ARDENNES 1944 – 5

The **Battle of the Ardennes** (1944–45), popularly known as the Battle of the Bulge, was Hitler's last fling, the German counter-offensive of December 1944, commanded by Von Rundstedt, against the weak Allied centre which had resulted from the decision to strike at Germany from Aachen in the N and Alsace in the south. On this centre, which ran along the German border from Monschau to Wasserbillig, the American 8th Corps was holding a front of 120km, and it was here that Hitler planned to break through, split the Allied front, and seize Antwerp. The Germans attacked on 16 December, and by 25 December the confused front line ran roughly as shown on the above map. Thus the 'bulge' had been formed, isolated within it being the important crossroads of *Bastogne* to which the 101st Airborne Division had been sent. However both American and British reinforcements were now reaching the Ardennes; on 23 December there was a major Allied air offensive against the German lines of supply and during the last week of the month, in snow and bitter weather, Patton's counter-attack launched from Arlon was approaching Bastogne. On 3 January Montgomery started his offensive from the N, the two counter-attacks meeting at *Houffalize* on 16 January. By the end of January the Germans were back behind their frontier, having lost 120,000 men.

22 Tournai to Brussels

Total distance 75km.—**Tournai**.—*16km Leuze* (for **Beloeil**).—*12km* **Ath** (for **Chièvres** and **Cambron-Casteau**).—*7km Ghislenghien* (for **Lessines**).—*12km* **Enghien**.—*14km* **Halle**.—*14km* **Brussels**.

TOURNAI (Flem. **Doornik**. 67,000 inhab. Tourist Information: 14 Vieux Marché aux Potteries, by the Belfry) is an ancient town on the

Escaut (Scheldt), with a colourful history a feature of which is a long and close association with France, a magnificent cathedral generally accepted as the finest in Belgium, and an outstanding art gallery. The town, the main part of which lies on the W. bank of the river, is encircled by ring boulevards of c 1860 following the course of the second ramparts (13C), sections of which can still be seen. At various periods Tournai has been known for its sculpture, tapestry and porcelain.

History. The Roman Tornacrum was a post on the road from Boulogne to Cologne. Christianised by the Italian evangelist St. Piat, who was martyred here in c 286, Tournai had by the end of the 4C become a Frankish royal city and capital. Clovis is thought to have been born here in 465 and Childeric almost certainly died here in 481. In c 486 Eleutherius, a locally born man and successful priest, was made bishop, building the first church here in c 501, outside which he was beaten to death by heretics in 532. After belonging in turn to the counts of Flanders and Hainaut, Tournai came into the hands of the French kings in 1187, an allegiance to which it remained faithful throughout the Hundred Years War and until the 16C. In 1340 the town withstood a siege by England's Edward III, this finally being raised as the result of a treaty between Edward III and Philip VI of France signed at Esplechin (6km SW). England's Henry VIII, during his war against France, seized Tournai in 1513 and gave the bishopric to Wolsey, who, however, preferring to gain French favour, sold the town back to the French in 1518. Only three years later (1521), after a siege of a month, the town was taken by the army of Charles V and thus became a part of the Spanish Netherlands. In 1581, in an effort to throw off the Spanish yoke, Tournai was bravely but unsuccessfully defended against Parma by Christine de Lalaing, Princess of Epinoy. Taken in 1667 by Louis XIV and fortified by Vauban, but retaken by the Allies in 1709, Tournai was handed over by the Treaty of Utrecht of 1713 to Austria under whom it remained (except for three years following the Battle of Fontenoy, 1745) until the French conquests of 1792–94.

During the First World War Tournai suffered some damage, notably in November 1918 when the retreating Germans blew up the bridges. In the Second World War, in May 1940 when crowded with refugees, the town was subjected to vicious air bombardment by the Germans and most of the old houses in the Grand-Place were destroyed. In September 1944 Tournai was the first Belgian town to be liberated, by British troops.

The painters Robert Campin (Master of Flémalle) and Roger van der Weyden were natives of Tournai, as were also, in more recent times, Piat Sauvage and Louis Gallait. Perkin Warbeck (1474–99), the pretender to the English throne, was the son of a Tournai official. Gabrielle Petit, the First World War heroine, was born here in 1893.

The slate-coloured **Tournai marble** has been well known since Roman times for both building and carving, and the sculptors of Tournai in the 14th and 15C were celebrated far and wide. Fonts of Tournai marble are frequently found in England, and the cathedral of Pamplona in Spain possesses a fine monument by a Tournai artist. In Tournai itself the work of its sculptors was in large part mutilated in the religious troubles of the 16C and later by the French revolutionaries, but examples can be seen in the cathedral.

The ****Cathédrale Notre-Dame** (Daily, 10.00 to 12.00, 14.00 to 18.00 or 16.30 from November–Easter) is the outstanding example in Belgium of the development of Romanesque and early Gothic architecture. The best general view is from a small square below the N transept (Place Paul Emile Janson, named in honour of a Tournai deputy who died in the concentration camp at Buchenwald in 1944). Here, beside the cathedral, there is a sculpture group, 'The Blind' by G. Charlier (1908).

The church built here in c 501 by St. Eleutherius was during the 9C replaced by a Carolingian basilica, soon however wrecked by the Norsemen (881). The present building was consecrated in 1175. The oldest part, the great Romanes que nave, was probably finished by 1150 while the apsed and aisled transepts, the most original feature of the cathedral, date mainly from 1150–71, though they were apparently not completed until 1200 when the vault was built

Tournai, the Cathédrale Notre-Dame

by Bishop Etienne. In 1245–55 Bishop Walter de Marvis, a great builder, reconstructed the choir in northern French style. Much internal damage was done by iconoclasts in 1566 and 1797, and the upper part of the Gothic W front was made 'Romanesque' in the 19C.

The cathedral's most distinctive exterior feature is its five towers, the oldest (80m high) being the central one. Of the others the two on the E are Romanesque (12C); the NW tower, which once contained the chapter prison, is Transitional (12–13C); and the SW tower is 13C Gothic. The pyramidal spires were added during the 16C. The two external aspects of more detailed interest are the N door (the Porte Mantile, named after one Mantilus who was cured of blindness by St. Eleutherius) and the W façade. The *Carvings on the former, with their moral message, are, though badly worn, among the most important in Belgium of their period (12C); here Virtue fights Vice, while Avarice, complete with purse, is carried off by the Devil. The W façade, rebuilt in the 13C, is preceded by a 14C portico, and the upper part, including a fake Romanesque window, was altered during the 19C. The carvings nevertheless are of interest. The lowest row (Adam and Eve, prophets, etc.) dates from the 14C; above are 16C reliefs of the history of the see; and at the top 17C figures of Apostles and saints flank a statue of Notre-Dame des Malades (14C; restored in 1609).

Here by the W façade the corner of the cathedral is connected with the *Evêché* (Bishop's Palace) by an archway with vaulting of 1189, some of the earliest Gothic work in Belgium, supporting a chapel. The palace itself, burnt in 1940 but preserving Romanesque cellars and a slender turret of 1643, occupies the site of the Merovingian palace.

An interesting feature of the cathedral's interior is that the length of the NAVE (58m) is the same as that of the choir. The height of the nave, vaulted with brick of 1774, is 22m and the triforium is almost equal in height to the main arcade; above are a smaller gallery and a plain clerestory. The carved capitals deserve close study, and in the Chapelle Saint Louis (1299; built in honour of a visit in 1257 by Louis IX of France), off the S aisle, there are restored stained-glass windows with 14th and 15C fragments and also a Crucifixion by Jordaens. Off the S triforium (sometimes used for special exhibitions) there is a chapel with 13C murals (Life of St. Catherine. Crucifixion).

As noted above, the TRANSEPTS are most unusual in being both apsed and aisled. In the S Transept the stained-glass of the main window tells a two-part story, the lower panels recording something of the shadowy local history of about 570 to 615, the unsettied period which followed the death of Clotaire, successor of Clovis. The Frankish realm was then divided between Clotaire's sons, Sigebert receiving Austrasia in the E (capital Rheims and then Metz) and Chilpéric receiving Neustria, with its capital at Soissons to which Tournai was subordinate. The brothers then married the two daughters of the king of the Visigoths, respectively Brunehaut and Galswinthe, the latter, however, promptly being murdered by Chilpéric's mistress, Frédégonde. Determined to avenge her sister, Brunehaut urged her husband Sigebert into war (1st panel), which he won (2nd panel) while Chilpéric fled to Tournai (3rd panel). But Frédégonde would have none of this, arming soldiers with a poisoned dagger (4th panel) with which they murdered Sigebert (5th panel). Now the master, Chilpéric conferred temporal powers, symbolised by a key, on the bishopric of Tournai (6th panel), one result being that the magistracy had annually to swear loyalty (7th panel). The upper part of the window continues the story by illustrating how the bishops made use of their temporal powers, one panel ironically making clear that a tax was levied on every head of cattle crossing the river while other panels show other taxes.—The N Transept is equally interesting for late 12C or early 13C *Murals, in part in glorious blue, generally accepted as the most important Romanesque murals in Belgium. The story told is that of St. Margaret (a shepherdess of Antioch) who, on confessing her Christianity to the local governor, was whipped. Refusing to sacrifice to the gods, she was then tortured and beheaded, an angel then carrying off her head. Note the fourth picture, bearing a red Lancastrian rose placed here by England's Henry VIII in about 1513. A Calvary has now taken the place of the throne which Henry placed in this transept for his use during services.

In front of the CHOIR the great rood-screen of 1572 is a Renaissance work by Cornelis Floris, while in the choir itself the daringly slender piers have had to be doubled in thickness except in the apse.

The AMBULATORY chapels contain (N side) 15C Tournai memorial sculptures (some from other churches), many mutilated at the time of the French Revolution. Behind the high-altar (1727), taken from the old abbey church of St. Martin (see below), there is a composite monument to the bishops of Tournai, with the effigy of Bishop Villain de Gand (died 1644) and sculptures from various other 17C tombs.

Note in this part of the ambulatory the painted walls, pillars and roof. In the S ambulatory are a Raising of Lazarus by Pieter Pourbus and Our lady of the Seven Sorrows by Wenceslas Coeberger, while in a chapel of c 1300 hangs Souls in Purgatory by Rubens; the stained-glasss here of 1526 was originally in the great W window. Especially notable in the *TREASURY are an ivory Diptych of St. Nicasius (8C); a 13C ivory Madonna; a Byzantine cross-reliquary (6th or 7C), lavishly decorated with gems and pearls; a reliquary of St. Eleutherius (1247); an Arras tapestry of 1402 depicting the stories of St. Eleutherius and St. Piat; 16C Brussels and Tournai tapestries.

The visit to the rest of Tournai can conveniently start at the GRAND-PLACE in which there is a statue (1863) of the heroic Christine de Lalaing. The **Halle aux Draps**, on the S side, originally a Renaissance building of 1611 by Quentin Rate, has been rebuilt after its destruction in 1940. At the SE end of the square rises the **Belfry** (Daily except Tuesday, 10.00 to 12.00, 14.00 to 17.30), the oldest in Belgium, a detached tower 72m high dating from 1200 (lower level) to 1294. The carillon has 43 bells (16–19C). The **Eglise Saint Quentin**, on the W side of the Grand-Place, dating from c 1200 but with a choir extended in 1464, traces predecessors on this same site back to the 7C. The interior, unusual in having a transept composed of two round chapels, contains the tomb of Jacques Kastangnes (1327), an early provost of the town. Just S of the church, No. 10 Rue des Maux (1633) was the tithe barn of the abbey which is now the Hôtel de Ville (see below).

The Reduit des Sions leads along the side of the Halle aux Draps to the Maison Tournaisienne (façade of 1677), now housing the **Musée de Folklore**, a collection illustrating old Tournai trades and interiors and including some good 18th and 19C local porcelain (April–October: daily except Tuesday, 10.00 to 12.00, 14.00 to 17.30. November–March: Saturday, Sunday, Holidays, 10.00 to 12.00, 14.00 to 17.30).

Close to the Grand-Place stand four towers of the first (11–12C) walls. These are in a cul-de-sac off the Rue du Cygne (N); in the Rue Perdue (NW); in the Rue Saint Georges (SW); and off the Place Reine Astrid (SE). Those in the Rue Perdue and the Rue Saint Georges are the nearest (c 150m).

NORTH AND WEST OF THE GRAND-PLACE. Leaving the Grand-Place at its N corner, the Rue de l'Yser, Rue Tête d'Argent and Rue du Cygne (the last with, right, one of the 11–12C towers referred to above) lead down to the river, which, 400m downstream, is crossed by the **Pont des Trous**, a 13C bridge of three arches guarded by towers, part of the 13C ramparts (river trips from jetty near here). From the Pont des Trous, Rue des Foulons, running S, soon reaches the *Eglise Sainte Marie Madeleine*, built by Bishop Marvis in 1252, and, 300m SE, the *Eglise Saint Jacques* with a 12C tower, a 13C nave and a 14C choir. Just SW of the church, in the Rue des Carmes (left), the **Musée d'Histoire et d'Archéologie** occupies the former Mont de Piété (Pawnshop) of 1622 (founded by Wenceslas Coeberger), with a tall slender turret. The museum includes a prehistory section, rooms devoted to the development of Tournai sculpture (12–16C), Roman material, manuscripts and books, and examples of Tournai tapestry and porcelain (April–October: daily except Tuesday, 10.00 to 12.00, 14.00 to 17.30. November–March: Saturday, Sunday, Holidays, 10.00 to 12.00, 14.00 to 17.30). To the SW again are (200m) the *Eglise Sainte Marguerite* of 1363 and (another 600m by Avenue de Gaulle) the small *Chapelle de la Ladrerie du Val d'Orcq* of 1163.

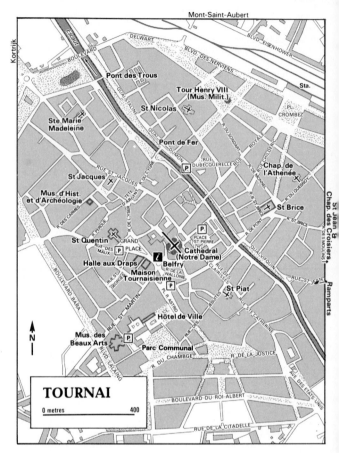

SOUTH OF THE GRAND-PLACE. The Rue Saint Martin in 250m reaches the pleasant ensemble made up of the Hôtel de Ville with its courtyard, the Parc Communal and the Musée des Beaux Arts, all once part of the abbey of St. Martin, founded in 1095, becoming by the 13C one of the wealthiest abbeys in western Europe, and disestablished at the time of the French Revolution. A plan of the abbey can be seen on the wall of a building to the left of the entrance to the Musée des Beaux Arts. The **Hôtel de ville** (L. Dewez, 1763), together with an annexe now housing a small natural history museum, occupies the site of the abbot's palace of which some Romanesque cellars survive. Gutted by German bombing in 1940, the building was restored after the war, what was left of the 15C abbey cloister being incorporated.

The *Musée des Beaux Arts, housed in a light and spacious building of 1928 by Horta, shows pictures spanning from early Flemish to the present century, the emphasis being on Belgian and French artists, the former including natives of Tournai such as Roger van der Weyden and, from more modern times and particularly well represented, Piat Sauvage and Louis Gallait. The museum is open April–October: daily except Tuesday, 10.00 to 12.00, 14.00 to 17.30. November–March: Saturday, Sunday, Holidays, 10.00 to 12.00, 14.00 to 17.30.

The visitor enters a central hall showing sculpture, many of the pieces being admirable works by *Guillaume Charlier*. Terraces and rooms, haphazardly numbered, surround the hall and, though there is frequent change as also disruption by temporary exhibitions, the Old Masters will probably mostly be found in a room at the far left corner; the well-known *Piat Sauvage* trompe l'oeil works are in an adjacent room; and Louis Gallait monopolises a large hall to the left of the entrance.

The Old Masters room, together with the nearby terrace, is likely to include most of the following. *Jan Brueghel*: Two small landscapes, the detail of which repays study. *Pieter Brueghel the Younger*: The Fowler. *Gaspard de Crayer*: Adoration of the Shepherds. *Frans Francken the Younger*: Concert of the Muses. *Abel Grimmer*: The Good Shepherd. *Jacob Jordaens*: Jesus teaching Nicodemus (until recently attributed to Rubens). The King Drinks. Jesus with Martha and Mary. *Jan Fyt*: Dog guarding Game. *Adriaen Key*: Portrait of a Gentleman. *Joos de Momper*: Mountain scenes. *Pieter Paul Rubens*: A small sketch. *Roger van der Weyden*: Triptych.

As noted above, a hall to the left of the entrance is devoted to *Louis Gallait*, the room being dominated by two huge and very effective historical canvases, *Plague in Tournai in 1092 and Abdication of Charles Quint. Among several other works by this artist the *Last Rites over Counts Egmont and Horn is especially striking.

More modern works, frequently changed, will be found around the other rooms. Among the artists may well be such as: *Edouard Agneessens*: *several portraits of ladies. *Hippolyte Boulenger*: several works. *Henri de Braekeleer*: The Laundry. The Studio. Several typically detailed interiors. *Emile Claus*: Lady at a Table. *James Ensor*: Still-life. *Fantin-Latour*: Girl Reading. Study (a lady artist about to paint flowers). *Charles de Groux*: Typical strong works such as Pilgrimage at Diegem, The Lost Harvest, The Drunkard, and, in different mood, a Study for the Head of a Benedictine. *Edouard Manet*: Argenteuil. At the Père Lathuille. Moorland. *Claude Monet*: Marine scene. *Théo Rysselberghe*: Nude in a Tub. *Guillaume van Strydonck*: Several works. *Jan Toorop*: Two studies for a man's head. *Theodoor Verstraete*: Departing Fishermen, Funeral in Kempen.— The upper floor is for contemporary art and temporary exhibitions.

To the N of the Parc Communal, in which there are two figures by Charlier, one a bronze of 1891 of the painter Louis Gallait, is the Place Reine Astrid, off the far side of which will be found one of the 11–12C towers. Just E of here the Rue des Jésuites passes (right) first the former Jesuit church (1603) and house (1619–72) and then the **Eglise Saint Piat** on an ancient site occupied since the 6C by a church, traces of which were discovered during restoration work in 1971 (see plaque and model, inside by NW door). The tower is 12C and the choir 13C with a 14C apse; inside there is a lectern of 1403 and, above the high-altar, a Crucifixion attributed to J. van Oost the Elder.

EAST OF THE RIVER. From the Belfry the Rue de la Wallonie, followed by others, curves down to the river, beyond which the Rue de Pont leads to the **Eglise Saint Brice** (600m from the Belfry) dedicated to the successor of St. Martin of Tours; forced to flee because of his arrogance and licentiousness, he went to Rome, repented, and then returned to Tours where his flock were so impressed at the change that they acclaimed him a saint. The nave is 12C, the choir 13C but extended eastwards in 1405, and below the church there is a 12C crypt discovered in 1941. In the Rue Barre-Saint-Brice, immediately W of the church, Nos 12–14 are two ancient houses the façades of which date from 1172–1200 and are among the oldest citizens' houses surviving in western Europe. On No. 8 Place Clovis, immediately N of the church, a plaque records the discovery here in 1653 of the tomb of the Frankish king Childeric (died 481).

The tomb contained Childeric's sword and other relics. These, including the 'golden bees' with which the royal robes are supposed to have been studded and which were adopted as symbols by Napoleon in preference to the fleur-de-lys, are now in the Bibliothèque Nationale, Paris.

To the E of the church a memorial honours the First World War heroine Gabrielle Petit, a native of Tournai, while in the Rue du Quesnoy running NE from here the *Chapelle de l'Athénée* has a façade of 1612. Well to the SE of the church (350m; reached by Rue Saint Brice, then right into the Rue des Moulins) is the *Eglise Saint Jean*, rebuilt in 1780 but still with its graceful tower of 1367. Nearby in the Rue des Croisiers the *Chapelle des Croisiers* (Crutched Friars) dates from 1466. Rue des Croisiers ends at the ring boulevard, c 350m S down which (Avenue de Craene) good sections of the 13C ramparts, with two towers (*Marvis* and *Saint Jean*), run down to the river.

NW from the Eglise Saint Brice, the Rue de Monnel extended by the Rue du Sondart in 450m reaches the area (PLACE VERTE and its surrounds) where in 1513–18 England's Henry VIII established a citadel for his garrison. This was demolished by Louis XIV except for the massive **Tour Henri VIII**, a cylindrical keep with walls 7m thick at their base. The interior (*Musée d'Armes*) is worth visiting for its unusual construction with a conical, brick-vaulted roof. The museum includes a section devoted to the Resistance (April–October: daily except Tuesday, 10.00 to 12.00, 14.00 to 17.30. November–March: Saturday, Sunday, Holidays, 10.00 to 12.00, 14.00 to 17.30). The *Eglise Saint Nicholas*, to the NW of the Place Verte and included within the citadel, was completed in 1213.

ENVIRONS OF TOURNAI. The *Mont Saint Aubert*, 5km N, is an isolated hill (147m) commanding a view of the Scheldt valley; the name recalls a 7C bishop known for his enthusiasm for founding religious houses throughout Hainaut and Flanders. Along the road to Courtrai (27km), *Esquelmes* (6km) has a little Romanesque church (11C) and *Pecq* (3km farther N) one of the 13C.—The road to Roubaix (14km), in France, runs through *Templeuve* (8km), the reputed birthplace of St. Eleutherius. At *Royère*, 4km N of here, there are ruins of a 13C castle.—The great French town of *Lille* is 20km W of Tournai. At *Hertain* (7km), just before the border, a memorial commemorates the entry of British liberating troops into Belgium on 3 September 1944.—At *Rumes*, 8km S of Tournai, there is a small Gallo-Roman museum.

For Tournai to *Mons*, see Rte 25.

16km Leuze, 10km N of which is the 16C château of *Anvaing* where the Belgian capitulation of 27 May 1940 was signed. **Beloeil**, 10km SE of Leuze, is known for its imposing Château which traces its origins back to the 12C and has been in the possession of the princely family of Ligne since the 14C.

Arenberg, Croy and Ligne are three linked families, branches of which not infrequently appear as owners of estates in Belgium. In the 12C Arenberg was a duchy to the W of Cologne. In 1547 the lordship of Arenberg passed to Jean de Brabançon, of the house of Ligne, through his marriage to the sister of the childless Robert d'Arenberg. Jean's son Charles (died 1618) married Anne de Croy, heiress of Croy and Chimay, thus much increasing the wealth and lands of the family; he was created Prince de Ligne in 1576. An interesting member of the family was Prince Charles Joseph (1735–1814), distinguished both as soldier and writer; it was he who made the cynical observation of the Congress of Vienna 'Le Congrès danse mais ne marche pas'.

The wings of the present building date from 1682–95, but the main central portion was completely rebuilt after a fire in 1900. The interior contains antique furniture, tapestry, objets d'art of the 15–19C, and souvenirs of the family. The *Park, one of the finest in Belgium, is sometimes attributed to Le Nôtre, designer of that of Versailles. The Orangery, arranged as a recreation area, includes a restaurant and a camping and caravan site. (Château: April–September, daily, 10.00 to 12.00; 13.30 to 18.00. Park: All year 09.00 to 20.00 or dusk.)

At *Moulbaix* (7km from Leuze and 2km S of the main road) a windmill of 1624 is one of the last in Belgium still in active use (visits).—*5km* (from Moulbaix) **Ath** (24,000 inhab.) is a busy town in which the principal corner of interest is the *Tour de Burbant*, 100m from the Grand-Place down the narrow Rue du Gouvernement. A relic of the castle of c 1150 and the oldest surviving example of military architecture in Hainaut, the tower is now surrounded by an attractive group of 15C buildings. In the Grand-Place the *Hôtel de Ville* of 1614–24 is by Coeberger. The *Eglise Saint Julien*, founded in 1393, was in 1817 destroyed by lightning except for the E end and the tower.

There are several places of interest either side of the Ath to Mons road (N56).

WEST OF THE ROAD. At **Chièvres** there is a military airfield, much used by German bombers during the Second World War. In the little town, which traces its story back to the 9C, there are the late Gothic 16C *Eglise Saint Martin* with a chapel of the 12C; against the wall of the churchyard the 15C *Tour de Gavre*, flanked by two lengths of ramparts of the same period; and the *Chapelle de la Ladrerie* (lazar house) of 1112.—At **Tongre Notre-Dame**, 2km W of Chièvres, the church of 1777 is known for its miraculous Virgin (1081), patron of universities, poets and writers.—At **Herchies**, 6km S of Chièvres, the delightful small red-brick 14C keep of the lords of Egmont, with its pepperpot towers, is pleasantly situated in gardens and trees; the adjacent château, dating from 1511, was built by Charles de Berlaymont.

EAST OF THE ROAD. The **Château d'Attre**, 5km from Ath, built in 1752 near the site of a medieval predecessor by the Count de Gomegnies, retains intact its original decoration and furnishings and houses collections of silver, ivory and porcelain as well as paintings by Watteau, Snyders and others. In the park there are the remains of a 10C tower, known as the Tour de Vignon, the lair, the story goes, of one Vignon who, masquerading as a hermit, robbed and murdered his visitors; the former village pillory; a 17C dovecot; an artificial rock built by Gomegnies as a pavilion for the Archduchess Marie-Christine of Saxe-Teschen who was Marie Theresa's governor in the southern Netherlands; and a 19C artificial hill with a Swiss chalet. (Visits April–October: Saturday, Sunday, Holidays, 10.00 to 12.00, 14.00 to 18.00. Open daily except Wednesday in July and August.)—**Cambron Casteau**, 4km SE of Attre, is known for its ruined Cistercian abbey (Daily, 08.00 to 18.00 or dusk), founded in 1148 and suppressed in 1797. Beyond the entrance gate of 1722 are the 18C farm buildings with an octagonal dovecot. The ruined church (1190–1240) survives largely as parts of columns, parts of a cloister, and some Tournai recumbent figures in niches in the cloister wall; the tower (56m) was built in 1774 but the undercroft dates from the 12C. In the park, crossed by the Dendre, the main feature is a balustraded stairway and bridge (1776) over the river.

7km Ghislengehien, 6km N of which is **Lessiness** (16,000 inhab.), known for its porphyry quarries, first exploited in 1707. The *Hôpital Notre-Dame à la Rose*, founded in 1242 by Alix du Rosoit, widow of a lord of Lessines, was restored in the early 17C to which period today's buildings mainly belong (April–September, Sunday and Holidays at 15.00). The *Eglise Saint Pierre* was badly damaged in 1940 and largely rebuilt, but part of the central nave dates from the late 12C and much of the choir is 14C. Near the town centre there is a small medicinal herb garden. At *Bois de Lessines*, 4km SE, a tree by the church was planted in 1793 as a symbol of liberty. At *Deux-Acren*, 2km N of Lessines and in a district known for its herbal gardens, the church has a 12C tower while, inside, the font is a fine example of 12C Tournai stonework.

12km **Enghien** (Flem. **Edingen**. 10,000 inhab.), on the language frontier with Flemish-speaking Brabant just to the N, was long an appanage of the Bourbon family until sold by Henry IV of France in 1607 to the Count of Arenberg. The *Chapelle des Capucins* (17C) contains the alabaster tomb, by Jean Mone, of Guillaume de Croy (died 1521) Archbishop of Toledo, and also material on the Arenberg family. The counts' château, apart from its 15–16C chapel, was destroyed at the French Revolution.—*9km* **Saintes** (Flem. **Sint Renelde**), in Brabant, is where in c 680 St. Renelde (sister of St. Gudule), her priest Grimoald and their servant were martyred, the saint and priest being beheaded while the servant had nails driven into his skull. Inside the church of 1553 are a wooden figure of St. Renelde (c 1500 and possibly by Jan Borman), her silver shrine, and a curious painting on wood detailing her family tree.

At **Rebecq-Rognon**, 5km SW of Saintes, a small steam train operates in summer over a stretch of 6km. The local museum (of local history and porphyry) is housed in an old mill (rebuilt after a fire in 1858) which straddles the Senne.

5km **Halle**. See Rte 23 for Halle, for Halle to Mons, and for Halle to (*14km*) **Brussels** (Rte 1).

23 Brussels to Mons

The direct road is the main N6 (50km), but between Brussels and Halle and again between Tubize and Braine-le-Comte this Rte follows minor, more interesting roads to the east.

Total distance 73km.—*10km* **Beersel**.—*9km* **Halle**.—*4km* **Tubize**.— *5km* **Braine-le-Château**.—*12km* **Ronquières**.—*6km* **Ecaussinnes**.— *6km* **Braine-le-Comte**.—*6km* **Soignies**.—*15km* **Mons**.

Brussels, see Rte 1. From the Porte de Hal the Chaussée d'Alsemberg is followed to (*10km*) **Beersel** with its large ruined castle (March–mid November: daily, 10.00 to 12.00, 14.00 to 18.00. Other months: Saturday, Sunday, 14.00 to 17.00). Dating from the 14C, Beersel was much damaged in 1489 when the then owners, the Wittem family, supported Maximilian in his struggle against the towns. Though soon rebuilt, the castle ceased to be occupied after 1544 and was neglected until 1932 when it came into the care of the Association Royale des

Demeures Historiques. The place retains its medieval aspect, with a moat and three towers linked by walls surrounding a circular courtyard. The moat is crossed by a small drawbridge, and the towers are interesting for being defensively rounded to the outside but of typical Flemish stepped construction above the courtyard.

3km **Alsemberg** where the 15C church preserves some murals and also contains a noteworthy pulpit of 1837 by Van Geel and Van Hool. The theme of the carving is Christ teaching, the figures being particularly well observed; note, for instance, the mother with two children, one of whom is pulling away to catch a tortoise. Also in the church are a 12C font; a Descent from the Cross by Theodoor Rombouts; and a 13C figure of the Virgin.

Between Alsemberg and Halle the provincial recreational estate of *Huizingen* has gardens, deer enclosures, and a château converted to a restaurant.

6km **Halle** (Fr. **Hal**. 32,000 inhab.) is noted for its large Gothic *Onze Lieve Vrouwebasiliek*, dating in part from 1341–1409 and long a place of pilgrimage on account of its 'black' Virgin (13C), originally probably sheltered by a chapel on this site. External features are the heavy tower (18C); the curious balloon which sits above the octagonal baptistry; and, over the S portal, a 15C group of the Virgin and musician angels. The interior contains much of interest, starting with a recess to the right of the porch in which there are 33 cannon balls traditionally aimed at the church during a siege of 1580 and caught by the Virgin in her robe. Traditionally also the Virgin, above the high-altar, owes her blackness to gunpowder, although more probably the black is a combination of the smoke from centuries of candles and the oxydisation of the silver which once covered the figure. The chapel off the N aisle, built by Gilles de Trazegnies in c 1647, contains an alabaster reredos of 1533 by Jean Mone. In the choir the figures of the Apostles are dated 1410, and in the Lady Chapel (left of the choir), in a niche on the right, is the tiny black marble effigy (1460) of Joachim, son of Louis XI and Dauphin of France. Adjacent hangs a naive and amusing picture showing a dramatic rescue, the success of which was attributed to the Virgin. The octagonal baptistry, with stained-glass of 1408, contains a brass font of 1446 by Jean de Febvre of Tournai; the crypt, carried by a single column, houses the Treasury; and there is a collection of bells in the tower.

For Halle to Tournai, see Rte 22.

At (*4km*) **Tubize** (Flem. **Tubeke**), just across the language frontier, the *Musée de la Porte* shows Gallo-Roman material, religious art, fossils, coins, etc. (Saturday, Sunday, 10.00 to 12.00, 14.00 to 18.00. Tuesday, Thursday, 09.30 to 11.30, 18.30 to 20.00. Wednesday, Friday, 15.00 to 17.00). The small town merges with *Clabecq* (*Klabbeek*) where steelworks lining the river Sennette and the Charleroi canal were founded in 1828 by Edouard Goffin whose statue stands in the Grand-Place. From Tubize the main N6 continues direct to Braine-le-Comte (10km) but this Rte bears E for (*5km*) **Braine-le-Château (Kasteelbrakel)**, a small town which preserves its pillory erected in 1521 by Maximilian de Hornes whose tomb is in the church. The entrance to the château of the counts Horn is across the road from the pillory, and an old water mill at 4 Rue des Comtes de Robian has been restored as a museum (April–September: Saturday, Sunday, 14.00 to 18.00).—This Rte now bears S for (*4km*) *Ittre*, a secluded village with a forge (Museum. Easter–October: Sunday, 14.00 to 18.00) of 1701.

8km ***Ronquières**, with its interesting Sloping Lock, is in the province of Hainaut. The lock (1963), on the Charleroi to Brussels canal, comprises two large water tanks each capable of carrying barges up to a total of 1350 tonnes up or down a change of level of 68m over a distance of 1432m. The tanks, each with 236 rollers and running on rails, are each 91m long, 12m broad and with a water depth of between 3m and 4m. At the upper end of the slope there is a bridge dock, 300m long, 60m broad, and standing on 70 pillars, each nearly 20m high and 2m in diameter. The construction of this lock reduced the average barge time from Charleroi to Brussels by seven hours (from 25 to 18). Roads and paths line this impressive complex, at the top of which soars the Tower (150m) where visitors are offered an explantory film, an audio-visual presentation on the province of Hainaut, a look into the winch room, and of course a fine view from the top (May–August: daily, 10.00 to 18.00. Around one hour should be allowed for the visit to the tower, to which the last admission is 45 minutes before closing time). In summer there are boat excursions to the lock at Ittre and back (About one hour. May–August: daily except Wednesday and Saturday, unless Holiday, 12.00, 15.00, 17.00).

6km **Ecaussinnes** (20,000 inhab.) is divided into two, Ecaussinnes-Lalaing on the E side of the valley, and Ecaussinnes d'Enghien on the other, each taking the name of its former lord. The latter is mainly industrial, but **Ecaussinnes-Lalaing** is of interest chiefly for its large *Castle* (April–October: daily except Tuesday and Wednesday, unless Holiday, 10.00 to 12.00, 14.00 to 18.00), dating from the 12C but much altered up to the 18C. It preserves a 15C kitchen, restored to its then appearance, and also a chapel of the same period with a 14C Madonna ascribed to André Beauneveu. In the hall and armoury there are two early 16C chimneypieces, furniture, glass and Tournai porcelain. The *Eglise Sainte Aldegonde* (15C; dedicated to the sister of St. Waudru of Mons) contains the tomb of Blandine Rubens, sister of the painter, and also an Assumption by De Crayer. The *Château de la Folie* ('feuillie', meaning leafy), on the N edge of the town, is the 16–18C successor to the 14C castle of the lords of Enghien; the attractive 16C court can be seen from the road.

At *Arquennes*, 6km E, there is a Renaissance chapel of 1622, and at *Feluy*, 2km S of Arquennes, a moated château beside the road has the remains of its medieval predecessor alongside. **Seneffe**, 4km farther S, has given its name to two battles: Condé's victory over William of Orange in 1674, and the French defeat of the Austrians in 1794. The 18C château here (L. Dewez; under restoration) has in its grounds an orangery and an attractive small Palladian theatre.

'**Petit Granit**'. A feature of the Ecaussinnes district, extending across to Soignies, is the 'little granite' or 'bluestone' quarries, since at least the 8C producing a stone of which many Belgian buildings and monuments are made (e.g. the Collégiale Sainte Waudru at Mons and several of the houses in the Grand-Place in Brussels).

6km **Braine-le-Comte** (Flem. '**s Gravenbrakel**. 16,500 inhab.) is on the main N6. At the N entrance to the town by N6 the *Eglise Saint Géry* (mainly 16C), named after the founder of Brussels, contains a Renaissance high-altar of 1577 and a tall (3.40m) 15C statue of St. Christopher, carved from a single piece of walnut and standing on an octagonal base of 'petit granit'. Across the main road from the church a small structure marks the site of a section of the 12C fortifications, and remains of ramparts of the same period may be seen in the Ruelle Larcée behind the 17C Hôtel de Ville.

6km **Soignies** (Flem. **Zinnik**. 23,000 inhab.) is best known for its venerable Romanesque **Collégiale Saint Vincent*, dedicated to St. Vincent Madelgar, governor of Hainaut and husband of St. Waudru of Mons. After fathering his fourth child he became a monk and founded here a Benedictine house where he died in 677. In the 9C the house was destroyed by the Norsemen, but it was rebuilt soon afterwards. The choir and a section of the cloister are the oldest parts of the church (c 960); the transepts, now with 17C vaulting, and the central tower were built in the 11C, and the nave with its plain arcades in the next century. The W tower is a 13C rebuilding, to which the main portal was added in c 1620. The three outstanding features of the interior are the 60 superb Renaissance **Choir-stalls* of 1576 by Jacques Laurent and David Mulpas; on the S side of the choir, a 15C **Entombment* with terracotta figures; and, immediately below the rood-loft, a French 14C polychrome **Virgin*. The Shrine of St. Vincent can be seen above the high-altar; originally of the 13C, the shrine was buried in a nearby garden at the time of the French Revolution (see plaque in Latin on the wall in the Rue de la Régence beside the church) and when retrieved in 1799 was found to be so damaged that what is seen today is mostly a reconstruction of 1803. The Chapel of St. Vincent houses the Treasury, in which are the crozier of St. Landry (son and successor here of Vincent Madelgar) and a reliquary of St. Vincent, both of the 13C. The E walk of the 10C cloister is accessible either from the church or from the Rue de la Régence.

A short way to the N of the church the ancient chapel (in part 9th or 10C) of the old cemetery now houses a small archaeological museum. Soignies was famous for its Song School (15–18C), served by the Englishman Peter Philipps (born 1560, canon here in 1610) and other noted musicians, and the tradition is continued by a modern school.

8km Casteau-Maisières has its place in the history of the First World War. A memorial by the W side of the road, shortly before SHAPE (see below), commemorates the first British rifle-shot and also the first British mounted action against the Germans. The shot was fired at daybreak on 22 August 1914 by Corporal Thomas of the 4th Royal Irish Dragoon Guards, his target being the outposts of the German 4th Cuirassiers. A little over four years later, with the cease-fire at 11.00 on 11 November 1918, Canadian troops halted at this same spot. *SHAPE* (*Supreme Headquarters Allied Powers in Europe*) is the overall military headquarters within NATO. Previously in France, near Versailles, SHAPE, like NATO, moved in 1967 on French insistence.

7km **MONS** (Flem. **Bergen**. 90,000 inhab.), capital of the province of Hainaut, sprawls over the hill from which it derives its name and is encircled by boulevards which have replaced the former ramparts. The town is of interest to the visitor mainly for its great church, the Collégiale Sainte Waudru, and for the part it played in both world wars (museums).

Tourist Information. *Mons*: 20 Grand-Place. *Province of Hainaut*: 31 Rue des Clercs.

History. Although in origin probably a Roman military post on the road from Bavay to Utrecht, Mons is first mentioned in a 7C document, at which time it would have been a settlement around the convent founded here in the same century by Waudru, daughter of Count Walbert of Hainaut and wife of Madelgar (Vincent of Soignies). Tradition says that men of Mons fought on the English side at Crécy (1346). It was at Mons in 1433 that Jacqueline of Hainaut surrendered to Philip the Good. A century later, under Charles V, the town enjoyed a period of great commercial prosperity, being specially renowned for its cloth. It was taken in 1572 by Louis of Nassau, but soon recaptured by Alva; in 1691 by Louis XIV; in 1709 by Marlborough after Malplaquet; in 1746, after Fontenoy, by the Prince of Conti; and in 1792 by Dumouriez.

Among natives of Mons were Philippa of Hainaut (c 1314–69), queen of England's Edward III, and Louise of Stolberg, Countess of Albany (1752–1824), wife of the Young Pretender.—The painter Vincent van Gogh, during his mission among the miners of the nearby Borinage (1878–79), lived at Pâturages and Wasmes (7km SW). The following year he returned, living at Cuesmes just S of Mons.

Mons during the World Wars

At the opening of the **First World War** the British army, supporting the general French offensive, moved to Mons and by the morning of 23 August 1914 was in position, with one flank facing NE between the town and the river Sambre and the other facing N along the line of the Canal du Centre running W from Mons. Despite much gallantry (the first two Victoria Crosses of the war were won here by Lieutenant Dease and Private Godley) this long front of some 45km proved impossible to hold against a German superiority of twenty to one, particularly after French withdrawal on the right flank. The battle (sometimes called the First Battle of Mons) opened at 09.00; by early afternoon Mons had to be evacuated, and by the following morning the historic retreat to Le Cateau and the Marne was under way. (The story of the 'Angels of Mons' belongs to this battle; it is told that at one crucial point angels appeared in the sky, whereupon the British turned and for a while it was the Germans who fell back. A painting hangs in the Hôtel de Ville.)—Mons remained in German hands until freed by the Canadians on 11 November 1918 (Second Battle of Mons).

In the **Second World War** French troops entered Mons on 10 May 1940 and the Germans subjected the town to several air attacks during the following week, two bombs hitting the Collégiale Sainte Waudru. The French then withdrew, the inhabitants fled, and on 19 May the Germans took over what was a virtually empty town.—In 1944 Mons again came in for severe air attack, this time Allied. The town was freed on 2 September by American forces which had driven straight through from Meaux near Paris. There followed two days of fierce fighting to the S as large German rearguard elements attempted to isolate the Americans; this fighting ended with the destruction of the German force and the taking of 27,000 prisoners.

The heart of the town is the GRAND-PLACE in which stands the **Hôtel de Ville**, built by De Layens (1458) but since much altered and with a tower of 1718. On the front can be seen the 'Grande Garde' iron monkey (15C); perhaps once part of a children's pillory, the monkey is a bringer of good fortune to all who stroke his head. The elaborate lock, also seen here and representing the now demolished castle, is a copy of an original which is inside the building. Beneath the porch there are various memorials, these including one to the 5th Royal Irish Lancers; one commemorating the Canadian liberation of Mons in 1918; and a plaque in gratitude for food sent to Belgium by America during the First World War. The interior (normally open in working hours if no civic function) contains early chimneypieces, 17th and 18C tapestries, and a painting of the Angels of Mons by Marcel Gillis (1934).

Beyond the Hôtel de Ville porch is the pleasant JARDIN DU MAYEUR, in a corner of which and housed in a building which was once the 16C pawnshop are the **Musées du Centenaire** (Daily except Monday, 10.00 to 12.30, 14.00 to 18.00. In October–April, closes Sunday at 17.00. In May–September, closes Friday at 17.00). In front stand a prehistoric menhir and the American tank which was the first to enter Mons on 2 September 1944. The complex comprises four museums, the *War Museum*, in two parts, occupying the ground and third floors. The ground floor, devoted almost entirely to Mons during the First

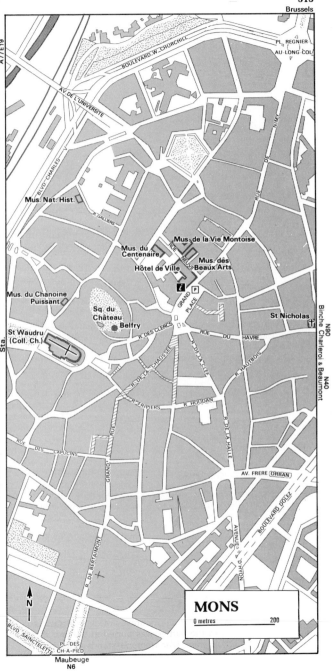

A7/E19

PL. REGNIER
AU LONG COL.

BOULEVARD W. CHURCHILL

AV. DE L'UNIVERSITE

BLVD. CHARLES

Mus. Nat. Hist.

R. GALLIERS

Mus. de la Vie Montoise

Mus. du Centenaire

RUE NEUVE

Mus. des Beaux Arts

Hôtel de Ville

GRAND PLACE

Mus. du Chanoine Puissant

Sq. du Château

St Nicholas

Belfry

St Waudru (Coll. Ch.)

R. DES CLERCS

RUE DU HAVRE

Sta.

R. DE LA CHAUSSÉE

R. DE LA CLEF

R. HAUTBOIS

R. FRIPIERS

R. HOUDAN

R. DE LA HALLE

RUE DES CAPUCINS

GRAND RUE

RUE

AV. FRERE ORBAN

AVENUE D'HYON

BOULEVARD DOLEZ

R. DE BERTAIMONT

N
↑

MONS

0 metres   200

BLVD. SAINCTELETTE

PL. DES CH-A-PIED

RUE DE NIMY

N90
Binche Charleroi & Beaumont

N40

World War, includes five national sections (British, French, Canadian, Belgian, German) as well as sections covering life in occupied Mons; the story of the Mons civic guard (1830–1914); and the Italian front. The third floor is concerned with the Second World War, the emphasis being on the liberation of September 1944.—The *Ceramic Museum* (1st floor) owes its origin to Henri Glépin, a wealthy citizen who on his death in 1898 bequeathed his collections to the town. Since much enlarged, the collections are now spread over four rooms, the first of which is devoted to material of later than 1850, special attention being given to Belgian products. The second room shows older porcelain from Belgium (Mons, Tournai, Brussels) as also from other European countries. The principal feature of the third room is a fine collection of over 500 pieces of Delftware, while the fourth room is devoted to French faience, over thirty factories being represented.—In the *Numismatic Museum* (2nd Floor), also owing its origin to Henri Glépin, are shown some 18,000 coins and medals of wide provenance, and also a large and interesting collection of engravings of historical people and events.—The *Museum of Prehistory* (2nd Floor) covers from prehistoric to Gallo-Roman and Frankish times.

Also accessible from the Jardin du Mayeur, but fronting on to the Rue d'Enghien, is the *Conciergerie* (April–September; apply Musées du Centenaire), a prison of 1512.

The Rue Neuve, out of the N corner of the Grand-Place, at once reaches the **Musée des Beaux Arts** (Daily except Monday, 10.00 to 12.30, 14.00 to 18.00. In October–April, closes Sunday at 17.00. In May–September, closes Friday at 17.00), owing its foundation to a bequest by Henri Glépin (see above). Opened in 1913, and much enlarged and modernised in 1970, the museum mounts frequent temporary exhibitions during which the permanent collections may in whole or in part be closed. The permanent collections (the many works shown in rotation) are arranged as seven sections as follows (a few representative artists' names are given). *Primitives and 16C Flemish* (Cornelis de Vos. Jan Gossaert. Jan Metsys. Paul Bril. Antoine Moro. Otto Venius). *French, 17C and 18C. Dutch, 17C and 18C. Italian, 18C. Late 19C* (Louis Gallait. F.J. Navez. Jan Portaels. H. Boulenger. T. Baron). *Early 20C and Contemporary* (Paul Delvaux. Edgard Tytgat. Léon Frederic. Also artists of the Nervia and Maka groups). *Modern Sculpture*.

Just beyond this museum, the **Musée de la Vie Montoise** (Daily except Monday, 10.00 to 12.30, 14.00 to 18.00), a museum of life and custom in the Mons district, occupies a former 17C convent.

The Rue de Havré, from the S corner of the Grand-Place, passes the 17C *Eglise Saint Nicholas*, with good contemporary woodcarving, and ends at the Place de Flandres in which there is an equestrian statue of Count Baldwin of Flanders (1171–1206) who in 1204 became Emperor of Constantinople.

From the W corner of the Grand-Place the Rue des Clercs climbs to the SQUARE DU CHATEAU, a park laid out on the site of the castle of the counts of Hainaut, pulled down in 1866. Here stands the Baroque **Belfry** (Daily except Monday, 10.00 to 12.30, 14.00 to 18.00 or earlier in September–April), built in 1662–72 by the local architect Louis Ledoux and containing a carillon. It is 86m high and the top, with panorama models of the battle of Mons, commands a wide view. At a ceremony in 1935 earth taken from the graves of every British and Canadian soldier killed in the battles was buried at the foot of the belfry. The *British and Canadian War Memorial* stands on the edge of the park; designed by Lutyens, the monument was unveiled in 1952 by Field Marshal Lord Alexander who himself fought here in 1914. Also in the park are a small tower, survivor of the 11C ramparts; the undercroft (12C) of the castle; and the basically 11C but much altered *Chapelle Saint Calixte* (Daily except Monday, 10.00 to 12.30. 14.00 to 18.00 or 17.00 in September–April). Founded in 1051 by the then Countess of Hainaut to house the relics of St. Calixtus (a slave who became pope in 217), which had been given to her by her aunt, abbess of a convent near Cologne, the chapel is at least in part the oldest building in Mons and, apart from the undercroft, all that survives of the castle. Here can be seen murals, reconstituted in 1951 from 11th or 12C originals still identifiable when discovered in 1872; effigies of the 12–14C (transferred here from Saint Ghislain and Cambron-Casteau); a large collection of flagstones of the 11C to 17C, once part of the flooring of the castle; and (Iconographical Museum, 9C to 1436) pictures of churches, castles, etc.; maps, plans and other documents relating to Mons and Hainaut.

From below the Square du Château the Rue des Clercs, passing the Province of Hainaut Tourist Information offices, continues to the *Collégiale Sainte Waudru which, though lacking a proper tower, is an outstanding example of the late Gothic style.

St. Waudru founded her convent and built her primitive chapel on this site during the later 7C, but of this building and of the three that followed it over a period of some 800 years there is no trace, though it is known that a Romanesque church stood here in 1450, the year in which work began on the present building. The early architects were Jean Spiskin and Mathys de Layens. The choir was completed in 1502, the transepts by 1527, and the nave by about the end of the century. In 1547 the decision was taken to build a tower and the plans, still held in the town archives, were for one similar to but even higher than that at Mechelen (it was to be 190m high). But work stopped on the death of the architect (Jean de Thuin) in c 1570, and it was eventually decided that the tower (completed c 1686) should not be higher than the nave.

The vast interior (115m long, 32m wide, 24m high), notable for its structural simplicity and unity of style, contains much of beauty and interest, most celebrated being the *Sculptures by the local artist Jacques Du Broeucq (c 1505–84). His work will be found in many parts of the church, outstanding being the various pieces of his great rood-loft (1535–39) which was broken up in 1797. These include the reliefs in the transepts (on the N, Resurrection, Ascension and Pentecost, with, on the first close to the right foot of Christ, a rare example of the sculptor's signature; on the S, Flagellation, Bearing of the Cross); the statues surrounding the choir; and the reliefs on the high-altar as also in the chapels. Note especially, in the fourth ambulatory chapel on the N, the unusual and effective rendering of the Last Supper. The sculptor's memorial (S transept) has three medallions on the themes Creation, Triumph of the Church, and Last Judgement.

In three adjacent chapels off the N aisle, as also elsewhere in the church, there are some beautifully preserved 15C funerary reliefs, while in the E chapel of the S aisle a heraldic painting of 1577 sets out the genealogy of St. Waudru. In the choir the stalls of 1707, from another church now demolished, are surmounted by medallion-heads from the abbey of Cambron-Casteau. The church houses the Car d'Or (1780) and the dragon, both used in ceremonies of Trinity Sunday when the remains of St. Waudru (reliquary of 1887 above the high-altar) are paraded around the town. The Treasury (July and

August, 14.00 to 17.00), in the former chapter house, contains the ring and brooch of St. Waudru and also a 13C reliquary attributed to Hugo d'Oignies.

The **Musées du Chanoine Puissant** (Daily except Monday, 10.00 to 12.00, 13.30 to 18.00), just NE of the church and entered at 22 Rue Notre-Dame Debonnaire, occupy a 16C house (Le Vieux Logis), once in part a refuge of the abbey of Ghislenghien, and also the 13C Chapelle Sainte Marguerite. The collections are those of Canon Edmond Puissant (1880–1934) who, by special dispensation, rests in the chapel. The varied material includes, in Le Vieux Logis, 16C chimneypieces, furniture, weapons and ironwork, while in the chapel are 15–17C wood statues, religious objects of many kinds, vestments, incunabula, and textiles and lace. The **Musée d'Histoire Naturelle** (Monday–Friday, 08.30 to 12.00, 14.00 to 17.00; Saturday, 10.00 to 12.00, 14.00 to 18.00. Closed Holidays) is some 200m farther N in the Rue Galliers. A curiosity here is the skeleton of Julius Koch (died 1902, age 30); known as Giant Constantin he measured 2.59m and may well have been the world's tallest man.

It was to *Cuesmes* (3km SW of the Grand-Place) that the painter Van Gogh came in August 1879, staying over a year and practising the basic principles of art. The small house at which he lived is beautifully set in a wood on the northern edge of Cuesmes, just under 2km from Mons station (daily except Monday, 10.00 to 18.00).

Mont Panisel and *Bois de Mons* are two hillocks in the SE outskirts of Mons. Throughout the afternoon of 23 August 1914 three British battalions here held a whole German corps, thus making possible the withdrawal of the main British force (see also memorial at La Bascule, the junction of N90 and N40). At the war's end, on 9 and 10 November 1918, German rearguards on these hillocks stubbornly held out against the attacking Canadians.

Between Mons and France

MONS TO QUIEVRAIN (18km). For much of the way this road traverses the Borinage, a thickly populated district where coal has been won since the 13C but which is now being forced to embark on major industrial diversification.—At *(3km) Jemappes* the French under Dumouriez defeated the Austrians in 1792 (memorial), and here also on 23 August 1914 the crossing of the canal was fiercely contested by British 9th Brigade.—*5km* **Hornu**, where there is a specially built 'miners' township' (Grand Hornu), the concept in 1820–32 of Bruno Renard and Henri de Gorge, now restored and listed as an industrial archaeological site (apply Hôtel de Ville). *Saint Ghislain*, 2km N of Hornu, was another place where in 1914 the canal crossing was gallantly defended. The town, largely rebuilt after the First World War, owes its name to St. Gislenus (died 680) who founded a Benedictine abbey here. The adjoining towns of *Pâturages* and *Wasmes*, just S of Hornu, are where Van Gogh lived in 1878–79 as missionary and pastor to the Borinage miners, going first to Pâturages as an independent pastor before being given an official appointment to Wasmes. He lived in poverty, gave away his clothes, preached, taught, and nursed the victims of typhus, but was dismissed for over-zealousness especially in pestering the authorities and the mine owners to improve the miners' lot (monument at Wasmes by Zadkine). Today mining is well recalled by the Musée des Mines (14 Rue du Pont d'Arcole. Daily except Wednesday afternoon, Saturday, Sunday, 09.00 to 12.00, 13.00 to 16.00) using galleries specially built in 1932 for mining instruction.—*2km Boussu* was the lordship of Maximilien de

Hennin (1542–79), known in Dutch history as 'Bossu' (Hunchback), who served the States General in 1576–77 in their struggle against Don John of Austria.—*8km* **Quiévrain** is the Belgian frontier town. *Audregnies*, 4km SE of here, was where in 1914 the 9th Lancers made a gallant charge and the Victoria Cross was won by Captain Grenfell. *Roisin*, on the border 6km farther S, was the home of the poet Emile Verhaeren (1855–1916); his house, burnt in 1914, was restored and is open to visitors (Daily except Friday, 10.00 to 12.00, 14.00 to 18.00).

MONS TO BOIS-BOURDON (10km). For *Cuesmes*, just to the W on leaving Mons, see above. To the E of the road (c 2km from the Mons ring boulevard) can be seen the remains of the abbey of *Bélian*, headquarters of Louis XIV in 1691 and of Marlborough in 1709.—*6km* (from Mons) the *Cheval Blanc* crossroads, and, *4km* farther at the border, *Bois-Bourdon*, both saw heavy fighting in September 1944 when the Germans tried to cut off the Americans who had reached Mons. The Château de Warelles, just W of the road about halfway between Cheval Blanc and Bois-Bourdon, was the American headquarters. Nearly surrounded here, the American commander's call for help brought massive air support as the result of which the short stretch of Roman road running W from Bois-Bourdon to the village of Goegnies-Chaussée was blocked by over a thousand destroyed German vehicles. A memorial to the American 1st Infantry Division stands by the road at Bois-Bourdon.—*Sars-la-Bruyère*, 7km NW of Bois-Bourdon, was the British headquarters (Château de la Haie) before the 1st Battle of Mons. *Malplaquet*, where Marlborough and Prince Eugene defeated the French marshals Villars and Boufflers on 11 September 1709, is just in France, 8km S of Sars-la-Bruyère.

For Mons to *Tournai*, and Mons to *Charleroi*, see Rte 25.

24 Brussels to Charleroi

Total distance 45km.—*14km* **Waterloo**.—*2km Mont Saint Jean.*—*9km* **Genappe**.—*4km* **Quatre-Bras** (with *Ligny*).—*16km* **Charleroi**.

This is the road across the battlefield of Waterloo. Also the road along which between 15 and 19 June 1815 Wellington advanced to Quatre-Bras, then withdrew to Waterloo; along which Napoleon both advanced and fled; and down which finally Blücher's Prussians chased the beaten French.—An alternative road branches SW at Mont Saint Jean to reach Charleroi via Nivelles; but since Nivelles is the only place of interest along this road, this town is included below as one of two diversions from Genappe.

Brussels, see Rte 1.—*14km* **Waterloo** and *2km Mont St. Jean*. See Rte 1 G. for Brussels to Waterloo, for the battlefield, and for the Charleroi road as far as *Belle Alliance* and *Ferme du Caillou*.

9km **Genappe** was the home between 1456–61 of the future Louis XI of France who found refuge here during his struggle with his father, Charles VII. More recently the small town was the scene of a fierce skirmish on 17 June 1815 as, in a violent thunderstorm, Wellington's cavalry, closely pursued by French lancers, tried to retire through the narrow street. Napoleon himself was recognised among the French; the following night he was here again, this time fleeing and hurriedly changing from his carriage to a horse and narrowly avoiding capture by the Prussians. Wellington spent some of the night of 16–17 June at the Auberge du Roi d'Espagne, and here on 20 June died General Duhesme, commander of Napoleon's Young Guard (plaque).

DIVERSIONS FROM GENAPPE. There follow two important diversions: to Villers-la-Ville (SE) and Nivelles (W). The main Rte S on N5 continues on p 322 after the description of Nivelles.—**Villers-la-Ville** (7300 inhab.), 5km SE, is known for its great ruined Cistercian *Abbey*, founded in 1146 on a nearby height but moved the following year to the present site beside the river, reputedly on the advice of St. Bernard himself who was visiting. The abbey was sacked by the French revolutionaries in 1794 and formally suppressed two years later. Long neglected (the central nave of the church collapsed in 1884), the site was acquired by the Belgian government in 1893 and is now managed by the Royal Belgian Touring Club. The abbey is open mid March–September: 10.00 to 18.00, or 22.00 in May–August. October–mid March: Sunday, Holidays, 11.00 to 17.00.

In a lovely hilly and wooded setting the extensive and impressive ruins form two main parts, the older spanning the 12–14C and the newer the 17th and 18C. Visitors may wander at will, but the following suggested route, starting with the older parts, takes in all places of principal interest (most buildings carry identification notices with dates). The entrance is at the S of the site, a track from here leading NW to a group of domestic buildings which include the 14C Romanesque Warming Room, the Transitional Refectory, and the 12–13C kitchen. On the N are the Cloisters, originally Romanesque, later rebuilt in Gothic style, but today almost wholly in ruins. Of the Romanesque period all that survives are twin 12C windows in the E walk. Other features of interest around the cloisters are the collection of graveslabs in the S walk; the various rooms opening off the E walk, these being (S to N) the stairway to the dormitory, the Parlour, Chapter House and Mortuary; the tomb (NE corner) of Gobert d'Aspremont, a crusader knight who became a monk here and died in 1263; and (NW corner) the Crypt (dark and often flooded) and a Transitional doorway with a three-cusped arch. The huge ruined Church is adjacent to the N walk of the cloisters and remains impressive despite neglect, spoliation and the collapse of the nave in 1884. The large 13C Brewhouse is to the NW of the church, while the area immediately E of the apse was the burial ground, now unrecognisable as such and in any case cut by the railway. The 17–18C part of the complex lies to the SE of the church and cloisters, or to the NE of the site entrance, and comprises what is left of the Abbot's Palace and, to the E, what was the kitchen garden but is now ornamental. Beyond this, steps ascend across the railway to a chapel of 1615.

In the village a hotel opposite the abbey entrance was its mill, while in the parish church there are two *Retables from the abbey (the lower 15C, the upper 16C), both with exquisitely detailed carving.

Tilly, 3km S of Villers-la-Ville and with a 12C keep, was the birthplace of Jean 't Serclaes (1559–1632), commander of the Catholic League during the Thirty Years War. For *Gentinnes*, 5km E, see Rte 27.

Nivelles (Flem. **Nijvel**. 22,000 inhab. Tourist Information: Waux-Hall, Place Albert I), 7km W of Genappe, is the chief town of the 'Roman Pays', the French-speaking part of the province of Brabant. Although much of its centre was destroyed by fire during bombing of May 1940, the town remains a place of some character and still has a number of dignified 17–19C buildings and houses. Its origins are those of its great church, the *Collégiale Sainte Gertrude* (Daily, 09.00 to 12.00, 14.00 to 17.00).

Nivelles, the Collégiale Sainte Gertrude

A convent was founded here in c 650 by St. Itte, the widow of Pepin of Landen, who brought her husband's remains here and appointed her daughter (St. Gertrude) as the first abbess. The convent's church, originally dedicated to St. Peter, gradually changed its name after Gertrude had been buried here. Building of the present church began at the end of the 10C, but later centuries brought much destruction, alteration and addition, largely because the building was burnt some nineteen times, the last occasion being in the bombing of May 1940. Restoration, including the reconstruction of the upper part of the Romanesque tower, was completed by the mid 1980s.

Despite much rebuilding the church remains a notable example of a double-ended (transepts and choirs at opposing ends) Romanesque structure, with a 12C W addition which had an apse until demolished in 1619 and which was given a somewhat incongruous Baroque portal in 1664. The W tower is flanked by two 12C turrets, on one of which (S) is the figure of an armed knight known as Jean de Nivelles; dating from the 15C the figure was on the early town hall (demolished 18C) until placed here in the early 17C. The other turret is called the Tour Madame from the fact that it adjoined the palace of the abbess.—The Cloister is entered from the N aisle of the church; the NE angle is 11–12C and the N walk 13C, but the remainder is poor rebuilding of 1846.

Entry to the church is normally at the W end through one of two aisle doors with finely carved lintels, the Portail de Samson (N) being more elaborate than the other. The nave and E choir—the former with a pulpit of 1772 by Laurent Delvaux; the latter dominated by the magnificent 13C Shrine of St. Gertrude, meticulaously restored after almost melting away in the fire of 1940—are pleasing in their simplicity and proportion. Guided visits (Daily except Saturday and Sunday mornings, at 10.00, 11.00, 14.00, 15.00 and 16.00) include the large Crypt of c 1100, with its three aisles and six vaulted bays, and the even more ancient Sous-sol Archéologique where traces have been identified of no fewer than five earlier churches. These are the early funerary chapel (7C); the first church (late 7C), with the tomb of St. Gertrude; the first Carolingian church (late 9C); the second Carolingian church (10C); and the third Carolingian church (also 10C). Here, too, amid much other venerable material, there are shadowy links to St. Foillon, the Irish monk who founded the abbey of Fosses-la-Ville in about 650 (on land given to him by that same widow of Pepin of Landen who founded this convent at Nivelles) and who with his three companions was later murdered near today's Le Roeulx; a stone here suggests his name and there is also a (?) 7C sarcophagus in which the bones of four people were found.

The *Musée d'Archéologie* (Daily except Tuesday, 09.30 to 12.30, 14.30 to 17.00), in the Rue de Bruxelles immediately NE of the church, is housed in the 18C refuge of the abbey of Orval and contains mixed collections, some coming from the Collégiale Sainte Gertrude. The scope includes archaeological material spanning from prehistoric to Merovingian times; religious figures, and sculpture of the 15–18C, including works by Laurent Delvaux; Flemish paintings, some attributed to Rubens; furniture; Brussels tapestry; locks, keys, weapons and musical instruments. Opposite the museum entrance a plaque on a house reminds that the Gestapo was active here. In the Rue Seutin, running W from the church, No. 38 is the *Tour Simonne*, the last survivor of the eleven towers which formed part of the 12C ramparts, while in the SW part of the town (Avenue de la Tour de Guet) *La Tourette* is a tower of 1620 which was used as a country retreat by the Jesuits.

The motor-racing circuit of *Nivelles-Baulers* is 2km N of Nivelles. At *Bois-Seigneur-Isaac*, 2km farther N, there is a Premonstratensian abbey, rebuilt in 1903 on old foundations but with an entrance of 1764. The richly decorated chapel (1550–80) is beside the road.

Baisy-Thy (*2km* S of Genappe) was the birthplace of Godfrey de Bouillon (1060–1100), leader of the First Crusade and first king of Jerusalem (monument of 1855 in the church).—*2km* **Quatre-Bras**, and (9km to the SE in the province of Namur) **Ligny**, are the sites of the two important battles which on 16 June 1815 set the stage for Waterloo.

On learning that the French were approaching Quatre-Bras, Wellington left the Duchess of Richmond's ball in Brussels in the early hours of 16 June and ordered his army to concentrate at Quatre-Bras, where he arrived at 10.00. At this moment, though neither side was aware of it, Marshal Ney's force before Frasnes, 3km S, had a vast superiority in both men and guns. Around noon Wellington rode to Ligny to confer with Blücher, concentrated here with his Prussian army. Across the small river Wellington and Blücher could clearly see Napoleon and his massed troops, and Wellington observed that Blücher would be 'damnably mauled', with his men drawn up as they were on an exposed forward slope. By 14.30 Wellington was back at Quatre-Bras, only to find that battle had not only been joined but almost lost; at the same time he heard the cannon which signalled the start of the fighting at Ligny. At Quatre-Bras Allied reinforcements were now arriving, Wellington was able to hold Ney, and by 21.00 the battle had petered out. Early next morning (17 June) Wellington sent his aide-de-camp, Alexander Gordon, to find out what had happened at Ligny. Gordon returned with the grim news that the Prussians had been defeated and had fallen back on Wavre. Wellington then had no choice but to order a retreat to the position he had already selected S of Waterloo.

At Quatre-Bras, where the fighting was in open country, the Duke of Brunswick was killed (monument), and Wellington narrowly escaped capture, jumping his horse clear over the Gordon Highlanders lining a bank. At Ligny the battle raged for five hours in narrow village streets; the Ferme d'en Haut (plaque) in the village was a typical defensive point. Blücher too narrowly avoided capture; leading a dashing but useless final cavalry charge, he fell and was twice ridden over, probably being saved by his aide-de-camp who covered his chief's medals to hide his identity. Blücher was carried to *Mellery* (7km N) where for several vital hours he lay virtually unconscious.

Fleurus, 2km S of Ligny (or Presles, see Rte 25), may have been the site of Caesar's crushing defeat of the Nervii in 57 BC. The town has given its name to other battles. In 1690 the French under Marshal Luxembourg defeated the Germans and Dutch here; more memorable was the victory of the French revolutionary army (under Marshal Jourdan) on 26 June 1794 over the Austrians, indifferently led by the Prince of Coburg.

4km Frasnes-lez-Gosselies is the first village in Hainaut.—*6km Gosselies* is an industrial extension of Charleroi. The airfield is beside the road.

6km **CHARLEROI** (212,000 inhab. Tourist Information: Square de la Gare du Sud), partly on a hill and partly in the valley of the Sambre, and the centre of the principal industrial zone of Belgium, is visited for its two outstanding museums, the Musée des Beaux Arts and the Musée du Verre (Glass).

Charleroi sprang from a colliery village which the Spaniards developed into a fortress (1666) and named in honour of Charles II of Spain. From then on it saw much of war. Louis XIV seized the town within nine months and Vauban built defences (replaced in 1868 by boulevards); it was four times besieged by the French in 1794; Napoleon crossed the Sambre here in 1815, driving out the Prussians and advancing up the roads to Quatre-Bras and Ligny; in August 1914 French troops vainly defended the Sambre bridgehead against overwhelming German strength; finally the town was again taken by the Germans in May 1940, remaining occupied until liberated by the Americans on 3 September 1944.

The town centre is the PLACE CHARLES II on the hilltop, here being the *Basilique Saint Christophe*, with a front of 1667 but much extended in 1968, and the *Hôtel de Ville* (1936) occupying a triangular block between Place Charles II and the large rectangular PLACE DU MANEGE.

The *Musée des Beaux Arts (Tuesday–Saturday, 09.00 to 17.00. Also Sunday in July and August. Closed Holidays), opened in 1980 on an upper floor of the Hôtel de Ville, exhibits mainly works by native Hainaut artists but also by other artists who worked in or were inspired by the province and in particular by the district around

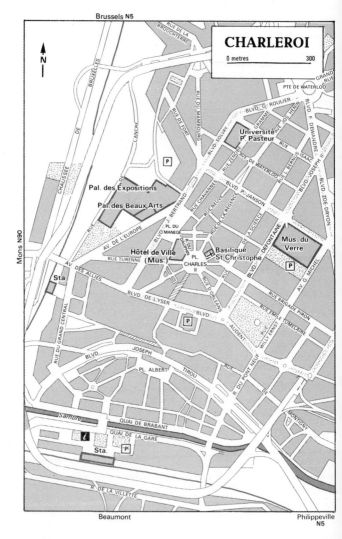

Charleroi. This is a vivid gallery, likely to appeal in particular to three chronologically successive tastes—the warm portraiture and other themes of the Charleroi artist François Joseph Navez (1787–1869) and pupils such as Jan Portaels; the realistic portrayal of Hainaut mining and industrial life as recorded by several artists, outstandingly Constantin Meunier; and, in total contrast, the colourful fantasy world of such as Paul Delvaux and René Margritte. Additionally there are several works by Nervia, not so much a school or movement as a loose association of 1928–38 formed to encourage Walloon art.

The museum round starts with two rooms showing Walloon ceramic, stonework, furniture, pewter and suchlike. Beyond comes the Galerie Navez in which the emphasis is on F.J. Navez with a brilliant selection of his works among which the two girls with a bird's nest is one of particular appeal. Here too are works by Navez's pupils and other 19C artists, such as the widely travelled Jan Portaels (son-in-law of Navez) whose Portrait of a North African Girl is typical of a theme he made popular. Beyond, the visitor meets the harsher world of the Hainaut black country (Pays Noir). Constantin Meunier is outstanding here with his pictures and figures of manual workers, but there are several other artists, such as Marius Carion, an orphan who painted the Borinage of his impoverished childhood; Xavier Mellery (Scene in a Mine); Maximilien Luce, a neo-Impressionist who specialised in mines and factories and those who worked in them; Alex-Louis Martin, a miner's son whose early deprivations are reflected in his portrayals; and P.P. de Chatelet who, springing from a comfortable artistic background, was fired, when on a visit in 1909, by the harsh contrasts of the Pays Noir.

The Pays Noir is left for the 'Monde de l'Irrationel', a fantasy world light-years away from the down-to-earth labour and poverty of the Pays Noir. Here, for instance, are Paul Delvaux, with his cynical bright blue Annunciation; René Magritte (La Liberté de l'Esprit); and Jean Ransy, showing an amusing if confused La Maison d'Ange. Lastly there is Nervia (see above), represented by the contrasting styles of such as Louis Buisseret, Anto Carte and Rodolphe Strebelle.

On the W of the Place du Manège are the *Palais des Beaux Arts* and the *Palais des Expositions*, the former used for cultural purposes and the latter for technical, commercial and industrial exhibitions. The *Université Paul Pasteur*, a short way N, is a technological university.

The *Musée du Verre is in a modern building in Boulevard Defontaine, some 200m E of Place Charles II. All aspects of glasswork are covered from antiquity to the present day. Roman, Chinese, Islamic, Byzantine, Venetian and Bohemian glass is displayed, as well as glass from other parts of Europe. Other sections explain manufacture, shaping, decoration, etc. (Tuesday–Saturday, 09.00 to 17.00. May be open Sunday in July and August. Closed Holidays).

For Charleroi to *Mons*, and Charleroi to *Namur*, see Rte 25. For Charleroi to *Chimay* (Botte du Hainaut), and Charleroi to *Couvin*, see Rte 26B and C.

25   Tournai to Mons, Charleroi and Namur

Total Distance 123km.—*6km* **Antoing**.—*13km* **Péruwelz-Bonsecours**.—*30km* **Mons**.—*15km* **Binche** (or *17km* **La Louvière**).—*21km* (from Binche) or *19km* (from La Louvière) **Charleroi**.—*9km* **Châtelet**.—*13km* **Fosses-la-Ville**.—*7km* **Floreffe**.—*9km* **Namur**.

Tournai, see Rte 22.—There are three choices of road to Mons: the main N7/N50 through Barry and Basècles, of little interest; the motorway; or this Rte which, as far as Péruwelz (19km from Tournai), follows minor but more interesting roads to the south. After Péruwelz there is little of note and the motorway to Mons is recommended.

From Tournai the road SE along the S bank of the Escaut (Scheldt) is taken, this soon running into the dusty PAYS BLANC, a district so named because of the limestone which has been quarried here since Roman times or earlier.—*4km* Calonne where there is a château in which Louis XV lodged at the time of the Battle of Fontenoy.—The river is crossed to (*2km*) **Antoing** (8000 inhab.) with a *Hôtel de Ville* of 1565 and an imposing *Château* which, although largely a reconstruction of the 19C, preserves 12C walls, a 15C keep and a 16C tower (mid May–September: Sunday, Holidays, guided tours at 15.00, 15.30, 16.30, 17.00 and 17.30).

The château is of some historical interest. Long the home of the Melun family, princes of Epinoy, it eventually passed by marriage to the princes of Ligne. In 1565 the wedding ceremonies here of Floris de Montmorency were used to concert the first moves of the nobles' rebellion against Spain. Counts Egmont and Horn (the latter brother of the bridegroom) and Jean de Glymes were all present, and all, including Floris, had by 1568 been executed or assassinated.—A corner tower contains fine graveslabs of the Melun and Ligne families, some of these being Tournai sculpture of the 11–16C.

Fontenoy, 2km E of Antoing, has given its name to the battle fought in this area in May 1745, when the French under Marshal Saxe defeated a British, Hanoverian, Austrian and Dutch army under the Duke of Cumberland.

The main French line, facing S, was between Antoing and Fontenoy, with an important fortified redoubt to the rear a short way N of the latter. After unsuccessful early attacks aimed at turning the French line, Cumberland decided to assault between Fontenoy and the redoubt, he himself leading and his army following with drums beating and colours unfurled. As the armies met, Captain Lord Charles Hay, Grenadier Guards, ran forward, drank to the French, and called for three cheers. Astonished, the French cheered in reply and, according to some reports, invited the English to fire first. This at any rate the English did, advancing and soon finding themselves deep into the French lines and apparently the victors. However, although deserted by his court, Louis XV stood firm, while Marshal Saxe, despite suffering from dropsy, rallied himself sufficiently to bring his artillery into action. This shattered the Allied square which, still fighting, fell back on Vezon.—A Celtic cross (1907) commemorates the Irish Brigade which fought for the French.

Near Hollain, 2km S of Antoing on the W side of the river, the *Pierre Brunehault* (1km SW) is a large menhir 4.40m high.

From Antoing the Mons road winds across country for *13km* to **Péruwelz-Bonsecours** (17,000 inhab.), in the latter (S) part of the town, on the French border, being the château of L'Hermitage, built by Marshal de Croy in 1749, and also a large *Basilica* of 1885–92 which is an important pilgrimage objective. The story goes that in the 16C a pious girl came to this place to pray to a figure of the Virgin she had placed on an oak. In 1636, threatened by the plague, the people of Péruwelz successfully begged this Virgin to save them and in gratitude built a chapel. This, enlarged in 1642, was pulled down in 1885 to be replaced by the present basilica, the high-altar of which is said to stand on the site of the oak.

Bernissart, 4km SE, is where in 1878 the 250 million-years-old fossil iguanodons were found which are now in the Institut des Sciences Naturelles at Brussels (local museum; April–October: Sunday, 15.30 to 17.30). At *Blaton*, 2km N of Bernissart, the Romanesque church of c 1183 has since 1470 been dedicated to All the Saints, the only such dedication in Belgium.

30km (by motorway) **Mons**, see Rte 23.

There is a choice of two roads, both virtually the same distance (36km), between Mons and Charleroi. The main N90 runs through the pleasant and interesting town of Binche; the more northerly choice, through La Louvière with the fine park and museum of Mariemont, wanders through industrial patches but includes the great hydraulic lift-locks on the Canal du Centre.

Mons to Charleroi via Binche

6km Villers-Saint Ghislain was in August 1944 the headquarters of General Allenby, commander of the British cavalry, the first important cavalry action of the war being fought on the rise to the W of Péronnes (7km E) on 22 August.

9km **Binche** (35,000 inhab. Tourist Information: Hôtel de Ville), an attractive old fortified town on a hill, is perhaps best known on account of its carnival.

The first fortifications seem to have been built in c 1150 by Count Baldwin IV of Hainaut, these being enlarged and strengthened in the following centuries, notably in 1491 by Margaret of York, widow of Charles the Bold. In 1545 Mary of Hungary, regent of the Netherlands and sister of Charles V, demolished a part of the fortifications to make place for the palace she required here; and it was here in 1549 that, in the presence of Charles V, she organised a great festival to celebrate the Spanish conquest of Peru. Nine years later, in 1554, Henry II of France, at war with Charles V, destroyed most of the town, but rebuilding soon followed. Louis XIV razed much of the ramparts in 1675.

The **Carnival** dates from the 14C, but seems to have taken on much of its present form from Mary of Hungary's festival of 1549. The important days are Shrove Tuesday and the preceding Sunday and Monday, but festivities start to build up from January. The outstanding feature (Shrove Tuesday only) is the dance of the 'Gilles', clowns special to Binche and said to owe something of their costume to nobles who, at Mary's festival, dressed as Peruvian Incas.

The southern part of Binche is the oldest and the most interesting. The *Hôtel de Ville*, in the Grand-Place, was started by Jacques Du Broeucq in c 1555 to replace the building destroyed by the French the year before; further work, notably the stucco façade, was carried out by Laurent Dewez in 1735. The *Collégiale Saint Ursmer*, S of the Grand-Place and dedicated to the builder of the abbey at Aulne, was first built in the 12C, but only the base of the tower and the Romanesque main portal survive from this time. Adjacent to the church are a figure of a 'Gille' (1952) and the *Musée International Carnaval et Masque* (May–October: daily except Friday, 10.00 to 12.00, 14.00 to 18.00). At the E end of the church is the entrance to a park in which a fragment of ruin is all that is left of the palace of Mary of Hungary; in part rebuilt by Du Broeucq after the destruction of 1544, the building was used for municipal purposes until the 18C, after which it fell into neglect. The farther end of the park lies along the ramparts, with a steep drop to the river. To the W of the church the little *Chapelle Saint André* (16C) contains good woodwork and sculpture. The old ramparts, with their towers, run below the chapel.

The abbey of *Bonne Espérance*, now a seminary, is 3km south. The buildings are mainly 17–18C, but the church (Dewez, 1770–76) incorporates a 15C tower and a cloister in which there is some 13C work.—At *Carnières*, 5km NE of Binche, the town hall exhibits material on the painter A.L. Martin (Monday–Thursday, 08.00 to 12.00. 13.00 to 16.00).

At *(11km)* **Fontaine-l'Evêque** (19,000 inhab.) the *Hôtel de Ville* is in a château of 1558 but with a chapel and towers of the 13–14C, the former in summer used for exhibitions by local artists. The towers are linked by an underground gallery which has been converted into an imaginative *Musée de la Mine*, an extensive section of a coal-mine complete with working machinery (Tuesday, Thursday, Saturday, Sunday, 10.00 to 12.00, 14.00 to 18.00).—*10km* **Charleroi**, see Rte 24.

Mons to Charleroi via La Louvière

At *(5km)* **Havré** the ruins of a château of 1603 stand on 12C foundations. Jean Dunois, the 'Bastard of Orleans' and companion of

Binche, the dance of the 'Gilles'

Joan of Arc, was lord of Havré in 1452–68, and later the estate belonged to the family of Croy-Havré who here entertained Marlborough and Eugene in 1709.

The Canal du Centre, between *Thieu* (*2km* beyond Havré) and (*7km*) *Houdeng-Goegnies*, has long been served by four unusual and impressive lift-locks (at Thieu, where the road crosses the canal at the lock; and at Bracquegnies, Houdeng-Aimeries and Houdeng-Goegnies). Built in 1885–1919, and with a daily limit of 12 barges of 380 tonnes, these locks are now being superseded (1982–89) by a single giant lock, with 1350 tonnes capacity the world's largest. This is at *Strépy-Thieu* (signed from motorway exit 21) where there is a Visitor Centre (May–September: Monday–Friday, 14.00 to 18.00; Saturday, Sunday, Holidays, 10.30 to 18.30).

The château of *Le Roeulx* (Easter–September: daily except Wednesday, 10.00 to 12.00, 13.30 to 18.00), 4km NW of Houdeng-Goegnies, dates from the 14–15C but was refronted and given other alterations between 1713 and 1760. Since the 15C it has belonged to the Croy family and the interior shows their varied collections. The park, by one tradition the place where St. Foillan and his companions were murdered during the 7C, is noted for its rose garden and magnificent trees.

3km **La Louvière** (78,000 inhab.) is a busy industrial and commercial town, of most interest to the visitor for the park and museum of *Mariemont*, 3km SE of the town centre. The name derives from Mary of Hungary, sister of Charles V and regent of the Netherlands, who built a palace here in 1546. This was destroyed by Henry II of France as soon afterwards as 1554, no successor following until Charles of Lorraine built again in 1756, this château (some ruins of which can be seen) also only lasting a short while until burnt by French revolutionaries in 1794. The third château (1831) was owned by the Warocqué family and in 1917 bequeathed to the state by Raoul Warocqué, together with the collections he had assembled. After fire damage in 1960, a fine new museum was built, this being in two sections, one devoted to European, Asian and Oriental antiquities and the other to regional archaeology and history, Tournai porcelain being an outstanding feature. The fine park, with glasshouses, a rose garden and the ruins of the palace of Charles of Lorraine, also shows 19C and contemporary sculpture. (Museum: daily except Monday, 10.00 to 18.00. Closed 1 January, 25 December. Park: 09.00 to 18.00 or 16.00.)

10km Trazegnies, where there is a small château, first built in the 12C, rebuilt in the 16–17C and enlarged in 1854. The 16C church contains two mausoleums (one by Luc Fayd'herbe) of the lords of Trazegnies.—*9km* **Charleroi**, see Rte 24.

9km **Châtelet** is roughly the SE corner of the industrial complex around Charleroi.—*4km Presles* claims (with Fleurus) to be the place where Caesar defeated the Nervii in 57 BC.—*9km* **Fosses-la-Ville** (7000 inhab.), in the province of Namur, is an ancient and mellow small town tracing its origins to Celtic times when this place was known as Biberona, the valley of the beavers. By the Gallo-Roman period, though, the Latin name Fossa was in more common use. Later, in about 650, the widow of Pepin of Landen gave land here to the Irish monk St. Foillan (Feuillen) for the foundation of an abbey. This was later ravaged by the Norsemen, but in c 974 Bishop Notger of Liège built fortifications within which was a new abbey church, today's *Collégiale Saint Feuillen* (mainly 18C but with foundations in part of the 9–10C and a slightly later Romanesque tower and crypt) being the successor of these earlier churches. In the pleasant Place du Chapitre, beside the church, may be seen some of the later canons' houses and the largely 16C Maison du Doyen du Chapitre incorporating part of the ramparts.

Tamines, an industrial centre 7km NW, is notorious for being the scene of one of the worst of the German massacres of 1914 when, on 20 August, 384 civilians were mowed down in front of the church. A monument records the tragedy, and the victims rest beside the church. *Oignies*, on the other side of the river from Tamines, is famous for the abbey, now a glassworks, of which Hugo d'Oignies, the medieval goldsmith, was a monk.

The *Lac du Bambois*, 2km S of Fosses-la-Ville, is a recreational area, while *Mettet*, 5km farther S, is known as a motor-cycling centre.

7km **Floreffe**, a small town on the Sambre, is visited for its grottoes
and its great abbey. The *Grottoes* (Easter–mid October, daily 09.00 to
19.00), beside the main road, are the only dolomitic caves in Belgium.
Human and bear bones have been found here (the latter are shown)
as well as other evidence of prehistoric occupation. Above the
grottoes there is a slim 16C tower. The imposing buildings of the
Abbey (March–November: daily, 11.00 to 19.00 or 20.00 at weekends), now a school, straddle a ridge between the main road and the
Sambre.

In 1120 St. Norbert, passing through Namur on his way back from Cologne
where he had been to negotiate for relics, was invited by the local lord to build a
monastery here. Between its foundation and its suppression at the French
Revolution the abbey was many times wrecked; in 1188 by the Count of Hainaut,
in 1232 and 1237 by counts of Flanders, and in 1683 by the French.

Today's domestic buildings are largely of the 18C, but the architecture of the church spans five or six centuries. Choir, transepts and
nave are 12–13C, the tower is 16C, the eastward extension of the choir
was built in 1638, and during the 18C the Baroque W front was added
while at the same time Laurent Dewez converted the interior, facing
the walls with stucco. The outstanding feature of the interior are the
*Baroque Stalls (1632–48) by Peter Enderlin, a German who lived in
Namur; his little signature self-carving is shown. A leaflet details the
subjects of the carvings, and a room is set aside for an audio-visual
description of the abbey. By the church entrance, the small vaulted
Salle des Frères Convers (c 1150), the oldest surviving part of the
abbey, contains 12C murals. Below the abbey can be seen the 13C
mill and brewhouse, the latter still used as a brasserie and claiming to
be the oldest commercial building in Belgium.—In (*3km*) *Malonne*, a
small place straggling up a steep-sided and wooded valley, the
mainly 17C church is successor to an abbey church founded here
before 698 by the Anglo-Saxon monk and missionary St. Bertuin.—
6km **Namur**, see Rte 28.

26   Between Sambre and Meuse

This Route, broken into three sections, covers the area roughly
bounded on the N by the Mons, Charleroi, Namur road; on the S by
the French border; and on the W and E by the Sambre and Meuse
rivers. It should be noted that Rte 26A below (Mons to Dinant) is
crossed by the N–S Rtes 26B and 26C at Beaumont and Philippeville
respectively.—Once the largely industrial environs of Charleroi are
left, the country, which can be regarded as a westwards extension of
the Ardennes, is either open, agricultural upland with wide vistas, or,
towards the S, forest.

A. Mons to Dinant

Total distance 79km.—*21km Solre-sur-Sambre.*—*10km*
Beaumont.—*12km Silenrieux* (for **Walcourt**).—*10km*
Philippeville.—*26km* **Dinant.**

Leaving **Mons** (see Rte 23), the right fork (N40) is taken at La Bascule
from where Rte 25 runs E to Binche.—*5km Spiennes*, just beyond

which (W) an area of open field known as Camp à Cailloux is a site of Neolithic flint mines (no admission until further notice).—*5km Givry*, immediately after which the Roman road from Bavai to Binche is crossed.—*11km Solre-sur-Sambre* where the moated castle, one of the finest feudal strongholds in Hainaut, comprises a 12C keep (the original fortified house) and a square court enclosed by walls with 14C cylindrical towers at the corners.—*4km Montignies-Saint-Christophe*, on the French border, preserves, in a quiet setting a short way S of the main road, an attractive Roman bridge spanning the little river Hantes; this is just about the last trace of their road from Bavai to Trier.—At (*6km*) **Beaumont** (5800 inhab.), an ancient small town on a hill, there are still lengths of the 11–12C fortifications, the best part to visit being the *Tour Salamandre* (small museum) a short walk from the Grand-Place, all that is left of the castle of the counts of Hainaut, built in c 1051 and demolished in 1691 (May–September: daily, 09.00 to 12.00, 14.00 to 19.00). For places N and S of Beaumont, see Rte 26B.

10km Boussu-lez-Walcourt is 1km short of the border of the province of Namur. Between here and *Cerfontaine* (6km S; local museum in the old station; Easter–mid September: Sunday, 15.00 to 18.00) stretches the attractive and impressive complex of the **Barrages de l'Eau d'Heure**, a system of dams and reservoirs, together with over 70km of roads, walkers' paths, picnic sites, view-points, recreational and water sports facilities, etc. There is an Information Centre (Easter–September: 09.00 to 17.00) near the Plate Taille dam and a belvedere overlooks that of Eau d'Heure.

The scheme (capacity 47 million cubic metres of water) has three main purposes: to feed the Brussels-Charleroi canal; to dilute urban and industrial pollution; and, indirectly, to maintain the flow of the Meuse. The two main dams, the latter with a power station, are *Eau d'Heure* in the N and *Plate Taille* in the S, named for their respective rivers. To ensure a constant water level there are three pre-dams, these being *Feronval*, close to Eau d'Heure, and *Ry Jaune* and *Falemprise*, both on the east.

2km Silenrieux, in the province of Namur, is 3km S of the ancient little town of **Walcourt** in which the Place de la Poste now occupies the site of what was successively a Gallo-Roman camp and a medieval castle. Tradition holds that St. Maternus of Tongeren (4C), incensed at finding a pagan altar here, built a Christian chapel. This would have been an early predecessor of today's *Basilique Saint Materne*, most of which was built between 1250 and 1447, the older part being the choir and transepts. However, the base of the tower and the narthex belong to an earlier church of 990–1026, while the upper part of the tower, with its strange 17C steeple, is of c 1200. The interior is notable for a marble *Rood-loft of 1531, an elaborate masterpiece in Flamboyant style presented by Charles V on the occasion of his pilgrimage to the miraculous Virgin of Walcourt, a wooden figure plated with silver, generally accepted as of the 11C (silver 1626) although local tradition insists on a much earlier date, even claiming that Maternus may have been the artist. The Treasury contains work attributed to Hugo d'Oignies, a native of Walcourt.

For *Thy-le-Château*, 4km N, see Rte 26C.

10km **Philippeville** (7000 inhab.) was built as a fortress in 1555 by Charles V, after the French had taken Mariembourg (12km S) the previous year, and named for his son Philip II (see stone on first left pillar of the church). It was not until 1620 that the place received civilian inhabitants. The town retains its star-shaped fortress plan and the defensive galleries ('souterrains') can be visited (July and August: daily, 13.00 to 18.00). The former powder magazine is now the Chapelle des Remparts. (For places N and S of Philippeville, see Rte 26C.)

Florennes (8km NE) claims to be the birthplace of Arletta, daughter of a tanner and mother of William the Conqueror of England. The 18C Eglise Saint Gangulphe (dedicated to a Burgundian nobleman who became a recluse but was nevertheless murdered in c 760 by his wife's lover) stands on foundations of 1001.—*Senzeille*, 8km SW of Philippeville, is visited for the remarkable astronomical clock built by a local craftsman at the beginning of this century (tel: 071–644105).

20km Onhaye where the church contains the tomb of St. Walhere, an early priest here, murdered by another priest whom he was chiding for his dissolute life.—*6km* **Dinant**, see Rte 29.

B. Charleroi to Chimay

Total distance 47km.—*12km Gozée* (for W **Aulne**, **Thuin** and **Lobbes**; and E **Ham-sur-Heure**).—*13km* **Beaumont**.—*12km Rance*.—*10km* **Chimay**.—South of Beaumont this Rte runs down the centre of the wooded BOTTE DU HAINAUT, a narrow 'boot' of land bounded by France to the W and S, and by the province of Namur to the east.

The direct road to Beaumont is N53 through Gozée and Strée, the latter name deriving from the Latin 'strata' and recalling that this was a Roman road. The main places of interest, the abbeys of Aulne and Lobbes and the town of Thuin, are to the W along the Sambre. Close to one another, they may be reached either from Gozée or by following minor roads along the Sambre from Charleroi.

12km Gozée, 3km E of which is **Ham-sur-Heure** with an imposing castle, dating from the 11C but virtually rebuilt in the 18–19C and now used for municipal purposes. The *Eglise Saint Martin* contains a 12C font and, in the porch, a 15C carved 'Apostles' beam.

The ruins of the abbey of **Aulne** (Mid April–mid October: Monday–Friday or Saturday, 09.00 to 12.00, 13.30 to 20.00. Mid October–mid April: Monday–Friday or Saturday, 13.30 to 16.00; Sunday, 09.30 to 12.30, 13.30 to 16.00), 3km NW of Gozée, are pleasantly sited in wooded surroundings beside the Sambre. Founded in 657 in an alder ('aune') grove by monks from Lobbes, led by St. Ursmer with possibly also St. Landelin, the abbey became Cistercian in 1144 and prospered sufficiently to earn the name 'Aulne-la-Riche'. Though sacked in the 15th and 16C and largely burnt by French revolutionaries in 1794, some of the domestic buildings (mainly 18C) were saved and have been restored as a home for the aged. The now ruined church was built between 1214 and 1250, the original plan and a Romanesque doorway from this surviving. The most conspicuous remains are the 16C apse and parts of the transepts and something of the W front of 1728.

Thuin (13,000 inhab.), 6km S of Aulne, sprawls over high ground above the Sambre. Once a strongly fortified place, the town's walls were razed in 1408 on the orders of John the Fearless after he had crushed Liège, until then overlord of Thuin. The Place du Chapitre, with a view-point, is the town centre, here standing the tower of the *Belfry* (1638), all that now remains of the former collegiate church. Across the road the building known as the *Tour Notger* has as its base a relic of the fortifications built by Bishop Notger of Liège in c 1000. A short way up the main street the post office occupies the 16C refuge of the abbey of Lobbes, while opposite is that of the abbey of Aulne of about the same date. The S-shaped 300m-long viaduct bridge over the Sambre is a noteworthy modern feature.

Lobbes (5000 inhab.), 2km NW of Thuin across the Sambre, is known for its Benedictine abbey, founded in c 654 by St. Landelin, a repentant brigand of noble birth associated also with Aulne. Destroyed by the French in 1794, all that survives of the mainly 18C domestic buildings are a gateway and a wing of a farm near the station. The abbey's hilltop *Eglise Saint Ursmer*, dedicated to the builder of Aulne who was a monk here, dates in part from c 825 and is an outstanding example of pre-Romanesque and Romanesque building. The E crypt, chancel and W tower are all 11C, but the central tower and the roof of the W tower are additions of 1865.

Immediately S of Gozée, the menhir known as the *Pierre de Zeupire* stands to the E of the road.—*13km* (from Gozée) **Beaumont**, see Rte 26A.—*8km Sautin*, 1km SW of which are two menhirs called the *Pierres-qui-tournent*. At *Renlies*, 3km NE of Sautin, the church of 1572 houses a particularly fine retable of 1530 and at *Sivry*, 3km W of Sautin, there is a natural history museum (Monday–Saturday, 10.00 to 17.00; Sunday and Holidays in Easter–September, 14.00 to 18.00; closed mid December–mid January).—*4km Rance* is known for the red marble quarried here, used, for example, in the chimneypieces at Versailles and the columns of St. Peter's at Rome (Museum. April–October: Monday–Saturday, 09.30 to 18.00; Sunday, 14.00 to 18.00. November–March: Monday–Saturday, 08.30 to 17.00).

10km **Chimay** (9000 inhab. Tourist Information: 1 Grand-Place) is a pleasant town above the Eau Blanche. The chronicler Froissart, canon and treasurer of the collegiate church, died here in 1410 and is commemorated by a statue in the Place Froissart. In the Grand-Place, with a monument to the princes of Chimay, stands the *Collégiale Saints Pierre et Paul*, the three E bays of the choir dating from the 13C but the remainder of the church being largely 16C with a tower of 1732. Inside are the mausoleum of Charles de Croy (died 1525), first Prince of Chimay, and the tombstone of Mme Tallien (see below). A stone arch in the Grand-Place marks the entrance to an attractive, short and narrow street at the end of which stands the *Château* (Easter–October: daily, 09.00 to 12.00, 14.00 to 18.00), high above the river. Dating from the 15C, the château was much modified in 1607, badly damaged by fire in 1935, and then rebuilt on the original lines.

The property passed to the De Croy family at the start of the 15C, and in 1486 Charles de Croy was created Prince of Chimay by Maximilian. Here in 1835 died the lady best know as Madame Tallien (Jeanne Marie Ignace Thérèse Cabarrus, born 1773), a colourful figure of the French revolutionary period. Daughter of a Spanish banker, she married and was divorced from the Marquis de Fontenay and in 1793 found herself a prisoner in Bordeaux. Here Jean Tallien, in charge of the Terror, fell in love with his prisoner, who then helped him in his Thermidor coup against Robespierre, whom she hated. Tallien married her and she gained the name of 'Notre-Dame de Thermidor', becoming a leading figure in the revolutionary salons. In 1802 Tallien divorced her and three years later she married the Prince de Chimay.

Most of the valuable contents of the château were saved from the fire of 1935. These include family portraits, including one of Mme Tallien, and also many souvenirs of the 18–19C. The small Rococo theatre, used now during Chimay's summer festival, was built for Mme Tallien by her son Prince Joseph. Some Louis XI banners hang in the chapel.

The *Etang de Virelles*, 3km NE, arranged for water sports and as a recreation area, is the largest lake in Belgium (125ha).

C. Charleroi to Couvin

Total distance 38km.—*10km Somzée.*—*12km* **Philippeville**.—*12km* **Mariembourg**.—*4km* **Couvin**.

10km Somzée is in the province of Namur. At *Thy-le-Château*, 3km W, the great feudal castle of the 10–12C houses a collection of paintings by Charles Delporte (May–mid September: Saturday, Sunday and Holidays, 14.00 to 18.00).—*12km* **Philippeville**, see Rte 26A.—To the E, rather over halfway between Philippeville and Mariembourg, lies the village of *Roly* where a fortified farm (small museum) dates in part from the 12C and where the estate is a nature reserve with waymarked walks and drives.—*12km* **Mariembourg** was built as a fortress in 1542 by Charles V and named for his sister Mary of Hungary. Supposed to be impregnable, it was taken by the French in 1554, a loss which led to the building of Philippeville. Little trace now remains of the place's military past, but from an earlier period the *Chapelle Notre-Dame de la Brouffe* is a survival from a priory of 1134. A steam train which runs between Mariembourg and Treignes in the valley of the Viroin is a spring and summer attraction (round trip 2 hours; three or more trains daily between April and September: Saturday, Sunday, Holidays; also Tuesday, Wednesday, Thursday in July and August).

4km **Couvin** (5000 inhab.), a pleasant small town on the Eau Noire, is a popular centre for drives and walks in the surrounding countryside of forest and rocky and wooded hills. In the *Cavernes de l'Abîme* (June–August: daily, 10.00 to 12.00, 14.00 to 18.00; April, May, September: Sunday, same times. Duration 45 minutes) have long served both as home and refuge; to prehistoric man, to the Romans, throughout medieval times and in 1940 to most of the people of Couvin. Today the visitor is offered an exhibition on prehistory and an audio-visual show.

A small road runs E from Couvin, following the valley of the Viroin (the combined Eau Noire and Eau Blanche) close to this being several attractive small places within c 10km of Couvin. The first is **Petigny**, where the *Grotte de Neptune* (Easter–September: daily, 09.30 to 12.00, 13.30 to 18.00. Also Sunday in October. Duration 45 minutes) was discovered at the end of the 19C. The visit includes a boat ride on the underground Eau Noire followed by a Son et Lumière close to a waterfall. The *Barrage du Ry de Rome*, 3km S of Petigny, is a large reservoir (24ha) in a forest setting.—Beyond Petigny, along the Viroin valley, *Nismes, Olloy* and *Dourbes* are all pleasant small resorts offering local attractions (castle ruins, rock formations, geological features such as the holes known as the Fondry des Chiens etc., and signed walks).

Forest extends to the S of Couvin. Here *Brûly-de-Pesche* (6km SW) was the site of Hitler's bunker headquarters in 1940 (Easter–September: daily 09.00 to 12.00. 13.00 to 18.30. Also Sunday in October). The main N5 runs S from Couvin to reach the French border in 10km.

27 Brussels to Namur

Total distance 53km.—*13km* **Overijse**.—*8km* **Wavre**.—*16km* **Gembloux**.—*16km* **Namur**.—This Rte roughly parallels the motorway A4/E411.

Brussels, see Rte 1, is left by the Chaussée de Wavre, the road crossing a corner of the Forêt de Soignes (Rte 1 F.).—*13km* **Overijse** (12,000 inhab.), on the southern edge of a grape growing district, sprawls down a steep hill into the valley of the Ijse. The town centre is the Justus Lipsiusplein, named for the scholar (1547–1606) born here; mainly a classical historian, he taught at Louvain, Jena, Cologne, Antwerp and Leiden. Behind the *Stadhuis* (16C, perhaps to a design by Antoon Keldermans), No. 10 Isidoor Taymansstraat was the birthplace of Lipsius. The *Château*, now a school, is mainly 17C. Of the *Begijnhof* (founded before 1267), in the W part of the town close to a sports complex, only the restored 15C chapel survives.

Huldenberg (3km NE) has a church of the 11–14C, containing statues of c 1400 of the Virgin, St. Catherine and St. Barbara and also an Assumption attributed to De Crayer. The château, much altered, dates from 1514.

La Hulpe, Genval and **Rixensart**. Other than Tombeek (see below) there is little of interest along the main road to Wavre. Instead, a short detour (some 8km extra) may be made through wooded country to the W, following N253 across the motorway to **La Hulpe** (**Terhulpen**) where the partly 13C church contains the gravestone of Charles Baillie (1542–1625), a secretary of Mary, Queen of Scots. **Genval**, immediately SE and with a lake, is a holiday and recreation centre, here too being a spring giving Schweppes mineral water. **Rixensart**, immediately SE again, is best known for its large *Château de Mérode* (Easter–October: Saturday, Sunday, Holidays, 14.00 to 18.00; also daily in July), built between 1631–62 and since 1787 the property of the De Mérode family. The attractive court is laid out in the form of a cloister with galleries of flattened arches, and inside the château may be seen tapestries; family portraits; a collection of Arab weapons brought from Egypt by Gaspard Monge who had directed archaeological and scientific studies during Napoleon's campaign in that country; and the lance-pennon of Frédéric de Mérode, killed during the 1830 revolution, whose memorial is in the Place des Martyrs in Brussels.—Wavre, on the main Rte, is reached through Bierges, see below.

2km (from Overijse) *Tombeek*. Just beyond the village is the Belgian broadcasting station, opposite being the Ferme des Templiers, an estate given to the Templars in c 1180 by Godfrey III of Brabant. After the suppression of the Order in 1312 the property passed to the Knights of Malta in whose hands it remained until the French Revolution. Except for a chapel of 1643 today's buildings (private) are 18th and 19C.—The language frontier is crossed just beyond Tombeek.

6km **Wavre** (Flem. **Waver**. 26,000 inhab. Tourist Information: Hôtel de Ville), an old and pleasant town on the Dyle, was much destroyed by bombing in 1940 but rebuilding has in part been in the old style.

On a site known to have been occupied in prehistoric and Roman times, the present town traces its origins to the 11C when a trading centre grew at this important crossroads and river crossing. A charter was granted in 1222, but from the 15C onwards Wavre saw much of war. In 1489, after rebelling against Maximilian, it was pillaged and burnt; in the late 16th and early 17C it again suffered, this time at the hands of the Spanish; in 1647 it was sacked by the Dutch;

in 1815, on the day of Waterloo, it was the scene of a battle between the French under Grouchy (see below) and the Prussians; and in May 1940 150 houses and the Hôtel de Ville were destroyed by bombing.

Marshal (Marquis de) Grouchy, in command of Napoleon's right flank, pursued Blücher's Prussians as they retreated from Ligny to Wavre. Through his rigid adherence to ill-drafted and contradictory orders he pressed on to Wavre instead of turning W towards Waterloo and thus both cutting off the Prussians and bringing Napoleon badly needed support. Later he was held partly responsible for the French defeat, court-martialled, and for a while exiled. See also Walhain, below.

The *Hôtel de Ville* is of unusual interest, occupying as it does the buildings of a Carmelite friary. Built in 1715–26, the friary was disestablished in 1797, the town soon afterwards acquiring the buildings. The friary church was only closed as such in 1856, later being used as a public hall. Largely destroyed in 1940, the building was carefully restored and officially reopened in 1961. The window on the soaring façade pictures the lords of Wavre handing over the keys. The *Eglise Saint Jean-Baptiste*, down the Rue Haute opposite the Hôtel de Ville, was built in c 1476 but later three times ravaged by fire: in 1489 during the uprising against Maximilian, in 1582 during the wars of religion, and in 1604 at the hands of mutinous Spanish soldiery. The tower, striped in white stone, grew in stages between the 15–17C. A curiosity of the interior is a French bullet of 1815 which remains lodged in one of the pillars. The *Musée Historique et Archéologique* (Wednesday and Saturday, 14.00 to 16.00), at 23 Rue de l'Ermitage, includes material on a Roman villa excavated near Basse Wavre in 1904 (nothing now to be seen on site).

Bierges (2km W) saw heavy fighting on the afternoon of 18 June 1815 as the French tried to cross the river. A memorial by the mill records that the French General Gérard was wounded here. *Walibi*, nearby, is a popular recreation park with many attractions for children.—At *Basse Wavre*, 2km NE of Wavre, the 18C church owns a copper-gilt reliquary, a gift from the Archbishop of Mechelen in 1628 to replace one destroyed by iconoclasts in 1580; it contains relics of various saints and martyrs. The high ground NW of the railway was the site of a Roman settlement, and the villa referred to above lay on the slope.

A diversion may be made into the rural district to the SE of Wavre and N of the motorway. Here at *Chaumont-Gistoux* (9km from Wavre) there are tumuli and earthwork traces of a prehistoric settlement (Bois de Chaumont, NW of the village) and there are more tumuli between this site and (NW) *Bonlez* where the château is in part of 1230. The hamlet of *Dion Valmont* (W of Bonlez) was mentioned in a document of 987.

5km ***Louvain-la-Neuve** is a new and fast growing university complex and town started for French-speaking students after the language-split at Louvain university in 1970. Sprawling over a district of small hills towards Ottignies the project is offering scope for daring and imaginative planning and architecture, with, in large part, an upper level town for pedestrians and cyclists while the ground level is for roads and car parks. The buildings are of pleasing light brickwork and to a variety of modern designs which give some interesting architectural vistas.—*2km Corbais*. In the village stand the remains of a 12th or 13C defensive keep, the Tour Griffon. A better preserved keep (1324), once forming part of a manor house, will be found on a river islet at *Alvaux*, reached by continuing along N4 for 1km and then following a narrow road W for 1.5km.—*4km Walhain* (1.5km E of the main road) is associated with Marshal Grouchy (see under Wavre). On 18 June he arrived here in time for a late breakfast, disturbed by the sound of the opening cannonade at Waterloo; but, although urged by his staff to 'march to the guns', Grouchy refused, instead obstinately sticking to Napoleon's woolly instruction that he should 'head for Wavre'. Out of the village the Rue du Château leads S past the overgrown remains of a (?13C) castle. *Baudeset*, just beyond, is thought to cover the site of a Roman fort.

Gentinnes is 7km SW of the Walhain crossroads. The château here was given in 1903 to the Order of Saint Esprit and used for the training of missionaries for the Congo. The château is still the house of the Order, in front standing a striking sculpture by Raf Mailleux and the austere but effective chapel (Charles Jeandrain) which together form a monument (1967) to the missionaries who lost their lives in the troubles at the time of the granting of independence in 1962. The façade bears the names of 181 Catholic missionaries and of 30 Protestant victims. Inside the chapel the altar is of Congo granite and the benches of Congo wood.

5km **Gembloux** (17,500 inhab. Tourist Information: Ancien Hôtel de Ville), in the province of Namur, is an agricultural and sugar-refining centre, also known for cutlery. The once powerful and learned Benedictine *Abbey*, founded in 940 by St. Guibert (a Lotharingian military leader who became a hermit on his estate here) and last rebuilt by Dewez in 1760–79, is now a college of agronomy. Beside the main entrance stands a section of the old wall. The parish church (Dewez, 1779), formerly the abbey church, has an 11C crypt. In the Rue de Mazy in the S of the town a restored 17C chapel commemorates a victory of Don John of Austria over the 'Gueux' (1577). The great castle of *Corroy-le-Château* (May–September: Saturday, Sunday, Holidays, 10.00 to 12.00, 14.00 to 18.00), 3km SW of Gembloux, was started in c 1270 and has seven solid round towers, linked by massive walls which, though now roofed, were formerly crenallated. Built as part of a defensive system for southern Brabant, the castle in fact saw little fighting and has thus little changed in outward appearance. The interior shows furniture, portraits, a painting by Van Dyck and a collection of dolls. In the village, the church, also little altered, dates from the early 12C; it is known that St. Norbert preached here in 1119.

The Château of *Mielmont* (approx. Easter–September: Saturday, Sunday and Holidays, 14.00 to 18.00) is 5km S of Corroy-le-Château and immediately N of the E42 motorway. Dating from 1160, the castle has since been much rebuilt; the interior shows pictures mainly concerned with the history of Belgium.

16km **Namur**, see Rte 28.

28 Namur

NAMUR (Flem. **Namen**. 102,000 inhab.), capital of the province of the same name and a town of both character and interest, lies largely to the N of the confluence of the Meuse and the Sambre, this point being below a steep hill crowned by the fortifications of the citadel. Although of ancient origin, the town's strategic position and its defences have cursed it with a violent history which has obliterated most traces of medieval and earlier times. Much, however, survives from the 17th and 18C, thanks in part to edicts of 1687 and 1708 forbidding timbered housing and thatch.

Tourist Information. *Town:* Square Léopold, close to the station. *Province of Namur:* 3 Rue Notre-Dame, across the Sambre beyond the Pont du Musée.

Teleferic to the Citadel from S end of Pont du Musée. April–mid November: daily, 10.00 to 18.00, but Sunday only after mid September.

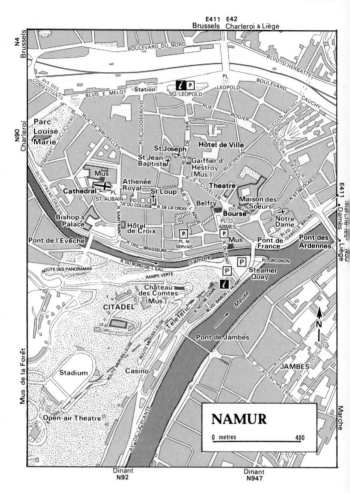

NAMUR

0 metres _____ 400

Boats. Local Sambre et Meuse cruise. Mid April–mid September: five times daily between 10.00 and 17.00, but afternoon only in April and September. Duration 45 minutes.—To *Dinant*. July and August: Sunday, 10.00 or 11.00. Duration 9 hours. It is advisable to check on round-trip timings between Namur and Dinant as these are liable to change.—To *Wépion*. July and August: Tuesday, Thursday, Saturday, 14.30. Duration 2 hours.

History. Namur has been suggested as being the site of the stronghold of the Aduatuci tribe mentioned by Caesar, but the place enters authentic history in the Merovingian period as Namurcum Castrum, at this time simply the citadel and the spit of land between the rivers. Early becoming a commercial centre, Namur had by the 10C developed into a feudal holding, the rulers of which soon styled themselves counts. In 1421 Count Jean III de Dampierre sold the county to Philip the Good of Burgundy. Of the town's many sieges the three most notorious are those of 1577 when it fell to Don John of Austria; of 1692 when taken by Vauban for Louis XIV, who was himself present; and of 1695 when the place was retaken by William of Orange. It was seized by French revolutionary forces in 1792 and 1794, thereafter until 1814 being the capital of the French department of Sambre-et-Meuse. In 1815 there was a gallant stand here by Grouchy's rearguard. The fortifications, dismantled by Joseph II in 1782–84, were rebuilt by the Dutch (United Kingdom of the Netherlands) in 1816, only to be razed in 1862–65 and replaced by boulevards and gardens. In 1887, however, the construction of an outer ring of nine forts made Namur once more an important fortress; but its supposed impregnability was disproved in August 1914 when the Germans silenced the forts in three days, afterwards burning and looting parts of the town. More damage, notably the destruction of bridges, was suffered in the Second World War. In April 1975, after perhaps 2000 years, the last army unit left the citadel and the keys were handed over to the town.—Charles de Berlaymont (1510–78), councillor to Margaret of Parma, was a native, as was also in more recent times the painter and engraver Félicien Rops (1833–98).

The main artery of the town is the Rue de Fer, prolonged by the Rue de l'Ange, the two linking Square Léopold near the station with the Place d'Armes close to the confluence of the rivers. These two roads cover a direct distance of 1km, but the tour suggested below, including the cathedral and other places to the W, is, as far as the Place d'Armes, rather over 2km in length.

In the Rue de Fer there are a number of 18C mansions, including the *Hôtel de Ville* (left, best seen from the garden) and at No. 24, also on the left, the *Hôtel Gaiffier d'Hestroy*, now housing two museums. The *Musée Félicien Rops* (Monday–Friday except Tuesday, 10.00 to 12.00, 14.00 to 17.00, Saturday, 10.00 to 12.00, Sunday, 14.00 to 17.00. Closed 23 December–3 January) contains many examples of the work of this versatile artist: paintings, drawings, engravings, small sculpture, and book illustrations which include those for Charles de Coster's 'Ulenspiegel'. The *Musée des Arts Anciens du Namurois* (Monday–Friday except Tuesday, 10.00 to 12.00, 14.00 to 17.00; Saturday 14.00 to 17.00; Sunday, 10.00 to 12.00. Closed 23 December–3 January) exhibits local painting, sculpture, metalwork, etc., largely of the 14–17C. The *Eglise Saint Joseph* opposite is of 1650. Beyond the next intersection the road becomes the Rue de l'Ange at once leading into the Place de l'Ange with a fountain of 1791.

To the right, a little farther on, the *Eglise Saint Jean Baptiste* stands in the quiet little Marché aux Légumes. In part the oldest church in Namur (13C), today's building is mainly 16C with restoration and additions of 1616 and 1890. Of the early furnishing only the font survives.

The Rue de la Croix leads W past the Baroque **Eglise Saint Loup**, built for the Jesuits in 1621–45. Features of the interior are the extensive use of marble of different colours and the carved sandstone vaulting. The altar is of wood painted as marble, this deception being necessary because the ship bringing the marble altar from Italy was wrecked at Calais where the altar was seized and placed in that town's church. Farther on, in the Rue du Collège, the *Athénée Royal* of 1614 was the Jesuit college. The Rue du Collège ends at the PLACE SAINT AUBAIN, with the offices of the *Provincial Government* in the former episcopal palace (1726–40) and, opposite, the **Cathédrale Saint Aubain**, a Neo-Classical work by Gaetano Pizzoni (stucco by the Moretti brothers), built in 1751–67 on the site of a succession of older churches the first of which was consecrated in the 3C. The tower (1388, heightened 1648) behind the apse is all that is left of the church pulled down in 1751. Among features of the interior are pictures by artists of the school of Rubens (the Jesuit priest J. Nicolai, and Nicolas Roose); a Calvary attributed to Van Dyck; works by Jacques Baudin and (attributed) Gaspard de Crayer; and, behind the high-altar, a tablet

covering the heart of Don John of Austria who died in camp at Bouge,
just NE of Namur, soon after his successful assault on the town.

The **Musée Diocésain** is the cathedral treasury (Easter–October:
daily except Monday, 10.00 to 12.00, 14.30 to 18.00. November–
Easter: daily except Monday, 14.00 to 16.30. Closed all Sunday
afternoon). Outstanding here are a golden crown-reliquary (13C)
with two thorns from the Crown of Thorns; a 14C silver-gilt statuette
of St. Blaise (died c 316), a physician saint from Armenia who became
known in Europe through returning crusaders; a 12C portable altar
with 11C ivory panels; a silver-gilt reliquary arm, attributed to Hugo
d'Oignies; and a 9C reliquary from Andenne.

From the cathedral the Rue Saintraint leads S, with on the left the
18C **Hôtel de Croix** (Daily except Tuesday. Guided tours at 10.00,
11.00, 14.00, 15.00, 16.00. Closed 23 December–3 January), successor
to a building of 1605 which was a refuge of the abbey of Villers. The
mansion now serves as a museum illustrating artistic achievement in
the Namur region during the 18C. The material includes furniture;
portraits; paintings of the sieges of Namur; flower paintings by
Joseph Redouté; sculpture and porcelain by Jacques Richardot;
Vonèche glass; Namur clocks, notably a grandfather in marble
(1759); silver; sculpture by Laurent Delvaux; porcelain, largely from
Saint Servais and Andenne; and an 18C game of Lotto with delightful
cards illustrating trades of the period. In the kitchen the fireplace is in

The Citadel at Namur

part from the original refuge.

Beyond the Hôtel de Croix, the Rue des Brasseurs, with several 17–19C houses which include (168–177) the home of Félicien Rops, bears E to cross the Place Maurice Servais, with more period houses, and end at the Rue du Pont.

The PLACE D'ARMES is a few paces to the left. Here the *Bourse* has replaced the 19C Hôtel de Ville, burnt down in 1914. Behind is the *Tour Saint Jacques* (or *Beffroi*, belfry), a surviving tower of the late 14C walls, provided with a bells-chamber in 1746. Immediately NE of the Bourse is the PLACE DU THEATRE, off which the Rue de la Tour and the Rue Julie Billiart respectively run S and SE, in the former being a small ramparts-tower known as the *Tour Spillar* and in the latter the **Maison des Soeurs de Notre-Dame** sheltering the **Treasury of the Priory of Oignies*, hidden from the revolutionaries when the priory was sacked in 1794. Here can be seen superb examples of the early 13C work of Hugo d'Oignies, including an evangelistery cover, a silver-gilt chalice, a reliquary for St. Peter's rib, two magnificent double-crosses (one bearing enamel portraits) and several phylacteries (Daily except Sunday morning and Tuesday, 10.00 to 12.00, 14.00 to 17.00. Closed Holidays and 11 November–25 December). A short way beyond (right) there survives a 17C portal of what was once a refuge of the abbey of Floreffe, while, beyond again (100m E by the Rue de

Gravière), is the **Eglise Notre-Dame** (1775, but successor to others), built by Franciscan Recollects. Inside, a figure of St. Anthony is by Laurent Delvaux and the high-altar is by Denis Bayart, while an inscription to the left of the latter records that counts William I (died 1391) and William II (died 1418) of Namur are buried here. By the church entrance can be seen the old façade of the *Hospice d'Harscamp,* the former Franciscan convent, with the modern hospital buildings behind.

The modern hospital fronts on to the Boulevard Isabelle Brunell (Countess of Harscamp), the name commemorating the hospital's founder (1805), a statue of whom (Willem Geefs, 1872) stands in the quayside garden. To the E, by the Pont des Ardennes of 1957, a striking modern sculpture by Rodolphe Strebelle depicts the Quatre Fils Aymon and their horse Bayard.

From the Place d'Armes the Rue du Pont soon reaches the Sambre, on the left before the bridge being the **Ancienne Boucherie** (1560), the one-time meat hall, now used for municipal purposes and also housing the *Musée Archéologique* (Daily, 10.00 to 17.00, but closed Friday between Easter and 1 November and Tuesday between 1 November–Easter; open 11.00 on Saturday, Sunday, Holidays). The museum contains notable prehistoric, Gallo-Roman, Merovingian and Early Christian collections, most from the province of Namur. The glass-walled building behind the Ancienne Boucherie is the *Palais de la Culture* (1961); and on the river bank below stands the *Porte de Sambre-et-Meuse* (D. Bayart, 1728).

Between the Rivers

To the S of the Place d'Armes two bridges cross the Sambre at its mouth, these being the Pont du Musée (Rue du Pont) on the W and the Pont de France to the east. Beyond, open space, gardens, and some busy roads fill the pointed spit formed by the confluence of the two rivers. Where the rivers meet (Place Grognon) there is an equestrian statue of King Albert while, facing the square, two figures symbolise the union of the rivers. The boat excursions quay is a short way S on the Meuse. The road ascending the Meuse (Boulevard Baron L. Huart) passes the Pont de Jambes, also known as the Pont de Meuse, first built in the 11C but now a new bridge replacing a predecessor blown up in 1944, and then (right) the *Casino* (from 14.00, or 13.00 on Sunday), behind which ascends the Route Merveilleuse, one of the approaches to the citadel.

The small road parallel to Boulevard Baron L. Huart is the Rue Notre-Dame, at the N end of which (No. 3), opposite the citadel teleferic, is the Province of Namur Tourist Information. The building here separating the two roads was the 17C *Hospice Saint Gilles.*

The N side of the citadel hill is skirted by the Rue du Bord-de-l'Eau along the S bank of the Sambre, on the left being the *Rampe Verte,* a footway to the citadel, and, farther on, the *Porte Bordiale* (1766), the only survivor of the town gates. Just beyond, the Route des Panoramas ascends to the citadel, while, opposite, the Pont de l'Evêché crosses the Sambre to the *Evêché* (Bishop's Palace), occupying the former refuge of the abbey of Malonnes.

The CITADEL divides broadly into two areas, the Mediane to the E, this including the ancient stronghold of the counts and the fortifications of the 15th and 16C, and the Terra Nova to the W, with later defences. It can be reached by either of the two roads mentioned above (Route Merveilleuse, Route des Panoramas), by the Rampe

Verte, by the teleferic, or in summer by a bus service (roughly hourly) starting from the station. There is also a 'Tourist Train' which during the season covers much of the area.

The Route des Panoramas winds upwards into the 'Terra Nova' to skirt (left, near the top) the area of the *Fort d'Orange*, built in 1690 but largely demolished by the Dutch in 1816 when they rebuilt the whole citadel, preserving only the older foundations; on the E is the *Centre Attractif Reine Fabiola*, a children's recreation area. At this point the road becomes the Route Merveilleuse, soon passing the **Musée de la Forêt** (April–October: daily, 09.00 to 12.00, 14.00 to 17.00. Closed Friday, other than Easter and from mid June to mid September) occupying a building of 1910 in hunting-lodge style standing on the site of a former fort. The material, which includes some fine dioramas and a vivarium, covers most aspects of Belgium's forests.

Beyond, the road rounds the sports stadium, passing an open-air theatre and the upper station of the teleferic, and then drops to the Mediane area with the *Château des Comtes*, now simply two towers only the foundations of which are original. Here is the historic fortified heart of the Citadel. In season visits (by the light of flares) may be made to the casemates and lower fortifications, and there is also the **Musée d'Armes et d'Histoire Militaire** (Easter–September: daily, 10.00 to 18.00) with a large and varied collection, among the sections being the military history of Europe with particular reference to Namur, the sieges of Namur, the Middle Ages, the First and Second World Wars, Africa, and the Orient.

The road now snakes round under itself, offering a view of the confluence of the rivers before winding down to the Meuse near the Casino.

For the suburb of **Jambes**, on the right bank of the Meuse, see Rte 31.

For Namur to *Brussels*, see Rte 27; to *Charleroi*, see Rte 25; to *Dinant*, see Rte 29; to *Bastogne, Arlon* and *Luxembourg*, see Rte 33; to *Liège*, see Rte 31.

29 Namur to Dinant (Continuing to Givet, and to Rochefort and Han)

As far as Dinant (24km) this Route is in two parts: the main road up the left bank of the Meuse, and the smaller and rather winding road up the right bank. Both roads are scenic, keeping close to the river which flows between steep rock- and wood-covered hills. There are road bridges N and S of Profondeville, at Annevoie and at Yvoir; also a footbridge beside the railway 1km S of the Yvoir road bridge. For boat travel, see Rte 28 and under Dinant below.

South of Dinant this Route continues to Givet in France (21km), and to Rochefort and Han-sur-Lesse (37km).

A. Left Bank of the Meuse

Total distance 24km.—*5km Wépion.*—*5km Profondeville.*—*4km* **Annevoie.**—*4km Anhée,* for **Molignée Valley.**—*4km* **Bouvignes.**— *2km* **Dinant.**

Namur, see Rte 28, is left by Rue Baron L. Huart passing the Casino.—*5km Wépion*, a small resort straggling along the river, has since 1895 been known for its strawberries (museum).—*5km Profondeville*, another riverside resort and standing opposite picturesque and rocky cliffs, traces its origins to Roman times and claims also that it was here that the monks of Fosses-la-Ville hid the relics of St. Foillan when their abbey was sacked by the Norsemen.—*4km* **Annevoie** is best known for its beautiful *Château Gardens* (Gardens: April–October: daily, 09.00 to 19.00. Château: Easter–June, and September: Saturday, Sunday, Holidays, 09.30 to 13.00, 14.00 to 18.30. July and August: daily, same times). Laid out in 1775, with lakes and fountains, the gardens are in French, Italian and English styles, and special floral displays are mounted according to the season. The château (18C but with a 17C tower) has stucco work by the Moretti brothers.—*4km Anhée* is an attractive small resort at the foot of the picturesque Molignée valley.

MOLIGNEE VALLEY. This narrow, winding and wooded valley offers a worthwhile scenic diversion at least as far as Maredret (15km). After a little under 2km a large farm building, once an abbey, is passed (left).—*6km* (from Anhée) the ruined castle of *Montaigle* (left, and look backwards) clings to a spur of rock. Built in the 13C by Guy de Dampierre, it was blown up by the French in 1554.—At (*4km*) *Falaen* there is a particularly good fortified farm of 1670; local art exhibitions are held here in summer.—*4km*. The imposing Neo-Gothic buildings of the Benedictine abbey complex of **Maredsous**, founded in 1872, cover a high ridge. The large, austere church is normally open, and in the Centre Grégoire Fournier there are an audio-visual presentation on monastic life and a cultural exhibition (May–August: Monday–Saturday, 10.00 to 12.30, 13.30 to 18.00. September: Sunday, 11.00 to 13.00, 14.00 to 19.00). The sister convent (1891) of *Maredret* is a short way farther W, in the village here being craft exhibitions and also a Musée du Bois showing 18–20C woodwork (Daily except Wednesday, but open Wednesday in July and August, 09.30 to 12.30, 14.00 to 18.00).

4km **Bouvignes**, where the visitor should turn off the through-road and into this small town which, although now something of a backwater, has a story reaching back to 882 when the place was first mentioned. A fortress here built in the 11C by the Count of Namur was strengthened by town walls in 1176, while in 1320 the castle of *Crèvecoeur*, now no more than a ruin above the town, was built. All this fortification grew largely out of a deep enmity and commercial rivalry between Bouvignes (belonging to Namur) and Dinant (belonging to Liège), a rivalry accentuated by the granting of a charter to the former in 1213 and finally 'resolved' only in 1964 when Dinant officially absorbed Bouvignes; but an indication of local feeling is clear from an inscription above the entrance to the Maison Espagnole (see below), '1213 Bouvignons nous étions. 1964 Bouvignons nous resterons.'

Both towns were sacked and burnt by the French in 1554, an occasion from which stems the tale of the three ladies of Crèvecoeur, widows of the castle's defenders, who heroically took over until, finding themselves without ammunition, they leapt hand-in-hand from the battlements. In the square stands the 16C *Hôtel de Ville*, also known as the *Maison Espagnole* or the Baillage; inside there is an exhibition of local history and crafts (Easter–October: daily, 09.00 to 12.00, 14.00 to 18.00). The *Eglise Saint Lambert* dates from c 1200 but was altered in the 15C, again after the French siege of 1554 and yet again during the 18C; after war damage in 1914 the restoration aimed at achieving the pre-1554 appearance. Particularly noteworthy inside

are an early 16C polychrome Antwerp *Retable, a lively representation of the Passion, with over 50 figures, showing a curious mixture of
East and West in their costume; and a poignant wooden *Bon Dieu de
Pitié (early 16C). On the N side of the church stands the main town
gate, flanked by two small fortified towers. Bouvignes may have been
the birthplace of St. Walhere, and was that in 1480 of the painter Herri
met de Bles.

2km **Dinant**, see below.

B. Right Bank of the Meuse

Total distance 24km.—*11km Lustin Station.*—6km **Yvoir**.—*7km*
Dinant.

Namur, see Rte 28, is left through the suburb of *Jambes* (see Rte
31).—*11km Lustin Station* from where a road climbs the Rochers de
Frênes to a café-belvedere offering a view of the Meuse and where
there is also a small grotto. Lustin village is just beyond.—*6km* **Yvoir**,
a small riverside resort, is at the foot of the winding Bocq valley. (For
Crupet, 6km NE, and *Spontin*, 10km E, see beginning of Rte 33). Out
of Yvoir a road leads in 4km to the ruins of the castle of *Poilvache*
which may also be reached by footpath from Houx, on the river 2km S
of Yvoir. The extensive ruins, 125m above the Meuse, offer oubliettes,
a rock-well and some fine views. By tradition built by the Quatre Fils
Aymon, the castle was certainly in existence in the 10C, serving as a
stronghold of the counts of Namur and of John the Blind of Luxembourg until finally destroyed by Liège in 1430. The castle's name,
meaning 'cow's skin', derives from a successful assault by men who
disguised themselves in skins and hid among the cattle.—Between
Yvoir and Houx will be found the *Musée Vivant de la Forêt* or *Oasis
Nature*, an educational centre and park devoted to the fauna of
Belgium (April–October and Sunday in November: 10.00 to 18.00 or
19.00 in June–August. Sometimes open only to groups). To the S of
Houx there is a good view across the river to the ruins of Crèvecoeur
above Bouvignes.—*6km* (from Yvoir) *Leffe* has a much restored
Premonstratensian abbey, founded in 1152, dissolved in 1794 and
reoccupied in 1902. Today's buildings are 17–20C.—*1km* **Dinant**.

DINANT (12,000 inhab.), picturesquely situated on the Meuse
beneath its almost vertical citadel-cliff and a place with a long and
violent history, is today a very popular tourist centre both for local
attractions as also for excursions on the river and into the western
Ardennes.

Tourist Information. 37 Rue Grande, adjacent to the Casino some 300m S of the
bridge.

Boat Excursions can be made to Anseremme, at the confluence of the Meuse
and Lesse; farther S to Waulsort, Hastière and Heer-Agimont on the French
border, with, sometimes, an extension to Givet; and to Namur. Timings are
generally as below, but there may be additional services on some holidays.
    To *Anseremme*. Easter–mid October: daily every 30 minutes from 10.00 to
11.30 and every 20 minutes from 13.00 to 18.00. Return trip, 45 minutes.
    To *Waulsort, Hastière* and *Heer-Agimont*. Sunday in June, and daily July and
August. Leave Dinant at 14.00, return by 19.00. One hour stop at Heer-Agimont.
Passengers may disembark at Waulsort or Hastière and then catch the return
boat, this allowing about 2½ hours at Waulsort or about 1½ hours at Hastière.
For Waulsort and Hastière, see below under Dinant to Givet.

To *Namur*. June–August, Saturday depart Dinant at 15.00, arrive Namur at 18.30. (Namur to Dinant. June–August: Sunday depart Namur at 10.00 or 11.00.)

Descent of the Lesse. For the popular boat descent of the Lesse (Houyet to Anseremme), see Rte 30.

History. Tradition is that Dinant owes its name to Diana, Roman goddess and huntress. Certainly this place was inhabited in Roman times, later becoming a prosperous medieval town known especially for its 'dinanderie' (articles for domestic or church use made of copper, brass or bronze; by the 14C the population numbered some 50,000 of whom perhaps 7500 were engaged in 'dinanderie'. The industry began to die out during the 19C, but efforts are now being made to revive it). The first fortress on the cliff was built in c 1050 and from then on Dinant was to suffer much from war, some of the early fighting being due to the rivalry with Bouvignes (see Rte 29A). In 1466 Dinant was pillaged and burnt by Charles the Bold, 800 of the inhabitants being bound in couples back to back and thrown into the Meuse. In 1554 the town was again sacked, this time by the French who came again in 1675 when Louis XIV marched in.

In August 1914 the French came as allies, heroically defending the citadel, but on 23 August the Germans occupied the town. Alleging that their troops had been fired on by civilians, they executed 674 citizens, deported 400 more and sacked and burnt the town. Dinant again saw bitter fighting in May 1940, and in September 1944 the town became the target of American artillery during the three days it took to dislodge the Germans from the Citadel.

The painters Joachim Patinir (c 1475–1524) and Antoine Wiertz (1806–65) were natives of Dinant, as was also Adolphe Sax (1814–94) who in 1846 patented the saxophone.

The main town is on the right bank below the Citadel, the Meuse being crossed by a bridge first built by monks from Waulsort in 1080 and which was blown up in 1914 and again in 1944; some of the original piers can be seen in the Citadel. The Gothic **Eglise Notre-Dame** was consecrated in 1240, but has since been several times destroyed and rebuilt, always to the original plan. It stands on the site of a succession of predecessors, by tradition reaching back to a chapel founded by St. Maternus in 320; the last of these was destroyed by a fall of rock in 1227 although some parts can still be seen, notably a sandstone arch on the N exterior and, inside the church (baptistry, right of S entrance), a porch of three carved Romanesque arches. In the S transept there are two pictures by Antoine Wiertz and also a fine modern window by Perot.

The station of the teleferic to the Citadel (see below) is beside the church, and just upstream from the bridge are the embarkation quays for river excursions. The road running S from the church, the narrow Rue Grande, passes (right) the *Hôtel de Ville* (17C; rebuilt after 1918) and then (left in a small garden) an allegorical group called La Triomphe de la Lumière by Antoine Wiertz. Tourist Information is adjacent on Rue Grande, just behind in the hill being the *Grotte de Montfort* (Easter–October: 10.00 to 18.30 or later), a cave associated with the worship of Diana; here a chair-lift (Easter–October) ascends to the *Tour de Montfort* (14C; restored 1910) around which there is a garden and recreation area. From Tourist Information the Rue Grande continues S, becoming Rue Léopold and then Rue Daoust in which an inscription marks the *Mur des Fusillés* commemorating those massacred in August 1914.

Across the river bridge from the Eglise Notre-Dame are the railway station and, some 500m from the bridge, the **Grotte la Merveilleuse** (April–mid October: daily, 11.00 to 16.00 or 10.00 to 17.00 in May–August), known for the whiteness of its formations.

The **Citadel** (Daily, 09.00 to 18.30, but shorter hours out of season), over 100m sheer above the Meuse and offering magnificent views, can be reached by teleferic, by a path of 408 steps cut by the French in

1577, or by road (3km). The main area is shown only by conducted tour (30 minutes), likely to be very crowded in summer. The teleferic is included in the fee which is slightly reduced for those using the steps or who come by car.

It is thought that there was some kind of fortification here by the 4C but that whatever may have been here was wrecked during the 9C by Norsemen. New defensive works were built by the Bishop of Liège in 1051, successive fortresses being many times destroyed and rebuilt until the last major dismantlement by the French in 1707. What is seen today is in all essentials the fort built by the Dutch in 1818–21.

The guided tour includes a part of the casemates; the gallery in which in 1914 trapped French soldiers held out against the Germans for five hours; a memorial commemorating the French and German dead of 1914; prison cells used by the Dutch (today showing a guillotine, instruments of torture, etc.); the Dutch forge, kitchen and bakery; the piers of the 11C Meuse bridge, built by the monks of Waulsort and taken from the river in 1952; the carriage of Mme de Maintenon who stayed at Dinant in 1692 while Louis XIV was besieging Namur; historical dioramas, including one of the visit by Mme de Maintenon; and a small museum of 17–19C arms.

Dinant to Givet (France)

Total distance 21km.—*6km Freyr.—4km Waulsort.—3km*
Hastière.—*5km Heer-Agimont* (frontier).—*3km* **Givet** (France).—
This Rte follows the beautiful left bank of the Meuse; as far as
Heer-Agimont (and, sometimes, Givet) it may be travelled by boat.

Across the river are seen first the Rocher Bayard (see below) and then Anseremme (see Rte 30).—*6km Freyr* has a Château mainly of the 18C, known for its beautiful French-style gardens.—At (*4km*) *Waulsort* a 17C château occupies the site of an abbey established in c 962 by the Irish missionary St. Forannan. It was the monks from here who in 1080 built the first bridge at Dinant (see Citadel, above).—*3km* **Hastière** is a small place in two parts, *Hastière-Lavaux* being on the left bank, with the Grottes du Pont d'Arcole (all year except January and February: daily, 09.00 to 17.00. Closed Tuesday out of season). Across the bridge, *Hastière-Par-Delà* is known for its mixed Romanesque and Gothic church, once belonging to a priory which was subordinate to Waulsort. The church, now much restored, was built between c 1033 and 1260, the crypt being the oldest part. Noteworthy inside are the misericords of the stalls in the apse, some being of the 13C and, with those at Celles, the oldest in Belgium; the tomb of Abbot Allard, responsible for much of the later building; a vivid triptych (1914) by Auguste Donnay depicting the martyrdom of St. Walhere; and an unusual and interesting Vietnamese Stations of the Cross.—*5km Heer-Agimont* is the frontier.—*3km* **Givet**.

Dinant to Rochefort and Han-sur-Lesse

Total distance 37km.—*7km* **Furfooz Park.**—*4km Vêves.—2km*
Celles.—*18km* **Rochefort.**—*6km* **Han-sur-Lesse.**—This Rte traverses
the W part of the Ardennes, known as FAMENNE.

Dinant is left southwards by the right bank of the Meuse, the road soon reaching the *Rocher Bayard*, a detached needle 60m high named after the horse of the Quatre Fils Aymon who dislodged it with his hoof when leaping the river. The road beside the rock was cut by Louis XIV when on his way to seize Dinant in 1675, and a plaque records that King Albert climbed the needle in 1933. Rte 30, through Anseremme, continues S, while this Rte bears E, soon diverting S on to minor roads through Furfooz and Vêves before returning to the main road at Celles.

7km (from Dinant) **Furfooz National Park** (Mid March–mid November: daily, 10.00 to 2 hours before sunset; allow 1½ hours) sprawls over a high cliff promontory within a loop of the Lesse, one stream of which in fact runs underground below the promontory. Cars must be parked outside, and waymarked paths lead past perched view-points, Roman baths (reconstructed on original foundations), earthworks and other traces of a Roman camp, and several 'trous' (deep holes) of both geological and archaeological interest. In the Trou du Frontal, for instance, bones were found of a Mesolithic people.

Small roads lead in *4km* to the dramatic castle of *Vêves* (Easter–All Saints: daily, 11.00 to 12.00, 13.00 to 18.30), standing on a ridge above its village. This site may first have been fortified in c 640, but the castle seen today is 15–16C and much restored, the 17C half-timbered balconies around the court being the perhaps most noteworthy feature. In c 1770 the then owner, the Comte de Beaufort, moved out to his small manor house of Noisy. However his grandson, the Comte de Liedekerke Beaufort (1816–90), found this to be too modest and built the huge 'Scottish-Baronial' *Château de Noisy*, the turrets of which can be glimpsed across the valley; today a part of the château houses a museum of 19C life (Easter–All Saints: daily, 11.00 to 18.30). The park has a picnic area, walks, and a children's playground.—*2km* **Celles**, where the crossroads is a point at which Von Rundstedt was forced to halt his advance in December 1944. The village is known for its part-fortified Romanesque *Eglise Saint Hadelin*, built in c 1035 and an outstanding example of Mosan construction. Hadelin (see also Rte 39), a Merovingian courtier who in c 670 decided to withdraw from the world, established a hermitage here which grew into a monastery the monks of which four centuries later built the present church out of local stone. Inside, the stalls (13C) are, with those at Hastière, the oldest in Belgium; also noteworthy are the splendid marble gravestone of Louis de Beaufort and his wife, and the two crypts, one of the 11C and the other smaller one below the tower possibly of the 8C.

The village of *Foy Notre-Dame*, 2km NW of Celles, is entered through an arch formed by old houses. Behind the church, a short way down the Ciney road, a stone marks a limit of the German advance of December 1944. The church (1623) owes its construction to the Virgin of Foy, a small figure carved in local stone found in 1609 by a woodman inside an oak he had felled on this spot. Soon several miracles occurred and in 1619 Albert and Isabella made a pilgrimage here, as a direct result of which the church was built. The lime in front of the church is said to have been planted on the site of the original oak. The authentic Virgin (14–15C) is rarely seen, a replica often being used since the real figure was stolen (and recovered) in 1974. The church is much visited for its superb and unusual panelled *Ceiling*, with 147 individual portraits, the work of the 17C Dinant artist Michel Stilmant, a pupil of Rubens, also responsible for the design of the church and much of its woodcarving.

4km S of Celles a road forks W and drops 5km through woods to *Houyet* on the Lesse, the starting place for boat trips down the river (see Rte 30).

14km **Rochefort** (10,700 inhab.), on the river Lomme and a popular holiday centre, is known for its *Grotto* (Easter–September: daily, 09.30

to 17.15, roughly hourly). Discovered in 1865 the grotto has marble as well as limestone formations, the main feature being the great Salle du Sabbat, 125m by 65m and 85m high; here, as part of a Son et Lumière and to demonstrate the vastness of the cavern, a small fire-balloon is released. Opposite the road up to the grotto the remains of a feudal castle stand adjacent to a 19C mansion. A monument beside the road recalls the arrest here in 1792 of La Fayette by the Austrians. (He had commanded one of the three French revolutionary armies formed to attack Austria; but his intention was to use this to restore the French monarchy and, declared a traitor, he had to flee France.)

For Rochefort N to *Liège* and S to *Bouillon*, see Rte 35.

6km **Han-sur-Lesse** is a small Ardennes town almost entirely occupied with the tourist business brought by its famous grottoes and its safari park, for which a combined ticket can be bought at a reduced price. Roughly 3½ to 4 hours should be allowed for the combined visit. The *Musée du Monde Souterrain* (Easter–mid October: daily, 10.00 to 12.30, 13.30 to 18.00), by the main car park from where the grottoes tram starts, is devoted to the geology of the local caves and to archaeological finds in or near them.

**Grottoes (Easter–August: daily, every 30 minutes, 09.30 to 11.30, 13.00 to 17.30 or 18.00 in July and August. September–October: daily, hourly, 09.30 to 11.30, 13.00 to 17.00. November–Easter: daily, 2-hourly, 09.30 to 15.30. Closed January and February). Tickets are bought at the office in the town, the caves being reached by a special tram and the visit requiring about two hours. The complex, a series of caverns in Devonian limestone below carboniferous rock first explored in 1814, is some 8km in length, but only a part is visited. Among the caves shown are the Salle du Trophée, 20m high and with the largest stalagmite; the Galerie Lannoy (250m long) leading to the Mystérieuses, four small caves particularly rich in limestone formations; the Salle d'Armes (refreshments), a circular cave 50m across; and the vast Salle du Dôme, 129m high and its lower part filled by a small lake. From here the complex is left by boat along the Lesse, the exit being close to the town.

The *Safari Park* (March–December: daily, 09.30 to 11.30, 13.00 to 17.30 in summer or 15.30 in winter), covering some 250ha of beautiful country, is visited by safari car, the round requiring 1½ hours.

There are two places of interest close to Han-sur-Lesse. *Lessive* (4km NW) is the site of the Belgian Space Communications Centre (May–September: daily, 09.30 to 17.00, or 17.30 in July and August. Duration 1½ hours including film). Features of particular interest are the antennae, a full-scale model of a communications satellite, and the control room.—The château of *Lavaux-Sainte-Anne* (7km W), with massive squat round towers and surrounded by a moat, dates from the 14–17C and today houses a museum of nature and hunting (Daily, 09.00 to 12.00, 13.00 to 18.00).

30 Dinant to Bouillon via the Valley of the Semois

Total distance 81km.—*4km* **Anseremme**.—*15km* **Beauraing**.—*15km Gribelle*.—*18km Bohan*.—*15km Rochehaut*.—*14km* **Bouillon**.

Dinant (see Rte 29) is left southward by the right bank of the Meuse, the road soon passing the *Rocher Bayard* (Rte 29).—*4km* **Anseremme** is a small resort at the mouth of the Lesse, here crossed by a 16C bridge. A railway bridge (footpath) crosses the Meuse.

DESCENT OF THE LESSE. The Lesse is a beautiful river which for much of its lower course (21km between Houyet and Anseremme) flows below steep and wooded hills. The descent of the river by boat (Kayak or crewed larger boat) is a popular excursion, offered by three firms, namely Lesse-Kayaks M.M. Pitance, 2 Place de l'Eglise, Anseremme; Meuse et Lesse Libert Frères, 13–15 Rue Coussin, Dinant; Kayaks Ansiaux, 15 rue du Velodrome, Anseremme. The excursion operates generally May–September and advance booking is strongly advised. Trains leave Aneremme between roughly 08.00 to 10.45 for *Houyet*, starting point for the descent (21km. 5 or more hours), and on the way down the river a number of stops may be made. The best stretch scenically is below *Gendron* (starting point for a shorter trip), beneath the rocky slopes of Furfooz National Park and the castle of Walzin, dating from the 13C but rebuilt in 1581.

At (*3km*) *Falmignoul* there is a private museum on the development of the cycle and motorcycle.—*12km* **Beauraing** (7500 inhab.) has become an important pilgrimage objective since 1932–33 when the Virgin several times appeared before five children. The *Sanctuaire Marial* has in one corner the Jardin de l'Aubépine (Hawthorn Garden), where the appearances took place, and around this has grown a complex which includes a large crypt and upper church and also a museum. The castle, reserved for pilgrims, dates back to the 12C but has 16C towers.—*15km Gribelle*. The direct road to Bouillon (25km) is N95 through Bièvre. This Route bears SW for the *VALLEY OF THE SEMOIS, in 12km touching the French border, near which a right fork leads down a wooded valley to *Bohan* (*18km* from Gribelle) just below which the river flows into France to become called the Semoy. The road (SE) now climbs and descends, generally following the beautiful, winding valley through pleasant villages such as *Membre, Vresse* and *Alle*, all, though decreasingly, occupied with the tobacco industry; drying houses can be seen and there is a museum at Vresse. Just beyond Alle, the border is crossed into the province of Luxembourg.—At (*15km* from Bohan) *Rochehaut* there is a viewpoint beside the road, offering a vista down to the village of Frahan, far below, and a great loop of the river.—*4km Poupehan* where the river is crossed.—*10km* **Bouillon**, see Rte 35.

31   Namur to Liège

Below **Namur** (Rte 28) there are good roads along both banks of the Meuse as far as Namèche (9km; bridge), the main road being that on the S bank.

NORTH BANK. Between *Beez* and *Marche-les-Dames* (7km from Namur) the road runs below the Rocher du Roi where Albert I fell to his death in 1934 while rock-climbing (cross; museum). Marche-les-Dames is a straggling village which by tradition owes the second part of its name to crusaders' wives who settled here in the 11C and may have been the founders of the abbey. This, a short way along the

Gelbressée road, is now a school with buildings largely of the 18C although the church, with a 13C figure of Our Lady, dates from about the 14C. The nearby château of Arenberg, a rebuilding of 1917, is now military property.

The road up the Gelbressée valley, the scene of heavy fighting in 1914, in 3km reaches *Gelbressée* with a Romanesque church. Beyond, well seen from the road, is the attractive moated château of *Franc-Waret* (June–September: Saturday, Sunday, Holidays, 14.00 to 17.30). Rebuilt in 1748, but retaining its early 17C tower, the château houses period furniture, Brussels tapestries (from designs by Bernard van Orley), Flemish paintings, etc.

Namèche, with a bridge across the Meuse, is 2km beyond Marche-les-Dames. Below Namèche minor roads serve the N bank, but these are in places rough and cobbled and lead through unpleasant industrial districts.

SOUTH BANK. Namur is left through the suburb of *Jambes*, at the E edge of which (right, at the rear of a supermarket car park) is the small keep of the Château d'Enhaive which was in existence in 1283 when Jean of Flanders, Bishop of Liège, lived here; he died here in 1291, after which the château became a fortified farm the remains of which, with a 16C round tower, are adjacent.—*9km Namèche* is on the N bank.

The village of *Samson*, on the S bank roughly opposite Namèche, lies below a group of rocks crowned by fragments of a 13C ruin, once the residence of Sibylle de Lusignan, mother of Baldwin V, King of Jerusalem.

A pleasant road ascends the VALLEY OF THE SAMSON, soon passing an animal park (beavers) and after 2km reaching the *Grotte de Goyet* (April–September: daily, 09.00 to 18.00), once the home of prehistoric man, now represented by reconstructed scenes. At *Faulx-les-Tombes*, 3km above Goyet, the road runs below an extraordinary turreted folly of 1870, standing on 10C foundations, and, 1km farther on, above the remains of the Cistercian abbey of *Grand-Pré*, now forming part of a large farm.

9km **Andenne** (22,000 inhab.) owes its origin to a convent founded here in c 690 by St. Begga (died 698), daughter of Pepin of Landen. (Her son, when hunting, found a hen protecting her seven chicks from his hounds, so, regarding this as a sign from Heaven, Begga built her convent and seven churches.) Of this ancient past nothing survives in this largely industrial town, but the 18C *Collégiale Sainte Begge* (by Dewez), in the S of the town against the hill, houses the saint's tomb and a bust-reliquary. At 29 Rue Charles Lapierre, near the church, the *Musée de la Céramique* shows material dating from Gallo-Roman times (May–September: Tuesday, Saturday, Sunday, 14.30 to 17.30.). On the E outskirts of the town, in the suburb of Andenelle, the Romanesque *Eglise Saint Pierre* dates from 1100.

Beyond Andenne the province of Liège is entered.

12km **Huy** (18,000 inhab. Tourist Information: 1 Quai de Namur, near S end of bridge) stands on both banks of the Meuse, below (on the S side) its citadel, site in the 11C or earlier of the first episcopal castle around which the town grew. The bridge replaces one blown up in 1944. Local river excursions.

SOUTH BANK. The *Collégiale Notre-Dame*, begun in 1311, completed in 1536 and the third church to occupy this site, is an outstanding Gothic building on which the magnificent *Rose Window and the tall, slender lancets of the apse are especially noteworthy. The Treasury (Daily except Friday and during services, 09.00 to 12.00, 14.00 to 17.00) is known for four beautiful shrines: Our Lady (1240); St. Mark (c 1200); and St. Domitian (1173) and St. Mengold (1175), both these by Godefroid de Huy. (Domitian, died c 560, evangelised along the Meuse and became Bishop of Tongeren. Mengold, fl. 892, may have been a nobleman warrior of Huy, said to have been of English origin, who spent seven years in penitence for all the blood he had shed; but there was also a hermit here of similar name and date, and it may well be that the two have become one.)

A lane, lined with old graveslabs, runs along the S wall of the church to the former canons' entrance, the restored *Porte de Bethléem* bearing 14C reliefs of the Nativity. The Avenue des Ardennes is crossed to reach the Grand-Place in which there is a fountain with a bronze basin (1406) and bearing figures of saints (Mengold, Domitian and Catherine) as also of Ansfrid, last Count of Huy, who in 985 gifted the town to Bishop Notger of Liège. Behind the Hôtel de Ville of 1766 the 14C *Eglise Saint Mengold* shelters the tomb of its patron. A high-walled lane behind the church soon reaches the *Justice de la Paix*, preserving the cloister (1664–87) of a Franciscan friary and housing the *Musée Communal* (April–mid October: Monday–Saturday, 14.00 to 18.00; Sunday and Holidays, 10.00 to 12.00, 14.00 to 18.00). The collections include archaeological material; money of the prince-bishopric of Liège, minted at Huy; ceramic, metal and glasswork; and religious art, notable being the 'Beau Dieu de Huy', an oak figure of 1240.

In a park, to the right of the main Liège road (Quai d'Arona) are the scanty remains of the abbey of *Neufmoustier*, founded by Peter the Hermit who died here in 1115.

The CITADEL (Easter and May–September: daily, 10.00 to 18.00 or 19.00 in July and August) may be reached by a steep path from the waterfront or by teleferic (Easter–September: Sunday, but daily in July and August, 10.00 to 19.00) from the N river bank. The teleferic, 1400m in length and offering a unique view of the town and its surrounds, continues to La Sarte with a recreation area. The Citadel as seen today was built by the Dutch in 1818–23 and during the Second World War was used by the Germans as an internment camp. Visitors can see camp cells, photographs, and a small military museum.

NORTH BANK. Two old buildings on the quay are noteworthy: downstream the *Hôtel de la Poste* was once the staging-post for the 'river-coaches' to Liège, while upstream the *Maison Batta* (1575) was formerly the refuge of the abbey of Val Saint Lambert. From the bridge the Rue Neuve leads NW, in 150m reaching (right) the Rue Saint Pierre in which the church of the same name contains a Romanesque font.

Between Huy and Liège either bank of the Meuse may be followed. There is more of interest along the N bank, but the S bank road is better and less industrialised. There are several bridges.

HUY TO LIEGE BY THE NORTH BANK. The abbey of *Val Notre-Dame* (3km N of Huy and W of N64) was founded in c 1210 by Count Albert of Moha, the last of this line of counts, traditionally because his two sons ran one another through while playing at jousting. A convent until suppressed in 1796, the site was reoccupied in 1901 since when it has housed nuns of the Order of the Assumption. The entrance, flanked by towers, and the attractive dovecot just inside date from 1629; the farm buildings are mainly 16C, but the remainder is of 1741–45 apart from the church which replaced one destroyed by fire in 1932. The remains of the castle of the counts of Moha (11C) are just N of *Moha*, 3km W of the abbey.

At (*7km* from Huy) **Amay** the Romanesque *Collégiale Sainte Ode* stands on a site which has revealed evidence of both prehistoric and Roman occupation. Dedicated to a French princess (died 723) who married a Duke of Aquitaine and on his death devoted her time and wealth to the care of the sick and needy, the church has a nave of 1098, towers of 1525 and other parts of the 17–18C. It is known for its reliquary (c 1230) of St. Ode and St. George, a decorated work in gilt and enamelled copper, with reliefs of the Apostles and silver plaques depicting scenes from the lives of the two saints. The château of *Jehay-Bodegnée* (Easter Saturday–mid September: Saturday, Sunday, Holidays, 14.00 to 18.00), 4km N of Amay, is a curious chequered and turreted building (mainly 16C) which can be well seen from the road. Excavations here have produced Mesolithic remains and evidence that the château probably stands on the site of a Roman fort. The interior contains 15–17C tapestries, including Brussels, Gobelins and Aubusson; pictures, among these works by A. van Ostade, Frans Snyders, Murillo, Peter Lely (a portrait of Nell Gwynn) and Cornelis de Vos; furniture of many periods; lace, porcelain and religious statuary; and, in a special room devoted to the Duke of Marlborough, unique manuscript maps, orders of battle and suchlike. Additionally, in the cellars, there is an archaeological museum which includes material excavated locally. *Jehay* village was the birthplace of Zénobe Gramme (1826–1901; monument), physicist and inventor of the dynamo.

8km Engis, high above which is the château of *Aigremont* (Easter, Whitsun, July and August: daily except Monday, about 10.00 to 12.00, 14.00 to 18.00). Successor to a fortress of William de la Marck, the present château is mainly of the early 18C and is furnished in the style of the same period, an outstanding feature being the entrance hall and staircase with striking wall and ceiling paintings by the Huy artist Jean Delloye. The château is much used for exhibitions and receptions, and these may restrict access.— Above (*3km*) *Chokier* the 18C château preserves one medieval tower.—*13km* **Liège**, see Rte 34.

HUY TO LIEGE BY THE SOUTH BANK. The road traverses increasingly industrial districts with little of interest.—*16km* The *Grottes de Ramioul* (May–September: Sunday and Holidays, 14.00 to 18.00), discovered in 1911, are on two levels and include a small museum (prehistory and speliology.)—*5km* The glassworks (Cristallerie) of *Val Saint Lambert* occupy a former Cistercian abbey; founded in 1202, the abbey was suppressed in 1796 and the glassworks took over the mainly 18C buildings in 1826. The younger brothers of Louis XVI, the counts of Provence (later Louis XVIII) and Artois (later Charles X), were given shelter here when they fled the French Revolution.—*3km* **Seraing** is the home of the huge Société Cockerill (ironworks, etc.), founded here in 1817 by John Cockerill as an extension to the works his father William, a mechanic from Lancashire, had started at Liège in 1807. These Seraing works were the first on the Continent to build locomotives (1835), and the first

to use the Bessemer process in the production of steel (1863).—*7km*
Liège, see Rte 34.

32 Dinant to Liège

Total distance 69km.—*6km Sorinnes.*—*9km* **Ciney.**—*4km
Emptinne.*—*11km Havelange.*—*8km Pont de Bonne.*—*8km Scry*
(**Villers-le-Temple**).—*5km Saint Séverin.*—*4km Neuville-en-
Condroz.*—*14km* **Liège**.

Dinant, see Rte 29.—*6km Sorinnes*, some of the furnishings of
whose church (restored 1777; enlarged 1890) come from the abbey
of Leffe near Dinant. *Foy-Notre-Dame* (Rte 29) is 2km S, while the
church at *Thynes*, 2km N, has an 11C Romanesque crypt.—*9km*
Ciney (13,000 inhab.) is the capital of the CONDROZ, the pastoral
NW part of the Ardennes lying between the Ourthe and the Meuse.
The church, said to be successor to one founded by St. Maternus,
was wrecked in a storm in 1618 but the Romanesque tower and
crypt survive. At *Chevetogne*, 8km S, there is an Orthodox
Benedictine monastery (1925), dedicated to the theme of Christian
unity and with an 'Oriental' church of 1957 containing modern
frescoes (Cretan and Macedonian schools).—At (*4km*) *Emptinne*
Rte 33 is crossed.—*11km Havelange* is just before the border of the
province of Liège.

Here a pleasant diversion, adding 7km, may be made to the W through
Evelette, thence descending the valley of the Vyle to rejoin the main road at
Pont de Bonne. This wooded country road passes particularly attractive
fortified farms at *Libois* and *Tahier*.

8km Pont de Bonne, 1km SE of which is the château of *Modave*
(April–mid November: daily, 09.00 to 12.00, 14.00 to 18.00)
standing at the end of a long avenue and built on a cliff 80m above
the little Hoyoux river. The walls of the keep are 12C but the
remainder of the château is largely of c 1649, the rich decoration of
the interior being mainly the work of J.C. Hansche. Also shown
here (daily at 14.00) is the ingenious 17C wooden device which
brought river water up to the château.—*8km Scry*, just N of which
is **Villers-le-Temple** where the 13C church contains the tomb of a
Templar, Gerard de Villiers (died 1273), founder of the local
commandery; the church was much altered in the 18C when it was
given its Baroque apse. Remains survive of the fortified house of
the Knights Hospitallers who took over the Templars' properties
when the latter were suppressed in 1312.—At *Quatre-Bras*, just
beyond Scry, this Route joins Rte 35, Liège to Bouillon.—*5km Saint
Séverin*, where the church, attractively set above the village green
beside old farm buildings, was once part of an abbey; built in c
1140, the church has a font of the same date, of an unusual design
with multiple supports.—In (*4km*) the village of *Neuville-en-
Condroz* there is a 16C manor house. The American Ardennes
Cemetery here contains over 5000 Second World War graves and a
monument to the Supply Services, while wall maps in marble
illustrate the campaign.—*10km* At *Sart-Tilman* the road passes the
University of Liège, with interesting modern architecture and

sculpture and also the university's botanic gardens.—*4km* **Liège**, see
Rte 34.

33 Namur to Luxembourg via La Roche-en-Ardenne and Arlon

Total distance 149km.—*43km* **Marche-en-Famenne**.—*20km*
La Roche-en-Ardenne.—*25km* **Bastogne**.—*37km* **Arlon**.—*24km*
Luxembourg.

This is the principal W to E Route across the ARDENNES, between
Marche-en-Famenne and Bastogne leaving the main N4 and instead
taking the road N888 through La Roche-en-Ardenne, scenically and in
other respects the heart of the region. This Rte crosses three N to S
Ardennes Rtes, all starting from Liège, at Marche-en-Famenne (Rte
35), La Roche-en-Ardenne (Rte 36A) and Bastogne (Rte 36B).

Namur, see Rte 28, is left by the suburb of *Jambes* (Rte 31).—At
(*8km*) *Wierde* there is an 11C Romanesque church which is unusual
for the way in which its tower is loopholed.—*2km Sart-Bernard*, just
beyond which a diversion can be recommended southwards through
Crupet and Spontin.

At **Crupet** there is a particularly attractive 14–16C manor house,
with its old tower standing on its own, surrounded by water and
linked to the main house only by a small bridge. In the 14C church
there are some good graveslabs, notably one immediately left on
entering which well shows the formal dress of the period.—**Spontin**,
5km SE of Crupet, is known for its *Château* (daily, 09.00 to 18.00), the
oldest inhabited castle in Belgium, belonging to the Beaufort-Spontin
family from the 13–19C and thereafter to others. The château, beyond
a reconstructed farm courtyard, is an interesting example of the way
in which a feudal stronghold is combined with a manorial home. First
built in the 11C (lower keep), the castle was largely destroyed in 1466
and again in 1555, after this being rebuilt and, though still fortified in
appearance, serving only as a manor.

The main road can be rejoined at (*14km*, from Sart-Bernard)
Emptinne where Rte 32 is crossed.—*8km* The château of *Jannée*
(Easter–September: daily, 09.30 to 18.30), on the site of a 12C keep
and surrounded by a fine park, was built in an unusual horseshoe
shape during the 17–19C. The interior shows furniture of this period,
pictures, porcelain and hunting trophies.—*6km Hogne* is on the
border of the province of Luxembourg.—*5km* **Marche-en-Famenne**
(15,000 inhab.) owes its name to its position on the march, or border, of
Luxembourg and Liège. It was here in 1577 that Don John of Austria
signed the 'Perpetual Edict' with the States General, the town as a
result being honoured with the Order of the Golden Fleece. There is a
local museum (de la Tourelle. Prehistoric material, local lace. Open
July, August: daily. Other months: Tuesday–Saturday, 09.00 to 12.00,
14.00 to 17.00) in a tower called the *Rempart des Jésuites*, the only
surviving part of the fortifications. The village of *Waha*, 2km S, merits
a visit for its 11C Romanesque church, interesting for its simplicity (it
was built by village masons) and because it preserves its consecration
stone of 1050; inside there are some curious primitive 11C wooden
figures.

For N and S of Marche, see Rte 35 which is crossed here.

The direct road to Bastogne (38km) is N4, across forest and open upland. This Rte bears E along N888.—*20km* **La Roche-en-Ardenne** (4000 inhab. Tourist Information: Hôtel de Ville. For Province of Luxembourg, 9 Quai de l'Ourthe), in the heart of the Ardennes and the region's most popular summer resort, is beautifully situated within a loop of the Ourthe at the foot of steep, wooded hills. Above the town, the road splits (parking and view-point) offering a choice of descents. The main and most obvious tourist attraction is the ruined *Castle* (May–September: daily except Tuesday, 11.00 to 17.00. October–April: Sunday, 11.00 to 13.00, 14.00 to 16.00; other days except Tuesday, 14.00 to 16.00), in origin perhaps of the 9C but today's remains of the 11C or later. The castle belonged to the counts of La Roche, a junior branch of the family of the counts of Namur; later it was held by the dukes of Burgundy, and later still by Louis XIV who rebuilt the defences. Another visit that may be made is to a factory making a coarse blue-grey pottery (Grès) for which La Roche is known (*Poterie-Centre Artisanal*, 28 Rue Rompré. Open Monday–Friday, 09.00 to 18.00. Closed January and Holidays). Above all, perhaps, La Roche is popular as a centre for walking, several routes being numbered and signed. Special mention may be made of Nos 9 and 10 which include the view-point of the *Croix de Beausaint* (4km from the town), and of No. 5, a round of 5.5km, passing the 17C *Chapelle Sainte Marguerite*, the *Parc à Gibier* (deer, boar and other animals), and the *Diable-Château* rocks resembling a ruined castle.

Some of the scenically best parts of the VALLEY OF THE OURTHE are close to La Roche and a circuit of some 23km can be recommended. The route suggested follows N834 SE, after 5km bearing left for the *Belvédère de Nisramont* with a fine view of the Ourthe and its dam. Just above here the river splits into its E and W streams. The road crosses the river, then climbs to *Nadrin* on N860, 2km W of which is the tower of the *Belvédère des Six Ourthe* on a rocky ridge above six loops of the river. From Nadrin it is 12km to La Roche. Alternatively N860 can be followed E to join Rte 36B at Houffalize.

The small *Tramway Touristique de l'Aisne*, an old country tramway, runs through some 10km of typical scenery between Erezée (14km N of La Roche) and Lamorménil, just N of Dochamps (Easter–September or October: Sunday, Holidays, but daily except Monday morning in July and August, 10.30 to 17.00).

For La Roche N to *Liège* and S to *Florenville*, see Rte 36A.

25km **Bastogne** (11,000 inhab. Tourist Information: Place MacAuliffe), though an old town, preserves only its 13C *Porte de Trèves* and the *Eglise Saint Pierre* with a 12C tower and a Gothic nave (about 15C) with elaborate and colourful vaulting. Since at least the 15C it has been famous for its smoked hams, but in modern history the town is known for the heroic American stand during the Battle of the Ardennes in December 1944.

Mentioned as early as 634, Bastogne was many times besieged, notably in 1236 by Liège when the town was sacked; in 1318 when Louis of Nassau was repulsed; in 1688 when Louis XIV razed the ramparts; and in December 1944 when the Germans encircled the town defended by the American 101st Airborne Division commanded by General MacAuliffe. To the German commander's summons to surrender, MacAuliffe returned the laconic reply 'Nuts'. Despite heavy bombardment and much destruction, Bastogne held out until Allied pressure on both flanks forced the Germans to withdraw.

In the main square, the Place MacAuliffe, are a tank and a bust of the general. The *American Memorial* (Georges Dedoyard, 1950), standing on the hill of Mardasson 2km NE of the town, takes the form of a five-pointed star, with colonnades, and an upper gallery surrounding a central opening. The story of the battle is told in gold letters on the memorial's pillars. Adjacent, and also a star-shaped building, is the *Bastogne Historical Centre* (1975), where the Battle of the Ardennes is explained by a film and other presentations (mid February–May and September: daily, 09.00 to 18.00. June–August: daily, 08.30 to 18.30. October–November: daily, 10.00 to 17.00).

For Bastogne N to *Liège* and S to *Florenville*, see Rte 36B.—For *Wiltz* and *Esch-sur-Sûre*, to the E in the Grand-Duchy of Luxembourg, see Rte 44B.

19km Martelange (1500 inhab.) is curious because the border of the Grand-Duchy of Luxembourg runs along the immediate E side of the road, which, since petrol is normally cheaper in the Grand-Duchy, is lined with petrol stations. The small Musée de l'Haute Sûre includes an interior of the home of a slate worker.

18km **Arlon** (22,000 inhab. Tourist Information: Place Léopold), the capital of the province of Luxembourg and one of the oldest towns in Belgium, offers Roman remains and a particularly good archaeological museum. 'Maitrank', a local drink made of Moselle wine, cognac and fruit, is popular in early summer.

In the 2C Orolaunum Vicus was a trading post on the Roman road from Rheims to Trèves (Trier). It was walled in the 4C against attacks from the east and stood at the limit of the area where the invading Franks were not absorbed by the Gallo-Romans; a Germanic dialect still survives in the surrounding villages. In 1226 the marquessate of Arlon was attached to the county (later duchy) of Luxembourg through the marriage of Marquess Waleran IV with Ermesinda of Luxembourg. The town suffered French invasions in 1552–54 and 1558. In 1671 the ramparts were pulled down, but the French refortified the place during their occupation of 1681–97. In 1785 much of the town was destroyed by a fire. It was from Arlon at the end of 1944 that the American General Patton launched the counter-offensive that relieved Bastogne.

The modern centre of the town is not, as might be expected, the Grand-Place, but PLACE LEOPOLD, with the post office and other public buildings; also a tank memorial to the Americans who liberated Arlon on 10 September 1944, and a wall plaque honouring the victims of concentration camps and the members of the Resistance. The archaeological museum is 200m NW of here, and the Grand-Place is 150m NE, higher up the hill which was occupied successively by the castle of the marquesses, a Capuchin convent (1626), and a citadel built for Louis XIV. The hill is now crowned by the *Eglise Saint Donat*, once the 17C chapel of the Capuchins, established as parish church in 1825, and considerably altered in 1858 and 1900. Inside, frescoes of the 17th or 18C in the chapel of St. Blaise depict the story of a Roman legion, commanded by Donat, which was saved from thirst when its Christian members successfully prayed for rain. The view from the tower (orientation table) embraces Belgium, France and Luxembourg. By the SE external corner of the church there are some relics of the medieval parish church, which used to stand in the Grande Rue until demolished in 1935, and below there is a doorway of 1634. The gate (1700) from the convent of Clairefontaine (4km SE) has been placed at the NE external corner of the church.

At No. 18 Grand-Place can be seen remains of a 4C *Roman Wall and Bastion* (Daily except Sunday and Monday, 09.00 to 18.30), hurriedly constructed of graveslabs, and in the Grande Rue, just S, a 16C vaulted passage and some cellars below are the sole relics of medieval Arlon; a tablet in the passage records a visit by Goethe in 1792. Remains of 4C *Roman Baths* are in grounds off the Rue des Thermes, some 400m SE of the Grand-Place (May–September: daily, 09.00 to 12.00, 14.00 to 17.00).

The *Musée Luxembourgeois* (The archaeological museum. Monday–Saturday, 09.00 to 12.00, 14.00 to 17.00. Sunday, Holidays, From mid June–mid September, 10.00 to 12.00, 14.00 to 16.00 or 17.00. Closed all other Sundays and Holidays), 200m NW of Place Léopold in the Rue des Martyrs, is best known for its outstanding collection of Gallo-Roman sculpture and stonework. The material, which is particularly well and imaginatively displayed, is largely regional and builds up an excellent picture of the life and clothing of the times, models or drawings in many cases completing and explaining what to the layman are no more than stone fragments. Visitors planning to go to nearby Montauban (end of Rte 36B) should note the interesting Harvester relief, with its extension drawing). Excavated in Arlon in 1854, what this relief represented remained a puzzle until the discovery of the Montauban stone in 1958. Upstairs are Prehistoric and Frankish antiquities, and also an instructive section on Roman building methods. Additionally, the museum displays a collection of religious art which includes a good 16C retable.

For *Virton* (28km SW) and the surrounding district of *Gaume*, see end of Rte 36B.

The Luxembourg road out of Arlon passes on the outskirts of the town (left; sign) the *Source of the Semois*, with, beside the spring, a replica of a Roman statue in the museum.—*8km* the border is crossed into the Grand-Duchy of Luxembourg, to the N being the scenic and interesting touring district of the valleys of the Eisch and Mamer (see Rte 44A).—*10km* **Mamer**, the Roman Mambra. On the E outskirts of the town, road CR101 (for Mersch) branches N, on the left about 300m along this road being the remains of *Roman Baths* of the 1C, much damaged by the Franks in 275; the adjacent tomb, in which two skeletons were found, is medieval. This pleasant site, explained by diagrams and pictures, well rewards the short diversion.—*6km* **Luxembourg**, see Rte 40.

34 Liège

LIEGE (Flem. *Luik*. German *Lüttich*), ancient and historic capital of the province of the same name, spreads along the valley of the Meuse just below the confluence with the Ourthe. Although one of Europe's major industrial centres (202,000 inhab.), industry is generally confined to the perimeter, leaving the inner city (the left bank being touristically the more important), as a lively, even elegant place, offering much of interest. A minor but pleasing local feature is that many street-name plaques carry an explanatory note. Place Saint Lambert can be regarded as the city centre.

Tourist Information. *City*: 92 En Féronstrée, 500m NE of Place Saint Lambert. Also at Gare des Guillemins (May–September). *Province of Liège*: 77 Boulevard de la Sauvenière.

Main Railway Station. Gare des Guillemins, over 2km S of Place Saint Lambert.

Boats. Operator: Li Trembleur. Tel: 04187–4332. Embarcation City Centre, right bank. To Visé and Maastricht. 10 hours, with 2½ hours in Maastricht. July and August: Monday, Tuesday, Thursday, Friday, except Holidays.—Also via Visé to the Li Trembleur complex at Blégny (see Rte 39). 10 hours. July and August: daily except Wednesday.

History. Probably deriving its name from the Légie brook, a tributary of the Meuse now long hidden underground, Liège dates its birth to the building of a chapel here in 558 by St. Monulphus, Bishop of Maastricht. In 705, when St. Lambert, also Bishop of Maastricht, was murdered here (traditionally because he had accused Pepin of Herstal of incest), his successor, St. Hubert, at once erected a basilica in his memory. Soon afterwards (720) St. Hubert moved his see to Liège and thenceforth for 1000 years the town was a centre of ecclesiastical power occupying a commanding political and geographical position between the spheres of influence of France, the Netherlands and the Holy Roman Empire. Already in the 9C a centre of learning, Liège reached material eminence under the vigorous Bishop Notger. Appointed in 972, by his acquisitive policy he raised the see to a position of real territorial power, as a result being nominated Prince-Bishop by Otto I, a title and authority that were to last nearly 800 years. Notger fortified his city and encouraged trade, and soon after his death in 1008 the first bridge across the Meuse was built, the seventh successor of which is today's Pont des Arches. Quarrels between the bishops, the municipal authorities, the wealthy merchants, the landed gentry and the tradesmen were continuous, except when Liège was threatened from outside. Such occasions were in 1213, when Liège defeated Duke Henry II of Brabant, and in 1343 when the people supported Bishop Adolphe de la Marck against Brabant, but in return exacted the appointment of a representative council.

The coal mines were already being exploited by the 12C, but, though a metallurgical industry developed and social conditions improved, the rise to power of the dukes of Burgundy was for a time fatal to the growth of civil liberty. John the Fearless crushed Liège at Othée in 1408; Philip the Good again defeated the Liégeois at Montenaken in 1465; and in 1468 Charles the Bold won the battle of Brustem, sacking the city, annulling civil liberties, and carrying off their symbol, the Perron, to Bruges. Nine years later, however, Mary of Burgundy restored the city's privileges, and thereafter for three centuries the principality preserved neutrality in the wars between France and the Empire. In 1482 William de la Marck, the 'Wild Boar of the Ardennes', captured and killed the bishop (Louis de Bourbon), but the latter's successor, Jean de Hornes, invited the 'Wild Boar' to a feast, then seized him and sent him to Maastricht for execution (see Sir Walter Scott's 'Quentin Durward').

During the religious wars Liège maintained its neutrality. But in 1702 the citadel was stormed by Marlborough, and in 1794 Dumouriez captured Liège for revolutionary France, expelling the last prince-bishop, Antoine de Méan.

At the outbreak of the First World War Liège, under General Leman (p 294), guarding the gap between Holland and the Ardennes, put up a stubborn resistance for ten days (5–14 August). Throughout the war the men working in the small-arms factories refused to make weapons. At the end of the Second World War the bridges were blown by the retreating Germans, and the city was hit by over 1500 flying-bombs and rockets.

Industry. Liège is the centre of a mining district rich in coal, lead, zinc, and iron, this forming the basis of a vast metallurgical industry, the origins of which reach back to the 12C. The 19C saw great expansion and the firm establishment of heavy industry. Among the important factories were the Cockerill works in Liège and at *Seraing*, the blast furnaces at *Ougrée*, the ironworks at *Sclessin*, and the Usines de la Vieille-Montagne at *Angleur*. Among other industries are armaments, glass, electronics, and petro-chemicals.

Port. Largely due to the completion in 1939 of the Albert Canal, linking Liège and the Meuse to Antwerp and the Scheldt, the port of Liège is, after Paris and Duisberg, the third largest inland port in western Europe. Installations stretch from *Herstal*, downstream, the length of the city to *Chokier*, upstream. The main port area is downstream at *Monsin*, where the start of the Albert Canal is marked by a memorial to King Albert, incorporating a tower 45m high and a 14m high figure of the king.

Art. In medieval times Liège was known for its metalwork and ivories, and later (16–18C) for architecture and woodwork, in particular cabinet-making. In music the city was famous for its 14C Song School, which supplied most of the singers for the refounded Sistine Chapel at the Vatican (1376). Among musicians native of Liège were André Grétry, César Franck, and the violinist Eugène Ysaye.

The PLACE SAINT LAMBERT, a traffic cauldron but at the same time the focus of bold and imaginative planning, has long known man. Excavations have shown that Mesolithic people of six or more

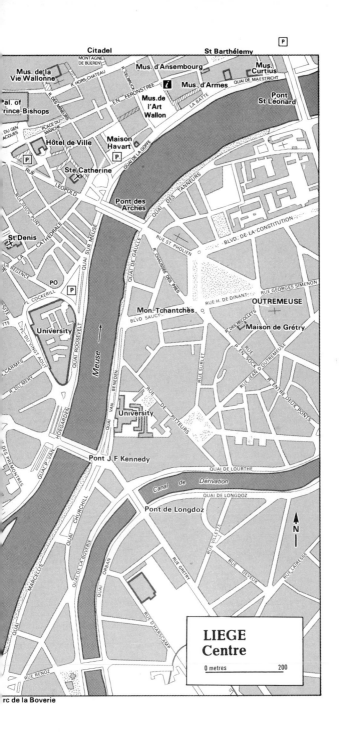

Citadel   St Barthélemy

Mus. de la
Vie Wallonne

Mus. d'Ansembourg   Mus.
Curtius

QUAI DE MAESTRICHT

MONTAGNE
DE BÜEREN

R. HORS-CHATEAU

R. VELBRUCK

EN FERONSTREE

Mus.
d'Armes   Pont
St Léonard

al. of
rince-Bishops

Mus.de
l'Art
Wallon

LA BATTE

R DES MINEURS

DU GEN
ACQUES

PLACE DU
MARCHE

Hôtel de Ville   Maison
Havart

RUE

Ste Catherine

QUAI DE LA GOFFE

P

LEOPOLD   Pont des
Arches   QUAI DES TANNEURS

RUE SOUS-PONT

St Denis   CATHEDRALE   QUAI SUR MEUSE   RUE ST PHOLIEN   BLVD. DE LA CONSTITUTION

E REGENCE   QUAI DE GAULLE   R. CHAUSSEE DES PRES   RUE GEORGES SIMENON

PO   P   RUE H. DE DINANT   OUTREMEUSE

PL. COCKERILL   Mon Tchantchès   Maison de Grétry

SITE   BLVD SAUCY   R DES RECOLLETS

University   QUAI ROOSEVELT   Meuse   RUE SURLET   RUE EN SOCK D'OUTREMEUSE

CARMES   QUAI VAN BENEDEN   RUE DE PITEURS   RUE JEAN D'OUTREMEUSE   RUE ENTRE DEUX PONTS

R. DU MERY   HOEGAARDEN   University

DES PREMONTRES   QUAI P. VAN

Pont J F Kennedy   QUAI DE LOURTHE

QUAI CHURCHILL   Canal   de   Dérivation   QUAI DE LONGDOZ

Pont de Longdoz

MARCELLIS   QUAI ORBAN   RUE VILLETTE   N

QUAI DE LA BOVERIE   RUE GRETRY   RUE DEVEUX   RUE CLAIRESSE

RUE D'HARSCAMP

LIEGE
Centre

0 metres   200

RUE RENOZ

rc de la Boverie

millenia ago were here, as were also their Neolithic and Gallo-Roman successors, these last leaving clear traces of their villa. Then from early Christian times there is a steady succession; a chapel, perhaps that of St. Lambert, followed by the sanctuary built by St. Hubert to shelter St. Lambert's relics, these followed again in the 10C by Notger's cathedral, burnt down in 1185. Then from the 13C to the 19C this was the site of the great Gothic Cathedral of St. Lambert which sprawled over most of the area in front of the palace of the prince-bishops. Destroyed in 1794 (as being an unacceptable symbol of the power of the now expelled prince-bishops), the ruins served for 30 years as a quarry while the Place slowly began to assume its present shape and purpose. (A Sous-sol Archéologique, closed during the 1980s' major works, may be reopened.)

On the N side stands the huge **Palais des Princes-Evêques**, the Palace of the Prince-Bishops, today housing the law courts. Bishop Notger's original building having been burnt in 1505, the palace was rebuilt in 1526–33 by Bishop Erard de la Marck, this new palace however suffering another serious fire after which the façade giving on to Place Saint Lambert was rebuilt in 1737. The whole building was restored in 1848–83, a W wing then being added for the provincial government. The two 16C courtyards are open to visitors. In the first, each of the columns is carved with different grotesques; the second, reached by a passage off the SE corner of the first, though smaller, is pleasanter, with grass, a fountain and a collection of old stonework (Galerie Lapidaire).

West of Place Saint Lambert

Three churches in this part of the town merit mention. The **Eglise Saint Servais** (Servatius), a short way NW above Place Saint Lambert, is a basically 13C building (successor of an even earlier one) which was much altered in the 16C. It contains some good Renaissance stained-glass, a 13C figure of the saint (4C Bishop of Tongeren and Maastricht), and a 14C Visitation. The Rue Saint Pierre, with at No. 13 the birthplace in 1822 of the composer César Franck, in 150m reaches the triple-nave **Eglise Sainte-Croix** of the late 12C (tower and baptistry) and 14C although a vestige of wall survives from 979. The baptistry, which forms a kind of W apse, contains a 15C polyptych, and in the Treasury can be seen a symbolical key given by Pope Gregory II to St. Hubert in 722. These keys, of which only two survive in Europe, the other being at Maastricht, were given by the Pope to distinguished visitors to Rome as a symbol of the right of entry to the vault of St. Peter. The **Eglise Saint Martin**, 500m W of Sainte Croix and standing on the Publémont, the hill where coal was first won in the Liège district, is celebrated as the church where in 1246 the feast of Corpus Christi was first observed, on the orders of Bishop Robert de Torote acting under pressure from the Blessed Juliana, prioress of a nearby convent, who had a vision after her veneration of the Sacrament. The church was founded in 965 by Bishop Eracle as the result of a vow made when, after praying at the tomb of St. Martin, he was cured of an illness (see pictures in the choir). It was, however, burnt down in 1312 and, apart from its early 15C tower, today's church dates from the 16C.

North East of Place Saint Lambert

The short Rue du Bex leads into the PLACE DU MARCHE, in the centre of which stands the *Perron*, symbol of the liberty of Liège. Erected in

1697, this perron, incorporating a fountain, is successor to one destroyed in a storm. The group of the Three Graces is by Del Cour. On the S side of the square is the **Hôtel de Ville** (1718), still often referred to as 'La Violette', a name going back to the 13C when the municipal authorities met in a house here of that name; the present building, the fourth to enjoy this name, contains statues by Del Cour and rich 18C decoration. The domed *Bourse* on the N side of the Place was formerly a church (1722), and at the square's E end the *Fontaine de la Tradition* (1719) bears an armorial door of the same date and bronze reliefs (1930) of Liège folklore characters.

Beyond the NE end of the Place du Marché, the Rue des Mineurs ends at the Cour des Mineurs, the name recalling that this was once the site of a Franciscan house. The buildings, destroyed by a flying bomb in 1945, have been rebuilt and now house the **Musée de la Vie Wallonne** containing a very complete collection illustrating many aspects of Walloon life, past and present (Tuesday–Saturday, 10.00 to 12.00, 14.00 to 17.00; Sunday, Holidays, 10.00 to 16.00. Closed 1 January, 1 May, 1 November, 25 December). Just NE of here, at 14 Impasse des Ursulines, the *Musée d'Architecture* (Daily except Monday and Thursday, 13.00 to 18.30 or 18.00 on Sunday. Closed 1 January, 1 May, 1 November, 25 December) is mainly a documentation centre but also incorporates the reconstructed studio of the violinist Eugène Ysaye (1858–1931). Also adjacent, in the Rue Mère-Dieu, there is the **Musée d'Art Religieux et Mosan** (Daily except Monday, 12.00 to 17.00. Closed 1 January, 1 May, 1 November, 25 December), a wide-ranging gallery showing many forms of exquisite religious and Mosan art spanning from medieval to modern times. A painting of about 1475 (Notre Dame 'a la Donatrice'), attributed to the Master of St. Gudule, ranks with the most important of the museum's treasures, among which there is also a sensitively carved oak Christ Enthroned of c 1240.

The narrow Rue Hors-Château (Outside the Castle), running NE below the citadel slopes, retains a number of old alleys and courts. Off this road the 407 steps of the *Montagne de Bueren* (honouring a hero of the defence of 1468 against Charles the Bold) climb to the CITADEL, with a hospital, public park and war memorials. The view (orientation table) can be disappointing due to a screen of bushes and trees. The citadel can also be reached by road.

EN FERONSTREE (i.e. Rue des Ferroniers, the ironworkers) runs NE out of the Place du Marché. The city *Tourist Information* is on the right at No. 92, virtually alongside up steps (No. 86) being the **Musée de L'Art Wallon** (Tuesday–Saturday, 13.00 to 18.00; Sunday, Holidays, 11.00 to 16.30. Closed 1 January, 1 May, 1 November, 25 December) showing works mainly by Walloon artists from the 16C Old Masters to contemporary works. Artists range from, for example, Lambert Lombard (a self-portrait) and Joachim Patinir through Pierre Paulus (Pays Noir) and Antoine Wiertz to Paul Delvaux and contemporists (changing exhibitions). Just beyond Tourist Information, at 114 En Féronstrée, the fine patrician mansion (1735–41) of the **Musée d'Ansembourg** provides a sumptuous setting for magnificent decorative art collections which include furniture, spectacular chandeliers, porcelain, tapestry, Mechelen leather and tilework of Delft and Liège (Monday, Wednesday–Saturday, 10.00 to 12.30, 14.00 to 17.00; Sunday, Holidays, 10.00 to 13.00; Thursday also 19.00 to 21.00. Closed 1 January, 1 May, 1 November, 25 December). Roughly opposite, the **Eglise Saint Barthélemy** (end of 12C) is Romanesque in external appearance but, except for the narthex, was internally completely disguised at the beginning ot the 18C. The church is visited for its splendid *Font*, cast in bronze in 1118, almost certainly by Renier de Huy. At this time only one Liège church, Notre Dame aux Fonts, was permitted to celebrate baptism and it was for this church that the font was commissioned. Notre Dame aux Fonts was destroyed during the French period, the font then being hidden until the concordat of 1804 allowed it to be placed where it is now. Resting on ten half-figures of oxen, the font is decorated with baptismal groups in relief (Monday–Saturday, 10.00 to 12.30, 14.00 to 17.00; Sunday, Holidays, 10.00 to 16.00).

The return to Place Saint Lambert is made along the quays, starting at the Quai de Maestricht by the Pont Saint Léonard.

The *Musée Curtius* (Monday, Wednesday–Saturday, 10.00 to 12.30, 14.00 to 17.00; Sunday, Holidays, 10.00 to 13.00; Wednesday also 19.00 to 21.00. Closed 1 January, 1 May, 1 November, 25 December) occupies the mansion, with a very distinctive high-pitched roof and tower, built in c 1600–10 for the wealthy merchant Jean de Corte (or Curtius). The museum, opened as such at the beginning of this century, offers archaeological, decorative art, glass and general collections, all, except for the glass, largely of local provenance. The Archaeological material includes prehistoric articles, amongst these small finds from the Place Saint Lambert; Roman antiquities such as glass, pottery and some bronze figurines; Roman and Frankish ornaments from tombs in the Hesbaye district; and Gallo-Roman bronzes from the Liège suburb of Angleur. The Decorative Arts collection is notable for the religious material, here being, for example, a Virgin in alabaster (English, c 1400); a 16C Pietà from Eben-Emael; German carved wooden groups of the 15C (Death of the Virgin. Last Supper); Byzantine ivories and icons; the Arenberg Evangelistery (11–12C); ivories of the 13–17C, and a pre-Roman example from Amay; sculpture from the destroyed cathedral; a Sedes Sapientiae from Xhoris; and *Bishop Notger's Evangelistery, a 10C manuscript with a binding of ivory (1008), Mosan enamels (c 1170) and copper plaques (1506), the whole completed in the early 17C. Additionally there are a number of exhibits of General Interest, these including Liège woodwork and tapestries (17–18C); Renaissance chimneypieces bearing the arms of Erard de la Marck; the Moxhon Collection of miniatures, paintings and 18C silver, here too (Grande Salle Moxhon) being an astonishing 18–19C six-face clock by Hubert Sarton of Liège; weapons, coins, medals and seals from the Gallo-Roman period up to the mid 19C; series of old plans of Liège (note how dominating this Maison Curtius once was) and also reliefs (courtyard) showing three earlier versions of the Pont des Arches.

The Glass section, off the courtyard and ranking as a separate *Musée de Verre*, and of international repute, tells the story of glass from earliest times up to and including the 20C, the over 9000 examples being of worldwide provenance.

The **Musée d'Armes** (Tuesday–Saturday, 10.00 to 12.30, 14.00 to 17.00; Sunday, Holidays, 10.00 to 14.00. Closed 1 January, 1 May, 1 November, 25 December), a short way farther along the quay, occupies a mansion of c 1775 which served as the French prefecture of the Ourthe in 1800–14 and as the seat of the Dutch governor in 1815–30. Among those who visited here were Napoleon and Blücher, the former's visit (1803) remembered by a portrait by Ingres. The museum, founded in 1885, exhibits the most complete collection of small-arms in Europe. Beyond the museum an attractive tile-plaque on a wall recalls that here was the diligence (coach) station in 1750.

The Quai de Maestricht becomes first the Quai de la Batte and then the Quai de la Goffe, these quays being the scene of a lively Sunday morning general market, the Marché Dominical de la Batte, the word 'batte' being old Walloon for 'quay'.

As early as the 12th or 13C this area was the home of cloth workers and other artisans associated with this trade, but even in the early 16C the waterfront here was little more than a frequently flooded meadow. Change started in the mid 16C when a trading quay was built. Commercial activity then quickly expanded, the cattle market arriving first, soon followed by facilities for other merchants, including in 1663 a horse market. At this time all three quays were known as the 'Batte', the division into three dating only from 1863.

On the Quai de la Goffe the *Maison Havart* (16C) is largely of wood, while diagonally across the quay is the *Vieille Boucherie* of 1545. The **Pont des Arches**, opened in its present form in 1947, is seventh in a line reaching back to 1026 when the first bridge was put across the river. The name recalls the seven arches of the first bridges, what is thought to be one of these appearing in a painting by Jan van Eyck (Madonna, with Chancellor Rolin) now in the Louvre in Paris. Interesting reliefs showing earlier bridges can be seen at the Musée Curtius. The statues on today's bridge represent resistance to invaders (upstream, right bank); the town's resistance to the Burgundians (upstream, left bank); the revolutionary spirit of 1789 and 1830 (downstream, right bank); and the birth of Liège at the time of Bishop Notger (downstream, left bank).

From the Pont des Arches, Rue Léopold leads back to Place Saint Lambert, to the right being the domed *Eglise Sainte Catherine*, a rebuilding of 1691.

South of the Place Saint Lambert

In the district to the south of Place Saint Lambert most places of interest lie within the area enclosed by the Meuse and, on the W, the loop formed by the boulevards de la Sauvenière and d'Avroy, wide roads following the course of a former arm of the river (see old plans in the Musée Curtius). A good starting point is the PLACE DE LA REPUBLIQUE FRANCAISE, 250m SW of the Place Saint Lambert. From here the Place du Roi Albert, the Rue Pont d'Avroy (a main shopping street) and the cathedral are some 350m to the south. The Parc d'Avroy, with its sculpture and terraces, is about 700m S of the cathedral while the Gare des Guillemins is nearly 1km S again.

The **Théâtre Royal**, on the Place de la République Française, stands on the site of a Dominican convent and was built in 1818 using material from the convent and from two demolished churches, one of these being that of the Carthusians eight marble columns from which now decorate the façade of the theatre. In front there is a statue (Willem Geefs) of André Grétry (1741–1813) whose heart lies within the plinth.

To the SE (250m) the **Eglise Saint Denis**, dedicated to the first bishop of Paris and the second of the churches founded in Liège in the 10C by Bishop Notger, in large part (nave, aisles, tower base) reaches back to this period (987), the rest of the structure however being alteration or addition spanning the 14–18C. The church, which may be entered either from the Rue de la Cathédrale by way of an 18C cloister or from the small Place Saint Denis, contains (S transept) a good early 16C Brabant retable.—To the SE of the church is the *Post Office*, a curious building of 1901 in 16C Gothic style, to the S of this being the **University**, founded in 1817 by William I, built in 1820–24 incorporating part of the former Jesuit church, and since much enlarged. The library and various scientific collections are open to the public on application, the most popular being the *Musée de la Préhistoire* (Wednesday, Friday, 10.00 to 17.30), located here, and, across the river on the Quai E. van Beneden, the *Musée de Zoologie (Aquarium)* (Daily, 10.30 to 12.30. 14.30 to 18.00).

From Place de la République Française, Rue Hamal and Place Xavier-Neujean leading SW soon reach the **Eglise Saint Jean**, founded in c 997 by Bishop Notger and built on the plan of the Carolingian basilica in Aachen. The tower, not finished until 1200, is all that survives of the early church although the nave and choir (both 18C) rest on 10C foundations. The tower is well seen from the 16–17C cloister on the west. In the entrance there are two 13C polychrome wood figures of the Virgin and St. John, while inside are a Sedes Sapientiae of c 1200 and the 14C doors of the treasury.

Boulevard de la Sauvenière runs SE to reach (left) Rue Pont d'Avroy, a busy shopping street (with to its N a 'popular' district of narrow streets) which soon arrives at PLACE DU ROI ALBERT. Here, on the N side by the start of the pedestrian precinct Vinave d'Ile, the *Fontaine de la Vierge* (1695) is by Jean Del Cour.

The **Cathédrale Saint Paul**, a church promoted to cathedral in 1801 to replace that of St. Lambert destroyed by revolutionaries in 1794, was founded in 971 but demolished in the 13C, the present structure being rebuilding spanning from the 14C (apse and lower part of the tower) up to the 19C when the tower was completed with materials taken from St. Lambert's. The interior contains several sculptures by Del Cour and a roof painted with arabesques of 1570, all that the 19C restorers left of the original decoration. The Treasury (Closed 12.30 to 14.00 and at 17.00), in the 15C cloisters entered from the S transept, has a doorway incorporating early 13C wrought-iron. The most notable treasures are a silver-gilt reliquary of 1505 containing the skull of St. Lambert, a 10C Byzantine painting of the Virgin and a 9C book of the Gospels.

In the pleasant little Place Saint Paul, immediately SW of the cathedral, the *Monument Jean Del Cour* (1911) honours this sculptor who worked in Liège and died here in 1707. The **Eglise Saint Jacques** (Daily, 08.00 to 12.00, but sometimes longer hours in July and August), reached from Place Saint Paul by the Rue Saint Rémy, was the church of a Benedictine abbey. Because it was independent of the bishops' jurisdiction, this abbey was charged with guarding the town's charters and for the same reason it was here that the burgomasters took their oaths; the abbey was closed in c 1750 at the request of its own monks. Architecturally the church is interesting for the way in which it combines a span of styles: a Romanesque façade, which has lost its towers (one through lightning and one demolished) as of 1170; the main church, begun in the 15C, reached window-level by 1421, work then stopping until 1518–38 when it continued in Flamboyant style (note the change in the colour of the stone); the N portal, Renaissance work of 1558 forming a kind of outwork, leads into a Gothic vestibule at the end of which, above the entrance, there is a Coronation of the Virgin of 1380. Features of the interior are the elaborate carved and painted decoration, especially the nave vaulting, the rood-screen of 1600, and the grotesques on the 14C stalls. A stair ascends to the Burgomasters' Gallery where the oath was taken.

Rue Eugène Ysaye, beside the church of St. Jacques, soon reaches Boulevard Piercot with the *Conservatoire de Musique* (1881) beyond a garden containing busts of musicians. Inside there is a monument

(1922) to César Franck. An equestrian statue of Charlemagne (Louis Jehotte, 1868) stands beyond the W end of Boulevard Piercot and at the N limit of the PARC D'AVROY known for its many reproductions of ancient sculptures. Avenue Rogier skirts the E side of the park to reach (right) the *Monument National à la Résistance* (P. Etienne and L. Dupont, 1955) with figures representing armed and intellectual resistance. Opposite are the *Terraces*, gardens containing sculpture, beyond which the Meuse is crossed by the Pont Albert I leading to the Parc de la Boverie. From the Resistance monument, Avenue Rogier continues S to a crossroads where there is a memorial to Charles Rogier (1800–85), a leader of the 1830 revolution and later the man who did most to give Belgium a railway system. From here, Rue des Guillemins reaches the *Gare des Guillemins* in 600m.

Outer Liège

The PARC DE COINTE (sports grounds, etc.) spreads over the hill to the S of the Gare des Guillemins, offering the best general views over Liège and its suburbs (orientation table beside road to the N of the sports grounds). In the E part of the park the *Basilique Sacré-Coeur* stands beside the tall (83m) *Allied War Memorial* (1936). Below the park the *Pont de Fragnée*, at the junction of the Meuse and the Ourthe, has four piers which survived the destruction of 1944 and is the only Liège bridge to have been rebuilt to its pre-war design. In the little garden on the point between the two rivers there is a monument (Vinçotte, 1905) to Zénobe Gramme, the inventor of the dynamo, who worked in Liège between 1849 and 1855.

The PARC DE LA BOVERIE is on the right bank of the Meuse immediately across the Pont Albert I, at the N end standing the large *Palais des Congrès* (1958) and towards the S the **Musée d'Art Moderne** (Tuesday–Saturday, 13.00 to 18.00; Sunday, 11.00 to 16.30. Closed 1 January, 1 May, 1 November, 25 December). Although largely used for temporary exhibitions, there is also a permanent collection of modern works from the Impressionists onward (including works by Gauguin, Picasso, Chagall, Kokoschka and Ensor), while the Cabinet des Estampes here contains some 25,000 works spanning from the 16C to modern times. The Canal de Dérivation bounds the E side of the park, across this at 17 Boulevard R. Poincaré being the unusual and interesting **Musée du Fer et du Charbon** (Saturday, 14.00 to 17.00), devoted to iron and coal. A principal feature, on the ground floor, is a largely authentic Walloon forge of the 17th and 18C, complete with its huge bellows turned by waterwheel (not however now functioning). The museum also offers a magnificent display of ironwork, notably elaborately patterned and illustrated firebacks, one of these dating from 1584; models; locks and keys, including Roman, Merovingian and Carolingian; and several interesting pictures of many sorts of industrial activity. A taped commentary in English is played on request.

OUTREMEUSE is the name given to the 'popular' quarter on the right bank across the Pont des Arches. The Rue Chaussée-des-Prés leads to a square (Pont Saint Nicholas) in which stands the *Monument Tchantchès*, a folklore figure representative of the true Liégois. In the streets around there are several 'potales' (niches with a Virgin or a saint), domestic shrines several of which date from the 17C; a tour of these may be made with the aid of a detailed guide obtainable from Tourist Information. The *Maison Grétry* (by appointment only, 14.00

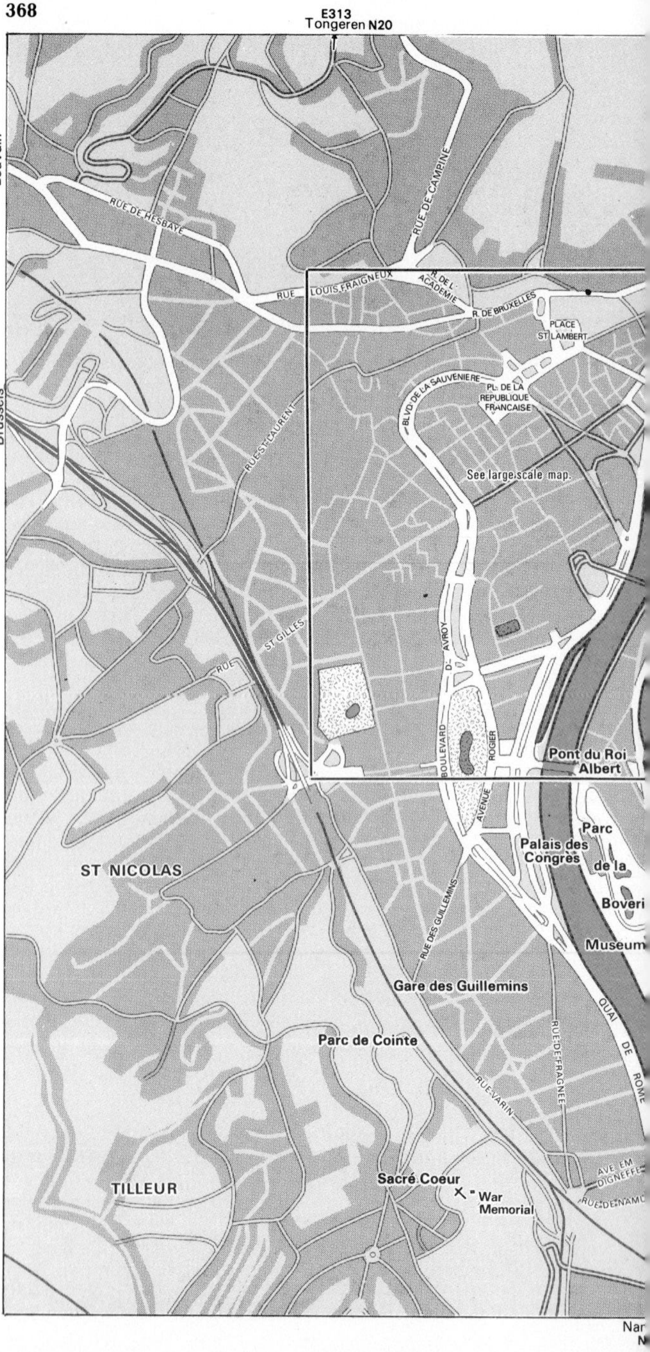

E313
Tongeren N20

N3
Louvain

E40
Brussels

RUE DE HESBAYE

RUE DE CAMBRE

RUE

RUE ST-LAURENT

RUE LOUIS-FRAIGNEUX

R. DE L'ACADÉMIE

R. DE BRUXELLES

PLACE ST LAMBERT

BLVD DE LA SAUVENIÈRE

PL. DE LA RÉPUBLIQUE FRANÇAISE

See large-scale map

ST GILLES

D'AVROY

BOULEVARD

AVENUE ROGER

Pont du Roi Albert

RUE

ST NICOLAS

RUE DES GUILLEMINS

Palais des Congrès

Parc de la Boverie

Museum

Gare des Guillemins

RUE D'FRAGNÉE

QUAI DE ROME

Parc de Cointe

RUE VARIN

TILLEUR

Sacré Coeur

× War Memorial

AVE EM DIGNEFFE

RUE DE NAMUR

Nar N

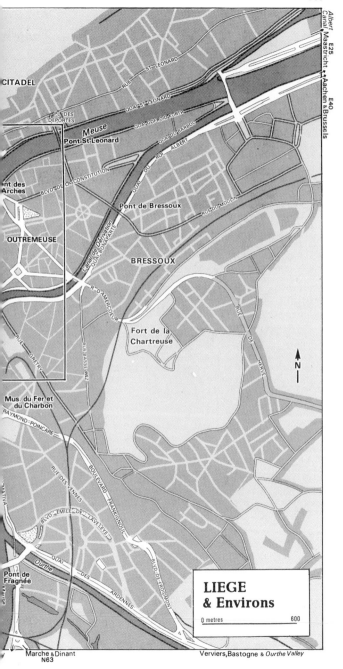

CITADEL

RUE ST-LEONARD

QUAI ST-LEONARD

PL. DES
DEPORTES

Meuse
Pont St-Leonard

QUAI-GOF/OIX-KURTH

QUAI-DU-ROI-ALBERT

nt des
Arches

BLVD-DE-LA-CONSTITUTION

QUAI DU ROI ALBERT

Pont de Bressoux

RUE-DU-MOULIN

OUTREMEUSE

Canal de Derivation
QUAI-BONAPARTE

BRESSOUX

R-D'AMERCOEUR

RUE-GRETRY

RUE-BASSE-WEZ

Fort de la
Chartreuse

RUE DE HERVE

N

Mus. du Fer et
du Charbon

RAYMOND-POINCARE

RUE DES VENNES

BOULEVARD FRANTIGNONU

MATIVA

BLVD-EMILE-DE-LAVELEYE

BLVD-DE-FROIDMONT

QUAI

Ourthe

DES

ARDENNES

Pont de
Fragnée

Meuse

LIEGE
& Environs

0 metres   600

Marche & Dinant
N63

Verviers, Bastogne & Ourthe Valley

to 17.00), at 34 Rue des Récollets 100m SE of the Monument Tcchantchès, is where the composer lived as a young man. Farther S, at 56 Rue Surlet, the *Musée Tchantchès* (Wednesday, Thursday, 14.30 to 16.00) is devoted to Liège folklore.

For the CITADEL, see p 363. For the PORT, see p 359.

From Liège to *Brussels*, see Rte 21; to *Namur*, see Rte 31; to *Dinant*, see Rte 32; to *Rochefort* and *Bouillon*, see Rte 35; to *Florenville*, see Rte 36; to *Luxembourg*, see Rte 37; to the *Cantons de l'Est*, see Rte 38; for between Liège, *Maastricht* and *Aachen*, see Rte 39.

35 Liège to Rochefort and Bouillon

Total distance 106km.—*20km Quatre-Bras.*—*33km* **Marche-en-Famenne.**—*11km* **Rochefort.**—*18km Transinne.*—*21km Noirefontaine.*—*3km* **Bouillon**.

Liège (see Rte 34) is left by the right bank of the Meuse and then, after the railway bridge, the winding Route du Condroz which soon ascends through woods. Rte 32 is followed past *Sart-Tilman*, *Neuville-en-Condroz* and *Saint Séverin* as far as (*20km*) the road fork of *Quatre-Bras.*—*12km Bois-et-Borsu* has a late 9C church containing 14C carvings and frescoes, the latter, in the nave, telling the stories of St. Lambert and St. Hubert. The Romanesque church at *Ocquier* (2km E) dates from 1017 and stands on the foundations of perhaps three predecessors.—*4km Méan* is in the province of Namur, which, however, is left 4km before (*17km*) **Marche-en-Famenne** in the province of Luxembourg (see Rte 33, which is crossed here, for Marche-en-Famenne and nearby Waha).—*4km* The castle of *Jemeppe* dates in part from the 12C.—At (*4km*) *Jemelle* the province of Namur is again entered. The station here is the nearest for Rochefort and Han-sur-Lesse (bus connection).

3km **Rochefort**, see Rte 29. From here the direct road S through *Tellin* in Luxembourg may be taken. An alternative, slightly more westerly road enables *Lessive, Han-sur-Lesse* and *Lavaux-Sainte-Anne* to be visited, for all of which see Rte 29. Both roads meet at (*18km* from Rochefort) *Transinne*, from where on there is much forest, but still sufficient open country to afford some fine vistas.—*4km Maissin* where (NW) a 16C Breton Calvary adjoining a war cemetery commemorates 3000 Bretons and over 200 Germans who fell here on 22–23 August 1914.—*7km Paliseul* was the childhood home of the poet Verlaine, and (as 'Palatidum') a hunting-seat of the early Merovingian kings.—*10km Noirefontaine.*

From here diversions can be made either W to *Botassart* (4km), just S of which there is a well-known view across the Semois to the *Tombeau du Géant*, a large natural mound enclosed by a sharp bend in the river; or E through the villages of the upper Semois, either continuing to *Herbeumont* (Rte 36A) or returning, part of the way S of the river, to Noirefontaine.

3km **Bouillon** (5600 inhab. Tourist Information: Porte de France), with its ancient castle perched high above the town and scenically situated near the best stretches of the lovely Semois valley, is a very popular tourist centre. There are fine views from the castle terrace and the castle itself.

From the 8C a castle here was held by the counts (later dukes) of an independent territory. All were called Godfrey (Godefroid), the fifth being the leader of the First Crusade (1096) and first King of Jerusalem. Before leaving, this Godfrey sold his lands to the prince-bishop of Liège, whose successors, however, were only able to rule through virtually independent lords, later styling themselves princes. These princely families were first La Marck and later La Tour d'Auvergne. In 1678 Bouillon was ceded to Louis XIV under the Peace of Nijmegen.—Prince Charles Edward, the Young Pretender, lived here with Clementina Walkinshaw from 1755 to about 1760; and in 1870 Napoleon III, as prisoner of the Prussians, spent the night of 3 September at the Hôtel de la Poste.

The *Castle (January, February: Saturday, Sunday, 10.00 to 17.00; March–December: daily, 10.00 to 17.00, 18.00 or 19.00. Closed Monday and Tuesday in December. In July and August, torchlight visit nightly at 22.00) dates in its present massive form largely from the 16th and 17C, the latter century seeing considerable modification by Vauban. The various parts are marked by numbers, these referring to the explanations given in the official guide, an English version of which is available. Parts of especial interest are indicated below. No. 1 is the second of three bridged cuts by which the castle was defended, the last being No. 3, stoned over in 1686 and with a moat that could be filled at will. No. 5 is the so-called Room of Godfrey de Bouillon, hewn out of the rock; the ancient wooden cross on the floor, of unknown age, was discovered in 1962, and the room also contains a statue of Godfrey, armour and medieval weapons. No. 6: the main courtyard in which once stood the lord's residence. Note the bell of 1563 and the twin-level triple-slitted loopholes, these latter very likely Vauban's work as is also certainly the present form of the rampart walk (No. 10) and the semicircular tower (No. 11). The Clock-Tower at the end of the rampart walk is a rebuilding by Vauban of an earlier watch-tower; the present clock is of 1810 but the hour bell was that of the earlier clock of 1606. The Tower of Austria, to the right of the clock-tower, is so named after George of Austria, Prince-Bishop of Liège, who converted it into a caponier in c 1551; in its earliest form this tower was designed to protect this end of the castle. No. 12: Godfrey de Bouillon's Chair, a double lookout hewn from the rock and one of the oldest parts of the castle since it could only have fulfilled its purpose prior to the building of the clock-tower and the construction to the south. No. 13, the top of the Tower of Austria, affords a view of both the castle and of much of the town below (for the dam across the river, see No. 24). No. 14, the basement of the Tower of Austria and once a guard-room, exhibits medieval weapons. No. 20, popularly called the Torture Room and showing instruments of torture, was more probably the armourer's workshop. Nos 21 and 22 were dungeons. No. 24 is a doorway (no entry) beyond which 396 steps descend to the site of a water mill of the 15C; what was left of the mill disappeared during the Second World War but its dam across the Semois survives. No. 25, with a large cistern at one end, is a gallery some 90m in length; as the castle's main corridor it was lined with storerooms. No. 27 is the well, much widened and deepened by Vauban.

The *Musée Ducal* (April–June and September–October: daily, 09.30 to 17.30. July and August: daily, 09.00 to 19.30), occupying an 18C house on the road up to the castle, is in two main sections; explanations in the rooms are in English, and a taped English commentary will be played on request. The History and Folklore section includes a small 16C living-room and adjoining kitchen; a 'Historic Room' with a model of Bouillon in 1690; a room devoted to hunting; a nursery, clogmaker's workroom, and a carding and weaving room. The Godefroid de Bouillon section of the museum is concerned largely with the crusades and exhibits Eastern applied art of the period and several interesting models of war engines and weapons. This section also shows medieval ecclesiastical material, notably Limoges work of the 13C, ivories of the 13th and 14C, a remarkably well-preserved 14C belt, and a 14C Shrine-Virgin.

For Bouillon via the VALLEY OF THE SEMOIS to *Dinant*, see Rte 30.

36   Liège to Florenville (Continuing to Virton and the district of Gaume)

Two roads are described. The first (Rte 36A) as far as La Roche-en-Ardenne generally follows the winding VALLEY OF THE OURTHE as it ascends from Liège into the Ardennes. Always scenic, and along many stretches flanked by steep wooded hills or cliffs, the valley is a favourite excursion and holiday objective, particularly for walkers. The other road (Rte 36B), through Bastogne, though rather shorter and faster, does not compare scenically and passes fewer places of general interest. Beyond La Roche-en-Ardenne (A.) and Neufchâteau (B.) both roads climb to the higher levels of the Ardennes, traversing forest broken by open upland permitting wide vistas.

A. Via the Ourthe Valley and La Roche-en-Ardenne

Total distance 148km.—*13km* **Esneux**.—*9km* **Comblain-au-Pont**.—*8km* Hamoir.—*15km* Barvaux.—*6km* **Durbuy**.—*10km* **Hotton**.—*15km* **La Roche-en-Ardenne**.—*23km* **Saint Hubert**.—*13km* Recogne.—*12km* Bertrix.—*10km* Herbeumont.—*14km* **Florenville**.

Liège (see Rte 34) is left by the right bank of the Ourthe which is crossed in the suburb of *Angleur* and again just before (*8km*) *Tilff* where there is a museum of bee-keeping in the château (April, May, September: Saturday, Sunday, Holidays, 10.00 to 12.00, 14.00 to 18.00. Daily in June–August).—*5km* **Esneux**, below steep wooded hills, has a large and pleasant riverside area with cafés and parking space, while the Parc du Mary is a visitor complex offering picnic sites, walks, view-points and an arboretum. For the next 17km (to Hamoir) the road keeps to the left bank of the Ourthe up a narrow, wooded and winding valley.—*9km* **Comblain-au-Pont** is a small town just above the confluence with the Amblève known for its deep '*Chantoire*', a chasm and grotto-complex of some twenty 'rooms' with typical limestone formations (July and August: daily, 09.00 to 18.00, but may be closed). The stump of an old tower stands above the town. From Comblain-au-Pont a diversion may be made 5km W to *Antisthenes* where the 'Avouerie', comprising a 12C keep and residential additions of 1648, is used for receptions and exhibitions and houses also a beer museum (April–October: daily except Monday 10.00 to 12.00. 14.00 to 19.00). At *Comblain-la-Tour*, across the river and S of Comblain-au-Pont, there is a 14C tower. *8km* Hamoir where there is a monument to the sculptor Jean Del Cour, born here in 1627.

This Rte now diverges eastwards, generally following the Ourthe and rejoining the main road at Durbuy. At *Tohogne* on the main road there is a Romanesque 11C church.

From Hamoir N66 is followed E to (*3km*) *Filot* beyond which N86 is taken S to (*5km*) **Vieuxville** (3000 inhab.). Here *La Bouverie* (just W), an attractive farm built in 1570 by the monks of Stavelot-Malmédy, now houses a local museum, information office and crafts boutique (July, August: daily except Monday, 10.00 to 13.00, 14.00 to 18.00). The nearby ruined castle of *Logne*, on a site used both by prehistoric peoples and the Romans and later a stronghold of the 'Wild Boar of the Ardennes', was destroyed in 1521 by Henry of Nassau in the service of Charles V (May, June, September, October: Sunday, 13.00 to 18.00. July and August: daily, 10.00 to 12.00, 14.00 to 18.00. Holidays, 13.00 to 16.00. Guided visit, 1 hour).

A road NW out of Vieuxville leads towards *Sy* (4km) at the head of a scenic Ourthe ravine.

N86 winds above the castle of Logne to cross into the province of Luxembourg and reach (*3km*) *Bomal* (7500 inhab.), twinned with the wine district of Beaujolais and offering wine-tasting, and then (*4km*) the small holiday centre of *Barvaux* (7500 inhab.), popular for being close to the meeting point of the three contrasting districts of Condroz (farming), Famenne (pastoral) and the Ardennes. Here too there is a Beaujolais tasting and from here also walkers have a path along one of the loveliest stretches of the river to Durbuy (7km).

Those interested in prehistory will wish to make a short diversion 4km SE to *Wéris*. If the Wéris road is followed out of Barvaux, a menhir is passed beside this road just SW of Wéris. At Wéris itself, beside the road just NW of the village, there is a dolmen (tomb) with a massive roof slab, one of the finest in Belgium, and there are other stones and tombs in the district. The church at Wéris is in part of the 11C and contains a 13C stone tabernacle.

From Barvaux, Durbuy is reached by a winding road through *Bohon* known as the Route Touristique.—*6km* **Durbuy** (7600 inhab.), which stands on Roman foundations and is a most attractive small town close to a spot where the Ourthe flows through a ravine with oddly twisted strata, is known for its old quarter (adjacent to a large parking area) in which the 16C *Halle aux Blés*, the former corn market, houses a local museum. The *Château des Comtes*, of 9C origin and victim of numerous sieges, is today mainly of the 19C though an 11C turret survives.—*10km* **Hotton** (3500 inhab.) lies below an escarpment known to have been occupied by prehistoric man and also to have served as a Roman strongpoint. The *Grottes de Hotton* ('Thousand and One Nights'. April–October: daily, 09.00 to 18.00), discovered in 1958, are exceptionally beautiful and endowed with some notable formations. The visit goes as far as the so-called Balcony, from where the river, some 30m below, can be heard.

The château of *Deulin*, 5km NW and dating from 1760, is used for concerts, exhibitions and other cultural activities.

For the *Tramway de l'Aisne*, see Rte 33 after La Roche-en-Ardenne.

8km Marcourt was until the 11C the capital of the counts of Montaigu on the site of whose stronghold above the village now stands a chapel of 1637.—*7km* **La Roche-en-Ardenne**, see Rte 33 which is crossed here. The road ascends through forest, reaching the important crossroads of *Barrière de Champlon* and continuing across the marshy Forêt de Freyr.

23km **Saint Hubert** (5500 inhab. Tourist Information: Place de l'Abbaye) is traditionally the place, at that time deep forest, where St. Hubert was converted to piety. The town was also the birthplace in 1759 of the painter of flowers Joseph Redouté.

Hubert was born of noble family in c 656. On Good Friday 683, when out hunting, his hounds cornered a stag. At bay, the animal turned and was seen to bear the Cross between its horns while at the same time a voice reproached Hubert for his profanity in hunting on Good Friday. He at once renounced the world, entering the abbey of Stavelot. In 705, when in Rome, he learnt of the murder at Liège of Bishop Lambert of Maastricht and Tongeren. The Pope then offered Hubert the bishopric, which he at first refused on grounds of unworthiness but later accepted when an angel appeared and draped him with a white episcopal stole. St. Hubert died in 727, and in 823 his remains were brought to the abbey (founded 7C) which stood near the site of his conversion, from that day onwards both the abbey and the town growing around it being known as Saint Hubert. Later the saint became the patron of hunters. His remains have long since disappeared, but the abbey remains a place of pilgrimage.

The abbey (rebuilt 1729) survived as such until the French Revolution, its domestic buildings on the main square now being a cultural centre. Its church, the *Basilique Saint Hubert*, in Flamboyant style of 1526–60, has an Italianate W façade of 1702 with a St. Hubert medallion between the towers. Inside, the lofty brick vaulting of 1683 is successor to shingle vaulting destroyed by Huguenots in 1568. The crypt below the choir is in part of the 11C. The stalls, Liège work of 1733, are carved with the stories of St. Hubert and St. Benedict, and in the S ambulatory a *Retable with Limoges enamels (1560), after Dürer's Small Passion, is one of the few furnishings to have survived, albeit damaged, the destruction by the Huguenots. The saint's cenotaph (1847) was a gift from King Leopold I who was a lover of the hunt.

There is a *Parc à Gibier* (game animals) off N849 2km NW of the town, and in the forest beyond (signed off N849) a squat pyramid in a lonely clearing recalls that King Albert often visited this spot, the last occasion being shortly before his death. N849 continues to (8km from Saint Hubert) *Fourneau Saint Michel* which has been arranged as a complex for ironwork up to the 18C. Here, beside the road, are an 18C forge built by the last abbot of Saint Hubert and also a barn showing a fine collection of firebacks. Tools and other equipment are shown in the lower section where there is also a museum (March–June; September–December: daily, 09.00 to 17.00 or 18.00 on Sunday; July, August: daily, 09.00 to 19.00).—The *Musée de la Vie Rurale en Wallonie*, a short distance farther N, is an open air museum illustrating Walloon rural life of the 16–18C through preserved and re-erected buildings—schools, chapel, cottages, tobacco hall, wash-house—generally arranged topographically and by themes (week before Easter–mid September: daily, 09.00 to 17.00 or 18.00 in July and August).

From Saint Hubert the road (N89) continues S through forest.—*13km Recogne* where Napoleon III stayed in 1870 after his defeat at Sedan; the poet Verlaine claimed descent from the lords of Verlaine, 3km southeast.—Near (*12km*) *Bertrix* this Rte leaves the main N89, which continues to Bouillon, and a lovely wooded and winding descent is made down to the valley of the Semois. On the left, about halfway between Bertrix and Mortehan, the 'Château des Fées' is a defensive work which seems to have been in use from the 4C until perhaps the 11C—*6km Mortehan*. Near Cugnon (just NW) there are traces of a Gallic camp of the 1C BC. and also grottoes by tradition associated with St. Remaclus, said to have been offered land here for a monastery and to have dug the grottoes to serve as a chapel.—*4km Herbeumont*, with, perched high above the river, the ruins of the 12C castle of the local counts, destroyed by Louis XIV in 1658. The view alone repays the short climb up from the village. South of the village the road crosses the river, beyond which (left) a hotel occupies the site of the 18C abbey of Conques.—*10km Chassepierre* (off the main N83) has a well-known view-point and is popular with artists. The village is said to have existed in prehistoric times when primitive fishermen used its grotto, and in Roman times to have been known as 'Casa Petra'. At *Azy*, 3km N within a loop of the Semois, there is a dolmen.—*4km* **Florenville**, see Rte 36B below.

B. Via Bastogne

Total distance 127km.—*10km Beaufays.*—*11km* **Aywaille**.—*28km Baraque de Fraiture.*—*15km* **Houffalize**.—*15km* **Bastogne**.—*27km Neufchâteau.*—*21km* **Florenville**.

Liège (see Rte 34) is left by the right bank of the Ourthe which is followed as far as the suburb of *Chênée* where Rte 38B continues E for Chaudfontaine and the Cantons de l'Est. This Rte ascends S to (*10km*) *Beaufays*, where Rte 37 to the Grand-Duchy of Luxembourg diverges SE, and then (*7km*) *Sprimont* where the Musée Régional de la Pierre (Monday–Friday, except Tuesday, 09.00 to 17.00; Saturday, Sunday, except mid November–mid March, 14.00 to 17.00), in the former generator house of the local quarries, tells the story of stones from their mining to their use for industrial or decorative purposes. After Sprimont the road drops to the Amblève valley at (*4km*) **Aywaille** (8000 inhab.). The *Château d'Amblève*, a fragment of ruin seen on the N cliff 2km downstream, was traditionally once a stronghold of the Quatre Fils Aymon and, later, belonged to the 'Wild Boar of the Ardennes'; it was demolished by Parma in 1587. For *Remouchamps*, 3km E of Aywaille, see Rte 37.—At (*4km*) *Harzé* the road curves round the restored 12–17C château (Easter–October: 10.00 to 12.00, 13.00 to 17.00). The gardens and a part of the building can be visited, the Salle des Comtes with walls hung with Cordoba leather being the room of principal interest.—*7km Werbomont*, just beyond which the province of Luxembourg is entered.—*17km Baraque de Fraiture*, a somewhat bleak spot, is the second highest place in Belgium (636m).

15km **Houffalize** (4000 inhab.), the name deriving from 'haute falaise' (high cliff), sprawls over both sides of the steep valley of the eastern arm of the upper Ourthe. The town was largely destroyed during the Battle of the Ardennes during which it was the place at which Patton's and Montgomery's counter-offensives met. The *Eglise Sainte Catherine*, with a 13C tower, was formerly the church of a priory founded in 1248 by Thierry, lord of Houffalize, whose tomb is here, as is also a fine brass lectern of 1372 by Jehans Josès of Dinant.

At *Tavigny*, 4km SE, there is a particularly fine fortified-farm. For *Hachiville*, 6km farther E in the Grand-Duchy of Luxembourg, see Rte 44B.

For the next 42km the road traverses open, rather dull country through (*15km*) **Bastogne**, on Rte 33 which is crossed here, to (*27km*) *Neufchâteau* (6000 inhab.) where the Tour Griffon is a relic of a castle destroyed in 1555.—The country now becomes more attractive as the road enters forest. At (*14km*) *Epioux* the château of 1650 was in 1862–71 the home of Pierre Bonaparte, nephew of Napoleon.—*4 km*

Lacuisine is a summer resort beautifully situated within a loop of the Semois, the glorious scenery here being best enjoyed by making the boat descent (Défile du Paradis) from *Chiny*, 4km N by road or 3km walk (April–September: daily 09.00 to 18.00. Time required, c 1½ hours).—*3km* **Florenville** (5500 inhab. Tourist Information: Place Albert I) is a small frontier town on a hill commanding a wide view to the N. across the valley of the Semois; this is best appreciated from a terrace behind the church (orientation table and multi-language taped commentary) or, even better, from the top of the tower. The church, rebuilt in 1950 after the destruction of half the town in 1940, houses a modern carillon of 48 bells of which one was presented by No. 1 Fighter Wing, Royal Canadian Air Force, in thanks for hospitality received from Florenville.

The Gaume

The GAUME, also known as Belgian Lorraine, is the southernmost corner of Belgium. While scenically it is one third forest, and in this respect an extension of the Ardennes, ethnically this is a melting pot in which Walloon, Lorraine and Luxembourg dialects and customs mingle. Ironworking, long the principal activity, has left its mark in the form of many abandoned forges but excellent examples of this often beautiful work can be seen in the Musée Gaumais at Virton. There are also many caves, large and small, sometimes called 'Trou des Nutons' (or 'des Fées'), the home of gnomes and fairies who, though they never show themselves, are famed for their hard work and helpfulness; it is said that tasks left near the caves—washing, mending and suchlike—are often meticulously carried out.

The principal town is *Virton*, and the two places of main tourist interest are the abbey of *Orval* and the archaeological site of *Montauban*. The description below starts from Florenville and follows an anticlockwise route through Orval, Virton and Montauban to Etalle on the Florenville-Arlon road. The total distance is 44km to Etalle, from where Arlon is 16km E or Florenville 23km west.

8km The **Abbey of Orval**, graciously set across a green and wooded valley, comprises the ruins of the ancient abbey and the buildings (1948) of the new one. Visitors are admitted to the medieval ruins and to the museum in the 18C cellars of the modern abbey. (Guided tours. Sunday before Easter–September: daily, 09.00 to 12.00, 13.30 to 18.00. Other months: daily, 10.00 to 12.00, 13.30 to 17.00).

Legend tells that Matilda of Lorraine (1046–1115), when sitting beside a spring here, lost her gold ring in the water. After praying at a nearby oratory, she returned to the spring and a fish swam up with her ring. Hence the abbey's name, an inversion of Val d'Or. Further tradition is that Benedictine monks founded an abbey here in 1020 and that, when they abandoned it, Cistercians took over in c 1132. Whatever its origins, Orval quickly became one of the richest Cistercian houses in Europe, famed for its ironwork. In the 18C the abbey was largely rebuilt (by Dewez), only to be virtually destroyed by the French in 1794. In 1926 Trappists acquired the estate, their new buildings being completed by 1948.

A detailed plan and guide in English is provided with the entrance ticket. The main feature of the ruins is the 12–13C part Romanesque and part Gothic church, with a notable rose window and pillars with Romanesque capitals, these last being among the best of their kind in Belgium. Near the ambulatory are the foundations of two very early buildings; a late 11C church and an even earlier oratory, perhaps that at which Matilda prayed so successfully. The visit also includes an audio-visual explanation of modern monastic life, this (20 minutes) being given in the former guest-house which preserves a 13C gable; the Matilda Fountain; remains of the cloisters; the museum; the gallery of the modern church; and a garden of medicinal plants.

17km **Virton** (3700 inhab.), the chief town of the Gaume, was known in Roman times as Vertunum but dates its more modern history from a stronghold built by a count of Chiny in c 1060. At the entrance to the municipal park, an Indian totem pole was a gift from Canadian forces earlier stationed at a nearby NATO base. The *Musée Gaumais* (April–October: daily except Tuesday, 09.30 to 12.00, 14.00 to 18.00), in the Rue d'Arlon in the NE part of the town, occupies a part of a 17C Franciscan (Recollect) convent. Along the approach-path is a machine into which a coin can be placed to cause the Franciscan on the tower to strike the bell, while opposite there is a reconstruction of a Gallo-Roman pottery. The museum covers a wide range of regional themes, these including archaeology (prehistory and the Gallo-Roman period); local custom and crafts; period rooms; and, especially, ironwork with a large display of firebacks bearing a great variety of designs.

At *Montquintin*, 6km SW, an 18C farm has been converted to a museum of country life (April–mid September: Sunday, but daily in July and August, 14.00 to 18.00).—At *Latour*, 4km SE, there is a museum of local history, with particular reference to the local regiment of Dragoons (Easter–November: Sunday, but daily in July and August, 15.00 to 18.00).—At *Gomery*, 5km E, there is a dolmen.

Vallus, Arlon and Montauban

Croix-Rouge, with a Trou des Fées, is a crossroads in forest *10km* N of

Virton. Near here (1.5km N) is the little Humbois Potter Museum with a 1C Gallo-Roman kiln (normally open only for groups).—The (*4km*) **Archaeological Park of Montauban** may be reached either by continuing N through *Buzenol*, or by bearing E at Croix-Rouge and then in 3km turning N towards Buzenol. A path climbs (c 10 minutes) to the quiet, wooded promontory across which sprawls this extensive and long fortified site, well worth a visit, at any rate in fine weather, even though there is not a great deal to be seen and some imagination is required. An Iron Age earth rampart of c 500 BC was replaced in the 2C BC by a stone wall, part of which, together with traces of huts, survives. Later, in the 3–4C, a Gallo-Roman wall was built as defence against the Franks, and, later again, a medieval fortress arose, part of the keep of which can be seen. Archaeologically the Gallo-Roman wall is the most important feature, this having been strengthened with carved Roman funerary and other stone blocks, probably hurriedly collected from surrounding abandoned settlements. These blocks have now for the most part been replaced by replicas, the originals, with other Gallo-Roman stonework, being shown in the windows of the exhibition building. Of these carved blocks the most interesting, though incomplete, is that of the Harvester (vallus), illustrating, together with another incomplete block in the Arlon museum, an agricultural device described by the elder Pliny in his 'Historia Naturalis' but not identified until this block (excavated 1958) enabled the Arlon block (excavated 1854) to be identified; a donkey pushes a wheeled container, edged with teeth, these teeth tearing off the ears of corn which then drop into the container. A wooden reconstruction of the device stands just above the exhibition building (Park always open. To enter the building arrangements must be made through the Musée Gaumais at Virton). Across the road from the car park can be seen the remains of ironworks which flourished here between the 16C and 19C.

From Montauban the main Florenville-Arlon road is reached in *5km* at *Etalle*.

37 Liège via the Valleys of the Amblève and the Salm to the Grand-Duchy of Luxembourg

Total distance 81km.—*10km Beaufays.—6km Louveigné* (for **Banneux-Notre-Dame**).—*6km* **Remouchamps**.—*19km* **La Gleize**.— *6km Coo.—3km* **Trois-Ponts**.—*13km* **Vielsalm**.—*18km Frontier of Grand-Duchy*.

For **Liège** (Rte 34) to (*10km*) *Beaufays*, see Rte 36B.—*6km Louveigné*, 2km NE of which is **Banneux-Notre-Dame**, the place where in 1933 the Virgin appeared eight times to a girl aged 12 and which has since developed into a pilgrimage complex with a hospital and many chapels. The Chapel of the Appearances is immediately left on entering, while set back from the other side of the road is the Magnificat Altar. The Source (spring), a short way farther along the road, incorporates a fragment from the grotto of Lourdes.

After Louveigné this Rte turns S along N666 (the Vallon des Chantoirs, so named for the numerous 'chantoirs' or 'holes' in the limestone) to descend to the valley of the Amblève at (*6km*) **Remou-**

champs, a riverside resort whose pleasant position in a wooded valley is now somewhat marred by the admittedly impressive spans of a motorway. The *Grotto* here, carved out by the Rubicon, a little tributary of the Amblève, is known to have been lived in by prehistoric man. The visit requires a good hour, the main features being the Salle de la Cathédrale and a 1km-long subterranean boat ride, claiming to be the world's longest (May–August: daily, 09.00 to 18.00. March, April, September, October: daily, 09.30 to 17.00. Last departure 1 hour before above closing times). *Sougné*, just below Remouchamps, is a village at the foot of a rock-rampart called the Heid des Gattes from which the French dislodged the Austrians in 1794.

The road (N633) now ascends S along the winding valley of the Amblève—*19km* **La Gleize** is a bleak, perched and severe mountain village in which a German Tiger tank and a museum combine to recall that it was here that the infamous Kampfgruppe Peiper (see Rte 38B, Baugnez) made its last stand during the Battle of the Ardennes. At *Cheneux*, 3km SW, there is a memorial to the American 509th Parachute Infantry Regiment of 82nd Division who stormed and retook La Gleize.—*6km Coo*, where the river flows in a loop of c 4km the narrow neck of which was cut by the monks of Stavelot in the 18C. The cut forms a small cascade which today has served as excuse to turn this spot into an excursion objective (cafés, go-karts, souvenir stalls, etc.). A chair-lift ascends to the height of the *Montagne de Lancre* (450m) with an extensive view (mid March–mid November: daily, 09.00 to 20.00).—*3km* **Trois-Ponts** (2000 inhab.) is at the hub of the two loops of the *Circuit des Panoramas* (signs), offering ever-changing views across wooded country. The W loop, through Haute-Badeux, Reharmont and Bergeval is 21km; the E loop through Wanne is 15km. For *Stavelot*, 5km NE, see Rte 38B.

During the Battle of the Ardennes, Trois Ponts witnessed one of the most gallant and cleanly decisive incidents along the advance of Kampfgruppe Peiper (see La Gleize above). It was approaching midday on 18 December that the German battle-group's advance guard tanks (coming from Stavelot) clattered under the railway viaduct to swing left for the vital Amblève bridge—only to be faced by a lone American anti-tank gun which at once picked off the lead tank. There followed a brief, uneven contest, inevitably ended by the destruction of the gun and the deaths of its crew of four. But the gallantry of these four gained the seconds needed for the demolition of the bridge, and the demolition too of Peiper's hopes for a dash to the Meuse. Instead now he had to turn N for La Gleize and Defeat.

The road now winds past wooded cliffs up the valley of the Salm, in 5km entering the province of Luxembourg.—*6km* (from Trois-Ponts) *Grand Halleux*, to the S of which is the *Parc du Monti*, a game park in which forest fauna may be seen in semi-liberty.—*7km* **Vielsalm** (7000 inhab.), an American headquarters during the Battle of the Ardennes and today with memorials. One, immediately below a church beside the road from Trois Ponts, is to the Ardennes Secret Army. Another, in the S part of the town within a road junction and comprising a small fountain and a rough, dark stone, remembers the American 7th Armoured Division, while, alongside, another stone recalls that this is Square General Bruce C. Clarke, a combat commander within the division. By way of contrast another memorial, on the left leaving Vielsalm for (*2km*), *Salmchâteau*, recalls the many people of this region who fought against slavery in the Congo. In Salmchâteau are the ruins of the castle of the counts of Salm, first built in the 9C, while for those interested in local geology there is the Musée de Coticule (April–October: Tuesday–Sunday, 13.00 to 17.00. In July and August, same days but also 10.00 to 12.00). This rare stone, also known as razor-stone or hone-stone and exploited only in this district, was much in demand during the 19th and earlier 20C; but as markets declined quarrying ceased by 1980.—*11km Beho*, at 500m on the Ardennes plateau, is where the British vanguard crossed the then German frontier on 1 December 1918. The church here, with a 12C tower but otherwise a rebuilding of 1712, contains some good Baroque furnishings.—*5km Frontier of the Grand-Duchy of Luxembourg.*—To **Luxembourg** (c 75km), see Rte 44.

38 Liège to the Cantons de L'Est

The largely German-speaking CANTONS DE L'EST (**Eupen, Malmédy, Sankt Vith**) together make up an eastern bulge of Belgium bounded on the E by Germany and on the W by a line running roughly from Eupen, through Baraque Michel and Malmédy, to the border of the Grand-Duchy of Luxembourg near Beho. Before the French Revolution these lands belonged to a variety of immediate overlords: Eupen was a district of the duchy of Limburg; Malmédy belonged in part to the ecclesiastical principality of Stavelot-Malmédy and in part to the duchy of Luxembourg; Sankt Vith also was divided, part adhering to the duchy of Luxembourg, but the communes of Schönberg and Manderfeld depending on the prince-bishop of Trèves (Trier). All this ended with the French Revolution when Belgium was absorbed into republican France. In 1815 the Congress of Vienna gave the Cantons (less the district of Moresnet and the town of Stavelot) to Prussia, and a vigorous policy of Germanisation was pursued until the First World War, after which (1920) the League of Nations awarded the Cantons to Belgium, where they have since remained, apart from 1940–45 when Hitler declared them reunited to Germany. Today the Cantons have no administrative significance as such and all form a part of the province of Liège.

The pleasant and often interesting small towns and villages, many very German in atmosphere, lie amid scenery much of which is upland forest and lakes or reservoirs. Between Eupen and Malmédy the Hautes Fagnes (with Belgium's highest point, Signal de Botrange, 694m) is a large area a main feature of which is peat bog and sphagnum moss holding reserves of very pure water. The plants are of low Alpine and Nordic type, and the indigenous trees are beech, oak, birch and alder; spruce has been introduced for environmental purposes. Pillars and crosses seen here were guides along ancient trails.

A. Liège to Verviers and Eupen

Total distance 43km.—*30km* **Verviers**.—*7km* **Limbourg**.—*6km* **Eupen**.

Liège, see Rte 34.—*30km* **Verviers** (54,000 inhab. Tourist Information: 11 Rue Vielle Xhavée) is most easily reached by motorway (A25/E25 down the right bank of the Meuse, followed by A3/E40 and A27/E42). A more interesting if slower alternative is to follow Rte 38B as far as Pepinster. Today still an important textiles centre, Verviers was as early as 1480 granted the right to sell cloth in Liège, although, curiously, it was not given official town status until 1651. The town has three good museums.

The town centres around the PLACE VERTE and the adjacent PLACE DU MARTYR. From the former the Rue Crapaurue, a main shopping street, rises to the Neo-Classical *Hôtel de Ville* (J.B. Renoz, 1780). The martyr commemorated by the Place du Martyr in which his memorial stands was Dr Grégoire Chapuis, a doctor who served the poor and was later attached to the magistrature only to be executed in 1794 because he confirmed a civil marriage, an act which the Prince-Bishop, briefly back in power after the Austrian defeat of Dumouriez at Neerwinden, condemned as fomenting anarchy. At the NW corner of this square the *Eglise Notre-Dame* dates from 1647. From the E end of the square the Rue du Collège leads to the Rue des Raines in which, among other 17–18C houses, No. 42 is the *Musée d'Archéologie et Folklore* (Tuesday, Thursday, 14.00 to 17.00; Saturday, 09.00 to 12.00; Sunday, 10.00 to 13.00). The ground and first floors have rooms showing 17–18C furniture, pictures (largely by local artists), and objets d'art; also souvenirs of Henri Vieuxtemps (1821–81), the violinist, born in Verviers and honoured by the Place Vieuxtemps in the S part of the town. On the second floor there are weapons, a small local archaeological collection which includes Roman coins found near the museum, and a room devoted to lace.

The *Musée des Beaux-Arts et de la Céramique*, a short distance NW in the Rue Renier beside the river Vesdre, occupies a former alsmhouse of the late 17C (Monday, Wednesday, Saturday, 14.00 to 17.00; Sunday, 15.00 to 18.00). The most important collections are the ceramics and the pictures, both old and modern. The Old Masters include works by Joachim Patinir (Landscape and St. Christopher); Pieter Pourbus the Elder (Punishment of Annanias); Jan van Goyen (Landscape); Nicolas de Largillière (two portraits); Roelant Savery (Landscape with a white Horse. Animals in a Landscape); Cornelis de Vos (Portrait of a Child); Gerrit Dou (Adoration of the Magi); Daniel Seghers (Virgin among Flowers); Jan Weenix (Portrait of Admiral van Heemskerk); Gerard de Lairesse (Council of the Gods). Among the later artists on this floor are Joshua Reynolds (Head of a Child); Marie Louise Vigée-Lebrun (Self-portrait); Henri de Braekeleer (Inn by a Lake); Johann Barthold Jongkind (Skaters. Canal Bridge). On the first floor are carved and sculpted 15th and 16C religious figures and also the gallery of modern art. The pictures are sometimes removed to allow space for temporary exhibitions, but the many artists represented include Gustave Courbet, Jacob Smits, Constantin Meunier, Hippolyte Boulenger, René Magritte, Paul Delvaux, Edouard Tytgat, and Emile Claus. The passage leading to the basement shows stonework and graveslabs.

The town's third museum is the *Musée de Laine* (Monday–Saturday, 14.00 to 17.00 or 18.00 on Wednesday), at, though perhaps temporarily, the Institut Supérieure Industriel in the Rue de Séroule in the SW of the town; the museum tells the story of the local textiles industry, generally prior to 1800.

7km **Limbourg** (3700 inhab.) stands on a ridge 275m above the Vesdre. A former fortress, and capital of the duchy of Limburg from feudal times until 1648, the town was many times besieged and sacked. Now a quiet little place, it is worth visiting for its old walls and picturesque streets, notably the broad cobbled main street. The church, mainly 15–16C, has a tower of 1300. The *Barrage de la Gileppe*, 4km SE, a beautiful sheet of water with hilly, thickly wooded sides, offers a good view from the Belvédère, and also a tourist path (Sentier Touristique) which descends to the dam, built to provide a reservoir for Verviers in 1869–78 and heightened in 1967–71.

2km Baelen where the church has a curious spiral steeple of 1773.—*4km* **Eupen** (17,000 inhab. Tourist Information: 6 Bergstrasze), mainly German-speaking and, thanks to the water of the Vesdre, a textiles town since the 14C, only really developed in the 17–18C after persecuted French Calvinists had settled here. The Baroque *Eglise Saint Nicholas* (1721–26) is known for its rich furnishings, notably its altar of 1744. The *Barrage de la Vesdre* (5km E), completed in 1950 and the largest dam in Belgium, has a Panoramic Tower (lift) from which there is a superb view of the reservoir and the great forest of Hertogenwald which surrounds it.

A road (N67) cuts through the Hertogenwald to the small German town of *Monschau*.

Raeren (8km NE of Eupen) was from the 15C to the 19C a thriving pottery centre whose products were known both locally and as far afield as Ireland and Sweden. The castle (in origin 14C) houses a museum of pottery spanning the 12–19C (Daily except Monday, 14.00 to 16.45).

For the HAUTES FAGNES to the S of Eupen, see the introduction to this Rte and also below (Rte 38B, Malmédy to the Hautes Fagnes and Eupen).

B. Liège to Spa, Stavelot, Malmédy, the Hautes Fagnes and the Canton of Sankt Vith

Total distance (to Malmédy) 61km.—*10km* **Chaudfontaine**.—*15km* *Pepinster*.—*5km* **Theux**.—*7km* **Spa**. 8km Francorchamps. 8km **Stavelot**.—*8km* **Malmédy**.

Liège, see Rte 34, is left by the right bank of the Ourthe to the suburb of *Chênée* where the Vesdre is crossed at its mouth and its narrow, winding valley then ascended. On the N bank the hill of *Chèvremont* is crowned by a pilgrimage-church of 1697.—*10km* **Chaudfontaine** (19,500 inhab. Tourist Information: Maison Sauveur, Parc des Sources) is a pleasant little spa which was much admired by Victor Hugo. Just behind the large car park visitors may help themselves to water from the warm spring (36.5°), since 1676 used for the alleviation of rheumatism. There is an audio-visual presentation in the Maison Sauveur, site of the town's first thermal baths.—*15km* *Pepinster* is 4km SW of *Verviers* (see Rte 39A). At *Tancrémont*, 4km SW of Pepinster, a chapel houses a striking and unusual 11C robed Christ.

5km **Theux** traces its origin to a Roman settlement, later being owned in turn by the Carolingian kings and the prince-bishop of Liège and formally receiving town status in 1456. The church, with a fortified tower and dating in part (walls and nave) from 1000 or earlier, contains a 12C font the middle section of which may be Roman. In the pleasant small square there are 17–18C houses, including the *Hôtel de Ville* of 1770, and also the *Perron* (1769), successor to that of 1456 which was destroyed by Charles the Bold only 12 years later. The town's early story is essentially that of its castle of *Franchimont*, the ruins of which are on the hill above (Daily, 09.00 to 19.00 or dusk if earlier. Closed Tuesday in October–March). A pentagonal fortress with corner towers, it dates basically from the 14C, and it was from here in 1468 that there sallied out a heroic 600 men who vainly attacked the army of Charles the Bold after his victory over Liège at Brustem; in revenge Charles sacked Theux and destroyed its perron. Later a stronghold of William de la Marck, the 'Wild Boar of the Ardennes', the castle was after his execution successfully held by his brothers besieged here by the Bishop of Liège. The principal features are all numbered and a key in English is provided with the entry ticket which is also valid for the adjacent museum which outlines the local history by means of maps and some interesting illustrations.

7km **Spa** (9700 inhab. Tourist Information: 43 Place Royale, by the Casino), the father of Europe's spas and still a popular resort with mineral springs ('pouhons') and a casino, today has only faded reminders of the elegance which led Joseph II to describe it as the 'Café of Europe'; some echo of this past can be caught by studying the fascinating list of distinguished visitors (16–19C) inscribed on the semicircular monument just S of the Pouhon Pierre-le-Grand. Lying in a valley beneath wooded hills and moors, and with good amusement and other facilities, Spa is a convenient centre for touring.

History. The first notable foreign visitor was Augustino, the Venetian physician of Henry VIII of England. Other early distinguished visitors were Henry III of France, Marguerite of Valois, Charles II of England, Christina of Sweden, and Peter the Great of Russia, and by the 18C the gaming tables had become as much a fashionable as a gambling attraction. In 1918 Spa saw much of the closing German moves of the First World War. In March the German General Headquarters was established here in the Hôtel Britannique (now a school) and here on 26 October Ludendorff's dismissal was agreed by the Kaiser who was living at the Château de Neubois, 2km east. Later the Kaiser moved to La Fraineuse, and it was here during the afternoon of 9 November that he learnt that in Berlin the chancellor Prince Max von Baden had on his own initiative announced the abdication. Early the next morning the Kaiser left for Holland from Spa station. After the Armistice a German military mission remained in Spa for several months in conference with the Allies.

'**Baladeuses**' are open 'road-trains' which, starting from the Place Royale and the Jardin du Casino and offering a choice of routes, provide a pleasant method of enjoying the town and its environs (July and August: daily, 09.00 to 19.00. Also May, June, September, October: weekends in fine weather).

The *Pouhon Pierre-le-Grand*, at the town centre, is, after Sauvenière, the oldest spring, known since at least the 16C. For long no more than an open niche, the spring was given a colonnaded shelter in 1822 and then its present building in 1880. Inside, a medallion with the arms of Russia was a gift by Peter the Great in gratitude for a successful cure here in 1717, while the Livre d'Or, a work of 1894 by the local artist Antoine Fontaine, portrays 93 of Spa's best known visitors of earlier centuries. On the rear outside wall there is a memorial in gratitude to the US 1st Army which liberated Spa on 10 September 1944, while just S stands the semicircular monument listing distinguished visitors from the 16–19C.

The *Hôtel de Ville* (J.B. Renoz, 1768), 200m N, has in turn been the Grand Hotel, a factory, three different schools, and the municipal library.—In the Rue de la Sauvenière, leading SE from the Pouhon Pierre-le-Grand, is the *Hôtel Britannique* (see above).

The *Casino*, immediately W of the Pouhon Pierre-le-Grand, was founded in 1763 and rebuilt in 1919. In addition to gaming tables, it provides gardens, a restaurant, a theatre, and reception and exhibition rooms. The *Etablissement des Bains* (1862–68) is next door.

The waters of Spa are cold and aerated, containing iron and bicarbonate of soda, and are mainly used for drinking. They are good for a number of complaints, notably heart and respiratory troubles as also rheumatism. The chief springs are

Pouhon Pierre-le-Grand in the town centre, and the Tonnelet, Sauvenière, Groesbeek, Géronstère and Barisart, all to the south (see Tour des Fontaines, below). The bottling works of Spa Monopole are near the station.

Off the NW corner of the PLACE ROYALE (the open area roughly opposite the Etablissement des Bains) is the *Parc de Sept Heures*, originally laid out in 1758, which became the elegant evening meeting-place of the town's visitors; it contains a number of memorials and is now in part used for recreational purposes. Farther W along Avenue Reine Astrid (right, 400m from Place Royale) the *Villa Royale*, once a favourite home of Queen Marie-Henriette (died 1902), now in part houses the *Musée de la Ville d'Eau* showing collections of articles made by Spa craftsmen, notably 'jolités', little boxes and other articles of lacquered and painted wood dating from the late 16C. On request the attendant will loan an English description of Spa work and its origins and purposes. The museum also includes a section on equestrianism. Mid June–mid September: daily, 14.30 to 17.30. Mid March–mid June and mid September–December: Saturday, Sunday, Holidays, 14.30 to 17.30. The station is 400m SW of the museum, above it being the bottling works of Spa Monopole (visits).

The TOUR DES FONTAINES (Circuit of the Springs) is normally made by 'baladeuse', the round lasting about one hour. The *Tonnelet*, which became popular in the early 17C, is so named because the water was once piped into a small barrel. The *Sauvenière* is the oldest spring, traditionally said to have been known to St. Remaclus and already by 1300 believed to provide a cure for sterility. Adjacent there is an arboretum. The *Groesbeek* is named after Baron Groesbeek who paid for the marble niche in 1651. The *Géronstère*, with rather sulpherous water, was patronised by Peter the Great to alleviate his indigestion. The *Barisart*, although known since at least 1559, was not in popular use until 1850.

The *Lac de Warfaz* is 2km NE of the town and reached by car or 'baladeuse', road names on the way (Boulevard des Anglais, Route de Balmoral and others) recalling the popularity of Spa with the 19C British. Off the road to the lake the estate of *Fraineuse* (see History, above), now a large sports complex, is passed. The lake (boating, fishing), in a hilly and wooded setting, was formed by a dam built in 1890.

At *La Reid*, 6km W of Spa, there is a game park with deer, boar, etc. (Daily, 09.00 to dusk).

8km Francorchamps owes its name (Francorum Campus) to a battle won here by Charles Martel, grandfather of Charlemagne. Today the place is known for its 14km-long motor-racing circuit (for museum see Stavelot below).

Stavelot and **Malmédy**, described individually below, may historically be regarded as one.

Both places owe their origins to abbeys founded in 650 and 648 respectively by St. Remaclus. These twin abbeys became, and remained right up to the French Revolution, the centre of a principality under the lordship of a powerful line of prince-abbots. Politically these prince-abbots owed allegiance to the Holy Roman (German) Empire. Ecclesiastically, however, there was a split, with Malmédy answerable to Cologne and Stavelot to Liège. Later this split had the important result that when in 1815 the Congress of Vienna awarded the Cantons de l'Est to Prussia Stavelot was excluded and, with Belgium, became a part of the United Kingdom of the Netherlands.

8km **Stavelot** (5500 inhab. Tourist Information: Ancienne Abbaye) is a pleasant and interesting town on a hill with some narrow streets and several 18C houses.

Stavelot was viciously fought over and badly damaged during the Battle of the Ardennes, notably on 18 December when Allied failure to demolish the Amblève bridge below the abbey (possibly because of sabotage by German commando groups wearing American uniforms) enabled the spearhead Kampfgruppe Peiper (see also Baugnez below) to cross and then, despite American success in holding the Place Saint Remacle for about two hours, swing SW for Trois Ponts. It was in Stavelot and Trois Ponts, and at hamlets and farms in between (Ster, Renardmont, Parfondruy, Hurlet) that the worst of the atrocities against civilians took place, largely the crimes of SS youths, enraged by their inability to advance in the face of American artillery and hysterically convinced that every house sheltered Belgian and American snipers.

Of the abbey buildings there survive two 18C quadrangles, approached beside a huge 16C archway, in fact the lower part of the tower-arch of the now demolished church. From the garden beyond the archway, steps descend to the main quadrangle with the Hôtel de Ville and three museums. The *Musée Regional d'Art Religieux et de l'Ancienne Abbaye* (Easter–mid October: daily, 10.00 to 12.30, 14.30 to 17.30) is in four principal sections, these being religious art of the 14–19C (plate, jewellery, small statuary, vestments, liturgical books); the story of the abbey and its excavations; tanning, which was an important local industry until 1939; and contemporary Belgian ceramic. The Romanesque cellars of the abbey now house the *Musée Circuit de Spa-Francorchamps* (Easter–mid October: daily, 10.00 to 12.30, 14.30 to 17.30. Mid October–Easter: daily, 10.00 to 12.00, 14.00 to 16.30), showing cars, posters and much else reflecting the Francorchamps circuit since 1907. Finally, in the Hôtel de Ville, there is the *Musée Guillaume Apollinaire* (July–August: daily, 10.30 to 12.00, 14.00 to 17.30) with souvenirs of this Franco-Polish poet(1880–1918) who lived in Stavelot in 1899 (tablet on the Hôtel de Luxembourg) and decamped without paying his bill.

Above the abbey, the sloping Place Saint Remacle, the 18C market-square, has a perron of 1769 and a stone commemorating the halting of Von Rundstedt. The *Eglise Saint Sébastien* (1751), with a pulpit and medallions from the abbey, is known for its Treasury which contains the *Shrine of St. Remaclus (1263), in gilt and enamelled copper; a reliquary bust (Jean Gossin, 1626) of St. Poppo (died 1048), abbot of Stavelot-Malmédy; another reliquary sheltering a part of the skull of St. Poppo; and a 19C reliquary with the skull of St. Remaclus.

On the left of the road to Malmédy: stands the national monument to Bomb Disposal Units.

8km **Malmédy** (10,000 inhab. Tourist Information: 11 Place de Rome), lying by the junction of two small rivers at the foot of wooded hills, was much damaged by Allied bombing in December 1944. Apart from the cathedral little of interest has survived, and the town is best known as a centre for walks and other excursions into the local countryside. The *Cathedral* (of St. Peter, St. Paul and St. Quirinus), the latest in a line reaching back to St. Remaclus's abbey church, dates from 1775–84 and has a somewhat bleak interior with a lofty domed crossing and half-domed transepts. A curiosity (on the altar) is the set of four silver busts of Roman soldiers, reliquaries of martyred members of the Theban Legion.

According to early chronicles, the Theban Legion, commanded by Mauritius (later canonised) and composed largely of Christians, was sent to northern Italy and ordered to assist in the persecution of Christians there. The legion refused and was slaughtered at Martigny in what is now Switzerland. One company,

detached to Cologne, suffered the same fate, and it is presumably these martyrs
whose relics are here.

The abbey domestic buildings of c 1701 are now a school and offices.
Just W off Place Albert I, in Chemin-Rue, the *Maison Villers* (1724)
survived the bombing of 1944.

MALMEDY TO THE HAUTES FAGNES AND EUPEN (N, 32km). The direct
road (N68) zigzags above the valley of the Warche. A more interesting
road ascends to (*9km*) **Robertville** (5600 inhab.) close to the beautifully set reservoir formed by the *Barrage de la Warche* below which
there is a very steep valley. A path (c 800m) from the dam, or a road
from the village, leads to the castle of *Rénastène* (or Reinhardstein),
dating from 1354 and largely in ruins until restored and furnished in
1969 (normally open only to groups). Beyond Robertville the road
ascends to the **Hautes Fagnes** (see introduction to this Rte).—*7km
Signal de Botrange*, on a forest plateau, is the highest point in Belgium
(694m; tower with orientation table).—At (*3km*) *Baraque Michel*, a
bleak spot at the heart of the Hautes Fagnes, there is a statue to Albert
Bonjean (1858–1939) who wrote about this district. From here the
road drops through the Hertogenwald to (*13km*) **Eupen**.

MALMEDY TO BUTGENBACH AND BULLINGEN (E 19km). Road N62 is
taken as far as (*4km*) the hamlet of **Baugnez** whence N62 continues S
while N632 breaks away NE for Waismes. At this road junction,
sometimes known as the *Croix des Américains*, stands a memorial
recalling that this was the scene of the worst (at any rate in terms of
the number of prisoners murdered, some 107) of the atrocities
committed by Kampfgruppe Peiper, the German Battle of the Ardennes spearhead led by the ruthless SS Lieutenant Colonel Joachim
(Jochen) Peiper. Its poignancy apart, this road fork is interesting for
the fact that, although there have been some changes, and although
also a snow-covered landscape must be imagined, the skirmish which
led to the massacre can nevertheless still be well pictured.

Soon after noon on 17 December the German combat group was advancing N
along the minor road from Thirimont (2km SE of Baugnez), while at the same
time B Battery of 285th Field Artillery Observation Battalion, having just left
Malmédy, reached Baugnez where they were directed S along what is now N62.
Almost at once, and taken wholly by surprise, the Americans came under tank
fire from the German column, whose infantry then stormed across the (then
open) fields between the two more or less parallel roads while their tanks swung
the short distance W and then S through Baugnez. It was quickly obvious that the
American situation was hopeless, their only protection being the roadside ditch
(it is still there, its inadequacy still obvious) and their rifles useless against tanks
and machine guns. So they surrendered. Marched back the few yards to the road
fork, they were lined up in rows in the open field (now in part built over)
immediately S of the café and, soon afterwards, mown down by fire from two
tanks. Miraculously 43 survived out of a total of some 150.

After the war a temporary memorial was erected in what is now the
car park of the café. Today's memorial, a wall along the length of a
stretch of green, is on the other side of the road. Individual plaques
bear the names of the victims, and at one end there is a chapel shrine.
   10km Bütgenbach (5000 inhab.) is a scattered township with an
attractive fortified-farm. To the E is the Barrage de la Warche; the
reservoir (boating, fishing), less wooded and steep-sided than others,
is not scenically noteworthy.—N632 continues SE, passing a
memorial to the America 1st Infantry Division, to reach (*5km*)

Büllingen (Fr. Bullange. 5000 inhab.) a place of ancient origin which stood at the crossing of the Roman roads from Maastricht to Trier (the Via Mansuerisca) and from Rheims to Cologne, and which was also the site of a Carolingian royal villa.

MALMEDY TO SANKT VITH, REULAND AND OUREN (S, 42km). To (*4km*) the *Croix des Américains*, see immediately above.—4km Ligneuville, where the Amblève is crossed, is mentioned in documents of the 9th and 10C. A more modern record is provided by a memorial (by the Moulin hotel) to American soldiers shot while prisoners of war.— *12km* **Sankt Vith** (8300 inhab.) traces its name to the fact that in c 836 the remains of St. Vitus (died c 300) rested near here while being carried from Paris to Corvey in Westphalia, a settlement then growing up around the chapel built to honour the site. The small town was virtually obliterated by bombing in 1944, but the *Büchel-turm*, mainly rebuilding of 1961 but with a base in part dating from 1350, stands as a reminder of the medieval fortifications. There is a small regional museum at 2 Rue Hecking (Sunday, 09.00 to 12.00).— At (*12km*) *Reuland* there are the ruins of an 11C castle, successor to one mentioned as early as 963. From here a minor road winds along the valley of the Our into a narrow pocket of Belgium lying between the Grand-Duchy of Luxembourg and Germany.—10km Ouren is a village with some slight remains of its medieval castle. Just beyond, where the little river is crossed, the three frontiers meet. From here the Grand-Duchy's main N–S road (N7; see Rte 44) can be reached in 6km; also a footpath descends the Our for 14km to *Dasburg* (Rte 44D).

39 Between Liège, Maastricht and Aachen

The little-visited triangle of Belgium lying between roughly Liège, Maastricht in Holland, and Aachen (or Aix-la-Chapelle) in Germany offers some quiet upland scenery, a number of places worth a visit, and a mingling of Walloon, Flemish and German customs and language. The route described below travels N from Liège to Visé, then E towards Aachen, a total distance of 50km.

From **Liège** (see Rte 34) either bank of the Meuse may be followed, the W side being the more interesting and on the edge of the city passing the port area and the start of the Albert Canal with its statue of King Albert.—*6km* **Herstal**, birthplace of Pepin of Herstal, is today a large industrial extension of Liège and the home of the Fabrique Nationale (small arms). Beyond Herstal the road passes below the A3/E40 motorway, the landscape now becoming less industrial.—At (*4km*) *Oupeye* there is a 17–18C château, originally built by the same Jean de Corte who owned the mansion in Liège now occupied by the Musée Curtius; today the château houses a museum of local archaeology.—Around the churchyard at (*4km*) *Haccourt* there is a good but much restored medieval wall probably built with stones already used by the Romans.

Eben-Emael, 7km N, had a supposedly impregnable casemated fort, which though, despite a gallant defence, was taken by the German paratroops in their invasion of 1940; something of the fort (no adm.) can be seen from the memorial (sign) just E of the village.

2km **Visé**, on the E bank of the Meuse, traces its origin to a bridge
built here during the 8C. Over the centuries the town changed hands
many times and was repeatedly sacked, a recent occasion being 1914
when it was burnt by the invading Germans. The town is visited for its
Eglise Saint Martin (16C in origin) which houses the *Châsse Saint
Hadelin, a silver and gold coffin-reliquary of the 11–12C depicting
scenes from the life of the saint. The shrine, which came from Celles
where Hadelin died in 690, contains not only the saint's remains but
also some of his ceremonial garments. The adjacent silver bust is of
1650. The *Hôtel de Ville*, rebuilt in the original style of 1612, houses a
local museum (Thursday, 10.00 to 12.00).

From the frontier, 2km N, a narrow tongue of the province of Limburg extends E
for 15km. Known as the VOERSTREEK (or Région des Fourons), this now quiet,
pastoral and rather lost district with its six villages along the little rivers Berwijn,
Voer and Gulp, was the subject of bitter dispute during the language-frontier
negotiations of 1962. *Sint Martens-Voeren* and *Sint Pieters-Voeren* both have
11C churches.

At *(5km)* *Warsage* the church has a Romanesque tower.—*8km* The
Abbaye Val Dieu, in a quiet, rural setting, was founded in c 1216,
disestablished in 1798, reoccupied in 1844 and is still the home of a
Cistercian community. The choir of the church, the fourth on this site,
may be 13C, and parts of the nave and transepts are 14–15C, but the
remainder of the church is rebuilding of 1870. Inside there is a 12C
statue of St. Bernard. It is worth going through the archway beside the
church to look at the 18C domestic buildings.

A diversion may be made to **Blégny**, 7km SW of the abbey, where there is a
tourist complex at which a visit may be made to a now disused coal mine, with an
associated museum (April–mid October: daily. Duration up to 2½ hours). There
is also a small train (Li Trembleu) which runs (11km) to Mortroux and back
through Dalhem and the Berwinne tunnel, the excursion including three
museums (Vehicles. Cheese. Rural Life). Also boat cruise link with Liège.

4km *Aubel*, 3km E of which is a large Second World War cemetery
(American and German), resting place mostly of soldiers killed in the
attack on Aachen in September and October 1944. The American
colonnade-memorial (by Holabind, Root and Burgee) has at one end a
chapel and at the other maps and a four-language text telling the
story of the campaign leading to the final drive into Germany.—*8km*
Moresnet and *2km Neu-Moresnet*.

The tiny district of MORESNET, with important zinc (calamine) mines, was at
the northern tip of the Cantons de l'Est. Unlike most of the rest of the Cantons
territory it was not awarded to Prussia in 1815 but instead left to the joint
administration of Prussia and the United Kingdom of the Netherlands, Belgium
taking the place of the latter after the revolution of 1830. The district became
fully Belgian in 1920.

The *Drielandenbos*, N of Neu-Moresnet and spreading into Germany
and Holland, once a Carolingian hunting forest, is now a popular
walking area with waymarked paths. The frontiers of the three
countries meet at the *Drielandenpunt* (322m).—The German border is
crossed *2km* beyond Neu-Moresnet, and **Aachen** is *5km* beyond.

GRAND-DUCHY OF LUXEMBOURG

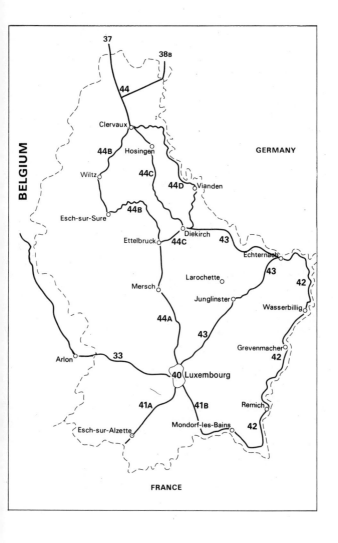

Background and Practical Information

Introduction to the Grand-Duchy

The Grand-Duchy of Luxembourg, an independent country with a population of about 364,000 and an area of 2586 sq km, measures some 80km from N to S and some 55km across its central and broadest part. The capital, the city of Luxembourg, is in the southern part of the country. Bounded by Belgium, France and Germany, and with a history which has brought not infrequent change of rule by all three, the country is a mingling of cultures and languages.

This mixture apart, interesting enough in itself, the main attractions of the Grand-Duchy for the visitor are its dramatically situated capital, the wine valley of the Moselle, and the beautiful, often rugged scenery, particularly that of the more northern part of the country. Here the Sûre river cuts Luxembourg from W to E, from the Belgian border to the German, its sinuous course and those of its tributaries (notably the Wiltz, the Clerve and the Our) offering glorious valleys with rocks, cliffs and romantically perched castles. Between the valleys there is upland plateau with extensive vistas. Two places meriting special mention are *Esch-sur-Sûre* nestling at one end of its long lake, and, on the E frontier, the valley of the Our in which the town of *Vianden* overhung by a massive castle is perhaps the most spectacular place in the Grand-Duchy. To the S of the Sûre the country is generally undulating and agricultural, while to the S of the city of Luxembourg lies the *Bassin Minier*, a mining and heavy industry region not without an interest of its own.

Aspects of The Grand-Duchy

Constitution. Luxembourg is a constitutional 'monarchy', under a Grand-Duke. Executive power rests with the Cabinet, legislative power with the Chamber of Deputies, and there is an independent judiciary. The Chamber of Deputies is elected by universal franchise over the age of 18 on a basis of one deputy to represent every 5500 electors.

The **Grand-Ducal Family** is that of Nassau (see under History, below). On the throne since 1964 are Grand-Duke Jean and Grand-Duchess Joséphine Charlotte, daughter of King Leopold III and Queen Astrid of Belgium. They have five children, of whom Prince Henri (born 1955) is the heir, himself the father of a son, Prince Guillaume, born in 1981.

Language. There are three languages—German, French and the local language—these being used throughout the country and all being understood. The local language (Letzeburgesch, a German dialect), the normal spoken language, is also written and has a literature of its own. French is the official language of the civil service, the law and the government (though this does not preclude the use of others, e.g. in legal proceedings), but German is more often the language of the press. Education is in both German and French, the former being mainly used at primary level and French at secondary level.

Industry. The main industries are iron and steel, agriculture, tourism and wine.

Wine is the industry of the Moselle valley, both still and sparkling white wine being made and many 'caves' being open to visitors (see Rte 42). Authenticity and quality are protected by the State Viticulture Institute which is at Remich.

Walking is a very popular activity and an admirable way in which to enjoy the magnificent countryside. Many of the best walks are arranged as signed paths, these being either on a national (yellow signs) or local basis. A choice of maps is available, particularly popular being the 'Circuits Auto-Pédestres', published by the Ministry of Tourism and obtainable at bookshops. Many towns also provide their own more local maps.

Archaeological Sites. Although minor and comparatively little known, Luxembourg has a number of not uninteresting archaeological sites (Gallo-Roman and earlier) which, although mostly accessible by car, still have the merit of lying off the beaten track. Among such sites are the Gallo-Roman baths near Mamer (Rte 33); the Titelberg Gallic and later vestiges (Rte 41A); the Gallo-Roman complex at Echternach (Rte 43); and four sites (Goeblange, Steinsel, Mersch and Bill), all on Rte 44A.

History of the Grand-Duchy

Note: Broadly the expression 'Luxembourg' (except when referring simply to the city) can until 1839 be taken to include the territory of today's Grand-Duchy together with that of the Belgian province of Luxembourg. The History below should be read with that of Belgium.

The Roman roads from Paris to Trèves (Trier) and from Metz to Liège crossed at a point which is now in the centre of the city of Luxembourg, and the Roman station of Andethana (probably now Niederanven, between the city and the Moselle) is recorded in the Antonine Itinerary. The iron ore of the Alzette valley was already being worked in Roman times, and in the 3C a tower, later known as *Lucilinburh*, is said to have been built where Luxembourg now stands. The Frankish invasions of the 3–5C, and the evangelisation of the 6–7C, followed the same pattern as in eastern Belgium.

963. Sigefroi of Lorraine built the first castle on the Rocher du Bock in Luxembourg, he and his successors holding it and the surrounding lands as a fief of the Holy Roman Empire. Either Conrad (died 1086) or William (died 1129) was the first ruler to assume the title of Count of Luxembourg.

1136. Henry IV (the Blind) of Namur succeeded to the county, ruling over Namur, La Roche, Durbuy, and Luxembourg.

1196–1247. Countess Ermesinda gained the marquessate of Arlon, but only retained Namur E of the Meuse. She granted charters to the more important towns, including Luxembourg in 1244 and Echternach in 1236.

1288–1310. Reign of Henry VII, elected emperor in 1308.

1310. Bohemia was added to the possessions of the House of Luxembourg. The county was ceded to Henry's son, John the Blind.

1346–54. John's eldest son, Charles IV, was elected emperor. John was killed at Crécy, being succeeded by his son Wenceslas, but Charles IV usurped the government. In 1354 he returned the county to Wenceslas, at the same time creating it a duchy.

1353–83. Wenceslas acquired Brabant, Limburg, and Chiny. At this period Luxembourg extended almost to Malmédy in the N, to Metz in the S, to the Saar in the E, and to around Sedan in the west.

1383. Wenceslas II, becoming Emperor and Duke of Luxembourg, used the duchy simply as a means of raising money.

1411–43. Civil war between the legal sovereigns and the 'engagistes', to whom the duchy had been pledged by Wenceslas II. Emperor Sigismund, last male of the House of Luxembourg, died in 1437. In 1443 Luxembourg was bought by Philip the Good of Burgundy.

15–18C. Luxembourg's history was much the same as that of the Spanish and Austrian Netherlands. During the Revolt of the Netherlands Luxembourg remained loyal to Catholicism and Spain. During the 17C the duchy suffered appallingly from the Thirty Years War. In 1684 (Chambres de Réunion) Louis XIV annexed the duchy, holding it until 1697 when it was returned to Spain; during this period Vauban fortified the city. In 1714, at the close of the War of the Spanish Succession, Luxembourg went to Austria, whose rule lasted until 1795. From 1795 until the fall of Napoleon in 1814, Luxembourg was, with the rest of the Netherlands, incorporated into revolutionary France.

After the fall of Napoleon the Congress of Vienna agreed that Luxembourg should become a **Grand-Duchy**, and (in exchange for the German possessions of the House of Orange-Nassau, confiscated by Napoleon in 1806 and which the powers now gave to Prussia) the throne was offered to William I (of Orange-Nassau), first king of the new United Kingdom of the Netherlands. At the same time all territory E of the Moselle and Our was joined to Prussia, while in compensation the new Grand-Duchy received the greater part of the duchy of Bouillon and part also of the former prince-bishopric of Liège. Although sharing the same sovereign, there was no political link between the United Kingdom of the Netherlands and Luxembourg, the powers having decided that Luxembourg should be a member of the Germanic Confederation and that the city of Luxembourg should be a Confederation fortress manned by Prussians.

Major change came in 1830 with the Belgian revolution and secession from the United Kingdom of the Netherlands, the Grand-Duchy revolting also and placing itself under Belgian authority, although the city of Luxembourg, controlled by its Prussian garrison, could not join the revolt and thus remained under William I. In 1839, under the Treaty of London, the Grand-Duchy was divided into two. The larger, French-speaking western part went to Belgium to become the province of Luxembourg, and the smaller eastern part was retained by William I. Thus the Grand-Duchy assumed its present frontiers. .

In 1842 Luxembourg was incorporated into the German Zollverein (Customs Union). In 1867, with the dissolution of the Germanic Confederation, the Prussian garrison was withdrawn from Luxembourg city, the fortifications were dismantled, and the powers guaranteed the Grand-Duchy's neutrality.

A succession problem arose with the death without male heir of William III in 1890. While his daughter Wilhelmina could succeed to the throne of Holland, an Orange-Nassau family pact did not allow her to succeed in Luxembourg. The latter throne therefore went to the last in the male line, Duke Adolf of Nassau. (Under the pact a woman could not succeed if there was a male heir in any branch of the House of Nassau).

In 1914, despite the guarantee of neutrality, Germany occupied Luxembourg. After the war Grand-Duchess Marie-Adelaide abdicated in favour of her sister, Charlotte. In 1939 Luxembourg proclaimed her neutrality, but was invaded by the Germans in 1940.

1950 et seq. Luxembourg, with Belgium and Holland, formed the Benelux customs union, and later joined NATO and the Common Market, from 1952 becoming the home of various international institutions. Relations with Belgium were strengthened in 1953 when Prince Jean married Princess Joséphine-Charlotte of Belgium. On the abdication of Grand-Duchess Charlotte in 1964 this pair ascended the throne. (See also Grand-Ducal Family, above.)

Practical Information

Note: Only points particular to the Grand-Duchy appear below. Some practical points (e.g. Medical) included under Belgium, Practical Information, apply also to Luxembourg.

Office National du Tourisme. *Grand-Duchy*: PO Box 1001, Luxembourg 1010. For personal visits, Place de la Gare, Luxembourg. Tel: 481199. Open daily 09.00 to 12.00, 14.00 to 18.00, but in July–mid September, open 09.00 to 19.30. Closed Sunday in December to March. *United Kingdom*: 36–37 Piccadilly, London, W1V 9PA. Tel: 01–434 2800. *United States*: 801 2nd Avenue, New York, NY 10017. Tel: 212–370 9850.

Motoring. Generally speaking the points included under Belgium apply. The address of the *Automobile Club du Grand-Duché de Luxembourg*, offering reciprocal services to members of affiliated clubs, is 13 Route de Longwy, Luxembourg–Helfenterbruck (tel: 311031). The club operates a round-the-clock assistance service (yellow vehicles marked Automobile Club, Service Routier) throughout the country. Tel: 311031.

Speed Limits are 60km/h in built-up areas; 90km/h elsewhere, but 120km/h when so signed. Lower speed limits are frequently imposed.

Coach Tours operate during the season out of Luxembourg, Echternach and Mondorf-les-Bains.

Railway and Bus. A combined train and bus network (Luxembourg National Railways) covers some 1500km. Various reduced-fare plans are offered, these including a reduction of 50 per cent for people over the age of 65 (but there are restrictions on the use of frontier stations).

Accommodation and Restaurants. A national guide to hotels, pensions and restaurants is published annually by the Office National du Tourisme. *Camping and Caravanning*: The Office also publishes an annual guide to sites.

Food in Luxembourg tends to be rich, generally similar to that of the Belgian Ardennes but with German influence. Among specialities are Black Pudding (treipen); smoked pork with beans; Ardennes ham; jellied sucking pig ('gras-double'); and calf's liver dumplings (quenelles).

Public Holidays. New Year's Day (1 January). Easter Monday. May Day (1 May). Ascension Day. Whit Monday. National Day (23 June). Assumption Day (15 August). All Saints Day (1 November). Christmas Day (25 December). St. Stephen's Day (26 December). When public holidays fall on a Sunday, the following day is usually declared to be a holiday. Carnival Monday (February) and All Souls (November) are also treated as holidays.

Currency and Banking. The unit is the Luxembourg franc, which closely resembles and is tied to the Belgian franc. While the latter is accepted in both countries, the reverse may not apply. Normal banking hours are Monday–Friday, 08.30 or 09.00 to 12.00, 13.30 or 14.00 to 16.30 or 17.00.

40 City of Luxembourg

LUXEMBOURG (79,000 inhab.), the capital of the Grand-Duchy, occupies a dramatic and picturesque situation on a high bluff above precipitous cliffs dropping to the narrow valleys of the Alzette and the Pétrusse. Because of this site Luxembourg was for long one of the strongest fortresses in Europe, with ramparts and casemates lining the rims of the bluff. Although demolished in 1867, something of this defensive system survives, offering exciting view-points and the opportunity to visit the casemates hewn into the rock. Newer quarters have today spread far beyond the bluff, notably towards and around the station on the S side of the Pétrusse ravine, and in the N on the Plateau de Kirchberg, which since 1952 has become the site of various European political institutions.

Tourist Information. *City*: Place d'Armes. *Grand-Duchy*: Place de la Gare.

City Tours. In summer from the station, or Place de la Constitution.

Station. In the S of the city, c 1.5km from the Place d'Armes; frequent bus services.

Airport. Findel, 6km east. Terminal at the station.

Consulates. *United Kingdom*: 28 Boulevard Royal. Tel: 29864. *USA*: 22 Boulevard Emmanuel-Servais. Tel: 40123.

History. The city's history, particularly as regards its many wars and changes of ruler, is substantially the same as that of the lands which now make up the Grand-Duchy. Luxembourg traces its name to a Roman tower, later named Luculinburh, said to have been built here in the 3C. Although there is evidence of earlier settlement in the Alzette valley, it was around the fortress built on the Rocher du Bock by Count Sigefroi in c 963 that the walled town began to grow which some 300 years later (1244) would receive its charter from Countess Ermesinda. In the centuries that followed, as the fortress was extended and strengthened by successive rulers, the town spread until by the end of the 15C it covered practically the whole area today occupied by the older quarters. Taken by the French in 1684, the fortifications were remodelled by Vauban. In 1815 Luxembourg became capital of the new Grand-Duchy under the personal sovereignty of William I of the Netherlands but, as capital of a country linked to the Germanic Confederation, the town had a Prussian garrison. When in 1830 Belgium split from Holland and the Grand-Duchy allied itself with Belgium, the town was prevented from so doing by the Prussian garrison and thus remained under William I. Only in 1839, under the arrangements of the Treaty of London, was the town rejoined to the Grand-Duchy in the form the latter then took. After the dissolution in 1866 of the Germanic Confederation, the Prussians left and the town's fortifications were dismantled the following year, the conversion of the defences into boulevards being completed by 1870. Since the Second World War, Luxembourg has become home to many European institutions, these including the Court of Justice, Investment Bank, Monetary Fund, and Parliament Secretariat.

The part of the city of main tourist interest is compact and can comfortably all be visited on foot. The description below starts from the PLACE D'ARMES (cafés and restaurants) in which are *Tourist Information* and also the *Cercle*; completed by 1909 and much used for municipal and private functions, the latter building bears a frieze depicting Countess Ermesinda conferring the charter of 1244. The Grand' Rue, just N of the Place d'Armes, today a main shopping street, is in origin a Roman road.

South of the Place d'Armes a passage from the Rue du Curé leads into the PLACE GUILLAUME, once covered by a Franciscan house, but today a market. Here are a central statue of William II and a pleasing memorial to the poet Michel Rodange (1827–76), with figures recalling his version in local dialect of 'Reynard the Fox'. The Rue de la Reine (E) soon reaches the **Palais Grand-Ducal** (mid July–August: daily except Wednesday and Sunday at varying times), originally the town hall (and on a site believed to have been occupied by a town hall since perhaps 1244), which dates in part from the 16C, has a Renaissance façade with strapwork decoration, and was enlarged in 1891–94. Immediately S is the *Chamber of Deputies* building of 1859. From here Rue de l'Eau leads back SW into Rue Notre-Dame running directly below Place Guillaume, reached by steps either side of the *Hôtel de Ville* of 1830–38. Opposite the Hôtel de Ville, flanking the cathedral, are (E) government offices of 1751, previously the refuge of an abbey at Trèves, and (W) the *Bibliothèque Nationale* (1611), a former Jesuit College.

The **Cathédrale Notre-Dame** was built as a Jesuit church in 1613–18 by Jean du Blocq, still in the Gothic manner but with a Renaissance portal. Noteworthy inside are the massive nave pillars with their curious strapwork decoration and also, in the unusually broad choir, the arms of the chief cities of the duchy when its boundaries were at their widest. By the modern crypt is the tomb of John the Blind, killed at Crécy in 1346.

The S side of the cathedral is skirted by the Boulevard Franklin Roosevelt, across which (W) is the PLACE DE LA CONSTITUTION, with a monument to the fallen of the two world wars and also the entrance to the *Casemates de la Pétrusse* dug by the Spanish in 1674 (Easter, Whitsun, July–September). From here there is an excellent view across the ravine of the Pétrusse, to the right bridged by the Pont Adolphe of 1903. To the E Boulevard Franklin Roosevelt reaches the PLACE DU SAINT ESPRIT, with on the left the *Citadelle du Saint Esprit* built by Vauban on the site of a convent (see also below). Here stands the *Monument de la Solidarité Nationale* (1971), commemorating the dead of the Second World War as also the resistance of the people of Luxembourg to the Nazi occupier. The design conveys the concentration camps and barracks which were the fate of so many citizens; the chapel, with stained-glass walls, shelters a rock as symbol of the victims' tomb. Ahead the valley is crossed by La Passerelle, a viaduct built in 1859–61 to link the town to its railway station; below, partly hollowed out of the rock, can be seen the 14C *Chapelle Saint Quirinus.*

From the Place du Saint Esprit the *Promenade de la Corniche* (pedestrians only; views) follows the course of the 17C ramparts northward to the ***Rocher du Bock**, which, with remains of the ancient castle of the counts, juts out high above a loop of the Alzette. This, the place where Sigefroi built his fortress in 963, is the most ancient corner of the city. A plan describes the various fortifications which, in addition to the remains of the castle, include something of Vauban's work of 1685 and also the *Casemates du Bock* of 1737–46 (March–October: daily, 10.00 to 17.00 or 18.00). A memorial recalls a visit by Goethe in 1792.

The view includes to the left the *Plateau de Kirchberg* (see below). Ahead, the extension of the Rocher du Bock is known as the *Plateau Altmunster*, named for an abbey destroyed in 1544. To the right can be seen the *Tour Jacob*, the *Porte de Trèves*, and (barely visible on the skyline) the three '*Spanish Towers*' of the ramparts of c 1400 which protected the Plateau du Rham. Below, in the district of GRUND, are the mainly 17C buildings of the former abbey of Neumunster (founded 1083) and of the former Hospice Saint Jean (founded 1309).

From the Rocher du Bock, Rue Sigefroi leads W past the *Eglise Saint Michel* (17C), founded as the castle chapel in 987 but many times destroyed and rebuilt; some Romanesque windows have survived on the N side. The MARCHE AUX POISSONS, with some old houses (see small print below), was once the Roman crossroads and then later the hub of the early town which grew around the castle. The **Musée de l'Etat** here (Tuesday–Friday, 10.00 to 12.00, 13.00 to 17.00; Saturday, 14.00 to 18.00; Sunday, 10.00 to 12.00, 14.00 to 18.00), in the former governor's house, contains good and varied collections spanning from

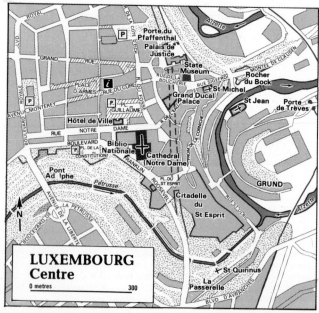

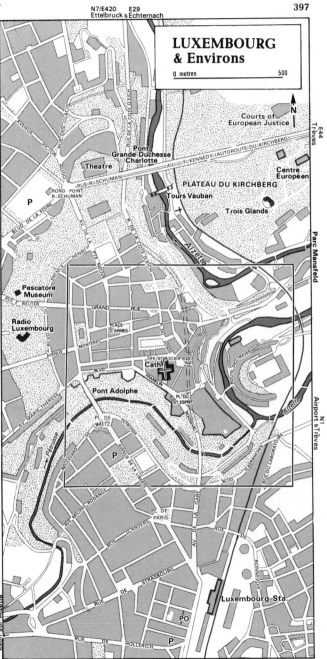

LUXEMBOURG
& Environs

0 metres ⎯⎯⎯⎯⎯⎯⎯⎯ 500

N

E44
Trèves

Courts of
European Justice

Pont
Grande-Duchesse
Charlotte

Theatre

AV. J.-F. KENNEDY (AUTOROUTE-DU-KIRCHBERG)

Centre
Européen

RUE R.-SCHUMAN

ROND POINT
R.-SCHUMAN

PLATEAU DU KIRCHBERG

Tours Vauban

Trois Glands

P

BLVD. DE LA FOIRE

AV. DE LA PTE. NEUVE

R. DE LA CÔTE D'EICH

Alzette

Parc Mansfeld

AVE DE E. REUTER

Pescatore
Museum

Radio
Luxembourg

AVENUE MONTEREY

GRAND

RUE

PLACE
D'ARMES

R. DU FOSSÉ

See large scale map

Cath†

BLVD.

FRANKLIN

ROUTE DE TRÈVES

Alzette

N1
Airport & Trèves

AVE MARIE-THÉRÈSE

Pont Adolphe

PL. DU
ST. ESPRIT

RUE DU LABORATOIRE

Pétrusse

PL. DE
METZ

P

AV. DE LA LIBERTÉ

BLVD.

RUE D'AVRANCHES

AV. MICHEL-RODANGE

PL. DE
PARIS.

RUE

DE

RUE

D'ANVERS

AV. DE LA GARE

RUE

DE

BONNEVOIE

N4
Esch-sur-Alzette

RUE

DE

STRASBOURG

RUE DE HOLLERICH

PO

P

Luxembourg Sta.

prehistoric to modern times. The Gallo-Roman material is outstanding and, from both this and other periods, there are some excellent models and illustrations of archaeological sites which the visitor may take in during his tour of the Grand-Duchy (e.g. the baths at Mamer, the palace at Echternach). Among other themes are coins (in the Trésor room) where an interesting small book of 1546 illustrating the legal tender of the day may especially be noted; medieval sculpture, some pieces of particular interest for the way in which they illustrate the dress of their time; a replica of the Hachiville retable (Rte 44A); well-displayed ceramic; arms and armour; and geology and natural history.

There is also a small but artistically excellent art gallery, among the artists and works being Pieter Brueghel the Younger (Calvary); Pieter Brueghel the Third (Village Wedding); Lucas Cranach the Elder (Caritas); Gerard David (Group around the dead Christ); Antoon van Dyck (Portrait of a Man); Jacob Jordaens (St. Simon); Cornelis Metsys (St. Jerome); Joachim Patinir (Descent from the Cross); David Teniers the Younger (After the Meal).

Old houses around the Marché aux Poissons have been restored, and, as part of the museum, show 18th and 19C interiors and also local industrial and popular art work.

Luxembourg, Trois Tours

The *Palais de Justice* of the 16–17C is immediately N of the museum. Here it is worth descending the lane, once a Roman road, through the *Porte du Pfaffenthal* (1685; on the site of a 10C gate) and then the second gateway, called the *Trois Tours* (11C, but altered in the 14–16C), to reach a point offering a good view across the Alzette.

To the left the road passes the remains of two old gateways. The valley is spanned by the *Pont Grande-Duchesse Charlotte* (1966), carrying the city's ring road, below this being the *Tours Vauban*, a fortified footbridge across the river. Above is the *Plateau de Kirchberg* (see below). Near the river is the *Hospice Civil* (1684), formerly the convent of Saint Esprit, built here by Louis XIV when Vauban converted the convent's original site into the Citadelle du Saint Esprit.

The remainder of this description covers districts further afield.

On the W side of the city extends a wooded park, laid out on the site of this sector of Vauban's fortifications. In the centre *Radio Luxembourg* occupies the position of what was once Fort Louvigny, while to the N of Avenue E. Reuter the *Musée J.P. Pescatore*, in a 19C mansion, shows 17–19C Dutch and French paintings (Late June–early September: Monday, Wednesday, Thursday, Friday, 13.00 to 18.00; Saturday, Sunday, 09.00 to 12.00, 15.00 to 19.00).

To the N, the ROND-POINT ROBERT SCHUMAN is an important traffic roundabout named after the man who promoted the plan for pooling Europe's steel and coal resources (1951), precursor of today's Common Market. The *Théâtre Municipal* here is a striking building of 1964 by Alain Bourbonnais, while to the E rises the equally striking monument to Robert Schuman, the six points of which represents the founder members of the Coal and Steel Community.

Beyond the memorial, the Pont Grande-Duchesse Charlotte (1966), crossing the valley of the Alzette at a height of 85m, leads to the PLATEAU DE KIRCHBERG with, to the immediate S, the *Trois Glands*, the three redoubts of an Austrian fortification of 1732. The plateau is the home of various European institutions, to the N of the road being the Investment Bank, the Court of Justice, and the Jean Monnet building housing various departments; to the S of the road are the Robert Schuman building (parliamentary secretariat) and the European Centre, this latter in two main parts, an administrative skyscraper and a conference and parliament complex.

At *Hamm*, off the road to the airport, there is an American military cemetery in which General George Patton (1885–1945), commander of the American 3rd Army, is buried.

For Luxembourg to *Esch-sur-Alzette* and *Mondorf-les-Bains*, see Rte 41; to *Echternach*, see Rte 43; to *Ettelbruck* and the N of the country, see Rte 44. For Luxembourg to *Arlon* and *Namur*, see Rte 33; to *Liège*, see Rtes 37 and 44.

41 South from Luxembourg

A. South-West

The roads SW out of Luxembourg soon reach the BASSIN MINIER, also known as the 'red earth' district, stretching for over 20km along the French border from Dudelange in the E to Pétange in the W and with Esch-sur-Alzette as the principal town. Rich in iron ore, exploited here since Roman if not earlier times, the district is one of ore mining and associated industry and is thus unlikely to attract many visitors. Nevertheless the glimpses of heavy industry have a character of their own and there are also some places of interest. The round described is one of c 50km.

18km **Esch-sur-Alzette** (25,000 inhab. Tourist Information: Hôtel de Ville) can claim ancient origin from the fact that its name derives from the Celtic 'esk', meaning a stream. In the SW part of the town (Place du Bril) there is a combined war and Resistance shrine and museum. At *Rumelange*, 6km SE, will be found the Musée National des Mines, housed in a disused gallery and illustrating mining of the 19th and 20C (Easter–October: daily, 14.00 to 17.00, when the last tour begins. Other months: second Saturday and Sunday of each month, 14.00 to 17.00).—*12km* (NW of Esch-sur-Alzette) **Pétange** forms with *Rodange* and *Lamadeleine* an industrial community of some 12,000 people lying close to the foot of the *Titelberg* with traces of Gallic presence of the 1C BC and of later Gallo-Roman occupation lasting until the beginning of the 5C. From Rodange an excursion may be made on the small steam 'Train 1900' (May–September: Sunday and Holidays, at 15.00, 16.15 and 17.40).—*3km* (NE of Pétange) *Bascharage* is a brewing town.—*16km* **Luxembourg**.

B. South-East

Total distance 19km.—*5km Hespérange.*—*10km Aspelt* (for *Dalheim*).—*4km* **Mondorf-les-Bains**.

5km Hespérange (2600 inhab.) has the ruins of an 11C castle, enlarged in the 14C; destroyed in 1483 by Maximilian, it was rebuilt but battered down again by the French in 1679.—*7km Frisange*, 5km W of which is the *Parc Merveilleux de Bettembourg*, a large and popular recreational park with many attractions for both adults and children (Easter–October: daily, 09.30 to 19.00). Frisange is on the French border and this Rte bears east.—*3km Aspelt* where a diversion may be made 2km NE towards *Dalheim*, just short of which a pillar, crowned by an eagle and erected in 1855, commemorates the five centuries of Gallo-Roman civilisation in this district; knocked down by the Germans in 1940, the pillar was put up again in 1957. An adjacent board records that this is the site of a Gallo-Roman town of the 1C on a crossroads along the great highway between Metz and Trier. First discovered during road construction in the 19C, later aerial reconnaissance revealed a street system and both public and domestic buildings. Excavation was started in 1977, but at present there is no admission to the site where in any case little is visible to the lay eye.—*4km* **Mondorf-les-Bains** (2000 inhab.) is the Grand-Duchy's thermal spa, with, in a beautiful park, two springs used for the alleviation of liver and similar complaints as also for rheumatism. The *Casino* is open from 16.00 daily except December 23 and 24.

From Mondorf-les-Bains the Moselle (Rte 42) may be reached at *Schengen* (8km SE) or *Remich* (8km NE).

42 The Moselle and Lower Sure Valleys (Schengen to Wasserbillig and Echternach)

Total distance 57km.—*10km* **Remich.**—*21km* **Grevenmacher.**—*6km*
Wasserbillig.—*20km* **Echternach.**

This scenic and interesting Rte descends the length of the Luxembourg Moselle (Schengen to Wasserbillig), the opposite bank
throughout being Germany. The scenery here, as also up the first part
of the Sûre, is vine-clad slopes. Some wine 'caves' are open to visitors,
though for a fee which however includes a drink. Behind the main
road many of the smaller towns have retained something of their late
medieval character.—The 'Princesse Marie-Astrid' plies between
roughly May–September, the normal run being between Schengen
and Wasserbillig with many stops. On some days the boat continues to
Trier (Trèves) and Bernkastel, both in Germany.

Schengen, with adjacent *Remerschen* and *Wintrange*, is a wine
centre. The village is close to the borders of both France and Germany
and there is a bridge across to Perl in the latter.—*8km Schwebsange,
Wellenstein* (off the main road) and *Bech-Kleinmacher* together form
another wine grouping which is one of the most important along the
Luxembourg Moselle (the Caves Cooperatives at Wellenstein may be
visited. May–August: daily, 09.00 to 11.00, 13.00 to 16.00). At
Bech-Kleinmacher there is a wine and folklore museum in a 17C wine
grower's house ('A Possen': Easter–October: daily except Monday,
14.00 to 19.00).—*2km* **Remich** (3000 inhab. Tourist Information: Bus
Station) is the seat of the State Viticulture Institute and is known for its
sparkling wine (Caves Saint Martin. April–October: daily, 09.00 to
11.30, 14.00 to 17.30). A bridge crosses the river here, and at the
German village of Nennig (3km) there is a Roman pavement.—*10km
Ehnen*, lying behind a pleasant, wide and green river front, is a
particularly attractive village with old, narrow cobbled streets, the
only round church in the Grand-Duchy, and a Wine Museum
(April–October: daily except Monday, 09.30 to 11.30, 14.00 to
17.00).—*2km Wormeldange* (1100 inhab.) forms, with Ehnen, Ahn
and Machtum, another wine grouping, Wormeldange styling itself
the 'Capital of the Riesling' (visits to Caves Cooperatives, April–
October: daily, 09.30 to 11.30, 13.30 to 17.00).—*9km* **Grevenmacher**
(3000 inhab. Tourist Information: 32 Route de Thionville), the chief
town of the Luxembourg Moselle district, produces sparkling wine
(Caves Bernard-Massard. April–October: daily, 09.00 to 11.30, 14.00
to 17.30). The Caves Cooperatives are also open to visitors (May–
August: daily, 09.00 to 11.00, 13.00 to 16.00). For those interested in
prehistory there is a dolmen 2km N of Grevenmacher on the minor
road CR137 to Manternach. The road from Grevenmacher back to
Luxembourg was the Roman road from Trèves to Arlon, *Niederanven*
(10km short of Luxembourg) being the most probable site of the
Roman 'Andethana', the halfway station.

6km **Wasserbillig** (2000 inhab.) is a frontier town at the mouth of the
Sûre where the Moselle curves away E into Germany. The famous
Roman funerary column of *Igel* (probably 3C) is 4km E in Germany
and Trier (Trèves) is 9km beyond.—This Rte now ascends the winding
valley of the Sûre, at first with vines but later narrowing and wooded.
Germany lies across the river. *15km Rosport* where there is a

hydro-electric dam forming a reservoir popular for water sports.—
5km **Echternach**, see Rte 43.

43 Luxembourg to Echternach
(Continuing to Diekirch)

Total distance 35km.—*15km Junglinster* (for **Larochette**).—*10km*
Consdorf (for **Suisse Luxembourgeoise**).—*10km* **Echternach**.

13km Bourglinster where there is an attractive turreted château.—
2km Junglinster, just beyond which are the masts of Radio Luxembourg's transmitters.

Larochette (1200 inhab. Tourist Information: Place de la Gare), 12km N of
Junglinster, is a particularly attractive small town set in the narrow and rocky
valley of the Ernz Blanche where this valley is joined by two others. On a crag
above, with traces of prehistoric occupation, stand the remains of a double castle,
the first dating from the 11C, the other being 14C, and both being destroyed
during the 16C.

10km Consdorf is a village at the S end of the misleadingly named
SUISSE LUXEMBOURGEOISE, a rather gloomy area of thick woods,
narrow valleys, and ravines, rocks and cliffs which stretches N almost
to the valley of the Sûre. The district is well served by a network of
minor roads and the motorist will see its best if he drives from
Consdorf up the Müllerthal to the Sûre or to the village of *Berdorf*
where the church has an unusual altar the table of which rests on a
large Roman stone bearing reliefs of Hercules, Apollo, Minerva and
Juno. The area is especially popular with walkers for whom there are
numerous waymarked tracks to ravines, caverns, rocks and view-
points.

10km **Echternach** (4000 inhab. Tourist Information: Porte Saint
Willibrord), an ancient place on the Sûre with an abbey, a good length
of medieval ramparts and also Roman remains, is one of Luxembourg's principal tourist centres, in summer crowded with coaches
and day-visitors, particularly from Germany which is just across the
river. Collectors of odd information may note that Echternach was the
first place in the Grand-Duchy to be lit by electricity, a claim recorded
by a plaque on the abbey wall.

With early Roman associations (see below), the town sprang up around the
abbey founded here in 698 by the Northumbrian monk St. Willibrord on land
gifted by St. Irmina of Ouren (died c 710), daughter of the Frankish king
Dagobert II. Willibrord (died 739) was the first Anglo-Saxon missionary working
on the Continent, and from its founding until the time of the French Revolution
the abbey was the effective local power. An important date was 1444 when a fire
destroyed much of the town, though not the abbey.—Echternach is known for its
Dancing Procession (Whit Tuesday) which attracts many thousands of pilgrims
and others. Dating from the 13C, the procession commemorates St. Willibrord's
cures of both epilepsy and plagues affecting cattle.

In the Place du Marché is the 15C *Old Town Hall*, with an arcaded
porch of 1520–30 where justice was once administered. An inscription
records the granting of town status in 1236 by Countess Ermesinda of
Luxembourg; the 18C new town hall is next door. Off the Place du
Marché spreads the large complex of the *Abbey*, its considerable 18C
domestic buildings now occupied by municipal offices and schools. Its
Romanesque *Basilique Saint Willibrord* dates, apart from its crypt,

from the 11C, but has Gothic additions of the 13C and was completely restored in 1862–68 and again after war damage of 1944. The crypt of c 900, with its five aisles and plain Romanesque vaulting, is architecturally the most interesting part of the interior, down here too being 11–12C murals and the white marble mausoleum (1906) of the saint. In front of the basilica the *Porte Saint Willibrord* (Tourist Information) leads to the Orangery of 1761, bearing figures of the four seasons.

To the SE of the abbey complex the *Eglise Saint Pierre et Saint Paul*, with Romanesque towers, stands on a hillock occupied in turn by a Roman camp and then a 7C chapel and hospice, and adjacent to the church the *Musée de Préhistoire* (April–September: Tuesday–Sunday, 10.00 to 12.00, 14.00 to 17.00) is housed in a building in origin of the 11C and well worth visiting if only for its immense beams and splendid internal roof. Roughly opposite, the four-arched river bridge rests on Roman foundations. Along the S of the town a good length of the medieval ramparts has been preserved, but the wall between the bridge and the abbey is a later defence erected to protect abbey territory.

Just SW of the town centre (1km; off the Luxembourg road) there is a large recreational lake off the approach road to which are the extensive remains of a Gallo-Roman property ('palace') which developed between c AD 50 and c 400 into a large complex. What is seen today is the outline formed by largely reconstructed lower courses, although some of the original stonework is still visible.

For Echternach to *Wasserbillig* and *Schengen*, see Rte 42.

For the SUISSE LUXEMBOURGEOISE, a main excursion from Echternach, see above. Here *Berdorf* (see also above) can be reached on foot (c 8km) by a path which passes the *Gorge du Loup*, the best gorge in the district (10m wide, 150m long) and other rock formations.

ECHTERNACH TO DIEKIRCH. 30km. A winding and scenic road ascending the Sûre.—*10km Grundhof* is at the mouth of the Ernz Noire, the valley of which leads a road into the Suisse Luxembourgeoise.—*3km Dillingen*, from where a road ascends to the ruined castle of **Beaufort**, beautifully sited on a steep, wooded slope (April–mid October: daily, 09.00 to 18.00). Its foundations resting on the site of a Roman camp (Castellum Belfurti), the castle, which has known many changes of ownership, is of three periods, the oldest dating from 1150; there followed in 1380 an extension on the valley side, and in c 1500 the addition of the wing with high Renaissance windows. The tour of the ruins is by a numbered route, illustrations, captioned in English, identifying the various parts. After 1646 the castle was abandoned, the then owner, Baron de Beck, building the adjacent Renaissance château but never living in it since he was killed in battle before he could do so. It is of interest that the castle apparently saw nothing of war until hit by shells during Von Rundstedt's offensive of 1944. Blackcurrant wine is a local speciality.—*5km Wallendorf-Pont* is by the confluence of the Ernz Blanche, Our and Sûre, this last here turning W and ceasing to be the frontier with Germany. Roads ascend the Our to *Vianden* (10km; see Rte 44D) and the Ernz Blanche to *Larochette*, see above.—*12km* **Diekirch**, see Rte 44C.

44   North from Luxembourg

A. Luxembourg to Ettelbruck

Total distance 28km.—*7km Steinsel.—9km* **Mersch**.—*12km*
Ettelbruck.

Apart possibly from Steinsel (see below), the main road to Mersch is
without much interest. To the W, though, lies the little visited district
of the valleys of the Mamer and Eisch which, with its upland views
and wooded valleys, quiet roads and isolated villages, Gallo-Roman
remains and medieval castles, offers up to a day's rewarding touring
and an alternative approach to Mersch (c 50km by this diversion).

VALLEYS OF THE MAMER AND EISCH. Luxembourg is left by N12
running NW through woodland to *Kopstal* on the Mamer (for the
Roman baths at Mamer, 4km S, see end of Rte 33). Beyond Kopstal
(2km), just before reaching the crossroads of Quatre-Vents, a left turn
leads immediately to a chapel and cemetery (*Schoenberg-Kehlen*).
Within the cemetery many old crosses (mainly 17C) have been
planted around the wall, while outside stands a replica of a Roman
Four Divinities Stone, the original of which, now in the Luxembourg
museum, probably once stood here. Two of the gods were removed,
probably when the stone became a Christian altar, but Hercules and
Apollo remain, the former, judging by the carved word, in Christian
times doubling as St. Anthony. In *Kehlen* village there is a little tower
of 1576.—*Nospelt*, 2km W, was long known for its pottery (Museum.
Easter, July, August: daily except Monday, 14.00 to 18.00).—
Continuing W from here, a road fork is reached on the edge of the
village of *Goeblange*, in the woods 2km along the road to the right
being the remains of two Gallo-Roman villas. Part of an agricultural
settlement, they date from the 1–4C and foundations, wells, traces of a
stair and, in the more eastern villa, something of the heating system
can all be seen.—At *Koerich*, 1km W of Goeblange, there is a ruined
castle incorporating work of the 14–18C. The village church of 1750
contains a magnificent Baroque altar.

From Koerich the road drops NW into the wooded valley of the
Eisch (Valley of the Seven Castles) which is followed N to *Septfon-
taines* with a modern seven-mouthed fountain and, above the village,
the 13–17C castle. Facing the 13C church door are two unusually well
preserved and detailed graveslabs of 1540, while inside the church
are a painted sculpture group (Christ Descended), with strikingly
alive faces, and also a wooden Pietà.—The road now bears E to reach
in 7km *Ansembourg* with a fine castle ruin (12–16C) perched above
the thickly wooded valley and, beyond the village, a large 17C
château with an ornate Baroque gateway and small round tower.—
From *Marienthal* (just E of Ansembourg), with a convent straddling
the valley, a road climbs steeply to *Hollenfels*, whose castle houses a
youth hostel, then continues to *Tuntange* where the church has a
sensitive Pietà and some effective modern stained-glass.—At *Saeul*,
2km NW, there is a 12C church. From here *Mersch* is reached in
10km.

The Castle at Hollenfels

7km (from central Luxembourg) *Steinsel* where there is a small site, not easy to find, likely to be of interest to Gallo-Roman enthusiasts. A small road angles steeply up the wooded hill on the W of the town, near the top curving right, here leaving the wood and passing (right) a large private property, after which (c 200m) the wood starts again. The car should be left here and a track (right, sign) followed for 300m to the lower-course remains of what was once an important woodland sanctuary (1–4C) comprising a temple and several surrounding buildings.—*9km* **Mersch** (4000 inhab. Tourist Information: Mairie, or

nearby Tour Saint Michel in July and August) stands at the confluence of the Eisch and the Mamer with the Alzette. The *Tour Saint
Michel*, with a bulbous top, is all that is left of the old church
demolished in 1851, while, opposite, the castle, in origin 12–13C, is
largely rebuilding of the 16C. Mersch is known for its *Gallo-Roman
Villa* (apply 1A Rue des Romains, nearby, or the Mairie for key), some
500m SW of the Tour Saint Michel and reached by rounding the N
side of the church with its twin bulb-towers and then following the
Rue des Romains, the villa being within a building on a green plot c
200m beyond No. 1A. Much of the villa area is now covered by
housing, but a furnace area and heated room have been preserved
and given some reconstructed hypocaust.

From Mersch a diversion may be made NW through *Fensterdall* to (8km) the
hamlet of *Bill* on CR115. Here, in woods just S of the hamlet and just W of the
road (sign), there is a large Gallo-Roman tumulus (3C), 24m in diameter,
originally 6–7m high, and surrounded by a low stone wall, now largely
reconstruction.—At *Useldange*, on the river Attert 5km NW of Fensterdall, there
is a ruined 11C castle.

For *Larochette*, 10km NE of Mersch, see Rte 43.

8km The château of *Berg* is now the grand-ducal residence. Dating
from 11–12C, the castle was acquired by William II of Holland in 1845
and rebuilt by his son.—*4km* **Ettelbruck** (6500 inhab. Tourist Information: 13 Grand' Rue), at the meeting of three valleys, is an important
road and rail junction. The town was much damaged in 1944, and a
statue to General Patton, on the Sûre bridge E of the town, marks the
point where the German southward advance was checked by the
Americans (Museum. April–May: Monday–Friday, 10.00 to 11.45,
14.00 to 16.45. June–September: daily, 09.00 to 11.45, 13.00 to 16.45.
October–March: Tuesday, Friday, 10.00 to 11.45, 14.00 to 16.45).

B. Ettelbruck to Clervaux
via Esch-sur-Sûre and Wiltz

Total distance (direct) 53km.—*17km* **Esch-sur-Sûre**.—*10km*
Wiltz.—*26km* **Clervaux**.

The distances given above assume use of the direct road (N15)
between Ettelbruck and Esch-sur-Sûre. Apart however from an
unusual small octagonal church at *Heiderscheidergrund* (c 3km short
of Esch-sur-Sûre) this road is without especial interest and the choice
of one of the two other roads described below (via Bourscheid for
scenery; via Rindschleiden for frescoes) is suggested. This Rte,
especially if the road through Bourscheid is chosen, traverses some of
the finest scenery in the Grand-Duchy.

ESCH-SUR-SURE VIA BOURSCHEID (34km). The scenic wooded valley
of the Sûre is followed through *Michelau*, where the great castle of
Bourscheid comes into view on the heights above, as far as
Bourscheid-Moulin. Here the valley is left and a small road taken
which winds up to the stark ruins of the castle of *Bourscheid*
(March–September: daily, 10.00 to 19.00), in a spectacular position
155m above the valley. Of roughly triangular shape, the castle is
entered through a 16C barbican to reach the upper castle, dating from
the 11–15C; the lower part of the castle, the so-called Maison des

Stolzembourg (museum), was built in 1384 and has been restored. Beyond the village of Bourscheid, the road drops back down to the Sûre at *Göbelsmühle* from where the valley is ascended to Esch.

Bourscheid Castle above the Valley of the Sûre

ESCH-SUR-SURE VIA RINDSCHLEIDEN (30km). The main N15 is followed for 5km to *Feulen*, after which smaller roads lead westward through the villages of Mertzig and Grosbous to the isolated hamlet of **Rindschleiden**, the smallest local government community in the Grand-Duchy, with a simple, small Romanesque church of the 12–15C built on the foundations of a 10C chapel and known for the 15C **Frescoes which cover its vaulting as also much of its walls. Also noteworthy are the small sculpted Pietà forming the central vault boss and the ancient font; this latter, thought to date from c 900 and to have belonged to the earlier chapel, was discovered (inverted and serving as the base of a wayside shrine) during nearby roadworks in 1954 (Church open Monday–Saturday, 08.00 to 18.00. Place coin in box-switch to illuminate frescoes. Readers of German wishing to study the frescoes in detail may obtain a guide from the sacristan).— From Rindschleiden, Esch-sur-Sûre may be reached either by taking the road NE to join N15, or alternatively by following smaller roads N to Insenborn on the Lac de la Haute-Sûre (see below).

17km (direct from Ettelbruck) **Esch-sur-Sûre**, reached through a short tunnel of 1850, is a small fortified town in a loop of the Sûre, romantically sited on and below steep crags on which stand the ruins of its castle. This castle, the keep of which is probably 10C in origin, was largely demolished at the French Revolution; the detached round tower, across a ravine, served as an outpost.

Esch-sur-Sûre

Immediately above Esch the river has been dammed to form a hydro-electric reservoir (1937), the **Lac de la Haute-Sûre**, extending some 10km up the valley. A visit to the dam is worthwhile. From the dam a road, with many attractively sited parking and picnic areas, skirts the S side of the snaking lake to (5km) *Insenborn*; another road crosses the dam to climb to a large parking area with views down to the lake.

10km **Wiltz** (4100 inhab. Tourist Information: Château), on a steep hillside and divided into a lower and an upper town, has close associations with the Boy Scout movement (chalets and camping grounds). In the upper town the *Château*, standing on foundations of the 12C, was built between 1631–1727; today it serves various municipal purposes, housing Tourist Information, a home for the aged, and two museums: Battle of the Bulge (Easter: 14.00 to 17.00; mid June–mid September: daily, 10.00 to 12.00, 13.00 to 17.00) and Arts et Métiers, or Arts and Crafts (Whitsun–August: daily, 10.00 to 12.00, 13.00 to 17.00). In summer the château gardens are used for an international festival (music and theatre). Near the château entrance are the *Cross of Justice* (1502 but with later statues) and, beside the main road, a memorial commemorating the American 28th Infantry Division which liberated Wiltz on 10 September 1944. Between the upper and lower towns a memorial incorporating an observation tower commemorates a strike of 1942 in protest against the German introduction of military service, six people being shot for their participation. The church in the lower town, dating from 1510 but with a much older tower which may have been part of a castle, contains tombs of the lords of Wiltz and also heraldic decoration.

17km Antonuishaff is a hamlet at a road fork.

Here a diversion northwards is suggested, first along minor roads to (5km) *Hachiville* where the church contains a lovely, coloured *Retable of several panels, each crowded with small carved figures playing out the Crucifixion and other biblical scenes. At *Troisvierges*, 5km farther NE, the altar of the former Franciscan church of 1640 bears statues of the three virgins, Faith, Hope and Charity, long the objectives of pilgrimage. The Belgian frontier (Rte 37) is 5km north.

At Antoniushaff this Rte bears E for (*9km*) **Clervaux**, see Rte 44C.

C. Ettelbruck to Clervaux
via Diekirch and Hosingen

Total distance 36km.—*5km* **Diekirch**.—*20km* Hosingen.—*11km* **Clervaux**.

5km **Diekirch** (5600 inhab. Tourist Information: Place Guillaume), a tourist and commercial centre on the Süre, is known for its beer and its Roman mosaics. The *Mosaics Museum* is on the main square, the Place Guillaume (Easter–mid October: daily except Tuesday, 10.00 to 12.00, 14.00 to 18.00. Mid October–mid November: Saturday, Sunday, same times). The three mosaics, all of the 3C, were the flooring of a Gallo-Roman villa, thought to have been burnt by the Franks. Two were discovered in 1926 in the course of excavation in the Esplanade, the main road just E of Place Guillaume; one of these (3 by 3.5m) bears the head of a lion, while the other, larger (9 by 4m) but less well preserved, was the cover of a hypocaust. The third and best mosaic was found near the same place in 1950; measuring 3.50 by 4.75m the design includes a curious double-faced Medusa. The *Eglise Saint Laurent* (Easter–mid October: daily, 10.00 to 12.00, 15.00 to 17.00), a short distance E of Place Guillaume, is a 5C foundation which dates in part from the 9C and has an 11C turret, restored in 1913. Inside there are the remains of frescoes, and an opening in the nave allows a glimpse of some medieval tombs. About 1km to the S of the town a sign beside the Larochette road indicates a path (10–15 minutes walk) to the *Deiwelselter* (Devil's Altar), a dolmen reconstructed to a fanciful vertical form in 1892.—*5km* The ruins of the castle of *Brandenbourg*, 2km E of the main road (N7), stand above the valley of the Blees; the keep was built in the 12C, other parts were added until c 1500, and the castle was destroyed in 1668.—*7km Hoscheid*, from where small roads leading E in c 8km reach the upper reservoir of the Our hydro-electric complex (Rte 44D).

5km N of Hoscheid, N7 is crossed by the small CR322. To the W this is a delightful, wooded, twisting road, generally following the valley of the Wiltz, the town of Wiltz being reached in 21km. About halfway, *Kautenbach*, a village in beautiful mountain and forest surroundings, is the scene of international canoe competitions.

8km Hosingen was the site of an Augustinian abbey of about the 12C, its church now surviving as the parish church (17C with older traces).—*11km* **Clervaux** (1000 inhab. Tourist Information: Châteaux), on a loop of the Clerve, lies in a romantic valley setting dominated by a large Neo-Romanesque church (1910) and the ancient but reconstructed massive, squat *Castle*; with parts dating from the 12C, it was rebuilt in the 17C and again after serious war damage in 1944 and today houses exhibitions (Easter. Whitsun–mid September, Christmas: daily, 10.00 to 17.00. Mid September–Whitsun except January and February: Sunday, Holidays, 13.00 to 17.00). Above the station a chapel of 1786 contains tombs of the lords of Clervaux. The *Abbey of Saint Maurice and Saint Maur*, standing high above the town to the W, was founded in 1890, the buildings of the warm local stone dating from 1910; it can be reached by road or footpath and contains an exhibition on modern monastic life.

From Clervaux the Belgian border (Rte 37) is reached by N7 in 19km. From the hamlet of *Lausdorn* (on N7, 13km from Clervaux), a small road drops E into the valley of the Our at a place where the frontiers of Luxembourg, Belgium and Germany meet (see end of Rte 38B).

For Clervaux to *Wiltz*, see Rte 44B; to *Vianden*, see Rte 44D.

D. Ettelbruck to Clervaux via Diekirch and Vianden

Total distance 48km.—*5km* **Diekirch**.—*11km* **Vianden**—*21km* *Dasburg*.—*11km* **Clervaux**.

5km **Diekirch**, see Rte 44C.—*2km* N19 continues E for Echternach (see Rte 43), while this Rte bears N along N17, climbing out of the Sûre valley to reach (*6km*) Fouhren beyond which starts the winding and steep descent to the valley of the Our. Immediately above Vianden a road bears left, a short distance up this being a parking area offering what is probably the best view of the town's great castle in its dramatic setting.

3km **Vianden** (1600 inhab. Tourist Information: Musée Victor Hugo), the most picturesque and, after Luxembourg itself, the most spectacular town in the Grand-Duchy and surrounded by rugged scenery, crowds around its little river crossing and climbs steeply to the W up narrow cobbled streets. Although for most of its course the Our is the border between the Grand-Duchy and Germany, here there is a Luxembourg enclave on the E bank. Signed walks lead to view-points, sections of ramparts, etc.; a map showing recommended walks is on a wall by the bridge.

On the descent into the town the Route de Diekirch hairpins to become the Grande Rue, with a group of places of interest, including the *Croix de Justice* (1902), a replica of a 14C predecessor, and the *Eglise des Trinitaires* (1250), with a notable Rococo altar of 1758. Now the parish church, this was formerly that of a Trinitarian abbey and on the S side can be seen the 14C (restored in 1955) cloister of the abbey with some ancient tombs and also a long, lively stone carving showing

St. Hubert erring on Good Friday. A lane leads to the *Hockelstour*, a relic of the ramparts. The *Hôtel de Ville* occupies a patrician mansion of 1579.

On the river bridge are a statuette its coof St. John Nepomuk, the patron of bridges, and a bust by Rodin of Victor Hugo, opposite the latter being the *Musée Victor Hugo*, occupying the house, reconstructed after war damage in 1944, in which the writer stayed on five occasions between 1862 and 1871 (April–October: daily, 09.30 to 12.00, 14.00 to 18.00. Closes Wednesday out of high season). From this E side of the river a chairlift (Easter–September: daily, 09.30 to 19.00 or 11.00 to 18.00 out of high season) ascends to a belvedere and café 200m above the town.

The huge *Castle (January–March: Saturday, Sunday, Holidays, 10.00 to 12.00, 13.00 to 16.00. April: daily, 10.00 to 17.00. May–September: daily, 09.00 to 19.00 or 18.00 in September. October: daily, 10.00 to 16.00), once largely ruined but now the focus of major restoration, spectacularly occupies a promontory above the town known to have been the site of a Roman fortification. The present castle dates from the 11C onwards and shows both Romanesque and Gothic features. The earliest count was one Gerard (1096), but in 1417 the county passed through the female line to Engelbert of Nassau and today the castle is still owned by the grand-ducal family.

On approaching the gateway, note (above left) a balcony from which official proclamations were made and also, above the gateway, the chutes through which boiling oil could be poured. Within the complex the first principal features include the Wine Cellar (a large store with two aisles and Romanesque arches), an oubliette, the chief watchtower, and the Count's Hall of the 13C, one of the largest surviving of its kind; there was another hall above, and, above again, a granary. Beyond, the Romanesque Chapel is of particular interest, both because of its decagonal shape and because of the opening down to a lower chapel which, though small, is thought to have been for prisoners and servants; the narrow terrace surrounding and lighting the main chapel is also an unusual feature. Another interesting room is the Byzantine Room, so called because of its large trefoil windows. Beyond, and now forming a single unit with Gothic vaulting, were a reception room, an armoury, and the private room of the Count. Magnificent views over the town and surrounding country are had from the castle's many terraces.

The **Centrale-Electrique de Pompage**, using a lower and an upper reservoir connected by pipes through the mountain, is an international undertaking completed during the 1960s. The lower reservoir (8km long) has been formed by damming the Our just above Vianden (*Barrage de Lohmühle*). The road N out of the town skirts and crosses this lower lake (parking and view-points), in *4km* reaching the *Caverne* (Daily 09.00 or 10.00 to 17.00), the pumping station in the mountain where a Visitor Gallery with models and pictures explains the operation of the complex. Farther into the tunnel the turbines and control room can be seen through observation windows.—The *Bassin Supérieure* is a large reservoir on Mont Saint Nicolas (330m) above; from the approach roads there are extensive views over both Luxembourg and Germany.

2km (from the Caverne) *Stolzembourg* has a château of 1898 grafted on to a medieval predecessor.—*15km Dasburg*, above which the narrowing valley of the Our is roadless but has a footpath to (14km) *Ouren*, see end of Rte 38B.—*11km* **Clervaux**, see Rte 44C.

INDEX OF ARTISTS

A = Architect
G = Glassworker (including stained-glass)
M = Metalworker
P = Painter (including etching, drawing, engraving, etc.)
S = Sculptor (stone or wood)
Place names, where appropriate, indicate where most active.

BOGART, BRAM (Abraham Boogart; 1921–), P.—67

BOL, HANS (1534–93), P.—249

BONDT, J.A. DE (20C), S.—219

BONNARD, PIERRE (1867–1947), P.—120

BONNECROY, J.B. DE (1618–79), P. Antwerp—242

BONNET, ANNE (1908–60), P.—66

BORCHMAN, JAN (16C), S.—279

BORCHT, PIETER VAN DER (1545–1608), P. Antwerp—261

BORMAN or BORREMANS, JAN (fl. 1479–1520), S. Brussels—55, 56, 292, 310

BORREMANS, PASQUIER (fl. 1510–36), S. Louvain, Brussels—274

BOSCH, HIERONYMUS (fl. 1474–1516), P. 's Hertogenbosch—44, 117, 125, 181, 217

BOSSCHAERT, T.W. (1614–54). P. Antwerp—261, 262

BOTH, JAN (c1618–52), P. Uticcht.—118

BOUDIN, LOUIS EUGENE (1824–98), P.—120

BOULENGER, HIPPOLYTE (1837–74), P.—63, 307, 316, 381

BOULLAIN, SYLVANUS (early 17C), A.—145

BOURBONNAIS, ALAIN (20C), A.—399

BOURGEOIS, VICTOR (1897–1962), A.—64, 137

BOURLA, BRUNO (1783–1866), A. Antwerp—250

BOUTS, ALBERT (c 1460–1549), P. Louvain—117, 123, 266

BOUTS, DIRK (c 1415–75), P. Louvain—43, 116, 125, 187, 217, 285, 287

BRAECKE, PIERRE (1859–1938), S.—141

BRAEKELEER, F. DE (1792–1883), P. Antwerp—60

BRAEKELEER, HENRI DE (1840–88), P.—60, 111, 119, 124, 222, 268, 307, 381

BRANGWYN, SIR FRANK (1867–1956), P.—181, 182

BRAY, JAN DE (c 1626–97), P.—218

BREE, M.I. VAN (1773–1839), P. Antwerp—60

BREITNER, GEORGE HENDRIK (1857–1923), P.—268

BRIL, PAUL (1554–1626), P. Rome—46, 268, 316

BROEUCQ, JACQUES (d. 1584), S. Mons.—56, 317, 327

BROODTHAERS, MARCEL (1924–76), P.—67

BROUWER, ADRIAEN (1605–38), P. Haarlem, Antwerp—49, 80, 118, 197, 198, 268

BRUEGHEL, AMBROOS (1617–75), P. Antwerp—252

BRUEGHEL, JAN (1568–1625; 'Velvet'), P. Antwerp, Brussels—46, 50, 249, 250, 267, 276, 307

BRUEGEL, PIETER THE ELDER (c 1525–69), P. Antwerp, Brussels—46, 97, 110, 117 (Brussels Gallery), 249 (Dulle Griet)

BRUEGHEL, PIETER THE YOUNGER (1564–1638; 'Hellfire'), P. Brussels, Antwerp—46, 110, 117, 218, 249, 267, 276, 307, 398

BRUEGHEL, PIETER THE THIRD (b. 1589), P. Antwerp—267, 398

BRUSSELMANS, JEAN (JAN) (1884–1953), P.—66, 181, 218, 268

BRUYN, WILLEM DE (fl. 1695), A.—99

BUISSERET, LOUIS (1888–1956), P.—66, 325

BURY, POL (1922–), P.—67

BUYSSE, GEORGES (1864–1916), P.—63

CAMP, CAMILLE VAN (1834–91), P.—176

CAMPIN, ROBERT (1378/9–1444; Master of Flémalle), P. Tournai—43, 54, 116, 302

CANTRE, JOSEPH (1870–1957), S.—137

CAPRONNIER, J.B. (1814–91), G.—106, 247

CARABAIN, JACQUES (1834–after 1889), P.—232

CARAVAGGIO, MICHELANGELO (1571–1610), P.—47, 183, 244

CARRIER BELEUSE, (19C), S.—61

CARTE, ANTO (1886–1954), P.—66, 325

CELS, CORNELIS (1778–1859), P. Antwerp, Brussels—230, 244

CHAGALL, MARC (1889–1985), P.—367

CHAINAYE, ACHILLE (19C), S.—61

CHAMPAIGNE, JEAN-BAPTISTE DE (1631–81), P.—105, 211

CHAMPAIGNE, PHILIPPE DE (1602–74), P. Paris—119, 217

CHARLIER, GUILLAUME (19–20C), S.—61, 111, 302, 307

CHATELET, PIERRE PAULUS DE (1881–1959), P.—325

CHEVRON, J.N. (19C), A. Liège—60

CHRISTUS, PETRUS (d. 1472), P. Bruges—43, 116

CLAESSINS, ANTHONY (1536–1613), P. Bruges—187

CLAESSINS, PIETER (c 1550–1623), P. Bruges—186

CLAESZ, JACOB (early 16C), P.—265

CLAUS, EMILE (1849–1924), P.—63, 119, 148, 181, 218, 268, 307, 381

CLAYS, JEAN-PAUL (1819–1900), P.—63

CLEEF, JOOS VAN (c 1485–1541), P. Antwerp—44, 216

GOES, HUGO VAN DER (c 1445–82), P. Ghent, Brussels—43, 116, 125, 180, 187

GOGH, VINCENT VAN (1853–90), P.—314, 318

GOSSAERT, JAN ('Mabuse', c 1478–c 1536), P. Antwerp—44, 117, 227, 316

GOSSIN, JEAN (fl. 1625), M. S. Liège—385

GOYEN, JAN VAN (1596–1656), P.—118, 181, 218, 268, 381

GRANGE, LOUIS (1686–c 1739), P. Brussels—97

GRIMMER, ABEL (fl. 1592–1618), A. P. Antwerp—117, 181, 267, 307

GRIMMER, JACOB (c 1525–90), P.—267

GROOT, GUILLAUME DE (19C), S.—115

GROOTWERC, NICOLAS (fl. c 1300), M.—172

GROUX, C. DE (1825–70), P.—62, 119, 268, 307

GRUPELLO, GABRIEL (1644–1730), S. Brussels, Geraardsbergen—58, 59, 108

GUARDI, FRANCESCO (1712–93), P. Venice—118

GUIMARD, BARNABE (fl.1765–92), A. Brussels—42, 106, 107, 255

HAECHT, WILLEM VAN (fl. 1552), P. E. Antwerp—264

HAECK, JAN (fl. 1516–50), G. Antwerp—105

HAEGHEN, J.B. VAN DER (fl. end 17C), S.—200

HALS, FRANS (?1580–1666), P. Haarlem—118, 218, 227, 249, 268

HANKAR, PAUL (1859–1902), A.—64

HANSCHE, JAN (fl. 1672–9). S. Louvain—279, 290, 354

HAYEZ, J. (20C), P.—106

HEDA, WILLEM (1594–1680), P.—249

HEEM, JAN DAVIDSZ DE (c 1616–c 84), P.—50

HEEMSKERK, MARTEN VAN (1498–1574), P. Haarlem, Rome—46, 117, 217

HEERE, LUCAS DE (1534–84), P. Ghent—202

HEIL, LEO VAN (1605–c 80), A. Brussels—105

HEINRICH OF CONSTANCE (early 14C), S.—249

HELMONT, MATTHIJS VAN (1632–c 79), P. Antwerp—261

HEMONY, PIETER (fl. c 1600), M. Zutphen—207

HERBOSCH, PIETER (fl. end 17C), A.—99

HERMANS, CHARLES (1839–1924), P.—62

HERREGOUDTS, J.B. (c 1690–1721), P. Bruges—190

HERREYNS, G.J. (1743–1827), P. Antwerp—230, 246, 272

HERRI MET DE BLES (1480–1550), P. Namur, Antwerp—46, 249, 345

HESDIN, JACQUEMART DE (working from 1384, d. c 1409), P.—42

HESSIUS, WILLEM (1601–90), A. Antwerp—41, 288

HEY, JEAN (?Master of Moulens, fl. 15C), P.—116

HEYMANS, ADRIAAN JOSEF (1839–1921), P. Kalmthout.—63

HILLEWERVE, F. VAN (1621–62), A. Bruges—173

HOBBEMA, MEINDERT (1638–1709), P. Amsterdam—118, 268

HOFFMANN, JOSEPH (20C), A.—129

HOGENBERG, NIKLAAS (d. 1539), E. Mechelen—262

HOLABIND, ROOT and BURGEE (20C), As. USA—388

HOLLEBEKE, BRUNO VAN (1817–92), P.—176

HONTHORST, GERARD (VAN) (1590–1656), P. Utrecht, Rome—206, 252

HOOL, J. VAN (1769–1837), S.—311

HOORENBAUT, GHEERAERT, (16C), P.—217

HOORENBAUT, LUCAS (d. 1626), P. Ghent—219

HOREMANS THE ELDER, J.J. (1682–1759), P.—51

HORST, NIKLAAS VAN DER (c 1590–1646), P. Antwerp, Brussels—261

HORTA, VICTOR (1861–1947), A.—64, 106, 124, 306

HOSTE, H. (1881–1957), A.—65

HOUBRAKEN, JAN VAN (17C), P.—122

HOVE, E. VAN (18C), P.—181

HUBERTI, EUGENE (1819–80), P.—62

HUFFEL, A. VAN (20C), A.—126

HUGO D'OIGNIES (14C), M.—54, 297, 329, 331, 340, 341

HUMBEECK, PIERRE VAN (1891–1964), P—290

HUYS, PIETER (c 1519–c 81), P. Antwerp—117

HUYSSENS, PIETER (1577–1637), A. Bruges—40, 190, 219, 250

INGELS, DOMIEN (20C), S.—219

INGRES, JEAN A.D. (1780–1867), P.—364

ISENBRANT, ADRIAEN (fl. 1510–51), P. Bruges—181, 183, 187, 217, 249

JAMAER, VICTOR (late 19C), A.—97

JANKEVITSJ (20C), S.—225

JANSSENS, ABRAHAM (1575–1632), P. Antwerp—47, 96, 186, 193, 203, 229, 267

418 INDEX OF ARTISTS

GENERAL INDEX

Topographical names are in **bold** print; names of persons in *italics*; other entries, including city indexes, in Roman print. Where there are two or more references the most important are in appropriate cases printed bold.

Numbered Military Formations and Units

NOTES

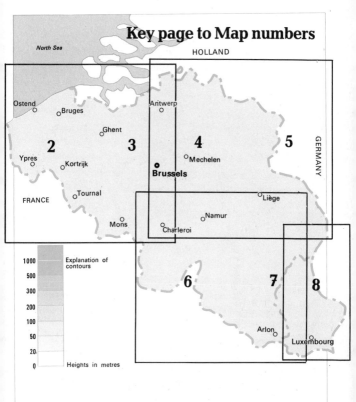

Key page to Map numbers

North Sea

HOLLAND

Ostend

Bruges

Ghent

Antwerp

2

3

4

5

Ypres

Kortrijk

Mechelen

GERMANY

Brussels

Tournai

FRANCE

Liège

Namur

Mons

Charleroi

6

7

8

Arlon

Luxembourg

	Explanation of contours
1000	
500	
300	
200	
100	
50	
20	
0	Heights in metres

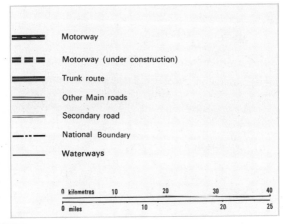

	Motorway
	Motorway (under construction)
	Trunk route
	Other Main roads
	Secondary road
	National Boundary
	Waterways

0 kilometres	10	20	30	40
0 miles	10		20	25

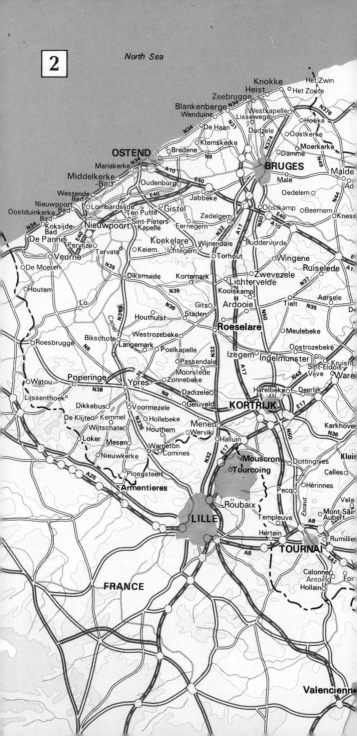

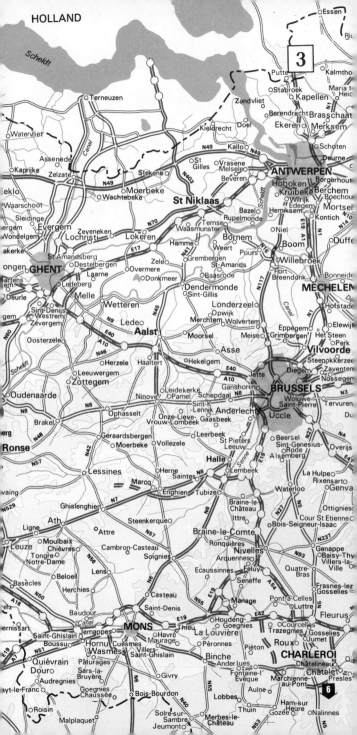

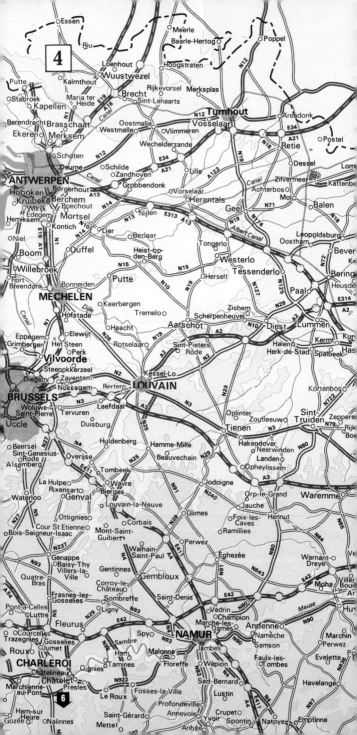

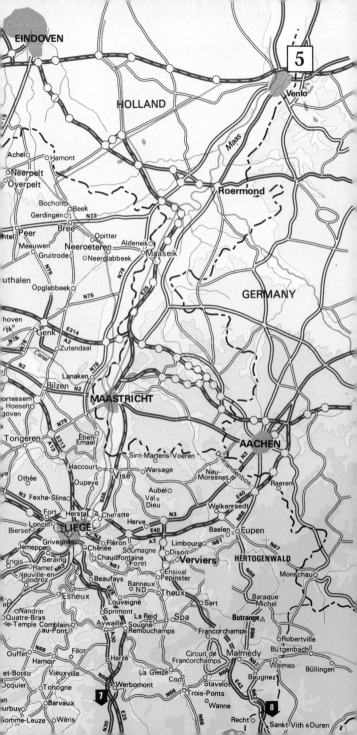